Systems Approaches to Knowledge Management, Transfer, and Resource Development

W.B. Lee
The Hong Kong Polytechnic University, Hong Kong

Managing Director:	Lindsay Johnston
Senior Editorial Director:	Heather A. Probst
Book Production Manager:	Sean Woznicki
Development Manager:	Joel Gamon
Assistant Acquisitions Editor:	Kayla Wolfe
Cover Design:	Nick Newcomer

Published in the United States of America by
Information Science Reference (an imprint of IGI Global)
701 E. Chocolate Avenue
Hershey PA 17033
Tel: 717-533-8845
Fax: 717-533-8661
E-mail: cust@igi-global.com
Web site: http://www.igi-global.com

Library of Congress Cataloging-in-Publication Data

Systems approaches to knowledge management, transfer, and resource development / W.B. Lee, editor.
    p. cm.
  Includes bibliographical references and index.
  Summary: "This book provides a new view of knowledge management through the lens of systems approach, which looks at each part of the knowledge management system as a section of the full overview"--Provided by publisher.
  ISBN 978-1-4666-1782-7 (hardcover) -- ISBN 978-1-4666-1783-4 (ebook) -- ISBN 978-1-4666-1784-1 (print & perpetual access) 1. Knowledge management. I. Lee, W. B.
  HD30.2.S952 2012
  658.4'038011--dc23
                                    2012002479

British Cataloguing in Publication Data
A Cataloguing in Publication record for this book is available from the British Library.

The views expressed in this book are those of the authors, but not necessarily of the publisher.

Table of Contents

Section 1
Theory and Model

Section 2
Knowledge Management

Section 3
Knowledge Technology

Section 4
Applications

Detailed Table of Contents

Section 1
Theory and Model

Yoshiteru Nakamori, Japan Advanced Institute of Science and Technology, Japan

Andrzej P. Wierzbicki, National Institute of Telecommunications, Poland

This article presents a systems approach to knowledge synthesis or construction, starting with a new systems thinking named the informed systems thinking, which should serve as the basic tool of knowledge integration and support creativity. Based on this new systems thinking, a new systems approach to knowledge synthesis or construction has been developed as a systems methodology that consists of three fundamental parts: how to collect and synthesize knowledge, how to use our abilities in collecting knowledge, and how to justify the synthesized knowledge. This article first describes the informed systems thinking and then introduces a new systems approach to knowledge synthesis and the features of this new approach from a viewpoint of knowledge creation.

Leif Edvinsson, Lund University, Sweden & The Hong Kong Polytechnic University, Hong Kong

Today we are bombarded by information and news signals, including health, meteorological, and financial issues. The interpretation of many of these signals will call for a new dimension of Systems Science for enterprises and society, which can be called Intellectual Capital (IC) Science. This article will look into the evolution of IC Science during the past 20 years and emerging signals for its future applications.

Social sciences have been in crisis for a long time, partly by being the captive of the Newtonian para-digm, and partly through the effects of this paradigm on practice. This crisis was recognized in the past by the Russian psychologist and philosopher Lev Vygotsky, and continues to this day. The educational crisis is just one instance. It is hard to imagine how to escape this crisis, and a real shift of paradigm is needed. In this article, such a shift toward the paradigm of complexity is advocated. The shift implies a reframing of complexity and a new kind of thinking in complexity. The new paradigm implies the development of a causally generative complexity theory of change and development. Ultimately, the fundamental challenge is to harness the complexity of complex, generative learning in the communities of learners in learning organizations.

The usual horizon of knowledge science is limited to nominalism, empiricism, and naturalistic and evolutionary epistemologies. I propose to broaden this horizon by applying some other philosophical attitudes, such as a non-nominalistic philosophy of language. A basic methodology for the new epis-teme, including (non-nominalistic) typology and a definition of knowledge and of tacit knowledge, is proposed. Several types of knowledge and the corresponding tacit knowledge are discussed within a broadened philosophical context. There are many types of knowledge and tacit knowledge using dif-ferent methods of sharing. The main problem with the effective sharing of tacit knowledge is sharing knowledge *relevant* to the given problem. The transfer, change and transformation of tacit knowledge into explicit knowledge are possible. An example of such a transition, which I call *conceptualization*, is described. Conceptualization exemplifies *how* new knowledge can be created with the use of tacit knowledge. A need also exists for a professional collaboration between knowledge science, knowledge management and philosophy.

Section 2
Knowledge Management

This is a conceptual paper offering an approach to apparent practitioner and academic dissatisfaction with the field of Knowledge Management (KM). Discussing definitions of knowledge, the drivers for its value as an organisational resource and comparing these against definitions of Knowledge Management, this paper suggests a divergence between operational needs and KM as the medium for coordination. Offering an historical perspective of knowledge as a resource it suggests KM to be too broad a concept to be effective in fulfilling the needs of organisations. The authors suggest a continuum for knowledge resource development from which Strategic Knowledge Resource Development is offered as a potential solution for current unsatisfaction.

Chapter 6
David A. Griffiths, University of Edinburgh, Scotland
Serge Koukpaki, University of Edinburgh, Scotland
Brian Martin, University of Edinburgh, Scotland

This paper derives from a research project, which sets out to address practitioner dissatisfaction in the area of Knowledge Management. The author discusses common weaknesses in existing thinking about Knowledge Management and in prevailing models in particular. Modelling processes are considered and underlying assumptions that are required to be addressed in any attempt to create a Knowledge Management Model are examined. An overview is provided of the initial stages in the development of a new, synthetic and general model, The Knowledge Core©, with assumptions underlying this signposted and their influences upon modelling are discussed.

Chapter 7
Jean-Louis Ermine, TELECOM Business School, France

Population ageing is a phenomenon that is quite new and irreversible in the history of mankind. Every country and every organisation is concerned while it is not certain that all the risks and challenges have been clearly identified. Clearly, there is a risk of massive knowledge loss, i.e., "Knowledge Crash", due to massive retirements, but not exclusively for this reason. This risk is not evaluated at the right level, and in this regard, this article, by including the problem of "Knowledge Crash" in the more general framework of "Knowledge Management", enlarges the concepts of knowledge, generation, and knowledge transfer. The author proposes a global approach, starting from a strategic analysis of a knowledge capital and ending in the implementation of socio-technical devices for inter-generational knowledge transfer.

Chapter 8
Hepu Deng, RMIT University, Australia

This paper investigates the role of information and communication technologies in enabling and facilitating the conversion of knowledge objects in knowledge management and explores how these roles might be affected in an organization. Such an investigation is based on a critical analysis of the relationships between data, information and knowledge, leading to the development of a transformation model between data, information and knowledge. Using a multi-method approach, in this paper, the author presents a conceptual framework for effective knowledge management in an organization. The author discusses the implications of the proposed framework for designing and developing knowledge management systems in an organization.

Section 3
Knowledge Technology

Chapter 9

Gu Jifa, Academy of Mathematics and Systems Sciences, CAS, China

Meta-synthesis knowledge system (MSKS) is based on the meta-synthesis system approach and knowledge science. This article introduces the basic theory of meta-synthesis knowledge system like DMTMC system, model integration, opinion synthesis, consensus building and expert mining. Similar MSKS systems are illustrated. Case studies and examples are also explored in this article.

Chapter 10

Tatyana Ivanova, Technical University of Sofia, Bulgaria

A grand number of ontologies have been developed and are publicly accessible on the Web making techniques for mapping between various ontologies more significant. Research has been made in the area of ontology alignment, a grand number of approaches, algorithms, and tools have been developed in recent years, but are still not "perfect" and excellent knowledge. In this article, the author makes an overall view of the state of ontology alignment, including the latest research, comparing many approaches, and analyzing their strengths and drawbacks. The main motivation behind this work is the fact that despite many component matching solutions that have been developed so far, there is no integrated solution that is a clear success, which can be used for ontology mapping in all cases, making knowledge about developed ontology mapping methods and their clear classification needed.

Chapter 11

Weisen Guo, University of Tokyo, Japan
Steven B. Kraines, University of Tokyo, Japan

To promote global knowledge sharing, one should solve the problem that knowledge representation in diverse natural languages restricts knowledge sharing effectively. Traditional knowledge sharing models are based on natural language processing (NLP) technologies. The ambiguity of natural language is a problem for NLP; however, semantic web technologies can circumvent the problem by enabling human authors to specify meaning in a computer-interpretable form. In this paper, the authors propose a cross-language semantic model (SEMCL) for knowledge sharing, which uses semantic web technologies to provide a potential solution to the problem of ambiguity. Also, this model can match knowledge descriptions in diverse languages. First, the methods used to support searches at the semantic predicate level are given, and the authors present a cross-language approach. Finally, an implementation of the model for the general engineering domain is discussed, and a scenario describing how the model implementation handles semantic cross-language knowledge sharing is given.

Chapter 12

Haoxiang Xia, Dalian University of Technology, China

With the rapid proliferation of all sorts of online communities, the knowledge creation and dissemination in these online communities have become a prominent social phenomenon. In this paper, one typical Open Source Software community—the online community of Linux kernel developers—is studied from the perspective of collective intelligence, to explore the social dynamics behind the success of the Linux kernel project. The Linux kernel developer community is modeled as a supernetwork of triple interwoven networks, namely a technological media network, a collaboration network of the developers, and a knowledge network. The development of the LDC is then an evolutionary process through which the supernetwork expands and the collective intelligence of the community develops. In this paper, a bottom-up approach is attempted to unravel this evolutionary process.

In previous studies on coordinating exploration-exploitation activities, much attention has been paid on network structures while the roles played by actors' strategic behavior have been largely ignored. In this paper, the authors extend March's simulation model on parallel problem solving by adding structurally equivalent imitation. In this way, one can examine how the interaction of network structure with agent behavior affects the knowledge process and finally influence group performance. This simulation experiment suggests that under the condition of regular network, the classical trade-off between exploration and exploitation will appear in the case of the preferentially attached network when agents adopt structure equivalence imitation. The whole organization implicitly would be divided into independent sub-groups that converge on different performance level and lead the organization to a lower performance level. The authors also explored the performance in the mixed organization and the management implication.

Wikis are quickly emerging as a new corporate medium for communication and collaboration. They allow dispersed groups of collaborators to asynchronously engage in persistent conversations, the result of which is stored on a common server as a single, shared truth. To gauge the enterprise value of wikis, the authors draw on Media Choice Theories (MCTs) as an evaluation framework. MCTs reveal core capabilities of communication media and their fit with the communication task. Based on the evaluation, the authors argue that wikis are equivalent or superior to existing asynchronous communication media in key characteristics. Additionally argued is the notion that wiki technology challenges some of the held beliefs of existing media choice theories, as wikis introduce media characteristics not previously envisioned. The authors thus predict a promising future for wiki use in enterprises.

Recently, information is being used to enhance supporting technologies in conference management systems, which greatly improves the efficiency of conference organizing affairs and promotes extensive communication and cooperation between researchers. The on-line conferencing ba (OLCB) serves as a conference management system and provides an environment for knowledge creation. CorMap analysis is a technique for qualitative meta-synthesis, which can carry out series mining from qualitative data. The early OLCB system pushes the visualized results of CorMap analysis to users by images. In this paper, the authors introduce an interactive CorMap analysis to enhance the OLCB system, which enables users to conduct the conference mining process directly and acquire more clear and structured information. The working process of interactive CorMap analysis is shown with the application of the 7th International Workshop on Meta-synthesis and Complex Systems (MCS'2007).

Section 4
Applications

Chapter 16

Gu Jifa, Chinese Academy of Sciences, China
Song Wuqi, Dalian University of Technology, China
Zhu Zhengxiang, Dalian University of Technology, China
Gao Rui, China Academy of Chinese Medical Sciences, China
Liu Yijun, Chinese Academy of Sciences, China

Expert mining is an emergent theory and technique that is useful for collecting the ideas, experiences, knowledge and wisdom from experts. Thus, in this paper, the authors have applied expert mining to solve problems related to social system and knowledge systems pertaining to specific types of information. TCM (Traditional Chinese Medicine) masters accumulated useful knowledge in medicine from ancient China paying close attention to collecting and maintaining the ideas, experiences, knowledge and wisdom from famous elder masters in TCM. In collecting this information, a large project was conducted from 100 famous elder masters in TCM supported by the Ministry of Science and Technology of China, State Administration of Traditional Chinese Medicine. Due to the enormity of this project, subprojects have been established using advanced IT technology, Artificial Intelligence, Knowledge Science and Systems Science to analyze and express these masters' experiences and theories. One of the subprojects uses expert mining and other techniques to analyze both individual and group ideas and knowledge. This paper will describe results and future planning in how this subproject will be conducted while introducing methods and tools used for expert mining.

Chapter 17

Ching-Chieh Kiu, Multimedia University, Malaysia
Lai-Yung Yuen, The Hong Kong Polytechnic University, China
Eric Tsui, The Hong Kong Polytechnic University, China

E-Government emerges from web sites that offer static information, documents and forms for employees and citizens, enquiries, and process automations to many types of stakeholders. Increasingly, different layers of government services are being consolidated into a knowledge portal, providing on time and online services. Such knowledge portals not only provide a platform for integrating applications and information from all government sources, but also provide platforms for knowledge sharing and learning to the public with the objective to improve the efficiency and the quality of E-Government processes and services. However, due to the heterogeneity of applications and information across different levels of government agencies, a significant amount of work is needed to re-configure such applications and services into a new platform. However, semantics are often deficient, which results in problems establishing effective knowledge sharing and learning in E-Government. This paper confers how knowledge intensive portals can be used for enhancing sharing and learning in E-Government. The authors discuss innovative information on how the Semantic Web and Web 2.0 technologies can be applied in providing interoperability to leverage knowledge sharing and learning activities.

Chapter 18
Mike Brownsword, Atego, UK
Rossitza Setchi, Cardiff University, UK

Taking pragmatic, systems engineering approach, this paper identifies a number of fundamental issues that presently arise in risk management, primarily as a result of the overly complex approach conventionally taken in process definition and a lack of coherence within the current risk management vocabulary. The aim of the paper is to enable a fundamental simplification of the risk management process and an improved understanding of the associated terminology. The outcome of this work is a formalised but pragmatic approach to risk management resulting in the development of a conceptual framework and an associated ontology, which emphasises the understanding of people and their environment as part of risk management. The approach has been validated in a number of case studies of varying depth and breadth from the IT domain, defence, rail industry, and education, covering health and safety, business, project and individual needs.

Chapter 19
Gang Xie, Chinese Academy of Sciences, China
Wuyi Yue, Konan University, Japan
Shouyang Wang, Chinese Academy of Sciences, China

From the perspective of risk response in petroleum project investment, the authors use a group decision-making (GDM) approach based on a variable precision rough set (VPRS) model for risk knowledge discovery, where experts were invited to identify risk indices and evaluate risk exposure (RE) of individual projects. First, the approach of VPRS-based GDM is introduced. Next, while considering multiple risks in petroleum project investment, the authors use multi-objective programming to obtain the optimal selection of project portfolio with minimum RE, where the significance of risk indices is assigned to each of corresponding multi-objective functions as a weight. Then, a numerical example on a Chinese petroleum company's investments in overseas projects is presented to illustrate the proposed approach, and some important issues are analyzed. Finally, conclusions are drawn and some topics for future work are suggested.

Chapter 20
Hongli Ju, Japan Advanced Institute of Science and Technology, Japan
Yoshiteru Nakamori, Japan Advanced Institute of Science and Technology, Japan

This paper proposes a Kansei modeling technique by using the Rough-sets Theory based on a set of evaluation data for Kutani-ware coffee cups. Kutani-ware is a famous traditional craft that is a very important traditional industry in Japan. However, it has been shrinking recently because of the changes in lifestyle or the appearance of more functional modern products. To reactivate this industry by developing and recommending products that attract people's feelings, this study develops a modeling technique for identifying relations between design and feeling by obtaining some if-and-then rules. An important contribution of the paper is that the proposed technique can suggest new designs by analyzing customers' Kansei requirements, which are not used in the evaluation experiment. This makes the recommendation successful by determining people's Kansei into data instead of attempts.

Chapter 21
Lei Wang, Kyoto University, Japan
Yajie Tian, Kyoto University, Japan
Tetsuo Sawaragi, Kyoto University, Japan
Yukio Horiguchi, Kyoto University, Japan

A critical problem in robotic manufacturing is that the task of teaching robotics is rather time-consuming. This has become a serious problem in the present age of cost reduction. Collaboration with a company in the field has revealed that the root cause of this problem is that there is not a common knowledge base in this domain, which can serve as shared and reused knowledge. In robotic manufacturing, the skills and experiences of skilled workers are a form of tacit knowledge that is difficult to be acquired and transferred to other workers and robots. This paper proposes a knowledge-based system for sharing and reusing tacit knowledge in the robotic assembly domain. In this system, a modified EBL (Explanation-based Learning) method is proposed to generalize tacit knowledge from specific robotic programs made by skilled workers. A newly operational criterion is proposed for the generalized tacit knowledge, which demands that it should be expressed understandably by human workers and be reusable by robots to generate programs automatically.

Preface

Background

It gives me a great pleasure and honour to introduce the first book in the Advances in Knowledge and Systems Science series published by IGI Global. This is an unique book of its kind devoted to explore the different aspects of knowledge and systems science from a multi-dimension perspective.

Looking back, our knowledge in every field of human activities has been ever exploding as well as fragmented since the industrial revolution. These encompass almost every field we know today from natural, physical, bio-medical, cognitive, information, and management, to social and philosophical sciences. Whereas on one hand we see the intensification and specialization of many subject areas which were unheard of before, on the other hand, there is also a significant parallel development in the cross-diffusion and synthesis of many domains of knowledge which sounds seemingly unrelated, but bears high resemblance in their methodologies or even ontologies. It is under such historical background where Systems Science evolves. Starting with the study of open system of Bertalanffy in the 70s, the living systems of Axelrod and Kauffman in the 90s as the nature unfolds to us, to the more recent study of complex social systems of Stacey and Snowden through a better understanding of the human interactions.

The Birth of Knowledge and Systems Science

Since the establishment of the Santa Fe Institute from a group of top scientists from Los Alamos National Laboratory in the 80s devoted to the study of complex adaptive systems, it has attracted scientists everywhere from the world, and created a new kind of scientific research community, which emphasizes multi-disciplinary collaboration in pursuit of understanding the common themes that arise in natural, artificial, and social systems. Paralleling with this development is the rapid advancements in information and communication technologies, the branch of computer science called Artificial Intelligence, AI (from the study of machine intelligence in the early years to the study of intelligent agents and systems) has found applications in many technology in autonomous vehicle, aviation, medical diagnosis, advanced user interface, and scientific classification and its application in experts systems of numerous knowledge domains. The study of AI and expert systems has also branched out and spun off into many sub-studies of knowledge representation and knowledge engineering, and knowledge science, which deals with the scientific aspects of how knowledge are represented (ontology and semantics), acquired, communicated, and learnt from different perspectives of the researchers. The modern approach in the study of AI and knowledge science has moved from formal logic and deductive reasoning to complex decision making, communication, and learning behavior in human systems.

It is based on these development that we find there is a common ground emerging from these two disciplines and a great opportunity to bring scientists from the systems science and knowledge scientist together to discuss, debate, and learn from one another on how these know-how and development can be used to synthesize in the design of advanced decision support systems and knowledge systems, and to adopt the latest findings in various applications such as ontology based learning system, medicine and healthcare, financial and risk management, et cetera.

From Wikipedia, the free encyclopedia, Systems Science is an **interdisciplinary** field of science that studies **complex systems** in nature, **society**, and **science**, and covers **formal sciences** fields like **complex systems, cybernetics, dynamical systems theory**, and **systems theory**. It is of interest to note that there is no formal entry of what is knowledge science yet, the nearest of which is knowledge engineering and epistemology. The former has a tradition of building knowledge-based systems through software engineering approach, and the latter has two thousand years of history in philosophical discourse on what knowledge is, how knowledge is acquired, and how we know what we know. Nevertheless, a lot of classical debates on the nature of knowledge has something in common with the modern Knowledge Engineering (KE), which also tries to explore how human reasoning and logic work. The overlapping areas of KE and epistemology thus constitute the legitimate study of this young knowledge science. The intimate connectedness of these two disciplines is best dealt with by the systems approach, and hence the idea of the need to bundle knowledge and systems science as the 21st century epistemology, with a parallel development in neurotronics (combining cognitive science with electronic computing) and social informatics (combining the study of social systems with information sciences). The potential for cross-diffusion, applications, and challenges ahead is huge!

The Content of Knowledge and Systems Science

The above interwoven view on the development of knowledge and systems science is reflected in the content of this book. The articles in this book is a collection of most recent papers published in the *International Journal of Knowledge and Systems Science*. These are grouped into four sections. The first part is devoted to theory and model of knowledge and systems science, the second part deals with knowledge management, the third part on various knowledge technologies and the last part on specific applications. The arrangement is as below.

Theory

Y. Nakamori and A.P. Wierzbicki introduce the system approach for the study of knowledge creation from both the social, scientific, and creative dimension so as to collapse the wall between hard and soft in systems science, and to integrate the above three fields in the establishment of a new academic system. They plead for the education of a new generation of young talents as knowledge coordinators who can act as an intermediary agents in managing technology and innovation. Such emphasis on both knowledge and social is futher explored by L. Edvinsson, one of the pioneers of the intellectual capital movement. His paper is non-traditional but one that takes us through a journey to navigate what Intellectual Capital is and its significance to the knowledge enterprises and nations. He calls for a new dimension of Systems Science, that is, the Intellectual Capital (IC) Science, for the re-organization of enterprises as well as mind, as embodied now in the experimental projects on Future Centres in Europe. To Edvinsson, the cultivation of IC stands for derived insights about the most important value for our Future.

The recognition from Edvinsson that our traditional educational system does not seem to give enough cultivation of our brains is echoed in Ton Jörg's review article on advocating a new theory of learning for the creation of new knowledge and new value. He points out that an adequate theory of learning embedding the role of communicative human interaction is still very much lacking, as much of our thinking is still captive of the Newtonian paradigm, with a strong reductionist view of reality. There is a need to develop a new theory about complex, generative learning for the creation and management of knowledge in learning organizations, to foster their self-generative, self-sustaining capabilities for growth and development. The complex relationship between epistemology, ontology, and methodology in knowledge science as pointed out by Jörg is elaborated further by Z. Król, Knowledge Science and Systems Thinking which are comparatively young scientific disciplines are the "equivalent" of philosophy and epistemology that are more than 2000 years, is limited by nominalism in the philosophy of language. Without any conscious person (not necessarily a human), there is no knowledge at all. In his article, some consequences of the application of a non-nominalistic philosophy of language to the definition and classification of knowledge and tacit knowledge, and effective transfer and sharing of tacit knowledge are discussed. He urges the need for a professional collaboration between knowledge science, knowledge management, and philosophy in its next stage of development.

Knowledge Management

The discussion on the future role of knowledge management is grouped around the second part of this book. If a simple distinction is to be made between Knowledge Science (KS), Knowledge Engineering (KE), and Knowledge Management (KM), the difference is that KS deals with knowledge representation and interpretation, KE which deals with extraction, classification, storage and retrieval of unstructured information embedded in various sources and format, and KM which deals with organizational knowledge creation, development and assessment. These three areas are not independent of one another. For example the building of a taxonomy for classifying and retrieving useful information invokes a good working knowledge of ontology and semantics (KS). For the systems to be successfully designed and built, one needs to be aware of the strategic needs of the organization and the human factors involved (KM). Although the importance of Knowledge Management to create an organization's competitive advantage has been widely recognized, there are different views as to what is the essence of KM to make this into a reputable discipline as distinct from information management. David Griffiths addresses the dissatisfaction of both academics and practitioners in the area of Knowledge Management and the common weaknesses in existing thinking about KM. A new model of knowledge management is proposed. On the other hand, Jean-Louis Ermine raised the risk of massive knowledge loss problem as a result of the global aging population. Such a "knowledge crash" should be included in the general framework of any knowledge management program to be implemented. In order to retain knowledge, the importance of inter-organizational knowledge transfer is emphasized by Hepu Deng who presents a conceptual framework for the effective management of knowledge in an organization, and the development of a transformation model between data, information and knowledge.

Knowledge Technology and Applications

In the subsequent part addressing on knowledge technology, J. Gu throws light on the on the research direction of knowledge science and management by showing how a meta-synthesis knowledge system based on the meta-synthesis system approach and knowledge science can be developed for solving problems related to the open, complex and giant systems. Essential feature of the system is that it combines human brain and computer (man-machine), synthesize opinions from experts (group knowledge), the left brain and right brain (quantitative and qualitative analysis), the reality and virtual reality (reality and virtual), and the reduction and holism (analysis and synthesis). It is well known to information scientists that ontology and semantics are the cornerstones in building knowledge systems. The state of art of the ontology mapping methods is addressed by Tatyana Ivanova, and in this section a semantic model to match knowledge descriptions in diverse language based on semantic technologies is introduced by Weisen Guo and Steven B. Kraines.

The rapid advances in Internet and Communication Technology (ICT) over the last decades does not only change the speed at which business are run, but also has profound effect on the way how information is shared and how knowledge is generated in on-line and virtual communities. Social Network and its analysis play an important role in understanding the interactions and social dynamics of these communities, The network modeling of on-line community such as the open source software community as a supernetwork is analyzed by Haoxiang Xia, whereas the effect of network structure on knowledge process and group performance are tracked by Hua Zhang and Younim Xi. Wiki technology and on-line conference are widely used nowadays to enhance communication and collaboration. The adoption of Wiki is evaluated by Christian Wagner et al. based on Media Choices Theories and come up with new insights in running an enterprise, whereas the use of a qualitative modeling and visualization tool to achieve the Web-based human-machine interaction in on-line conferencing among researchers is described by Bin Luo and Xijin Tang in details.

The last part of the book deals with the applications of various knowledge tools and methods. These include expert mining of Traditional Chinese Medicine (TCM) by Gu Jifa et al., use of semantics in government portal services by C.C. Kui et al., systems engineering approach to risk management by Mike Brownsword, group decision-making for risk response in petroleum investment by Gang Xie, modeling technique for identifying relations between design and feeling by analyzing customer requirements by Hongli Ju and J. Nakamori, and sharing and reusing tacit knowledge in robotic manufacturing by Lei Wang et al.

W.B. Lee
Hong Kong Polytechnic University, Hong Kong

Acknowledgment

I would like to thank the authors for their contributions to share their insights and thoughts in this book series. I hope this volume continues to be a source of valuable information for academics and practitioners to develop the disciplinarily of knowledge and systems science as well as to inspire their research.

W.B. Lee
Hong Kong Polytechnic University, Hong Kong

Section 1
Theory and Model

Chapter 1
Systems Approach to Knowledge Synthesis

Yoshiteru Nakamori
Japan Advanced Institute of Science and Technology, Japan

Andrzej P. Wierzbicki
National Institute of Telecommunications, Poland

ABSTRACT

This article presents a systems approach to knowledge synthesis or construction, starting with a new systems thinking named the informed systems thinking, which should serve as the basic tool of knowledge integration and support creativity. Based on this new systems thinking, a new systems approach to knowledge synthesis or construction has been developed as a systems methodology that consists of three fundamental parts: how to collect and synthesize knowledge, how to use our abilities in collecting knowledge, and how to justify the synthesized knowledge. This article first describes the informed systems thinking and then introduces a new systems approach to knowledge synthesis and the features of this new approach from a viewpoint of knowledge creation.

INTRODUCTION

An important concept in the theory of organizational knowledge creation (Nonaka, 1991, 1994; Nonaka & Takeuchi, 1995) is 'Ba' which is a Japanese word meaning 'place'. Nonaka uses it as 'creative environment'; actually Nonaka (Nonaka & Konno, 1998; Nonaka et al., 2000) called the dynamic context which is shared and

redefined in the knowledge creation process 'Ba' which does not refer just to a physical space, but includes virtual spaces based on the Internet, for instance, and more mental spaces which involve sharing experiences and ideas. They stated that knowledge is not something which can exist independently; it can only exist in a form embedded in 'Ba', which acts as a context that is constantly shared by people.

Similar ideas exist in systems theory: for instance, Churchman (1970) states that *all knowl-*

DOI: 10.4018/978-1-4666-1782-7.ch001

edge is dependent on boundary judgments. This article follows this idea in such a way that our theory chooses three important dimensions (or subsystems) from the high-dimensional *Creative Space* (Wierzbicki & Nakamori, 2006) and require actors to work well in each dimension (or subsystem) in collecting and organizing distributed, tacit knowledge. These are *Intelligence* (a subsystem or a scientific dimension), *Involvement* (a subsystem or a social dimension) and *Imagination* (a subsystem or a creative dimension). When the theory is interpreted from a viewpoint of sociology, the *Creative Space* is considered as *Social Structure* which constrains and enables human action, and consists of *a scientific-actual front*, *a social-relational front* and *a cognitive-mental front* corresponding respectively to the three dimensions or subsystems.

Our theory introduces two more dimensions or subsystems: *Intervention* and *Integration*, which correspond to 'social action' and 'knowledge' from a sociological point of view. This article follows the definition of 'systemic intervention' in Midgley (2000, 2004) that *systemic intervention is purposeful action by an agent to create change in relation to reflection upon boundaries*. Our actors collect knowledge on all three structural dimensions or fronts, with a certain purpose, and synthesize those distributed knowledge to construct new knowledge. In this sense, the subsystem *Intervention* together with *Integration* corresponds to Midgley's 'systemic intervention'. As Wang Yang-Ming the 14th-century Confucianist contends that *knowledge and action are one, for purpose, and with consequences* (Zhu, 2000).

The theory to be presented in this article aims at integrating 'systematic approach' and 'systemic (holistic) thinking'; the former is mainly used in the dimensions or subsystems *Intelligence*, *Involvement* and *Imagination*, and the latter is required in the dimensions or subsystems *Intervention* and *Integration*. Leading systems thinkers today often emphasize 'holistic thinking' (Jackson, 2003; Mulej, 2007), or 'meta-synthesis' (Gu &

Tang, 2005). They recommend and require 'systems thinking' for a holistic understanding of the emergent characteristic of a complex system, and for creating a new systemic knowledge about a difficult problem confronted. Our theory aims at synthesizing objective knowledge and subjective knowledge, which inevitably requires intuitive, holistic integration.

With a similar idea, Wierzbicki, et al. (2006) proposed an informed, creative systemic approach, named *Informed Systems Thinking*, which should serve as the basic tool of knowledge integration and should support creativity. This systems thinking emphasizes three basic principles: *the principle of cultural sovereignty*, *the principle of informed responsibility*, and *the principle of systemic integration*. If the first is a thesis, then the second is an antithesis and the third is a synthesis. The problem here is: how are we to fulfill a systemic integration in the context of knowledge synthesis? One of the answers to this is *Theory of Knowledge Construction Systems*, the topic of this article, which consists of three fundamental parts: *a knowledge construction system* (Nakamori, 2000, 2003), *a structure-agency-action paradigm* (Nakamori & Zhu, 2004), and *evolutionally constructive objectivism* (Wierzbicki & Nakamori, 2007). The main features of this theory are *fusion of the purposiveness paradigm and purposefulness paradigm, interaction of explicit knowledge and tacit knowledge*, and *requisition for knowledge coordinators*.

The article is organized as follows: First, our basic systems approach is introduced briefly, which is called *Informed Systems Thinking*. Then a summary of the theory of knowledge construction systems is given. Second, the main model for knowledge synthesis, called *i*-System, is introduced, with a special emphasis on the types of integration: specialized, interdisciplinary and intercultural. Third, a sociological interpretation of the *i*-System is presented, which refers to the ability of actors in collecting and synthesizing knowledge. Fourth, a new episteme to justify collected and synthesized knowledge is explained, which is important in evaluating actions in collecting knowledge as well as knowledge synthesized or constructed. Fifth, we propose a new systems theory for knowledge construction, which is based on the above three factors: system (or model), agency (or ability), and episteme (or justification). Finally, concluding remarks are given, which emphasizes the importance of knowledge science to nurture knowledge coordinators.

Summary of a New Systems Approach

Wierzbicki et al. (2006) proposed to redefine systems science as the discipline concerned with methods for the *intercultural* and *interdisciplinary* integration of knowledge, including soft intersubjective and hard objective approaches, *open* and, above all, *informed*. *Intercultural* means an explicit accounting for and analysis of national, regional, even disciplinary cultures, means trying to overcome the incommensurability of cultural perspectives by explicit debate of the different concepts and metaphors used by diverse cultures. *Interdisciplinary* approach has been a defining feature of systems analysis since Comte (1844), but has been gradually lost in the division between soft and hard approaches. *Open* means pluralist, as stressed by soft systems approaches, not excluding by design any cultural or disciplinary perspectives (Linstone, 1984; Jackson & Key, 1984; Flood & Jackson, 1991). *Informed* means pluralist as stressed by hard systems approaches, not excluding any perspectives by ignorance or by disciplinary paradigmatic belief, and is most difficult to achieve.

A basic novel understanding related to this approach is the essential extension of the skeleton of science (Boulding, 1956). Wierzbicki, et al. (2006) named this approach *Informed Systems Thinking* which consists of three principles:

- *The principle of cultural sovereignty*: We can treat all separate levels of systemic complexity as independent cultures, and generalize the old basic cultural anthropology: no culture shall be judged when using concepts from a different culture.

- *The principle of informed responsibility*: No culture is justified in creating a cultural separation of its own area; it is the responsibility of each culture to inform other cultures about its own development and be informed about development of other cultures.

- *The principle of systemic integration*: Whenever needed, knowledge from diverse cultures and disciplines might be synthesized by systemic methods, be they soft or hard, without a prior prejudice against any of them, following the principle of open and informed systemic integration.

It is, however, quite difficult to perform the principle of systemic integration unless we have theories or methods for knowledge construction. We summarize here *the theory of knowledge construction systems*, the main proposal of this article, which consists of three fundamental parts:

- *The knowledge construction system*: A basic system of the theory called the *i*-System to collect and organize a variety of knowledge, which itself is a systems methodology (Nakamori, 2000, 2003).

- *The structure-agency-action paradigm*: A sociological interpretation of the *i*-System to emphasize the necessary abilities of actors when collecting and organizing knowledge (Nakamori & Zhu, 2004).

- *The evolutionally constructive objectivism*: A new episteme to create knowledge and justify collected, organized, and created knowledge (Wierzbicki & Nakamori, 2007).

The main features of this theory are *fusion of the purposiveness paradigm and purposefulness paradigm, interaction of explicit knowledge and tacit knowledge*, and *requisition for knowledge coordinators*. The detail explanation of these features will be given later. Here we just give a brief summary. With the *i*-System we always start with searching and defining the problem following to the purposiveness paradigm. Since the *i*-System is a spiral-type knowledge construction model, in the second turn we use the *i*-System to find solutions following the purposefulness paradigm. However, it is almost always the case that when we find an approximate solution we face new problems.

This article accepts the idea of Nonaka and Takeuchi (1995) that *new knowledge can be obtained by the interaction between the explicit knowledge and the tacit knowledge*. The use of the *i*-System means that we have to inevitably treat the objective knowledge such as scientific theories, available technologies, social-economical trends, etc. as well as the subjective knowledge such as experience, technical skill, hidden assumptions, paradigms, etc. The theory requires people who accomplish the knowledge synthesis. Such persons need to have the abilities of knowledge workers in wide-ranging areas and of innovators. However they cannot achieve satisfactory results unless they possess the ability to coordinate the opinions and values of diverse knowledge and people. We should establish an educational system to train human resources who will promote knowledge synthesis in a systemic manner.

Collecting and Synthesizing Knowledge

A knowledge construction system called the *i*-System was proposed in Nakamori (2000, 2003), which is a systemic and processual approach to knowledge creation. The five ontological elements or subsystems of the *i*-System are *Intervention* (the will to solve problems), *Intelligence* (existing scientific knowledge), *Involvement* (social moti-

vation), *Imagination* (other aspects of creativity), and *Integration* (systemic knowledge), and they might correspond actually to five diverse dimensions of *Creative Space*.

These five ontological elements were originally interpreted as nodes, as illustrated in Figure 1. Because the *i*-System is intended as a synthesis of systemic approaches, *Integration* is, in a sense, its final dimension (in Figure 1 all arrows converge to *Integration* interpreted as a node; links without arrows denote the possibility of impact in both directions). The beginning node is *Intervention*, where problems or issues perceived by the individual or the group motivate their further inquiry and the entire creative process. The node *Intelligence* corresponds to various types of knowledge, the node *Involvement* represents social aspects, and the creative aspects are represented mostly in the node *Imagination*.

Intelligence and Involvement

Observe that the node *Intelligence*, together with all existing scientific knowledge, corresponds roughly to the basic epistemological dimension (with three levels: *Emotive Knowledge - Intuitive Knowledge - Rational Knowledge*) of *Creative Space*. The node *Involvement* stresses the social motivation and corresponds roughly to the basic social dimension (with three levels: *Individual - Group - Humanity Heritage*) of *Creative Space*. It is not only necessary to distinguish between the knowledge on the level of *individual, group* and *humanity heritage*; it is also important to distinguish motivation related to the interests of individual, group and humanity. While an organization operating in the commercial market rightly stresses the interests of the group of people employed by it (or of its shareholders), educational research activity at universities might be best promoted when stressing the individual interests of students and young researchers; on the other hand, the interests of humanity must be protected

Figure 1. The i-System (from a systems scientific viewpoint)

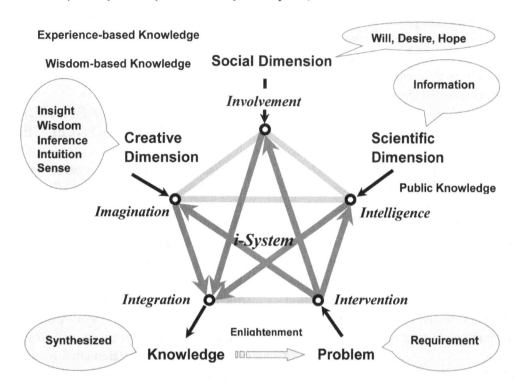

when facing the prospect of privatization of basic knowledge.

Imagination

Other nodes presented in Figure 1 indicate the need to consider other dimensions of *Creative Space*, and additional dimensions result in additional complexity. The node *Imagination* seems to be an essential element of only individual intuition; but it could include inter-subjective emotions and intuition. All creative processes can be related to three levels of imagination: *Routine - Diversity - Fantasy*. We utilize imagination in diverse degrees depending on the character of a creative process. The lowest level is *Routine* that involves imagination, but in a standard, well-trained fashion. We are able to use imagination more strongly, to involve an element of *Diversity*, but we must be motivated to do this by professional pride, pure

curiosity, monetary rewards, etc. Finally, we have also the highest level of imagination, which might be called *Fantasy*. The 20th Century tradition of not speaking about metaphysics (started by Wittgenstein, 1922) relegated *Fantasy* to the arts and the emotions. However, *Fantasy* is an essential element of any highly creative process, including the construction of technological devices and systems.

Intervention

The node *Intervention* is difficult to consider separately in Oriental philosophy and culture, with their concepts of 'unity of mind and body', and 'unity of man and nature': the will to do something is not considered as a separate phenomenon, it is simply a part of being, and being should be such as not to destroy the unity of man and nature. In a culture seeking consensus and harmony, such an explanation and such principles are sufficient. Western culture pays more attention to the problems related to human intervention and will. The concept of will, of freedom to act and intervene, has been for many centuries and still remains one of the central ideas of Western culture. Concerning any creative activity, it is clear that the role of motivation, of the will to create new ideas, objects of art, technological devices, etc. is a central condition of success. Without *Drive*, *Determination*, *Dedication* no creative process will be completed. By *Drive* we understand here the basic fact that creativity is one of the most fundamental components of self-realization of mankind. *Determination* is the concentrated Nietzschean will to overcome obstacles in realizing the creative process. *Dedication* is a conviction that completing a creative process is right in terms of Kantian transcendental moral law.

Integration

Integration in the original *i*-System is a node intended to represent the final stage, the systemic synthesis of the creative process. Thus, in this stage we should use all systemic knowledge; applying systemic concepts to newly created knowledge is certainly the only explicit, rational knowledge tool that can be used in order to achieve integration. Thus, any teaching of creative abilities must include a strong component of systems science. The apparently simplest is *Specialized Integration*, when the task consists of integrating several elements of knowledge in some specialized field. But even this task can be very difficult as, for example, the task of integrating knowledge about the diverse functions of contemporary computer networks. It becomes more complex when its character is *Interdisciplinary*, as in the case of the analysis of environmental policy models. However, the contemporary trends of globalization result today in new, even more complex challenges related to *Intercultural Integration*, as in the case of integration of diverse theories of

knowledge and technology creation. In fact, the *Intercultural Integration* of knowledge might be considered a defining feature of a new interpretation of systems science.

UTILIZING ACTORS' ABILITIES IN COLLECTING KNOWLEDGE

The structure-agency-action paradigm was adopted when understanding the *i*-System from a social science viewpoint (Nakamori & Zhu, 2004). The *i*-System can be interpreted as a structurationist model for knowledge management. Viewed through the *i*-System, knowledge is constructed by actors, who are constrained and enabled by structures that consist of *a scientific-actual*, *a cognitive-mental* and *a social-relational front*, mobilize and realize the agency of themselves and of others that can be differentiated as *Intelligence*, *Imagination* and *Involvement* clusters, engage in rational-inertial, postrational-projective and arational-evaluative actions in pursuing sectional interests. Note that here we identify the elements *Intelligence*, *Imagination* and *Involvement* with agencies of actors (see Figure 2).

The *i*-System differentiates human agency into *Intelligence*, *Imagination* and *Involvement* clusters, so that agency can be understood in an organized way, not treated as a black-box. By *Intelligence* we mean the intellectual faculty and capability of actors: experience, technical skill, functional expertise, etc. The vocabulary related to intelligence addresses logic, rationality, objectivity, observation, monitoring and reflexivity. The accumulation and application of intelligence are mission-led and rational-focused (Chia, 2004), discipline- and paradigm-bound, confined within the boundary of 'normal science' (Kuhn 1962), which leads to 'knowing the game' and incremental, component improvement (Tushman & Anderson, 1986).

Seeing *Intelligence* as inertial and paradigm-bound though, the *i*-System does not regard

Figure 2. A sociological interpretation of the i-System.

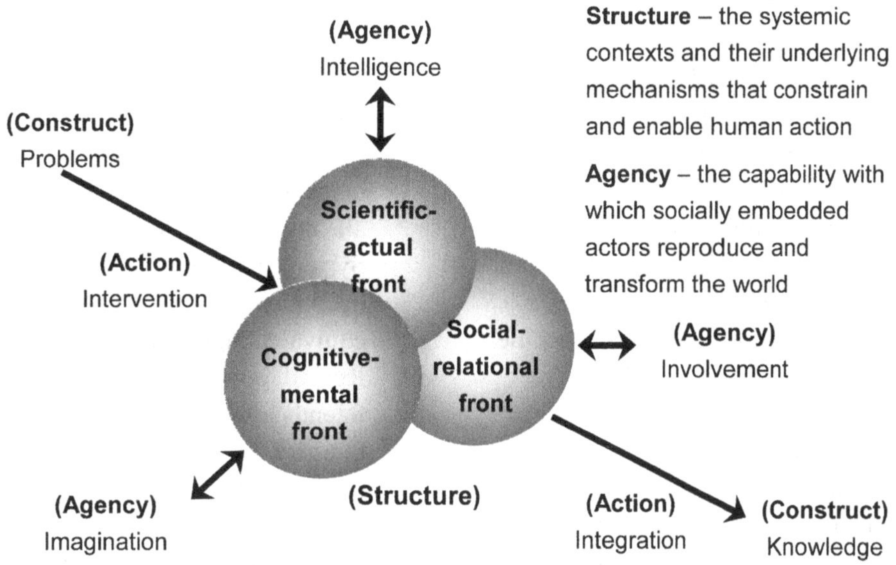

Intelligence as negative per se. Rather, to the *i*-System, *Intelligence* is indispensable for creativity. As Polanyi (1958) puts it, 'science is operated by the skill of the scientist and it is through the exercise of this skill that he shapes his scientific knowledge'. Following Sewell (1992), we see the search for intelligence as a process of 'transposition': actors apply and extend codified rules and procedures 'to a wide and not fully predictable range of cases outside the context in which they are initially learned'. *Intelligence* becomes liability to innovation only when it blocks actors from seeing alternatives.

In the *Imagination* cluster we include intuition, innocence, ignorance, enlightenmental skill and post-rationality, which leads to a vocabulary of 'feeling the game', playful, fun, chaotic, illogic, forgetting, upsetting, competency-destroying, knowledge-obsoleting and risk-taking. This brings us beyond the 'thoroughly-knowledgeable' (Archer, 1995) and 'over-rationalized' agents (Mestrovic, 1998) that are portrayed in Giddens's structuration theory (Giddens, 1979). We turn to the naturalist Taoism, the transcendental Zen Buddhism and the pragmatic Confucianism.

Zhuang Zi the Taoist sage famously proclaims 'Great knowledge is like a child's ignorance'. He distinguishes three kinds of knowledge: pre-rationality (child's knowledge, or 'primary ignorance'), rationality (adult's knowledge, i.e., 'great artifice', which denotes established theories, concepts, categories, 'normal science' and associated findings), and post-rationality (absence of knowledge, or 'true knowledge', i.e., the knowledge of the 'True-man').

Involvement is the cluster in human agency that consists of interest, faith, emotion and passion, which are intrinsically related to intentionality and 'habits of the heart' (Bellah, et al., 1985), as well as the social capital (Bourdieu, 1985), social skill and political skill (Garud, et al., 2002) that make intentionality and 'the heart' being felt. As human agency, involvement can produce managerial and institutional effects, particularly in dealing with the *social-relational front*, in that it helps or hampers researchers' efforts to 'make the game'.

Note that even if the actors work well using their agencies, this does not guarantee the validity of the obtained knowledge. We need 'a theory for knowledge justification', which will be given later by the name of *Evolutionary Constructive Objectivism*.

Nakamori and Zhu (2004) unpacked the structure, agency and action black boxes, discussing their internal complexity as well as that implicated in the relationships between them. For this, they drew from, in addition to Western social theories as well as Taoism and Buddhism, the realist Cheng-Zhu and the idealist Lu-Wang schools of neo-Confucianism (see Zhu, 1998, 1999, 2000). Their key propositions are summarized in the following:

- Both knowledge-as-construct (the realist Confucianism) and knowing-in-practice (the idealist Confucianism) are indispensable for knowledge construction. Knowledge, stabilized in structure and agency at focal empirical moments, provides actors material, intellectual as well as social capacities and contexts to conduct social action, whereas knowing as that action transforms knowledge, for the better or the worse, which is embodied 'back' into structure and agency, over time.

- *Construction* is meant to be practical, temporal and relational. As Wang Yang-Ming the 14th-century Confucianist contends that *knowledge and action are one, for purpose, and with consequences* (Zhu, 2000). Knowledge is not 'created' if creation means, as it does in popular 'knowledge creation' models, well-ordered, linearly progressive, interest-free, politically neutral and intellectually beyond dispute. Rather, knowledge is better seen as always and constantly ambiguous, contextual, provisional, contestable, negotiated, agreed upon, informing, constituting and legitimating.

- The *i*-System brings 'the heart' back in knowledge agendas, rather than shies away from it or takes it for granted. While knowledge enhances material well-being and spiritual sophistication, at least for some on the globe, it also grants humans awesome power to do all the ugly things to Nature and among human ourselves. Are knowledge, technology and innovation necessarily a good thing? How and who to manage it for good, good for Nature and all, not just the few? These are, to the *i*-System, legitimate and relevant questions in 'knowledge management' that is not equivalent to knowledge commodification.

- Rooted in systems science, the *i*-System intends to be integrative in spirit. A system to us is a set of components connected such that properties emerging from which cannot be found in components. *Yin* and *yang* never melt down into a 'synthesis', the lost of opposites means death. Hence, integration is about openness, tolerance, interdisciplinary and intercultural, is an interactive and reciprocal process of perspective-making and -taking (Boland & Tenkasi, 1995) and -sharing and -enriching, not of programming heterogeneity into homogeneity by the magic hand of 'system experts'.

Justifying Collected and Synthesized Knowledge

There is a general agreement that we are living in times of an informational revolution which leads to a new era. Knowledge in this era plays an even more important role than just information, thus the new epoch might be called *Knowledge Civilization Era*. Among many changes, the most important one might be the changing *episteme* - the way of constructing and justifying knowledge, characteristic for a given era and culture (Foucault, 1972).

The destruction of the industrial episteme and the construction of a new one started with relativism of Einstein, indeterminism of Heisenberg, with the concept of feedback and that of deterministic chaos, of order emerging out of chaos, complexity theories, finally with the emergence principle. The destruction of the industrial era episteme resulted in divergent developments of the episteme of three cultural spheres: hard and natural sciences, technology, and social sciences with humanities:

- *Paradigmatism* in hard and natural sciences (Kuhn, 1962): Theories should fit to observations or outcomes of empirical tests, but such theories that are consistent with the paradigm are welcome, while theories that contradict the paradigm are rejected, even if they would better fit observations or empirical outcomes.
- *Falsificationism* in technology (Popper, 1934, 1972): Knowledge and theories evolve and the measure of their evolutionary fitness is the number of attempted falsification tests they have successfully passed.
- *Postmodern subjectivism* in social sciences and humanities: Knowledge is constructed by people, thus subjective, and its justification occurs only through inter-subjective discourse.

The episteme of knowledge civilization era is not formed yet, but it must include integration, a synthesis of the divergent episteme of these three cultural spheres, as well as a synthesis of different aspects of Oriental and Western episteme. The integration must be based upon a holistic understanding of human nature; here humanity is defined not only by language and communicating, but also by tool making, and by curiosity.

This article considers *Evolutionary Constructive Objectivism* as a possible episteme in the knowledge-based society, and adopts it as one of the elements of the theory of knowledge construction systems. It is originally considered for testing knowledge creation theories (Wierzbicki & Nakamori, 2007), consisting of three principles:

- *Evolutionary falsification principle*: Hypotheses, theories, models and tools develop evolutionarily, and the measure of their evolutionary fitness is the number of either attempted falsification tests that they have successfully passed, or of critical discussion tests leading to an inter-subjective agreement about their validity, which corresponds to the *group tacit knowledge* in Nonaka theory.
- *Emergence principle*: New properties of a system emerge with increased levels of complexity, and these properties are qualitatively different than and irreducible to the properties of its parts.
- *Multimedia principle*: Language is just an approximate code to describe a much more complex reality, visual and preverbal information in general is much more powerful and relates to intuitive knowledge and reasoning; the future records of the intellectual heritage of humanity will have a multi-media character, thus stimulating creativity.

Although these principles were developed with the purpose of validating knowledge creation models such as the *i*-System, this article reuses them as principles to test the obtained knowledge. Because it usually takes time to evaluate new knowledge, the idea here is to evaluate the models, methods or processes through which the new knowledge emerges. Figure 3 shows the concept of justification of knowledge through evaluation of models, tools, etc. for obtaining that knowledge as well as through evaluation of attitudes and agencies of actors or analysts in collecting that knowledge.

Based on these three fundamental principles, we can give a detailed description of an epistemological position of *constructive evolutionary objectivism*, closer in fact to the current episteme of technology than to that of hard sciences.

- The innate curiosity of people about other people and Nature results in their constructing hypotheses about reality, thus

Figure 3. Justification of knowledge through evaluation of tools to get it.

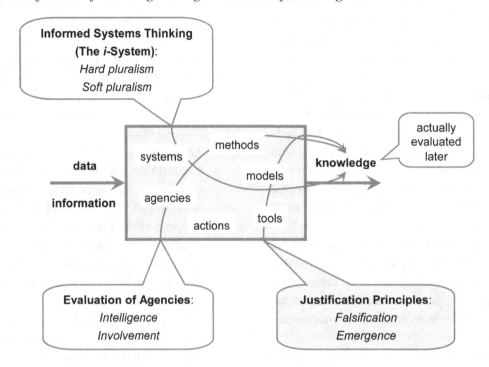

creating a structure and diverse models of the world. Until now, all such hypotheses turned out to be only approximations; but we learn evolutionarily about their validity by following the *falsification principle*.

- Since we perceive reality as more and more complex, and thus devise concepts on higher and higher levels of complexity according to the *emergence principle*, we shall probably always work with approximate hypotheses.
- According to the *multimedia principle*, language is a simplified code used to describe a much more complex reality, while human senses (starting with vision) enable people to perceive the more complex aspects of reality. This more comprehensive perception of reality is the basis of human intuition; for example, tool making is always based on intuition and a more comprehensive perception of reality than just language.

- A prescriptive interpretation of objectivity is the *falsification principle*; when faced cognitively with increasing complexity, we apply the *emergence principle*. The sources of our cognitive power are related to the *multimedia principle*.

Features of the Approach

As explained above the theory of knowledge construction systems consists of three fundamental elements: (1) The knowledge construction system (the *i*-System), (2) The structure-agency-action paradigm, and (3) The evolutionarily constructive objectivism. The main features of this theory are:

- Fusion of the purposiveness paradigm and purposefulness paradigm,
- Interaction of explicit knowledge and tacit knowledge, and
- Requisition for knowledge coordinators.

With the *i*-System we always start with searching and defining the problem following the purposiveness paradigm. Since the *i*-System is a spiral-type knowledge construction model, in the second turn we use the *i*-System to find solutions following the purposefulness paradigm. However, it is almost always the case that when we find just an approximate solution we face new problems. By introducing a viewpoint of knowledge construction, the *i*-System enables us to have purposiveness and purposefulness paradigms simultaneously:

1. We start any problem solving with a desire to collect some knowledge. Let us denote this knowledge by *A*.
2. The first use of the *i*-System is to investigate what kind of knowledge actually available. Actors usually obtain integrated knowledge, which might consist of explicit intellectual assets, implicit or tacit knowledge among people, and knowledge that actors already have. Denote this integrated knowledge by *B*.
3. Almost always there is a difference between *A* and *B*. There must be knowledge that actors cannot obtain despite their best endeavor. This pursuit is a trade-off with limited time.
4. Actors have to create new knowledge *C* to fill in the gap between *A* and *B*. The *i*-System cannot have *C* in advance. The creation of *C* is the work of actors who are embedded in the *i*-System. If the creation of *C* is difficult, actors have to restart searching it with the *i*-System.

This article accepts the idea of Nonaka and Takeuchi (1995) that the new knowledge can be obtained by the interaction between explicit knowledge and tacit knowledge. The use of the *i*-System means that we have to inevitably treat objective knowledge such as scientific theories, available technologies, social-economical trends, etc. as well as subjective knowledge such as experience, technical skill, hidden assumptions and paradigms, etc., and most importantly we have to integrate them for a certain purpose.

The theory requires people who accomplish the knowledge synthesis. Such persons need to have the abilities of knowledge workers in wide-ranging areas. However, they cannot achieve satisfactory results unless they possess the ability to coordinate the opinions of people and diverse knowledge. We should establish an education system to train human resources who will promote the knowledge synthesis in a systemic manner.

CONCLUSION

This article proposes a theory of knowledge construction systems, which consists of three fundamental parts: the knowledge construction system, the structure-agency-action paradigm, and evolutionarily constructive objectivism. The first is a model of collecting and synthesizing knowledge, the second relates to necessary abilities when collecting knowledge in individual domains, and the third comprises a set of principles to justify collected and synthesized knowledge. This article reached a conclusion that we should nurture talented people called the knowledge coordinators. How can we nurture such people? One of the answers is that we should establish knowledge science, educate young students by this discipline, and encourage learning by doing.

However, at the present stage, knowledge science is more a theme-oriented interdisciplinary academic field than a 'normal science'. We believe that its mission is to organize and process human-dependent information and to feed it back to society with added value. Its central guideline is the creation of new value (knowledge)—such innovation being the driving force of society, but it mainly deals with the research area involving social innovation (organizations, systems, or reorganization of the mind). However, society's progress is underpinned by technology and the joint progress of society (needs) and technology (seeds) is essential, so it also bears the duty to act as a coordinator (intermediary) in extensive technological and social innovations.

In order to fulfill the above mission, knowledge science should focus its research on observing and modeling the actual process of carrying out the mission as well as developing methods to carry out the mission. The methods can be developed mainly through the existing three fields. These are the application of information technology/artistic methods (knowledge discovery methods, ways to support creation, knowledge engineering, cognitive science, etc.), the application of business science/organizational theories (practical uses of tacit knowledge, management of technology, innovation theory, etc.) and the application of mathematical science/systems theory (systems thinking, the emergence principle, epistemology, etc.).

However, it will take some time to integrate the above three fields and establish a new academic system. We should first attempt their integration in practical use (problem-solving projects), accumulate actual results and then to establish them as a discipline in a new field. Finally we believe that the concepts and directions of knowledge science will collapse the wall between hard and soft in systems science.

REFERENCES

Archer, M. S. (1995). *Realist social theory: The morphogenetic approach*. Cambridge, UK: University of Cambridge Press.

Bellah, R. N., Madsen, R., Sullivan, M. M., Swidler, A., & Tipton, S. M. (Eds.). (1985). *Habits of the heart*. Berkeley, CA: University of California Press.

Boland, R. J., & Tenkasi, R. V. (1995). Perspective making and perspective taking in communities of knowing. *Organization Science, 6*, 350–372. doi:10.1287/orsc.6.4.350

Boulding, K. (1956). General systems theory: The skeleton of science. *Management Science, 2*, 197–208. doi:10.1287/mnsc.2.3.197

Bourdieu, P. (1985). The forms of capital. In J.G. Richardson (Ed.), *Handbook of theory and research for the sociology of dducation* (pp. 241-258). New York: Greenwood.

Chia, R. (2004). Strategy-as-practice: Reflections on the research agenda. *European Management Review, 1*, 29–34. doi:10.1057/palgrave.emr.1500012

Churchman, C. W. (1970). Operations research as a profession. *Management Science, 17*, 37–53.

Comte, A. (1844). *A general view of positivism*. London: Reeves and Turner.

Flood, R. L., & Jackson, M. C. (1991). *Creative problem solving: Total systems intervention*. New York: John Wiley & Sons.

Foucault, M. (1972). *The order of things: An archeology of human sciences*. New York: Routledge.

Garud, R., Jain, S., & Kumaraswamy, A. (2002). Institutional entrepreneurship in the sponsorship of common technological standards: The case of Sun Microsystems and Java. *Academy of Management Review, 45*(1), 196–214. doi:10.2307/3069292

Giddens, A. (1979). *Central problems in social theory: Action, structure and contradiction in social analysis*. London: Macmilian.

Gu, J. F., & Tang, X. J. (2005). Meta-synthesis approach to complex system modeling. *European Journal of Operational Research, 166*(3), 597–614. doi:10.1016/j.ejor.2004.03.036

Jackson, M. C. (2003). *Systems thinking: Creative holism for managers*. Chichester, UK: John Wiley & Sons.

Jackson, M. C., & Keys, P. (1984). Towards a system of systems methodologies. *The Journal of the Operational Research Society, 35*, 473–486.

Kuhn, T. S. (1962). *The structure of scientific revolutions*. Chicago: Chicago University Press.

Linstone, H. A. (1984). *Multiple perspectives for decision making*. Amsterdam, The Netherlands: North-Holland.

Mestrovic, S. G. (1998). *Anthony giddens: The last modernist*. London: Routledge.

Midgley, G. (2000). *Systems intervention: Philosophy, methodology and practice*. New York: Kluwer/Plenum.

Midgley, G. (2004). Systems thinking for the 21st century. *International Journal of Knowledge and Systems Science, 1*(1), 63–69.

Mulej, M. (2007). Systems theory - a world view and/or a methodology aimed at requisite holism/realism of human's thinking, decisions and action. *Systems Research and Behavioral Science, 24*(3), 347–357. doi:10.1002/sres.810

Nakamori, Y. (2000, September 25-27). Knowledge management system toward sustainable society. In *Proceedings of the 1st International Symposium on Knowledge and System Sciences,* Ishikawa, Japan (pp. 57-64).

Nakamori, Y. (2003). Systems methodology and mathematical models for knowledge management. *Journal of Systems Science and Systems Engineering, 12*(1), 49–72. doi:10.1007/s11518-006-0120-z

Nakamori, Y., & Zhu, Z. C. (2004). Exploring a sociologist understanding for the i-System. *International Journal of Knowledge and Systems Science, 1*(1), 1–8.

Nonaka, I. (1991). The knowledge-creating company. *Harvard Business Review, 69*(6), 96–104.

Nonaka, I. (1994). A dynamic theory of organizational knowledge creation. *Organization Science, 1*, 14–37. doi:10.1287/orsc.5.1.14

Nonaka, I., & Konno, N. (1998). The concept of 'Ba': Building a foundation for knowledge creation. *California Management Review, 40*(3), 40–54.

Nonaka, I., & Takeuchi, H. (1995). *The knowledge-creating company: How Japanese companies create the dynamics of innovation*. New York: Oxford University Press.

Nonaka, I., Toyama, R., & Konno, N. (2000). SECI, ba and leadership: A unified model of dynamic knowledge creation. *Long Range Planning, 33*, 5–34. doi:10.1016/S0024-6301(99)00115-6

Polanyi, M. (1958). *Personal knowledge: Towards a post-critical philosophy*. London: Routledge & Kegan Paul.

Popper, K. R. (1934). *Logik der Forschung*. Vienna, Austria: Julius Springer Verlag.

Popper, K. R. (1972). *Objective knowledge*. Oxford: Oxford University Press.

Sewell, W. H. Jr. (1992). A theory of structure: Duality, agency, and transformation. *American Journal of Sociology, 98*(1), 1–29. doi:10.1086/229967

Tushman, M. L., & Anderson, P. (1986). Technological discontinuities and organizational environments. *Administrative Science Quarterly, 31*, 439–465. doi:10.2307/2392832

Wierzbicki, A. P., & Nakamori, Y. (2006). *Creative space: Models of creative processes for the knowledge civilization Age*. Springer-Verlag: Berlin-Hidelberg.

Wierzbicki, A. P., & Nakamori, Y. (2007, July 23-27). *Testing knowledge creation theories*. Paper presented at IFIP-TC7 Conference, Cracow, Poland.

Wierzbicki, A. P., Zhu, Z. C., & Nakamori, Y. (2006). A new role of systems science: informed systems approach. In A. P. Wierzbicki & Y. Nakamori (Eds₊), *Creative space: Models of creative processes for the knowledge civilization Age* (pp. 161-215). Berlin-Heidelberg: Springer-Verlag.

Wittgenstein, L. (1922). *Tractatus logico-philosophicus*. Cambridge, UK: Cambridge University Press.

Zhu, Z. C. (1998). Conscious mind, forgetting mind: Two approaches in multimethodology. *Systemic Practice and Action Research, 11*(6), 669–690. doi:10.1023/A:1022140405046

Zhu, Z. C. (1999). The practice of multimodal approaches, The challenge of cross-cultural communication, and the search for responses. *Human Relations, 52*(5), 579–607.

Zhu, Z. C. (2000). Dealing with a differentiated whole: The philosophy of the WSR approach. *Systemic Practice and Action Research, 13*(1), 21–57. doi:10.1023/A:1009519505326

This work was previously published in the International Journal of Knowledge and Systems Science, Volume 1, Issue 1, edited by W.B. Lee, pp. 1-13 copyright 2010 by IGI Publishing (an imprint of IGI Global).

Chapter 2
Evolution of IC Science and Beyond

Leif Edvinsson
Lund University, Sweden & The Hong Kong Polytechnic University, Hong Kong

ABSTRACT

Today we are bombarded by information and news signals, including health, meteorological, and financial issues. The interpretation of many of these signals will call for a new dimension of Systems Science for enterprises and society, which can be called Intellectual Capital (IC) Science. This article will look into the evolution of IC Science during the past 20 years and emerging signals for its future applications.

INTRODUCTION

We are on the edge to something in the World Economy. But what? Can system science give another holistic understanding? What is the core of the new actuality?

Recently we have seen the problems and failures as signals of emerging new realities. Famous cases from the financial sector are Fannie Mae, Lehman Brothers in the United States, UBS in Switzerland, Royal Bank of Scotland in UK, and many more.

There are also very prominent and interesting positive cases like Microsoft, Google, Skype, and IKEA. Is there a new type of value chain? Perhaps, as stated by late professor Richard Normann, this value chain can be reframed into a new Value Constellation (Normann, 2001) or an inverted value chain as suggested by research from among others E. Ossiansson, Gothenburg University, Sweden.

It is time to both observe the signals and tentative pattern. For this we need to phrase a kind of Quizzics that will help us to see and understand what is happening from several perspectives—a holistic intelligence for better Knowledge Navigation. Knowledge Navigation might be seen as

DOI: 10.4018/978-1-4666-1782-7.ch002

a way to remove the barriers and obstacles in uncovering new opportunity spaces and the many doors around.

The problems we are facing are also calling for another ecological approach to economics, not just harvesting maximum. For the IC we need to go to the epistemological dimensions, meaning that IC stands for *Derived Insights about the most important /Head Value for our Future*. IC can then be differentiated to different types such as Intellectual Capability, Intellectual Capacity, Intellectual Competencies, etc. If knowledge is not just in our heads or an object, but seen as a relationship, we need to discover new ways for navigating into the unknown, especially related to the intangibles, to be able to develop a universe of not value chains but value stars, as stated by late R. Normann.

Will the Knowledge Era be replaced by some other era? Early signs indicate that we are moving into more and more intangible perspectives; therefore, the next era might be called the *Mind Era*, according to Professor Csaba Varga, at the Institute of Strategic Research in Budapest, Hungary (Varga & Ugrin, 2008).

Will there emerge on the national level some new dimensions of knowledge democracy? Emerging research and prototyping is already under way in Hungary, Croatia, UK and many other places. This could be another interesting space for Systems Science, and for societal innovations.

Knowledge Navigation is a complex and compounded challenging issue, especially when the global knowledge flow, like multiple waves at the sea is rolling in on the beach every 24 hour. At Lund University the late professor Stefan Dedijer inspired a starting point for the subject on *Quizzics*—the art and science of questioning. This is a fundamental dimension for both the navigation in the knowledge based economy as well as the future. A good question is triggering the brain to develop new connections or synapses. A good question might be more focused on whom than what, i.e. relationship rather than object.

Intellectual Capital (IC)

The use of images has become part of the pedagogy of Knowledge Leadership. One of the very first images, but still valid, is the tree of knowledge (Figure 1), which illustrates the holistic perspective and ecosystem of Intellectual Capital (IC) as well as its hidden dimensions. In this tree, the fruits are highlighted as assets, based on a flow through the tree of nutrition based on the capabilities of the roots. The soil is the enabling cultural context for continuous renewal and knowledge growth (Edvinsson & Malone, 1997).

However, two major dimensions related to the Knowledge Era can be added—a time line as well as logic. The time line is the present surrounded by the past and the future. The logic is based on, among others, research from Professor Karl-Erik Sveiby, with Human Capital, Organizational Capital and Relational Capital (Sveiby, 1997). IC is then, from a systems science perspective, a larger concept, as well as containing the concept of Intellectual Property (IP) and IP Rights, which are legally packaged and protected intangible assets.

Furthermore, if the perspective is to prepare for the future, then the tree dimensions might be turned upside down, to amplify the strategic perspective shift of this cultivating ecosystem, as illustrated below. This is also closely related to the way the word Intellectual Capital is written in Chinese, where the meaning of capital is close to the meaning of the roots and ground.

This will take us to the Quizzics of understanding different levels of IC, IC of the human being, i.e., Human Capital. Here the deeper understanding of Neuroscience and Brain Research will give further insights. Here we also find the intangibles of values, and thought patterns, with questions around the correlation of wealth and values. On the macro perspectives we are facing the deeper understanding of IC of nations, such as the evolution of Singapore and Finland versus Indonesia and China. But also IC of cities and

Figure 1. The tree of knowledge

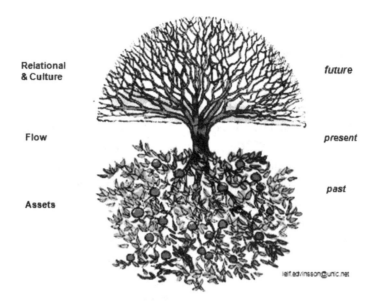

Relational
& Culture

Flow

Assets

future

present

past

leif.edvinsson@unic.net

regions, leading to the Quizzics of what is behind the concept of Knowledge Cities or Knowledge Harbor? Furthermore, we see the pattern of health and economical evolution as so pedagogically visualized by professor Hans Rosling, Karolinska Institute (www.gapminder.org).

IC History

With a longer time perspective it is now 500 years since Amerigo Vespucci drew his discovery map of a new continent, later called America, following the female name tradition. In the same way, globalization discovery has been at the forefront both by China as well as Portugal. The history of studying human intellectual starts from Aristotle and his quest for Phronesis (practical wisdom) and is now being applied in modern context by Professor Nonaka in Japan (Nonaka et al., 2008).

Today, in every corner of the world, there is something going on with a relationship to the Knowledge Era, research, education, consulting, networking, seminars, conferences, projects and enterprises. Much of this started in the 1980s, when the investment in the major economies became more intangible, focused on knowledge investment.

For the intensified flow of knowledge, there is the evolution of internet and media online. It is not only the mobile phones, but now smart phones and mobile media devices. The World Wide Web is still young, but has a great impact on the networking of brains and thoughts.

How will this impact the Knowledge Era dimensions? Will the phenomena of blog and wiki, as a knowledge sharing tool lead to a new level? The well acknowledged professor Dave Snowden, earlier at the IBM Knowledge Management Center, and Cynefin, now on Cognitive Edge sees blogging as a social global knowledge sharing tool, resulting in improved knowledge productivity (see www.cognitive-edge.com).

With a time line and the navigation metaphor, it might be easy to think of Longitude. This is a special dimension, actually a third dimension beyond altitude and latitude to describe position. The unit of measurement is time. Thus, IC is a relative three dimensional position. Could it be that knowledge is of the same character?

IC of Nations

More than ten years ago, I started to look for an enlarged perspective, on how to view Intellectual Capital - IC of nations. If we take a perspective of Future Earnings, i.e. a future outlook and capabilities view, this becomes especially challenging.

Among others, Nick Bontis in Canada followed up on this concept. Later, Carol Lin at TICRC—Taiwan Intellectual Capital Research Centre—and her colleagues alsot started to do interesting research (Lin & Edvinsson, 2008). A benchmark report from 2009 lists the following countries at the top countries regarding Intellectual Capital:

- Finland
- Sweden
- Switzerland
- USA
- Denmark
- Norway
- Singapore
- Netherlands
- Canada

This is leading to many interesting questions. How sustainable is such an IC of Nation position? What kind of knowledge policy is needed? Why are so many on the list from Northern Europe? Is there a reason behind why many of them are rather small scale nations? Why isn't the United States on top? Where is IC of China? What are the emerging IC trends? METI in Japan is also addressing these new national macroeconomic dimensions of IC and intangibles, and as one of the very few countries of the world, arranging annually an Intellectual Asset week.

Recently China has started to address this. This large part of the world has in terms of IC of nations

- Human Capital 1.3 billion or about 20% of world population, and expected 2015 to supply 5 million University graduates an-

nually at the same volume as USA and EU together
- Relational Capital, a growing proportion of world trade, and is now soon the largest exporter in the world, with impact on among others trade flows, currency reserves, investments flows.
- Structural Capital, still in progress, but today with the largest harbors in the world, as well as the nation with the most Internet users in the world, i.e., more than 210 million.

Quizzics still needs to be elaborated by more research. But some emerging patterns indicate that island nations are scoring higher. Why? Furthermore the density of Human Capital as knowledge workers is a critical issue. Why? But even more is the surrounding infrastructure and structural capital. Why? Here systems science can be very instrumental to give cross disciplinary systematized perspectives to increase a kind of IC consciousness and new national attention.

For the further development of more refined Agenda of Knowledge Era Politics a group of knowledge oriented volunteers have gathered in the name of The New Club of Paris (NCP) (www.the-new-club-of-paris.org). The NCP is among others arranging Round Table dialogues on Knowledge Agenda for nations.

A Movement on IC Accounting and Measurement

One of the starting areas for the KM movement was the measurement of Invisible Balance Sheet and the pioneering work of Professor K. E. Sveiby in a project group in Sweden called Conrad Group. This was more than 20 years ago.

In Skandia, I started in 1991 the work on reporting by the famous Skandia IC Navigator (see Figure 2), a kind of visualized complexity of intangibles. The model was then the basis for

Figure 2. Skandia IC Navigator (Source: Edvinsson, 1993)

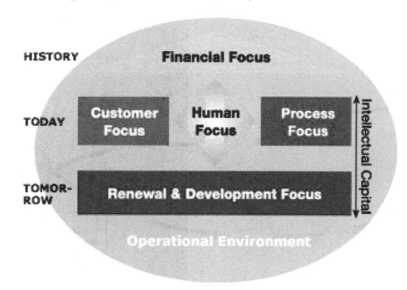

the very first official publication of a corporate IC Annual Report in the world in 1994.

This was then followed by the work on benchmarking IC, and the shaping of a special company for IC rating (see www.icrating.com for a global network and methodology).

The work on IC reporting escalated in many countries in the 1990`s, with among others pioneering work in Denmark. Now this has grown into a world community of measuring Intangibles, Intangible Assets and IC. Some of the early important contributions are around IC efficiency and the work of Nick Bontis, Canada on IC value dynamics, Jan Mouritsen on Knowledge Reporting, Goran Roos on IC index and Ante Pulic on VAIC—Value added IC.

Recent Developments

European countries are currently experiencing a number of new developments.

- RICARDIS—Reporting on Intellectual Capital to Augment Research, Development and Innovation in SMEs—is a European Commission project finished in 2006.

- In March 2008 EFFAS—European Federation of Financial Analysts—officially published the 'Principles for Effective Communication of Intellectual Capital'.
- WICI- World Intellectual Capital Initiative is a consortium of public/private sectors on research and development of IC Accounting and Reporting, with the major accounting firms behind as well as leading IC scholars on IC accounting (see www.worldici.com).
- More specifically and with a practical application approach, the Stock Exchange in Poland is pioneering a kind of IC index for enterprises to be listed on their stock exchange.

Germany also started a now very successful project in 2004 called Wissensbilanz. Made in Germany, under the leadership of BMWA—BundesMinisterium fur Wirtschaft unt Arbeit. It has now evolved to incorporate small as well as large German enterprises, both public and private. It has resulted in open software to download on www.akwissensbilanz.org, today done by more than 20,000 enterprises in Germany.

Figure 3. A process view: Generators and time flow

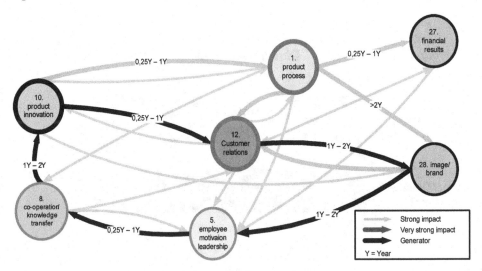

This work is a pioneering work, close to systems science perspectives, as Wissensbilanz is going from reporting of IC as a position to a process view of the non hierarchical interaction and interdependencies between the IC components to shape value. It has a lot of benefits from leadership viewpoint. This systems dynamics approach is also described in articles and research papers, among others, IC or Wissensbilanz Process—some German experiences (Edvinsson & Kivikas, 2007)

As a follow up, another EU project was launched called InCas-Intellectual Capital Statements made in Europe, 2007. It is focused on expanding the learning from the German Wissensbilanz project and expands it to five countries with a target for 50,000 EU SME's to be using InCaS knowledge tools and techniques by the end of the project dissemination phase. In this project is also now a "Wiki", or special InCapedia emerging since Spring 2008, being developed at LSE within the InCaS project. It provides an emerging interactive encyclopaedia about everything to do with Intellectual Capital and Intellectual Capital Statements. See www.incas-europe.org

InCaS is now being followed by another European Commission project called CADIC—Cross

Organizational Assessment and Development of IC, with a strong focus on IC Flows.

In Asia, there is also a lot of progress, especially in Japan with METI—Ministry of Economy, Trade and Industry. South Korea, Malaysia, and China also have progressed on the measurement and reporting of IC, Knowledge Capital. Australia is among others in the forefront based on early input from Professor Karl-Erik Sveiby and Professor Goran Roos. In Hong Kong, the KM Research Center at The Hong Kong Polytechnic University is a dynamic pioneering unit with both KM and IC management development. In Hong Kong also the IPD- Intellectual Property Department at the Hong Kong SAR Government is pioneering a governmental sponsored program on IC Management for SMEs.

Early IC Movements Focusing on Measuring and Metrics

Accounting and measuring has since long been an instrument of and for assessing knowledge, directly or indirectly. The core of this measuring might now be refined to a dynamic navigational dimension, me-assuring, meaning to be on the right track with the right direction and speed.

This is a kind of Longitude Leadership for which systems dynamics can give a lot of more depth and support for the dynamics eco process of value creation (Edvinsson, 2002). The Wissensbilanz work in Germany is a very good start. It can be seen from a great interest by a growing number of enterprises of different size in several European countries as well as in Asia, called InCaS—Intellectual Capital Statements.

In the next phase of IC evolution is the forecasting of IC. This is a kind of mapping the tentative outcomes of IC processes into a landscape format. It is a patented prototyping work in progress in Sweden. See www.tvk.se

IC Eco System of Values

What should be the aim of economic activities? Maximizing resource utilization? Explaining human choices? Mapping future well-being? The economics has now to go from control of numbers to cultivation of relational nanoroots. How can the traditional IC approach based on HC; SC and RC be reframed to a phronesis of today with a deeper understanding of a higher form of capital (Edvinsson & Yu, 2008)?

A deeper and more intangible eco system dimension of the Knowledge Era is presented by culture and values. Is culture and values the soil or context for value creating activities as well as standard of living? What culture or context will then shape future well being and sustainable wealth? What would be a link to systems science on these intangible drivers?

A special and very interesting mapping has been designed and elaborated by Inglehart and Welzel from the World Values Surveys (see www. worldvaluessurvey.com).

What they find is that 70% of cross national differences is described by evolution in the dimensions of traditional/secular values versus survival/self expression values. This might imply a shift from the tangible survival economy to the culture of intangible Knowledge Relational Economy

dimensions. Societies ranked high on self expression is also ranking high on interpersonal trust, tolerance and political moderation. This is said to shape a culture of high individual freedom and with self expression values for participation in environmental protection, tolerance of diversity and rising demand for participation in decision making in economic as well as political life.

It is interesting to note the nations at the top of the ranks, including Sweden, Norway, Denmark, The Netherlands, and Finland, as well as Japan and Hong Kong. It seems to correlate with the earlier mentioned study of IC of nations as well as more common economical wealth statistics. Another interesting observation can be made related to the position for China versus the United States on the map.

If the above map is relevant for nations, could then the same values dimensions be relevant for enterprises? If so, then management and leadership in the Knowledge Era need a more refined management approach to value creation based on culture and values. The traditional economics approach is too narrow.

The difference in values is also what the recent work of Andriessen and van den Boom is looking into, with a special focus on West versus East (2007). In short the Asian perspective is more focused on the relationship dimensions while the West is focused on the object and intellectual property or copyright dimension.

Furthermore it looks from work by Ruut Veenhoven's world database of happiness that happiness has been growing in many of the top listed countries (see http://worlddatabaseofhappiness.eur.nl).

Could this be a signal for a new type of reward system, based on more intangible dimension? Here Neuroscience will navigate us to more understanding around the dopamine, endorphins and serotonin dimensions for the mind satisfaction.

From this follows a lot of different approaches for the Knowledge Navigation, Knowledge Management and Knowledge Leadership. A new

Bottom Line approach will emerge (see more on www.bottomline.se).

For Board of Directors it will require a closer look at the past as well as present culture, but also take culturally oriented leadership actions on these intangible mapping dimensions for a new actuality (Bennet & Bennet, 2007). This has also recently been put forward by the famous U.S. investor Warren Buffett, as well as professor Gordon Redding, INSEAD, France.

The emphasis on wealth generation might move into another Eco system. Perhaps the insights from Scandinavia and parts of Asia might give us insights for our future Systems Navigation and a shift from the orthodox "Economic Man" to *"IC man or Insightful Man"*. This is also in line with the shift from "Theory of the Firm" to the new theory, as touch upon above, the "Theory of the Un-Firm", as illustrated by networked enterprises for example Google or IKEA. This has also been called the "hollow enterprise".

New IC Indicators

The traditional economical tools are too limited to capture the flow of knowledge, the impact of the flow and value creating dimensions over time. Professor Nonaka is pointing to the importance to manage this flow (Nonaka et al., 2008).

For the Knowledge Era with an understating of knowledge as a social process as well as a knowing dimension, Social Network Analyses are becoming more used as a tool. Especially for Science and R& D communities this seem to be a good starting point for understanding knowledge flow as well as getting a base for further investigation and investment.

IC is not a zero sum system, but rather an exponential growth systems, or in simplified terms 1+1=11. This is due to the Relational Capital multiplier effect.

One of the core dimensions for the Knowledge Era seems to be in the Relational Capital. If we are looking upon knowledge as an interactive

issue, and put networking and contactivity into the forefront of knowledge leadership, then new types of relational capital mapping emerge. This is being done now as a kind of Value Networking, by among others Allee (2002). See more on www.valuenetworks.com, as well as research by Professor Z. Wang at Dalian University of Technology in China on Super Networks of People, Content and Knowledge.

In CMM—Center for Molecular Medicine, at Karolinska Institute in Stockholm—network mapping is presented in their Annual IC report. CMM is a world leading research group and community of scientist, ranked as number three in the world in its field. A special structural capital context is shaped for the around 400 in-house scientists, of which around 50% are Ph.D graduates. However it is the networking between the scientists that shape different kinds of productivity, illustrated by Figure 4 (see also www.cmm.ki.se).

Next step is to start to go deeper into this internal perspective and then add the external perspective. Especially as the knowledge flow is done on a global base in more and more virtual networking enterprises and so called Social Networking (Figure 4). Below are also some of the recent global phenomena and IT systems for the global connectivity of knowing (Figure 5). New Creative Commons are emerging as value creating spaces based on creative talented individuals, but in connected systems. They know whom might be of high productivity value for rapid knowing and thereby gives another value dimension of Relational Capital.

This is also a starting to shape another understanding and consciousness of also Knowledge intensive nations, regions as well as cities. The old paradigm was that the city was a place for exchange of goods, and trade. Today it is becoming more and more a place and space for exchange of contacts. This is also referred to as Knowledge Cities. See more on World Capital Institute. In November 2009 there was a second Global Knowledge City Summit organized in Shenzhen

Figure 4. Publications pattern of the CMM research groups, based data produced by Catharina Rehn, Koralinska Institutet Library, www.cmm.ki.se

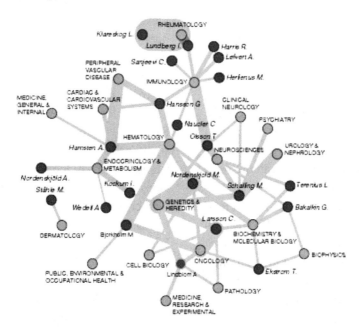

Figure 5. Examples of social media and social networking

(see www.kcsummit.com to address many of these issues).

We can today see the emergence of Intelligent Regions, such as Öresund as the Borderline Zone between Sweden and Denmark, as well as the new Innovation Region between Hong Kong and Shenzhen. Such a space is characterized by Societal Renewal based on social innovation, the future and engagements of volunteers and global digital commons. Special Economic Zones are being upgraded by Knowledge Innovation Zones (see www.inthekzone.com).

In those, a key role is emerging for societal entrepreneurship. It might have started in UK with initiatives from among others the government of Tony Blair, and now the Swedish Governmental Knowledge Foundation has since 2008 a special program on this (see www.kks.se).

A special summer training camp will also be organized during 2010 at the Aalto Innovation University in Helsinki, Finland with a focus on societal entrepreneurship and societal innovations.

For the mapping and understanding of above we need the new indicators. Systems Science will assist in looking for these indicators, including:

- Space of ignorance in relation of knowledge stock
- Market opportunity share versus market share
- Number of open quizzics per day
- Opportunity cost versus transaction costs
- Friction indicators instead of transaction indicators
- Intellectual capital units as the new currency
- Time spent per day on social space
- IDA-identity assets/spaces
- Knowledge Innovation and Future Centers

Knowledge Innovation has become a recent much elaborated concept. It started among others with Dr. Debra Amidon as a concept 1993. It is now a registered trademark of Entovation International Ltd with the following distinction: the creation, exchange and application of new ideas into goods and services, as stated in her book The Innovation Super Highway (Amidon 2003). It has been refined into many dimensions (see www.entovation.com).

In my work in Skandia we also launched 1996 an arena for such Knowledge Innovation, called Skandia Future Center. It became one of the world's first prototyping labs for Organizational Capital. We were focusing the innovation dimensions as an organizational issue. In this work we also collaborated with Dr. Debra Amidon. The critical question became how to build a bridge between brains inside, called Human Capital, and brains outside the enterprise, called Relational Capital. This bridge, as Organizational Capital, was and is the channel for flow of knowledge. So the Organizational Capital Renewal and Innovation dimensions became a very essential eco system perspective.

After us came many more such places, however with different context and aspirations, such as ABB Future Center. Sweden, EON Future Center, Sweden, Minc for Malmö City, Sweden, Mindlab, Denmark, Future Center, Norway, Mobilion/LEF and many more in The Netherlands, Innovation Lab for Royal Mail, UK, Scottish Intangible Asset Centre, UK, Beér Sheva in Israel, Mind Tree in India. Today there are more than 30 such hubs for knowledge innovations and more in progress among others in Asia. One of the most elaborated ones was launched in November 2007 by ABN Amro Bank as a special hub for dialogue, learning, prototyping and incubators (see www.dialogueshouse.nl).

The learning from some 30 or more Future Centers has now been captured in a European Commission funded project called Open Futures, describing the operating systems for such Hubs. The report as a Future Center Recipe book for many of the tools is now available (see www.futurecenters.eu).

Some of the FC design learning is related to among others the following aspects

- In sourcing of outside intelligence
- Experiental Knowledge Exploration
- Dialoguing across disciplines and Generations
- Reduction of fear for collaboration and meeting the Future
- Location, space design and furniture
- Psycho social supportive architecture
- Icons for timeline of past –present-future

Although Future Center (FC) carries the word future, the essence is to bring the attention of the brain (mind) to the present, by stimulating environmental impact with the 5 known senses, that is in the FC context. If we use our brain to project into the future, we cannot escape the influences of "old wiring" in our brain. Through new stimulation in the "now" we can reach another consciousness in our brain. Totally new possibilities do seldom have its roots in the past, rather in brilliant failures. So a FC systems approach differs from the well known scenario planning, which is much more based on projection of past into the future.

An efficient Future Centre actually should give the shocking effect (to frozen the time and thus stop the "logical brain" from working) and try to build new circuits/synapses in the brain (by unlearning), as pseudo-future. It should have a strong effect to remove prejudice, pre-hold assumptions, etc, that the brain is good at. That's how Future Centre should lead to emergence of new intellectual capability. This is then supported by a cross disciplinary new intellectual science! As stated by Professor WB Lee (Lee, 2008) on the article " On the Relationship between Innovation, Intellectual Capital and Organizational Unlearning", knowledge neuronomics (the study of brain activities and rational choices) and knowledge ergonomics (the study of human-environment system to enhance knowledge sharing and building) give us a better understanding on the development of human capital needed for innovation, and would open up a new paradigm of research in Intellectual Capital Science.

Close to this is also the Japanese concept of BA, developed by Professor I. Nonaka. Ba is a special place that bridges the sharing of information and knowledge. Ba means context, circumstances and connections in which knowledge is created, shared, utilized and stored. A Ba is an arena where knowledge becomes "visible". Different types of Ba exist related to the famous SECI model, to originate dialogue, systematize and apply or internalize knowledge. The concept is now used for workplace design in among others Hitachi. Ba is a concept, while Future Center can be seen as a systems science tool to nurture and grew individual, organizational and social innovation capabilities into developing true sustainable IC.

Based on the research from professor I. Nonaka the famous SECI model above (Figure 6) can be related to the various types of area for Knowledge Creation, as done by Y. Yoshimoto. It highlights among others different models for different focus and context. It also relates to Systems Science as both a stretching and evolving growth spiral of insights for the brewing of new ideas and extended knowledge sharing and knowledge flow.

As Noburo Konno write, closely collaborating with professor Nonaka, most enterprises today have designed their offices for administrative work, based on old paradigms and inadequate understanding of knowledge creation (Konno, 2008). Now it is time to look for cognitive design, social knowledge dimensions and knowledge campus models. So we might learn from another type of eco system that is adequate for less for administrative functions and more apt for knowledge innovation. He is also very instrumental in now shaping a special FC network in Japan around Fuji Future Center, Tokyo, during the autumn 2009.

In Hong Kong Science and Technology Park there is now in progress a Special Inno Nest based on the above model, which will open officially in

Figure 6. FCs and other centers in SECI Model

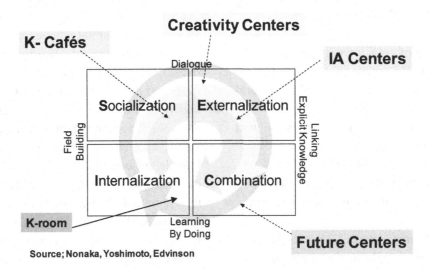

Source; Nonaka, Yoshimoto, Edvinson

January 2010. A global network of Future Center pioneers is in shaping called FCA (Future Center Alliance), as network for bench learning.

Talents and IC Science

Talent is an old unit of measurement. It stands for among others weight. Talents might be a core component. But it is not alone. It operates in context and in collaboration. Therefore a deeper understanding of the ecology becomes important. Perhaps this can be called IC Systems Science.

Our traditional educational system does not seem to give enough of the cultivation of our brains. The implication is that we have a growing space of Capital in Waiting, i.e. untapped potential.

IC Science is a systematic cross disciplinary study of how intellectual resources can be identified, nurtured, shared and utilized for the larger good:

• On individual level; ability to unlearn to find out what we do not know.
• On organizational level; trust building and leverage of collective capacity to reach 1+1=11.

• On societal level; social networking to grow density of talents for quality of life.

This will also highlight the Capital in Waiting as the opportunity space/room as well as the evolving systems perspective for future well being and wealth creation, as the new actuality challenge. Talents will be the connecting unit to enlarge, to co-create the most strategic Intangible Capacity we know.

REFERENCES

Allee, V. (2002). *The future of knowledge: Increasing prosperity through value networks*. Boston: Butterworth-Heinemann.

Amidon, D. (2003). *The innovation superhighway: Harnessing Intellectual Capital for sustainable collaborative advantage*. New York: Butterworth and Heinemann.

Andriessen, D., & van den Boom, M. (2007). East is East, and West is West, and (n)ever its intellectual capital shall meet. *Journal of Intellectual Capital, 8*(4), 641–652. doi:10.1108/14691930710830800

Bennet, A., & Bennet, D. (2007). *Knowledge mobilization in the social sciences and humanities: Moving from research to action.* Frost, WV: MQI Press.

Edvinsson, L. (2002). *Corporate longitude: Navigating the knowledge economy.* Stockholm, Sweden: Bookhouse & Pearson.

Edvinsson, L., & Kivikas, M. (2007). IC or Wissensbilanz process: Some German experiences. *Journal of Intellectual Capital, 8*(3), 376-385. Edvinsson, L., & Yu, A. (2008, December 11-12). *Some Intellectual Capital (IC) perspectives from a Chinese point of view.* Paper presented at the 4th Asia-Pacific International Conference on Knowledge Management (KMAP 2008), Guangzhou, China.

Edvinsson, L., & Malone, M. A. (1997). *Intellectual Capital: Realizing your company's true value by finding its hidden brain power.* New York: Harper.

Konno, N. (2008, October). Knowledge workplace: Knowledge management and office design. *Happy Workplace.* Retrieved October 2008, from http://www.happyworkplace.jp/en/

Lee, W. B. (2008). On the relationship between innovation, Intellectual Capital and Organizational Unlearning. In G. Ahonen (Ed.), *Inspired by knowledge organizations: Essays in honour of Professor K Sveiby on his 60 Birthdy.* The Swedish School of Management, Helsinki, Finland.Lin, Y. Y., & Edvinsson, L. (2008). National intellectual capital: Comparison of the Nordic Countries. *Journal of Intellectual Capital, 9*(4), 525-545.

Nonaka, I., Toyama, R., Hirata, T., & Kohlbacher, F. (2008). *Managing flow: A process theory of the knowledge-based firm.* Basingstoke, UK: Palgrave Macmillan.

Normann, R. (2001). *Reframing business: When the map changes the landscape.* Chichester, UK: John Wiley & Sons.

Sveiby, K. E. (1997). *The new organizational wealth: Managing and measuring knowledge-based Assets.* San Francisco: Berrett-Koehler Publishers.

Varga, C., & Ugrin, E. (2008). *New theory of state and democracy.* Budapest, Hungary: Institute for Strategic Research.

This work was previously published in the International Journal of Knowledge and Systems Science, Volume 1, Issue 1, edited by W.B. Lee, pp.14-26 copyright 2010 by IGI Publishing (an imprint of IGI Global).

Chapter 3

A Theory of Learning for the Creation and Management of Knowledge in Learning Communities and Organizations

Ton Jörg
University of Utrecht, The Netherlands

ABSTRACT

Social sciences have been in crisis for a long time, partly by being the captive of the Newtonian paradigm, and partly through the effects of this paradigm on practice. This crisis was recognized in the past by the Russian psychologist and philosopher Lev Vygotsky, and continues to this day. The educational crisis is just one instance. It is hard to imagine how to escape this crisis, and a real shift of paradigm is needed. In this article, such a shift toward the paradigm of complexity is advocated. The shift implies a reframing of complexity and a new kind of thinking in complexity. The new paradigm implies the development of a causally generative complexity theory of change and development. Ultimately, the fundamental challenge is to harness the complexity of complex, generative learning in the communities of learners in learning organizations.

DOI: 10.4018/978-1-4666-1782-7.ch003

INTRODUCTION

Social sciences has been in crisis since long, partly by being the captive of what may be called "the blinding paradigms", and partly by the effects of these paradigms on practice. The corresponding dominant view takes a strong reductionist view of reality, which implies an objectivistic, rationalistic stance in viewing and doing science. This crisis in the field of psychology and education was already recognized by the Russian psychologist and philosopher Lev Vygotsky; it is the crisis which is still the crisis of our days. To escape the crisis we are still in, we strongly need a paradigm shift. This, however, is not an easy task, as history has shown us. This view is in line with Kuhnian thinking on the role of paradigms and paradigm shifts in science (Kuhn, 1970). The question, in our case, then, is "what is the very nature of this crisis?" And, linked to that question, what paradigm shift we may speak about? What role may this crisis have for the kind of shift of paradigm needed?

It still seems true what Kuhn remarked about the role and the nature of crisis in the field of science in general and the tools of thought as essential elements of a paradigm: "The significance of crisis is the indication they (the tools of the previous paradigm) provide that an occasion for *retooling* has arrived" (see Kuhn, 1970, p. 76, emphasis added)

So, the first problem is to recognize a crisis, and to get it recognized and 'accepted' as *real* by scholars in the field. To my mind, this has been the essence of the early work of Vygotsky. For him, it was one of the preconditions for a paradigm shift in his field of study to formulate a so-called 'theory of the crisis' (see Vygotsky, 1997, for his work on the crisis in psychology, which was unpublished during his lifetime). By describing and formulating such a theory in the field of education, we may be able to view the crisis as real and take the effects of that crisis seriously. Thus, we may dis-cover new phenomena that we have not yet seen, 'simply' because we were not able to look

for it. Only by taking such a change of perspective, we may become able to start to 'solve' the crisis in psychology and the crisis in education. Of course, this is not an easy job to do. For the crisis never is a given, self-evident crisis for all of the scholars involved in the field of science, as history of science has shown us.

The crisis we speak about, now, is a crisis unrecognized or even denied by many educators in the field of education. This crisis is, in our view, strongly related to what the French pedagogue and philosopher Edgar Morin has called 'the epistemological problem' (Morin, 2001: 39). In Jörg (2009), we have sketched the complex tri-partite relationship between epistemology, ontology, and methodology, and the relationship with a potential new (enlarged) worldview. This relationship is constitutive for the paradigm 'in use' in viewing and doing science. This paradigm is not always beneficial for science and society, as history has shown (see Kuhn, 1970). However, we strongly believe that staying un-reflective of this position of viewing and doing science runs the risk of getting into a state of crisis (see Jörg, 2009). To put it rather boldly, we may refer to Morin, again, who stated that the crisis can be viewed as a *result* of what he has called "blinding paradigms" (Morin, 2001: 21). We want to argue here that they are still operative in the field of learning and education. The consequence of this view and their effects is that education and pedagogy may still show blind spots and myopia (Van der Veer & Valsiner, 1994, p. 5-6). They correspond with the prejudices and habits of thinking noticed by Vygotsky (1997), in his analysis of the crisis in psychology in his days (the twenties of the last century). He tried to formulate an adequate theory of learning and development, as an inherently complex process, stressing the role of the other in the communicative human interaction. Although being very critical about the state of art, he did not fully succeeded in his efforts of building a new science of learning and development. He 'simply' lacked the tools for it!

An adequate theory of learning and the role of the other in this are still very much lacking. Mostly, it is the case that "the 'otherness' of the other, ….., is left *unexplored*" (Akkerman, 2006; emphasis added). We may wonder why this is the case. Once becoming reflective about this situation, we may become more aware that

We exist in relation to others and at the heart of the complex nexus of forces that attract and repel us to and from each other is the need to know that others cannot ignore our existence (Rosenfield, 2000, as cited in Nowotny, 2005, p. 26)

This kind of awareness of the (potential, admitted) role of the other in complex, learning demonstrates, in a way, that education and pedagogy are not innocent, and can "never be innocent" (Bruner, 1996, p. 63).

We agree with Edgar Morin that the fundamental problem of the crisis of our time seems to be that "the crisis worsens as fast as the incapacity to reflect on the crisis increases" (Morin, 2001: 35). The effects of the crisis are persistently overlooked! This brings with it the fundamental 'ethical question'; a question, which can be viewed as related to the new paradigm of complexity, the study of complex systems, and the ethics of our sciences with their ethical consequences (see Mainzer, 2004, pp. 406, 411; cf. Cilliers, 2005, p. 264). The notion of complexity is, therefore, not neutral (see Cilliers, 2005: 256). Edgar Morin is very clear on this point: "complexifying, that is humanizing the sciences" (Morin, 2002, p. 9). Klaus Mainzer (2004, p. 410) shows a similar humanizing view; he argues to consider humans as complex nonlinear entities of mind and body. In his view, the ethical consequences "depend on our knowledge about complex nonlinear dynamics in nature and society." (ibid.: 411) For us, the challenge of such humanizing by complexifying is in making reality richer in all aspects (see also Morin, 1992, p. 383). It may be regarded as a way to overcome the deleterious effects of old habits

of thinking, as effects of blinding paradigms. This shows the possibility of starting new thinking, of new thinking in complexity *for* the social sciences (Jörg, 2009). Doing so, we may become able to recognize the *seemingly* hidden "deprivation of our culture," hidden by the myths we live (Midgley, 2004; cf. Akkerman, 2006). This makes it possible to start with escaping this deprived culture: a culture, which is characteristic of both our science and practice of education. This culture is leading to the detrimental effect of a *trivialization* of the learner as a human being (see von Foerster, 1993). Complexifying may overcome such detrimental effects and lead to a humanizing of the science and practice of education. Consequently, we are able to sketch the significant 'human benefits' for the field of education and all people involved in it, i.e. the benefits for the students in that field, who are strongly dependent on the view of practice and the organization of educational practice in that very field of education, a view which is *not innocent at all*:

The costs of our educational crisis, in terms of alienation, psychological rootlessness, and ignorance of the world and the possibilities of human experience within it, are incalculable and heartbreaking. (Egan, 1997, p. 1)

Complexifying of our viewing and doing science may thus lead to loosing our innocence in this field of education. This is not a neutral position; not at all! We want to argue about complexity and take an assertive position in this; an assertive position which is based on a reflective position. In taking these positions, we reject the view of Cilliers (2005, p. 256) about their opposition, in a rather nuanced, but strong way. Of course, the knowledge of complexity is always provisional (Cilliers, 2005). But this does not prevent to use thinking in complexity for modelling of the performance of the complex dynamics of the subject of study, i.e. of the system to be studied (cf. Mainzer, 2004).

Our ultimate aim of new thinking in complexity is to enter new domains of potentialities for the field of learning and education and to open up new spaces of possibilities for learners (cf. Davis & Sumara, 2006). We want to develop a new theory about complex, generative learning in communicative human interaction within communities of learners, showing their unexpected potentially nonlinear effects over time. By creating a new theory, we may also develop a new language. Doing so, we may "create new realities" (Senge, et al., 2005; cf. Davis, 2004). This is also the real challenge for the creation and management of knowledge in learning organizations, to foster their self-generative, self-sustaining capabilities for growth and development.

A (Very) Short Theory of the Crisis We Are In

Social sciences has been in crisis since long, partly by being both the captives of what Edgar Morin has called 'blinding paradigms' (Morin, 2001), and partly by being the victims of what Elkana (2001) has called 'Enlightenment fundamentalism'. This is a fundamentalism with positivistic, objectivistic, deterministic, individualistic, dualistic, and reductionistic characteristics. All of these characteristics are characteristics of the 'calculable' in the age of Enlightenment (see Starobinski, 2003; cf. Mainzer, 2004). These characteristics can be ascribed to the historical tendency of social science trying to be scientific by copying natural science, i.e. of physics. Such a tendency has been called 'physicalism' in the history of science. This physicalism is not innocent as Mary Midgley has stated in her book on the myths of science we live by: "The Enlightenment notion of physical science was imperialistic from the outset" (Midgley, 2004, p. 23). This notion of science is still dominating social science. Social sciences still seem unable to escape those old ideas, remaining blind for what learning may be, showing a fundamental inability to recognize the complexity of it (see Lakoff,

1987; Van Geert, 1994; Luhmann & Schorr, 2000). Once, we become aware of the crisis we are still in, we may continue our efforts of new thinking in complexity, recognizing as well that "the best time to be working in a science is when it is in a crisis state" (Edelman, 1992, p. 65).

The position to be defended here is that to "really step into a new awareness" (Senge et al., 2005, p. 45), we have to start with recognizing the crisis and become reflective on the very crisis we are in. Only then, we may be able to make an end to the rhetoric in the field of education (see MIT, 2005). It is only through the recognition of the crisis, and its causes, that we may deal with the problems this crisis brings with it. Doing so, it may lead to a very different view of reality. We take the work of Darwin, who liquefied and complexified the notion of reality in his days, as a real source of inspiration. He was clearly able "to escape dear old habits of thoughts" and ways of seeing (Vygotsky, 1997; Dennett, 2003, p. 212; Senge et al., 2005). Darwin's work showed that science itself is not an 'independent variable' (Alvin Toffler, cited in Prigogine & Stengers, 1984, p. xii). He showed that reality can be very different for those viewing and doing science. So, he was able to escape "the deeply engrained orthodoxy about scientific reality" (Davis, 2004, p. 16). In line with this reasoning, Mary Midgley argued that "we need to stop treating 'science' as if it were a single monolithic entity." Midgley (2004, p. 22)

We need a new science, with a new theory of complexity, with a focus on the complex, temporal, spatial and organizational perspective of development of structures and processes (cf. Cilliers, 2005, p. 257; Rescher, 1998, p. 34). For this reason, this science will and must be a science of being through becoming, encompassing the role of time and complexity (see Prigogine & Stengers, 1984, p. 8). We need, therefore, new "tools of thought" to go beyond our trained thinking in terms of linear causality (Prigogine & Stengers, 1984, p. 203), as *a lever to change science*! The new science may lead to an expanding notion of reality: into a more adequate view of real-world complexity. What we need is a kind of reinvention of the reality, habitually 'delivered' by educational scientists. We may take up the challenge of *reinventing* reality of learning and education, by complexification, to 'produce' a *richer* version of reality by new thinking in complexity about real-world complexity (cf. Morin, 2002b, p. 383, emphasis added; cf. Rescher, 1998, pp. 6-7).

The challenge will be to invent a new science, with a new theory of learning and education, by new thinking in complexity, which shows *how* to turn the dynamics of complexity into *effective*, advantageous complexity in the field of learning and education. We may grasp the complexity of real-world complexity by reducing it (Cilliers, 2005; Akkerman, 2006). At the same time, however, we may need complexity of thinking to deal with complexity (see also Nowotny, 2005: 15, for these opposite tendencies). This leads us to a pragmatist view of dealing with complexity, for the sake of understanding and performing the complex dynamics in practice. Ultimately, therefore, we might be able to harness the complexity of this real-world complexity, by a better understanding and managing of the complexities involved in the dynamics of interaction within an ensemble of two learners as a dynamic, cyclical-helical unity (Jörg, 2009). We may discover some hitherto unknown laws of generating effects in and through mutual interaction between learners. All of this may finally lead to a new, *possibility*-oriented, instead of an *ends*-oriented approach in education (Jörg et al., 2007, 2008).

A New Theory

We may start our theorizing by becoming aware that there is no clear notion of a single paradigm operating in the field of education. It seems to be the case that many paradigms are operating in practice without questioning (see Dills & Romiszowski, 1997). It can also be stated that there is not a clear unifying theory on learning in

the field of education. The truth is that we may find more than 50 different theories of learning in the field of educational research (see Atherton, 2005). The presence of so many theories of learning may be interpreted as a kind of diversity we may, or even should, celebrate. But this blunt fact can also be interpreted in a very different way: as *both* demonstrating *and* hiding the complexities of learning. These are the complexities of a reality which are mostly taken for granted (Bak, 1997, p. 1). Consequently, there is neither an adequate definition of complexity, nor a theory of complexity (Nowotny, 2005; Davis & Sumara, 2006). It can be stated that it is through the very lack of critical reflection about the real-world complexity that there still is no clear theory and no clear thinking about practice of education (cf. Jörg, 2009). The view of constructivism as a dominant theory in this field, for instance, does not enable us "to design down to how students learn" (Sergiovanni, 1996, p. 38). The role of theory as theory *for* practice, therefore, is still unclear. In especial this may be the case "when linear theory meets the real world" (Sergiovanni, 1996, p. 159). For example, in the case of linear causality, with its misleading cause-effect logic (see Davis & Sumara, 2006, p. 12; Nowotny, 2005, p. 16). We need to open our eyes to see that "the world of (school) practice is *nonlinear*" (emphasis added). This view implies that the nonlinearity of that very practice may be "a practice which you cannot bring down from theorizing on education in general or theories of learning and of curriculum design in particular" (Jörg, 2003). The unexpected practice may bring with it unexpected processes and effects, which can be nonlinear *in practice*!

So, the question we may formulate now is what reality of practice is about? What kind of possibilities and unexpected potentialities reality may be shown in practice? It seems common practice that one does *not* recognize what real-world complexity of practice really is or can be. That's why the complexity of that practice is too easily taken for granted. This is true for the complexity of learning, and also for "the processes of knowledge formation, which are *not at all well understood*" (Desforges, 2001, p. 33, emphasis added). It seems to be the plain truth that we are leaving these processes without any adequate theory on the design science agenda (Desforges, 2001, p. 31; Maturana, 1978, p. 45). Such a view makes clear why pedagogy, with characteristics like these mentioned above, can 'never be innocent' (Bruner, 1996, p. 21). One may conclude from this kind of reflection about learning and knowledge formation that education seems to be based on common flaws in thinking and fallacies of reasoning. The crisis education is in is the crisis which is unrecognized or simply denied. James Wertsch explained that a situation like this can be the case because of "the 'learned incapacities' and 'disciplinary pathologies' that restrict the horizons of modern academic discourse" (Wertsch, 1998, p. 11).

What we badly need is an adequate theory about the complexity of learning and knowledge formation. This should be a theory which links with practice: with how complexity may 'work' in practice. We may start by theorizing on how learners may actually bootstrap each other in small communities (Bruner, 1996, p. 21) or how learners "collectively are making one another" (Kauffman, 1993, p. 371). These phenomena can be linked with the so-called 'Snowball Phenomenon', conceived as "the spread of ways of talking and ways of thinking across groups of children" (Anderson et al., 2001). This links with the aims for practice, like those for professional development of teachers in professional communities, as formulated by Brian Lord, who speaks about "achieving collective generativity", in terms of 'knowing how to go on' (Lord, 1994, p. 193, referring to Wittgenstein, 1958), as a state of being. This state of being may also be regarded as a state of 'knowingness' (Bohm & Peat, 2000, p. 212), or of 'generativeness' (Senge, 1990, p. 375). These states can be interpreted as states with a kind of *generative power*: the power to

generate creativity, novelty and innovation (see Jörg, 2009). We fully agree with Helga Nowotny that "novelty needs to be read and understood in a societal meaningful way, if it is to be appropriated" (Nowotny, 2005, p. 28). For such understanding we need "a selective reconstruction of complexity" indeed (Nowotny, 2005, p. 28), to be able to harness the very complexity of processes of novelty and innovation. We need not only to understand how complexity may thrive on interaction, but also how generative power thrives on the causal power of the causal forces exerted by the causal dynamics within the complex nexus of causal shaping forces of reciprocal influences in human interaction (see Jörg, 2009).

A Science for the Future

What we need for the building of a real science of education is not only 'a blue skies' research agenda, but also "research which think the unthinkable" (Blunkett, cited in Desforges, 2001:, p. 32). This, we think, is essentially what a shift of paradigm is about. To change paradigm is not an easy job, as history has clearly shown. It is impossible to derive the new paradigm from the old. On the contrary, an essential of a paradigm shift is that the new paradigm is incompatible with the old paradigm (Kuhn, 1970). That makes communication with those adhering to the 'old' paradigm of 'normal' science so difficult (cf. Davis & Sumara, 2006: 42). This is what history has shown to us, as scientists viewing and doing science as 'normal' science (Kuhn, 1970).

It still seems to be the case that for a new science of education we first have "to escape old ideas and habits of thought" (Dennett, 2003, p. 212; cf. Bohm, 2004, p. 44). So, to change the paradigm 'in use', we may need not only a theory of the crisis, of the state of the field as in a state of growing crisis (Kuhn, 1970, p. 66), but also for a better understanding of how to escape the very crisis we are in.

To escape old ways of thinking, and start viewing reality differently, we need to face the complexities of educational practice by "thinking in complexity" (Mainzer, 2004). Consequently we should develop new tools of thought, of thinking beyond dualism, beyond the poverty of reductionism, the destructive of reductionism, of the calculable and the computational (cf. Rose, 1997, p. 272; Bohm, 2004, p. 127; Nowotny, 2005, p. 16; Cilliers, 2005, p. 255). We should try to escape the strong wish of being in control of what happens in practice (see Prigogine & Stengers, 1984, p. 203). The challenge, therefore, is one of fostering a different kind of thinking in education.

A New Paradigm

We possibly may *invent* a new paradigm about complexity for new thinking in complexity. Only then we may be able to reinvent reality of learning and education. A good candidate for such a paradigm is a combination of the complexity and the evolutionary paradigm.

What we need for education is 'a science of being through becoming', with a corresponding generative complexity theory of change, involving the complex, generative transformative processes of growth and development (see Prigogine & Stengers, 1984; Webster & Goodwin, 1996). We may end with a generative science of education, which is similar to the generative biology of Webster and Goodwin (1996), and the generative social science, proposed by Joshua Epstein (2006). The generative complexity theory may be called a trans-disciplinary theory. The generative processes involved may imply complex, so-called states of being in the evolutionary processes of becoming (cf. Luhmann & Schorr, 2000, p. 245).

The generative complexity theory of change implies a need for rethinking social thinking about social interaction (cf. Vallacher & Nowak, 1994; Stacey, 2003). We have to escape the notions of action and reaction, of cause-effect logic, between fixed entities, and take a different view.

We should focus on a new unit of study and its dynamics: the dynamic unity of the ensemble of two persons in their interaction (cf. Granott, 1998; Wozniak, 1996). Stuart Kauffman has also argued for such a theory of the ensemble, of two entities evolving over time (Kauffman, 1993, pp. 426-427, 463-465). We may view this unit or unity of the ensemble as a 'cyclical-helical unity,' with its dynamics of interaction and the changes to be expected in the peers participating in that interaction (Valsiner, 1998, p. 251). The two entities of an ensemble may also be viewed as connected within a causal loop (see Jörg, 2009). Such loops may be connected to more complex, interconnected loop networks (Jörg, 2009; cf. Kauffman, 1993, pp. 426-427). This shows that thinking in complexity is strongly linked to network thinking indeed (Barabási, 2003, p. 238). We may view the effects on the entities in this unity, spiralling to higher level (see Vygotsky, 1978, p. 56). The spiralling dynamics may be described as a process of 'bootstrapping'. Jerome Bruner speaks specifically about learners who may 'bootstrap' each other in small (sub) communities (Bruner, 1996, p. 21). He is clear in his description but leaves explanation of such bootstrapping open to the reader. The same is true for the important work of Gerald Edelman in his description of processes of consciousness, implying a unity (of functioning of the brain as a whole) that embeds complexity (e.g. Edelman, 1992, 2004; Edelman & Tononi, 2000). But Edelman and Tononi are very clear in their stance that we should not keep on being the 'prisoners of description', but become explanatory about the processes involved in (causal) interaction (Edelman & Tononi, 2000, p. 207). For this reason, we believe that a theory of complexity is an *explanatory* theory (see Jörg, 2009; cf. Davis & Sumara, 2006, p. 7, for an opposing view). We agree with Stuart Kauffman that we want theories to be explanatory (Kauffman, 1993: 367). We also agree with Paul Cilliers that the description of the complexity of the subject of study is always a *reduction* of the complexity involved in the study of phenomena in the real world (cf. Cilliers, 2005, p. 258). We fully subscribe Vygotsky's statement that an explanation is causal or not an explanation at all, but only a metaphoric description. But it is a hard job to escape 'descriptionism', and become explanatory in our thinking in complexity. That's why we call it *new* thinking in complexity, within a *new* area of thought and investigation (cf. Kauffman, 1993, p. 367). It needs five fundamental steps of rethinking the basic assumptions in the social sciences, to open up this new area of thought and be able to start new thinking in complexity (see Jörg, 2009).

One of the results of all the rethinking is that if we speak about the complexity, we speak about the causal dynamics of the complexity involved. Next, we think the new thinking is about the new unit, of the ensemble, of coupled entities or systems, and the corresponding ensemble approach (Kauffman, 1993, p. 464). He fully recognizes the importance of the tri-partite relationship between epistemological, ontological and methodological consequences of his ensemble approach (Kauffman, 1993, p. 464). They are decisive for the explanation of the dynamic properties of ensembles, consisting of dynamic entities. This also implies a new style of modelling of the complex dynamics involved. The modelling needed for this process of change and their effects is, therefore, the modelling of the causal dynamics underlying them. The bootstrapping implies that whole persons, and their minds, are involved in the process of communicative human interaction, as functional wholes (Kauffman, 1993, p. 370). Kauffman opens the possibility of 'functional bootstrapping' (1993, p. 373). We may link this process with the creation of knowledge. We think this mutual process of bootstrapping may lead to "a total state of 'knowingness' of the individual", about 'what the individual knows all together' (Bohm & Peat, 2000, p. 212). To enable such a state we need to know how such a state can be generated in our theory of complex, generative learning through interaction. In our view this complex

process of bootstrapping should entail generative mechanisms, to explain the real complexity of bootstrapping. Such generative mechanisms may be regarded as hitherto unknown (Bhaskar, 1986). We should therefore *not* take the real complexity for granted, but take a more solid view of how complexity may 'work' in reality (Bak, 1997). This may imply a rethinking of interaction as a concept. We should have the courage to go beyond the orthodoxy of physicalism with its Newtonian view of action and reaction (Robins, 1999; Bohm & Peat, 2000; Starobinski, 2003; Midgley, 2004). The causal framework of LISREL, developed by Jöreskog & Sörbom in the last century, is a good candidate for this (Jöreskog & Sörbom, 1986, 1993). They describe the causal dynamics in terms of a "(causal) mechanism that generate the observable variables" (Jöreskog & Sörbom, 1986, p. I.1). This causal framework originates from the basic work of the mathematical biologist Sewall Wright, with publications ranging from the twenties to the sixties of the 20th Century (1921, 1934, 1960). This causal framework lends itself to modelling the interaction in terms of causal loops. The original work of Sewall Wright even shows how the coupling of two entities in a causal loop may grow in the real world. This answers a basic question, formulated by Stuart Kauffman: "why a given pair of variables are coupled" (Kauffman, 1993, p. 371). In practice, these are loops with reciprocal influences between the entities (latent variables in the causal framework) and their effects, with processes of potential enhancement of the causal effects 'produced' by these influences (Buckley, 1967; Hayduk, 1986, 1996). These total causal effects over time are called 'self-enhanced loop effects' (Hayduk, 1986, 1996). In 'normal' situations, these effects are linear, but the effects can become non-linear when conditions are met of stronger influences through the creation of stronger reciprocal relationships in practice (cf. Sidorkin, 2002, about creating dyadic learning relations among peers).

Based on this kind of causal modelling of interaction as sketched above, we may describe teaching as the art of bringing about those effects of stronger influences between persons during their reciprocal communicative interaction, as possibly 'explosive possibilities' (Barab & Kirshner, 2002), to be created by the building and encouraging of stronger relationships between the peers involved. We may take the stance of encouraging such learning through creating the conditions for the loops of learning demanded for such effects in educational practice (cf. Nixon et al., 1996, pp. 124-125). This view may encompass creating a kind of complex, generative learning which is central for fostering the learning of a learning school, to enable the prospects of a learning organization and, ultimately, of a learning society: "Unless schools develop the qualities of the learning organization then their capacity to lead the reconstruction of agency and contribute to the learning society will be considerably reduced" (Nixon et al., 1996, pp. 124-125).

The causal model of learners and their interaction, bootstrapping each other in small (sub) communities, enables the possibility to speak about the emergent patterns of causal interaction within the web-like structure of interconnected causal loops (cf. Nowotny, 2005, p. 24). The causal interaction involved has the characteristics of what has been called 'circular causality' (e.g. Minsky, 1988, p. 45; Morin, 1997, p. 2). This description can be broadened to that of an entangled web of circular causality (Nowotny, 2005, p. 24), of interconnected causal loop networks, with nested loops. We may speak, then, about the complex dynamic interaction between the variables which may be involved in the tremendous complexity of mind-to-mind causation (Buller, 2005, p. 452), as a complex, nested network of networks (Jörg, 2009). The causal modelling of bootstrapping each other shows why it can be true, in a real sense, that "two minds are better than one" (Frawley, 1997, p. 89). They can become functional, generative wholes through functional bootstrapping

within the cyclical-helical unit of the ensemble (cf. Kauffman, 1993).

The description of bootstrapping each other in interaction is very much in line with the paradox mentioned by Ralph Stacey, in his book on complexity and group processes: "the paradox of individual minds forming and being formed by the social at the same time" (Stacey, 2003, p. 327). It is also in line with the description of the nature of the processes of knowing and learning, given by Barab and Kirshner (2002), pointing to the dynamic generativity of knowing and learning, which they see as basic for engendering what they call "explosive possibilities" for the learning and knowing. Such dynamic generativity may be viewed as being *both* the cause *and* effect of individualization of each of the learners in time (Sassone, 1996). This very generativity might be the key building stone for the foundation of a complex, fully integrated interactive, communicative, relational, generative pedagogy (see Jörg, 2005). This will be a complex generative pedagogy (CGP), which integrates the notion of 'interactive pedagogy' of Bruner (1996), the 'communicative pedagogy' of Biesta (1995), and the 'relational pedagogy' of Sidorkin (2002). It will be possible, then, to use this integrated complex generative pedagogy for building a community of learners, or community of practice, in their practice of learning in ensembles of persons, with their dynamically evolving relationships, and the network of relationships between the ensembles (Granott, 1998; Sidorkin, 2002). This is a network, which can be characterized as consisting of persons as weavers, being "both the weaver and the pattern it weaves" (Rose, 1997).

In recent work, bootstrapping processes through human (communicative) interaction have been modelled with unexpected, unpredictable effects (Jörg, 2004, 2005, 2009). It may be shown that modelling interaction within a causal framework, taking time into account, may show interaction as a nonlinear process with potential nonlinear effects in time. Doing so, we may overcome the myopic thinking within the causal framework, which promoted itself in the history of social sciences as LInear Structural RELationships, c. q. LISREL-modelling. We should expand the horizon of the causal framework and the use of it in different disciplines. We should, then, be better aware that causal interaction in fields like biology and learning and education is *very different* from causal interaction in physics with fixed entities like masses (see Buller, 2005).

Causal interaction, now, can be taken as a *trans-disciplinary* concept for use in different disciplines, like complexity itself, as a fundamental part of complexity theorizing and thinking in complexity. The dynamics of interaction as nonlinear is similar to the autocatalytic processes we may know from the field of chemistry, biology and neuroscience (e.g. Edelman, 1992, 2004; Kaneko, 2006), showing loops of enhancement and enhancement effects in time.

Taking causal interaction and its causal effects as potentially nonlinear, self-enhanced loop effects opens up a different view on a reality of learning and education, and the building of a new complexity theory in this field. We call this theory a theory about generative complexity as a distinctive mode of complexity (see Rescher, 1998, p. 9). A theory which diverges strongly from traditional ways of thinking, inspired by physicalism: e.g. the degeneration of thinking in terms of end states of education (see Luhmann & Schorr, 2000, p. 246). These authors are very clear on this view: "But the complexity of the process could not be sufficiently ordered by starting at the end." (Luhmann & Schorr, 2000, p. 246) It is a very wrong kind of thinking; a kind of thinking which may imply the what Edgar Morin has described as "the perverted thinking of noble ends in education" (Morin, 2001, p. 72), a thinking based on a rationality which seems "perverted into rationalization" (Morin, 2001, p. 20).

We, now, may strive to a *new* way of social thinking, of thinking in generative complexity processes and their effects in time, replacing the old determinism, by developing it to "the idea of laws of interaction," and "to a diversifying and evolutive view of *determinations*", and potentialities via relations (see Morin, cited in Prigogine & Stengers, 1984, p. xxiii).

The new kind of thinking in complexity and theorizing on the dynamics of complexity "points out that the way things unfold is *inherently unknowable* to the human mind, emerging through spontaneous self-organisation … rather than advanced planning" (Flood, 1999, p. 90, emphasis added). The new complexity paradigm and its related thinking and theorizing implies a complexity which should not be taken for granted, but better be taken as a serious option for the practice of learning and education. Thus, we may link learning and education, and the complexity of reality, with very different options for the reality of learning and education: "… we should be realistic in a complex way, understanding the uncertainty of reality, knowing that the real holds invisible potential" (Morin, 2001, p. 70). This is how, in our view, reality in learning and education could be, and should be expanded into Vygotskian hyperspaces of possibility of learning and development. These spaces are personal spaces in which learning and development takes place; but not only as simple gradual changes. We may think as well of the significance of mental states of being of partners involved in interaction. We may think as well of mental states like 'the passion to learn or to understand', or even of 'a passion for learning and/or understanding' (Kirshner, 2002). These may be or become real states of mind of the peers in their interaction as partners, with their minds engaged in educational practice (cf. Davis et al., 2000).

How Could the New Theory Be Encouraged in Practice?

This is really a hard question to answer, because the answer is linked to a shift of paradigm needed for a real change, and the question "how to bring about such a shift in practice?" We seem confronted here with the old question of why and how paradigm shifts have taken place in the past (cf. Kuhn, 1970). In history we have seen that a growing crisis is needed before the change of paradigm may really happen. This crisis means that we may expect quite a bit of uproar and resistance in the scientific field of learning and education when a new paradigm tries to get a solid position in the field at hand; me may, however, as well see the known phenomenon of simply negating the crisis and the significance of the new paradigm.

To deal with the crisis and overcome the resistance to be expected we may be able to do the next three steps:

1. Developing a 'theory of the crisis', elucidating the crisis we are in, including the potential origin of the crisis;
2. Elucidating the impact of the crisis on the field of education, and on society at large;
3. Showing the new tools of thought of the new paradigm, their unifying power, and their unexpected usefulness for (new) practice in the field of education and society at large.

All of these steps seems necessary to get rid of the effects of 'blinding paradigms' (Morin, 2001). We believe, with Thomas Kuhn, that, probably and possibly at an individual level, the new paradigm "emerges all at once, sometimes in the middle of the night, in the mind of a man deeply in crisis" (Kuhn, 1970, pp. 89-90).

We should, however, be very much aware that you cannot *find* a new science; *you have to invent it*! (see Vygotsky, 1997) Brent Davis has shown how 'inventions of teaching' have taken place in our Western history of education (Davis, 2004). Similarly, we may invent learning and education, again, and teaching as well, for our time and for the future of our society. Similarly, you cannot 'simply' *find* new practice. We agree with Thomas Sergiovanni (1997), that you have to *invent* practice as well. Only then, you can see

how the complex processes involved in learning and education may actually 'work' in the real, and have their effects on learners: "It is not likely that much progress will be made over time in improving schools ….., *unless we begin to invent our own practice*" (Sergiovanni, 1997, p. xiv, emphasis original).

We may also refer to Nixon and their concept of a 'learning school' where the encouraging of learning is central (Nixon et al., 1996). Doing so, we may encourage the learning of peers in their interaction as a potential nonlinear process of 'bootstrapping', fostering the learning of these learners as functional wholes within an ensemble (Kauffman, 1993). We may show how two learners may operate within such an ensemble, in which the learners "*collectively make one another*" (Kauffman, 1993, p. 371, emphasis original). We may discover that the effects of 'functional bootstrapping' each other, leading to explosive possibilities in communities of practice (Barab & Kirshner, 2002). Demonstrating of such effects over time is very important, because it can show the truth that "The only way to learn anything about the future of the system is to perform the dynamics." (Mainzer, 2004, p. 411) This, we may conclude, is the complex dynamics of coupling of two unities within an ensemble: of a complex, dynamic, cyclical-helical unity, with two entities evolving over time into their particular state of evolvability (Kauffman, 1995). It is through the causal dynamics of interaction that the entities involved in this unity can grow into these states trough the enabling effects of generativity, as the power to generate creativity, novelty, and innovation, as the condition for transformation of the learners as functional wholes. Generativity, understood this way, may be considered as both *a state of being* and a state of complex 'knowingness' (Bohm & Peat, 2000, p. 212; cf. Senge, 1990, p. 375, about the heightened experience of 'generativeness' as a creative state, enabled by forces shaping one's life). This rather complex state may also be considered as a *norm* for describing the desired state of development of individual learners in and through interaction (see Sassone, 1996, p. 519). Such a state may be described as a desired state for learners, bootstrapping each other in small communities of learners (cf. Bruner, 1996; Barab & Kirshner, 2002). For education this can be expressed as a norm of *being-for-the-other*, by the possibility of *coupling* of learners in practice. Such a norm transcends the spirit of capitalistic greed in educational practice (Nietzsche, cited in Sassone, 1996, p. 514). This seems also very true for the concept of a learning organization (cf. Senge, 1990; Senge et al., 2005).

Concluding the reasoning above, it seems to be the case that we need a new vocabulary and lexicon of complexity, with a lexical group of concepts like '(causal) reciprocal interaction,' 'interactivity,' 'connectivity,' 'generativity' and 'complexity' itself, with all of its inherent nonlinear dynamics and their potential nonlinear effects in time, like 'bootstrapping', 'multiplier effects', and 'deviation-amplifying effects' as resulting from reciprocal, generative processes of causation in peer-to-peer interaction (see Maruyama, 1963). We may 'simply' expand these notions of reciprocal causation to triadic reciprocal causation (Bandura, 1997, p. 7; Jörg, 2009), or larger web-like structures of causal reciprocal relations (Jörg, 1994, 1998, 2005, 2009). These larger structures, with their hitherto unknown hypercomplexity, can be modelled as so-called hyper-structures of hyper-cycles, with reciprocal causality within reciprocal relations (Jörg, 2009). Such structures and their effects may include so-called 'deviation-amplifying effects' (Maruyama, 1962). These effects can be shown as nonlinear trajectories within hyperspaces as dynamic landscapes of possibilities of the entities involved, like learning human beings (Jörg, 2005, 2009). By the use of all of these concepts, then, we may *really* be able to *re-invent* the description and explanation of common reality of learning and education (Jörg, 2004; cf. Rescher, 1998; Davis, 2004), and show that we may create a new reality; a reality which

can be taken as a language-effected reality (Davis, 2004, p. 99; cf. Rescher, 1998). We fully agree with Davis & Sumara in their theorizing about complexity and education, that "Theories of reality and the vocabularies developed to describe the world are not independent from it" (Davis & Sumara, 2006, p. 34). It may, therefore, be no surprise that Peter Senge has stressed the role of a *language for complexity*, for the creation of a new reality, by the invention of the new practice of the learning organization (Senge, 1990, p. 268; emphasis original). Thus, we must become aware that the new reality may not include our present reality.

If all of the steps mentioned above can be made successfully, a panorama of vista for a new science may emerge for the various scholars in the fields of concern, in especial the field of learning and education. In our view the complexity paradigm, linked with the Darwinian perspective (or evolutionary paradigm), should lead to the overcoming of the myths we live by, with their common rigid metaphors and rhetoric. All of these myths may be viewed as ultimately leading to the 'deprivation of our culture' (Midgley, 2001, p. 179), by the destruction of a (hidden) generative order (Bohm & Peat, 2000, p. 209). These myths, disregarding what is essential for creating possibilities and potentialities, can easily lead to a *perverted system of education*, with its blind focus on ends (see Morin, 2001, p. 72). By leaving behind the myths we live by, we may stand on the shoulders of a genius like Vygotsky, as one of the first thinkers in complexity (see Wertsch, 1996), and become the 'visitors of the future' of a new science of education and educational practice (see Bruner, 1987).

It seems not only wise but also very challenging for the invention of new practice, to show that "The only way to learn anything about the future of the system is to perform the dynamics." (Mainzer, 2004, p. 411) It is the dynamics involved in the system of two learners, coupled in a continuing communicative human interaction, that may show the potential bootstrapping as a mutual process, and the 'bootstrapping effects' as multiplier effects, modeled within the complex, causal framework (Jörg, 2009). This is part of the conceptual innovation and the introduction of a new vocabulary about real-world complexity, needed to describe a possible world which is still rather unknown. In this contribution, we have dis-covered the tools for building a new framework of complexity, as the building stone for a new science of complexity. This is the building stone for building a new possible world of professional communities of learners, from a possibility-oriented approach, opening spaces of possibility and domains of potentialities (Morgan, 1997). Thus, we may finally *dis*-cover what Nicholas Rescher has called 'the realm of possibility' (Rescher, 1998). We take this realm as a realm *for* new practice: that of self-generation of a new generative order (Rescher, 1998, p. 207; cf. Bohm & Peat, 2000). Once we understand how 'complex states of collective generativity and knowingness' can be achieved, *in* and *for* practice, and know the explosive possibilities of interaction within reciprocal relationships for creating novelty and innovation in professional communities of learners, we may become able to harness the real-world complexity involved in creating knowledge within these communities. We may, therefore, conclude that it is the path of (generative) complexity that may lead not only to novelty and innovation, but also to self-potentiating processes, generated by unexplored processes of functional bootstrapping within dynamic unities of interconnected networks of professional learners in organizations. By harnessing the very complexity of complex, generative learning we may open a different future for professional communities of learners and learning organizations.

REFERENCES

Akkerman, S. (2006). *Strangers in dialogue. Academic collaboration across organizational boundaries*. Unpublished doctoral dissertation, University of Utrecht, The Netherlands.

Anderson, R. C., Nguyen-Jahiel, K., McNurlen, B., Archodidou, A., So-young, K., & Reznitskaya, A. (2001). The Snowball Phenomenon: Spread of ways of talking and ways of thinking across groups of children. *Cognition and Instruction, 19*(1), 1–46. doi:10.1207/S1532690XCI1901_1

Atherton, J. S. (2005). *Learning and Teaching, Theories of Learning*. Retrieved January 19, 2005, from http://www.learningandteaching.info/learning/theories.htm

Bak, P. (1997). *How nature works. The science of self-organized criticality*. Oxford, UK: Oxford University Press.

Bandura, A. (1997). *Self-efficacy. The exercise of control*. New York: W. H. Freeman and Company.

Barab, S., & Kirshner, D. (2002). Rethinking methodology in the learning sciences. *Journal of the Learning Sciences, 10*, 5–15. doi:10.1207/S15327809JLS10-1-2_2

Barabási, A.-L. (2003). *Linked. How everything is connected to everything else and what it means for business, science, and everyday life*. New York: Penguin Group.

Biesta, G. (2006). *Beyond Learning. Democratic Education for a Human Future*. Boulder, CO: Paradigm Publishers.

Bohm, D., & Peat, D. (2000). *Science, order & creativity* (2nd ed.). London: Routledge.

Bruner, J. (1987). Foreword. In R. W. Rieber & A. S. Carton (Eds.), *The collected works of L. S. Vygotsky, Vol. 1. Problems of general psychology* (pp. 1-16). New York: Plenum Press.

Bruner, J. (1996). *The Culture of Education.* Cambridge, MA: Harvard University Press.

Buckley, W. (1967). *Sociology and modern systems theory.* Englewood Cliffs, NJ: Prentice-Hall.

Buller, D. J. (2005). *Adapting minds. Evolutionary Psychology and the persistent quest for human nature.* Cambridge, MA: MIT Press.

Cilliers, P. (2005). Complexity, deconstruction and relativism. *Theory, Culture & Society, 22*(5), 255–267. doi:10.1177/0263276405058052

CIRET-centre. (n.d.). Retrieved January 18, 2009, from http://nicol.club.fr/ciret/english/visionen.htm

Cohen (Eds.), *Boston Studies in the philosophy of science, Vol. 200.* Dordrecht, The Netherlands: Kluwer Academic Publishers.

Davis, B. (2004). *Inventions of teaching. A genealogy.* Mahwah, NJ: Lawrence Erlbaum.

Davis, B., & Sumara, D. (2006). *Complexity and education. Inquiries into learning, teaching, and research.* Mahwah, NJ: Lawrence Erlbaum.

Davis, B., Sumara, D., & Luce-Kapler, R. (2000). *Engaging minds. Learning and teaching in a complex world.* Mahwah, NJ: Lawrence Erlbaum.

Dennett, D. C. (2003). *Freedom evolves.* New York: Viking.

Desforges, C. (2001). Educational research and educational practice. 'What does educational research have to offer to education?' In A. Wald & H. Leenders (Eds.), *Wat heeft onderwijsonderzoek het onderwijs te bieden?* Den Haag, The Netherlands: NWO.

Dills, C. R., & Romiszowski, A. J. (Eds.). (1997). *Instructional developmental paradigms.* Englewood Cliffs, NJ: Educational Technology Publications.

Edelman, G. (1992). *Bright Air, Brilliant fire. On the Matter of the Mind.* London: Penguin Books.

Edelman, G. (2004). *Wider than the sky. A revolutionary view of consciousness.* London: Penguin Books.

Edelman, G., & Tononi, G. (2000). *Consciousness. How matter becomes imagination.* London: Penguin Books.

Egan, K. (1997). *The educated mind. How cognitive tools shape our understanding.* Chicago: University of Chicago Press.

Elkana, Y. (2000). Rethinking – not Unthinking – the Enlightenment. In W. Krull (Ed.), *Debates on Issues of Our Common Future.* Weilerswist, Germany: Velbruck Wissenschaft. Retrieved from http://www.ceu.hu/yehuda_rethinking_enlightnment.pdf

Epstein, J. M. (2006). *Generative social science: Studies in agent-based computational modelling.* Princeton, NJ: Princeton University Press.

Flood, R. L. (1999). *Rethinking the Fifth Discipline. Learning within the unknowable.* London: Routledge.

Frawley, W. (1997). *Vygotsky and cognitive science. Language and the unification of the social and computational mind.* Cambridge, MA: Harvard University Press.

Globus, G. (1995). *The postmodern brain.* Amsterdam, The Netherlands: John Benjamins Publishing.

Granott, N. (1998). Unit of Analysis in Transit. From the Individual's Knowledge to the Ensemble Process. *Mind, Culture, and Activity, 5*(1), 42–66. doi:10.1207/s15327884mca0501_4

Guba, E. G., & Lincoln, Y. S. (1985). *Naturalistic Enquiry.* Beverly Hills, CA: Sage.

Hayduk, L. A. (1987). *Structural Equation Modeling with LISREL: Essentials and advances.* Baltimore, MA: John Hopkins University Press.

Hayduk, L. A. (1996). *LISREL issues, debates, and strategies*. Baltimore, MA: John Hopkins University Press.

Jörg, T. (1998). *The development of a complex dynamic causal model for cyclically organized processes of cumulative advantage and disadvantage in education*. Paper presented at the annual meeting of the American Educational Research Association, San Diego, CA.

Jörg, T. (2003). Towards a Complex Generative Pedagogy. A European perspective. In *Proceedings of SIG Chaos and Complexity Theories, AERA Conference*, Chicago. Retrieved from http://ccaerasig.com/papers/03/JorgEuropean.htm

Jörg, T. (2004). A theory of Reciprocal Learning in dyads. *Cognitive Systems, 6-2*(3), 159-170.

Jörg, T. (2004). Complexity Theory and The Reinvention of Reality of Education. In B. Davis, R. Luce-Kapler, & R. Upitis (Eds.), *Proceedings of the Complexity Science and Educational Research Conference* (pp. 121-146). Edmonton, Alberta, Canada: University of Alberta. Retrieved from http://www.complexityandeducation.ca

Jörg, T. (2005). A generative complexity theory of minds evolving in peer interaction. In P. Bourgine, F. Képès, & M. Schoenauer (Eds.), *Towards a science of complex systems*: *Proceedings of the European Complex Systems Society. Abstracts Book* (p. 210). Paris: European Complex Systems Society.

Jörg, T. (2006). Minds in Evolution through Human Interaction. *Cognitive Systems, 6-4*, 363-386.

Jörg, T. (2007a). Visiting the future of learning and education from a complexity perspective. In C. Stary, F. Bacharini, & S. Hawamdeh (Eds.), *Knowledge management: Innovation, technology and cultures* (pp. 227-241). Singapore: World Scientific Publishing Company.

Jörg, T. (2008). *Rethinking the Learning Organization as a complex, generative learning network*. Paper presented at the conference on Small Business Networks, Beijing, China.

Jörg, T. (2009). Thinking in complexity about learning and education – A programmatic view. *Complicity, 6*(1). Retrieved from http://www.complexityandeducation.ualberta.ca/COMPLICITY6/Complicity6_TOC.htm

Jörg, T. (in press). *New thinking in complexity* for *the social sciences and humanities. A generative, trans-disciplinary approach*. New York: Springer.

Jörg, T., Davis, B., & Nickmans, G. (2007b). Towards a new, complexity science of learning and education. *Educational Research Review, 2*(2), 145–156.

Jörg, T., Davis, B., & Nickmans, G. (2008). About the outdated Newtonian paradigm in education and a complexity science of learning: How far are we from a paradigm shift? *Educational Research Review, 3*(1), 77–100. doi:10.1016/j.edurev.2008.02.002

Kaneko, K. (2006). *Life: An introduction to complex systems biology*. Berlin, Germany: Springer.

Kauffman, S. (1993). *The origins of order. Self-organization and selection in evolution*. New York: Oxford University Press.

Kauffman, S. (1995). *At home in the universe*. New York: Oxford University Press.

Kirshner, D. (2002). *Anh Linh's Shapes as an Instance of "Complex Pedagogy", A Historical Perspective*. Paper presented at the Annual Meeting of the AERA, New Orleans, LA.

Koizumi, H. (2001). Trans-disciplinarity. *Neuroendocrinology Letters, 22*, 219–221.

Koneko, K. (2004). *Life as a Complex System*. Paper presented at the First European Conference on Complex Systems, Torino, Italy.

Kuhn, T. S. (1970). *The structure of scientific revolutions* (2nd ed.). Chicago: University of Chicago Press.

Lakoff, G. (1987). *Women, fire, and dangerous things*. Chicago: University of Chicago Press.

Luhmann, N., & Schorr, K.-E. (2000). *Problems of reflection in the system of education*. In European studies in education (Vol. 13). Münster, Germany: Waxmann.

Mainzer, K. (2004). *Thinking in complexity. The computational dynamics of matter, Mind, and mankind*. Berlin, Germany: Springer.

Maruyama, M. (1963). The second cybernetics, deviation amplifying mutual causal Processes. *American Scientist, 51*, 179.

Maturana, H. R. (1978). Biology of language. The epistemology of reality. In G. A.

Midgley, M. (2001). *Science and Poetry*. London: Routledge.

Midgley, M. (2004). *The myths we live by*. London: Routledge.

Miller & E. Lenneberg (Ed.). *Psychology and Biology of Language and Thought. Essays in honor of Eric Lenneberg* (pp. 27-63). New York: Academic Press.

MIT. (2005). *Mission statement*. Retrieved at June 10, 2006, from http://learning.media.mit.edu/mid_mission.html

Morgan, G. (1997). *Images of organization*. Thousand Oaks, CA: Sage.

Morin, E. (1997). *Reformé de pensée, transdisciplinarité, réforme de l'Université*. Retrieved January 15, 2006, from http://nicol.club.fr/ciret/bulletin/b12/b12c1.htm

Morin, E. (2001). *Seven Complex Lessons in Education for the Future*. Paris: UNESCO.

Morin, E. (2002). *A propos de la complexité*. Retrieved January 15, 2006, from http://www.litt-and-co.org/philosophie/philo.textes.htm

Morin, E. (2002). From the Concept of System to the Paradigm of Complexity. *Journal of Social and Evolutionary Systems, 15*(4), 371–385. doi:10.1016/1061-7361(92)90024-8

Nowotny, H. (2005). The increase of complexity and its reduction: Emergent interfaces between the Natural Sciences, Humanities and Social Sciences. *Theory, Culture & Society, 22*(5), 15–31. doi:10.1177/0263276405057189

Peters, M. (2005). Editorial. New approaches in the philosophy of learning. *Educational Philosophy and Theory, 37*(5), 627–631. doi:10.1111/j.1469-5812.2005.00146.x

Prigogine, I., & Stengers, I. (1984). *Order out of chaos. Man's new dialogue with nature*. Glasgow, Scotland: Fontana Paperbacks.

Rescher, N. (1998). *Complexity. A philosophical overview*. New Brunswick, NJ: Transaction Publishers.

Robbins, G. (1999). Prologue. In *The collected works of L.S. Vygotsky, Vol.6*. New York: Plenum Press.

Rose, S. (1997). *Lifelines. Biology beyond determinism*. Oxford, UK: Oxford University Press.

Salmon, W. C. (1993). Causality: Production and propagation. In E. Sosa, & M. Tooley *Causation* (pp. 154-171). Oxford: Oxford University Press.

Sassone, L. A. (1996). Philosophy across the curriculum: A democratic Nietzschean pedagogy. *Educational Theory, 46*(4), 511–524. doi:10.1111/j.1741-5446.1996.00511.x

Senge, P., Scharmer, C. O., Jaworski, J., & Flowers, B. S. (2005). *Presence. Exploring profound change in people, organizations and society*. London: Nicholas Brealey Publishing.

Sergiovanni, T. J. (1996). *Leadership for the schoolhouse*. San Francisco: Jossey-Bass.

Sidorkin, A. M. (2002). *Learning relations: Impure education, deschooled schools & dialogue with evil*. New York: Counterpoints.

Stacey, R. D. (2003). *Complexity and group processes. A radically social understanding of individuals*. Hove, UK: Brunner-Routledge.

Starobinski, J. (2003). *Action and reaction. The life and adventures of a couple*. New York: Zone books.

Toffler, A. (1984). Science and change. Foreword. In I. Prigogine & I. Stengers (Eds.), *Order out of chaos. Man's new dialogue with nature* (pp. xi-xxxi). Glasgow, Scotland: Fontana Paperbacks.

Vallacher, R. R., & Nowak, A. (Eds.). (1994). *Dynamical systems in social psychology*. San Diego, CA: Academic Press.

Valsiner, J. (1998). *The Guided Mind*. Cambridge, MA: Harvard University Press.

Van der Veer, R., & Valsiner, J. (Eds.). (1994). *The Vygotsky reader*. London: Blackwell.

Van Geert, P. (1994). *Dynamic systems of development: Change between complexity and Chaos*. New York: Harvester Wheatsheaf.

Vico, G. (1744). *The new science of Giambattista Vico*. Ithaca, NY: Cornell University Press.

Von Foerster, H. (1993). *Understanding understanding*. New York: Springer-Verlag.

Vygotsky, L. (1987). In R. W. Rieber & A. S. Carton (Eds.), *Vol. 1: Problems of general psychology*. New York: Plenum Press.

Vygotsky, L. (1997). In R. W. Rieber & A. S. Wollock (Eds.). *Vol. 3: Problems of the theory and history of psychology*. New York: Plenum Press.

Wallerstein, I. (1996). *Opening the Social Sciences. Report of the Gulbenkian Commission on the restructuring of the Social Sciences*. Palo Alto, CA: Stanford University Press.

Webster, G., & Goodwin, B. (1996). *Form and Transformation. Generative and Relational Principles in Biology*. Cambridge, UK: Cambridge University Press.

Wertsch, J. V. (1998). *Mind as action*. New York: Oxford University Press.

Wozniak, R. H. (1996). Qu'est-ce que l'intelligence? Piaget, Vygotsky, and the 1920s crisis in psychology. In A. Tryphon & J. Vonèche (Eds.), *Piaget – Vygotsky. The social genesis of thought*. Hove, UK: Psychology Press.

Wright, S. (1932). The role of mutation, inbreeding and crossbreeding and selection in Evolution. In *Proceedings of the Sixth International Congress of Genetics* (Vol. 1, pp. 356-366).

Wright, S. (1934). The method of path coefficients. *Annals of Mathematical Statistics, 5*, 161–215. doi:10.1214/aoms/1177732676

Wright, S. (1960). The treatment of reciprocal interaction, with or without lag, in path analysis. *Biometrics, 16*(3), 423–445. doi:10.2307/2527693

Zilsel, E. (2000). The social origins of modern science. In D. Raven, W. Krohn, & R. S.

ENDNOTES

1. "complexifier, c'est humaniser les sciences"
2. cf. Enlightenment dualism, as an example of this, in Midgley (2001, p. 179); see also Flood (1999) on the Enlightenment and science.

This work was previously published in the International Journal of Knowledge and Systems Science, Volume 1, Issue 1, edited by W.B. Lee, pp. 27-42 copyright 2010 by IGI Publishing (an imprint of IGI Global).

Chapter 4
Towards The New Episteme:
Philosophy, Knowledge Science, Knowledge and Tacit Knowledge

Zbigniew Król

Japan Advanced Institute of Science and Technology, Japan & Institute of Philosophy and Sociology of The Polish Academy of Sciences, Poland

ABSTRACT

The usual horizon of knowledge science is limited to nominalism, empiricism, and naturalistic and evolutionary epistemologies. I propose to broaden this horizon by applying some other philosophical attitudes, such as a non-nominalistic philosophy of language. A basic methodology for the new episteme, including (non-nominalistic) typology and a definition of knowledge and of tacit knowledge, is proposed. Several types of knowledge and the corresponding tacit knowledge are discussed within a broadened philosophical context. There are many types of knowledge and tacit knowledge using different methods of sharing. The main problem with the effective sharing of tacit knowledge is sharing knowledge relevant to the given problem. The transfer, change and transformation of tacit knowledge into explicit knowledge are possible. An example of such a transition, which I call conceptualization, is described. Conceptualization exemplifies how new knowledge can be created with the use of tacit knowledge. A need also exists for a professional collaboration between knowledge science, knowledge management and philosophy.

DOI: 10.4018/978-1-4666-1782-7.ch004

INTRODUCTION

This article is divided into two parts. In the first part, I discuss some general connections between knowledge science and philosophy, cf. section 1. In the next sections, I present a philosophical and methodological discussion of the definitions of knowledge and tacit knowledge together with their possible classification. The minimal set of conditions which are necessary for an adequate grasp of the phenomena of knowledge and tacit knowledge is presented. Also, the conversion mechanism of tacit knowledge into explicit knowledge is described. The different types of knowledge with the corresponding kinds of the relevant tacit knowledge are given.

Part I: On the Possible Impact of Philosophy on Knowledge Science and Systems Methodology

Very important properties of the approach proposed by Knowledge Science (KS) as well as by Systems Thinking (ST) are methodological pluralism and perspective shifting, for instance Wierzbicki and Nakamori (2006, ch. 6) or Houghton(2008). KS and ST contain some purely philosophical considerations. For instance, on the JAIST website of KS, philosophy is mentioned as a part of the scientific base of KS. L. Houghton also starts with a philosophical definition of epistemology. On the website of KS, some questions are also listed, as the most important for KS, for instance, "what is knowledge?" and "how can knowledge be created?", which are exactly the same questions that are basic to epistemology, for instance, the definition of epistemology on the Wikipedia[1] (to avoid more professional, and spurious at the moment, explanations). KS and ST are comparatively young scientific disciplines. On the other hand, philosophy and epistemology are more than 2000 year old. Also, the best scientists usually were philosophers or were well informed regarding some philosophical problems.

As a philosopher, I would like to indicate that postulates of ST and KS of methodological pluralism, variegation, perspective shifting etc., or Creative Holism, are mostly only *verbal*, because a great variety of philosophical possibilities are not at all taken into consideration by KS- and ST-scientists, and both KS and ST are based on a very narrow and discerned special approach to epistemological and ontological problems. The horizon of this narrow approach is limited by nominalism in the philosophy of language, materialistic monism in ontology, and empiricism, naturalistic and evolutionary epistemologies. Other possibilities are almost unseen. Also, from the viewpoint of pure philosophy, modernism and post-modernism are only very special and very limited philosophical attitudes. Strictly speaking, they are rather some "philosophical fashions", popular in the public at large, and ideologies which are very easy to understand by non-philosophers.

As an example of the consequences of this situation, I present, in the next sections, a philosophical analysis of knowledge and tacit knowledge which is based on a non-nominalistic philosophy of language.

Many kinds of nominalism[2] exist. However, we can define nominalism as a philosophy of language which denies the existence of abstract objects, and which accepts only the existence of different linguistic forms which are some real physical objects. Avoiding a long philosophical explanation, I would like to indicate that nominalism was rejected in an exact way in the philosophy of mathematics. Therefore, there are at least some examples of languages in which it is *not* possible to eliminate the acceptance of some abstract objects.

For example, there was a philosophical debate between L. Henkin (a nominalist) and W.V.O. Quine (a Platonist). As a result of this discussion, we have the so-called Henkin's models and Henkin's method in logic and model theory, i.e. theories based on the finding of some interpretations of the given formal language in this language. Henkin tried to demonstrate that "language speaks only about itself" and that there are *not* two sides of language: expressions and abstract meanings. He was wrong (cf. Quine, 1947, 1951; Henkin, 1953). It appeared that the diagonal argument of Cantor is based on a kind of (unavoidable) anti-nominalistic attitude, and this argument is used in the construction of Henkin's models.

In this article, I would like to indicate one direction toward a possible enlargement of the hermeneutical horizon of KS and ST.

A very important problem which is still under discussion in epistemology is the problem of the source of knowledge. There are plenty of various viewpoints, and some *possible* answers to very basic philosophical questions are dependent on some other philosophical solutions in ontology, ethics, philosophy of language etc. Every *real* epistemologist should to know that there is, for instance, an argument about the source of knowledge.

The empiricists argue that the only source of knowledge is sense experience, sensory perception etc. The rationalists argue that there are some other sources of knowledge, independent from the senses, as for instance, purely rational or intellectual truths, e.g. *a priori* knowledge. The idealists (only some of them because there are many different kinds of idealism) neglect the sense experience, and they are followers of *a priori*, purely intellectual truths, intuition or revelation. There are also skeptics (and agnostics), who argue that we have no firm source for knowing even one thing. There are plenty of other possible solutions and great variety of theories considering every possible ascertainment "for and against" the given view. Therefore: if KS and ST are really pluralistic, *why* are these other views absent from their considerations?

A similar question is: a *negation* of pluralism is also a possible standpoint, therefore why is this possibility also not considered. There exist also large differences regarding possible kinds of pluralism. For instance, *variabilism* is also a kind of (a-rational) pluralism.

My questions are motivated not only by an encyclopedic attitude and the quest for a completeness and integrity of the scientific research in KS and ST, but mainly by the fact that nominalism, empiricism, monism etc., have many untenable properties and weak points from the *rational viewpoint*, and that there are some kinds of knowledge, as for instance mathematical knowledge, which are incompatible with them or which are inexplicable – in my opinion - within their conceptual frames. For instance, in philosophy of science, a well-known fact is that experience and experiment do not induce a single scientific theory. There are many possible competing theories and explanations of the same experiments, experimental facts, observations etc. Therefore, scientific theories are not only a simple rewiring of experience, but have some content that is independent from experience.

Therefore, philosophy as a very important part of the rational heritage of humanity should be a little more known to every KS- and ST-scientist. I do not suggest that every knowledge scientist should study philosophy to become a philosopher. I assert only the necessity of a scientific collaboration between some philosophers interested in KS, ST and knowledge management, and the scientists from these fields. A general introduction to philosophy and the philosophy of science should be provided to every student of KS, because knowledge about other theoretical possibilities is the *sine qua non* condition of real, i.e. not only verbal, methodological pluralism.

The next point of possible collaboration between KS, ST, knowledge management and philosophy is the problem of the rationality of scientific change. In my opinion, epistemological pluralism (in the sense of variabilism) and a mechanical synthesis of some views is ineffective in solving of some real scientific problems. The knowledge of as many scientific perspectives as possible is very important. In real science, there are many competing theories and not only one mixture of many disconnected views. We have to choose, and we can chose, something that is better and more effective. However, what is proposed by systems epistemology is only a random whimsical mixture: the mixture of only some views in which the contradiction, or even the lack of good sense, are the main advantages and virtues of such a "dialectical reality". In my opinion, it is ineffective in science to replace the scientific "art of cooking" by the method of random mixture of every kind of substances that is inadequate even for the non-rational animals.

Uncritical pluralism does not provide any means to discern between valuable science and some unscientific trifles. There is a real danger to create—I use here the famous term by R. Feynman (1974; Wikipedia, 2009c)—a *cargo cult science* theory within the framework of uncritical pluralism, variegation etc. We need to consider *the rational mechanisms* of the creation of knowledge.

Part II: Introductory Remarks

One essential property of the scientific effort is the drive for the precision of concepts and language used in science and in the humanities. Scientific knowledge *in statu nascendi*, however, makes using just sharp and well-defined concepts extremely difficult. Nevertheless, an explicit definition of a concept must satisfy elementary methodological conditions such as consistency, non-circularity and the ability to grasp and convey *essential*, i.e. necessary and sufficient, properties of the concept that is defined. Obviously, there are many kinds of definitions, and a possible one is a *metaphoric definition*, for instance: "knowledge is power". But adherence to *only* metaphoric definitions and an inability to recognize that some of them are pseudo-definitions is a real methodological disadvantage of the theory.

In general, there are two kinds of definition: a good one and a wrong one. For instance, the definition of a bird as "an animal which has wings and can fly" is wrong because there are many animals which are not birds which fly using wings, e. g. insects. Exactly for the same reason as the one in the example above, the following definitions of knowledge are equally wrong:

* knowledge is power,
* knowledge is an ability or a capacity to act.

Both definitions are wrong because there are many things which have power but have nothing in common with knowledge, and not every ability (or capacity) to act is connected with knowledge. (The Earth has the ability to rotate on itself and orbit the Sun, but, in my opinion, there is no knowledge present in this ability to act, and there is rather no ability to act in this knowledge of the Earth. A laser printer can print out definition 2, but, also in my humble opinion, has no knowledge, especially concerning the question "what is knowledge?".) Definitions 1 and 2 are metaphoric, and even in the case where every kind of knowledge has the property of power and is connected with an ability to act, they do not provide an adequate translation of the term "knowledge".

The lack of a mutual identity of scopes of *definiens* and *definiendum* disqualifies a definition. Even if (almost) everybody in some scientific field is satisfied with that definition; it is wrong.

One example of the importance of mutual translatability is the so-called Gettier's paradox, concerning the well-known *classical definition of knowledge*: "knowledge is justified true belief". Gettier's paradox is the construction of the counterexample of this definition, i.e. such a case (object, hypothetical situation) that somebody has justified true belief, but cannot be said to have knowledge. To find even one *hypothetical* and *rational* counterexample is enough to disqualify the definition altogether.

To the defenders of definitions 1 and 2, it is recommended that they learn from the debate concerning Gettier's paradox, and abandon their frequent self-satisfaction.

It is also possible to have definitions approaching the meaning of a concept "from the point of view of the given science", for example, what knowledge is from the viewpoint of economics. Let us call such definitions *partial*. But partial definitions can be wrong, as wrong, from the point of view of economics are definitions 1 and 2. Why? Because we have to determine what kind of *power* and *capacity to act* are important from the economic viewpoint. Much better is a partial definition of knowledge in economics as a specific kind of product (other specifications are necessary) which has important *economic* properties that are essential for the market and industry such as the property of following the laws of "demand and supply", or the price of a merchandise.

The last kind of definition to mention in this brief overview is a *definition by enumeration of cases*. An example of such a definition is that of the *emotive heritage (of humanity)*: "It consists of arts—music, paintings, but also [of] literature, of all fiction created by humanity. To this fiction belong also movies (…)" (cf. Wierzbicki & Nakamori, 2006, p. 44). Definitions by enumeration can be a composite of metaphoric, partial and *ostensive* definitions if the enumerated cases are discerned as such. (An *ostensive definition* is a definition by simple indication: "what is a table?"—"this is", i.e. we can define an object of the given type by showing one such object.) Another possible type of definition by enumeration is the *definition by example(s)*. Thus, ostensive definitions, definitions by enumeration and by examples can transfer mainly tacit knowledge.

The decision to indicate only the above definitions comes from the recognition that only these types of definitions are usually applied in knowledge economy, knowledge science, knowledge management, etc. Also, all these definitions are important in non-formal heuristics, in schools, in everyday life. However, their importance in mature science or the humanities is rather limited: they should be replaced, even partially, by other better kinds of definitions, well-known in the methodology and philosophy of science. There is also a need to analyze the content of definition by enumeration and the mutual relations between enumerated concepts. However, there is no possibility to avoid and eliminate them altogether, even in pure mathematics.

The absence of well-defined concepts at the beginning of the development of a given science is a common problem. It suffices to mention the well-known situation at the beginning of differential calculus or of quantum mechanics. Sometimes, it is simply impossible to give an exact definition of the given concept; however, the drive towards such a definition is invigorating for the development of science. One example of the last situation is the difficulty to define the concept of polyhedron in Euclidean geometry (cf. Król. 2007a).

From the methodological viewpoint, at the beginning of the development of a given new branch of knowledge – and we accept that the new episteme is *in statu nascendi*—when there are some difficulties in giving good definitions of the basic concepts, there is also a second possibility to develop an exact and methodologically consistent base of such a new theory: *the intuitive analysis of concepts* (cf. Król, 2007a) together with the *rational analysis and critique* of the extant approaches, both approaches being mechanisms of transfer and conversion of tacit knowledge into scientific knowledge.

Philosophical Primer

In this section, I would like to present some basic distinctions concerning language, concepts, conceptual knowledge etc., in order to explain the structure of knowledge and a tacit knowledge together with a possible classification (in section 4). The reader should remember that what follows is an extraordinarily brief account concerning some philosophically advanced theories that are extant in the literature (cf. Husserl, 1928, 1973, 1982, 1984; Król, 2005; Ryle, 1984). (However, I use rather the phenomenological concept of intentionality.)

Language, Symbols, Names, Meanings, Concepts, Imagination and Abstract Objects

The philosophical primer, necessary for the description of the conceptual content of *knowledge* and *tacit knowledge*, starts from the distinction between *names* and *meanings* or *concepts* and *senses*.

In language, we have a twofold structure consisting of some *names* and other *linguistic expressions* (such as different *predicates*) and *senses*. The same name can have two or more different *meanings*. We have also some synonyms, i.e. different names which *designate* the same meanings (i.e. "shut" and "close"). A meaning of a sentence is called *sense* (or *proposition*). A meaning of a (general) name is called *concept*. The theory of language which states that there are only names without meanings is called *nominalism*. Nominalism is not a true theory of language, and it is impossible—from a purely theoretical point of view—to defend it. For instance, even in the domain of pure strictly formalized languages in mathematics, it is impossible to avoid concepts. Thus, nominalism is false, because there are examples of languages which possess meanings that are not reducible to the meaningless names.

One can has a concept without the corresponding name. It is a common situation in science: we create new names for already *intellectually* recognized senses and concepts. Sometimes, we create only new names without any reasonable sense or, after consideration, it appears that, in the given theoretical context, there is no sense connected with the given name, i.e. logical and semantical antynomies. As an example of the possible situation of having a concept without any corresponding name, we can consider the entity shown in Figure 1.

Without any formal or explicit description and any name, we can answer the following questions: how many faces, vertices and edges are there? How many vertices are invisible?, etc. Thus, after

Figure 1. Small stellated dodecahedron (cf. Wikipedia, 2009d)

an *ostensive* definition of this *something*, one can grasp *intellectually* the corresponding concept. However, for the bushman, it is possible to see a flat figure. Therefore, there is a tacit knowledge corresponding to *abstract (intellectual) knowledge*. "To share abstract knowledge" means "to reconstruct the same meanings"; cf. the next sections. The identity of names is irrelevant. In the given example, one can speak about an "urchin" instead of a "small stellated dodecahedron". Therefore, we can operate with senses (concepts) without names and – sometimes - without words or language. We can speak about the same sense or concept in different languages or in the same language using different words.

Meanings are not imagination that is connected—only sometimes—to names or sentences. For example: there is a perfectly well-formed meaning of the concept designated by the name "square" as well as the sense "1000-angle polygon". It is easy to imagine a square, but rather impossible to imagine a polygon having 1000 angles. Nevertheless, almost everybody *understands* what a

"1000-angle polygon" means. This understanding indicates some purely intellectual (conscious) acts in which we grasp the given meaning. Sometimes, creating such an act of understanding is a very difficult task. Therefore, "to have a meaning" is not the same as "to be an object of imagination".

The same sense may be given in different acts (mental presentations). The same meaning of "urchin" is a part of the imagination of an urchin and of a recollection of the previous perception of the creature in Figure 1. There are many different acts of consciousness. There are also methods of analysis of such acts and for explaining their essence (cf. Król, 2007a).

Meanings are not physical objects. The theories treating meanings as physical objects (e.g. *monism*, *physicalism*, *psychologism*, *naturalistic* and *evolutionary epistemologies* etc.) are untenable. However, there is no need to accept *Platonism*. It is enough to be aware of the difference between physical objects and meanings, and to discern *abstract objects* and material or physical objects. (In *conceptualism*, such a distinction is expressed by differentiation between *mental* and *real objects*.)

A parallel situation occurs with the names and (linguistic) sentences. They are also abstract objects. There is a necessity to discern between a name (or a sentence) and a *physical representation* of this name (or sentence). Names and sentences are not physical sounds, acoustic waves, marks of ink on article, vibrations of air or impulses in the brain machinery. The actually spoken name "circle" is the physical realization via acoustic waves of "an ideal" and fixed abstract pattern (of the corresponding sound). A printed picture is a physical representation - consisting of many discrete points - of a mental object, constituted in some relevant conscious acts.

Therefore, strictly speaking, the relation between a name and the corresponding sense is the relation between two abstract objects. Names are "more" conventional than meanings: we can freely change the name of the given concept and, for instance, to speak of a "circle" (instead of a "square") and "having in mind" the sense "square". However, the main goal of language is to be a mean of communication, and usually, we retain the received relation name/meaning, determined in the given common natural language. On the other hand, meanings are not so freely opened to creation and convention. This means that there is a *pre-given* (tacit) rational structure and content of meanings.

Symbols and letters (e.g. an alphabet) are the next examples of abstract objects. They also may have corresponding *physical realizations*.

Probably, it seems strange - especially for a "naturalized economist" - that names, sentences and letters are abstract objects. However, it is absolutely necessary to recognize and accept their abstract non-physical nature, otherwise, we have to accept that – for instance – there is no *one* (given) book but as many as there are copies of it. Also, to be an author of such a "manifold book" it is necessary to write/print personally every item of the corresponding edition. We would have also many different books, without the acceptance of the *abstract* character of letters and symbols. The only possible and consistent (known to me) solution of the problem is to accept that there is only one (*abstract*) book having many physical representations.

In the same way, in every physical representation of the abstract book in "vestment" of abstract names, letters and symbols, there is a corresponding meaning. Usually, there is a spectrum of possible meanings corresponding to possible *interpretations* of the given book (or text), but one of them is privileged and discerned. Even in mathematics, we usually work in the so-called *intended model*, having an infinite number of possible non-isomorphic different models.

Also, in every copy of the given book, on every page of the text, we have many physical representations of *one and the same* abstract alphabet. As the reader can check personally using a microscope or magnifying glass, there are no (even only) two identical physical representations of – say – a letter "a", and the relation of their mutual similarity is tacit and undefined. It is only our (usually tacit) decision that different inscriptions designate and *represent* the same abstract letter. Also, when you print out this book on a paper 5 meters in size, it nothing changes in the abstract structure of letters, names, symbols and meanings. Hard discs of computers or the Internet contain also the same *one* book, however, in a quite different, "electronic" representation.

Representations are physical spatio-temporal objects. The main development and change in the new era concerns the extraordinary extension of the number and ways of the possible means, modes of storage and transformation of physical representations. However, in the computers, there is no *knowledge* at all. There are only physical representations and transfers of *information*.

Acts of Consciousness

Without any conscious person (not necessarily a human), there is no knowledge at all. Even in the best fully computerized library, there is no knowledge. We need a conscious subject to recreate and *intellectually* grasp abstract objects that are coded with the use of physical representations. Physical representations stored in libraries and computers can be "deciphered" as being meaningful only by some acts of consciousness. I do not demand that such a conscious subject must be only of the human-type, and not – for instance – a machine or an animal. However, I am absolutely sure that every machine known to us is not a conscious subject. From the theorems on Turing machines, Gödel's theorems, as well as from phenomenological observation, it follows that they never become conscious subjects.

The reader can easily consult the story of the deciphering of the Linear B scripture of Knossos by M. Ventris and J. Chadwick (cf. Chadwick, 1990). To see a physical representation of Linear B and to store the clay tablets, without the reconstruction of the underlying *abstract* structure, is

useless. First of all, it was necessary to recognize and reconstruct the alphabet, then the syntactical and semantical structure of this language. These structures *were not realized and present* "in" any (physical) "tablet". The scientist had to recognize and to be aware of the *consciously reconstructed* structure of meanings and language of the extant representations. In order to describe these structures, they had to *conceptualize* the language hidden in the tablets, i.e. it was necessary to create new concepts, unknown to the users in antiquity and to recreate others—everything, without any change "in the tablets". For the ancient users of Linear B, all grammatical structure of the language was tacit. However, such tacit structure is open to further *conceptualization*.

Every conscious act has a corresponding object, and every act is directed toward the object. The moment (property of the act) of being directed toward an object is called the *intention of the act*. Obviously, not every object of a conscious act is a real physical object. An act can "grasp" an object, and the object is *given to us* in this act. The same object can be given in different acts. An orange can be given in sensual perception, in the acts of the sense of touch, in the acts of recollection of the previous sensual perception, in the acts of imagination, etc.

Act is something different than object, however, there are also conscious acts having as objects other conscious acts. In every act of consciousness, the subject of cognition gets *cognition*. Knowledge is necessarily connected with cognition and should be founded on the real source-based cognition. In general, the subject matter of knowledge is *not* knowledge itself. A cow is not a part of zoology, a human being is not a part of psychology, medicine, sociology, etc. Nevertheless, there are some sciences and knowledge about knowledge: epistemology, philosophy of science, etc.

At the times of primitive naturalized epistemologies and behavioral psychology, the rudimentary facts concerning the role of consciousness and conscious *intellectual* acts in science and everyday life are totally unrecognized and ignored (cf. Król, 2007b).

What Is and What Is Not Knowledge and Tacit Knowledge?

Negative knowledge about what is *not* the given object is very valuable in enabling to avoid misinterpretations. The best starting point of the next considerations is the distinction between knowledge and physical representations of knowledge. Obviously, there are numerous definitions of knowledge and information; however, I would like to present some theoretical considerations rather than make a comparison of the corresponding definitions.

The main goal of this section is to give some examples of essentially different types of knowledge and corresponding tacit knowledge with a different mechanism of the sharing of tacit knowledge, contrary to that is presented in the literature axiom that "the best way to share tacit knowledge is an informal gathering, informal networks or informal personal contacts". From this point of view, the reader can recognize the uselessness of the definitions of knowledge such as definitions 1 and 2. On the other hand, the role of a correct definition, containing essential properties of knowledge and tacit knowledge, will become visible.

Personal, Abstract and Practical Knowledge with the Corresponding Types of Tacit Knowledge

Even if there is no possibility to give a methodologically correct and materially adequate definition of knowledge, as a result of the former considerations, we can provide some essential set of the necessary conditions for "knowledge". One can also determine some unnecessary and insufficient conditions for the definition of the concept of knowledge.

Condition 1. There is no knowledge out of a *conscious subject of cognition*. Thus, every knowledge must be personal knowledge. There is no knowledge in a stone, plant, computer, library, etc. Knowledge is necessarily connected with awareness. Even, if not all kinds of knowledge are conscious, there is no knowledge at all if there is no conscious "part" of knowledge. There is no knowledge without the conscious. However, there is also no knowledge and sharing of knowledge in society without physical representations. Every effort to define "knowledge" without the recognition of its *abstract intellectual character* is hopeless.

Condition 2. "To possess an ability to act" is not equivalent to the possession of knowledge. A plant can grow, but it does not know what "growing" is. Also, this ability is not any kind of tacit knowledge "inherited" in a plant. Only the conscious ability to act can be connected with knowledge.

Condition 3. There are numerous kinds of knowledge which have nothing in common with any "ability to act". It is possible to have knowledge without any action. It is one of the greatest achievements of Western culture and science to recognize *two* types of knowledge (cf. Plato and Aristotle): theoretical abstract (intellectual) knowledge not essentially connected with action and practical knowledge, connected with *every conscious* human action. *Phronesis* is (also) the *intellectual* ability of a human being.

As an illustration of the last principle, I can present an outline of a *typology of knowledge* indicating only the main types, and mention some examples rather than giving methodological divisions. First of all, personal knowledge can be *theoretical abstract knowledge* and *practical knowledge*. The reader should be aware that – in general – in the real human conscious act, these kinds of knowledge are not separated in a sterile manner.

Theoretical abstract knowledge is necessarily connected with the use of abstract objects such as meanings (concepts and senses, i.e. *conceptual knowledge*), symbols, names and other abstract linguistic objects. A sub-type in this group creates knowledge as theoretic, systematic, codified conscious knowledge together with a theoretical justification, e.g. *scientific knowledge*, philosophical knowledge—acquired via learning, study, mental effort, reasoning. There are also many types of informal and everyday non-scientific, though abstract, knowledge.

Practical knowledge is an ability, skill, competence etc., of a *conscious* subject, e.g. the ability to drive a car, a bicycle, to climb. It is behavior acquired by practice, training and experience. Thus, the ability to breathe or digest food does not constitute any kind of knowledge, because it is not consciously acquired through practice. However, there may be some knowledge connected with these abilities, because, there are many kinds of breathing training. Not everything is knowledge. In the same way, instincts are not practical knowledge but can constitute the base of some types of practical (as well as abstract) knowledge. In the same way, our living body does not constitute any kind of knowledge.

To every kind of knowledge corresponds a specific kind of tacit knowledge. It is impossible to present a complete justification of this thesis here in the limits imposed to this article. Nevertheless, I can give some other examples of mutually irreducible and different types of tacit knowledge with different methods of sharing. Such examples – if correct – fully justify the thesis.

Verbal abstract tacit knowledge is theoretical abstract knowledge for which there are no names in the given language, however, we have (or even only one person has) some meanings in mind, for example, "urchin". Thus, it is possible to create such names in the future and to convert such knowledge into *verbal explicit knowledge*.

Conceptual abstract tacit knowledge is theoretical abstract knowledge for which there are no names and no concepts formed in the given language. This kind of knowledge can be of two types:

1. a type of abstract knowledge for which cannot be conceptualized at all, and,
2. an abstract situation is open for further conceptualization.

For instance, one can analyze the object shown in Figure 1 through the creation and use of concepts of "dimension", "polyhedron", "face", "vertex", "edge" etc. In general, it is possible to replace Figure 1 by a long conceptual description. When we give names and definitions to the terms "face", "vertex" etc., it is possible to communicate this kind of knowledge to other conscious subjects of cognition without any kind of pictures. But, "at first", one can have some nonverbal and non-conceptual meaning of what an "urchin" is *on the base of conscious acts* connected with the *representation* shown in Figure 1.

An example of conceptual (and verbal) abstract tacit knowledge, which cannot be conceptualized "in full", is tacit knowledge connected with the use of mathematical symbols. There is not one handbook of mathematics in which the obvious conditions for "what symbol x is" are explicitly stated. Everybody (from elementary school) "knows" that it is irrelevant whether this symbol is printed, written on the blackboard, written with the use of a pencil, its size is also arbitrary, etc. Obviously, I can use a stone or a piece of wood and say: "this is our x". Thus, to be the symbol x, it is unnecessary to have physical representations of "similar shape". Precisely speaking, it is impossible to strictly formalize what a symbol in mathematics is, because every such trial results in theories of equal conceptual power as some systems of formal arithmetic, for example, so-called concatenation theories. To define "the shape of x", one needs (as one of many possibilities) a part of a 2-dimensional Euclidean geometry. For the usual development of mathematics, it is enough to have some tacit knowledge concerning how to operate the symbols, for instance, that—in every place or page of the given book—the different physical representations represent the same abstract symbol. This type of tacit knowledge is shared in *formal lessons* in schools and even an infinite number of informal gatherings, such as a barbecue party, is irrelevant in the sharing of such knowledge.

There is also tacit knowledge connected to the use of language, and concerning, for example, the grammatical structure of the given language. Many people can speak correctly without any knowledge about this structure. However, this hidden knowledge may be, and usually already is, verbalized, conceptualized etc.

It is seen now that there are many kinds of tacit knowledge which are "tacit" only for some members of society. For others, they have explicit abstract conceptual and verbal content. Even the same person at a given time can have tacit knowledge concerning something, and later, can conceptualize it. Thus, there are some mechanisms of transition and mutual conversion between tacit and explicit knowledge (such as "conceptualization"). "Informal gatherings" are the least effective way to share such tacit knowledge.

The same situation occurs with tacit knowledge connected with practical knowledge. The author of the present article was a consultant for one project on writing "a manual" for climbers. It was necessary to classify and to give new names for the possible position of fingers and hands during climbing that have no counterparts in any language and are "known" to climbers. Thus, even practical tacit knowledge is wide open to become explicit and verbal. This is the reason why there are some formal driving lessons and road tests. Nobody can acquire such knowledge by informal fishing or gardening.

Not every type of explicit conceptual knowledge is transferable by use of a verbal or linguistic apparatus. For instance, there are concepts corresponding to general English names such as "red", "white", "green", "blue", "color" and so on. It is impossible to share the corresponding concepts without previous personal experience as is easily seen during a talk about colors with a person who is blind since birth. It illustrates also the difference between name and abstract (intellectual) concept.

Then, we have several types of tacit knowledge according to the criteria: verbal *vs.* nonverbal, conceptual *vs.* non-conceptual knowledge. These are:

* Def. T_L1: tacit knowledge is nonverbal, non-linguistic knowledge;
* T_L1a: actually nonverbal, but potentially verbal;
* T_L1b: absolutely nonverbal;

and

* Def. T_C1: tacit knowledge is non-conceptual knowledge, i.e. this part of knowledge which is outside of the conceptual apparatus of the human mind ("beyond concepts").
* Def. T_C1a: actually ("at present") non-conceptual, but accessible for further conceptualization.
* a': non-transferable in words and concepts (impossible to pass on) but having "names" (previous experience is necessary to share this kind of tacit knowledge, for example, "colors").
* Def. T_C1b: absolutely non-conceptual (i.e. there are no concepts to speak about it):
  1. as above, but still rational (i.e. tacit purely rational knowledge),
  2. irrational, secret, mystic, etc. (i.e. a-rational, irrational tacit knowledge).

The term "group tacit knowledge" is very popular. This term can designate only the sum of personal tacit knowledge of the members of the given social group. This follows from the conditions 1 and 2 above. However, "to be a member of the given group" creates a quite new cognitive situation for problem solving and essentially extends creative possibilities.

We can speak of "group tacit knowledge of the ancient Greeks" or the Aztecs or "tacit knowledge in the Nakamori Lab in JAIST". The above types of tacit knowledge are connected with *personal theoretical* (**K_1**) and *practical knowledge* (**K_2**). I propose the term: *personal intellectual (or theoretical) tacit knowledge* (**PIT**). Different from **PIT** is personal tacit knowledge connected with **K_2**. I propose the term: *personal practical tacit knowledge* (**PPT**).

- ○ **PIT** + **PPT** = *personal tacit knowledge.*
- ○ There are corresponding types for *group personal* tacit knowledge: group **PIT**, group **PPT**.

An example of tacit group practical knowledge is the knowledge concerning the production of some stone tools in the Stone Age. The Oldowan technology of the production of stone tools lasted more than 1 million years and, what is very interesting, was created not only by one genus, but also by other species of hominids (from *Australopithecus* to early *Homo*). Scientists found the same methods of tools production in many places, from East, Central and South Africa to Pakistan, Israel, Iran, Spain, France, Germany, etc. We can identify this culture after the reconstruction (with the use of modern experiments), theoretical conceptualization and classification of the methods and tools, i.e. after a modern conceptualization of the ancient informal and tacit knowledge concerning the process of their production. For instance, there is a known classification of these tools given by Mary Leakey in terms of "Heavy Duty, Light Duty, Utilized Pieces and Debitage, or waste".

The tacit knowledge shared by practice and experience can be converted into explicit conceptualized and abstract theoretical knowledge and shared without any practice as the reader can find personally on the website (Wikipedia, 2008). Almost every prehistoric culture (Neolithic, pottery cultures, etc.) is identified with the use of such a conversion.

In the scope of the present article, it is impossible to present an extended classification of the possible types of knowledge and of tacit knowledge. I would like to mention only that, besides two pairs of already mentioned criteria, there are other possible:

- the conscious/unconscious *vs.* tacit knowledge,
- intuition *vs.* tacit knowledge,
- hermeneutical conditions of understanding *vs.* tacit knowledge,
- actual and potential knowledge *vs.* tacit knowledge,
- explicit and implicit knowledge *vs.* tacit knowledge.

Without the recognition of these other types (and many sub-types) of knowledge and tacit knowledge, it is impossible to create effective theories of knowledge creation. It is obvious now that there is not only one general method of sharing tacit knowledge, and not the only one model of transitions between tacit knowledge and (corresponding) knowledge.

It is also possible to inquire different types of knowledge: mathematical, physical, historical, biological etc., and to detect what I call the *hermeneutical horizon* (cf. Król, 2007a). For instance, in the hermeneutical horizon for mathematics, *all* possible types of tacit knowledge, formulated with the use of the above 7 pairs of criteria, are present. In the hermeneutical horizon, one can describe the process of historical changeability of the *relevant* tacit knowledge.

CONCLUSION

A broadening of the hermeneutical horizon of KS and ST is proposed. The usual background of KS and ST is based on nominalism, materialistic monism, empiricism, naturalistic and evolutionary epistemologies. In this article, I investigate some consequences of the application of a non-nominalistic philosophy of language to the definition and classification of knowledge and tacit knowledge. Some practical consequences for the effective transfer and sharing of tacit knowledge follow. It is also possible to consider in future work some other consequences of the broadening of the hermeneutical horizon of KS that are important, for example, for the multimedia principle.

Every type of knowledge and science has relevant tacit knowledge. Therefore, to obtain important and practically valuable information about the process of knowledge creation, it is necessary to *delimit* the area of study to the given problem or science. Theories concerning "everything" are too general and non-effective, especially, when we are unaware of the existence of so many different types of tacit knowledge and/or using unclear concepts and unstable methods with (only) an "intuitive" methodology. There is a necessity for a formal collaboration regarding these problems between philosophy and knowledge science.

The reader can compare the content of this article with other classifications of tacit knowledge presented in the literature (cf. Polanyi, 1974; Nonaka, & Takeuchi, 1995; Clement, 1994; Wierzbicki, & Nakamori, 2006).

The mechanisms of sharing tacit knowledge are various. A very important conclusion from the above consideration is that there are possible the transfer, change and transformation of tacit knowledge into explicit knowledge. I described an example of such transition which I call *conceptualization*. In general, conceptualization is an example of what is called codification or articulation (of tacit knowledge). However, without the description of conceptual content of knowledge codification (articulation) is only a slogan. Conceptualization exemplifies that, and explains also *how* new knowledge can be created with the use of tacit knowledge. However, usually we consider only the transfer of tacit knowledge in the form of tacit knowledge only, i.e. the starting and the ending points of such a transfer is tacit knowledge, what is totally inadequate. Therefore, it is not generally true that tacit knowledge always must be indefinite "in words". The best counterexample to this is that it is possible to conceptualized different types of tacit knowledge, i.e. to *speak* about tacit knowledge using explicit conceptualized knowledge. The explicit knowledge about tacit knowledge is possible.

The least efficient method of the transfer of tacit knowledge is informal gathering or informal contact without any theme. Such methods are the best in some situations only, as for team building. For the development of science, the main problem is to share *the relevant to the given problem or domain tacit knowledge* and to make it possible to convert this tacit knowledge into conceptualized knowledge. Therefore, we usually organize congresses, lectures, seminars *on the given problem or theme*. Also, informal contacts are effective only when the *relevant* tacit knowledge is shared. But how to explain the apparent effectiveness of such informal networks which seems to manifest itself in some experimental data?

These data simply show that, for the development of science, *free discussion and open rational critique* together with not officially "tied up" contacts are necessary. Real science and knowledge grow only in freedom and in opposition to the apparent *irrational* authorities for which only "power" is knowledge.

ACKNOWLEDGMENT

The grant from the Japan Society for the Promotion of Science (JSPS), as well as the resulting opportunity created by Prof. Yoshiteru Nakamori to do my work on the rational foundations of knowledge creation at JAIST, is gratefully acknowledged. I extend my thanks to Prof. A. P. Wierzbicki for many interesting philosophical discussions.

REFERENCES

Chadwick, J. (1990). *The decipherment of linear B* (2nd ed.). Cambridge, UK: Cambridge University Press.

Clement, J. (1994). Use of physical intuition and imagistic simulation in expert problem solving. In Tirosh, D. (Ed.), *Implicit and Explicit Knowledge*. Hillsdale, NJ: Ablex Publishing.

Feynman, R. P. (1974). *Cargo Cult Science*. Retrieved from http://www.lhup.edu/~DSIMANEK/cargocul.htm

Henkin, L. (1953). Some notes on nominalism. *Journal of Symbolic Logic, 18,* 19–29. doi:10.2307/2266323

Houghton, L. (2008). Generalization and systemic epistemology: Why should it make sense? *Systems Research and Behavioral Science, 26,* 99–108. doi:10.1002/sres.929

Husserl, E. (1928). *Logische untersuchungen. Erster Band: Prolegomena zur reinen Logik. Text der 1. und der 2. Auflage (Husserliana: Edmund Husserl Gesammelte Werke)*. Berlin, Germany: Springer.

Husserl, E. (1973). *Cartesianische Meditationen und Pariser Vorträge* [Cartesian meditations and the Paris lectures]. The Hague, The Netherlands: Martinus Nijhoff.

Husserl, E. (1982) Ideas Pertaining to a Pure Phenomenology and to a Phenomenological Philosophy, First Book: General Introduction to a Pure Phenomenology (Kersten, F., Trans.). In Husserl, E., *Collected Works: Volume 2*. The Hague, Netherlands: Martinus Nijhoff.

Husserl, E. (1984). *Logische untersuchungen. Zweiter Band: Untersuchungen zur Phänomenologie und Theorie der Erkenntnis. In zwei Bänden*. Berlin, Germany: Springer.

Król, Z. (2005). Intuition and history: Change and the growth of mathematical knowledge. *International Journal of Knowledge and Systems Science, 2*(3), 22–32.

Król, Z. (2007a). The emergence of new concepts in science. In Wierzbicki, A. P., & Nakamori, Y. (Eds.), *Creative Environments: Issues for Creativity Support for the Knowledge Civilization Age* (pp. 415–442). Berlin-Heidelberg, Germany: Springer Verlag. doi:10.1007/978-3-540-71562-7_17

Król, Z. (2007b). Is Science About Power and Money? In Y. Nakamori, Z. Wang, J. Gu, & T. Ma (Eds.), *Proceedings of the 8th International Symposium on Knowledge and Systems Sciences (KSS2007), 2nd International Conference on Knowledge, Information and Creativity Support Systems (KICSS2007)* (pp. 364-371). Nomi, Japan: Japan Advanced Institute of Science and Technology and International Society for Knowledge and Systems Sciences.

Nonaka, I., & Takeuchi, H. (1995). *The knowledge-creating company: How Japanese companies create then dynamics of innovation*. New York: Oxford University Press.

Polanyi, M. (1974). *Personal knowledge: Towards a post-critical philosophy*. Chicago: University of Chicago Press.

Quine, W. V. O. (1947). On universals. *Journal of Symbolic Logic, 12,* 74–84. doi:10.2307/2267212

Quine, W. V. O. (1951). Semantics and abstract objects. *Proceedings of the American Academy of Arts and Sciences, 80,* 90–96. doi:10.2307/20023638

Ryle, G. (1984). *Intensionality: An essay in the philosophy of mind*. New York: Cambridge University Press.

Wierzbicki, A. P., & Nakamori, Y. (Eds.). (2006). *Creative space: Models of creative processes for the knowledge civilization age*. Berlin-Heidelberg, Germany: Springer-Verlag.

Wierzbicki, A. P., & Nakamori, Y. (2007). The episteme of knowledge civilization. In Y. Nakamori, Z. Wang, J. Gu, & T. Ma (Eds.), *Proceedings of the 8th International Symposium on Knowledge and Systems Sciences (KSS2007), 2nd International Conference on Knowledge, Information and Creativity Support Systems (KICSS2007)* (pp. 8-21). Nomi, Japan: Japan Advanced Institute of Science and Technology and International Society for Knowledge and Systems Sciences.

Wikipedia. (2008). *Oldowan*. Retrieved May 21, 2009, from http://en.wikipedia.org/wiki/Oldowan

Wikipedia. (2009a). *Epistemology*. Retrieved May 26, 2009, from http://en.wikipedia.org/wiki/Epistemology

Wikipedia. (2009b). *Nominalism*. Retrieved May 22, 2009, from http://en.wikipedia.org/wiki/Nominalism

Wikipedia. (2009c). *Cargo cult science*. Retrieved May 7, 2009, from http://en.wikipedia.org/wiki/Cargo_cult_science

Wikipedia. (2009d). *Small_stellated_dodecahedron*. Retrieved June 7, 2009, from http://en.wikipedia.org/wiki/Small_stellated_dodecahedron

ENDNOTES

[1] Epistemology (from Greek ἐπιστήμη - episteme-, "knowledge, science" + λόγος, "logos") or theory of knowledge is the branch of philosophy concerned with the nature and scope (limitations) of knowledge. It addresses the questions: What is knowledge? How is knowledge acquired? What do people know? How do we know what we know? Why do we know what we know?; cf. (Wikipedia, 2009a).

[2] Cf. for instance (Wikipedia, 2009b).

Section 2
Knowledge Management

Chapter 5
Are We Stuck With Knowledge Management?
A Case for Strategic Knowledge Resource Development

David Griffiths
University of Edinburgh, UK

Serge Koukpaki
University of Edinburgh, UK

ABSTRACT

This is a conceptual paper offering an approach to apparent practitioner and academic dissatisfaction with the field of Knowledge Management (KM). Discussing definitions of knowledge, the drivers for its value as an organisational resource and comparing these against definitions of Knowledge Management, this paper suggests a divergence between operational needs and KM as the medium for coordination. Offering an historical perspective of knowledge as a resource it suggests KM to be too broad a concept to be effective in fulfilling the needs of organisations. The authors suggest a continuum for knowledge resource development from which Strategic Knowledge Resource Development is offered as a potential solution for current unsatisfaction.

DOI: 10.4018/978-1-4666-1782-7.ch005

INTRODUCTION

In a 2009 survey of 1430 global executives across sectors KM was found to be one of the least effective strategic management tools available to organisations today (Rigby & Bilodeau, 2009). This practitioner dissatisfaction appears to be mirrored by academics; 'Knowledge Management is a poor term, but we are stuck with it, I suppose' (Sveiby, 2001, cited in Wilson, 2002). We set out to address the complex issues that trouble both practitioners and academics in the KM field. From the perspective of value creation in organisations, we suggest that Sveiby is correct and Knowledge Management (KM) is in fact a poor term. However we refute the assertion that we are 'stuck with it'.

This is a conceptual paper that examines the current position of KM and finds a field at odds with itself. We begin by first establishing a working definition of knowledge and identify the Knowledge Economy drivers for value in organisations. We examine KM as the mediating force for the coordination of organisational knowledge resources, within an exploration of knowledge as an economic resource. Establishing a history that is easily traceable over 250 years, we question whether today's practitioners and theorists are actually speaking of Knowledge Management at all, which we believe is not the case. The argument evolves to present a continuum of perspective from HR-Centric (knowledge as a process) to Techno-Centric (knowledge as an object) views with an eye to the interface between the two as the point of value extraction for organisations. We suggest this to be the focus of organisations and propose Strategic Knowledge Resource Development to be the medium for maximising organisational assets and capital.

The paper concludes that, contrary to Sveiby's damning prognosis for the future, the field is not 'stuck with' KM but that there appears to be a case for a more focused field, being Strategic Knowledge Resource Development.

WHAT IS MEANT BY KNOWLEDGE?

Theorists such as Mingers (2008) have identified a lack of definition as a weakness in the field, where too many papers fail to establish a situated definition of knowledge, and thereby take an overly simplified view of its economic value.

Knowledge in its epistemological form is frequently referred to as 'justified true belief' (Plato, cited in Kakabadse et al., 2003, p. 76). It has also been described in the modern context as 'information combined with experience, context, interpretation and reflection' (Kulkarni et al., 2006). Wilson (2002) states that:

'Knowledge involves the mental processes of comprehension, understanding and learning that go on in the mind and only in the mind, however much they involve interaction with the world outside the mind and interaction with others.' (p. 2)

Others present an ontological position in suggesting that Knowledge exists in three states: 'Knowledge-as-data', 'Knowledge-as-meaning' and 'Knowledge-as-practice' (Spender, 2005). It is also said to be part of a flow or evolution process: 'Data – Information – Knowledge – Understanding – Wisdom' (Sarah & Haslet, 2003). Wilson (2002) makes an important differentiation between knowledge and information from an organisational perspective by positing that the externalisation of what we know outside of the mind constitutes information.

Popular theorists in the KM field argue there to be two fundamental types of knowledge, tacit and explicit (Nonaka & Takeuchi, 1995) - Explicit knowledge being described as 'knowing that', or codifiable and tacit knowledge as 'knowing how'; knowledge that exists within the mind of the individual or group collective therefore and is difficult to articulate or extract (Armstrong, 2006). This pervasive KM view of knowledge as being either tacit or explicit is perpetuated from the seminal work of Nonaka & Takeuchi, whose SECI (Socialisation, Externalisation, Combination, Internalisation) model is founded upon the work of Polanyi (1969). The work of Nonaka & Takeuchi receives critical treatment from Wilson (2002) who suggests that the authors misinterpreted or manipulated the founding work of Polanyi. Polanyi states that tacit knowledge is inexpressible, whereas the core of Nonaka & Takeuchi's (1995) work relies on the conversion of tacit to explicit knowledge. Wilson suggests that Nonaka & Takeuchi are referring to implicit knowledge, which is the demonstration of expressible knowledge. Wilson further posits that explicit knowledge is mere information and therefore we are not speaking of tacit and explicit knowledge, but only knowledge and information. Ironically, Nonaka et al. (2000) posit that 'The Knowledge Management that academics and people talk about often means just 'information management'' (p. 6). In short, Wilson's work fundamentally questions the foundations of today's KM theory, as developed by Nonaka and Takechi (1995), which suggests a need to look beyond the realms of SECI when developing an understanding of knowledge as a resource.

In our view, the work of Wilson (2002) exposes the potential of KM to become orientated towards Information Management, but fails to define what drives organisations to invest time and money in what could be seen as an ambiguous field. It could be suggested that the reason for this apparent weakness in his article is a failure to provide an ontological definition of knowledge as suggested earlier by Mingers (2008). His dramatic article 'The nonsense of Knowledge Management' may be true, but the core essence of organisational value that exists at the heart of KM appears to be understated or even missed.

Therefore our position is that knowledge could be classified by what Holsapple (2004) refers to as the 'Primary' types of knowledge: 'Know What', descriptive knowledge; 'Know How', procedural knowledge; 'Know Why', reasoning knowledge. Holsapple's approach appears to originate from the

work of Ryle (1949) who suggests that 'knowing what' is the declarative knowledge that provides an understanding of facts and 'knowing how' is the procedural knowledge that provides understanding of how to do things. Ryle's work is expanded upon extensively by Mingers (2008) in his discussion on the multiple forms of knowledge and truth – in which he moves beyond the discussion of 'know what', 'know how', 'know why', knowledge to discuss Propositional Knowledge ('generally explicit and propositional' p. 71) Experiential Knowledge ('memories, some aspects of which may be tacit embodied' p. 71) Performative Knowledge (personal experience or embodied knowledge) and Epistemological Knowledge ('explicit, discursive, 'objective', open to debate' p. 71). These variations in definition suggest knowledge to be illusive, which could bring into question the ability of an organisation to manage it as a knowledge resource.

Our view is that KM cannot be delineated through simple black and white definitions, such as knowledge and information. We subscribe to the broader definitions presented by Holsapple and Mingers, which would appear to be further representative of the resources that drive organisations.

KNOWLEDGE AS A RESOURCE

The importance of knowledge as a resource is demonstrated by theorists and practitioners, such as Ulrick (1997, 1998), Dicken (2007) and the Deputy Secretary General of the OECD (Organisation for Economic Cooperation and Development) (Asgeirsdottir, 2005), who states that competitive advantage is grounded in the ability of an organisation to be more efficient and effective than its competitors; knowledge being identified as something that needs to be harnessed in order to exploit the uniqueness of the organisation. This position is expanded upon by van den Hooff and de Ridder (2004) amongst many others when they declare knowledge to be a critical resource, the management of which is seen as one of the biggest challenges for modern organisations. This approach places knowledge within the resource based view of the organisation (Garavan, 2007). In this view competitive advantage is derived from the unique knowledge and skills held by the organisation, which are informed by its human capital (Garavan, 2007). This is supported by Davies *et al.* (2005) who posit that in the modern organisation value is determined more by its intellectual than physical assets, even though this can vary according to sector (Davies et al., 2005).

Knowledge is seen as a unique strategic resource in that it increases in value with use, directing the need to manage human capital and technologies to develop competitive advantage (Clark, 2001). It is linked to the intangible human and social assets of an organisation (Armstrong, 2006). The value of knowledge has dramatically increased over the last 80 years, rising from a 30% representation of company valuation in 1929 to recent times where companies, such as Google and Microsoft, are declaring as much as 90% (Ash, 2004).

Clark (2001) goes on to state that a perpetual state of development is required to enhance an organisation's adaptive capacity, 'in dynamic environments highly developed learning is necessary in order to keep knowledge current; an organisation's learning capability must keep pace with the changes in the competitive environment' (pp. 192-193). This situates learning and knowledge in terms of what the OECD view as the four pillars of the knowledge economy: Innovation, as a critical factor of competitive advantage; New Technologies, linking technology progress to growth in productivity; Human Capital, which is seen as essential to harness the benefits of the first two pillars; Enterprise Dynamics, the ability to flex according to evolving consumer needs (Asgeirsdottir, 2005). Human Capital as a catalytic driver is supported by Nonaka and Takeuchi (1995), who observe the socialisation of human resources as the key to developing tacit knowledge resources. This

is further explored by Gherardi (2009) who states that knowing is demonstrated in practice where people are 'able to participate with the requisite competence in the complex web of relationships among people, material artefacts and activities' (p. 118). The idea of knowledge as a resource for value creation within organisations is further discussed later in this paper.

Accepting knowledge as a resource within the Resource Based View of the organisation, it leads us to issues regarding its management or coordination.

THE NEED TO MANAGE KNOWLEDGE

Whilst the theorists thus far cited support this view of knowledge as a form of competitive advantage, the 'management' of this resource is steeped in debate, with theorists such as Gibson (2005) suggesting that it is not feasible to manage knowledge as a commodifiable resource. This view is damningly reinforced by theorists such as Sveiby, who states 'I don't believe knowledge can be managed' (www.sveiby.com) and Drucker (Cited in Wilson, 2002, p. 3) who is quoted as '[scoffing] at the notion of Knowledge Management. 'You can't manage knowledge,' he says'. Popular KM theorists such as Prusak (cited in Schutt, 2003) suggest that 'you cannot manage knowledge like you cannot manage love, patriotism or your children' (p. 45). This argument regarding the manageability of knowledge appears to be at the heart of disagreements within the field with authors such as Bouthillier and Shearer (2002) stating that knowledge itself cannot be managed, it is only the representations of knowledge that can be subjected to management principles. Mokyr (2002) provides an insight into the difficulties of managing those very representations:

'"Representations within the brain"…and the knowledge "this is how you do that" is twice

removed from the audience: First by the ability of the knower to map what he does into his own brain, and then by his ability to cast it in a language common with the audience.' (p. 11)

These complexities heat the debate surrounding the ability of an entity, whether an individual or an organisation, to manage knowledge, as summed up by Alvesson and Karreman (2001):

'Knowledge is an ambiguous, unspecific and dynamic phenomenon, intrinsically related to meaning, understanding and process and therefore difficult to manage.' (p. 995).

Fundamentally the issue of the management of knowledge is grounded in the fact that 'it originates and is applied in the minds of human beings....' (Grover & Davenport, 201, p. 6). Wenger et al. (2002) suggest that knowledge exists within the human act of knowing, which can be seen as knowledge in action. This links with Nonaka & Toyama's (2007) notion of knowledge emerging from a process of socialisation in which practice exists as the cornerstone for the process. Theorists such as Nonaka & Toyama (2007) and Rahe (2009) discusses the complexities of coordinating individual cognitive experiences that are influenced by personally situated reflections, perceptions and interpretations.

'In the literature, knowledge is defined as the result of a process which combines ideas, rules, procedures and information ... The outcome of this process is based on reasoning and understanding and therefore made by the mind, whereby the process itself reflects information through experience, learning or introspection.' (Rahe, 2009, p. 105)

If this can be accepted as true then it would seem that we are actually speaking in terms of 'Development' as opposed to 'Management'.

THE FOUNDING FATHERS OF KM

Theorists and practitioners appear to credit Drucker with the birth and exponential growth of the modern KM movement through his seminal article in 1988 'The coming of the new organisation' (Spender, 2005). Some suggest Sveiby to be the key figure in the field (Wilson, 2002), others credit Machlup (Mingers, 2008) and yet others credit Robert Buckman (and his work with Buckman Laboratories during the early 1980's) with being the 'father-figure' of KM due to his influence over the technological aspects of the field (Angus, 2003). This perception of Buckman as a patriarchal figure for KM appears to demonstrate a view of KM as something that technology does, whereas theorists such as Mokyr (2002) suggest that the evolution of technology is evidence of knowledge development.

KNOWLEDGE MANAGEMENT: THEORETICAL FOUNDATIONS

Models for KM are suggested to be found in the Cognitive, Philosophy, Community of Practice, Network or Quantum schools of thought. The Cognitive and Philosophy Models examine self-similar ideas, such as objectives, type and source of knowledge. But the Philosophy Model also looks at how knowledge links with other human instincts such as certainty, belief, causation and doubt. It examines questioning and doubt as key factors in knowledge generation, whilst also exploring the theory put forward by Polanyi that there is no divergence between tacit and explicit knowledge (Kakabadse et al., 2003): 'All knowledge is either tacit or rooted in tacit knowledge' (Polanyi, cited in Kakabadse et al., 2003, p. 78). This is in conflict with the Cognitive Model of KM. The Philosophy model centres on the individual and the interaction with the group or organisation, which is in common with the Cognitive model. Unlike the cognitive model, which promotes technology to regenerate and codify knowledge, it does not embrace technology; focusing on a Socratic definition of knowledge and the search for higher knowledge (Kakabadse et al., 2003). Community of Practice and Network Models amplify the need for social interaction with structural and cultural development to successfully acquire and co-ordinate knowledge. The Quantum Model is the antithesis of the Philosophy Model, entrenching itself in technology. Applying quantum physics theories and IT solutions it develops scenario algorithms to determine the decision-making outcome. It examines the interface between human and digital resources and shares elements with the Philosophy Model, in that it works to become an instrument of wisdom in the organisation's social architecture (Kakabadse et al., 2003).

As a consequence of this KM can be seen as intimidating by its sheer breadth and scale, caused by the variety of disciplines it encompasses, from social science to artificial intelligence (Kakabadse et al., 2003; Ray, 2005). Because of this diversity of influence, KM, much like knowledge itself, is difficult to define (Mekhilef & Flock, 2006)

KM DEFINITIONS

There is no accepted general definition of KM with theorists offering alternative definitions such as:

'...*a framework that builds on past experiences and creates new mechanisms for exchanging and creating knowledge'* (Kakabadse et al., 2003, p. 78)

and:

'...*the exploitation and development of the knowledge assets of an organisation with a view to furthering the organisation's objectives'* (Davenport & Prusak, cited in Mekhilef & Flock, 2006, p. 9)

Some posit that the definition is situated according to discipline and/or sector (Alavi & Leidner,

1999), whilst Kulkarne et al. (2006) suggest KM to be conditional according to a 'personalisation strategy' for tacit knowledge, or a 'codification strategy' for explicit knowledge. Sarah and Haslett (2003) suggest 'Knowledge as a product' and 'Knowledge as a process' and other authors, such as Kulkarne et al. (2006), discuss the management of knowledge or the management of knowledge workers.

The lack of agreed definition could be attributed to the breadth of theoretical foundations that underpin the field. It could also be seen as too broad and ill defined for practitioners attempting to extrapolate value from the field; a perspective that is explored further later in this paper.

KNOWLEDGE MANAGEMENT FUNCTIONS

The functions of organisational KM are identified through two independent meta synthesis studies of literature, which demonstrate KM to be focused on the acquisition, storage, use, dissemination and evolution of knowledge (Qureshi et al., 2006; Supyuenyong & Islam, 2006). This contributes to the organisational development of what Gold et al. (2001) refer to as 'absorptive capacity'; the ability to recognise existing knowledge, adapt it and apply it to develop new knowledge capability. This also relates to the OECD's fourth pillar of the Knowledge Economy; Adaptive Capacity.

Snowden (2002) stated that KM is situated in version 3.0, with version 1.0 only emerging during the late 1980s to mid 1990s. This 'recent' perspective on KM is reinforced in the mentioned work of Wilson (2002) in which he conducts extensive quantative analysis to suggest that KM literature demonstrates that KM didn't really emerge until 1986 and didn't demonstrate signs of maturity until 1997. In his paper 'The nonsense of "Knowledge Management"' he appears to suggest that KM emerged as an evolution of one of many strategies born of Taylor's Scientific Management – a perspective that we challenge later in this paper. It could be suggested that this puts forward a view of KM that could fuel some authors to consider KM as a fad (Stewart, 2002; Ray, 2005). The perception of KM as a fad has even led others to enquire into whether KM has reached its zenith (Schutt, 2003). If KM is this young it could be seen as a potential issue for the field.

KNOWLEDGE MANAGEMENT: ISSUES IN THE FIELD

Chiva and Alegre (2005) suggest that knowledge and its management within organisations is in a state of disorder, with no clearly defined architecture for its application. McElroy (2000) observes an early failure in KM in that there is not enough focus on how organisations generate knowledge. He believes that managers find it 'too scary a problem to tackle: too fuzzy; too controversial; too theoretical' (p. 44). Practitioner perceptions of performance are reflected in a 2006 survey of management tools utilised by 1221 global executives where Rigby and Bilodeau (2007) KM ranked 22 out of 25 for satisfaction and received the lowest rating of all management tools within respondents from large organisations. Though it ranked as the 8th most popular tool in European business, up from 15th in 2004, it only received a 17% satisfaction rating. A downward trend in satisfaction has been identified where, in a 2009 survey of 1430 global executives by the same authors and using the same methods, KM ranks 24th out of 25 for satisfaction (Rigby & Bilodeau, 2009). This suggests a lack of congruence between perceived value and actual performance. This appears to be echoed in the academic field where Smith (2003) cites Fahey & Prusak, amongst several others, in demonstrating the growing concerns of theorists that KM is failing to deliver value.

These arguments bring focus to bear on the fundamental ability of the field to deliver the value that lies at the core of its being. This said, perhaps

the issue is not in the need for organisations to coordinate knowledge resources and the micro-environment that stimulates human knowledge processes, but in the seemingly inflammatory terminology used to describe the activities that are actually happening in organisations? This position is presented by Kakabadse et al. (2003) who states that 'Knowledge Management is about exploitation, whilst 'knowledge' is all about exploration' (p. 83). Parallels can be drawn with the terminology of The Knowledge Economy, which the Guardian newspaper has been said to be misleading; though it stops short of qualifying that statement (Barkham, 2008). Stephen Overell, speaking on behalf of the Work Foundation, states that 'it is silly to focus on the jargon and not the very real changes taking place behind it' (www. theguardian.co.uk). In order to better understand what we are speaking of when discussing value in knowledge there would seem to be the need to explore the origins of today's knowledge economy within which Riley (2003) states that 'Technology and knowledge are now the key factors in production' (www.egovmonitor.com). In this way it might be possible to better understand whether knowledge is a relatively new resource for organisations, as suggested by the quantative research conducted by Wilson (2002), or whether it has been acknowledged before the 1980s. If this is the case then KM might be nothing more than a new label on an old bottle.

HISTORICAL POSITIONS ON KNOWLEDGE AS A RESOURCE

To research the background of knowledge as a resource, prior to 1980, an exploratory literature search was conducted utilising JSTOR, Emerald and Business Source Premier search engines, utilising the title keyword 'knowledge'. Literature was screened to exclude the following: popular article titles from around the turn of the twentieth century that included the phrase: 'A contribution

Table 1. Overview of exploratory search

Author	Year	Position
Mokyr	2005	Evidence of knowledge as a resource through technological advances during the First and Second Industrial Revolution – linked via our research to surge in new universities
The Lancet	1908	The need for knowledge sharing in medicine
Nutting	1918	Knowledge as a national resource
Fisher	1933	Tertiary stage of development – emphasis on knowledge based goods and services
Williams	1931	Knowledge collection and creation through problem solving in education
Barnard	1938	Need for organisations to create and disseminate knowledge
The Science Newsletter	1940	Knowledge as a resource for competitive advantage
Lusty	1942	Industrial Efficiency Engineers
Bush ASLIB	1945 1952	The knowledge explosion
Drucker	1959	Productive work involves work based on the mind
Machlup	1962	The production and distribution of knowledge
Carter	1967	Government involvement in the development and conservation of knowledge
Maxwell	1968	Information storage and retrieval
Havelock *et al.*	1969	Science Of Knowledge Utilisation
Farradane	1970	Importance of knowledge creation through education
Duncan	1972	Knowledge flow in organisations
Bell	1973	Knowledge usurping capital in organisations
Henry Gates *et al.*	1974 1975	Knowledge Management appears as a term in papers on Public Administration
Freeman	1977	Knowledge Management in Marine and Environmental sciences
Hillman	1977	Knowledge Management in Computer Sciences

to the knowledge on...' Harvard Law Review articles involving points of law; and psychology based returns investigating the foundations of knowledge. The search was guided by KM definition and focused directly on articles relating to the acquisition, application, storage, and sharing of knowledge as a resource. Table 1 provides an overview of our findings.

Pre- 20th Century

Initial research led us to Mokyr's (2002) acclaimed work into the links between knowledge and technology delivers an insight into the development of knowledge economies, the impact of which can be observed through surges in technological achievements, such as during the first and second industrial revolution. Mokyr posits that:

'The Industrial revolution...constitutes a stage in which the weight of the knowledge-induced component of economic growth increased markedly.' (p. 30)

He also alludes to the fact that knowledge-induced technological gains are available to 'any society that invests in institutions to encourage invention and enterprise' (p. 17). The first industrial revolution is commonly understood as starting around 1760-1780 and lasting until 1830-1850.

During this time the United Kingdom experienced technological surges that marked the empire as an industrial leader. A cursory search into United Kingdom universities, synthesising data from multiple academic websites, demonstrates that at the beginning of this period there were five Scottish universities and 2 English universities in existence. During the latter stages of this period six new universities were founded along with three civic or 'red brick' universities, that focused on civic science and engineering. What is interesting is it appears that that technological innovation spurred the need for educational institutions. This could be seen as spurring the onset of the second industrial revolution, which is seen as blending with the end of the first industrial revolution and lasting until the onset of The First World War.

The timing of the foundation of United Kingdom universities is interesting as the United Kingdom fell behind the rest of the world, particularly to the United States, during the second industrial revolution (Mokyr, 2002) – The emerging United Kingdom universities were founded in the latter part of the first industrial revolution, between 1810 and 1837 with one exception being 1796. A further synthesis of dates demonstrates that during the same period the United States founded approximately 40 universities with the majority being prior to 1800. This would appear to support Mokyr's assertion that the investment in institutions will bear fruit and appears to link technological advancement to a knowledge economy, which in turn elevates the importance of human knowledge and learning. Mokyr is supported in the literature by Adler (2001), amongst others, who states 'increasing knowledge intensity takes two forms: the rising education level of the workforce…and the growing scientific and technical knowledge materialised in new equipment and new products' (p. 216).

The 20th Century

The perceived value of knowledge to an organisation or sector becomes visible in this search over one hundred years ago, with The Lancet (1908) publishing an article, 'The Diffusion of Medical Knowledge' extolling the virtues of knowledge sharing within the discipline of Medicine & Health.

Knowledge has been discussed as a value driver for organisations, predominantly in North America, since 1918 with authors such as Nutting (1918) stating:

'The greatest problem for any nation is that of developing its resources to the utmost. The solution of this problem involves a thorough knowledge of all resources – natural, intellectual, manual and financial – and thorough knowledge of all means of making the most of them.' (p. 406).

This sentiment, which appears to still resonate in today's KM literature, is progressed by authors such as Fisher (1933) who recognised industry to be moving toward a tertiary stage, with an emphasis on knowledge based goods and services instead of traditional manufacturing and production. This was also recognised by Barnard (1938) in his book 'The Functions of the Executive' where he positioned the need for organisations to create and disseminate knowledge. It was also being discussed in the social sciences, with authors recognising the value of knowledge collection and creation through problem solving in higher education (Williams, 1931).

It would seem that issues of competitiveness ultimately brought focus to knowledge as a resource. This can be evidenced in literature from World War II, with authors calling for knowledge to be organised and implemented for national advantage (The Science newsletter, 1940).

'Primarily we need proved weapons, men, planes and ships to make America safe from attack.…Back of these defense lines lies knowledge, organised

and implemented by the searchings of human minds and hands.' (p. 47)

Literature from the period also offers us a glimpse of an early incarnation of the modern Knowledge Manager, in the form of Industrial Efficiency Engineers (Lusty, 1942). These Industrial Efficiency Engineers were seen by Lusty as specialists who could critically manage knowledge, brought about by what he described as:

'...An organisation, so arranged that the results of all its efforts are recorded and analysed. The lessons to be learned and the experience to be gained are thus made as much as a company's asset as more tangible things, and can be used in the direction of future undertakings.' (p. 201).

Subsequent to this period there appears to have been what Havelock et al. (1968) describe as a knowledge explosion. This is evident in literature such as Bush (1945) and ASLIB (1952), the latter acknowledging the value of knowledge in the post war recover of Britain. This appears to have brought a second incarnation of the Knowledge Manager through the advent of the 'Science of Knowledge Utilisation' where there was discussion of the need to coordinate such knowledge that was deemed useful to man (Havelock et al., 1968).

The production of knowledge was being discussed as a national asset in literature such as 'The production and distribution of knowledge in the US' (Machlup, 1962). A position championed by Carter (1968) as 'something with which the Federal Government must be vitally concerned... [as] it needs to guide the overall development and conservation of such an asset [knowledge]' (p. 13). The importance of Information Storage and Retrieval was also being progressed in the United Kingdom at this time by Maxwell (1968). Dun-

can (1972) progresses this through discussion on knowledge flow in organisations 'The knowledge flow system in management and organisation includes all resource and user subsystems involved in development and application of meaningful management knowledge' (p. 274).

It could be perceived that Drucker with his article in 1988 was a little behind the times. That would be misleading, as in 1959 Drucker stated, 'Productive work in today's society and economy is work that applies vision, knowledge and concepts – Work that is based on the mind rather than the hand' (p. 120).

It is during the 1970's that KM first appears in literature discussing Public Administration (Henry, 1974): 'By Knowledge Management, I mean public policy for the production, dissemination, and use of information as it applies to public policy formulation' (p.189). The discussion of knowledge was also ongoing in education through authors such as Farradane (1970). It was during this time that authors such as Bell (1973) recognised that knowledge was usurping capital in the battle for power within organisations. Freeman (1977) demonstrates the visibility of KM within marine and environmental science and Hillman (1977) positions KM as part of computer science, which aligns with the vision of Maxwell (1968).

It would therefore seem possible to trace the concept of managing knowledge resources to the turn of the twentieth century and beyond. If this can be accepted as true then theorists and practitioners have been attempting to extract economic value from knowledge for a period extending well over 250 years. Perhaps then, instead of resigning ourselves to being 'stuck with' KM, we should revisit the field to contemplate a paradigm shift to better accommodate the needs of organisations as they navigate the modern knowledge economy.

STRATEGIC KNOWLEDGE RESOURCE DEVELOPMENT: A PARADIGM SHIFT

The Assumptions of a Paradigm

A paradigm is seen as a framework that allows for common thought or a shared language allowing for the expression of beliefs, models, values and views focused toward the solution of an identified problem (Yolles, 1996; Arbnor & Bjerke, 2009). Yolles (1996) suggests that new paradigms evolve when creators of knowledge find existing paradigms to be inadequate in providing a solution to the problem at hand. This would seem to be the case for KM, based on the discussions of this article. However, Yolles suggests that a new view of knowledge is not enough justification for the announcement of a new paradigm, observing a paradigm as 'a group affair, rather than an individual one' (p. 558). This suggests that new knowledge cannot evolve into a paradigm without group validation and therefore we will only discuss conceptual paradigm shift.

The Case for a Paradigm Shift

KM literature presents a turbulent field. Issues of performance could be linked to a lack of agreed definition and scale of practice, which could appear as too cumbersome for organisations to derive true value.

From the evidence it is clear that over the past 250 years the development of knowledge, through educational, business or civic institutions has been seen as an important function has been a driver for national and organisational value well before the advent of KM and today's Knowledge Economy. Value appears to exist through two defined strands, being people and technology, which exist in a reciprocal relationship. Both of these strands intersect with the OECD's four pillars of the knowledge economy. This brings us to a fundamental question; what do we mean by

'knowledge assets', or 'knowledge resources' in the context of this article?

DEFINING KNOWLEDGE ASSETS OR RESOURCES

Simply put, the value of knowledge is seen as being linked to the organisation's intangible human and social assets (Armstrong, 2006). However, value, when associated with the ongoing development of knowledge resources, would appear much more complex than that. Research into value creation within the KM field brings one to the field of Intellectual Capital (IC), which is said to be driven by three strands: Human, Structural and Relationship Capital (Solitander & Solitander, 2010).

Diakoulakis et al. (2004) suggest a generic IC taxonomy, linking the value of organisation knowledge to the following capital markers: Intellectual (Human) Capital – The competencies and capabilities of its staff; Structural (Relationship) Capital – The strength of enterprise relations with external stakeholders; Organisational (Innovation) Capital – The capacity to develop existing knowledge and intangible assets such as culture; Process Capital – Value creating processes, procedures, management structure and IT infrastructure. This harmonises with the OECD pillars for the knowledge economy, blending the dynamics of people, their social environment and technology, and informs the practices that need to be developed in order for organisations to derive value from organisational knowledge resources. Solitander and Solitander (2010) stress that this type of model is not hierarchical, but sets out the markers that 'compliment each other creating value from the interplay' (p. 40). Sveiby (2008), in his criticism of IC, advocates the use of the term 'Intellectual Assets' instead of IC.

This lays the vista for the capitalisation of knowledge, but the literature appears to require a differentiation between capital and asset. This is succinctly defined by Nonaka et al. (2000) who state that 'At the base of knowledge-creating processes are knowledge assets. We define assets as 'firm specific' resources that are indispensable to create value for the firm' (p. 20). The authors speak of knowledge-assets as consisting of 'Experiential', 'Conceptual', 'Systematic' and 'Routine'.

Therefore capital can be seen to consist of both human and technology resources. This reflects the two strands identified by the KM literature and the key contributors to the OECD's four pillars of the Knowledge Economy. We will now explore the two strands as polar opposites on a continuum and discuss the place of the conceptual paradigm of Strategic Knowledge Resource Development (SKRD), illustrated in Figure 1.

THE HUMAN RESOURCE/ TECHNOLOGY RESOURCE CONTINUUM

Prusak and Weiss (2007) postulate KM to be traditionally more technology centric and learning as more Human Resource (HR) centric.

We examined this balance between the techno-centric (knowledge as an object) and HR-centric (knowledge as a process) views in Griffiths and Morse (2009). We discovered, through an evidence-based meta-analysis of 287 pieces of KM literature, that 45% was 'Interactionist', dealing with the interface between technology and human resources, with 32% being HR-centric and only 23% being techno-centric. This would seem to suggest that in discussing the development of knowl-

Figure 1. The Knowledge Resource Continuum

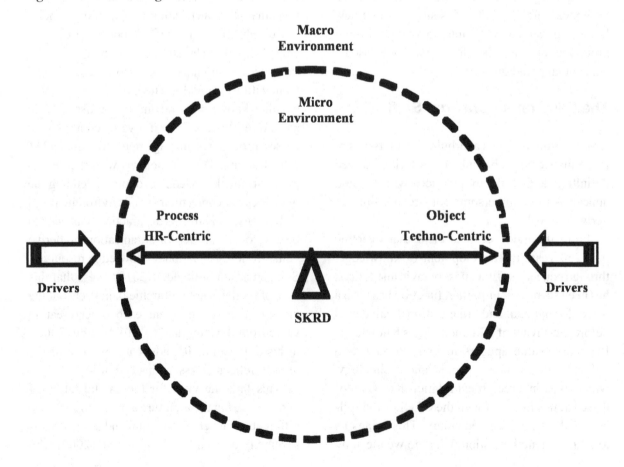

edge resource capabilities within an organisation that it is necessary to discuss the development of both technology and human resources and concurs with the OECD four pillars. It also demonstrates a balance between 'traditional' KM and learning discussed by Prusak and Weiss (2007).

HR-CENTRIC FOCUS: KNOWLEDGE AS A PROCESS

What is agreed is that the development of knowledge resources contributes to the enhancement of Adaptive Capacity through Technology, Innovation and Human Capital (Grover & Davenport 2001; Bournemann et al, 2003). Adaptive Capacity can further be seen as grounded in the sharing of knowing; being knowledge in action or practice (Nonaka & Toyama, 2007). Antonacopoulou (2006) criticises the current KM field in that it has managed to capture some of the forces that shape the nature of knowing, but has failed to deliver an understanding of the dynamic nature of knowing in action.

Adaptive Capacity, discussed earlier, has been linked in unified KM models, such as by Bournemmann et al.'s (2003) Wissenmanagement model, to principles of organisational learning; where organisational learning is seen as a process of analysis of the learning impetus, analysis of goals against the current environment, design of intervention and a development phase for implementation. Rahe (2009) proposes organisational learning theory to be one of the founding concepts of modern KM.

Edward and Rees (2006) state that knowledge needs to be maintained and developed by engaged and energised people to add true organisational value. 'It is clear that managing behaviour, learning and knowledge cannot be separated from one another' (Edward&Rees, 2006, p. 167). Sarah and Haslett (2003) observe learning as influencing organisational development in the area of strategic resources, which takes the form of new additions to the knowledge flow of data to wisdom. This is also emphasised by Prusak and Weiss (2007) suggest the need to blend knowledge and learning in order to deliver sustainable organisational development.

Smith (2003) champions KM through its ability to develop the critical element of organisational Social Capital, which links to the generic capital taxonomy model discussed earlier and which he believes has a pivotal influence in transforming Human Capital and Financial Capital into profit. Boxall (1996), Boxall and Steeneveld, (1999) demonstrates this, suggesting that Human Capital Advantage and Human Process Advantage generates Human Resource Advantage.

They state that Human Capital Advantage is gained through the employment and nourishment of workers with value adding tacit knowledge. Human Process Advantage is the dynamic that allows knowledge to interface with the environment through inimitable organisation structures and settings. Human Resource Advantage is the unique product brought about by the combination of people, environment, culture and structure. This also seems to be a further reflection of and Nonaka and Takeuchi (1995) in that socialisation or practice is at the heart of Human Resource value in organisations.

The concepts of Knowledge and learning have been argued to share many of the same fundamental theories and models, a position championed in extensive research by Chiva and Alegre (2005). This brings us to Strategic Human Resource Development (SHRD) (Garavan, 1991, 2007) and brings about the question of why KM isn't simply placed under the umbrella of SHRD.

This could be seen as appropriate, but when looking at the characteristics of SHRD as presented by McCracken and Wallace (2000) or Garavan (2007) it is clear that technology is not a focus for the concept. Garavan does present 'Technology Change' as a driver for SHRD in his 'Contextual and Dynamic Framework for SHRD', but the SHRD reaction message can only be described as discrete. This is a potential issue for both KM and SHRD as the OECD's four pillars suggest that it is the combination of ICT and Human Capital that delivers Innovation in the knowledge economy.

TECHNO-CENTRIC FOCUS: KNOWLEDGE AS AN OBJECT

Technological KM systems (KMS) have been developed to assist organisations with the codification, storage and distribution of its knowledge resources. The success of which have been linked to an increase in company valuation, an improvement in the focus of management on knowledge capability and in the justification of organisational knowledge activities. A successful KMS is seen as one that performs four key functions: knowledge creation; storage and retrieval; transfer; and application (Jennex & Olfman, 2004). This leads to the question of how technology based solutions can 'create knowledge'? Jennex and Olfman (2004) and Kulkarne et al., (2006) acknowledge factors external to technology ultimately affect its successful implementation:

- Senior Management support
- Delineated communication of organisational knowledge strategy
- Strategic alignment to organisational outcomes
- Motivational incentives
- A culture conducive to knowledge values
- A suitable organisational culture

KMS therefore appear to be a contentious issue for KM. Roth (2003) suggests that 'bought-in' KM tools attempt to centralise and deconstruct knowledge, which is against the understanding of knowledge as a complex entity that is difficult to store in a particular form or role, especially when discussing tacit knowledge. This could be seen as the causality behind the failure of KM as a strategic tool, as illustrated earlier by Rigby

and Bilodeau (2007; 2009) and why some authors could interpret KM as a fad. This perception of KM being driven by technology is demonstrated in the proliferation of technology based knowledge solutions evident in the 2009 International Data Corporation Report (Feldman, 2009), where it is stated that 'search and discovery' software, designed to streamline knowledge work, grew 19% to $2.1 billion in 2008.

Smith (2003) cites Fahey & Prusak; Newell & Scarborough; Storey & Barnett and Lindgren & Henfrisdsson in demonstrating the growing concerns over KM's ability to deliver organisational value. Watson & Hewitt (2006) discusses the causality of these claims, suggesting that many organisations see technology as the answer to KM, when it is in fact the individual and the social capital they create that is the true resource.

'It is clear that the success of a knowledge transfer system hinges in large part not only on the extent to which the system is accessed and used, but also on the willingness of individuals within the firm to contribute their valuable knowledge to the system' (Watson & Hewett, 2006, p. 170)

This argument appears to be negatively biased against technology, but this is not our intention. Technology is identified by the OECD as one of the pillars for the knowledge economy and, whilst technology companies appear to be exploiting definitional and understanding issues in the KM field, it should be embraced as a key aspect of value creation in organisations.

THE NEED FOR BALANCE

What is reinforced throughout the literature is the development of value through knowledge assets, of which very few are tangible. As stated earlier, much of an organisation's knowledge assets are derived from people participating in practice or dialogue within situated environments. Prusak and

Weiss (2007) cite the Nobel Prize Winner, Joseph Stiglitz, in stating 'The appropriation of global ideas and the ability to search, filter and socialise knowledge are the most important tasks for global organisations today' (p. 42). The terminology used in this statement could lead to support for a technology centric view of knowledge development for organisations, but when considering the need for uniqueness in competitive advantage, discussed earlier in this paper, one cannot dismiss the role and development of human resources. It also appears that the Stiglitz commentary fails to acknowledge the need for innovation or improvement, which theorists and practitioners such as Dicken (2007) and the OECD see as imperative for developing adaptive capacity.

Prusak and Weiss (2007) reflect the opinions of many theorists in opining the need for a balance between 'smart systems', being technology driven knowledge enablers, and the HR aspect of learning and development if future knowledge initiatives are to be successful. The danger is that organisations can be influenced by commentaries, such as that of Stiglitz, into believing that technology is the solution to the development of organisational knowledge resources.

We summarise the need for balance through Smith (2003) who suggests that 'significant breakthroughs and competitive advantage typically come from the social exchange, exploitation, and augmentation of current tacit knowledge, rather than codified explicit knowledge based on past contexts' (p. 1-2). Smith postulates that technology will fail if organisations do not recognise that cultural and social frameworks are the bedrock of success for any KM process. He also states that no amount of technical investment will overcome fundamental flaws in these pivotal areas.

STRATEGY: THE BINDING AGENT

Strategy is seen as being core to knowledge activities within organisations (Yang et al., 2009) and emerges as a binding agent for the two aspects of the HR-Centric and techno-Centric Continuum. This is supported through Sarah & Haslett (2003), who talked about learning being associated with 'strategic resources', and Kulkarne et al. (2006), who talked of the need for KM to have 'strategic alignment to organisational outcomes'.

Chiva and Alegre (2005) suggest that organisational strategists and academics in the field of strategic management study knowledge, whereas learning is studied and applied in the field of human resources. Strategy is supported by the International Institute for Sustainable Development (Creech, 2005) as being essential in order to provide direction for knowledge based initiatives. Prusak and Weiss (2007) posit that in the past KM has been disconnected from organisational strategy (perhaps due to there interpretation of the literature that positions KM as technology biased and anchored in hard systems thinking), relating failings in the field to issues where 'few people asked what knowledge was most important to the organisation's, or division's or unit's strategy' (p. 34-35). This is addressed by Nonaka and Toyama (2002) through their assertion that knowledge assets need to be mapped and dynamically used to maintain and develop value. Strategy as a contextualising driver for KM activity is evident as a global economic driver as demonstrated in Company Action Plans, such as the Asian Development Bank (ADB) Strategy 2020 Knowledge Management Action Plan (www.adb.org).

'ADB's edge in generating, disseminating, and applying knowledge stems from 3 comparative advantages: Strategic position in identifying trends within and across the region; Capacity for interdisciplinary and integrated approaches; ability to blend knowledge with large, concessional financing.' (www.adb.org)

Interestingly, ADB's method for generating knowledge is through utilisation of Communities of Practice and the development of individual learning and skills. ADB also discuss 'knowledge capture', which could suggest a technology based solution in tandem with a socialisation strategy. This approach reflects a response to all four of the OECD's pillars of the knowledge economy. It also exposes the blending of Human and Technology resources and the activity taking place at the interface of the two concepts.

STRATEGIC KNOWLEDGE RESOURCE DEVELOPMENT (SKRD)

By following the signposts from knowledge to learning to HRD, it could lead one to the conclusion that the issue at hand is not about KM, rooted in its turmoil of being, knowledge definition, commodifiability and manageability, but Strategic Knowledge Resource Development (SKRD). SKRD structurally couples itself with SHRD and associated functions and concepts, such as Organisational Learning, the Learning Organisation and Human resource Management. It applies a holistic view of the organisation in order to strategically bring knowledge resources to bear in a manner that creates competitive advantage.

The drivers for knowledge as a resource, as put forward by the OECD, appear to require a treatment of development as opposed to management or coordination. We believe KM to be too broad to deliver this function. The concepts of 'knowledge' and 'management' do not appear to comfortably coexist, which is clearly evidenced by practitioner and theoretical dissatisfaction within the field.

Theorists such as Heisig (2009) and Nonaka et al. (2000) support the notion that the true essence of what is seen as KM is actually about the coordination of resources:

'The systematic handling of knowledge at the operational level of an organisation is a core element of KM... its arrangement [knowledge] and increased orientation towards organisation goals demands more systematic handling of knowledge

in organisational practice in order to achieve better results.' (Heisig, p. 5)

These authors are further supported by Sveiby and Lloyd (1987) who suggests the management of organisational know-how to be about the structures and processes of knowledge production and transfer. We cannot talk about this without speaking of aspects such as learning and technology. These theorists would appear to be talking about value generating activities that contribute directly to the generic intellectual capital taxonomy discussed earlier.

KM appears to exist as an evolution of Industry Efficiency Engineers and the Science Of Knowledge Utilisation. SKRD is presented as a further evolution, a discipline that mediates the interface between the development of human and technology resources to generate organisational value. SKRD would operate as a transactional function between learning and knowledge, building on the links established by theorist such as Chiva and Alegre (2005). The discipline would also bring focus to strategy, which Prusak and Weiss (2007), amongst others, see as an aspect frequently missed in KM practice.

CONCLUSION

To end where we began; we set out to address issues of dissatisfaction that resonate with both practitioners and academics.

"I don't believe knowledge can be managed. Knowledge Management is a poor term, but we are stuck with it, I suppose. "Knowledge Focus" or "Knowledge Creation" (Nonaka) are better terms, because they describe a mindset, which sees knowledge as activity not an object. A is a human vision, not a technological one' (Sveiby, cited in Wilson, 2002)

Almost a decade ago Sveiby acknowledged that KM was the wrong term to describe the nature of the field, lamenting its label over the suggestions of other more HR-centric theorists. We set out to challenge the assertion that we are 'stuck' with this dissatisfaction. This paper has demonstrated that KM is a modern day variation on a theme that has existed for over a quarter of a century. Seminal theorists in the field have expressed their dissatisfaction with the terminology of KM and the concept of managing what essentially exists in the mind of human beings. What also seems to be true is that the field is experiencing practical difficulties that could be attributed to its sheer breadth and scale.

Isolating the value drivers for knowledge as an organizational resource, we have presented a continuum for KM and offered Strategic Knowledge Resource Development as a potential solution to the current practitioner and academic dissatisfaction in both practice and theory. Sitting at the interface between the Techno-Centric and HR-Centric views of KM, Strategic Knowledge Resource Development appears to provide a space for extracting value from organizational knowledge resources.

We acknowledge the shortcomings of this limited paper, but suggest further research in this area in order to address the trends of KM dissatisfaction and to ultimately provide value for organizations in their quest for advantage. Our next step will be a further exploration of epistemological and ontological issues of SKRD by exploring realism in KM.

REFERENCES

Adler, P. (2001). Market, hierarchy and trust: The knowledge economy and the future of capitalism. *Organization Science*, 214–234.

Alavi, N., & Leidner, D. (1999). Knowledge management systems: emerging views and practices from the field. In *Proceedings of the 32nd Hawaii international conference on system science.* Retrieved October 22, 2008, from http://www2.computer.org/portal/web/csdl/doi/10.1109/HICSS.1999.77 2754

Alvesson, M., & Karreman, D. (2002). Odd couple: coming to terms with knowledge management. *Journal of Management Studies, 38*(7), 995–1018. doi:10.1111/1467-6486.00269

Angus, J. (2003). KM's father figure: Robert Buckman. *Infoworld Magazine.* Retrieved December 18, 2008, from www.infoworld.com

Antonacopoulou, E. P. (2006). Modes of Knowing in Practice: The Relationship between Learning and Knowledge Revisited. In Renzl, B., Matzler, K., & Hinterhuber, H. (Eds.), *The Future of Knowledge Management.* London: Palgrave.

Arbnor, I., & Bjerke, B. (2009). *Methodology for creating business knowledge* (3rd ed.). London: Sage.

Armstrong, M. (2006). *A handbook Of Human Resource Management Practice* (10th ed.). Cambridge, UK: Cambridge University Press.

Asgeirsdottir, B. (2005). OECD work on knowledge and the knowledge economy. In *Proceedings of the OECD/NSF conference on 'Advancing knowledge and the knowledge economy.* Retrieved November 15, 2007, from http://www.flacso.edu.mx/openseminar/downloads/ocde_knowledge_speech.pdf

Ash, J. (2004). Knowledge works. *Inside knowledge magazine, 8*(2). Retrieved October 1, 2007, from http://www.ikmagazine.com/xq/asp/txtSearch.CRM/exactphrase.1/sid.0/articleid.9F1AD936-E784-4833-A566-E92BF3B92B6C/qx/display.htm

ASLIB. (1952). Harnessing knowledge. *Nature, 170*, 698–699. doi:10.1038/170698a0

Barkham, P. (2008, July). What is the knowledge economy. *The Guardian Newspaper*. Retrieved January 18, 2009, from http://www.guardian.co.uk/business/2008/jul/17/economics.economicgrowth

Barnard, C. (1938). *The function of the executive*. Cambridge, MA: Harvard University Press.

Bell, D. (1973). *The coming of post-industrial society: A venture in social forecasting*. New York: The Basic Press.

Bournemann, M., et al. (2003). *An illustrated guide to Knowledge Management*. Paper presented at the Wissenmanagement forum, Graz. Retrieved December 18, 2008, from www.wm-forum.org

Bouthiller, F., & Shearer, K. (2002). Understanding knowledge manageent and information management: the need for an empirical perspective. *Information research, 8*(1). Retrieved January 4, 2008, from http://informationr.net/ir/8-1/paper141.html

Boxall, P. (1996). The strategic HRM debate and the resource-based view of the firm. *Human Resource Management Journal, 6*(3), 59–75. doi:10.1111/j.1748-8583.1996.tb00412.x

Boxall, P., & Steeneveld, M. (1999). Human Resource strategy and competitive advantage: a longitudinal study of engineering consultancies. *Journal of Management Studies, 36*(4), 443–463. doi:10.1111/1467-6486.00144

Bush, V. (1945). As we may think. *The Atlantic Magazine*. Retrieved October 7, 2008, from http://www.theatlantic.com/magazine/archive/1969/12/as-we-may-think/3881/

Carter, L. F. (1968). Knowledge production and utilisation in contemporary organisations. In T. L. Eidell & J. M. Kitchel (Eds.), *Knowledge production and utilisation in educational administration 1969* (pp. 1-20). Columbus, Ohio: University council for educational administration.

Chiva, R., & Alegre, J. (2005). Organisational learning and organisational knowledge. *Management Learning, 36*(1), 49–68. doi:10.1177/1350507605049906

Clarke, T. (2001). The knowledge economy. *Education + Training, 43*(4/5), 189–196. doi:10.1108/00400910110399184

Creech, H. (2005). Mobilising IUCN's knowledge to secure a sustainable future. *The IUCN knowledge management study*. Retrieved December 18, 2008, from http://www.iisd.org/pdf/2008/km_study_full_report.pdf

Davies, J., Struder, R., Sure, Y., & Warren, P. W. (2005). Next generation knowledge management. *BT Technology Journal, 23*(3), 175–189. doi:10.1007/s10550-005-0040-3

Diakoulakis, I. E., Georpopoulos, N. B., Koulouriotis, D. E., & Emeris, D. M. (2004). Towards a holistic knowledge management model. *Journal of Knowledge Management, 8*(1), 32–46. doi:10.1108/13673270410523899

Dicken, P. (2007). *Global Shift: Mapping the changing contours of the world economy* (5th ed.). London: Sage Publications Limited.

Drucker, P. F. (1959). *Landmarks of tomorrow*. New York: Harper.

Duncan, W. J. (1972). The knowledge utilisation process in management and organisation. *Academy of Management Journal, 15*(3), 273–287. doi:10.2307/254853

Edward, T., & Rees, C. (2006). *International Human resource Management: Globalization, national systems and multinational companies* (pp. 151–167). Upper Saddle River, NJ: Pearson Education Limited.

Farradane, J. E. L. (1970). Analysis and organisation of knowledge for retrieval. In *Proceedings of the 44th Aslib conference, University of Aberdeen.* Retrieved October 8, 2008, from http://www.emeraldinsight.com.ezproxy.webfeat.lib.ed.ac.uk/Insight/viewPDF.jsp?Filename=html/Output/Published/EmeraldFullTextArticle/Pdf/2760221203.pdf

Feldman, S. (2009). *Worldwide search and discovery software 2009-2013 Forecast update and 2008 vendo shares (Doc. No. 219883).* International Data Corporation.

Fisher, A. G. B. (1933). Capital and the growth of knowledge. *The Economic Journal, 43*(71), 379–389. doi:10.2307/2224281

Freeman, R. R. (1977). Ocean and environmental information: The theory, policy and practice of knowledge management. *Marine Policy, 1*(3), 215–229. doi:10.1016/0308-597X(77)90028-8

Garavan, T. N. (1991). Strategic Human Resource Development. *Journal of European Industrial Training, 15*(1), 17–31. doi:10.1108/EUM0000000000219

Garavan, T. N. (2007). A strategic perspective on human resource development. *Advances in Developing Human Resources, 9*(1), 11–21. doi:10.1177/1523422306294492

Gherardi, S. (2009). The critical power of the 'practice lens'. *Management Learning, 40*(2), 115–128. doi:10.1177/1350507608101225

Gibson, J. (2005). *Community resources: Intellectual property, international trade and protection of traditional knowledge.* Burlington, VA: Ashgate Publishing.

Gold, A. H., Malhotra, A., & Segars, A. H. (2001). Knowledge Management: An organisational capabilities perspective. *Journal of Management Information Systems, 18*(1), 185–214.

Griffiths, D. A., & Morse, S. M. (2009). Knowledge Management: Towards overcoming dissatisfaction in the field. *World Academy of Science Engineering and Technology, 54,* 724–735.

Grover, V., & Davenport, T. H. (2001). General perspectives on knowledge management: Fostering a research agenda. *Journal of Management Information Systems, 18*(1), 5–21.

Havelock, R. G. (1968). Dissemination and translation roles. In T. L. Eidell & J. M. Kitchel (Eds.), *Knowledge production and utilisation in educational administration 1969* (p. 64-119). Columbus, OH: University council for educational administration.

Heisig, P. (2009). Harmonisation of knowledge management – comparing 160 KM frameworks around the globe. *Journal of Knowledge Management, 13*(4), 4–31. doi:10.1108/13673270910971798

Henry, N. L. (1974). Knowledge Management: A new concern for public administration. *Public Administration Review, 34*(3), 189–196. doi:10.2307/974902

Hillman, D. J. (1977). Model for the on-line management of knowledge transfer. *On-line Review, 1*(1), 23-30.

Holsapple, C. W. (2004). *Handbook on knowledge management: Knowledge Matters.* Berlin: Birkhauser.

Jennex, M. E., & Olfman, L. (2004). Assessing knowledge management success/effectiveness models. In *Proceedings of the 37th Hawaii international conference on system sciences.* Retrieved February 18, 2008, from http://ieeexplore.ieee.org/xpl/freeabs_all.jsp?arnumber=1265571

Kakabadse, N. K., Kakabadse, A., & Kouzmin, A. (2003). Reviewing the knowledge management literature: Towards a taxonomy. *Journal of Knowledge Management, 7*(4), 75–91. doi:10.1108/13673270310492967

Kulkarni, U. R., Ravindran, S., & Freeze, R. (2006). A knowledge management success model: Theoretical development and empirical validation. *Journal of Management Information Systems, 239*(3), 309–347.

Lusty, I. (1942). Air-line engineering management. *Aircraft engineering,* 201-202.

Machlup, F. (1962). *The production and distribution of knowledge in the United States.* Princeton, NJ: Princeton University Press.

Maxwell, R. (1968). Presentation speech. *Information storage and retrieval, 4*(2), 87-90.

McCracken, M., & Wallace, M. (2000). Towards a redefinition of strategic HRD. *Journal of European Industrial Training, 24*(5), 281–290. doi:10.1108/03090590010372056

McElroy, M. W. (2000). The new Knowledge Management. *Knowledge and innovation, Journal of the Knowledge Management Consortium International, 1*(1), 43–67.

Mekhilef, M., & Flock, C. (2006). Knowledge Management: A multidisciplinary survey. In Cunningham, P., & Cunningham, M. (Eds.), *Exploiting the knowledge economy: Issues, applications, case studies.* Amsterdam, The Netherlands: IOS Press.

Mingers, J. (2008). Management knowledge and knowledge management: realism and forms of truth. *Knowledge management research and practice, 6,* 62-76.

Mokyr, J. (2002). *The gifts of Athena: Historical origins of the knowledge economy.* Princeton, NJ: Princeton University Press.

Nonaka, I., & Takeuchi, H. (1995). *The knowledge creating company: How Japanese companies create the dynamics of innovation.* New York: Oxford University press.

Nonaka, I., & Toyama, R. (2002). A firm as a dialectic being: toward the dynamic theory of the firm. *Industrial and Corporate Change, 11,* 995–1109. doi:10.1093/icc/11.5.995

Nonaka, I., & Toyama, R. (2007). Why do firms differ? The theory of the knowledge creating firm. In Ichijo, K., & Nonaka, I. (Eds.), *Knowledge creation and management 2007* (pp. 13–31). New York: Oxford University Press.

Nonaka, I., Toyama, R., & Konno, N. (2000). SECI, Ba and leadership: a unified model of dynamic knowledge creation. *Long Range Planning, 33,* 5–34. doi:10.1016/S0024-6301(99)00115-6

Nutting, P. G. (1918). The application of organised knowledge to national welfare. *The Scientific Monthly, 6*(5), 406–416.

Polanyi, M. (1969). Knowing and Being. In Grene, M. (Ed.), *Essays by Michael Polanyi.* Chicago: University of Chicago.

Prusak, L., & Weiss, L. (2007). Knowledge in organisational settings. In Ichijo, K., & Nonaka, I. (Eds.), *Knowledge creation and management 2007* (pp. 32–43). New York: Oxford University Press.

Qureshi, S., Briggs, R. O., & Hlupic, V. (2006). Value creation from intellectual capital: convergence of knowledge management and collaboration in the intellectual bandwidth model. *Group Decision and Negotiation, 15*(3), 197–220. doi:10.1007/s10726-006-9018-x

Rahe, M. (2009). Subjectivity and cognition in knowledge management. *Journal of Knowledge Management, 13*(3), 102–117. doi:10.1108/13673270910962905

Ray, T. (2005). Making Sense Of Managing Knowledge. In S. Little & T. Ray (Eds.), *Managing Knowledge: An Essential Reader 2005* (pp. 1-6, 10). London: Sage.

Rigby, D., & Bilodeau, B. (2007). Management tools and trends 2007. *A survey from Bain and Company*. Retrieved June 17, 2008, from http://www.bain.com/management_tools/Management_Tools_and_Trends_2007.pdf

Rigby, D., & Bilodeau, B. (2009). *Management Tools and Trends 2009*. Retrieved October 8, 2009, from www.bain.com

Riley, T. B. (2003, August 4). An overview of the knowledge economy. *egov Monitor Weekly*. Retrieved February 22, 2009, from http://www.egovmonitor.com/features/riley07.html

Roth, J. (2003). Enabling knowledge creation: Learning from an R+D organisation. *Journal of Knowledge Management, 7*(1), 32–48. doi:10.1108/13673270310463608

Ryle, G. (1949). *The concept of the mind*. Chicago: University of Chicago press.

Sarah, R., & Haslett, T. (2003). *Learning is a process which changes the state of knowledge of an individual or organisation* (Tech. Rep. No. 72/03). Melbourne, Australia: Monash University. Retrieved February 16, 2008, from http://www.buseco.monash.edu.au/mgt/research/working-papers/2003/wp72-03.pdf

Schutt, P. (2003). The post Nonaka knowledge management. *Journal of universal computer science, 9*(6), 451-462.

Smith, P. A. C. (2003). *Successful knowledge management: The importance of relationships, Invited paper – Universidad Central de Chile*. Retrieved February 2, 2008, from www.tlainc.com/S&C%20A1%20N1%2003.doc

Snowden, D. J. (2002). Complex acts of knowing, paradox and descriptive self-awareness. *Journal of Knowledge Management, 6*(2), 100–111. doi:10.1108/13673270210424639

Solintander, M., & Solintander, N. (2010). The sharing, protection and thievery of intellectual assets: The case of the formula 1 industry. *Management Decision, 48*(1), 37–57. doi:10.1108/00251741011014445

Spender, J. C. (2005). An overview: What's new and important about knowledge management? Building new bridges between managers and academics. In Little, S., & Ray, T. (Eds.), *Managing Knowledge: An essential reader 2005* (2nd ed., pp. 126–128). Thousand Oaks, CA: Sage Publications.

Stewart, T. A. (2002). The case against Knowledge management. *Business 2.0 magazine*. Retrieved August 20, 2007, from http://money.cnn.com/magazines/business2/articles/mag/print/0,1643,36747,00.html

Supyuenyong, V., & Islam, N. (2006). Knowledge management architecture: building blocks and their relationships. In *Proceedings of the IEEE PICMT 2006 technology management for the global future* (pp. 1210-1219).

Sveiby, K. E. (2008). East and West do meet – that is the real issue! *Journal of Intellectual Capital, 9*(2).

Sveiby, K. E., & Lloyd, T. (1987). *Managing knowhow – Add value by valuing creativity*. New York: Bloomsbury.

The Lancet. (1908, January 4). The Diffusion of Medical Knowledge. *Lancet*, 33–34.

The Science Newsletter. (1940). Defense requires knowledge, organised and implemented. *Science News, 38*(3), 47. doi:10.2307/3916486

Ulrick, D. (1997). Organising around capabilities. In Hesselbein, F., Goldsmith, M., & Beckhard, R. (Eds.), *The organisation of the future*. San Francisco: Jossey-Bass.

Ulrick, D. (1998). The new mandate for HR. *Harvard Business Review*, 124–134.

van den Hoof, B., & de Ridder, J. A. (2004). Knowledge sharing in context: the influence of organizational commitment, communication climate and CMS use on knowledge sharing. *Journal of Knowledge Management*, *8*(6), 118.

Watson, S., & Hewett, K. (2006). A multi-theoretical model of knowledge transfer in organisations: determinants of knowledge contribution and knowledge reuse. *Journal of Management Studies*, *43*(2), 141–173. doi:10.1111/j.1467-6486.2006.00586.x

Wenger, E., McDermott, R., & Snyder, W. (2002). *Cultivating communities of practice: A guide to managing knowledge*. Boston: Harvard Business School Press.

Williams, S. R. (1931). The collection and creation of knowledge. *The Journal of Higher Education*, *2*(8), 415–419. doi:10.2307/1974428

Wilson, T. D. (2002). The nonsense of knowledge management. *Information research, 8*(1).

Yang, B., Zheng, W., & Viere, C. (2009). Holistic views of knowledge management models. *Advances in Developing Human Resources*, *11*(3), 273–289. doi:10.1177/1523422309338584

Yolles, M. I. (1996). Critical Systems Thinking, paradigms, and the modelling space. *Systems Practice*, *9*(6), 549–570. doi:10.1007/BF02169213

This work was previously published in the International Journal of Knowledge and Systems Science, Volume 1, Issue 4, edited by W.B. Lee, pp. 41-60 copyright 2010 by IGI Publishing (an imprint of IGI Global).

Chapter 6
The Knowledge CORE:
A New Model to Challenge the Knowledge Management Field

David A. Griffiths
University of Edinburgh, Scotland

Serge Koukpaki
University of Edinburgh, Scotland

Brian Martin
University of Edinburgh, Scotland

ABSTRACT

This paper derives from a research project, which sets out to address practitioner dissatisfaction in the area of Knowledge Management. The author discusses common weaknesses in existing thinking about Knowledge Management and in prevailing models in particular. Modelling processes are considered and underlying assumptions that are required to be addressed in any attempt to create a Knowledge Management Model are examined. An overview is provided of the initial stages in the development of a new, synthetic and general model, The Knowledge Core©, with assumptions underlying this signposted and their influences upon modelling are discussed.

INTRODUCTION

This is the second in a series of papers derived from an ongoing research project, the overall aims of which are to address practitioner dissatisfaction in the field of Knowledge Management (KM). The first paper presented the outcome from an enquiry into Critical Success Factors, comparing findings from an extensive review of literature with existing models and frameworks (Griffiths & Morse, 2009).

This second paper examines the underpinning values that might influence the construction of a new model, and how this might influence the construction of a new KM assessment tool for organisations. The narrative provides an overview and visualisation of our earlier findings before developing an Action Research based approach,

DOI: 10.4018/978-1-4666-1782-7.ch006

linking KM to Systems Thinking, Soft Systems Methodology and Logic Modelling spaces.

We conclude by identifying the next steps in pursuit of what could be seen as a general model for the field.

1. OVERVIEW

KM appears to be firmly established as a strategic management tool (Rigby & Bilodeau, 2007). However, practitioners and academics seem to be expressing dissatisfaction with its performance in organisational settings (e.g., Rigby & Bilodeau, 2007; Smith, 2003). Theorists have been discussing dissatisfaction and potential deficiencies in the field for some time, particularly the lack of common framework to bind the process to situated settings (Rubenstein-Montano et al., 2001; Holsapple & Joshi, 2004; Metaxiotis et al., 2005; Mekhilef & Flock, 2006; Limone & Bastias, 2006). This lack of satisfaction, where KM is ranked 22 of 25 strategic management tools in a survey of 1221 global executives (Rigby & Bilodeau, 2007), coupled with an identified gap in theory, could cause a critical loss of resource value for organisations. These problems are succinctly acknowledged by Chun et al. (2008) who state that 'despite the importance of knowledge as an asset, few organisations truly understand what it means to be a knowledge-based firm and how to manage knowledge to achieve its goals' (p. 1).

These apparent deficiencies led to an extensive enquiry into the field (Griffiths & Morse, 2009). Conducting an evidence-based meta-analysis of 287 pieces of academic and practitioner KM literature and 71 KM models and frameworks, we concluded that a common framework of KM appeared plausible, existing across the disciplines of Business & Management; Engineering; Decision Science; Computer Science; Medicine & Health; and Social Science. We further concluded that this framework consisted of 16 common CSFs. In a distillation of our results we proposed four

functions of KM (Capturing & Storing, Creating, Sharing and Applying) and twelve enablers (What Is Known, Extending What is Known, Reflecting, Context, Motivation, Artifacts, Space, Culture, Organisational Structure, Knowledge Structure, Catalysts, Transmission). Examining the sample of 71 models and frameworks we exposed a potential gap in current research where 0 (zero) models, and only 1% of the literature in the original meta-analysis, identified all 16 CSFs.

This paper attempts to progress our research by suggesting a general model for the field, represented through The Knowledge Core Model. The search for new models and frameworks has been criticised by some theorists as being a contributing factor to the apparent poor performance of KM as a strategic management tool: 'The profusion of terms...flippancy as to the way the concept is used, ignorance of the classical categories of thought and the frivolous abuse of fashions...are constructing a "Tower of Babel", provoking injustice and unease in the unnecessary formulation and accelerated substitution of propositions of new models and expressions without allowing them to mature and without making a minimal effort to contrast them to prior ones' (Bueno, translated from Spanish and cited in Limone & Bastias, 2006, p. 40).

The position of Bueno is interesting as he appears to discourage the improvement of scientific theory, specifically Popper's theory of Falsifiability, which would seem to demand a process of evolution in order to interrogate the efficiency and effectiveness of existing models and frameworks in order to determine not only when they work, but when and why they don't work (Blackman *et al.*, 2004). However, Bueno's stance would also appear to inhibit the field from advancing Argyris & Schon's double loop learning theory (1982), where not only the action strategies, but also the governing variables of theories are examined.

In addition, Meadows (1982) opines that addressing issues of process change can be politically challenging as it can be easier to point away from the cause, being, in the case of KM, current action strategies within models and frameworks, than to interrogate the core of the issue, being the governing variables. Meadows further suggests that thinking such as that of Bueno can produce a state where a culture of least resistance is perpetuated and the desired performance of the field is lost to an accepted state of lower standards and poor performance. In another interpretation perhaps Bueno could be seen to be asking theorists to take more care and give greater depth of thought to analysis.

In acknowledging the concerns of Bueno, it would seem important to point towards the depth of our research which, whilst echoing the concerns of disparate language, demonstrates that current models and frameworks appeared to be deficient in demonstrating the CSFs or governing variables that could influence success within organisations. This would seem to indicate that it is in the interests of the field to consider a new model.

2. THE MODEL

The Knowledge Core (Figure 1, Figure 2 and Figure 3) presents a visual representation of our findings. However, theorists have suggested that creators of knowledge should be prepared to state their assumptions or theories before mapping their view of the world (Yolles, 1996; Checkland, 2000; Knowlton & Phillips, 2009). Knowlton & Phillips suggest that a failure to do this offers the potential to pollute research and devalue the knowledge created: 'Too often...models are built without the benefit of explicitly naming the assumptions and underlying theories of change. This omission can help explain why tremendous conflict, even chaos can erupt during program development, planning and implementation, or assessment' (p. 36).

This is supported by Arbnor & Bjerke (2009) and Jackson (2001) who believes that the knowledge creator's view of the world has to be explicit if the knowledge created is to be explained, understood and validated. Jackson (2001) posits

that it is not possible to determine the strengths of the methodological approach unless the theoretical view of the knowledge creator is explicitly expressed. This view can again be linked to Popper's Principle of Falsifiability and the need for scientific theory to be transparent in its underpinnings in order to enhance its testability. In this way it is possible to subject the findings to refutation and by doing so confirm its scientific status (Crease, 2001). Therefore the narrative presented in this paper will attempt to clarify the underlying assumptions of the authors in order to develop a clear perspective of the inductive process. This clarification would also seem to address another criticism suggested by Bueno, cited earlier, being the 'ignorance of the classical categories of thought'.

The knowledge creator's view of the world also provides signposts towards appropriate methodology, or blend of methodology, for enquiry and evaluation, which in turn develops the language that will mould the modelling space. By unveiling this for the examination of structures within the research paradigm the uncertainty surrounding the structural elements and their interrelationships can be reduced (Yolles, 1996; Arbnor & Bjerke, 2009). This would seem important in order to overcome issues of clarity within the KM field, which we discussed in our original research. Therefore the remainder of this paper will look to set out the assumptions employed and the journey taken in the development of The Knowledge Core as a prospective new model.

3. CRITICISM OF MODEL BUILDING

Bueno (cited by Limone & Bastias, 2006) criticises new models for not making 'a minimal effort to contrast them to prior ones' (p. 40). However, we did demonstrate in our analysis of 71 models and frameworks that 0 (zero) identified the 16 CSFs identified in our analysis of 287 pieces of KM literature. We also suggested that existing models

Figure 1. Frontal plane

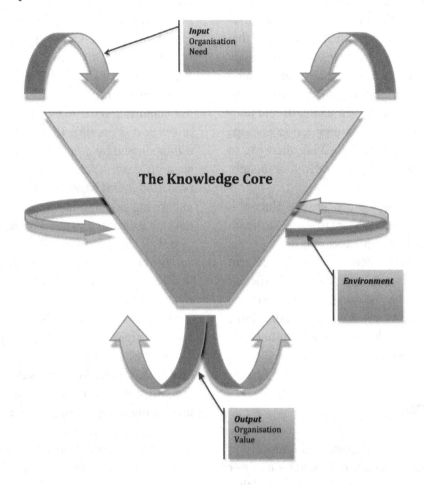

The Knowledge Core

Griffiths (2009) Edinburgh

failed in tests of 'Comprehensiveness', 'Correctness', 'Usefulness', 'Clarity' and 'Consciousness' synthesised from the work of Rasli (2004), Bacharach (1989) and Shanks (2003). The rigour applied to our research would appear to address Bueno's concerns and justify the development of a new model. Furthermore models are observed by Checkland (2000) as 'intellectual devices – whose role it is to help structure an exploration of the problem situation being addressed' (p. s26).

Model building has been criticised for attempting to be mathematical, where 'proof and formal analysis are aesthetic crafts' (Klein & Romero, 2007, p. 245) and Ludvall (2006) has stated that KM cannot be reduced to a set of techniques. However, Klein and Romero (2007) argue that model building brings discipline of mind and insight by applying formulaic models. They contend that proof will involve arguments that the model's formulation is of academic interest and importance with a purpose aimed at advancing knowledge and understanding of real-world issues.

Checkland (2000) offers a non-threatening view of models in suggesting that at this stage of

Figure 2. Upward view

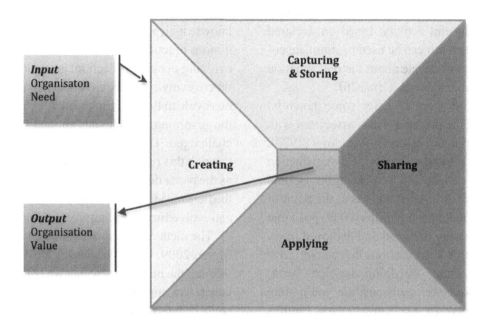

Figure 3. Transverse plane

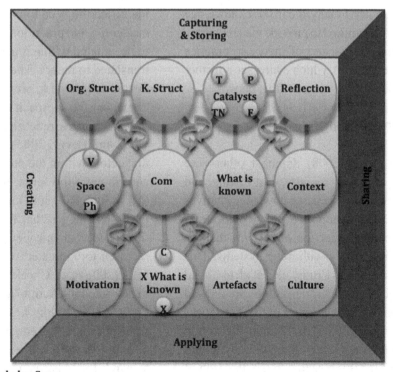

KM The Knowledge Core

Griffiths (2009) Edinburgh

Soft Systems research they are not actually models of anything: 'They are accounts of concepts of pure purposeful activity, based on declared world-views, which can be used to stimulate cogent questions in debate about the real situation and desirable changes to it' (p. s26).

This would seem to offer some potential resolution of the political issues associated with change as intimated earlier by Meadows (1982).

Further to this the signals of dissatisfaction signposted by Rigby and Bilodeau (2007) would appear to suggest ineffectiveness at the point of practice. Knowlton and Phillips (2009) posit that models need to be designed and deployed in order to overcome key questions that can improve effectiveness; 'are you doing the right work; can you make better decisions; are you getting superior results?' (p. 13). Knowlton and Phillips further suggest that models provide a critical link between strategy and results. This coupled with our findings suggests that a new model could assist in overcoming the dissatisfaction that lies at the core of this enquiry. Finally, theorists acknowledge that models are required to provide visual literacy in stimulating the transfer of theory to practice (Handzic et al., 2008), which addresses a further issue discussed at the outset of this paper.

4.1 Action Research

Cruywagen et al. (2008) amongst others see knowledge as being socially, historically and culturally bound and, because knowledge involves people, it leads the authors to relate the knowledge process to a collection of systems that are in constant interaction with other systems. This leads theorists such as Cruywagen et al. to Social Constructivism where 'organisations are viewed as a function of a particular set of circumstances and individuals' (p. 105). This fundamental notion of knowledge as a socially and culturally bound construct has led this research in the direction of Action Research (AR). Carr (2006) observes AR as having its foundation in the philosophy of human

action and the epistemological theories emanating from 'the personal and contextualised nature of knowledge' (p. 422). Schon (1983, 1987) provides a more practical description of AR as being an evolving cycle of reflection, grounded in action, where evolving research reflects upon the previous cycle to then inform the next cycle, allowing the governing variables and applied strategy to be challenged. This is the approach being pursued through this research, which will become clearer as the paper develops, where assumptions within the field are identified, reflected upon, challenged and evolved in an ongoing process of development.

The meta-analysis we conducted (Griffiths & Morse, 2009) was influenced by the AR paradigm through the manner by which we employed a co-generative approach to the data collection. This could be interpreted as being part of the Grounded Theory paradigm, where theories emerge from the collected data. However, we spoke of the need for a collaborative approach to the problems being experienced by the field and specifically identified the need to unblock the flow between academics and practitioners, as KM issues appear to be situated within practice, which is not being translated to theory. The initial research we conducted attempted to provide the foundation for a co-generative approach to the problem of KM in order to improve practitioner 'know how'. Greenwood and Levin (2005) support this suggesting that actors within the problem need to be able to contribute to the sense making process in order to develop successful 'know how'. Greenwood & Levin also suggest that this combination of practitioner and academic views formulates a powerful research tool situated within the AR paradigm. Carr (2006) and Checkland (2000) suggest AR to be rooted in 'Action' and 'Phronesis' and Carr (2006) proposes Phronesis as a form of reasoning where the journey of enquiry and outcome are open and subject to ethical reasoning and reflection in a search for 'what is good'. Carr posits that the co-generative link between academic and practitioner enables the progression of knowledge into knowing, through action. He further states that this link allows: 'practitioners who, in seeking to achieve the standard of excellence inherent in their practice, develop the capacity to make wise and prudent judgments about what, in a particular situation, would constitute an appropriate expression of the good' (p. 426).

Whether our original research is seen as Grounded Theory or AR, it would not seem to effect the development of the model or its future testing, to be discussed later, within the AR paradigm. This assertion is supported by Teram et al. (2005) and Dick (2003) who acknowledge that a Grounded Theory approach within the AR cycle improves the recoverability of research and therefore its validity in contributing to scientific knowledge.

4.2 AR and Soft Systems Methodology (SSM)

KM has been observed as being part of a system process (Cruywagen et al., 2008; Tiwana, 2000; Alavi & Leidner, 1999). A system has various definitions, such as 'a set of components interconnected for a purpose' (Open University, cited in Hebel, 2007, p. 499) or 'an entity which maintains its existence through the mutual interaction of its parts' (Chun et al., 2008) or 'a bounded system of linked components' (Carter et al., 1986, p. 4). The view of the system involving the whole is supported by authors such as Meadows (1982) who observes a system to be a bounded whole where one is able to analyse 'where things come from and where they go' (p. 102). This leads thinking to authors, such as Arbnor & Bjerke (2009), have discussed three methodological views of the world relating to organisational research: Analytical, Systems and Actors views. The Analytical view relies predominantly on quantitative evidence and tends to look at the individual parts of the whole. The Systems view, influenced by Holism, leans more towards a qualitative approach and examines reality from the perspective of the whole. In contrast, the Actors view examines the impact of the subject and enquirer upon the environment when viewed as a social construct (Arbnor & Bjerke, 2009). A clear line of sight has also been established between knowledge and learning (Pasteur et al., 2006; Chiva & Alegre, 2005). This exposes the field to the work of Senge (1997), who identifies Systems Thinking to be at the core of learning development in his seminal work 'The Fifth Discipline'. This suggests that Systems Thinking could have a major influence on the KM field.

In reviewing the 71 models and frameworks we examined it became apparent that KM solutions are usually developed via a Systems view of the world: Of 71 models, the foundation of 11 practitioner models could not be identified and 7 were computer based hard systems models, which whilst having their place were discarded for the purpose of this study; Of the remaining 53 models, 51 (96%) employed a Systems view and 2 (4%) utilised an Analytical view. This paper does not attempt to conclude upon a correct view of the world in relation to the KM field, it only reports that the Systems view appears to be the dominant view of knowledge creators within the field. However, this view would seem to be appropriate considering the nature of KM and its grounding in knowledge, which theorists such as (Carr, 2006) observe as being embedded in the situated context of the individual and therefore difficult to quantify. In further exploring the concerns of Knowlton and Phillips (2009), with regard to a lack of theoretical underpinning within modelling practice, a further enquiry was conducted of the sample to determine the number of papers that discussed the implications of underpinning theory upon the model presented. This enquiry found that 1 model (1.8%) discussed these implications. This, coupled with the dissatisfaction suggested by other authors, would seem to validate the concerns of Knowlton & Phillips and reinforces the argument highlighted at the outset of this paper.

The theory of the bounded whole is seen as providing well structured signposts for practitioner intervention (Jackson, 2001). However, if this is the case, with 96% of our literature subset utilising the Systems view, it would seem that there is an issue with the formulation of the model as 'well structured signposts for practitioner intervention' should not lead to the level of dissatisfaction being observed by Rigby and Bilodeau (2007). We emphasise this in our original research, where of the 71 models interrogated, only an average of 10 CSFs were identified per model. We suggest that this demonstrates a lack of 'know what' in literature, which impacts the performance of models in delivering 'know how'.

The systems view is further explored in relation to AR by the pre-eminent theorist, Checkland (2000) who developed a differentiated approach to systems methodology, being 'Soft' or 'Hard' systems. Checkland observes 'Hard Systems' as evolving from a systemic view of the world where systems can be engineered, as in the case for defined technical process related problems. Whereas with 'Soft Systems' the creator of knowledge observes complexity in the environment, usually related to social or cultural situations, and employs a system as a process of enquiry.

Theorists such as Senge (1997), Mehta (2007), Hebel (2007) and Handzic et al. (2008) suggest that solutions to issues such as those being experienced by KM need to be developed by exploring the patterns inherent to the process as a whole in order to identify enabling patterns that produce success. This appears to support a Soft Systems approach to the field as defined by Checkland (2000). The call for the application of Systems Thinking to overcome the lack of a common framework has been supported by authors such as Rubenstein-Montano et al. (2001) and is evidently being recognised given the fact that 96% of subset models sampled in our research employ the systems view.

KM could therefore be seen as an open network of existing processes that, through their interac-

tion, produce the whole that produced them in the first place. What is being suggested here, based on the work of authors such as Mingers (2002) and Cruywagen (2008), is that KM is made up of a network of existing processes consisting of the four functions of 'Collecting & Storing', 'Sharing', 'Creating' and 'Applying', and when they are combined they produce the output that is KM. This is furthered by theorists who suggest a coupled, autopoietic relationship between KM and the processes of the organisational macro and micro environment (Massey & Montaya-Weiss, 2003).

Criticism of current KM research suggests that practitioners and theorists are focused on the isolated functions of the KM process, such as knowledge sharing, whilst ignoring the interrelationships that contribute to the whole (Chun et al., 2008). However, this appears to be in conflict with the subset sample of models and frameworks investigated for this research, where only 4% employed an Analytical view compared to 96% that utilised a Systems view.

The systems view has been criticised by some authors for being indigenous to a 'Western' view of KM (Sharif, 2005). Sharif differentiates his views using the 'Western' and 'Eastern' descriptors. Sharif believes that 'Eastern' approaches to KM are founded upon communities of human interaction, which do not conform to a Western systems view. The human interaction view is supported by 'Western' authors such as Pasteur et al. (2006) who observe knowledge as being created through situated human interaction, which would appear to negate the East/West bias suggested by Sharif. 'Viewing knowledge...as a process or practice... brings people into the picture and thus tends to be more cognitive and behaviouristic in approach. It aims to understand how people acquire and apply knowledge and under what circumstances they learn and affect change' (p. 4).

This said Pasteur et al. advocate a Systems approach to KM processes, which also appears to challenge the systems/social interaction bias suggested by Sharif. However, in the interest of balance, the models examined in this paper were predominantly Western in origin and therefore would seem to support the claim of Sharif. Sharif also suggests the Eastern view of the world to involve communities of human interaction, which is incompatible with a Western Systems view. However, the work of Checkland (2000), discussed earlier, would seem to demonstrate that these environments can be investigated through Soft Systems methodology and therefore a systems approach. This would seem to address the criticisms of authors such as Sharif.

The Systems approach has also been criticised for overcomplicating what will happen naturally (Dawn et al., 2002). They posit that the learning process within an organisation will take place naturally, acting as a stimulus for continuous change in organisational cognitive structures. This said, it could be argued that in a modern global environment, which appears to truncate product life cycles and heighten demand for quality services (Dicken, 2007), the natural process needs to be understood in order to stimulate and manipulate it for competitive advantage.

Having established the rationale for developing research under the AR paradigm, the link between KM and Systems and the subsequent link between systems and Checkland's Soft Systems, it would seem appropriate to expand upon Soft Systems Methodology (SSM). Kemmis and McTaggart (2005) suggest that Soft Systems methodology provides a suitable framework for hypothesis testing. The authors state that the initial stages should comprise 'a process of problem identification'; this has been contextualised through our research, which is followed by a 'modelling phase' where a potential solution to the problem is developed and used to question the situation. This approach is supported by Checkland (2000) who provides a more detailed seven-step process for SSM. The steps relevant to this research include: 'The problem unstructured', provided by authors such as Rigby and Bilodeau (2007); 'The problem expressed', expressed in our first paper (Griffiths

& Morse, 2009); 'Root definition of the relevant system', again, expressed in our first paper; and finally, 'Development of conceptual models', which we generate through this paper.

The model building process will then be validated through Checkland's (2000) sixth step, being the examination of possible changes within the situated environment, and the seventh step, being the action taken to address the problem situation. This is further discussed in our conclusion.

4.3 The Logic Modelling Space

Checkland (2000), states that SSM involves a 'logic-based stream of analysis' (p. s21). This would appear to lead this research towards a Logic Modelling method as a tool to develop visual literacy as an expression of our research.

The Logic Modelling space offers a visual representation of the world in order to 'offer a way to describe and share an understanding of relationships among elements necessary to operate a program or change effort' (Knowlton & Phillips, 2009, p. 5). Knowlton & Phillips offer two distinct pallets in the Logic Modelling space, 'Theory of change' and 'Program'. The fundamental differences between the two pallets is that Theory of Change Models provide a high magnification, giving a simple view of the world, which is seen as a version of the truth that guides knowledge development. Whereas a Program Model provides a lower level of magnification that provides precise situated detail (Knowlton & Phillips, 2009).

There appears to be an issue of Logic Modelling definition when applied against the needs of this research. Theory of Change Models are seen as delivering plausible 'big picture' overviews which are designed to demonstrate the deliverables achievable through structured intervention (Knowlton & Phillips, 2009). However, we criticised existing models for a lack of demonstrable 'know how' in their construction. It would appear that a high level of magnification would not satisfy the current needs of the field. Program Logic Models 'help with more precise decisions about which activities in a given strategy are most effective' (Knowlton & Phillips, 2009, p. 14), but the authors state that these models are situated in their focus and are firmly grounded in validated knowledge of what is known. This is not the case at this stage of this enquiry. Theory of Change Models are observed by Knowlton & Phillips as 'drafts' that are subject to change as the model evolves, which would appear to support the Soft Systems methodology proposed by Checkland (2000) and the position of this research as an evolving reflective process. The core of the problem would seem to be that the Theory of Change modelling space does not provide for the details that affect planning, implementation and evaluation, all of which would appear necessary to overcome issues of 'know-how' identified in our first paper (Griffiths & Morse, 2009)

Therefore this research utilises a blended modelling space, landscaping the KM field through a Theory of Change Model, whilst using elements of lower magnification provided by Program Logic Models. Knowlton and Phillips (2009) offer three key characteristics that need to be present in a Theory of Change Model: 'Co-created with shared meaning; evidence based; appropriate scale' (p. 61). Our research applied a co-generative approach to their meta-analysis, which combined with the scope and scale of their research would seem to satisfy the first two requirements of Knowlton & Phillips. The third point will directly inform the design of The Knowledge Core.

Checkland (2000) offers a potential explanation for the plethora of models identified by Bueno and supported by our findings. Checkland suggests that problems can be subject to contextualised versions of the truth, which would seem to be the case in the KM field where a lack of a generalised framework would seem to increase demand for situated models that appear to be difficult to translate across disciplines. Checkland suggests that this is because 'interpretations of

purpose will always be many and various; there would always be a number of models in play, never simply one model purporting to describe "what is the case"' (p. s15). The field has been demonstrated to be systems based and linked to logic analysis, which can employ models that display one of many versions of the truth. This would appear to be a possible contributor to the dissatisfaction being experienced in the field. This paper therefore proposes The Knowledge Core to be a general model for KM, which can then be applied according to situated need.

5. INFLUENCES ON DESIGN

Carter et al. (1986) describe key principles in the construction of system boundaries; only include those elements or relationships that cause an impact upon the process; include elements that are inherently controlled by the system or its user, but similarly it is important to remove those elements that cannot be controlled by the system or user. Yolles (1996) suggests that this approach dissolves uncertainty, where system boundaries should avoid cutting across processes by either including or excluding them from the system's whole. Carter et al. (1986) develop this position stating that this approach removes uncertainty when examining the effect of elements upon the system. Carter et al. also suggest that a useful description is needed, in which the open or closed, or partial open/closed processes are clear to the user (an open process being one that interacts with the environment and a closed process being one that is insulated from the environment). This would seem to be supported by Senge (1995) who discusses the need for systems that are generative in nature. He suggests that these convey 'what causes the patterns of behaviour' (p. 53), which in turn allows the user to understand how changes to these patterns can produce different behaviours within the system. Senge promotes this approach over the 'responsive processes' (those which examine patterns of behaviour), or 'reactive processes' (those which examine events). Therefore the model sets out to demonstrate the 16 Critical Success Factors broken down into 4 functions and 12 enablers that we discussed in our first paper (Griffiths & Morse, 2009), along with an element of environmental interaction, which will be discussed later.

Meadows (1982) suggests that Systems Thinking determines a weighting towards the whole and not towards myths or perceived major factors – which could inhibit success through a failure to identify a limiting factor, having true influence over the process. With this being the case the model does not take into account the frequency of findings discussed in our meta-analysis, as limiting factors would seem to be situationally embedded and cannot be represented within the blended Theory of Change Model being applied in this paper. This has therefore informed the appropriate scale of the model as suggested earlier by Knowlton and Phillips (2009)

KM has been suggested in this paper to be a system of processes that interacts with the environment to produce its whole. This interaction would seem to suggest that it informs and is informed by the situated environment and would appear to require representation within the flows of the model process. Leonard (1999) posits that knowledge needs to be maintained in order to be of value and Markus (2001) suggests that knowledge reuse is of importance to the viability of knowledge as a value creating resource. This suggests the need for a KM tool that is designed to create a loop as opposed to a linear chain. McElroy (2000) reinforces this, stating that KM is a complex open system, influenced by complexity and System theory, which constantly interacts with its environment. Chowdhury (2006) links Bandura's Social Learning Theory to demonstrate that human behaviour develops in a 'continuous reciprocal interaction between cognitive, behavioural and environmental determinants (p. 5). This seems to underpin the need for a loop, where the system both influences and is influenced by the environment through its actions, and is demonstrated in diagram 1 (p. 3) as the flow through and around the model in a cyclic relationship.

Handzic et al. (2008) conducted narrative research into current KM models and suggested that many to be deficient in their use of double-loop feedback. Handzic et al. Support the link between knowledge and learning, discussed earlier, and consequently observe this omission as a critical flaw in the field. The need for a feedback loop is also discussed by Meadows (1982) who suggest that where systems experience situated failure it can often be directly attributed to structural behavioural issues. Meadows suggests that a feedback loop is required in order for the model to flex and overcome issues of situated failure. We also identified this, where we observe reflection or testing as one of our 16 CSFs (Griffiths & Morse, 2009). This also satisfies the need for a double loop approach to modelling, as suggested by Argyris and Schon (1982), where the governing variables and applied strategy are constantly challenged.

Feedback loops have been criticised for not providing an ongoing testing process, where proposed solutions are fed back into the process and continuously tested to determine effectiveness against other alternative solutions (Blackman et al. 2004). Blackman et al. link their theory back to the work of Popper to suggest that double-loop thinking fails the falsifiability test, in that is identifies when a system works, but fails to identify when it doesn't. However the Theory of Variety Attenuation suggests that variety overload can break down the system (Schwaninger, 2009). It could also be said that solutions are effective until a flaw is identified through application, at which time an optimised solution should be implemented. This could be linked to value and context, this was discussed in Griffiths and Morse (2009), where we cite the work of Hori et al. (2004) in overcoming issues such as variety overload through the following formula: Representational Context [Artefacts]

+ Conceptual Context [Existing in the mind] + Real world context [Situated Application] = Value.

Checkland (2000) suggest that defined arrows and boxes demonstrate a certainty in the process, which Soft Systems research at the stage of this paper is not able to offer. Checkland believes that visual representations of the proposed solution should reflect the volatility of the Action Research Process. However, this research is attempting to move towards a paradigm that can be viewed as 'what really exists' in an attempt to overcome uncertainty in the field. With this being the case the model is represented at the point of research conducted to date. This divergence from Checkland's approach to SSM would appear to be supported in the Logic Modelling space, where Theory of Change Models are represented with defined flows that reflect the certainty of the creator at that time (Knowlton & Phillips, 2009).

The Knowledge Core has been designed to demonstrate the interaction between the system and the environment. It has also been structured to demonstrate the interrelated support of the four main functions, which provide the parameters of the bounded whole. The enablers are demonstrated to be interlinked, but volatile, in that they are not stationery and will move according to the need of the function and the demand of the situated environment.

It is proposed that in order for an organisation is to create value it must look at the whole, being the bounded functions of 'Capturing & Storing', 'Sharing', 'Creating' and 'Applying'. From this position it would seem possible to enquire in to the efficiency and effectiveness of the function through the engagement of the enablers.

CONCLUSION

The Knowledge Core Model appears to provide an evidence based representation of 'know what', but for it to be an effective management tool it will need to transmit 'know how'. This is supported by authors such as Meadows (1982) who suggests that in order to heighten standards it is necessary to identify leverage points, which in the case of this research has been identified by the functions and enablers. However the 'know how' required to manipulate them would still appear to be ambiguous, which does not satisfy the current needs of the field. This is accented by Handzic et al. (2007) who find that many model processes detail the 'what' but appear to fail in transmitting the 'how', rendering them incomplete. This lack of identification of leverage points and 'know-how' is evident beyond the KM field, with social scientists being criticised for not extrapolating clearly signposted means of intervention to effect change at a practitioner level (Jackson, 2001).

It would therefore appear necessary to develop an assessment tool for organisations to evaluate their processes and their effectiveness as part of the KM system. However, it would first seem appropriate to gather a second data set to compare and contrast our findings against the situated views of practitioners. This approach can improve the quality of the research whilst providing the enquiry with prompts for the AR cycle where the data sets converge and diverge (Dick, 2003). A practitioner survey will therefore be deployed as part of a dual stream of research investigating Checkland's next step in Soft Systems Methodology, which involves the comparison of the proposed model against real world situations (Checkland, 2000). The second step in this enquiry will involve the development of a participatory assessment tool for use as part of an organisational enquiry. This process will use document analysis, interviews and surveys as a blended approach to identify gaps in existing practice. These gaps will then be addressed as part of an Action Learning activity within the organisation, the outcomes of which will then be used to inform strategic and operational plans for KM development. This will allow for the validation of the model through Checkland's (2000) sixth step in SSM, being the examination of possible changes within the situated environment and the seventh step, being the action taken to address the problem situation. This would also allow for the contextualisation of the situated issues through the development of a Programme Logic Model as suggest earlier in this paper.

This process may therefore have the potential to develop a model that has utility across sectors and cultures, with the model being designed for situated application and a participatory framework for implementation as part of the AR paradigm in a co-generative approach to situated problem identification (Teram et al. 2005), which we have suggested as being essential if KM is to shrug off its shroud of dissatisfaction.

This paper set out to present a new general model for the KM field. Expanding upon the findings from our earlier research, this paper has examined underlying assumptions to contextualise the presentation of a new KM model, The Knowledge Core. We have outlined these assumptions and signposted their influence upon the development of the model for testing. Criticism of the modelling process within the KM field has been discussed and addressed. Finally a pathway for the validation of The Knowledge Core has been developed as a progression in accordance with the AR paradigm and Soft Systems Methodology. This will be further addressed in our next paper, which will explore the situated views of KM and their potential contribution to a general model for the field.

REFERENCES

Alavi, M., & Leidner, D. E. (1999). Knowledge management systems: Issues, challenges and benefits. *Communications of the Association for Information Systems, 1*(7).

Arbnor, I., & Bjerke, B. (2009). *Methodology for creating business knowledge* (3rd ed.). London: Sage Publications.

Argyris, C., & Schon, D. (1982). *Reasoning, learning and action: Individual and organisational.* Reading, MA: Addison-Wesley.

Bacharach, S. B. (1989). Organizational theories: some criteria for evaluation. *Academy of Management Review, 14*(4), 496–515. doi:10.2307/258555

Blackman, D., Connelly, J., & Henderson, S. (2004). Does double loop learning create reliable knowledge. *The Learning Organization, 11*(1), 11–27. doi:10.1108/09696470410515706

Carr, W. (2006). Philosophy, methodology and action. *Journal of Philosophy of Education, 40*(4), 421–435. doi:10.1111/j.1467-9752.2006.00517.x

Carter, R., Martin, J., Mayblin, B., & Munday, M. (1986). *Systems, management and change.* London: The Open University.

Checkland, P. (2000). Soft systems methodology: A thirty year retrospective. *Systems Research and Behavioral Science, 17*, S11–S58. doi:10.1002/1099-1743(200011)17:1+<::AID-SRES374>3.0.CO;2-O

Chiva, R., & Alegre, J. (2005). Organisational learning and organisational knowledge. *management learning, 36*(1) 49-68.

Chowdhury, M. S. (2006). Human behaviour in the context of training: An overview of learning theories as applied to training and development. *Journal of knowledge management, 7*(2). Retrieved January 10, 2008, from http://www.tlainc.com/articl12.htm

Chun, M., Sohn, K., Arling, P., & Granados, N. F. (2008). Systems theory and knowledge management systems: The case of Pratt-Whitney Rocketdyne. In *proceedings of the 41st Hawaii International Conference on Systems Sciences* (pp. 1-10).

Crease. (2002). Finding the flaw in falsifiability. *Physics world online magazine*. Retrieved April 8, 2009, from www.physicsworld.com/cws/article/print/16478

Cruywagen, M., Swart, J., & Gevers, W. (2008). One size does not fit all – towards a typology of knowledge centric organisations. *Electronic Journal of Knowledge Management*, *6*(2), 101–110.

Dawn, J., Bodorik, P., & Dhaliwal, J. (2002). Supporting the e-business readiness of small and medium sized enterprises: approaches and metrics. *Internet research: Electronic networking applications and policy*, *12*(2), 139-164.

Dick, B. (2003). Action research and grounded theory. In *Proceedings of Refereed paper ALARPM/SCIAR conference*. Retrieved February, 8, 2009 from http://www.uq.net.au/~zzbdick/dlitt/DLitt_P60andgt.pdf

Dicken, P. (2007). *Global shift: Mapping the changing contours of the world economy* (5th ed.). London: Sage Publications.

Greenwood, D. J., & Levin, M. (2005). Reform of the social sciences and of universities through action research. In Denzin, N. K., & Lincoln, Y. S. (Eds.), *The sage handbook of qualitative research* (3rd ed., pp. 33–64). Thousand Oaks, CA: Sage.

Griffiths, D. A., & Morse, S. M. (2009). Knowledge Management: Towards overcoming dissatisfaction in the field. *World Academy of Science Engineering and Technology*, *57*(2), 724–735.

Handzic, M., Lagumdzija, A., & Celjo, A. (2008). Auditing knowledge management practices: model and application. *Knowledge management research and practice*, *6*, 90-99.

Hebel, M. (2007). Light bulbs and change: Systems Thinking and organisational learning for new ventures. *The Learning Organization*, *14*(6), 499–509. doi:10.1108/09696470710825114

Holsapple, C. W., & Joshi, K. D. (2004). A formal knowledge management ontology: conduct, activities, resources, and influences. *Journal of the American Society for Information Science and Technology*, *55*(7), 593–612. doi:10.1002/asi.20007

Hori, K., Kakakaji, K., Yamamoto, Y., & Ostwald, J. (2004). Organic perspectives of knowledge management: Knowledge evolution through a cycle of knowledge liquidisation and crystallisation. *Journal of universal computer science*, *10*(3), 252-261.

Jackson, M. C. (2001). critical Systems Thinking and practice. *European Journal of Operational Research*, *128*(2), 233–244. doi:10.1016/S0377-2217(00)00067-9

Kemmis, S., & McTaggart, R. (2005). Participatory Action Research: Communicative Action and the Public Sphere. In Denzin, N., & Lincoln, Y. (Eds.), *Handbook of Qualitative Research* (3rd ed., pp. 559–603). Thousand Oaks, CA: Sage Publications.

Klein, D. B., & Romero, P. P. (2007). Model building versus theorising: The paucity of theory in the journal of economic theory. *Econ Journal Watch*, *4*(2), 241–271.

Knowlton, L. W., & Phillips, C. C. (2009). *The Logic Model Guidebook – Better strategies for great results*. London: Sage publications.

Leonard, A. (1999). A viable systems model: consideration of knowledge management, *Journal of knowledge management practice*. Retrieved October 2007, from http://www.tlainc.com/articl12.htm

Limone, A., & Bastias, L. E. (2006). Autopoiesis and knowledge in the organisation: Conceptual foundation for authentic knowledge management. *Systems Research and Behavioral Science*, *23*, 39–49. doi:10.1002/sres.745

Lundvall. (2006). *Knowledge management in the learning economy* (Danish Research Unit for Industrial Dynamics working paper 06-6). Retrieved May 16, 2008, from http://www.druid.dk/wp/pdf_files/06-06.pdf

Markus, L. M. (2001). Toward a theory of knowledge reuse: Types of knowledge reuse situations and factors in reuse success. *Journal of Management Information Systems, 18*(1), 57–93.

Massey, A. P., & Montaya-Weiss, M. M. (2003). Enhancing performance through knowledge management. In *Handbook of business strategy* (pp. 147-151). New York: Thomson publishing.

McElroy, M. W. (2000). The new knowledge management. *Knowledge and innovation: Journal of the knowledge management consortium international, 1*(1), 43-67.

Meadows, D. H. (1982). Whole systems – Whole Earth models and systems. *The Coevolution Quarterly*, 98–108.

Mehta, N. (2007). The value creation cycle: moving towards a framework for knowledge management implementation. *Knowledge management research and practice, 5*, 126-135.

Mekhilef, M., & Flock, C. (2006). Knowledge Management: A multidisciplinary survey. In Cunningham, P., & Cunningham, M. (Eds.), *Exploiting the knowledge economy: Issues, applications, case studies*. Amsterdam: IOS Press.

Metaxiotis, K., Engazakis, K., & Psarras, J. (2005). Exploring the world of Knowledge management: agreements and disagreements in the academic/practitioner community. *Journal of Knowledge Management, 9*(2), 6–18. doi:10.1108/13673270510590182

Mingers, J. (2002). Can social systems be autopoietic? Assessing Luhmann's social theory. *The Sociological Review, 50*, 278–299. doi:10.1111/1467-954X.00367

Pasteur, K., Pettit, J., & van Schagen, B. (2006). *Knowledge management and organisational learning for development* (Workshop background paper). Retrieved January 11, 2009, from www.km4dev.org

Rasli, M. D. (2004). *Knowledge management framework for the Malaysian constructing companies* (IRPA Project No. 74320). Retrieved December 18, 2008, from http://eprints.utm.my/4121/

Rigby, D., & Bilodeau, B. (2007). Management tools and trends 2007. *A survey from Bain and Company.* Retrieved June 17, 2008, from http://www.bain.com/management_tools/Management_Tools_and_Trends_2007.pdf

Rubenstein-Montano, B., Liebowitz, J., Buchwalter, J., McCaw, D., Newman, B., & Rebeck, K. (2001). The Knowledge Management Methodology Team. A Systems Thinking framework for knowledge management. *Decision Support Systems, 31*, 5–16. doi:10.1016/S0167-9236(00)00116-0

Schon, D. A. (1983). *The reflective practitioner: How professionals think in action.* New York: Basic books.

Schön, D. A. (1987). *Educating the reflective practitioner.* San Francisco, CA: Jossey-Bass.

Schwaninger, M. (2009). Complex versus complicated: The how of coping with complexity. *Kybernetes, The international journal of systems and cybernetics, 38*(1-2), 83-92.

Senge, M. (1997). *The fifth discipline.* London: Century Business Publishing.

Shanks, G., Tansley, E., & Weber, R. (2003). Using ontology to validate conceptual models. *Communications of the ACM, 46*(10), 85–89. doi:10.1145/944217.944244

Sharif, A. M. (2006). Knowledge management: A neuro-hemispherical view of the field. *Knowledge management research and practice, 4*, 70-72.

Smith, P. A. C. (2003). *Successful knowledge management: The importance of relationships* (Tech. Rep.). Santiago, Chile: Universidad Central de Chile. Retrieved February 2, 2008, from www.tlainc.com/S&C%20A1%20N1%2003.doc

Teram, E., Schachter, C. L., & Stalker, C. A. (2005). The case for integrating grounded theory and participatory action research: Empowering clients to inform professional practice. *Qualitative Health Research*, *15*(8), 1129–1140. doi:10.1177/1049732305275882

Tiwana, A. (2000). *The Knowledge management Toolkit: practical techniques for building a knowledge management system.* Upper Saddle River, NJ: Prentice Hall.

Yolles, M. I. (1996). Critical Systems Thinking, paradigms, and the modelling space. *Systems Practice*, *9*(6), 549–570. doi:10.1007/BF02169213

This work was previously published in the International Journal of Knowledge and Systems Science, Volume 1, Issue 2, edited by W.B. Lee, pp. 1-14 copyright 2010 by IGI Publishing (an imprint of IGI Global).

Chapter 7
Knowledge Crash and Knowledge Management

Jean-Louis Ermine
TELECOM Business School, France

ABSTRACT

Population ageing is a phenomenon that is quite new and irreversible in the history of mankind. Every country and every organisation is concerned while it is not certain that all the risks and challenges have been clearly identified. Clearly, there is a risk of massive knowledge loss, i.e., "Knowledge Crash", due to massive retirements, but not exclusively for this reason. This risk is not evaluated at the right level, and in this regard, this article, by including the problem of "Knowledge Crash" in the more general framework of "Knowledge Management", enlarges the concepts of knowledge, generation, and knowledge transfer. The author proposes a global approach, starting from a strategic analysis of a knowledge capital and ending in the implementation of socio-technical devices for inter-generational knowledge transfer.

INTRODUCTION

Inter-generational knowledge transfer is a recent problem which is closely linked to the massive number of retirements expected in the next few years. These retirements are caused by "population ageing," which is the situation of societies where the ratio of elderly people is growing. This phenomenon has two characteristics that are not

well-known, and hence not really integrated into the solutions currently being put forward (OECD, 1996; UNFPA, 2002):

- *The phenomenon is worldwide:* one often wrongly thinks that this phenomenon (often assimilated with the so-called « Baby Boom » phenomenon, which is just a particular case) is only occurring in developed countries with a low birth rate. But nearly every country in the world is concerned:

DOI: 10.4018/978-1-4666-1782-7.ch007

it is sufficient to have a growing average lifetime, or a decreasing birth rate to have a population ageing phenomenon.

- *The phenomenon has never occurred before*: this is the first time in the history of mankind that ageing is growing like this, and, according to the UN, the process seems to be irreversible.

This phenomenon is worrying a lot of international, national, regional and local social groups, regarding the social, economical, cultural, political consequences. It will certainly change many things for investments, consumers, job markets, pensions, taxes, health, families, real estate, emigration and immigration etc. (Harper, 2006; Kohlbacher, Güttel, & Haltmeyer, 2009).

A consequence of population ageing is, of course, ageing of the working population. Employment policies (especially for seniors) will greatly change. If nothing is done, the number of retired people will grow rapidly in the next ten years, and conversely the number of employed people will stay constant. According to the OECD's studies, this will pose a great threat to the prosperity and the competitiveness of countries.

Related to competitiveness, population ageing raises an unexpected problem. We now know that we have entered the "Knowledge Economy" where the main competitive advantage is an intangible asset in organisations (private or public), called "knowledge", the definition and the status of which is still being discussed (Foray, 2004). The massive retirement of a lot of employees is also accompanied by the loss of a lot of knowledge and know-how. The Knowledge Management discipline says that nearly 70% of useful knowledge in companies is tacit. That means that knowledge and know-how are compiled in the employees' brains and are very little elicited by using information bases, documents, databases. There is also a theoretical difficulty to elicit this kind of tacit knowledge. If this knowledge, which is not well known, is critical in order to carry out some

processes in the organisation, its loss must be considered as a major risk for this organisation. One must say that, nowadays, very few organisations in the world are considering this risk. Three levels of risk (and risk perceptions) are possible:

- Knowledge Gap, due to a re-acquisition of knowledge which is not sufficiently fast. This implies more cost for acquiring knowledge, loss of efficiency, delays in evolution etc. This is not perceived as a major risk
- Knowledge Loss, due to a partial loss of the organisational memory. This implies loss of production, quality decreasing, loss of market shares or clients ... This is perceived as a serious risk, and has been already experienced by a lot of companies (DeLong, 2004)
- Knowledge Crash, due to a loss (often sudden) of a strategic capability of the organisation. This is a major risk for the organisation

Very few organisations are considering those risks, and envisage a catastrophe scenario from Knowledge Gap to Knowledge Crash (Streb, Voelpel, & Leibold, 2008).

However, some sectors are very preoccupied. The nuclear domain worldwide has been especially concerned since 2002 (IAEA, 2006). It is in fact seriously exposed to knowledge loss, because it is "knowledge intensive" (i.e., based on complex and varied know-how), because it has experienced a "knowledge gap" due to the non-interest of the young generation and a long period of non-recruitment. Moreover, the safety and geo-strategic constraints, which are well known in this domain, add to the criticality of a "Knowledge Crash".

The public sector is also very concerned, as population ageing is growing faster than in other sectors (OECD, 2007). Regarding the number of public agents retiring in the next decade, maintaining the capabilities for delivering the same efficiency and quality in public services is a very complex problem, and is closely linked to the risk of knowledge loss.

This issue is not really addressed in knowledge management literature (See for instance (Ebrahimi, Saives, & Holford, 2008); Joe & Yoong, 2006; Slagter, 2007). However, this is a true challenge for this domain (Kannan & Madden-Hallet, 2006).

Integrating the problem of the "Knowledge Crash" in the more general framework of "Knowledge Management" gives a new dimension to the inter-generational knowledge transfer problem. KM is a global approach for managing a knowledge capital and will allow a risk management in a reasonable, coherent and efficient way.

This is in fact a "symptom" of a more general and complex "disease". It gives new visions for the notion of generation and Knowledge transfer process: the risk of Knowledge Crash is also linked, to a lesser extent, to the phenomenon of staff turnover, the notion of generation is not only linked to age, for instance (Bourdelais, 2006) shows that the notion of ageing is a social construct, and that in our normalised societies, chronological age is unfortunately more and more a determining factor in the definition of the stages in a person's life ; the problem of knowledge transfer is very close to the problem of « Knowledge Sharing », which is a top issue for Knowledge Management.

This article addresses the question of using Knowledge Management methods for knowledge risk prevention. The main contribution of this research is a global methodology, starting from the highest level in the organisation (the strategy) to build step by step some operational solutions, in a coherent KM roadmap for the organisation. This methodology is complete, from strategy to information system, and then its implementation requires an important effort of the concerned organisation; it can be also partially implemented, depending the problem addressed. In this paper, we just give a brief description of the methodology.

That methodology has been experimented worldwide and continuously refined during the last ten years. Some experiments have been documented in different languages, and we give at the end of the article some selected published case studies in English. This approach, built with a constant cross-fertilisation between theory and practice, is now robust enough to be deployed on a very wide range of knowledge problems in the next few years, including especially inter-generational knowledge transfer (Van Berten & Ermine, 2006); Boughzala & Ermine, 2004).

DESCRIPTION OF THE METHOD FRAMEWORK

The proposed method to implement an inter-generational knowledge transfer approach is based on three principles that give a sound basis for the three basic phases in an inter-generational transfer plan. These principles are:

Principle 1: Any organisation has « organisational knowledge » as a specific sub-system.

This knowledge is much more than the addition of all individual knowledge and it is more or less preserved through time in training materials (documents, data-bases, software etc.) or through individual and/or collective exchanges/transfers. This organisational knowledge is accumulated within the organisation throughout its history, and constitutes what we shall call the « Knowledge Capital ». The concept of Knowledge Capital as an intangible sub-system of the organisation is still controversial, because it contradicts the classical vision of the organisation as a system that processes information for operational actors or decision makers. This new vision for an organisation, seen as a « knowledge processor », is formalised in a systemic and mathematical model, called AIK with the subsystems: A for Knowledge Actors, I for Information System, K for Knowledge Capital, which includes the knowledge flows circulating in the organisation. The full theoretical justification of that principle and complete model are given in Ermine (2005).

Principle 2: The organisational knowledge (the sub-system K) is a complex system.

The concept of "complex system" is the one given by the "General System Theory" (Von Bertalanffy, 2006). It is then intelligible and « manageable » by considering several essential points of view. We claim that these points of view are not numerous, and generic enough to be applied to any knowledge corpus, regardless of the domain of application. Moreover, as already said, the major part of the knowledge corpus is essentially tacit.

Principle 3: Knowledge transfer is a binary social process depending on the learning context.

Knowledge transfer is more complex than one might imagine at first sight. It must be defined according to two points of view (cf., for instance, Argote, 1999; Szulanski, 2000).

- A process based on a bilateral process between a transmitter and a receiver (individuals, groups, organisations) with an expected result and a given content as input.
- A social emerging process, depending on context and environment.

Based on these three principles, the intergenerational knowledge transfer approach must include three phases:

- Phase 1: Strategic analysis of the Knowledge Capital:

The Knowledge Capital of an organisation is now considered as one of its most strategic assets. As we have seen, this asset is vulnerable

and threatened by a Knowledge Crash (a massive loss of tacit knowledge, essentially). Therefore, a large plan of preservation and transfer must be designed and integrated as a strategic process of the organisation. But it asks a lot of « touchy » questions: what are the knowledge domains that are really threatened? Are they really strategic? Who has this knowledge? What are the possible and pertinent operational actions? How do you ensure the action plan that will be put into place in the medium term is aligned with the strategic objectives of the organisation etc?

To answer these questions, it is therefore necessary to perform an audit of the Knowledge Capital, guided by the strategy of the organisation and to propose a plan of action for knowledge preservation and transfer that is aligned with this strategy. This is this first phase, called the "strategic analysis of the Knowledge Capital", whose objective is to identify the knowledge domains that are "critical" in the organisation.

- Phase 2: Capitalisation of the Knowledge Capital:

Among the critical knowledge domains identified in the first phase, a large number are candidates for a capitalisation action. This phase concerns critical and strategic knowledge domains with an important tacit component, where the tacit part is primarily owned by identified experts. In this case, the capitalisation means the collection of knowledge from experts, in order to formalise their non-written knowledge, with the objective of sharing with other people having the same or very close activities.

- Phase 3: Transfer of the Knowledge Capital:

Capitalisation allows the added-value content of a knowledge domain to be collected and structured and thus to constitute a knowledge corpus (or repository) of the domain. One needs then to transfer this knowledge corpus to a community which must use it for its operational practices. The real problem of transfer arises here: how to design transfer devices from the capitalised knowledge corpus, depending on the objective, the target, the environment etc.?

In the following sections, we detail the three phases of the method, with the description of modelling tools and processes related to each phase.

PHASE 1: STRATEGIC ANALYSIS OF THE KNOWLEDGE CAPITAL

First tool for the strategic analysis: the cognitive maps

The strategic analysis is based on the modelling of the different components of the company, as described in AIK representation given above. The system A of knowledge actors is classically divided into two systems: the decision system (D), including the decision makers (especially top management), and the operating system (O), including the actors in the operational processes. In the proposed methodology, we give modelling tools for the subsystems A, O, D and K. We do not consider the information system I, because this system is fully analysed in information management or information engineering methods, which are complementary to knowledge management methods.

In the approach, we choose mapping as modelling tool. Mapping is an abstraction process which involves selection, classification, simplification, and symbolisation. When we want to represent our thinking, our experience, or our knowledge, we can construct a metaphorical map that adequately represents what is by nature invisible and intangible into something visible, concrete, and meaningful, which we call a cognitive map. The development of a map, in a general sense, is therefore the transcript in a graphic system of a set of data, processing these data to reveal the global information needed, and the construction

most suited to communicate this information. The approach proposed here, for the strategic analysis of Knowledge Capital, uses representations by "cognitive" maps, built on these principles, and validated by ergonomic studies.

To build a map from « cognitive » information, there is a famous methodology, called « Mind Mapping », created and popularised by Tony Buzan (Buzan & Buzan, 2003). This is the area of "Mind Maps", sometimes called mental maps, or heuristic maps or cognitive maps. This is an approach that permits the mental representation of one or several persons concerning a specific problem to be visualised graphically. Our method uses principles of Mind Mapping, but in a very controlled manner. There are four maps in our method, used within a strict framework, and with a strict use mode. Each map corresponds to a specific problematic, has a defined semantic and its own graphical symbolism.

In the strategic analysis of the Knowledge Capital, we build the cognitive maps of:

- The strategy, supported by the decision system of the organisation (D).

The strategy map is a simplified visual representation of the strategy of the company, as recommended in Kaplan and Norton (2004). This map is built from a central node, divided into different branches, called « strategic axes ». These strategic axes are then divided into sub-axes representing the "strategic guidelines", each being divided again into "strategic themes". The objective of this map is to represent the main strategic axes, guidelines and themes in a synthetic, mnemonic and intelligible way that is the best possible corporate strategy formulation.

- The processes, supported by the operating system (O).

The process map is a visual and tree-like representation of the business process of the or-

Knowledge Crash and Knowledge Management

ganisation. It starts from the central node which symbolises the business of the company, split into the different business processes, split again into activities and sub-activities. The objective of this map is to represent the main current activities of the organisation. It takes into account the different business processes existing when the cartography occurs.

- The strategic capabilities, supported by the knowledge actors system (A)

The strategic capabilities map is a tree-like representation of the capabilities required by the organisation in a business process to achieve a strategic objective. It is the result of the confrontation between the strategic objectives (symbolised by the strategy map) and the business processes implemented in the enterprise (symbolised by the process map). It is obtained by identifying and classifying the capabilities required by the strategy in different processes. The objective of this map is to highlight the capabilities required to achieve the strategic objectives of the organisation.

- The knowledge, available in the Knowledge Capital of the company (K)

The knowledge map (or knowledge domains map) is a representation, given by the knowledge actors, of how the knowledge domains are structured, the know-how or skills (the vocabulary is not yet set) which are useful and necessary to operate the different business processes. This map is broken down into knowledge axes (or themes), domains and then sub-domains. This map has the objective to represent the different knowledge domains (the « knowledge portfolio ») in the organisation in a clear and easily understandable way.

These four maps (strategy, processes, strategic capabilities, knowledge) are key tools in our approach (see one example in Figure 1).

Second tool for the strategic analysis: the critical knowledge factors

Our approach uses a set of critical knowledge factors, developed by the "French Knowledge Management Club". This set is composed of 20 criteria, grouped in 4 thematic axes. (cf., Figure 2).

Each criterion is evaluated on a scale from 1 to 4. To facilitate the analysis and the notation, each level of each criterion is described briefly. It is not a normative description, but only a rating description (see an example in Figure 3)

Evaluation of the criticality of one knowledge domain consists in rating every criterion for that domain. The higher the rate, the more critical the domain. Each domain is evaluated independently of the others. The method may lead to heavy implementation, regarding the number of domains and criteria used and if there are many evaluators. It is why we use tools to facilitate the evaluation task. Results are graphically synthesized in a "radar" (also called Kiviat) diagram and other Excel representations.

Finally, each knowledge domain is assigned a score that represents its criticality.

The process for the strategic analysis

- Step 1: the strategic capabilities analysis

The first draft of the strategy map is drawn up by using corporate documents (e.g., the strategic plan). It is then completed and validated by some actors of the strategy, such as heads of units or members of top management. The process map is drawn up by using quality documents describing the business processes.

Identification and evaluation of strategic capabilities consist in interviewing actors (2 to 3 hours) of the corporate strategy who have been identified and solicited beforehand (usually the members of the executive board).

The strategy and process maps are presented to the interviewee; they are used as tools of mediation. Then the interviewee is asked to consider each strategic axis, and indicate, axis by axis, what are

Figure 1. Example of a knowledge map (with the names of referring people for each domain – so-called "name dropping"-)

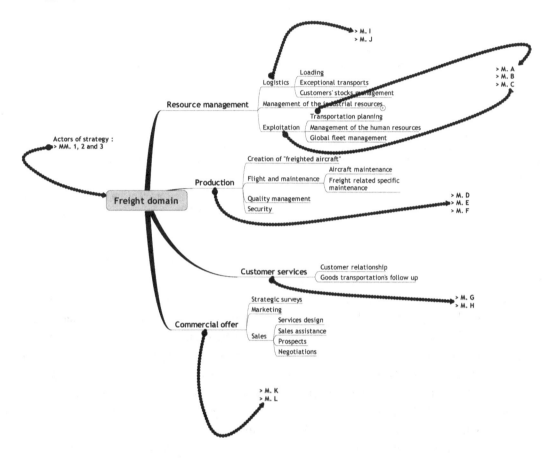

Figure 2. Grid of critical knowledge factors

Thematic axes	Criteria
Rareness	• Number and availability of possessors • Specific (non- subsidiary) character • Leadership • Originality • Confidentiality
Usefulness to company	• Appropriateness to business operations • Creation of value for parties involved • Emergence • Adaptability • Re-usability
Difficulty in acquiring knowledge	• Difficulty in identifying sources • Mobilization of networks • Tacit character of knowledge • Importance of tangible sources of knowledge • Rapidity of evolution
Difficulty in exploiting knowledge	• Depth • Complexity • Difficulty of appropriation • Knowledge background • Environmental dependency • Internal relational networks • External relational networks

Figure 3. Example of evaluation of one critical knowledge factor

TOPIC   DIFFICULTY OF USE OF KNOWLEDGE
Criteria 17   Complexity
What is the degree of complexity of the knowledge domain?

Level 1   **Complicated**
The domain is very specific to a scientific discipline. It handles many but well identified elements.

Level 2   **Low complexity**
The control of the knowledge domain involves the control of many parameters which come from various disciplines.

Level 3   **Complexity**
The control of the domain is not reduced to the control of variables, even if they are many and varied. It requires a total and qualitative comprehension, which is expressed by various points of view giving sense to the domain.

Level 4   **High complexity**
The study and the control of various points of view are essential for the control of the knowledge domain. Methods and models are used to explain and make the various points of view coherent.

the capabilities involved in the operational processes (described in the process map), according to his/her own perception, in order to achieve the strategic goals. At the end, each capability identified is qualitatively evaluated by its criticality level (is this capability very critical, moderately critical or little critical?), based on the themes of the criticality grid described above: a capability is more or less critical if it is more or less rare, useful for the company, difficult to acquire, difficult to implement. At the end of each interview, a synthesis of assessments and arguments is written up and submitted to the interviewee for validation.

When all evaluations are finished and validated, a summary is made to eliminate the redundancies, to homogenise the language, to group and to classify the capabilities. These capabilities, thus classified, are represented by a strategic capabilities map, and each capability is assigned a coefficient of criticality, developed through criticality assessments during the interviews.

This step of strategic capabilities analysis corresponds to the new theories of strategy, called CBV or KBV (« Competence Based View » or « Knowledge Based View ») (Kogut & Zander, 1996; Hamel & Prahalad, 1990; Teece, Pisano, & Shuen, 1997)

• Step 2: The critical knowledge analysis

The construction of the knowledge map begins by identifying the knowledge domains. Identification is performed from documentation reference and interviews, to highlight domains of knowledge (know-how, generic professional skills etc.) through successive analysis of activities, projects, products, etc. Formatting the map must be adequate to the operational vision of the people concerned. This map will be used as support for the interviews during the evaluation of the criticality of the knowledge domains.

Subsequently, for each domain of knowledge, one has to designate reference people that will be interviewed for the analysis of their domain criticality. This step (called "name dropping") may be difficult, especially in large organisations. The credibility of the analysis is based on the legitimacy of the people asked. A knowledge map can be very detailed, but one must choose a level of granularity in the map that does not require too many interviews.

Criticality analysis takes place systematically with the criticality grid and rating procedure described above (Ermine, Boughzala, & Tounkara, 2006).

- Step 3: Strategic alignment and action planning

This step aims to compare strategic visions and business visions, and make relevant recommendations on Knowledge Management actions/devices to be implemented. These recommendations stem from cross-analysis of the strategic capabilities analysis (characterized by the strategic map of the capabilities and their criticality) and the critical knowledge analysis (characterized by the map of the knowledge domains and their criticality). This cross-vision between strategy and business is called the strategic alignment. It allows "strategic dissonances" to be identified: from one side cognitive biases in the representation that business and knowledge workers have of the strategy and, on the other side, the representation the actors of the strategy have of the impacts of the objectives on professional knowledge in the business processes. Furthermore, the large amount of information collected during the interviews with stakeholders in strategy and business can be summarised, according to this strategic alignment, into recommendations for a Knowledge Management action plan.

This step involves several phases.

- Development of the influence matrix

To identify the influence potential of the strategic vision on the business vision and vice-versa, one writes a double entry array, a "matrix of influence" in which the correspondences between the knowledge domains and the strategic capabilities are marked.

Each domain and each capability having a criticality score, a simple weighted average can be attributed to each item. This score is characteristic of the strategic importance and of the criticality of the item. If a strategic capability is critical, if it impacts numerous critical knowledge domains, then its importance is high. Similarly, if a knowledge domain is critical, if it is affected by numerous critical strategic capabilities, then its importance is high. Finally, one can classify knowledge domains and strategic capabilities in ascending order of importance.

- Identification of knowledge management actions

The arguments collected throughout the analysis at the knowledge or strategic level are of a great richness, and comprise many suggestions. The axes of reflection concerning the actions of Knowledge Management to be set up are defined for each knowledge domain and each strategic capability.

These axes are argued:

- For the knowledge domains, on the basis of synthetic documents produced during the critical knowledge analysis and by striking points identified (they are about recurring elements highlighted during the interviews and which characterize the criticality of the domain: need for a knowledge sharing, tool, unsuitable training device, absence of knowledge capitalisation device, strong technicality of the domain, etc.)
- For the strategic capabilities, on the basis of arguments collected during the interviews with the actors of the strategy.

To provide better visibility, these various work axes can be grouped in topics:

- Organization, when they are managerial actions
- Training, when the actions relate to training devices
- Capitalisation-transfer when they are actions of safeguarding, collection, division, documentation etc.

Within each topic, the actions of knowledge management are prioritised according to the rank of importance of the involved knowledge domain (or the strategic capability according to the case)

In the next paragraph, we are interested, within the framework of inter-generational knowledge transfer, in the actions of capitalisation-transfer.

PHASE 2: CAPITALISATION OF THE KNOWLEDGE CAPITAL

In the audit conducted in phase 1, it very often appears that critical and strategic knowledge domains where the crucial knowledge is tacit, is embedded in the heads of a group of critical knowledge workers. That knowledge is threatened (by the departure of some people, for example) and must be transferred to other people. Our proposition is to collect this knowledge in an explicit form to obtain a "knowledge corpus" that is structured and tangible, which shall be the essential resource of any knowledge transfer device. This is called "capitalisation", as it puts a part of the Knowledge Capital, which was up to now invisible, into a tangible form. Therefore these actions require a process of converting tacit knowledge into explicit knowledge. This process, also called "externalisation" by Nonaka is central in the creation of organisational knowledge as Nonaka noted: "it is a process that is the quintessence of knowledge creation because tacit knowledge becomes explicit as metaphors, analogies, concepts, assumptions or models" (Nonaka & Takeuchi, 1995).

The tools for the capitalisation: the knowledge models

Our approach chooses to use graphical models. This is a method based on knowledge elicitation with knowledge models. Knowledge modelling is a technique which started in the 1970s and '80s for artificial intelligence purposes, and has now been considerably developed to constitute a new kind of engineering discipline, called "knowledge engineering". Our approach uses and adapts well-known knowledge models and offers some others

that are more original. This is a CommonKADS-like approach (Schreiber et al., 1999).

To analyse, represent and structure a knowledge capital with templates, the method is based on a theory of knowledge (adapted to the engineering) that is described in detail in Aries, Le Blanc and Ermine (2008); see also Matta et al. (2002). The knowledge is perceived as information that takes a given meaning in a given context. There are therefore three fundamental points of view to model knowledge: information, sense, and context (symbolised by the equation $K = ISC$). Each point of view is split into three other points of view: structure, function, evolution. This yields nine points of view. For information, the three points of views are classical: the structural aspect is modelled by the data structures, the functional aspect by the data processing, and the evolution aspect by dating and "versioning". Our method focuses on the other six points of view. From the point of view of meaning (sense, semantic), the structural aspect is modelled by concept networks, the functional aspect by cognitive tasks and the evolution aspect by lineages. From the point of view of context (pragmatic), the structural aspect is modelled by phenomena, the functional aspect by activities, and the evolution aspect by historical context. Here is a simplified description of models; an example is given in Figure 4.

The phenomena model

This is a description of the domain of expertise with general phenomena which is the basic knowledge related to the activity. These phenomena are the events that need to be controlled, known, triggered, optimised, inhibited, or moderated in the concerned business activity.

The activity model

It is built by an analysis of the activity of the system that uses or produces the knowledge. The *activity model* is broken down into major

Figure 4. An example of a knowledge model: the activity model

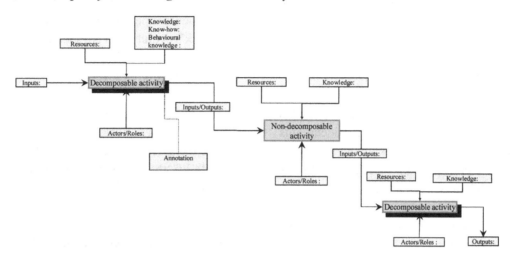

phases (sub-activities) of the business under consideration, these major phases being linked by exchanges of data flow, material flow, energy flow etc.

The concept model

The *concept model represents* the conceptual structuring of an expert, accustomed to working in a particular area. This structure is given in the form of a classification of concepts, the domain objects.

The task model

The *task* model is a representation of a problem solving method implemented in specific know-how.

The history model

The *history model* corresponds to the desire to learn more about what happened at certain times in the evolution of knowledge. It integrates the evolution of given knowledge in a context that is explanatory for this development, and allows the overall guidelines that led the knowledge to the currently perceived state to be understood.

The evolution model

The *evolution model*, linked to the previous one, describes the evolution of ideas, concepts, technical solutions etc. in the form of a genealogical tree that keeps the memory of the causes and reasons that led to these developments.

The capitalisation process

The final product of the capitalisation process is called a "Knowledge Book", a metaphorical term which designates a set of structured elements of knowledge, essentially diagrams representing knowledge diagrams, and the associated text, but also publications, electronic documents, references and all kinds of documentation, digital or not.

The development of a Knowledge Book follows a specific process:

• *Framing*

The purpose of the framing phase is to delimit the knowledge domain on which the Knowledge Book is built, to identify modelling phases that will be useful to the objective. It allows the feasibility of the project to be validated and a work plan to be set up.

• *Implementation of the Knowledge Book*

The realization of a knowledge book is a complex process. It takes several tasks:

- Co-construct the knowledge models with the knowledgeable stakeholders.

Interviewing the knowledge holders provides a set of models with possible attached documents or references. Grouping some knowledge models and diverse elements of knowledge, one builds "knowledge chunks".

- Build consensus between the knowledge contributors.
- Design and produce the Knowledge Book.

This is an important work to design the architecture of the book and its presentation.

- Legitimise the Knowledge Book's content.

The knowledge capitalised in the book must be legitimised by a Peer Committee composed of peers recognised by the company

- Approve the Knowledge Book.

The Knowledge Book must be finally approved by the hierarchy. This is important to ensure that the capitalised knowledge is well and truly recognized as the company's knowledge and that it must be used as such.

- *Share the Knowledge Book*

The phase of sharing is fundamental for the success of the knowledge transfer operation. It ensures that knowledge is available to those who need it, so that they can use it in their business practices and can make it evolve.

- *Evolution of the Knowledge Book*

Knowledge is always evolving, it is necessary to implement a supervising process for the Knowledge Book's evolution. It is a specific process that is not reducible to a simple classic maintenance operation. It requires several tasks:

- Identify new emerging knowledge
- Submit and validate the new knowledge to be integrated into the Knowledge Book
- Modify the Knowledge Book and validate its evolution

PHASE 3: TRANSFER OF THE KNOWLEDGE CAPITAL

The transfer process

Once the knowledge is capitalised in a Knowledge Book, which provides a consistent, structured and high added-value corpus, this book must not stay "on the shelf". The knowledge needs to be transferred to some specific people in the organization. As we have said in §2, knowledge transfer is an exchange process based on a binary relationship that depends on the contexts in which the actors act. A knowledge transfer action is therefore characterized by the target, the source that provides content and participates in the transfer, the knowledge content that is transferred, the description and the characteristics of the environment (technical, social, organisational, cultural etc.) in which this transfer takes place. A transfer process is easily described by a model (one of the models cited in the §3), and therefore provides a reference model for the approach of transfer operations. It is given in Figure 5.

This model allows for any transfer action, to be very precise concerning what items are to be taken into account in the implementation. It is extremely useful for the success of the transfer. It is possible to use a large number of criteria to characterize these processes. We shall give two examples.

Figure 5. The knowledge transfer process model

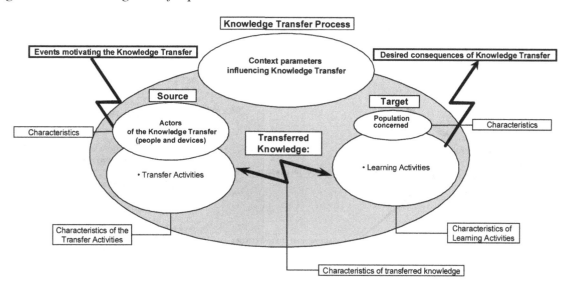

Generational profiling in an organisation

A study, made with the French Knowledge Management Club, has determined several classes of generational characteristics of the populations that may be source or target in a transfer process that can determine successes or failures depending on the terms of the transfer device used (Figure 5).

It is remarkable to see that the characterisation of a generation is far from simply being a reference to the age. This contradicts a persistent idea. According to this idea, a generation would be a set of people with approximately the same birth date. The generations follow one another at determined intervals; each generation would be characterized by a major innovation, destructive of the old corpus of innovation constructed by the previous generation. Then, the criteria for the characterisation of a generation would be the year of birth and the technical contribution, but this so-called positivist vision has been challenged for a long time (Manheim, 1928). A qualitative, non-measurable approach can define a generation as a set of people with the same structuring trends. To identify a generation, it is necessary to have a unified unit of generation, with a socialisation

based on structuring principles. This definition of a generation has an economic aspect, which is a factor of social dynamic, and a significant socio-spiritual aspect.

Thus the generational characteristics grid in Figure 6 includes quantitative and qualitative criteria, related to the individual (age, of course, but also training and professional background), related to the social environment, and related to mutations or changes people have experienced in the company. In some projects this grid was used to build the "generational profile" of a company and to determine the key success or failure factors for knowledge transfer factors between various generations (according to the meaning of the grid) in this company. "Generational profiling" in a company is still a little explored idea, but is very promising (for knowledge transfer, but also for internal communication, management of human resources etc.).

Key Factors of Transfer (KFT)

In an action of knowledge transfer, it is important to characterise the difficulties specific to the knowledge flow from the source to the target.

Figure 6. Generational characteristics

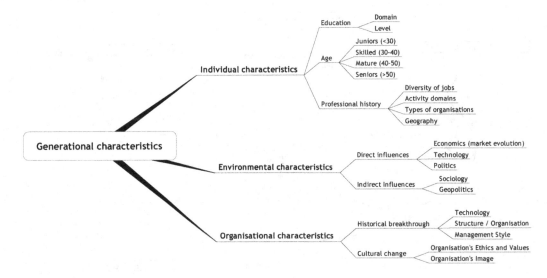

Figure 7. Key factors of transfer

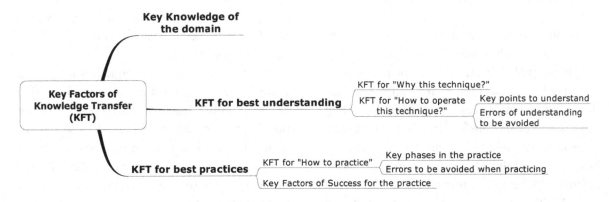

This characterisation of the transferred knowledge (cf., Figure 7) is to identify the difficult points in the involved knowledge domain.. This identification is essentially made with domain experts, who have always transmitted some knowledge to less experienced people, and who are familiar with the difficult points that generally cause problems for novices. To help this identification, one uses a grid which classifies so-called "Key Factors of Transfer". One example is given in Figure 7. These items are listed according to technique, practice or theory and are split in general into two classes: most frequent errors and key points to be learnt (Castillo et al., 2004). Identification of these characteristics is invaluable to any transfer device.

The transfer devices

The transfer of knowledge is a rich issue that has many tools. There are many methods for knowledge transfer (mentoring, tutoring, community of practices, training, learning etc.) supported by many technologies (CMS (Content Management System), blogs, shareware, e-learning platforms, portals or knowledge servers, etc.). Unfortunately, there is often confusion between the process, the method and the technology.

The approach proposed here is interested in transfer processes that use the Knowledge Book as the main support. It requires the design of a "socio-technical" system, modelled by the process described in Figure 7, and which uses a Knowledge Book as a basic corpus. It adapts often classic devices to the context of the Knowledge Books. This phase of the approach is currently under development and is the final brick. We give three significant examples:

• Transfer process based on the socialisation of a Knowledge Book

Two separate processes can be implemented:

• expert/novice co-modelling: an expert and one or several novices are together (with a knowledge engineer as moderator), with the aim of using modelling techniques (of § 4, for instance) to capitalise on the expert's knowledge. The expertise is represented on a common basis, which allows novices to learn.
• direct transfer of the Knowledge Book: models created during the design of the Knowledge Book provide a "condensed", intensive and rich structure of the knowledge corpus to be transferred. This is a representation of the expert's knowledge and it is useful to explain this knowledge in a structured and logical form. From this representation, the expert can easily and in a short time explain to novices, during training sessions, most of his/her know-how. This can be done with the help of a knowledge engineer. The knowledge engineer who drew up the Knowledge Book could even make a direct transfer session to the audience without the expert's presence.

More generally, a Knowledge Book, built with experts of a given knowledge community, may be entrusted to this community to ensure dissemination, maintenance and the sharing. The Knowledge Book is then fully socialised.

• Transfer process based on a Knowledge Server

A Knowledge Server is a website that provides a knowledge community with a knowledge corpus (a Knowledge Book for example) and provides access to all knowledge resources related to the corpus, in the framework of a profession (URL links, documentation, work groups, databases, software, collaborative spaces etc.). It is also known as a Knowledge Portal or a Business Portal.

The design of a Knowledge Server raises specific challenges compared to the design of a classic website. The problems are essentially cognitive usability problems, where browsing the site must follow mental schemes that match business logic. Design methods used currently have two steps: first designing a knowledge repository, where all resources are encapsulated (in the sense of object-oriented languages) in "knowledge chunks", then organising the knowledge chunks according to one business logic (or several, if one needs several websites for several use cases). It is only when implementing the site that one includes items for "usage", which cannot be encapsulated in knowledge chunks.

• Transfer process based on a learning system

The Knowledge Book, built with knowledge modelling, is organised to represent know-how in a specific domain. This is practical knowledge acquired from problem-solving experiences. In general, the Knowledge Book is not enough to ensure the transfer of the knowledge that it has capitalised. As often, the transfer can be classically done by an associated training device. The way that the book was designed greatly facilitates the pedagogical engineering necessary to design a training device (see for example Benmahamed & Ermine, 2007). It allows:

113

- the learning tracks to be designed for the learners according to their levels, the evolution of their learning etc.
- teaching materials to be created from a Knowledge Book, in the form of quizzes, level tests, assessment tests, etc.
- pedagogical tools to be specified that can be integrated into learning supports of e-learning type.

CONCLUSION

The ageing population is a phenomenon which few people or organisations have measured the extent and consequences of, nor envisaged answers proportional to the challenges.

One of the effects expected from this phenomenon is the "knowledge crash", which is the risk of losing a massive amount of knowledge, which may be strategic, or even vital, for all kinds of organisations (private, public, international) and social groups.

The integration of the "knowledge crash" in a "Knowledge Management" framework allows a general approach to be taken, at the macro-economic or (and above all) micro-economic level. This also allows the re-examination of the notions of knowledge, of generations, of knowledge transfer in operational and pragmatic perspectives.

In this paper, we proposed an approach built on three phases:

- *Strategic analysis of knowledge.* It identifies the strategic and critical knowledge in an organisation, proposes operational actions sets, and prioritises them. It is based on the strategy maps concepts (Kaplan & Norton 2004), and the « Competence Based View » or « Knowledge Based View » theories (Kogut & Zander 1996; Hamel & Prahalad, 1990; Teece, Pisano, & Shuen, 1997). The tools for that phase are inspired

by the Mind Mapping tools (Buzan & Buzan, 2003)
- *Capitalisation of knowledge.* It provides a structured method, based on knowledge modelling knowledge, to elicit the most critical tacit knowledge. It is based on the externalisation process of Nonaka and Takeuchi (1995). The tools for that phase are Knowledge modelling tools like in the CommonKADS-like approach (Schreiber et al., 1999).
- *Transfer of knowledge.* It develops inter-generational knowledge transfer devices based on the knowledge corpus capitalised in the second phase. It is based on the knowledge transfer vision as an exchange process based on a binary relationship that depends on the contexts in which the actors act (Argote, 1999; Szulanski, 2000). Various tools are used in that phase: IT tools like Knowledge Servers, learning tools like e-learning, socialisation tools etc.

We have given a very short description of that methodology. Implementation of that methodology is an important project that requires strong commitment of the concerned organisation, even for a partial implementation.

That methodology has been elaborated since more than ten years and applied and refined in numerous projects in public or private, international or national, small or big organisations. It being added value for the organisations by structuring their Knowledge Capital, in order to align their strategy with their knowledge resources, by preserving the tacit knowledge, hence reducing the knowledge risks (especially knowledge loss or crash), and by enhancing inter-generational knowledge transfer, in order to face the "baby boom" phenomena or the ageing population process (knowledge gap).

That methodology is now robust, and an industrial and commercial phase is planned for international deployment: creation of start-ups, development of a KM workbench, and commercial offers. In term of research, there is still a lot of domains to explore: the design and automatic generation of knowledge servers from the results of the capitalisation phase, the design of learning systems (using IMS-LD) from the knowledge models, the connection of the strategic analysis to HR-database (like PeopleSoft or HR Access) etc. Research programs are planned in those directions.

REFERENCES

Argote, L. (1999). *Organizational Learning: creating, retaining and transferring knowledge.* Norwell, MA: Kluwer Academics.

Aries, S., Le Blanc, B., & Ermine, J.-L. (2008). MASK: Une méthode d'ingénierie des connaissances pour l'analyse et la structuration des connaissances (MASK: A Knowledge Engineering Method for Analysing and Structuring Knowledge). In *J.-L. Ermine (Dir.), Management et ingénierie des connaissances, modèles et méthodes* (pp. 261–306). Paris: Hermes Lavoisier.

Benmahamed, D., & Ermine, J.-L. (2007). Knowledge Management Techniques for Know-How Transfer Systems Design. The Case of Oil Company. In *Creating Collaborative Advantage through Knowledge and Innovation* (pp. 15–34). New York: World Scientific Publishing Company. doi:10.1142/9789812707482_0002

Boughzala, I., & Ermine, J.-L. (Eds.). (2006). *Trends in Enterprise Knowledge Management.* London: Hermes Penton Science. doi:10.1002/9780470612132

Bourdelais, P. (1993). *L'âge de la vieillesse. Histoire du vieillissement (Age of ageing, the history of ageing).* Paris: Odile Jacob.

Buzan, B., & Buzan, T. (2003). *The Mind Map Book: Radiant Thinking - Major Evolution in Human Thought (Mind Set)* (3rd ed.). London: BBC Active.

Castillo, O., Matta, N., Ermine, J.-L., & Brutel-Mainaud, S. (2004). Knowledge Appropriation from Profession Memories. In *Proceedings of 16th European Conference on Artificial Intelligence, Workshop Knowledge Management and Organizational Memories*, Valencia, Spain.

DeLong, D. W. (2004). *Lost knowledge. Confronting the threat of an aging workforce.* Oxford, UK: Oxford University Press.

Ebrahimi, M., Saives, A. L., & Holford, W. D. (2008). Qualified ageing workers in the knowledge management process of high-tech businesses. *Journal of Knowledge Management, 12*(2), 124–140. doi:10.1108/13673270810859569

Ermine, J.-L. (2005). A Theoretical and formal model for Knowledge Management Systems. In Remenyi, D. (Ed.), *ICICKM'2005* (pp. 187–199). Reading, UK.

Ermine, J.-L., Boughzala, I., & Tounkara, T. (2006). Critical Knowledge Map as a Decision Tool for Knowledge Transfer Actions. *Electronic Journal of Knowledge Management, 4*(2), 129–140.

Foray, D. (2004). *The Economics of Knowledge.* Cambridge, MA: MIT Press.

Hamel, G., & Prahalad, C. K. (1990). The Core Competence of the Corporation. *Harvard Business Review, 68*(3), 79–9.

Harper, S. (2006). *Ageing Societies: Myths, Challenges and Opportunities.* London: Hodder.

IAEA. (2006). *Risk Management of Knowledge Loss in Nuclear Industry Organizations.* Vienna, Italy: IAEA Publications. Retrieved from http://www.iaea.org/inisnkm/nkm/nkmPublications.html

Inkpen, A. C., & Tsang, E. W. K. (2005). Social capital, networks, and knowledge transfer. *Academy of Management Review, 30*(1), 146–165. doi:10.5465/AMR.2005.15281445

Joe, C., & Yoong, P. (2006). Harnessing the expert knowledge of older workers: Issues and challenges. *Journal of Information and Knowledge Management, 5*(1), 63–72. doi:10.1142/S0219649206001323

Kannan, S., & Madden-Hallet. (2006). Population ageing challenges knowledge management and sustaining marketing culture. *International Journal of Knowledge. Culture and Change Management, 6*(3), 57–70.

Kaplan, R. S., & Norton, D. P. (2004). *Strategy Map: converting intangible assets into tangible outcomes.* Boston: Harvard Business School Press.

Kogut, B., & Zander, U. (1996). What do firms do? Coordination, identity, and learning. *Organization Science, 7*, 502–518. doi:10.1287/orsc.7.5.502

Kohlbacher, F., Güttel, W. H., & Haltmeyer, B. (2009). Special Issue on the Ageing Workforce and HRM – Challenges, Chances, Perspectives. *International Journal of Human Resources Development and Management, 9*(2/3).

Matta, N., Ermine, J.-L., Aubertin, G., & Trivin, J.-Y. (2002). Knowledge Capitalization with a knowledge engineering approach, the MASK method. In *Proceedings of the Knowledge Management and Organisational memories* (pp. 17-28). Boston: Kluwer Academic Press.

Nonaka, I., & Takeuchi, H. (1995). *The knowledge-Creating Company: How Japanese Companies Create the Dynamics of Innovation.* New York: Oxford University Press.

OECD. (1996). *Ageing in OECD Countries, a Critical Policy Challenge.* Paris: OECD Publishing.

OECD. (2007). *Ageing and the Public Service, Human Resource Challenges.* Paris: OECD Publishing.

Schreiber, G., Akkermans, H., Anjewierden, A., de Hoog, R., Shadbolt, N., Van de Velde, W., & Wielinga, B. (1999). *Knowledge Engineering and Management, The CommonKADS Methodology.* Cambridge, MA: MIT Press.

Slagter, F. (2007). Knowledge management among the older workforce. *Journal of Knowledge Management, 11*(4), 82–96. doi:10.1108/13673270710762738

Streb, C. K., Voelpel, S. C., & Leibold, M. (2008). Managing the aging workforce: Status quo and implications for the advancement of theory and practice. *European Management Journal, 26*, 1–10. doi:10.1016/j.emj.2007.08.004

Szulanski, G. (2000). The Process of Knowledge Transfer: A Diachronic Analysis of Stickiness. *Organizational Behavior and Human Decision Processes, 82*(1), 9–27. doi:10.1006/obhd.2000.2884

Teece, D. J., Pisano, G., & Shuen, A. (1997). Dynamic Capabilities and Strategic Management. *Strategic Management Journal, 18*(7), 509–533. doi:10.1002/(SICI)1097-0266(199708)18:7<509::AID-SMJ882>3.0.CO;2-Z

UNFPA. (2002). *Population Ageing and Development.* UNFPA Publishing. Retrieved from http://www.unfpa.org/publications/detail.cfm?ID=67&filterListType=3

Van Berten, P., & Ermine, J.-L. (2006). Applied Knowledge Management: a set of well-tried tools. *VINE: The Journal of Information and Knowledge Management Systems, 36*(4), 423–431.

Von Bertalanffy, L. (2006). *General System Theory: Foundations, Development, Applications* (Revised ed.). George Braziller.

This work was previously published in the International Journal of Knowledge and Systems Science, Volume 1, Issue 4, edited by W.B. Lee, pp. 79-95 copyright 2010 by IGI Publishing (an imprint of IGI Global).

Chapter 8
A Conceptual Framework for Effective Knowledge Management Using Information and Communication Technologies

Hepu Deng
RMIT University, Australia

ABSTRACT

This paper investigates the role of information and communication technologies in enabling and facilitating the conversion of knowledge objects in knowledge management and explores how these roles might be affected in an organization. Such an investigation is based on a critical analysis of the relationships between data, information and knowledge, leading to the development of a transformation model between data, information and knowledge. Using a multi-method approach, in this paper, the author presents a conceptual framework for effective knowledge management in an organization. The author discusses the implications of the proposed framework for designing and developing knowledge management systems in an organization.

DOI: 10.4018/978-1-4666-1782-7.ch008

INTRODUCTION

Knowledge management is a systematic process of managing knowledge assets, processes, and organizational environments to facilitate the creation, organization, sharing, and utilization of knowledge for achieving the strategic aim of an organization (Wiij, 1997; Alavi & Leidner, 2001; Kakabadse et al., 2003; Song et al., 2005). In today's dynamic environment, effectively managing organizational knowledge is of tremendous importance for an organization to gain and sustain its competitive advantage due to the advent of the knowledge economy, increased globalization, the rapid advance of technology, the changing demand of increasingly sophisticated customers, and the turbulent competition in the market (Liao, 2003; Beccerra-Fernandez & Sabherwal, 2006).

The importance of effective knowledge management in an organization has been increasingly being recognized both in business (Foy, 1999; Teleos, 2004, 2006) as well as in academy (Nonaka et al., 1995; Drucker, 1997; Davenport & Prusak, 2000; Prusak, 2006). This leads to the development of numerous knowledge management theories and practices (Martensson, 2000; Chauvel & Desprs, 2002; Desouza, 2003; Babcock, 2004) due to the tremendous benefits that effective knowledge management brings to an organization including (a) responding to customers quickly, (b) developing new products and services rapidly, (c) shortening the response time for client engagements, (d) improving project management practices, (e) increasing staff participation, (f) enhancing communication, (g) reducing problem-solving time, (h) better client services, and (i) better performance measurement (Alavi & Leidner, 2001; Chauvel & Desprs, 2002; Lehaney et al., 2004). As a result, much attention have been paid to design and develop strategies, policies, and technical tools for effective organizational knowledge management through making the full use of the available information and communication technologies (Spiegler, 2003; Tsui, 2003).

Knowledge, however, is an elusive concept (Blacker, 1995; Tuomi, 2000; Deng & martin, 2003; Song et al., 2005). The complex nature of knowledge offers many challenges, resulting in different approaches being developed (Nonaka et al., 1995; Davenport & Prusak, 2000; Alavi & Leidner, 2001; Bhatt, 2001). Among these, the technological approach to organizational knowledge management is one that is commonly adopted (Deng & Martin, 2003; Martin & Deng, 2003). This approach focuses on the application of information and communication technologies (ICT) for managing knowledge in an organization (Ruggles, 1998; Spiegler, 2003; Song et al., 2005).

The rapid advance of ICT offers unprecedented capacities and potentials for effective knowledge management (O'Leary, 1998; Beccerra-Fernandez & Sabherwal, 2006; Hasan & Crawford, 2003; Tsui, 2003). There are, however, still concerns about the role of ICT in organizational knowledge management. This is owing to the failure of numerous knowledge management initiatives using ICT in knowledge management (Desouza, 2003; Tsui, 2003; Song et al., 2005). This shows that it is desirable and necessary to further explore the role of ICT in organizational knowledge management in order to help organizations make use of the full potential of organizational knowledge management through the adoption of modern technologies.

This paper investigates the role that ICT plays in enabling and facilitating the conversion processes of knowledge objects in organizational knowledge management and explores how these roles might be affected in an organization. It critically analyzes the relationships between data, information and knowledge, resulting in the development of a novel transformation model between data, information and knowledge. Using a multi-method approach, the paper presents a conceptual framework for effective knowledge management in organizations. The implications of this new framework for designing and developing knowledge management systems are also discussed.

In what follows, we first discuss the knowledge transformation process through a comprehensive analysis on the relationship between data, information and knowledge. We then define the research questions for this study, followed by the discussion on the design and implementation of the research. The role of ICT in facilitating the conversion processes of knowledge objects in organizational knowledge management is then investigated through an empirical analysis of the collected data from three perspectives. This leads to the development of a novel transformation model between data, information and knowledge and results in the production of a conceptual framework for effective knowledge management in organizations

MODELING THE KNOWLEDGE TRANSFORMATION PROCESS

Knowledge is commonly referred to as the human ability to effectively use the information available in a specific context (Blacker, 1995; Davenport & Prusak, 2000; Alavi & Leidner, 2001). Information is organized data for specific purposes. Data are raw facts in relation to specific events, business transactions, and operations of our society. Data, information, and knowledge are an integral part of our daily lives (Damm & Schindler, 2002; Song et al., 2005).

The importance of knowledge has been recognized for a long time (Davenport & Prusak, 2000; Cepeda, 2006). This importance is represented in a simple, yet well-known statement, that is, *"Knowledge is power"* (Drunker, 1997; Alavi & Leidner, 2001; Song et al., 2005). From very early times, sustained succession of knowledge has been secured by transferring in-depth knowledge from one generation to the next. The study of human knowledge has been a central subject matter of philosophy and epistemology since the ancient Greeks (Nonaka et al., 1995; Kakabadse et al., 2003). In fact, knowledge is well recognized to

be the central to the achievements of the industrial revolution (Cepeda, 2006; Prusak, 2006).

Understanding the relationships between data, information and knowledge is of tremendous importance to effective organizational knowledge management (Tuomi, 2000; Deng & Martin, 2003). This is because such relationships are a cornerstone for understanding organizational knowledge management (Alavi & Leidner, 2001; Martin & Deng, 2003; Song et al., 2005). This understanding facilitates the transformation between data, information and knowledge in developing organizational knowledge management strategies and policies (O'Leary, 1998; Benbya et al., 2004). In general there are two dominant models for describing such relationships including the conventional hierarchical model (Song et al., 2005) and the reversed hierarchical model for describing such relationships (Tuomi, 2000). Figure 1 shows an overview of these two models for describing the complex relationships between data, information and knowledge.

With the conventional hierarchical model, data are seen as facts that can be structured to become information. Information, in turn, becomes knowledge when it is interpreted or put into context, or when meaning is added to it. The reversed hierarchical model recognizes that data only emerge after information is available, and that information only emerges after the required knowledge are present (Tuomi, 2000). Knowledge exists before information can be formulated and data can be measured. Knowledge exists which and when articulated and structured. It becomes information which, when assigned a fixed representation and interpretation.

Much confusion continues to surround the understanding of the relationships between data, information and knowledge despite the opportunities and challenges presented by the reversed hierarchical model for better understanding such relationships (Martin & Deng, 2003). This causes numerous problems for designing and developing knowledge management systems in the organi-

Figure 1. Knowledge transformation models

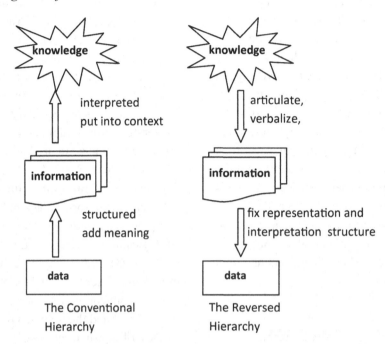

zational Endeavour to pursue technical solutions to effective knowledge management. As a result, enormous expenditure on technology initiatives for effectively managing organizational knowledge has rarely delivered what the expenditure originally promise (Tsui, 2003).

There are various propositions on how the existing confusion can be handled for better managing organizational knowledge. For example, some confusions can be eliminated if there is a better understanding of the difference between information and knowledge (Song et al., 2005). The key to effectively distinguishing between information and knowledge is not in the content, structure, accuracy, or utility of the information and knowledge. Rather the explanation may well lie in the similarities between the concepts (Alavi & Leidner, 2001). Accordingly systems designed to support knowledge management may not appear radically different from other information systems, but will be geared toward enabling users to assign meaning to information and to capture some of their knowledge in information and/or data.

Epistemology is one theory for describing knowledge in organizational knowledge management. Along this theory, there are two schools of thoughts including rationalism and empiricism. Rationalism believes that knowledge can be obtained deductively by reasoning (Martensson, 2000). Knowledge-information-data hierarchy reflects this thought (Song et al., 2005). It contends that existing knowledge can be formed into the premises of indubitable foundations, on which information and data are formalized by employing reasoning mechanisms. Whereas data-information-knowledge hierarchy reflects empiricism (Tuomi, 2000). It uses mathematical algorithms to extract knowledge from existing information systems.

The two hierarchies can be conceptual guides for designing and developing knowledge management systems in the process of pursuing technical solutions to organizational knowledge management (Song et al., 2005). For example, data mining techniques can be used to discover the pattern in a huge amount of data and extract valuable knowledge emerging from these patterns, based on the data-information-knowledge hierarchy (Fayyad et al., 1996; Deng & Martin, 2003). Knowledge transfer is an example for knowledge-information-data hierarchy through identifying the best practices and sharing such best practices in knowledge management (Teleos, 2004, 2006).

Two strategies, the push strategy and the pull strategy, are often adopted in designing and developing knowledge management systems (Deng & Martin, 2003). By using a pull strategy, employees can actively initiate the request for information and knowledge. With the use of a push strategy, available information and knowledge are automatically delivered to their destinations without the intervention of individual employees.

In the conventional model, the pull strategy is adopted. Using this strategy, employees request information and knowledge that are not guaranteed to be satisfied either because the information and knowledge are not available or they are not what employees exactly expect. As the amount of data gathered in an organization is increasingly immeasurable, information overload is becoming the problem (Martensson, 2000).

To help ease the problem of information overload, the push strategy is introduced (Song et al., 2005). In the knowledge-information-data model, the preferences, specific task and function in relation to specific employees can be identified and captured. Therefore, requisite information and data relevant to specific tasks and functions can be delivered to targeted specific employs proactively, which are what individual employees exactly need. This ability to push data to employees rather than making employees find and pull data themselves facilitate the conversion process between data, information an knowledge in a more effective manner. It enables employees to configure the information to be captured, stored, and gathered.

Knowledge can be classified into tacit and explicit knowledge (Nonaka et al., 1995; Drucker, 1997). Based on the transformation of these two types of knowledge, the knowledge life cycle is formed into knowledge socialization, combination, internalization and externalization (Nonaka et al., 1995). In a broad sense, data and information are subset of explicit knowledge. The conventional model reflects the process of internalization and combination, whereas the reversed hierarchy model reflects the process of externalization and combination.

Both models depict the complex relationships between data, information and knowledge. The two models, however, are only part of the complete picture of knowledge flow and transformation. Firstly, between data and knowledge there does not exist any relationship, which is not true in the knowledge conversion process. There are many evidences of the existence of such a relationship through the applications of data mining and knowledge management systems. Secondly, the transformation within each components are ignored. Such a transformation is an important part of knowledge management. Thirdly, both models start from a component and end at another without focusing on reuse of any components. Fourthly, the two models imply that one component is superior to another, which easily results in over emphasis on the superior one while other components are overlooked without awareness of interrelationship and interaction between these core constructs.

The two models discussed are opposing yet complementary. They can be merged into a knowledge transformation cycle for better understanding this relationship. Combining the two models together, a more complete reflection of the relationship between data, information, and knowledge can be achieved, leading to the development of a novel conceptual framework for describing such relationships as shown in Figure 2. Such a framework synthesizes the conventional hierarchy model and the reversed hierarchy model in a holistic manner.

Figure 2. A novel transformation model

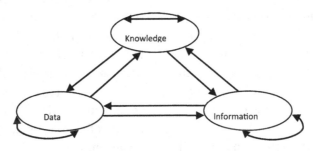

RESEARCH DESIGN AND IMPLEMENTATION

Knowledge management is of a trans-disciplinary nature involving a variety of disciplines (Earl, 2001; Kakabadse et al., 2003; Prat, 2006). These disciplines range from economics, management science, organizational theory, strategic management, human-resources management, information science, knowledge engineering, artificial intelligence, philosophy, and educational science, to cognitive science. Research into knowledge management often falls largely within the province of social, business and management science (Corbetta, 2003; Prusak, 2006). This suggests that this study should adopt a mixture of positivism and phenomenology (Creswell, 1994; Corbetta, 2003).

This study aims primarily to investigate the role of ICT in facilitating the conversion between knowledge objects in the knowledge management process. Such an investigation necessitates an understanding of the context and environment in which ICT is used to support organizational knowledge management. As such, both the deductive approach and the inductive approach are required. The main research question for this study is defined as follows: *What role can ICT play in* knowledge management *and how can ICT be effectively used in* knowledge management?

To answer this question, this study adopts a multi-method approach to investigate the role that ICT plays in enabling and facilitating the conversion processes of knowledge objects in knowledge

management and identify how these roles might be affected in an organizations as discussed above. The use of a multi-method approach allows the research to exploit the advantages of individual methods and minimize the negative effects that different methods might have on the research results (Creswell, 1994; Corbetta, 2003).

The quantitative research in this study employs an online survey method. The strength of using survey is focused on the versatility, efficiency and economy in the data collection process (Creswell, 1994). The survey is to investigate the conversion processes between information and knowledge in knowledge management. The distinction between information and knowledge is often treated theoretically. However, there has been little empirical research into the conversion processes between information and knowledge. To explore the mechanisms that facilitate the conversion between information and knowledge, 'what' and 'how' types of questions are posed. A survey is suitable for asking exploratory questions. It can provide a broad picture of respondents' experiences in the conversion processes.

The online survey has attracted 317 responses. After removing these repeat and invalid submissions, 305 valid responses remained for further analysis. In the remaining data, a few submissions were found to have missing responses to individual questions. These missing data were replaced with mean values during the course of data analysis.

The profile of the respondents is reflected in their job position, number of years in their current

Table 1. Industry groups of the business cases

Industry	Enterprise
Chemicals	BULABS
Consulting	McKinsey & Company
Electronics and electrical equipment	Siemens, General electric
Information technology	Hewlett-Packard, IBM, Microsoft, Xerox
Oil & gas	BP, Shell
Professional services	Ernst & Young, PricewaterhouseCoopers

position, their level of education, age, and gender. Most of the 305 respondents were females (55.7%), in the age group of 20 to 29 years (36.7%), and in their current position less than 5 years (82.3%). A majority of the respondents had university degrees (72.5%), with the rest having a TAFE-level and high school education. They included postgraduate students (39%), undergraduate students (38%), academic staff (13.1%), administrative staff (8.5%), and TAFE students (1.3%).

The qualitative research in this study employs a case study to gain a rich understanding of the context and the process of implementing a knowledge management project. The case study is related to an unsuccessful attempt at implementing a knowledge management portal (Mack et al., 2001; Benbya et al., 2004). The study focuses on the knowledge objects and knowledge processes in order to reveal the role that ICT plays in the knowledge conversion process and also to identify the critical factors for facilitating the knowledge conversion process.

To further validate the research findings from survey and case study, a document analysis method is applied on the twelve organizations recognized as Global MAKE Winners for being the best knowledge management practice organizations in the world since 1998. These organizations are from various business sectors. Their total return to shareholders is nearly double that of the Fortune 500 company median (Teleos, 2004, 2006).

The twelve organizations are actively engaged in knowledge management projects. These twelve organizations are distributed over some of the most knowledge-intensive sectors. Table 1 shows the distribution of industry groups that these companies are in (Teleos, 2004, 2006).

ROLES OF ICT IN KNOWLEDGE MANAGEMENT

Knowledge objects consist of data, information and knowledge (Davenport & Prusak, 2000; Alavi & Leidner, 2001; Song et al., 2005; Teleos, 2006). Effective knowledge management moves knowledge objects smoothly through generation, codification, and dissemination to application (Maier & Hadrich, 2006). Such practices streamline creating, capturing, classifying, organizing, transferring and reusing knowledge. While knowledge codification and dissemination are increasingly supported by ICT applications, the use of supportive technology for knowledge generation and application remains less extensive (Spiegler, 2003; Maier, 2004).

The online survey and the case study show that ICT can be used to effectively facilitate the conversion between data, information and knowledge. In fact, a majority of respondents believed that the use of ICT helps them gain new ideas and insights, to compare different views and to undertake research projects. The survey results show that ICT facilitates the conversion of knowledge objects. Furthermore, the survey shows that ICT facilitate the process of exchanging information and knowledge, leading to the creation of new information and knowledge.

The survey and the case study, however, also reveal that ICT currently cannot fully support the conversion process. Artificial intelligence, intelligent agents, and knowledge portals hold some potential (Fayyad et al., 1996; Spiegler, 2003; Tsui, 2003). This potential has not been fully tapped into in the current situation. It is still up to the human agents to analyze, understand, digest, absorb, synthesize, deduct, induct, and reflect on existing information and turn it into knowledge (Desouza, 2003; Beccerra-Fernandez & Sabherwal, 2006). Compared with converting knowledge into information, the number of respondents who are able to turn their knowledge into information is much lower in the survey. This involves the process of externalization (Nonaka et al., 1995), which is not fully supported by ICT. Although knowledge can partially be converted into information and explicit knowledge, the tacit knowledge and the context pertaining to the knowledge are usually lost. There exists a wide gap between information and knowledge. While the gap remains without ICT as a bridge, human agents need to actively use ICT to fill up the gap. In the mean time, there is clearly a need for developing new tools and technologies for facilitating the knowledge conversion process for effective knowledge management in an organization.

The in depth analysis of the twelve organizations in regard to the role of ICT in organizational knowledge management shows that ICT fully supports the conversion processes between data, information and knowledge (Spiegler, 2003). The twelve organizations are early adopters of ICT in their efforts to support knowledge management. For example, HP's involvement in a company intranet is almost as old as the Internet itself. By the late 1980s, HP had used Internet technologies and tools, such as email, ftp, and news groups for global electronic communications, for managing documents, for distributing software, and for training personnel (Information Services Advisory Council, 1998).

The use of ICT benefits these organizations in various ways including (a) developing a knowledge-based organization; (b) sharing documents and best practices organization-wide; and (c) improving customer relationship management. For IBM, technology is not a solution in itself. It helps provide solutions that meet the requirements of its users for sharing, re-using, and managing intellectual capital in a networked team environment. ICT tools such as the ICM AssetWeb, the enterprise knowledge infrastructure, and its related solutions, Knowledge Cafe and Knowledge Cockpit have helped to transform IBM's business to one that is knowledge based (Mack et al., 2001).

Intranet sites at another global company, General Electronic, contain sophisticated search engines capable of accessing thousands of documents (Detlor, 2000). Training modules are placed on the web, as well as best practices of various kinds in the organization. In addition, video-conferences are held frequently in which best practices are shared, and top executives communicate with employees in a timely manner. E-commerce and database technology provided the means for BULABS to collect large volumes of customer information, and to transfer accumulated expert knowledge to the point of customer interaction. This knowledge enables BULABS to quickly adapt to the specific requirements in customer relationship management with respect to individual customers. These practices reflect the fact that the use of knowledge management portals and advanced ICT is of tremendous potential for effective knowledge management (Tsui, 2003).

The case analysis shows that the application of ICT plays an important role in knowledge management initiatives. For example, Microsoft initiated a project early in 1995 to investigate information sharing and to identify the appropriate platform for facilitating sharing information. Until that time there had been little available as a central resource to house documents, findings, market research reports, and competitive intelligence information. The decision to use the Web enabled the organization to share information and knowledge. In BP AMOCO, the Internet made it possible to create a global procurement exchange by communicating information not just between one buyer and one seller, but between many individual participants simultaneously in real time. The scope and geographical distribution of the Ernst & Young knowledge base and its users meant that technology had to be used as an enabler wherever possible. Lotus Notes was selected as the primary technological platform for capturing and disseminating internal information and knowledge.

Many successful cases in knowledge management show that the data stored in database and data warehouse can be freely converted into meaningful information (Teleos, 2004, 2006). However, information must be carefully designed and well organized to cater for individual knowledge workers' needs in order to obviate the problem of information overload. ICT needs to be seamlessly integrated with information management to establish a knowledge platform for knowledge management (Detlor, 2000; Benbya et al., 2004).

New tools and technologies have been developed to enable and facilitate the conversion processes between data and knowledge (Liao, 2003). Data mining and knowledge discovery, for example, can extract patterns from the huge amounts of data collected and stored in organizational data warehouses. However, the prospect of turning knowledge into data is not so promising. A fundamental reason might be due to the complex nature of knowledge (Nonaka et al., 1995; Alavi & Leidner, 2001; Song et al., 2005). The context attached to knowledge and the tacit aspects of knowledge are difficult and at times impossible to capture and store when the technological approaches are applied to convert knowledge into data. This shows that ICT can enable and facilitate conversion processes between data and knowledge,.

Furthermore, tacit knowledge is often lost in the process of converting knowledge into information, albeit this loss is likely less than in the process of converting knowledge into data, where the separation of content and context, and the separation of data and metadata do occur. It is disappointing that ICT can do little in facilitating the conversion processes between information and knowledge. Artificial intelligence, electronic resources and knowledge portals hold some potential (Deng & Martin, 2003). Humans, however, play the key role in analyzing, understanding, digesting, absorbing, synthesizing, deducting, inducting, and reflecting on existing information and in turning it into knowledge (Blacker, 1995; Bhatt, 2001).

For the conversion processes between information and knowledge to be really effective, knowledge management requires new supportive tools and technologies (Deng & Martin, 2003; Maier, 2004). Where there is little technology to enable and facilitate the conversion processes between information and knowledge, humans need to play major role and actively interact with ICT. Overall ICT can enable and facilitate the conversion of knowledge objects. The needs of knowledge management cannot be fully met by ICT, the contribution of which remains enabling and supportive in nature. ICT still plays an important role in knowledge management, despite its limitations in supporting effective knowledge management. The majority of knowledge management projects use ICT as a backbone to achieve their knowledge management objectives (Teleos, 2004, 2006).

The success of knowledge management in an organization depends not only on the technologies used but also many other factors (Blacker, 1995; Drucker, 1997; Martensson, 2000). These factors can be grouped as organizational and cultural elements. Organizational element involves organizational strategy, management, resource, and structure. Cultural element involves beliefs, norms, values, assumptions, and behavior. These elements can directly impact on the success of technology-driven knowledge management proj-

Figure 3. Knowledge management framework

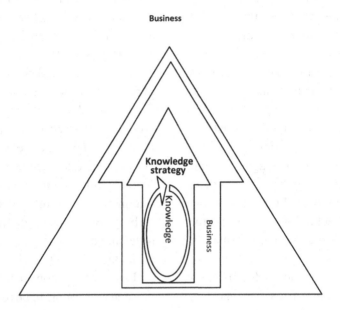

ects. The depth analysis of the twelve organizations shows that the critical success factors for effective knowledge management include strategy alignment, senior management support, resource allocation, structure flexibility, people participation and knowledge management friendly culture in an enterprise (Teleos, 2004, 2006).

A NOVEL FRAMEWORK FOR EFFECTIVE KNOWLEDGE MANAGEMENT

The new insights arising from this study extend our understanding of knowledge and of the relationship between ICT and knowledge management. Knowledge is an object that can be manipulated and the process of knowing, and the assets and capabilities that organizations must align with their business strategies to gain competitive edge (Martin & Deng, 2003; Song et al., 2005). knowledge management is essential for organizations to leverage their knowledge in a dynamic life cycle. The role of ICT in knowledge management is to enable and facilitate knowledge management

efforts (Alavi & Leidner, 2001; Early, 2001; Prusak, 2006).

Humans remain the major player in the dynamic cycle of knowledge management (Bhatt, 2001). ICT needs to support and integrate with people for effective knowledge management. The knowledge management strategy and processes must be aligned with business strategy and organizational processes (Maier et al., 2006; Prat, 2006). Organization management, structure and culture must be 'knowledge-friendly' for developing the capabilities that an organization needs to achieve its strategy.

The extended understanding of knowledge, of the relationship between ICT and knowledge management, and of the relationship between knowledge management and the internal knowledge management environment emerging from this research lead to a further development of the knowledge management process. Figure 3 shows a novel knowledge management framework with three tiers.

The outermost tier illustrates the boundary of an organization, the internal environment and the major components. The middle tier is the business process. An organization aims to establish its core business processes in order to achieve its business strategy (Earl, 2001). At the core tier, knowledge processes are embedded in business processes. Knowledge objects interact with knowledge processes. ICT is seamlessly integrated with people to convert knowledge objects and streamline knowledge processes, to accomplish the knowledge strategy, which must be in line with the business strategy.

The innermost of the core tier is composed of knowledge object conversion processes and knowledge processes including knowledge generation, codification, transfer and application. In the knowledge life cycle, knowledge objects are constantly converted into each other and transformed into different states or forms within the same component, with or without the support of ICT.

The conversion processes between data, information and knowledge integrate the conventional model and the reversed model. When new knowledge is abstracted from data and information, it can be explicated, captured and converted into new information and data. This reflects the process of internalization and combination (Nonaka et al., 1995; Song et al., 2005). When this knowledge is explicated, captured and converted into information and data, it can be the source of and basis from which new knowledge can be abstracted. This reflects the process of externalization and combination (Nonaka et al., 1995). The conversion within each component may be from one source to another, such as from people to system, or from one form to another. In this way, the conversion process from any component is continuous, iterative and evolving in a spiral fashion. The conversion processes between knowledge objects are closely related to the people who use them, and to the purposes, for which people use them. People are the major actors in the conversion processes and the knowledge management processes, with the support of ICT.

This framework can be used as a guide to direct knowledge management practitioners in knowledge management initiatives. A knowledge management project must start from its grounding in business strategy, business processes, organizational management, structure, culture, knowledge strategy, knowledge processes, knowledge objects, and people to ICT. The knowledge strategy must be aligned with business strategy. The knowledge processes must be embedded in business processes. The knowledge objects must be integrated with knowledge processes. The dynamic knowledge life cycle must be in harmony with the internal knowledge management environment characterized by organizational management, and organizational structure and organizational culture.

CONCLUSION

This study investigates the role of ICT in knowledge management. By employing a multi-method approach, the study confirms that ICT does play an enabling role in knowledge management. It shows that ICT enables and supports the conversion of knowledge objects in an organization. The study also shows that the potential for conversion between knowledge objects is limited in facilitation of the conversion of knowledge into data or information, and of information into knowledge. The knowledge life cycle is, therefore, only partially supported by ICT. To enhance such support, new technologies are required

The study further confirms that while necessary for the successful implementation of knowledge management projects, ICT is not in itself sufficient to ensure such success. Although ICT can play an important role in support of knowledge management, the effective use of ICT requires that knowledge management practitioners pay attention to a wide range of managerial, structural and cultural elements. It is essential that key alignments are obtained between knowledge strategy and business strategy. Without due attention to these elements in organizations, it is unlikely that knowledge management will succeed.

REFERENCES

Alavi, M., & Leidner, D. E. (2001). Review: Knowledge management and knowledge management systems: Conceptual foundations and research issues. *Management Information Systems Quarterly*, *25*(1), 107–136. doi:10.2307/3250961

Babcock, P. (2004). Shedding light on knowledge management. *HRMagazine*, *49*(5), 46–50.

Beccerra-Fernandez, I., & Sabherwal, R. (2006). ICT and knowledge management systems. In Schwartz, D. G. (Ed.), *Encyclopedia of Knowledge Management* (pp. 230–236). Hershey, PA: IGI Global.

Benbya, H., Passiante, G., & Belbaly, N. A. (2004). Corporate portal: a tool for knowledge management synchronization. *International Journal of Information Management*, *24*, 201–220. doi:10.1016/j.ijinfomgt.2003.12.012

Bhatt, G. (2001). Knowledge management in organizations: examining the interaction between technologies, techniques, and people. *Journal of Knowledge Management*, *5*(1), 68–75. doi:10.1108/13673270110384419

Blacker, F. (1995). Knowledge, knowledge workers and organizations: an overview and interpretation. *Organization Studies*, *16*(6), 1021–1046. doi:10.1177/017084069501600605

Cepeda, G. (2006). Competitive advantage of knowledge management. In Schwartz, D. G. (Ed.), *Encyclopedia of Knowledge Management* (pp. 34–43). Hershey, PA: IGI Global.

Chauvel, D., & Desprs, C. (2002). A review of survey research in knowledge management: 1997-2001. *Journal of Knowledge Management*, *6*(3), 207–223. doi:10.1108/13673270210434322

Corbetta, P. (2003). *Social Research: Theory, Methods and Techniques*. London: Sage.

Creswell, J. (1994). *Research Design: Quantitative and Qualitative Approaches*. Thousand Oaks, CA: Sage.

Damm, D., & Schindler, M. (2002). Security issues of a knowledge medium for distributed project work. *International Journal of Project Management*, *20*(1), 37–47. doi:10.1016/S0263-7863(00)00033-8

Davenport, T. H., & Prusak, L. (2000). *Working Knowledge: How Organizations Manage What They Know*. Boston, MA: Harvard Business School Press.

Deng, H., & Martin, B. (2003). A framework for intelligent organizational knowledge management. In *Proceedigns of Integrated Design and Process Technology, the 7th World Conference on Integrated Design and Process Technology*, Austin, TX.

Desouza, K. C. (2003). Janaury-February). Knowledge management barriers: Why the technology imperative seldom works. *Business Horizons*, 25–29. doi:10.1016/S0007-6813(02)00276-8

Detlor, B. (2000). The corporate portal as information infrastructure: towards a framework for portal design. *International Journal of Information Management*, *20*(2), 91–101. doi:10.1016/S0268-4012(99)00058-4

Drucker, P. F. (1997, September-October). The future that has already happened. *Harvard Business Review*, 20–24.

Earl, M. (2001). Knowledge management strategies: Toward a taxonomy. *Journal of Management Information Systems*, *18*(1), 215–233.

Fayyad, U., Piatetsky-Shapiro, G., & Smyth, P. (1996). From data mining to knowledge discovery: an overview. In Fayyad, U., & Piatetsky-Shapiro, G. (Eds.), *Advances in Knowledge Discovery and Data Mining* (pp. 1–34). Cambridge, MA: MIT Press.

Foy, P. S. (1999). Knowledge management in industry. In Liebowitz, J. (Ed.), *Knowledge Management Handbook*. Boca Raton, FL: CRC Press.

Hasan, H., & Crawford, K. (2003). Codifying or enabling: the challenge of knowledge management systems. *The Journal of the Operational Research Society*, *54*, 184–193. doi:10.1057/palgrave.jors.2601388

Information services advisory council. (1998). *Managing information as a strategic asset: corporate intranet development and the role of the company library*. Retrieved from www.conference-board.org/products/intranet-white-paper.cfm

Kakabadse, N. K., Kakabadse, A., & Kouzmin, A. (2003). Reviewing the knowledge management literature: towards a taxonomy. *Journal of Knowledge Management*, *7*(4), 75–91. doi:10.1108/13673270310492967

Lehaney, B., Clarke, S., Coakes, E., & Jack, G. (2004). *Beyond Knowledge Management*. Hershey, PA: IGI Global.

Liao, S. H. (2003). Knowledge management technologies and applications-literature review from 1995 to 2002. *Expert Systems with Applications*, *25*(2), 155–164.

Mack, R., Ravin, Y., & Byrd, R. J. (2001). Knowledge portals and the emerging digital knowledge workplace. *IBM Systems Journal*, *40*(4), 925–955. doi:10.1147/sj.404.0925

Maier, R. (2004). *Knowledge Management Systems: Information and Communication Technologies for Knowledge Management*. Berlin: Springer.

Maier, R., & Hadrich, T. (2006). Knowledge management systems. In Schwartz, D. G. (Ed.), *Encyclopaedia of Knowledge Management* (pp. 442–450). Hershey, PA: IGI Global.

Martensson, M. (2000). A critical review of knowledge management as a management tool. *Journal of Knowledge Management*, *4*(3), 204–216. doi:10.1108/13673270010350002

Martin, B., & Deng, H. (2003, December 17-19). Managing organizational knowledge in a socio-technical context. In P. Santiprabhob & J. Daengdej (Eds.), *Proceedings of the Fourth International Conference on Intelligent Technologies*, Chiangmai, Thailand.

Nonaka, I. O., & Takeuchi, H. (1995). *The knowledge-creating company: how Japanese companies create the dynamics of innovation*. New York: Oxford University Press.

O'Leary, D. E. (1998). Knowledge management systems: converting and connecting. *IEEE Intelligent Systems*, *13*(3), 30–33. doi:10.1109/MIS.1998.683179

Prat, N. (2006). A hierachical model for knowledge management. In Schwartz, D. G. (Ed.), *Encyclopaedia of Knowledge Management* (pp. 848–854). Hershey, PA: IGI Global.

Prusak, L. (2006). Foreword. In Schwartz, D. G. (Ed.), *Encyclopaedia of Knowledge Management*. Hershey, PA: IGI Global.

Ruggles, R. (1998). The state of the notion: knowledge management in practice. *California Management Review*, *40*, 80–89.

Song, H., Deng, H., & Martin, B. (2005). Technological approach to knowledge management. In *Proceedings of the Second International conference on Information Management and Science*, Kunming, China.

Spiegler, I. (2003). Technology and knowledge: bridging a "generating" gap. *Information & Management*, *40*(6), 533–539. doi:10.1016/S0378-7206(02)00069-1

Teleos. (2004). 2004 *Global Most Admired Knowledge Enterprises (MAKE) Report Executive Summary*. Retrieved from www.knowledgebusiness.com

Teleos. (2006). *2006 Global Most Admired Knowledge Enterprises (MAKE) Report Executive Summary*. Retrieved from www.knowledgebusiness.com

Tsui, E. (2003). Tracking the role and evolution of commercial Knowledge Management software. In Holsapple, C. W. (Ed.), *Handbook on Knowledge Management* (pp. 5–25). Heidelberg, Germany: Springer.

Tuomi, I. (2000). Data is more than knowledge: implications of the reversed hierarchy for knowledge management and organizational memory. *Journal of Management Information Systems*, *16*(3), 103–117.

Wiig, K. M. (1997). Knowledge management: where did it come from and where will it go. *Expert Systems with Applications*, *13*(1), 1–14. doi:10.1016/S0957-4174(97)00018-3

This work was previously published in the International Journal of Knowledge and Systems Science, Volume 1, Issue 2, edited by W.B. Lee, pp. 49-61 copyright 2010 by IGI Publishing (an imprint of IGI Global).

Section 3
Knowledge Technology

Chapter 9
Meta–Synthesis Knowledge System:
Basics and Practice

Gu Jifa
Academy of Mathematics and Systems Sciences, CAS, China

ABSTRACT

Meta-synthesis knowledge system (MSKS) is based on the meta-synthesis system approach and knowledge science. This article introduces the basic theory of meta-synthesis knowledge system like DMTMC system, model integration, opinion synthesis, consensus building and expert mining. Similar MSKS systems are illustrated. Case studies and examples are also explored in this article.

INTRODUCTION

Dealing with the different complex systems problems systems researchers developed a lot of various systems methodologies we may classified them as hard system methodologies, soft system methodologies and oriental system methodologies. The latest had been developed in the end of 1980' and the start of 1990. Within them author wishes emphasized the meta-synthesis system approach (MSA), which was developed by Qian, Yue and

Dai in 1990 for solving the open giant complex systems problems. From 1999 Gu involved in a major project supported by NSFC (Natural Science Foundation of China) related to MSA. At the May of 1999 Gu joined School of Knowledge Science in JAIST (Japan Advanced Institute of Science and Technology), continued this project research on MSA. But under the influence of atmosphere of knowledge science and author had learnt a lot of theories in knowledge science from Nonaka and his colleagues. As a system researcher Gu just wishes combine this knowledge science and systems science (especially theory of MSA). In

DOI: 10.4018/978-1-4666-1782-7.ch009

Figure 1. Movement of knowledge science research

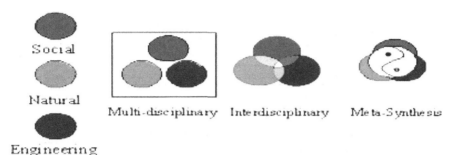

this School of Knowledge Science all professors come with the knowledge backgrounds from three aspects: natural science, engineering science and social science, so the school leaders wish them run research from multidisciplinary to interdisciplinary, then once in a school seminar Gu proposed colleagues to go forward from interdisciplinary research to interdisciplinary research with meta-synthesis (see Figure 1). Around 2001, Gu and Tang had proposed the Meta-synthesis knowledge system (2001a), which wishes use the help of a system with computer and a group of experts to integrate and synthesis all knowledge, which usually are used separately and individually.

META-SYNTHESIS SYSTEM APPROACH

Meta-synthesis System Approach is a Chinese system approach for solving problems related to the open, complex giant systems. MSA stands for combining the data, information, model, expert experience and wisdom. MSA helps people to utilize, discover and create knowledge combining with the computer.

The Essentials of MSA

1. Integrate data, information, knowledge, model, experiences and wisdom (D, I, K, M, E, W)
2. Combine human brain and computer (Man-Machine)
3. Synthesize all opinions from experts (Group knowledge)
4. Combine the left brain and right brain (Quantitative and Qualitative analysis)
5. Combine the reality and virtual reality (Reality and Virtual)
6. Combine the macroscopic and microscopic views (Macro and Micro)
7. Combine the reduction and holism (Analysis and Synthesis)

Meta-Synthesis Methods

MSA methods for different subjects we may use different methods (Gu, Wang, & Tang, 2007), see also Table 1.

Hall for Workshop of Meta-Synthetic Engineering (HWMSE)

HWMSE or discussion hall is an important tool for implementing the Meta-synthesis System approach. It consists of three systems: Knowledge system; Machine system; Experts system. Now in

Table 1. Meta-synthesis methods

Subject	Methods
Data	Data analysis, Data Base, Data Fusion, Data mining
Information	Information processing, Management Information System, Text mining, Web mining
Model	Modeling, Model Integration
Knowledge	Knowledge science, Knowledge Base
Experience,	SECI model, Opinion Synthesis, expert mining
Opinion	Opinion mining, Consensus building, Psychology mining
D, I, K, M, E,	System reconstruction

China several special HWMSE had been designed or installed for different purpose (Gu, Wang & Tang, 2007).

Flowchart of MSA

For realizing the MSA to solve complex problems we design a flowchart:

Synchronous (meeting I) -> Asynchronous (analysis) -> Synchronous (meeting II)

In the first stage the necessary data, information and knowledge are provided, the second stage various models are designed and integrated for the analysis, finally the methods for consensus building are prepared for use of convergence. If the problem is not solved, we will iterate this process again and again until getting some solution, or consensus.

Meta-Synthesis Knowledge System (MSKS): Basics

When the knowledge system consists of not only knowledge, but also data, information, model, experience from experts, wisdom from experts and decision makers, and the methods and tools for their total integration and synthesis (or in short Meta-synthesis) are emphasized, we call it Meta-synthesis knowledge system. To give a general description about the MSKS is a little bit difficult task for us. Next we just give some basic theories and methods for MSKS, which we had run some investigation. They are DMTMC system, model integration and consensus building.

DMTMC-System

In the MSKS the important thing is to convene the meeting often. In order to raise the efficiency and effectiveness for convening the meeting we propose the data-meeting--tool-method-consensus system (in short DMTMC system) (see Figure 1).

Furthermore when we combine the DMTMC and HWMSE, Tang gave the revised DMTMC system (Figure 2).

Model Integration

There are three approaches to model integration:

1. Top-Down Architecture: One object is broken into fundamental parts or modules and then assembled using functions
2. Bottom-up: It reflects distributed and decentralized activities during implementing model integration and management
3. System approach: It combines the human behavior and modeling techniques

There are also some integrated modeling environments (IME) to help in integrating models

Figure 2. DMTMC system

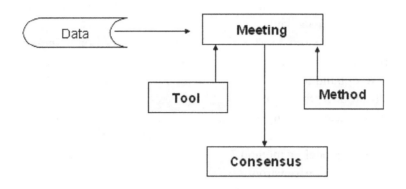

Figure 3. The revised DMTMC system

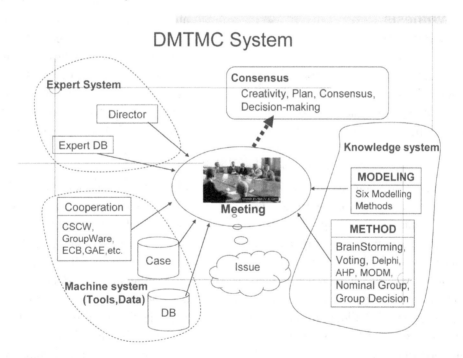

1. DOME (MIT),
2. SWARM (Santa Fe institute),
3. Modeling by 3MPCS (Ryobu, Fukawa and Sawaragi, Japan).

DOME means Distributed Object-based Modeling and Evaluation developed by CAD Lab, MIT... It may run collaborative product design in the network-centric design environment. Multi-agent simulation is a very important tool for using the multi-agent system. There are a lot of software packages for multi-agent simulation. The one of famous software packages for multi-agent simulation is SWARM developed at The Santa Fe Institute. It can simulate some complex adaptive system. It also can be a tool for meta-synthesis. Ryobu, Fukawa and Sawaragi proposed 3MPCS (The Modeling Method of Man's Participation for Complex System), they wish build the *artificial brain* which automatically produces the modeling equations that can take care of sudden changes in situations, only by the data given to the model, so they factually proposed the modeling method which can include the expert intuition, sensitivity and imagination. It means they can synthesis the hard mathematical models with the human wisdom by artificial brain. (Gu & Tang, 2005)

Opinions Synthesis (Consensus Building)

How can we synthesize the opinions from different experts or different information resources, we will use the theory and methods related to consensus building. People often use the voting method for reaching consensus, but as a matter of fact there is a lot of voting methods for selection in the different purpose, e.g. Borda method, Condorcet method which were based on making critique to the old election method for electing the French academicians. Besides of various voting method there are other methods for building consensus, e.g. statistical method, fuzzy method and Pareto method etc. There are some special research institutions in helping people to building the consensus, e.g. Consensus Building Institute, which got academic support from Harvard University and MIT. They had supported G77 in writing Kyoto Protocol, 2000, and published a "Consensus Building Handbook" in 1999. Then also some special software for building consensus, such as Mediator had been developed by Polish System Research Institute. And some advanced tools and methods designed for consensus building (Gu, 2001).

Some Similar Researches for MSKS

We had collected some similar researches and good examples developed by other researchers in the line of MSKS.

1. Synthesis of expert systems: China experiences large earthquakes, thus many cities run expert systems to forecast earthquakes. But there was often the case, different earthquake stations developed their own different expert systems, sometime these expert systems gave the different solutions for forecasting. Zhang and Zhang had proposed the methodologies and strategies of synthesis of solution in distributed expert system (1999).

2. Qualitative meta-synthesis (Comprehensive research synthesis): Researchers often wish they could summarize after reading a lot of literatures, and healthcare workers often wish they could diagnose some diseases or diagnosis after collecting a lot of evidence. There are three stages for processing such literatures and evidences:

    a. Traditional narrative reviews (Qualitative): This is a quite old method and many PhD students and researchers use it to describe their summary after collecting a evidence.

    b. Meta-analysis (Quantitative): A statistical method of research integration, which can quantitatively integrate and analyze the findings from all the empirical studies relevant to an issue and amenable to quantitative aggregation based on the "effect size" (Glass, 1976).

c. Qualitative meta-synthesis: (Combination of qualitative and quantitative)

The meta-analysis method now is widely used by health scholars, but in 1990's people find that how can we deal with if some literature, whose effect size is not so high but with the importance and novelty. For that reason some researchers started to find the improvement of meta- analysis by using the idea of synthesis, there are a lot of various methods for synthesis. e.g. "Best-evidence synthesis". In this method statistical analysis is supplemented with a rich literature review, which explains any discrepancies observed, and summarizes the results, which can not be quantified. There are some others methods, such as "reciprocal translational synthesis" and "refutational synthesis". In the early 2000s, Sandelowski and Borroso ran a project titled in "Analytic Techniques for Quantitative Meta-synthesis" supported by National Institutes of Health (NIH) and published a book "Handbook for Synthesizing Qualitative Research" (Sandelowski & Borroso, 2006) on this topic.

This kind of methods assumes that synthesis of qualitative research should be interpretive rather than aggregative. They consider the findings of individual studies, not only generate predictive theories, but to facilitate a fuller understanding of the phenomenon, context or culture under consideration.

3. Integration in Probability Risk Assessment (PRA): PRA has been applied in space programs (NASA, ESA) and nuclear power plants (U.S. Nuclear Regulatory Commission). Since the number of test samples for spacecrafts is small, its assessment of risk couldn't be expected by general statistical methods, which usually require a large number of samples. Instead, PRA combines the quantitative methods with the qualitative assessment methods by expert's judgment and experiences. It is an integration of FMEA (use for qualitative risk assessment), FTA (use for quantitative risk assessment) and other techniques to assess the potential for failure and help find ways to reduce risk.

PRA is similar methodology with a meta-synthesis from qualitative to quantitative, its analysis is based on data, information, knowledge and model. Expert opinions will also be collected. We applied the similar PRA techniques-CPRA to assess the safety of Chinese spacecraft (Zhao & Gu, 2000).

4. Environmental framework model (Environment knowledge management system): Nakamori had designed the environmental framework model, which tried to integrate the various energy, production and environment models altogether in order to solve some environment problems in Japan. Later it evolved into Environment knowledge management system. We usually analyze environmental problems with data, especially numerical data. Therefore, there are a few opportunities to utilize knowledge that people and society have, when we think of environmental problems. To solve the above-mentioned problems, it is necessary to build a system by which data, information and knowledge are collected, integrated and provided as new knowledge (see Figures 4-6) (Kawano & Nakamori, 2000).

5. Economic Meta-Synthesis Knowledge System: To investigate the Meta-Synthesis Knowledge System for macro-economic decision making which synthesizes the qualitative and quantitative information, model and knowledge using the environment

Figure 4. Knowledge creating model

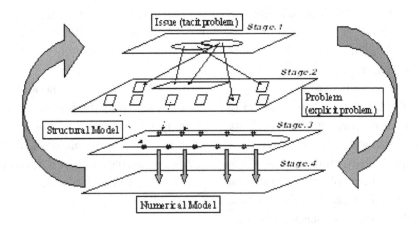

Figure 5. Environment framework model

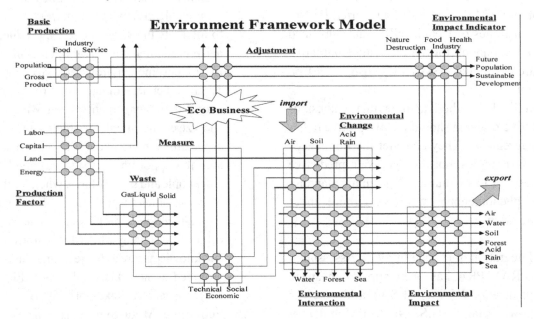

for developing knowledge, knowledge discovery techniques, especially with the participation from different fields of leaders, experts and system analysts in situ are provided. The main tasks are: Find the appropriate system methodology; Find the methods for meta-synthesis; Investigate the systematology with emphasizing the economic complex system; Provide the decision supporting (Gu, Wang & Tang, 2007).

Figure 6. Process of knowledge creation

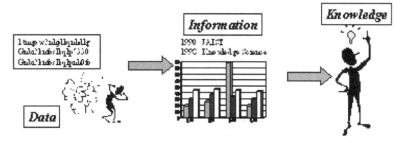

RECENT PROGRESS IN MSKS AND EXAMPLES

Six Mining

By six mining we mean data mining, text mining, web mining, model mining, psychology mining, and expert mining, which will be useful to MSKS. We may use the data mining to analyze a huge amount of data to discovery some useful knowledge. We may use text mining to extract some useful textual information from many texts in documents. We may use web mining to extract useful information from the internet, intranet, etc.

Expert Mining

Expert mining is a new emergent theory and technique, which is useful for collecting the ideas, experiences, knowledge and wisdom from experts. The source for mining mainly comes from live experts and group exchange by using computer and some special tools.

Besides of the mentioned five mining finally we will ask experts to analyze the all results which are sometimes contradicted each with other and also need expert to make final judgment for the obtained results, even more we will ask experts to create some new idea, methods, techniques and theory, new alternatives for decision, it means to use the wisdom to create something which originally does not exist (Gu et al., 2008a).

1. Meta-synthesis of Opinions
    1. Meta-synthesis of Opinions by text
    2. Meta-synthesis of Opinions by meeting (Ba, Facilitation, Mediation)
    3. Meta-synthesis of Opinions by interview deeply Psychology mining.
2. Meta-synthesis of wisdoms

We may combine the six mining and different sciences, such as knowledge science, systems science, noetic science, computer science, social science and political science altogether to solve complex problems, especially related to social complex problems (see Figure 7).

Figure 7. Meta-synthesis of wisdoms

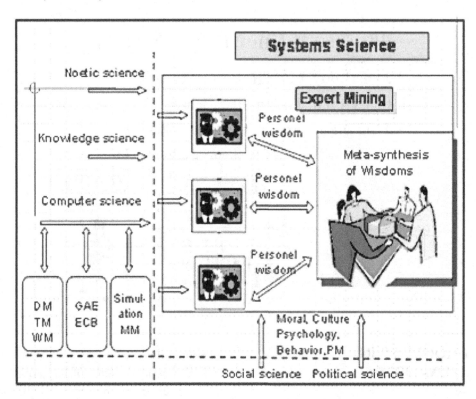

MSKS Platform

MSKS platform is designed for collecting different kinds of knowledge with the help of six mining and other techniques and tools, originally for the TCM case (Figure 8).

MSKS CASES AND EXAMPLES

Following cases and examples were done by my colleagues in recent years.

1. Social system: The social system is an open giant complex system. There are three kinds of channels to obtain information nowadays: formal society, informal society and network society. In order to collect and process useful information we have to use different mining techniques: data mining, text mining, web mining, model mining, psychology mining, and expert mining. The first four mining techniques deal with mainly the explicit data and information. The later two techniques mainly deal with the tacit information. We had run some case studies, e.g. MBA discussion for social harmony problems, Taxi driver's problem. Here we just wish mention the first case study-.MBA test-discussion about some social harmony problems, which had run in beginning of July, 2006. The main participants were the graduated students from MBA class, Graduate University, Chinese Academy of Sciences (CAS) during the period of 2006.6.27-7.13. The test was supported by the interdisciplinary study center of natural and social sciences, CAS. We divide all MBA students into six groups to attend the discussion on six selected topics separately: I. corruption, II. housing,

Figure 8. MSKS platform

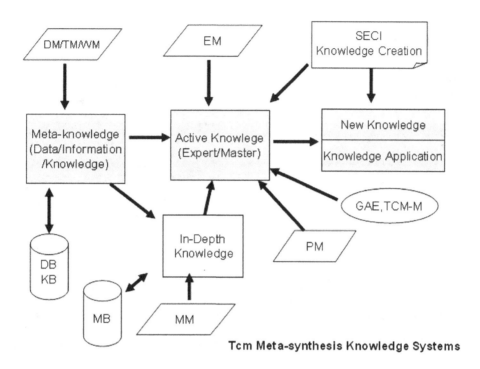

Tcm Meta-synthesis Knowledge Systems

III. health and insurance, IV. employment, V. peasant workers and VI. social safety. In each group we assign one facilitator using different discussion methods with some useful tools and methods, such as PathMaker, GAE, UciNet, GIS, interview and game theory. Most of participants satisfied such new scientific discussion test. There were some pictures used in the group on discussing housing problem (see Figures 9-13) and health problem (see Figure 14) (Gu, Liu & Song, 2007).

2. TCM system: From 2006 we participated in a major project supported by Ministry of Science and Technology of China for collecting and maintaining the idea, experiences, knowledge and wisdom from 100 elders and famous masters in TCM (Traditional Chinese Medicine). We use expert mining and knowledge synthesis to gain useful knowledge from individual and collective masters. We had applied a series of methods for expert mining, such as network analysis, GAE, correspondence analysis, machine learning etc. and designed a platform for TCM Meta-synthesis Knowledge system. Figure 15 just give one example for analyzing the usage of traditional medicine by masters (Gu et al., 2008b).

3. ADVISE (Analysis, Dissemination, Visualization, Insight, Semantic Enhancement) system: ADVISE was developed by some U.S. research institutes and universities funded by Department of Homeland Security starting from 2003 ended in September of 2007. This system as a platform may use the collection of different sources of data, information and make analysis by data mining, Semantic web etc tools and methods to analyze and forecast the terrorists information and events, especially it may got some insights and enhance

Figure 9. Housing problem (PathMaker)

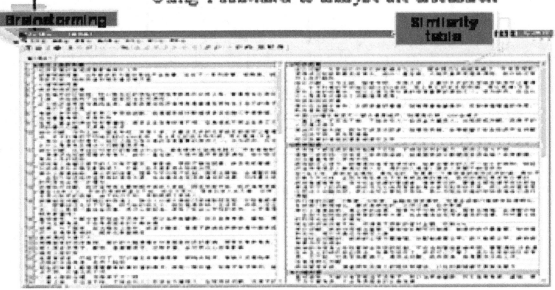

Figure 10. Housing problem (GAE)

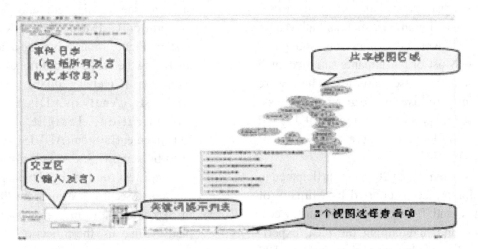

Figure 11. Housing problem (GAE-agreement)

Figure 12. Housing problem (GAE-Discrepceny)

Figure 13. Housing problem (Network analysis)

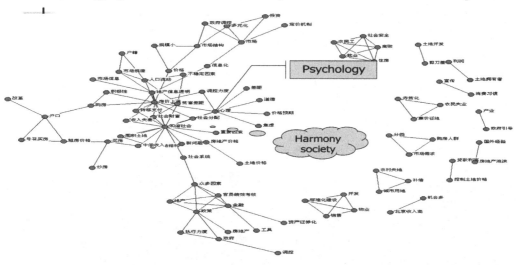

the semantic by knowledge utilization. It also uses visualization to help people to catch and understand some tacit knowledge (see Figure 16) (Kolda, Brown, Corones et al., 2005).

ACKNOWLEDGMENT

This article just introduces similar research on MSKS and some basics and case studies developed by my colleagues. I wish express my gratitude to all my colleagues who made contributions to this research, within them I wish specially to mention Nakamori from JAIST and Tang from Institute of Systems Science. My since-graduated PhD students Song and Zhu helped me format this article format and reprocess some figures.

Figure 14. Health and insurance (psychology mining)

Topic III: Health and insurance (Zheng R.,Inst.of Psychology)--Structure of samples

ÐÕ±ð

		Frequency	Percent	Valid Percent	Cumulative Percent
Valid	ÄÐ	22	59.5	61.1	61.1
	A®	14	37.8	38.9	100.0
	Total	36	97.3	100.0	
Missing	System	1	2.7		
Total		37	100.0		

ÄêÁä

		Frequency	Percent	Valid Percent	Cumulative Percent
Valid	20£30	16	43.2	44.4	44.4
	30£40	20	54.1	55.6	100.0
	Total	36	97.3	100.0	
Missing	System	1	2.7		
Total		37	100.0		

Ô°Òµ

		Frequency	Percent	Valid Percen	Cumulative Percent
Valid	'ýÒ²Æ óÊÀÒµµ¥Ì»¸É¹	3	8.1	10.0	10.0
	×¨Òµ¼¼ÊõÈÉÔ±	8	21.6	26.7	36.7
	Éý×É¡¢¼¯¯lá¡¢É½Ó°¡Òµ¹ÛÁÉÈÕ±	13	35.1	43.3	80.0
	'É·ÝÓÆÆóÒµ¹ÛÀÈ	5	13.5	16.7	96.7
	Ô°Òµ¶¶¶×ÊÕ߬	1	2.7	3.3	100.0
	Total	30	81.1	100.0	
Missing	System	7	18.9		
Total		37	100.0		

ÊÕÈ¸

		Frequency	Percent	Valid Percent	Cumulative Percent
Valid	500ÒÒÏÂ	1	2.7	2.9	2.9
	1000£2000	1	2.7	2.9	5.9
	2000£5000	18	48.6	52.9	58.8
	5000£8000	7	18.9	20.6	79.4
	8000ÒÕÉÏ	7	18.9	20.6	100.0
	Total	34	91.9	100.0	
Missing	System	3	8.1		
Total		37	100.0		

Figure 15. Analysis of usage of traditional medicine by network

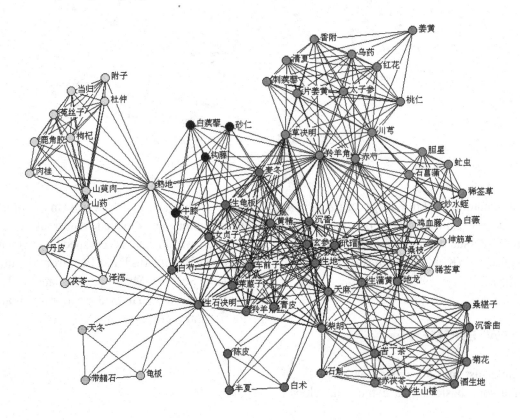

Figure 16. Architecture for ADVISE system

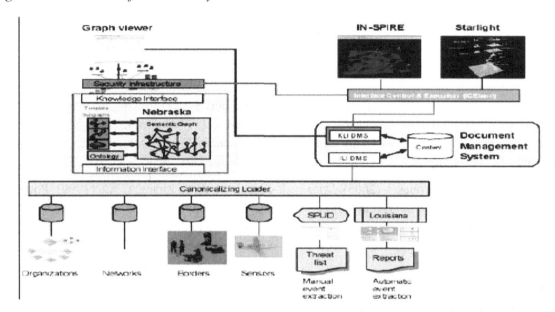

REFERENCES

Gu, J. F. (2001). On synthesizing opinions-how to reach consensus. *Journal of Systems Engineering, 16*(5), 340–348.

Gu, J. F. (2007). From hard to soft, from West to East. Panel discussion, Tokyo. In *Proceedings of ISSS2007*, Tokyo, Retrieved from http://isss.org/conferences/tokyo2007/20070807-isss-1100-gu.pdf

Gu, J. F. (2008, March 9-10). *Meta-synthesis knowledge system: Basics and practice.* Paper presented at the International Workshop on Knowledge Integration and Innovation, Dalian, China.

Gu, J. F., Liu, Y. J., & Song, W. Q. (2007, August 7-10). *A scientific discussion test on some social harmony problems.* Paper presented at ISSS2007, Tokyo.

Gu, J. F., Song, W. Q., & Zhu, Z. X. (2008a, October). Meta-synthesis and expert mining. In *Proceedings of the 2008 IEEE International Conference on Systems, Man, and Cybernetics* (pp. 467-471).

Gu, J. F., Song, W. Q., Zhu, Z. X., Gao, R., & Liu, Y. J. (2008b, December 11-13). *Expert mining and TCM knowledge.* Paper presented at KSS2008, Guangzhou, China.

Gu, J. F., & Tang, X. J. (2001a, September 21-23). *Meta-synthesis knowledge system (MSKS).* Paper presented at MCS2001, Beijing, China.

Gu, J. F., & Tang, X. J. (2001b). *Meta-Synthesis knowledge system for complex system* (Tech. Rep. AMSS-2001-11). Beijing, China: Academy of Mathematics and System Sciences, Chinese Academy of Sciences.

Gu, J. F., & Tang, X. J. (2002). Meta-synthesis and knowledge science, Systems engineering. *Theory into Practice, 22*(10), 2–7.

Gu, J. F., & Tang, X. J. (2005). Meta-synthesis approach to complex system modeling. *European Journal of Operational Research, 166*, 597–614. doi:10.1016/j.ejor.2004.03.036

Gu, J. F., & Tang, X. J. (2007). Meta-synthesis system approach to knowledge science. *International Journal of Information Technology and Decision Making, 6*(3), 559–572. doi:10.1142/S0219622007002629

Gu, J. F., Wang, H. C., & Tang, X. J. (2007). *Meta-synthesis method system and systematology research*. Beijing, China: Science Press.

Kawano, S., & Nakamori, Y. (2000, September 25-27). *Environment knowledge management using the framework model*. Paper presented at the International Symposium on Knowledge and Systems Sciences: Challenges to Complexity (KSS'2000), Ishikawa, Japan.

Kolda, T., Brown, D., & Corones, J. (2005). *Data Sciences Technology for homeland security information management and knowledge discovery* (Sandia Rep. SAND2004-6648). Livermore, CA: Sandia National Laboratories.

Qian, X. S., Yu, J. Y., & Dai, R. W. (1990). A New Discipline of Science: Open Complex Giant System and Its Methodology. *Chinese Journal of Nature, 13*(1), 3–10.

Sandelowski, M., & Barroso, J. (2006). *Handbook for Synthesizing Qualitative Research*. New York: Springer.

Song, W. Q., Liu, Y. J., Zhu, Z. X., & Gu, J. F. (2008). A Framework of Meta-Synthesis Consensus Support System for Group Decision-Making Problems. In *Proceedings of the 2008 Fifth International Conference on Fuzzy Systems and Knowledge Discovery* (Vol. 3, pp. 319-324).

Zhang, M. J., & Zhang, C. Q. (1999). Potential cases, methodologies and strategies of synthesis of solutions in distributed expert systems. *IEEE Transactions on Knowledge and Data Engineering, 11*(3), 498–503. doi:10.1109/69.774105

Zhao, L. Y., & Gu, J. F. (2000). The application of probabilistic risk assessment approach to the safety analysis of one specific type of launch vehicle in China. *Systems Engineering: Theory & Pratice, 20*(6), 91–97.

This work was previously published in the International Journal of Knowledge and Systems Science, Volume 1, Issue 1, edited by W.B. Lee, pp. 58-72 copyright 2010 by IGI Publishing (an imprint of IGI Global).

Chapter 10
Ontology Alignment:
State of the Art, Main Trends and Open Issues

Tatyana Ivanova
Technical University of Sofia, Bulgaria

ABSTRACT

A grand number of ontologies have been developed and are publicly accessible on the Web making techniques for mapping between various ontologies more significant. Research has been made in the area of ontology alignment, a grand number of approaches, algorithms, and tools have been developed in recent years, but are still not "perfect" and excellent knowledge. In this article, the author makes an overall view of the state of ontology alignment, including the latest research, comparing many approaches, and analyzing their strengths and drawbacks. The main motivation behind this work is the fact that despite many component matching solutions that have been developed so far, there is no integrated solution that is a clear success, which can be used for ontology mapping in all cases, making knowledge about developed ontology mapping methods and their clear classification needed.

INTRODUCTION

Ontology matching is the process of finding correspondences between entities belonging to different ontologies: classes, attributes, relationships, or value of attributes. The task of ontology alignment can be described as follows: given two ontologies, each of which describes a set of elements (classes, properties, rules, etc.), find the relationships (equivalence or subsumption), holding between these elements. More formally, an alignment between two ontologies O_1 and O_2 is a set of 4-tuple correspondences of type (e_1, e_2, R, n), where:

DOI: 10.4018/978-1-4666-1782-7.ch010

- e_1 and e_2 are the entities (e.g., formulas, terms, classes, individuals) of O_1 and O_2 between which a relation is asserted by the correspondence;
- R is the relation, between e_1 and e_2, asserted by the correspondence. This relation can be a simple set-theoretic relation (applied to entities seen as sets or their interpretation seen as sets), a fuzzy relation, a probabilistic distribution over a complete set of relations, a similarity measure, etc.;
- n is a degree of confidence in that correspondence (measure of the trust in the fact that the correspondence is appropriate);

Definitions of many concepts, related to ontology mapping can be found in (Choi et al., 2006). Much research has been made in the area of ontology alignment, a grand number of approaches, algorithms and tools have been developed in resent years, but mo one is "perfect" and choosing an alignment approaches, algorithms or tools for particular tack can be very difficult. Even when the needs are very clear, there are many criteria that can be used for choosing an adequate technique or matcher and all needed criteria cannot be assessed in the same way. It is also difficult to obtain all the information about each approach, technique or tool.

In this paper, I analyze and compare ontology mapping approaches (on the base mainly of results from a literature survey and according to many important for research and practical application criteria), merge and extend earlier good classifications by adding the newest research approaches, and discuss the principles behind ontology mapping, trends and perspectives in ontology alignment.

The contributions of this paper are classifications of ontology mapping approaches according various dimensions, comprehensive survey of latest approaches and discussion of the main trends and challenges in the ontology matching field.

The paper is discusses earlier (before 2008) research and classifications on ontology mapping and then discusses the newest ontology alignment approaches (proposed in 2007, 2008 or 2009). Next, the mapping evaluation approaches are analyzed, followed by a comparison of the mapping tools. Finally, the article is concluded.

THE STATE OF THE ART ON ONTOLOGY MATCHING

An important work on ontology mapping before 2008 has been conducted within the Knowledge Web project. Many approaches, algorithms and techniques are available for achieving ontology alignment and many systems have been developed, based on them. There are some good surveys (Euzenat et al., 2007; Euzenat et al., 2004; Euzenat & Shvaiko, 2007; Kalfoglou & Schorlemmer, 2005) but no one of them is comprehensive: every one describes different systems, classify and compare them according to its own criteria. This article aims to fill-in some of these gaps: lack of a comprehensive survey and unified criteria for comparison of approaches, techniques and tools. We critically reviewed works originating from a variety of fields to provide a comprehensive overview of ontology mapping work to date.

THE MAIN CHARACTERISTICS OF ONTOLOGY MATCHING APPROACHES AND ALGORITHMS

There are many independent dimensions along which approaches, algorithms or tools can be examined, classified or selected. After analyzing above mentioned surveys and many other published in the last few year materials we propose for discussing the following dimensions for comprehensive description and classification of ontology matching approaches, algorithms and tools:

1. The algorithm's input characteristics: size; input category as text, thesaurus, taxonomy, Web; input formality level; input model type, as domain ontology, tack ontology, application ontology; input natural language, input representation language as DAML, RDFS, OWL; input structure as tree, graph;

2. The characteristics of the matching process, which describes the matching approaches and algorithms themselves(manual or automatic, syntactic or semantic matching, matcher level, matcher ground, matcher type), scalability, automat ion degree, domain-dependence degree;

3. The output of the algorithms (output type, matching cardinality, execution completeness);

4. The main purpose of the matching approach takes into account the different situations where the approaches have been used (for using shared ontologies or for heuristic or machine-learning approaches in knowledge management, for local or network usage, application area, usage type, adaptation ability), making all possible alignments or only focal ones (Globality dimension);

5. Matching strategy – using one or many approaches and algorithms and usage strategy;

6. Documentation characteristics points out the existence and type of the documentation (documentation quality, documentation clarity, availability of examples);

7. Cost characteristics address the financial costs (license costs or algorithm sources cost) or computational efficiency and evaluation.

CLASSIFICATION OF ONTOLOGY MATCHING APPROACHES

As input and output characteristics are closely related to alignment tools, we will refer to them later in tool classification.

Since the characteristics of the matching process are of great importance for ontology alignment, we will analyze and classify mapping algorithms and approaches first. Mapping approaches in many cases include several (may be of different type) algorithms. We first classify the basic algorithms and approaches and then analyze the combined ones, including combination strategy.

Ontology alignment methods can be classified according to various dimensions: type, number, distribution of matching elements, matching criteria, used models or similarity measures etc.

Two main classes of ontology alignment methods depending on the matching elements, as it is shown on Figure 2, are schema based and instance-based.

Instance-based methods (called sometimes extensional) compare the extension of classes, i.e., their set of instances rather than their interpretation. They for example compare classes A and B by testting their intersection as sets of instances and concluding that these classes are very similar when $A \cap B = A = B$, more general when $A \cap B = B$ or $A \cap B = A$. In another cases they may used Similarity-based techniques, as Single linkage, Full linkage, Average linkage, Haussdorf distance, Matching-based comparison, Jaccard similarity and other statistical measures.

Schema matching (Figure 2) is usually performed with the help of techniques using the meaning encoded in the schemas, as classification, properties, taxonomic or non-taxonomic relations. Schema matching algorithms and technique are very reach and will be disused and classified below.

Depending from the scope of the alignment process approaches may be classified as local or global ones (Figure 1).

Local approaches aim to find to what entity or expression in the one ontology corresponds another one in the other ontology (contrary to global ones that aim at finding all correspondences between ontologies). In many cases, global methods are combination of local ones.

Figure 1. Classification of ontology mapping approaches

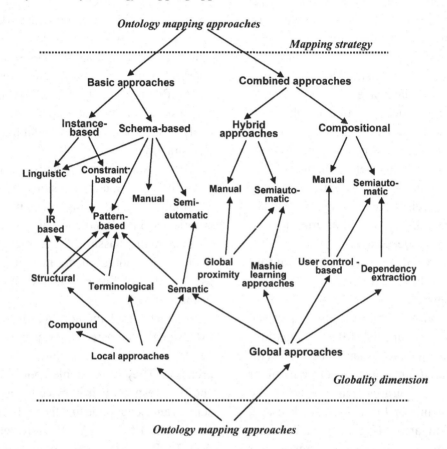

Local Approaches for Ontology Mapping

Understanding local approaches is very important because they are usually in the basis of global ones. Local approaches may be basic and compound (combination of basic ones).

Basic approaches usually enable to measure the correspondence between entities at a local level, i.e., only comparing one element with another and not working at the global scale of ontologies. They may be used various algorithms for best mapping selection, but their overall purpose is performing mapping only between isolated entities and never between all ontologies. The main subclasses of local approaches are Structural, Terminological and Semantic.

Terminological methods compare strings. They can be applied to the name, the label or the comments, concerning entities to find those which are similar. The main types of terminological methods are: String-based methods, as Normalization, String equality or similarity finding, distance calculating, Substring similarity; Language-based methods use Natural Language Processing (NLP) techniques to exploit morphological properties of the words (as tokenization or lemmatization), find associations between concepts or classes; Multilingual methods.

Structural and semantic methods are usually schema-based (Figure 2). Structural matching methods compare the structure of entities on the base of properties or interelement relationships that can be found in ontology, instead of comparing

Figure 2. classification of Schema-Based Matching Techniques

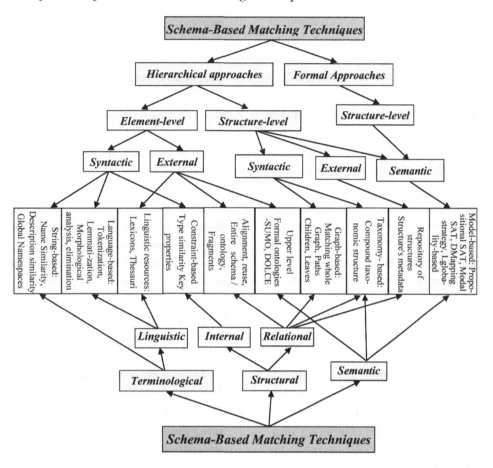

their names or identifiers. This comparison can be subdivided in a comparison of the internal structure of an entity (it's attributes or, for speaking OWL, the properties which takes their values in a data type) or the comparison of the entity with other entities to which it is related. Methods based on the internal structure of entities use criteria such as the range of their properties (attributes and relations), their cardinality, and the transitivity and/or symmetry of their properties to calculate the similarity between them. Internal structure based methods are sometimes referred to as constraint based approaches. Methods based on the external structure decide that the two entities are similar using the taxonomic or Mereologic schema structure. The similarity computation between entities can be also based on their relations.

The key characteristics of semantic methods are that they have model-theoretic semantics which is used to justify their results and they work with concepts (contrary to syntactical that analyze and manage strings). They use deductive reasoning as propositional satisfiability (SAT) and modal SAT techniques or description logic based techniques. SAT deciders are correct and complete decision procedures for propositional satisfiability, and will exhaustively check for all possible mappings, but it has very limited expressive power. Modal SAT can be used, for extending the methods related to propositional SAT to binary predicates. The key idea is to enhance propositional logics with modal logic (or a kind of description logics) operators. Therefore, the matching problem is translated into a modal logic formula which is further checked for its validity using sound and complete satisfiability search procedures. Description logics techniques (as subsumption and satisfability tests), can be used to establish the relations between classes in a purely semantic manner. Usually, first merging two ontologies and then testing each pair of concepts and role for subsumption or satisfability is enough for aligning terms with the same interpretation.Ppure semantic methods do not perform very well alone, they often need a preprocessing phase providing lexical, morphologic and syntactic analysis (stemming, using synonyms from external thesauruses).

Global Approaches for Ontology Mapping

Global approaches compare the whole ontologies (or valuable amount of elements, using not only their neighbors, but a valuable part of the whole ontology). Global approaches usually include aggregation of results of local methods in order to: compute the similarity between compound entities; develop a strategy for computing similarities in spite of cycles and non linearity in the constraints governing similarities; organize the combination of various similarity/alignment algorithms; involving the user in interactive mapping. The schema-based global approaches are usually structure-level techniques that incorporate graph-based information in compound measures or for matching strategy selection.

Using Compound Similarity Measures

Compound similarity is concerned with the aggregation of local (and compound) similarities. As some objects are understood as compound, their similarity depends on that holding between their components. For example, the similarity between two classes may depend on the similarity of their names, their super-classes, subclasses, properties. In case the difference between some

properties must be aggregated, the Minkowski distances, Weighted sums, Triangular norms, weighted averages and fuzzy aggregates may be used. The computation of compound similarity is local because it only provides similarity considering the neighbourhood of a node. However, real similarity involve the ontologies as a whole and the final similarity values ultimately depend on all the ontologies (or on the purpose is calculated to). For global similarity computation usually composition of several methods and its optimization is needed. For that purposes, strategies must be defined in order to compute the global similarity and the optimal strategy mast be discovered. Similarity flooding and machine learning approaches are usually used for estimating global similarity.

Strategies for Method Composition

Mapping and similarity assessment methods are also aggregated in order to compose a particular alignment algorithm. For instance, to map classes, we can first compute similarities between class names, then compute similarity between properties depending on how their names and classes to which they are attached are similar and then run a fix-point algorithm for computing interdependent similarities. We can distinguish three approaches to compose mapping methods: built-in composition, where the chaining of methods is part of the algorithm and is applied to any data set which is given to the system; opportunistic composition, where the system chooses the next method to run in function of the input data, and user-driven composition, in which the user has many different methods that can apply following his will.

Comprehensive multidimensional classification of ontology mapping techniques is shown in Figure 1, and of schema mapping techniques – in Figure 2.

Depending on usage of external resources during the mapping process, approaches can be classified as external or internal. Internal ones don't use additional resources as thesauruses, other ontologies, etc.

External Alignment Approaches

External (or background knowledge based) techniques aim to discover or evaluate correspondences by exploring an external resource to bridge the semantic gap between the matched ontologies. Using external resources usually increase precision and is recommended in such domains (as medical or biotechnology) where qualified resources are available. As depicted in Figure 3, matchers from this category exploit an external resource by replacing the original matching problem (between concepts A_1 and A_2) with two complementary matching and an inference step: the two concepts are first matched to so called anchor terms (A'_1, A'_2) in the background source, and then mappings are deduced from the semantic relations of these anchors. A pre-requisite for the success of such matchers is the availability of background knowledge sources with an appropriate coverage of the matched ontologies. Some approaches rely on readily available, large-scale, generic resources such as WordNet or Cyc. These resources cover a broad range of domains, but they might not cover specific domains (e.g., medicine, transportation planning) to the depth or granularity, required by the matching task. In these cases, appropriate domain ontology is either built manually, or selected prior to the matching process.

User Interaction

Depending on the degree of user intervention, ontology mapping approaches can be divided to manual, semi-automatic or automatic ones. As an effective fully automated alignment process is not attainable, the support of effective interaction of the user with the system components is is important for ontology alignment. User input can take place for assessing initial similarity be-

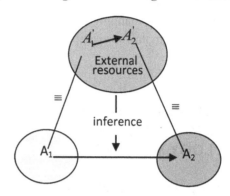

Figure 3. Background knowledge based matching

tween some terms; for invoking and composing alignment methods and for accepting or refusing similarity or alignment provided by the various methods. User feedback for each specific mapping extracted by the system could provide the alignment system with the ability of improving itself by changing the local alignment system parameters of the aggregation of the local alignments. However, asking users to specify this information is in general difficult since people conceptions change through their interaction with the alignment system, or user qualification often is not enough for working at this level of proficiency. Moreover, a lot of applications, as semantic web service composition inter-agent communication information integration, require no user participation.

Application Orientation

As most of the methods are developed, having in mind concrete ontologies, they have some degree of application dependence. Application orientation as a classification dimension may be classified as domain dependence, ontology type dependence, alignment goal dependence etc.

Domain dependence is very important ontology matching dimension. Some of the approaches as string-based ones are usable for every domain whereas external approaches are highly domain dependent. Knowledge structures and reasoning in different domains also differ significantly and as a result ontology mapping in biomedical and mathematical domain for example may be very different.

RECENT ACHIEVEMENTS AND CHALLENGES IN ONTOLOGY MAPPING

Apart from analyzing good surveys, we have explored a lot of scientific publications, issued during the last 3 years from digital libraries, electronic journals, and research projects in the area of ontology mapping to outline current trends in this dynamic and fast growing research and application domain. Most of them are combination of several (may be of different type) algorithms or approaches. We have classified them in subsequent groups:

1. Approaches, rely on complex mathematical models
2. Approaches, rely on background or context knowledge
3. Semantic alignment approaches
4. Pattern-based approaches
5. Approaches, having social orientation
6. Case-based approaches
7. Fuzzy or probabilistic ontology alignment approaches
8. Multistrategy approaches
9. Multiagent approaches

ALIGNMENT MODELS, USED NEW KNOWLEDGE-REPRESENTATION PARADIGMS, BASED ON COMPLEX MATHEMATICAL MODELS

A method for ontology matching, based on modeling two ontologies (for which the matching problem is of interest) in a single multi dimensional (N dimensional, N is the number of distinct concepts of two ontologies) vector space and estimating their similarity degree using vector-based techniques is presented in (Eidoon et al., 2008). Authors call it Vector Based Method of Ontology Matching (VBOM). This approach uses syntactic and structure-based (using labeled directed graphs) techniques to achieve semantic similarity measurement. Modeling ontologies in multi-dimensional vector spaces enable usage of vector matching methods for performing automatic structural ontology alignment. A post processing with two heuristic rules also has been employed to improve the results. The proposed method is successfully applied to the test suit of Ontology Alignment Evaluation Initiative. Results for precision are above 50% for all tests, but recall in some tests is very low (under 1%). Better results are obtained in mapping ontologies that contain similar concept names and similar structures. This method is best for determining global similarity between ontologies. Additional external semantic techniques (as using thesauruses or reference ontologies) may be added to increase the precision.

METHODS, USING BACKGROUND KNOWLEDGE OR CONTEXT KNOWLEDGE

Both Background Knowledge and Context provide additional information for semantic disambiguation during the mapping process. Comparing to the context, background knowledge provide more general and domain-related information as the context provides strictly specific (local according to the mapping elements) domain information or another application-specific information (as search type, author, date for example in the search domain)

Approaches, Using Background Knowledge

The idea of background and contextual knowledge usage in the ontology mapping process is not new, but significant results has achieved during recent few years. There are three main approaches to matching that rely on the use of background knowledge, depending on the type of the explored external resource: based on ontologies, on rules and on textual sources. Depending on the source of used resources it may be divided to ones, using local or web recourses. Ontology-based approaches may be divided to ones, based on upper or domain ontologies, depending on the type of used ontologies. Matchers, which exploit the particularities of the background ontology usually are domain-specific but there are some domain and ontology type, independent ones (Sabou et al., 2008).

Approaches, Using Reference Ontology (Indirect Alignment) as Background Knowledge

In many domains there is a significant amount of context independent knowledge. Much ontologies have been developed in the last years and some of them represent valuable context-independent knowledge (for example in mathematic, bioinformatics, medical domains). Such ontologies (called reference ontologies) are increasingly and successfully used as background knowledge to facilitate ontology mapping (especially in semi-automatic or automatic mapping). For example, a method, used reference ontology was successfully applied for automatically deriving a mapping between Mouse Anatomy (MA) and NCI from the two direct alignments MA-FMA and NCI-FMA in (Zhang & Bodenreider, 2007). When a FMA (Foundational Model of Anatomy) concept C_F is aligned with both a MA concept ({MA: C_M, FMA: C_F}) and a NCI concept ({NCI: C_N, FMA: C_F}), the concepts C_M and C_N are automatically aligned

({MA: C_M, NCI: C_N}). Automatic matching is usually limited to the detection of simple one to one correspondences to be further refined by the user. (Zhang & Bodenreider, 2007) presents a hybrid anatomical entities alignment strategy. It works by combining direct and indirect alignment techniques, both supported by the NLM Anatomy Ontology Alignment System (AOAS).

In many cases, when knowledge engineer haven't good reference ontology he may on some extent rely on that will find on the Internet some, that can be easily adapted, as there are freely available Web ontologies in almost every domain. Sabou et al. (2008) proposes an ontology matching paradigm, based on harvesting the Semantic Web, i.e., automatically finding and exploring multiple and heterogeneous online knowledge sources to derive mappings. It maximizes the coverage of the background knowledge by exploring multiple online ontologies, and minimizes any knowledge acquisition effort prior to matching through the automatic selection of the background knowledge by finding and selecting needed ontologies directly from internet, using semantic document search engines as Swoogle or Watson. Such an approach is domain independent and can be particularly helpful when a large, domain ontology does not exist but, nevertheless, the required knowledge is potentially spread over multiple different ontologies, or when the matched ontologies spread over several domains, requiring the use of a variety of ontologies. An experimental matching system, based on this approach has tested in the context of matching two real life, large-scale ontologies and experiments have yielded a promising baseline precision of 70% and have identified a set of critical issues that need to be considered to achieve the full potential of the paradigm.

A set of algorithms that exploit upper ontologies as semantic bridges in the ontology matching process and presents a systematic analysis of the relationships among features of matched ontologies (number of simple and composite concepts, stems, concepts at the top level, common English suffixes and prefixes, ontology depth), matching algorithms, used upper ontologies, and experiment results are presented in Mascardi et al. (2009) and Ou et al. (2008). This analysis allowed us to state under which circumstances the exploitation of upper ontologies gives significant advantages with respect to traditional approaches that do no use them.

Approaches, Used Association Rules

They use a background or context knowledge, represented as association rules applied to the concept hierarchies of the input ontologies. Such techniques as Ontology Mapping based on Association Rule Mining (ONARM) (Tatsiopoulos & Boutsinas, 2009), exploits a structural and linguistic similarity measure in order to automatically determine the mapping between two input ontologies. Association rules can be manually coded, periodically updated or automatically mined from web (for example in electronic commerce or web 2.0 tagging), and they guarantee a grand level of flexibility.

Context Based Approach

The exact matching of concepts is not only function of his labels or direct neighbors, but also of the current context, i.e., of the surrounding concepts and the situation, in which they are used. That is why some of the latest research is devoted to increase the precision of ontology mapping by using all available contextual information. Borgo and Lesmo (2008) present new method, which extracts the background knowledge from ontology, using new context similarity measure, for improving mapping results. This method is efficient when there is significant lexical overlap between the labels of the ontology entities or ontologies have rich or similar structures. It is efficient when the concept similarities cannot be discovered from syntactic or structural similarity, but becomes obvious when considering the meaning of the

concepts. Adding background or context knowledge to state of the art approaches in many cases significantly (up to 50%) increases the mapping recall. The approach has successfully tested with the public test cases of the Ontology Alignment Evaluation Initiative. Resent evaluations of mapping systems show that lack of background and context knowledge is one of the main problems of the mapping systems, leading to no such high values of recall.

SEMANTIC ALIGNMENT APPROACHES

Semantic matching is an approach for improving alignment quality (and performance) by reasoning. Semantic matching is based on two ideas: discovering mappings by computing semantic relations (e.g., equivalence, more general) and determining semantic relations by analyzing the meaning (concepts, not labels) which is codified in the elements and the structures of schemas. Basic and optimized algorithms for semantic matching, and their implementation within the S-Match system is presented in Giunchiglia et al. (2007).

Some research in semantic matching starts in 2003 (Giunchiglia & Shvaiko, 2003) using an iterative semantic matching approach based on SAT. Semantic mapping can't be used as a standalone method, but only as an upgrade to improve the results of other methods, and research in this area becomes very actual in the latest few years when mapping quality have become very important (especially in case of dynamic automatic mapping). Automated Semantic Matching of Ontologies with Verification (ASMOV) algorithm (Yves et al., 2009) for ontology matching is designed to combine a comprehensive set of element-level and structure-level measures of similarity with a technique that uses formal semantics to verify whether computed correspondences comply with desired characteristics. To remove the correspondences that are less likely to be satisfiability based on the information present in the ontologies, (Yves et al., 2009) presents a Semantic verification approach. The pre-alignment is passed through a process of semantic verification, designed to verify that certain axioms inferred from an alignment are actually asserted in ontology, removing correspondences that lead to inferences that cannot be verified. The presented experimental results show that ASMOV outperforms most existing ontology matching algorithms, and obtains accuracy values for the OAEI 2008 benchmarks on par with the best system in the contest. Tests on the alignment of a human anatomy with a mouse anatomy ontology show that the use of a specialized thesaurus such as UMLS significantly improves the alignment of ontologies of a particular knowledge domain.

Semantic methods (in the form of non-standard reasoning with mappings and about mappings) for supporting human experts in the task of revising automatically created mappings, and methods for detecting and propagating implications of expert decisions on the correctness of a mapping have proposed in Giunchiglia et al. (2007). It has implemented a graphical tool for manual revision that includes all of the methods mentioned in Giunchiglia et al. (2007). The experiments have shown that the revision methods proposed improve the revision process both in terms of the quality of mappings (in particular the precision is enhanced significantly) and in terms of the human effort.

In (Meilicke, 2008) is proposed the application of a reasoning based approach in different contexts for enrich and optimize ontology matching by reasoning about incoherence. It proposes an approach of reasoning with alignments, centered on the notion of alignment incoherence. It also proposes an approach for using incoherence to support manual alignment revision.

The approach followed in Meilicke (2008) is to interpret the problem of identifying wrong correspondences in an ontology alignment as a diagnosis task and analyzed the impact of each correspondence on the ontologies it connects. A correspondence that correctly states the semantic

relations between ontologies should not cause inconsistencies in any of the ontologies. If it does, the method computes sets of correspondences that jointly cause a symptom and repairs each symptom by removing correspondences from these sets.

Word Sense Disambiguation (WSD) approach (Locoro & Mascardi, 2009) is an automatic approach for repairing ontology alignments based on WSD techniques, using the Adapted Lesk algorithm, and upper ontologies to enrich the context, necessary to compute the meaning disambiguation of concepts to process the repairing task. The objective is to improve the results of background knowledge based Ontology Matching, by detecting and solving the ambiguity problems inherent to the use of heterogeneous sources of knowledge. It uses techniques from Word Sense Disambiguation to validate the mappings by exploring the semantics of the ontological terms involved in the matching process. Specifically it discusses how two techniques, which exploit the ontological context of the matched and anchor terms, and the information provided by WordNet, can be used to filter out mappings resulting from the incorrect anchoring of ambiguous terms. The experiments show that each of the proposed disambiguation techniques, and even more their combination, can lead to an important increase in precision, without having too negative an impact on recall. An initial evaluation of this method showed a 70% precision in obtaining mappings between ontologies. These experiments have also shown that more than half of the invalid mappings are due to ambiguity problems in the anchoring process.

PATTERN - BASED APPROACHES

State of the art ontology matching techniques are limited to detect simple correspondences between atomic concepts and properties. Sometimes, applications needed from complex correspondences, where at least one of the linked entities is non-atomic. Usually, complex relationships have described by means of predefined patterns. Shvaiko et al. (2007) Introduces several patterns describing complex correspondences and proposes methods for automatically detecting complex different types of correspondences. These methods are based on a combination of basic matching techniques. First results are promising, but generation of complex correspondences is significantly harder and pattern based approach will in most cases fail to generate highly precise alignments and the task of verifying the correctness of complex correspondences requires human interaction. The search space explodes and it becomes impossible for a human expert to evaluate each possible patterns. The proposed patterns usually covers only a small part of an infinite search space.

SOCIAL APPROACHES

There is much partly overlapping ontologies in open dynamic environment, such as the Web. To improve access to the related information, or web services, some elements of overlapping ontologies must be dynamically aligned. Despite significant advancement in automatic matching of ontologies, current systems can't perfectly match real-world ontologies automatically and human involvement is needed. This is only one of situations, where engagement of the usual user in the mapping process is of great importance. The spread of Web 2.0 approaches demonstrate the possibilities and the added value of using collaborative techniques for improving data sharing and consensus reaching. Social ontology alignment approach combines ontology mapping tools with social software techniques to enable users to collaborate on mapping ontologies. Emphasis is put on the reuse of user generated mappings to improve the accuracy of automatically generated ones. In Zhdanova and Shvaiko (2006) the authors proposed to use similarity of user and group profiles as a driver for suggesting ontology alignments reuse. The focus of that work was on building such profiles to personalize reuse of ontology mappings.

In Correndo and Alani (2007), OntoMediate, a prototype for collaborative ontology mapping and data sharing is proposed. It is exploring the use of collaborative features (discussions, voting, changed proposals) to facilitate the curation and reuse of mappings by the community. The approach is novel in the way it addresses the task of aligning ontologies, by extending and enhancing automatic mapping tools with a full community support. In this approach, alignments are seen as a resource, built and shared by a community. The community is able to investigate, argue, and correct individual mappings, using various supporting services provided by OntoMediate. The prototype has been designed to be extendible, allowing off-the-shelf tools to be integrated and is composed of three main subsystems: ontologies and datasets manager; ontology alignment environment; social interaction environment.

Community-driven ontology matching extends conventional ontology matching. It is a process that takes a direct contribution and personal profiles of an end user/ developer and two ontologies, as input and produces as output the relations (e.g., equivalence, subsumption) between entities of these ontologies. Alignments resulting from community-driven ontology matching are customized for the specific user and his/her specific task. In particular, community-driven ontology matching facilitates alignment discovery and satisfaction from alignment reuse via employing individual and community user profiles and social networking. The results are: More comprehensive representation of the domain and connection with other domains; Higher dynamicity and up-to-dateness; Improved treatment of alignment contexts by being user and community aware; Permanent improvement of existing ontology matching systems due to competition for the users. For an ordinary user to achieve semantic mappings gradually and over time between information models of interest to the user (Conroy, 2008) propose a mapping framework in support of ordinary people, making the ontology mapping process as natural as possible. It simplifies the end- user interaction in the process of constructing mappings (visualization, questionnaire, etc…), and propose the appropriate ways to engage the user over time.

GAMES FOR ONTOLOGY ALIGNMENT

For increasing the user interest to ontology mapping (Siorpaes & Hepp, 2008) proposes a new game-based paradigm for ontology alignment in web 2.0 environments. It recommends online semantic web games as a tool for soliciting the respective contributions from humans. Online games could support: spotting the most closely related conceptual elements in ontologies; selecting the most specific type of semantic relationships between two elements; validating the implications of a given semantic relationship between two conceptual elements.

An important advantage of game-based approach is easy balancing between expressivity and precision on one hand and the suitability for a large audience on the other. For example, a subset of the alignment relations defined by the W3C's Simple Knowledge Organization System (SKOS, www.w3.org/2004/02/skos) may be used because they're more suitable for broad audiences. This subset comprises these relations: equivalent, broaderThan, narrowerThan, related, partlyOverlappingWith. It may be paraphrased in simplified English to make these relations comprehensible to lay audiences. For the existing data sources, respective games to align ontologies in the Swoogle (http://swoogle.umbc.edu) or Watson (http://watson.kmi.open.ac.uk) repositories or to establish a mapping between eClassOWL and unspscOWL may be used. SpotTheLink is a game – tool for Mapping eCl@ss and the Unspsc, the two most important product and service categorization

standards, and establishing mappings between them for achieving data interoperability.

CASE-BASED RECOMMENDATION METHOD

Choosing a matching tool adapted to a particular application can be very difficult. To do this, (Euzenat et al., 2007) first identify basic application requirements based on a very general analysis of the application needs (input, output, usage, documentation, cost) and the corresponding characteristics of matchers (determine the characteristics on which matchers can be compared, and assess the value of these characteristics applying to matchers). Then (Euzenat et al., 2007) proposes a two-staged method for finding which matcher is usable for which application: the first stage is based on weighted aggregation of the characteristics depending on the expressed needs of applications and the second one is a case-based decision support method that take advantage of direct relative preference on criteria and a tool able to implement this process for making a decision. This method is based on a characterization of existing matching solutions obtained by the carefully crafted benchmark test of the Ontology Alignment Evaluation Initiative (OAEI). As a final conclusion for the appropriate alignment method selection proposes proceeding in two steps: first selecting systems for applications depending on application requirements and system measured performances, and then applying the findings to Knowledge web use cases depending on their identified class of application.

FUZZY ONTOLOGY MAPPING

The treatment of uncertainty plays a key role in the ontology mapping, as the degree of overlapping between concepts can not be represented logically. The main strength of Fuzzy ontology mapping is that during the mapping process a confidence value is assigned to every proposed mapping. Mappings are then classified not as valid or invalid but through a quantitative confidence value that can be easily managed during the alignment process. Usually the fuzzy logic techniques are used to determine the similarity between concepts from different ontologies. Several types of similarity measures are calculated: the Jaccard coefficient, and others, based on the linguistic relationship of concepts. Fuzzy rule-based systems are used to calculate combined similarities. Fuzzy approaches are

PROBABILISTIC APPROACHES

Probabilistic ontology matching model is widely used for interactive or automatic ontology matching, as it propose an easy-to-calculate or use metrics for probabilistic assessment of the quality of proposed mappings. The three topranked systems from the OAEI campaign 2008, i.e., RiMOM (Li et al., 2009), LILY (Wang & Xu, 2008) and ASMOV (Yves et al., 2008), differ from iMatch as they use graphical probabilistic models combined with other tools. RiMOM is a general ontology mapping system based on Bayesian decision theory. Probabilistic scheme for ontology matching based on Markov networks iMatch (Markov, 2009), has several advantages over other probabilistic schemes: it uses undirected networks, which better supports the non-causal nature of the dependencies, handles the high computational complexity by doing approximate reasoning, rather then by ad-hoc pruning, and the probabilities that it uses can be learned from matched data.

MATCHING STRATEGIES

Most real mapping algorithms in fact combine several approaches: usually first linguistic similarity is used (comparing labels or comments as strings), then a recursive computation of structural similarity, which exploits the semantics of terms (ontological context) until a certain depth is used, and finally the above values are combined to obtain the resultant synonymy measure.

The main aspects of building working effective matching system, discussed in Euzenat et al. (2007) are:

- aggregating the results of the basic measures and computing the compound similarity between entities;
- organizing the various matching algorithms;
- developing a strategy for compound similarity computing or organizing matching algorithms;
- learning from data the best method or matching parameters;
- using probabilistic methods to combine matchers;
- involving the user in matching process;

Usually global methods are realized using strategies to combine various matchers. Strategy selection may be static, but some valuable strategy selection parameters have been changed dynamically and that is who ability in dynamic strategy selection is important for many applications.

Matcher composition types are:

- Sequential combination;
- Parallel composition – running several matching algorithms independently and aggregating the results

Compound similarities are aggregations of heterogeneous similarities. Some aggregated similarities are triangular, Multidimensional distances and weighted sums, Fuzzy aggregation and weighted average, ordered weighted average.

Various ontology alignment strategies have been proposed, but few systems have explored how to automatically combine multiple strategies to improve the matching effectiveness. A dynamic Multistrategy ontology alignment framework, named RiMOM is presented in Li et al. (2009). The key insight in this framework is that similarity characteristics between ontologies may vary widely. It proposes a systematic approach to quantitatively estimate the similarity characteristics for each alignment task and proposes a strategy selection method to automatically combine the matching strategies based on two estimated factors.

Multi-Level Matching Approach (MLMA) (Alasoud et al., 2009) is a matching approach which uses different similarity measures at different levels. It assumes that the collection of similarity measures is partitioned by the user, and that there is a partial order on the partitions, also defined by the user. The important features of this method are that it benefits from existing individual matching techniques and "combines" their match results to provide enhanced ontology matching, and it matches a collection of n elements in the source ontology S to a collection of m elements in the target ontology T. MLMA, assumes that the collection of similarity measures are portioned by the user, and that there is a partial order on the partitions, also defined by the user. Assisting the user to find appropriate matching strategies is very important, as it often has little competence about the suitability of matching strategies for a given matching task. The quality and time of matching based on this approach have evaluated in the OAEI-06 and OAEI-07 and tests have shown that it is one of the best, proposed for testing in these years.

(Tan & Lambrix, 2007) Proposes a method that provides recommendations on alignment strategies for a given alignment problem. The method is based on the evaluation of the different available alignment strategies on several small selected pieces from the ontologies, and uses the evaluation results to provide recommendations.

Combining Matchers Using Machine Learning

This approach of combining different matchers (Eckert et al., 2009) is not to try to directly combine their output but to use machine learning techniques to train a classifier that decides whether two elements from different ontologies should be linked by an equivalence relation based on the output of different matching systems. The experiments have shown that it is not enough to base the learning step on the results of the matching systems alone, but that additional features representing and aggregating information about the mapping and the mapped ontology have to be taken into account. These features enable to put matcher results into appropriate context and get a better basis for deciding when to trust a certain matcher.

MULTIAGENT APPROACHES

Intelligent agents may by used in ontology mapping process to achieve flexibility and higher mapping quality in semi-automatic or automatic mapping. Agent usage concerns the practical (programming) realization of the process, rather than his main algorithm. Laera et al. (2007) proposes an approach for ontology alignment using an argumentation to provide a novel way for agents, with different ontologies, to work collaboratively. The mapping algorithm describes a process in which candidate correspondences are accepted or rejected, based on the ontological knowledge and the agent's preferences. This will give agents the ability to understand each other enough to carry out their objectives, for example to request a service, during interaction.

In Trojah et al. (2009) ontology mapping, using argumentation is used to combine different mapping approaches. The Value-based Argumentation Framework (VAF) represents arguments with confidence degrees, according to the similarity degree between the terms being mapped. The mappings are computed by agents using different mapping approaches. Based on their preferences and confidences, the agents compute their preferred mapping sets. The arguments in such preferred sets are viewed as the set of globally acceptable arguments. A threshold is used to reduce the set of mappings and adjust the values of precision.

In Silva et al. (2006) Ontology mapping negotiation aims to achieve consensus among real-world entities about the process of transforming information between different models (ontologies). A novel approach for ontology mapping negotiation, in which agents representing the real-world entities are able to achieve consensus among agents, about the mapping rules defined between two different ontologies. The proposed approach is based on utility functions that evaluate the confidence in a certain mapping rule. According to the confidence value, the mapping rule is accepted, rejected or negotiated. Since the negotiation process requires relaxation of the confidence value, a metautility function is applied, evaluating the effort made in relaxing (increasing) the confidence value, so that the mapping rule might be accepted. This convergence value is further applied by each agent in the evaluation of the global agreement

(Freddo & Tacla, 2009) presents a method to partially align ontologies in dialogues of agents. The method is a hybrid approach based on terminological, structural and extensional techniques. Differently from other methods, the proposed approach tries to find similarities between two concepts examining only their properties (or roles in description logic), producing property signature vectors for each concept, examining role/property restrictions for each pair of concepts and computing the distances between different vectors in a high dimensional space. This approach allows for identifying similarity between concepts where other methods cannot find similarities, for instance, between disjoint concepts. The method has two steps, property similarity computation and concepts similarity computation, and can also

be used as a pre-processing phase to semantic methods that need initial equivalence relations between concepts in order to work.

DSSim (Nagy et al., 2007; Nagy, 2008) is an ontology mapping algorithm based on the fact that ontology mappings contain inconsistencies, missing or overlapping elements and different entity meanings, and use a certain amount of uncertainty into the mapping process. In order to cope with these problems, the system adopted a multi-agent architecture, where each agent builds up a belief for the correctness of a particular mapping hypothesis. Beliefs or similarity assessments are the comparison results between all concepts and properties of two ontologies (the WordNet dictionary is used in this mapping process). These beliefs are stored into matrices and, after eliminating inconsistencies, they are combined into a more coherent view, in order to provide more refined mappings. It uses a specific technique (Dempster-Shafer theory of evidence) to handle missing data, as well as to model and reason uncertain information. This technique has recently incorporated a multiword ontology entity labels to provide compound term comparisons and abbreviations based on defined language rules. OAEI tests proved that when different similarity assessments have to be combined handling uncertainty can lead to a high precision. Since used Dempser's combination rule is computationally expensive operation it is needed to reduce the problem space (the number of additional variables per query fragment). This can lead to the loss of valuable information and consequently more irrelevant mappings.

DISCUSSION

As a result of the comprehensive analysis of all the previously mentioned approaches we may conclude that the main challenges in the area of ontology alignment are quality of the mappings, matcher selection strategies and self-configuration, user involvement (interactive, social and collaborative ontology matchin, explanation of matching results), strict evaluation and explicit showing of all the strengths and drawbacks of every approach.

Ontology matching is an important problem for which many algorithms have been provided. The increasing number of methods and tools available for schema/ontology matching suggests the need to establish a consensus for evaluation of these methods. In order to evaluate the performance of these algorithms it is necessary to confront them with test ontologies and to compare the results. Comparative evaluations of ontology alignment systems have been performed by some groups. The EU OntoWeb project (Kalfoglou & Schorlemmer, 2005) evaluated the systems Anchor-PROMPT, Chimaera, FCA-Merge and ODEMerge. In 2005 the Ontology Alignment Evaluation Initiative - OAEI was set up, which is a coordinated international initiative that organizes the evaluation of the increasing number of ontology matching systems. The main goal of OAEI is to support the comparison of the systems and algorithms on the same basis and to allow anyone to draw conclusions about the best matching strategies. OAEI campaigns have been occurred in 2005, 2006, 2007, 2008, 2009. OAEI is not a complete solution of ontology alignment evaluation and usage problem because of several drawbacks, including non perfect tests, non mashie-processable presentation of results, and the fat that non all developed tools have been evaluated.

Ontology alignment performance is of prime importance in many dynamic applications, for example, where a user or agent can not wait too long for the system to respond. Memory usage should also be taken into account. That is why optimization techniques (some of which rely on case-based approaches) are very important for practical applicability of alignment techniques and their increasing usage is one of the main trends to mature alignment tools.

Many efforts in improvement of ontology matching methods are addressed to matching quality improvement. Important trends in ontology alignment are: using as mach background or context knowledge as is possible (from domain specific corpus or querying the web, or using domain specific ontologies, or using ontologies available on the semantic web); modeling ontology matching as an uncertain process and reducing uncertainty iteratively or choose automatically the least one; implementing several matchers and strategies for dynamic choosing the best matcher for the specific case.

Collaborative and social approaches are the current challenge in ontology matching, relying on infrastructures allowing for sharing alignments and annotating them in a rich way to facilitate alignment reuse. The drawbacks of this approach are possibly contradictory and incomplete alignments and needs to deal with malicious users, and finding promising incentive schemas to facilitate user participation.

CONCLUSION AND FUTURE WORK

Despite the many component matching or integrated solutions that have been developed so far, there is no matured solution that is a clear success, which is robust enough to be used for universal practical ontology alignment or as a basis for future development, and before selecting the best approach, method or tool for concrete application the comprehensive exploration of grand number of variants is needed. Manual exploration is difficult, time consuming tack and is not suitable for ordinary users as well as not applicable in the cases of automatic Multistrategy or Multiagent mapping in dynamic environment. The exploration of several hundred of textual pages, describing the last research in this area would cost months working of professionals, and all this information is not processable for software agents.

Several classifications according to various dimensions have presented in this article. Our future research will be directed in extending and augmenting the proposed classifications to develop the comprehensive and severe classification of all the valuable ontology alignment algorithms methods and approaches according all valuable dimensions and represent them in machine-processable form as OWL ontology. Such ontology will be very useful for rapid introduction of specialists with developed valuable ontology alignment algorithms methods and approaches to make an easy and rapid selection to the best one for concrete application or research.

We recommend for all successful ontology mapping methods and algorithms implementations to be deployed as a web services for easy and effective usage by software agents, needed of ontology mapping. As all of them have various characteristics and are usable or effective in different situations, the above classification ontology is needed to describe and make them usable for software agents. By analogy with the existing Ontology Metadata Vocabulary (OMV) we will call this ontology *Ontology Alignment Classification Vocabulary* (OACV).

REFERENCES

Alasoud, A., et al. (2009). An Empirical Comparison of Ontology Matching Techniques. *Journal of Information Science, 35*(4), 379-397. Retrieved October 18, 2010, from http://jis.sagepub.com/cgi/content/abstract/35/4/379

Borgo, S., & Lesmo, L. (2008). Formal Ontologies Meet Industry. In *Frontiers in Artificial Intelligence and Applications Series* (*Vol. 174*). Amsterdam, The Netherlands: IOS Press.

Choi, N., et al. (2006). A Survey on Ontology Mapping. *ACM SIGMOD Record, 35*(3), 34-41. Retrieved October 18, 2010, from http://citeseerx.ist.psu.edu/viewdoc/download?doi=10.1.1.107.4316&rep=rep1&type=pdf

Conroy, C. (2008). *Towards Ontology Mapping for Ordinary People*. Paper presented at the European Semantic Web Conference, Tenerife, Spain. Retrieved October 18, 2010, from http://people.csail.mit.edu/pcm/ESWC08PHD/conroy.pdf

Correndo, G., & Alani, H. (2007). *Collaborative Ontology Mapping and Data Sharing*. (Tech. Rep. No. SO17 1BJ). Southampton, UK: University of Southampton, Electronic and Computer Science Department. Retrieved October 18, 2010, from http://eprints.ecs.soton.ac.uk/16676/1/correndo-Collaborative.pdf

Eckert, K., et al. (2009). Improving Ontology Matching using Meta-level Learning. In *Proceedings of the 6th European Semantic Web Conference on the Semantic Web (ESWC-2009)* (pp. 158-172). Berlin: Springer Verlag. Retrieved October 18, 2010, from http://ki.informatik.uni-mannheim.de/fileadmin/publication/Eckert09metalevel.pdf

Eidoon, Z., et al. (2007). A vector based method of ontology matching. *In Proceedings of Third International Conference on Semantics, Knowledge and Grid* (pp. 378-381). Retrieved October 18, 2010, from http://ro.uow.edu.au/cgi/viewcontent.cgi?article=1008&context= dubaipapers

Euzenat, J., et al. (2004). *D2.2.3: State of the art on ontology alignment* (IST Project IST-2004-507482). *Knowledge Web Consortium*. Retrieved October 18, 2010, from http://starlab.vub.ac.be/research/projects/knowledgeweb/kweb-223.pdf

Euzenat, J., et al. (2007). *Deliverable 1.2.2.2.1: Case-based recommendation of matching tools and techniques* (IST-2004-507482). *Knowledge Web Consortium*. Retrieved October 18, 2010, from http://knowledgeweb.semanticweb.org/semanticportal/deliverables/D1.2.2.2.1.pdf

Euzenat, J., & Shvaiko, P. (2007). *Ontology matching*. New York: Springer. Retrieved October 18, 2010, from http://www.springerlink.com/content/xl5g3g1774h84536/

Freddo, A., & Tacla, C. (2009). Evaluation of a method for partial ontology alignment in multi-agent system. [from http://inderscience.metapress.com/app/home/contribution. asp?referrer=parent&backto]. *International Journal of Reasoning-based Intelligent Systems, 1*(3/4), 132–146. Retrieved October 18, 2010. doi:10.1504/IJRIS.2009.028013

Giunchiglia, F., et al. (2007). Semantic matching: Algorithms and implementation. *Journal on Data Semantics, 9*, 1-38. Retrieved October 18, 2010, from http://www.cisa.inf.ed.ac.uk/OK/Publications/Algorithms%20and%20Implementation.pdf

Giunchiglia, F., & Shvaiko, P. (2003). Semantic Matching. *Knowledge Engineering Review journal, 18*(3), 265-280. Retrieved October 18, 2010, from http://citeseerx.ist.psu.edu/viewdoc/download?doi=10.1.1.69.8108&rep=rep1&type=pdf

Kalfoglou, Y., & Schorlemmer, M. (2005). Ontology Mapping: The State of the Art. *The Knowledge Engineering Review, 18*(1), 1-31. Retrieved October 18, 2010, from http://eprints.ecs.soton.ac.uk/10519/1/ ker02-ontomap.pdf

Laera, L., et al. (2007). Argumentation over Ontology Correspondences in MAS. In *Proceedings of the 6th International Conference on Autonomous Agents and Multi-Agent Systems*. Retrieved October 18, 2010, from http://citeseerx.ist.psu.edu/viewdoc/download?doi=10.1.1.97.3394&rep=rep 1&type=pdf

Li, J., et al. (2009). RiMOM: A Dynamic Multi-strategy Ontology Alignment Framework. *IEEE transactions on knowledge and data engineering, 21*(10). Retrieved October 18, 2010, from http://dit.unitn.it/~p2p/RelatedWork/Matching/RiMOM_TKDE.pdf

Locoro, A., & Mascardi, V. (2009). A Correspondence Repair Lgorithm Based On Word Sense Disambiguation And Upper Ontologies. In *Proceedings of the International Conference on Knowledge Engineering and Ontology Development (KEOD-09)*. Retrieved October 18, 2010, from http://didisi.disi.unige.it/person/MascardiV/Download/LocoroMascardiKeod2009.pdf

Markov, S. (2009). *Markov Network based Ontology Matching. Israel: Ben-Gurion University, Dept. of Computer Science*. Retrieved October 18, 2010, from http://ijcai.org/papers09/Papers/IJCAI09-312.pdf

Mascardi, V., et al. (2009). Automatic Ontology Matching Via Upper Ontologies: A Systematic Evaluation. *IEEE Transactions on Knowledge and Data Engineering, 22*(11). Retrieved October 18, 2010, from http://doi.ieeecomputersociety.org/10.1109/TKDE.2009.154

Meilicke, C. (2008). The Relevance of Reasoning and Alignment Incoherence in Ontology Matching. In *Proceedings of the ESWC2009 PhD Symposium*, Heraklion, Greece. Retrieved October 18, 2010, from http://www.springerlink.com/index/p56133140356v70g.pdf

Meilicke, C., Stuckenschmidt, H., & Tamilin, A. (2008). Reasoning support for mapping revision. *Journal of Logic and Computation*. Retrieved October 18, 2010, from http://logcom.oxfordjournals.org/content/19/5/807.short

Nagy, M. (2008). DSSim Results for OAEI 2008. In *Proceedings of 7th International Semantic Web Conference Ontology Matching (OM 2008)* (pp. 147-160). Retrieved October 18, 2010, from http://citeseerx.ist.psu.edu/viewdoc/download?doi=10.1.1.142.8474&rep=rep1&type=pdf#page=143

Nagy, M., et al. (2007). *DSSim: managing uncertainty on the semantic Web* (Tech. Rep.). Poznan, Poland: Poznan University of Economics, Department of Information Systems. Retrieved October 18, 2010, from [REMOVED HYPERLINK FIELD]http://citeseerx.ist.psu.edu/viewdoc/download?doi=10.1.1.104.9963&rep=rep1&type=pdf

Ou, S., et al. (2008). *Development and Alignment of a Domain-Specific Ontology for Question Answering*. Retrieved October 18, 2010, from http://www.lrecconf.org/proceedings/lrec2008/pdf/561_paper.pdf

Sabou, M., et al. (2008). Exploring the Semantic Web as Background Knowledge for Ontology Matching. *Journal on Data Semantics, 9*, 156-190. Retrieved October 18, 2010, from http://kmi.open.ac.uk/people/marta/papers/JoDS_2008.pdf

Silva, N., et al. (2006). *An approach to ontology mapping negotiation*. Paper Presented at the Third International Conference on Knowledge Capture Workshop on Integrating Ontologies, Banff, Canada. Retrieved October 18, 2010, from http://www.citeseerx.ist.psu.edu/viewdoc/download?doi=10.1.1.106.6079&rep=rep1&type=pdf#page=56

Siorpaes, K., & Hepp, M. (2008). Games with a Purpose for the Semantic Web. [from http://www.heppnetz.de/files/gwap-semweb-ieee-is.pdf]. *IEEE Intelligent Systems, 23*(3), 50–60. Retrieved October 18, 2010. doi:10.1109/MIS.2008.45

Tan, H., & Lambrix, P. (2007). A method for recommending ontology alignment strategies. In *Proceedings of the 6th international semantic web and 2nd Asian conference on Asian semantic web conference*, Busan, Korea (pp. 494-507). Retrieved October 18, 2010, from http://www.ida.liu.se/~patla/publications/ISWC07-preprint.pdf

Tatsiopoulos, C., & Boutsinas, B. (2009). *Ontology mapping based on association rule mining*. Paper Presented at 11th International Conference on Enterprise Information Systems, Milan, Italy. Retrieved October 18, 2010, from http://episgr.net23.net/docs/ontology_mapping_based_on_association_rule_mining.pdf

Trojah, C., et al. (2009). An Argumentation Framework based on strength for Ontology Mapping. In *Argumentation in Multi-Agent Systems* (LNCS 5384, pp. 57-71). Retrieved October 18, 2010, from www.di.uevora.pt/~pq/papers/argmas08.pdf

Wang, P., & Xu, B. (2008). Lily: Ontology Alignment Results for OAEI 2008. In *Proceedings of the 7th International Semantic Web Conference Ontology Matching (OM 2008)* (pp. 167-176). Retrieved October 18, 2010, from http://citeseerx.ist.psu.edu/viewdoc/download?doi=10.1.1.142.8474&rep=rep1&type=pdf#page=143

Yves, R., et al. (2008). ASMOV: Results for OAEI 2008, Monterrey. In *Proceedings of the 7th International Semantic Web Conference Ontology Matching (OM 2008)* (pp. 132-140). Retrieved October 18, 2010, from http://citeseerx.ist.psu.edu/viewdoc/download?doi=10.1.1.142.8474&rep=rep1&type=pdf#page=143

Yves, R., et al. (2009). Ontology matching with semantic verification. *Journal of Web Semantics: Science, Services and Agents on the World Wide Web*. Retrieved October 18, 2010, from http://www.dit.unitn.it/~p2p/RelatedWork/Matching/ontology_matching_with_ semantic_verification.pdf

Zhang, S., & Bodenreider, O. (2007). Hybrid Alignment Strategy for Anatomical Ontologies Results of the Ontology Alignment Contest. In *Proceedings of ISWC 2007 Ontology Matching Workshop,* Busan, Korea. Retrieved October 18, 2010, from http://mor.nlm.nih.gov/pubs/pdf/2007-oaei-sz.pdf

Zhdanova, A., & Shvaiko, P. (2006). Community-Driven Ontology Matching. In *Proceedings of ESWC'06* (LNCS 4011, pp. 34-49). New York: Springer. Retrieved October 18, 2010, from http://dit.unitn.it/~p2p/RelatedWork/Matching/eswc06_ontology_matching.pdf

This work was previously published in the International Journal of Knowledge and Systems Science, Volume 1, Issue 4, edited by W.B. Lee, pp. 22-40 copyright 2010 by IGI Publishing (an imprint of IGI Global).

Chapter 11
SEMCL:
A Cross–Language Semantic Model for Knowledge Sharing

Weisen Guo
University of Tokyo, Japan

Steven B. Kraines
University of Tokyo, Japan

ABSTRACT

To promote global knowledge sharing, one should solve the problem that knowledge representation in diverse natural languages restricts knowledge sharing effectively. Traditional knowledge sharing models are based on natural language processing (NLP) technologies. The ambiguity of natural language is a problem for NLP; however, semantic web technologies can circumvent the problem by enabling human authors to specify meaning in a computer-interpretable form. In this paper, the authors propose a cross-language semantic model (SEMCL) for knowledge sharing, which uses semantic web technologies to provide a potential solution to the problem of ambiguity. Also, this model can match knowledge descriptions in diverse languages. First, the methods used to support searches at the semantic predicate level are given, and the authors present a cross-language approach. Finally, an implementation of the model for the general engineering domain is discussed, and a scenario describing how the model implementation handles semantic cross-language knowledge sharing is given.

DOI: 10.4018/978-1-4666-1782-7.ch011

INTRODUCTION

In the age of information explosion, knowledge sharing can significantly increase social capital. The problem of knowledge sharing in the organizations was studied by many researchers of knowledge management field that indicated that the organization culture is more important aspect than technical problems (Widen-Wulff & Suomi, 2003; Widen-Wulff & Ginman, 2004; Tang, 2007; Tang & Zhang, 2008). But the technical problems of knowledge sharing on the Internet are critical issue, especially in the case of much of knowledge is represented in diverse languages that limits our ability to share and search knowledge globally. The traditional approach to share knowledge across diverse languages by manually translating each knowledge resource from the original language to all of the other languages is too slow and costly for tasks such as sharing scientific findings between researchers.

Automated cross-language technologies have been developed that use natural language processing (NLP) technologies to extract keywords for matching knowledge resources between different languages. However, NLP-based approaches cannot produce accurate matching results because of the ambiguity of natural language (Hunter & Cohen, 2006). Even thesauri or classification schemata are insufficient (Goldschmidt & Krishnamoorthy, 2008) because they do not support expressions of semantic relationships between keywords or named entities in text. Furthermore, the need to handle multiple languages in cross-language knowledge sharing models exacerbates the problem of natural language ambiguity. Some approaches to decrease the ambiguity have been reported in the literature. For example, Littman et al. (1998) used a latent semantic indexing technique to implement cross-language information retrieval. However, even these sophisticated NLP technologies do not address the fundamental issue of ambiguity in representing knowledge with natural language, an issue that is particularly problematic in a multilingual knowledge sharing situation.

Semantic Web technologies can be used to express knowledge in a computer-interpretable enable matching at a semantic predicate level, e.g., matching of both named entities and predicates stating the semantic relationships between them. Specifically, ontologies constructed in a language such as OWL-DL can represent domain knowledge within a description logic (DL) formalism (OWL, 2004). Then DL-based inference can be used in knowledge search to find more useful matching results (Guo & Kraines, 2008).

We present a cross-language knowledge sharing model in this paper that is based on ontologies and logical inference. Using this model, knowledge providers can publish knowledge resources in their native languages, and knowledge seekers can search for knowledge in different languages, thereby enabling cross-language knowledge sharing. Furthermore, both the descriptors of the knowledge resources and the search queries are represented in a form that can be interpreted semantically by a computer, which enables the computer to infer embedded meaning that is implied but not explicitly expressed. Therefore, the knowledge system implementing this model returns matching results represented in diverse languages that should be more accurate than those of conventional keyword based systems because matching is done at the semantic predicate level.

The rest of the paper is organized as follows. We review the state of the art of knowledge sharing on the Internet. We then present the cross-language knowledge sharing model and describe the cross-language method that we have developed to implement the model. We also discuss the related work.

KNOWLEDGE SHARING MODELS

There are many kinds of knowledge in our daily life, and there are many methods for classifying that knowledge. In this paper, we focus on knowl-

Figure 1. The TEM knowledge sharing model

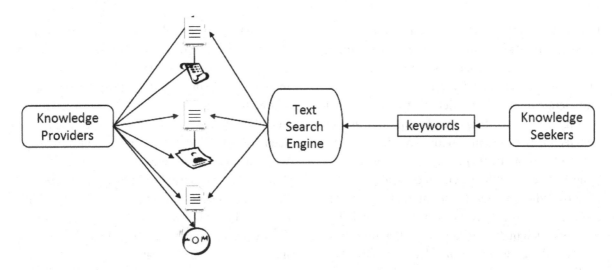

edge stored in the Internet, which is explicitly described in formats such as text, pictures, videos, and databases. The Internet environment makes it possible to share knowledge transparently across time and space. However, to make knowledge sharing and searching on the Internet more effective, we need to consider questions such as what knowledge sharing is, what the goal of the knowledge sharing is, and who participates in the knowledge sharing.

Knowledge sharing is an activity through which knowledge is exchanged among people and/or organizations (Lin, 2007). In this paper, we focus on knowledge existing in explicit digital form on the Internet. A knowledge sharing community consists of two main types of the knowledge users: knowledge providers and knowledge seekers. Community members can be both types: each knowledge user may both provide knowledge resources and seek knowledge resources. The goal of a knowledge sharing system is to return the correct knowledge resources to the knowledge seeker. A global-scale knowledge sharing community will invariably include knowledge users from different countries speaking different languages.

We classify the conventional knowledge sharing models into three types: TEM, TEMCL and

SEM. TEM and TEMCL models adopt Information Retrieval (IR) technologies. SEM model adopts Semantic Web (SW) technologies.

The TEM knowledge sharing model uses text keywords in natural language to represent the knowledge resources. Information Retrieval (IR) technologies are adopted to find matching results by matching keywords provided by knowledge seekers. In this approach, the matching system uses automatic techniques such as Natural Language Processing to determine which knowledge resources match the text keywords based on the natural language representations of those resources (Figure 1).

The TEMCL knowledge sharing model extends the TEM knowledge sharing model by supporting cross-language knowledge sharing (Figure 2). However, the problems of natural language ambiguity and grammatical complexity, which already make it difficult to determine matches with free-text in a single language, become even more serious when dealing with different languages, which results in a rapid decrease in matching precision and recall.

The problem of natural language ambiguity can be addressed by enabling people to create descriptions of knowledge resources in a com-

Figure 2. The TEMCL knowledge sharing model

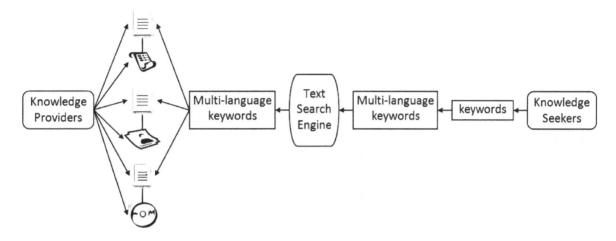

Figure 3. The SEM knowledge sharing model

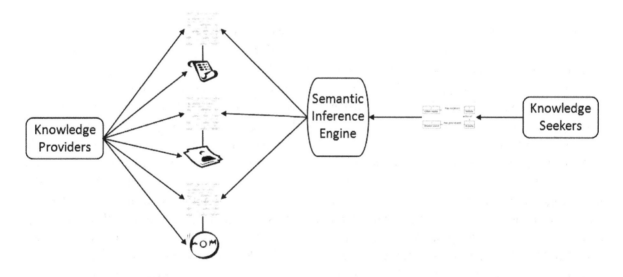

puter-understandable format. For example, accuracy of matching knowledge resources can be increased by considering predicate-level semantics (Hunter et al., 2008). In particular, Semantic Web technologies, such as ontologies and logical inference, can be used to implement knowledge sharing systems that can match knowledge resources with search descriptions at the level of a grammatical sentence. These systems, such as EKOSS (Kraines et al., 2006) and Annotea (Kahan et al., 2001; Koivunen, 2005), are based on a semantic model for matching knowledge resources, which we call Model SEM (Figure 3). In this model, the knowledge providers describe their knowledge resources using computer-interpretable semantic statements instead of natural language. The knowledge seekers also input their queries in a semantic way, rather than just listing keywords. For example, the EKOSS system uses semantic matching methods based on description logics (Kraines et al., 2006; Guo & Kraines, 2008) to match the descriptions of knowledge resourc-

Figure 4. The SEMCL knowledge sharing model. "Statement" denotes semantic statement information. "Query" denotes semantic query information. "Result" denotes matching result information.

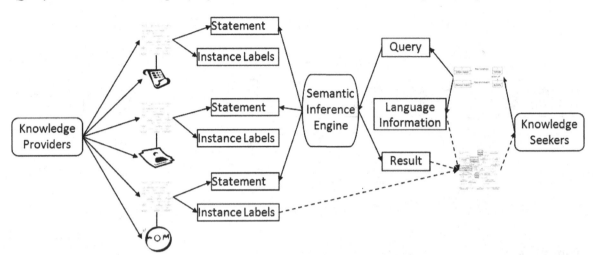

SEMCL KNOWLEDGE SHARING MODEL

es and the search queries. Because the EKOSS implementation of Model SEM supports semantic matching, it can help the knowledge seekers find more correct matching results by reducing the ambiguity in both descriptions of knowledge resources and search queries.

We suggest that the use of Semantic Web technologies to enable people to create computer-interpretable semantic statements describing knowledge resources and requirements could address the issues of ambiguity and grammatical complexity in cross-language knowledge sharing. Based on Model SEM, this paper presents a new model for cross-language knowledge sharing, which we call Model SEMCL. In this model, the knowledge providers describe their knowledge resources by creating computer-interpretable semantic statements using their preferred language. In the same way, the knowledge seekers use their preferred language to describe their queries. The system is able to infer semantic matches between the descriptions and the queries, and it then displays the matching results in the preferred language of the knowledge seeker (Figure 4).

Figure 5 shows the framework of SEMCL knowledge sharing model supporting three hypothetical languages: La, Lb, and Lc. Model SEMCL has four layers: the core semantic matching layer, the language layer, the user interface layer, and the human layer. At the center of Model SEMCL is the domain ontology, which is comprised of classes and properties together with labels in plain text. Translations of the class and property labels in the domain ontology to the other languages (Ontology(La), Ontology(Lb), and Ontology(Lc)) are made by a human or machine translator before running the knowledge sharing system.

At the human level, there are two types of users: Knowledge Providers and Knowledge Seekers. Knowledge Providers use the domain ontology to create computer-interpretable semantic descriptions of their knowledge resources, descriptions that are populated by instances of the ontology classes together with properties that describe specific relationships between those instances. Because these descriptions are free from the ambiguity of natural language and

Figure 5. The framework of SEMCL knowledge sharing model

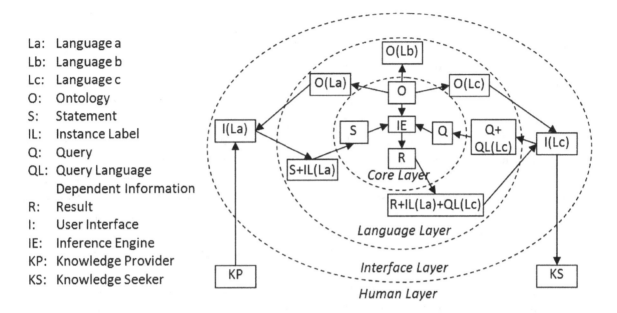

La: Language a
Lb: Language b
Lc: Language c
O: Ontology
S: Statement
IL: Instance Label
Q: Query
QL: Query Language
     Dependent Information
R: Result
I: User Interface
IE: Inference Engine
KP: Knowledge Provider
KS: Knowledge Seeker

grounded in the logic supported by the ontology, they can be used by computers for inference (Guo & Kraines, 2008). The language level of Model SEMCL supports the cross-language sharing and searching. The user interface level of Model SEMCL provides multi-language graphic user interfaces (GUIs), which users can use to provide or seek knowledge in their preferred language.

In Figure 5, a Knowledge Provider, who prefers to use language La, uses the GUI in language La (I(La)) to create a semantic description (S +IL(La)) of her/his knowledge resource in language La. A Knowledge Seeker, who prefers to use language Lc, uses the GUI in language Lc (I(Lc)) to create a semantic query (Q + QL(Lc)) in language Lc. The matching results produced by the Inference Engine at the core semantic matching level (R) are augmented with the language information for Lc from query and the language information for La from statement to create (R+IL(La)+QL(Lc)), which is shown to the Knowledge Seeker in I(Lc).

To make this kind of cross-language searching possible, each knowledge description has two parts: semantic statement (S) and language information (IL). Each search query also has two parts: semantic query (Q) and language information (QL). The language information is maintained in the language level. The semantic statement and semantic query go into the core level to be matched by the Inference Engine (IE), which uses reasoning in the supported logic as well as optional rule-based reasoning to match all the available semantic statements with each semantic query. When the Inference Engine finds some matching results (R), it returns them to the Knowledge Seeker. Language information (IL + QL) is added to the matching results when it goes through the language level to the user interface of the Knowledge Seeker. In summary, Model SEMCL uses ontologies to handle the ambiguity of natural language, logical inference for semantic matching, and the method of separating language from semantics to handle the cross-language issue. The following subsections give the details for each of these techniques.

KNOWLEDGE REPRESENTATION AND SEARCH

In Model SEMCL, there are two kinds of knowledge. The first kind is the domain knowledge: the basic concepts and their relationships in the targeted knowledge domain. The second kind is the knowledge that the Knowledge Providers want to share, which is described using the first kind of knowledge. In Model SEMCL, the first kind of knowledge must be created prior to the operation of the knowledge sharing system and kept relatively stable. It should also have sufficient detail to represent the second kind of knowledge, which makes up the contents of the knowledge base in Model SEMCL. Normally, the first kind of knowledge, i.e., the domain ontology, should be created by some experts of this domain. And also there are many ontologies are available on the Internet, such as the Suggested Upper Merged Ontology (SUMO, 2003), the Gene Ontology (GO, 1999), and so on. The knowledge sharing systems with Model SEMCL can create their own domain ontologies, or use the existing ontologies on the Internet. The key question is that the knowledge sharing community (including knowledge providers and knowledge seekers) should regard the domain ontologies are correct and can be used to describe their knowledge resources or search queries.

We have created an implementation of Model SEMCL for the domain of engineering knowledge. In our implementation, the first kind of knowledge is represented by using an OWL-DL ontology that we have created for that domain. There are five main classes in the ontology –substances (including elemental material, compound material, energy substance), activities (including human activity and natural activity), physical objects (including artificial physical objects and natural physical objects, actors and spatial locations are special kinds of physical objects), events (that mark the beginning or end of activities and physical objects), and classes of activities (including

method of activity, human failure activity, and organization failure activity), as well as several properties that can be used to specify relationships between the classes or instances of the classes. For example, an instance of the class "activity" can have a relationship with an instance of the class "class of activity" using the property "has activity class". Each main class is divided into subclasses to represent more specific concepts from the engineering domain.

The second kind of knowledge, knowledge shared by the Knowledge Providers, is represented using the classes and properties provided in the first kind of knowledge. Specifically, the entities described by each piece of shared knowledge are represented as instances of ontology classes, and the specific relationships that are described between those entities are represented using ontology properties. For example, consider the following accident report:

"A small explosion occurred at the No.2 oxygen tank of the support ship during the flight of Apollo 13. Apollo 13 was launched in 1970 for the purpose of making the third lunar landing. A portion of the outer shell was blown away, and several instruments that were stored in the support ship were also damaged by the explosion. In order to convert the oxygen tank of Apollo 10 for use in Apollo 13, the design was changed. The starting point of the cause was that the one of the technicians forgot to unfasten one screw when the tank was reinstalled. The plan for the landing on the moon was aborted, the Apollo 13 made a U-turn at the moon, and she barely made it back to the earth using the little oxygen, water and electric power that remained."

The knowledge that is expressed in this report can be represented using the domain ontology as shown in Figure 6.

In Model SEMCL, all knowledge resources are represented as knowledge descriptions in this way. When the Knowledge Seekers want to find

Figure 6. The knowledge description of "Apollo 13." Boxes show instances of classes from the domain ontology. The text above the line in a box is the instance label. The text below the line in a box is the class name of that instance. Arrows show properties expressing the asserted relationships between instances.

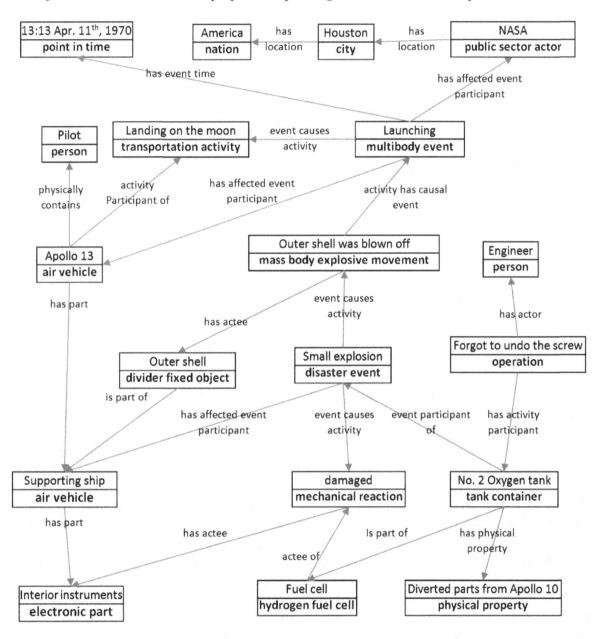

knowledge resources, they create semantic queries (an example is given as Figure 10), also based on the domain ontology, and send them to the Inference Engine.

Upon receiving a semantic query, the Inference Engine matches it with all the available semantic statements using a DL reasoner. First, the Inference Engine loads the domain ontology to the knowledge base. Then it loads the semantic statement for one knowledge resource. Finally, it evaluates the semantic query against the knowledge base that now contains the ontology and the

Figure 7. The Model SEMCL cross-language mechanism

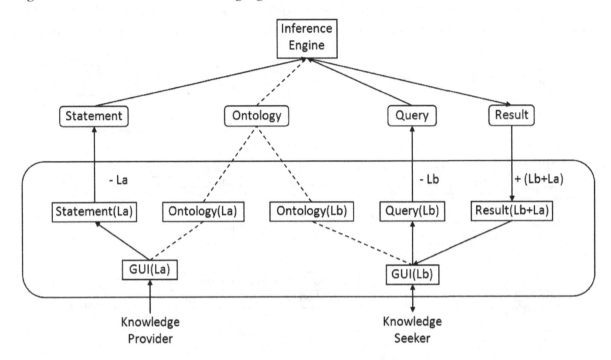

statement. If each ontology class in the query can be mapped to an instance in the knowledge base subject to the properties specified for that class in the query, then the semantic statement that was loaded to the knowledge base is said to match with the query.

CROSS-LANGUAGE KNOWLEDGE SHARING

Model SEMCL handles the cross-language issue by separating the language information from the semantic statement in the knowledge description that is created by the Knowledge Provider. Only the semantic statement is used by Inference Engine. The language information is added to the semantic statement of the matching results before showing them to the Knowledge Seeker. Because Model SEMCL uses a domain ontology instead of natural language to represent the knowledge, it

is easy to separate the language information from the semantic statement.

Figure 7 shows the overall Model SEMCL cross-language mechanism for two languages (La and Lb). In a real application, the number of languages can be more. The domain ontology and the user interface are created to form the infrastructure level and translated into each of the supported languages before running the knowledge sharing system. The interface language and ontology language are paired. In other words, if the interface language is changed to La, then the ontology language is changed to La automatically. We use dash line to show that the ontology language and interface language are pre-installed in the system that cannot be modified by regular users.

The Knowledge Provider uses the interface and ontology in her/his preferred language to create her/his knowledge descriptions. For example, if the preferred language is La, then "GUI(La)" and "Ontology(La)" are used, and the knowledge description "Statement(La)" is cre-

Box 1.

"1996年5月11日午後2時13分、フロリダ州マイアミからジョージア州アトランタに向かっていたA社航空A便（B社製B型機）が、離陸10分後、火災のため空港から19Kmのエヴァーグレーズ湿地帯に墜落した。この事故で運航乗務員2名、客室乗務員3名、乗客105名、計110名全員が死亡した。酸素発生装置（酸素ボンベ）のラベル表示ミスが原因で火災が発生し、同機は高度10000フィートから地上まで一気に落下した。墜落現場一帯は沼地であったため、残骸等は完全に水没し、墜落現場の確認に日数を要した。ラベル表示ミスは下請けの整備会社C社によるものだが、A社航空の大惨事は当社のコスト削減による安全確認およびメンテナンス不備から、起こるべくして起こった事故だと言われている。"

---

ated. The "Statement" is just the semantic information that remains when the language information in language La is removed. In the same way, the Knowledge Seeker uses the interface and ontology in her/his preferred language to create her/his search query. For example, if the preferred language is Lb, then "GUI(Lb)" and "Ontology(Lb)" are used, and "Query(Lb)" is created. The "Query" is the part that remains when the language information in language Lb is removed. The Inference Engine evaluates matches between the Statements and Queries using the ontology. If "Query" matches with "Statement", then the matching result "Result" is created by the Inference Engine. Because the preferred language of the Knowledge Seeker is Lb and the matched knowledge description "Statement(La)" is in La, so the language information for Lb from query side and the language information for La from statement side are added to create "Result(Lb+La)", which is displayed to the Knowledge Seeker.

SCENARIO

Here, we illustrate how Model SEMCL works by using a scenario involving three Knowledge Providers – Laura, Ichiro, and Zhao – who are sharing knowledge on a knowledge sharing system that supports three languages: English, Japanese and Chinese.

In our scenario, Laura is the person who provided the knowledge for the article about the accident described, and she prefers using English. She accesses the Model SEMCL knowledge sharing system and selects the English user interface

to create a description for this knowledge resource (see Figure 6). She adds the URL of the original news report to the description so that anyone finding this description to be of interest can access the knowledge resource (the news report) for details.

Ichiro is a scientist studying failure knowledge who prefers using Japanese. He created a video to explain the failure mechanism behind an airplane accident in Miami that he wants to share. He selects the Japanese user interface to create a description for this video, linked to the URL of the video. His description of the video in Japanese is shown in Box 1.

The corresponding English description is:

"The A flight of A company (B aircraft made by B) was headed from Miami to Atlanta at 2:13 pm on May 11, 1996. But 10 minutes after takeoff, the flight crashed at the Evagurezu wetlands, 19Km from the airport. The two flight crew, three flight attendants, and 105 passengers were killed in total. For the oxygen generators (oxygen tanks) caused fire due to the labelling mistake, the plane suddenly dropped to the ground from 10,000 feet altitude. Because the crash area was a swamp, and debris was completely under water, it took days to confirm the crash site. After investigation, the reason is the labelling subcontracting company C made a mistake to label Oxygen generating devices."

The description created by Ichiro is shown in Figure 8.

Zhao is a bridge architect who prefers using Chinese. After learning of the accident of bridge collapse in State of Texas, he created some il-

Figure 8. The knowledge description created by Ichiro in Japanese. Boxes and arrows have the same meanings as in Figure 6.

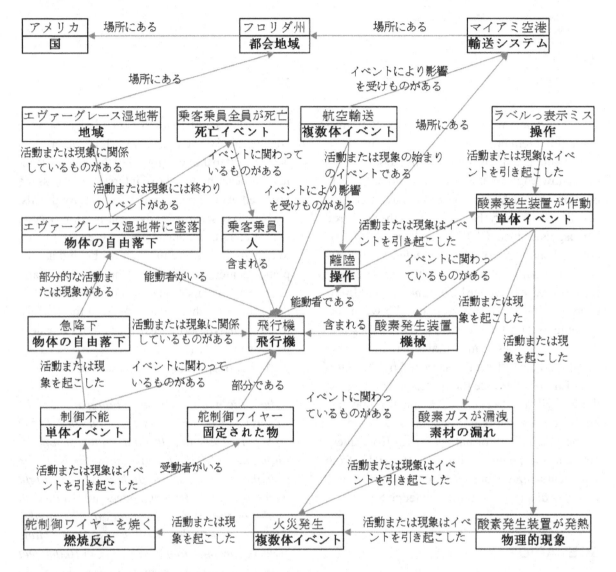

lustrations to show the accident from his professional perspective that he wants to share. He selects the Chinese user interface to create a description for these illustrations and links the description to the URL of the illustrations. His description of the content of the illustrations in Chinese is shown in Box 2.

The corresponding English translation is:

"In September 15, 2001, an accident of bridge collapse occurred at Isabella Bay, the State of Texas, U.S.A. Due to the strong current, the buoy scooted over, resulting in a tug boat being drag the barge ran over the sand bar, change direction and hit one of the Queen Isabella bridge supporting columns. Part of the bridge fell. Result of a sudden, a passenger car carrying eight people failed to stop in time, fell from the bridge. All the passengers were killed."

Box 2.

"2001年9月15日，美国得克萨斯州伊莎贝拉湾发生了一起塌桥事件。由于受巨流影响，浮标移动了很大距离，导致一艘正在拖动驳船的拖船辗过沙坝，改变方向，撞上了伊莎贝拉女王桥的柱子。桥的一部分断裂坠落。由于事发突然，一辆载客八人的汽车未能及时停下，从桥上坠落。所有乘客全部遇难。"

The description created by Zhao is shown in Figure 9.

A Knowledge Seeker named Rose, who prefers using English, is studying the accidents that some vehicles are actors in the urban region. In order to find some more knowledge, she wants to utilize the knowledge sharing system. She selects the English user interface to create her query for "A vehicle located in urban region is actor of activity, which activity has a disaster end event." (see Figure 10).

Rose sends her query to the Inference Engine of the Model SEMCL knowledge sharing system and waits for search results. The Inference Engine compares the semantic part of the query with the semantic statement part of Laura's description, Ichiro's description and Zhao's description.

Ichiro's description matches with Rose's query (see Figure 11). The "飛行機" is an instance of class "airplane" that is a sub class of "vehicle" through "air vehicle". The "エヴァーグレース湿地帯に墜落" is an instance of class "mass body freefalling" that is a sub class of "activity" through "mass body transport", "mass transport", "transport phenomenon", "physical activity", "natural activity". The "全員が死亡" is an instance of class "death event" that is a direct sub class of "disaster event". The "フロリダ州" is an instance of class "urban region". These four instances match with the entities of Rose's query.

The property "has actor" between "エヴァーグレース湿地帯に墜落" and "飛行機" in description matches with the property "actor of" between "vehicle" and "activity" in query for the inverse relationship between "has actor" and "actor of". The property "activity has end event" between "エヴァーグレース湿地帯に墜落"

and "乗客乗員全員が死亡" in description matches with the property "has end event" between "Activity" and "Disaster event" in query for that property "activity has end event" is a direct sub property of "has end event". The relationship between "飛行機" and "フロリダ州" is inferred from the rule that "if A has location B and A has activity participant C, then C has location B", the subsumption relationship between property "actor of" and property "activity participant of", the inverse relationship between property "activity participant of" and "has activity participant", and the transitivity of property "has location". In detail, the relationship "離陸 has location フロリダ州" is inferred from the relationship "離陸 has location マイアミ空港" and relationship "マイアミ空港 has location フロリダ州". The relationship "離陸 has activity participant 飛行機" is inferred from the relationship "飛行機 actor of 離陸", the subsumption relationship between "actor of" and "activity participant of", and the inverse relationship between "activity participant of" and "has activity participant". Based on above rule, "離陸" has location "フロリダ州" and "離陸 has activity participant 飛行機", the relationship "飛行機 has location フロリダ州" is inferred. The properties (including implied ones) among these four instances in the description are matched with the properties of Rose's query. So Ichiro's description matches with Rose's query.

Zhao's description matches with Rose's query (see Figure 12). The "灾难事件" is an instance of class "death event" that is a direct sub class of "disaster event". The "汽车从桥上掉下" is an instance of class "mass body freefalling" that is a sub class of "activity" through "mass body trans-

Figure 9. The knowledge description created by Zhao in Chinese. Boxes and arrows have the same meanings as in Figure 6.

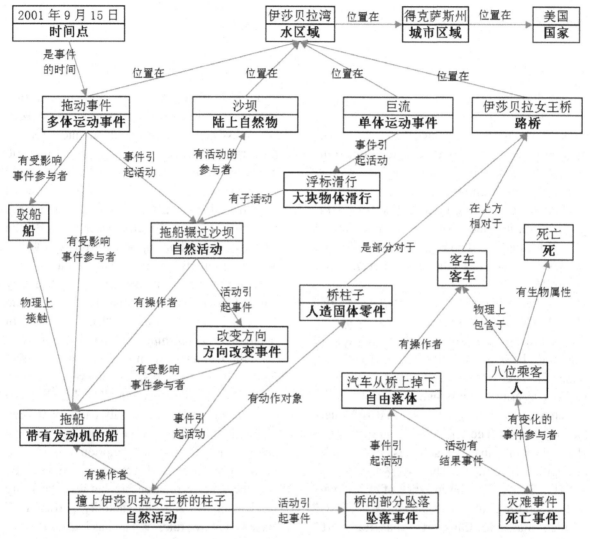

Figure 10. The search query created by Rose in English. Boxes and arrows have the same meanings as in Figure 6.

port", "mass transport", "transport phenomenon", "physical activity", "natural activity". The "客车" is an instance of class "passenger car" that is sub class of "vehicle" through "wheeled vehicle with engine", "vehicle with engine". The "得克萨斯州" is an instance of class "urban region". These four instances match with the entities of Rose's query.

Figure 11. Matching results of Rose's query with Ichiro's description. Boxes with thick borders show the mappings of instances in the description (upper side) with entities in the query (lower side). Arrows with dash line and italic label show the properties between the classes in the query. Other boxes and arrows have the same meanings in Figure 6.

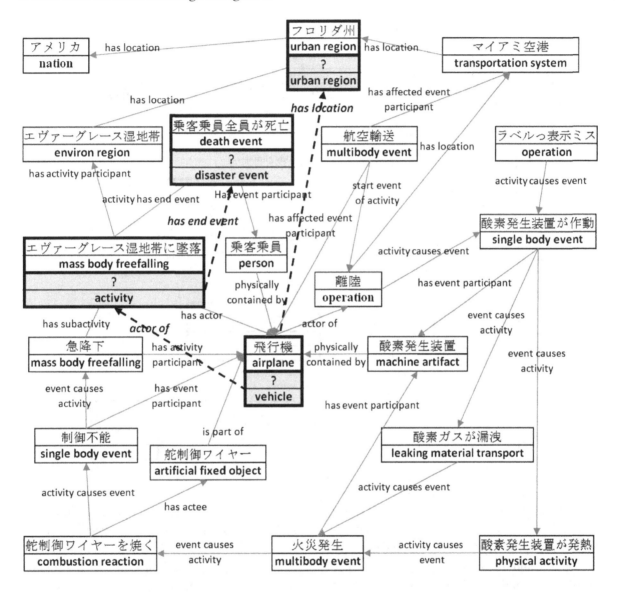

The property "activity has end event" between "汽车从桥上掉下" and "灾难事件" in description matches with the property "has end event" between "activity" and "disaster event" in query for the subsumption relationship between "activity has end event" and "has end event". The property "has actor" between "汽车从桥上掉下" and " 客车" in description matches with the property "actor of" between "vehicle" and "activity" for the inverse relationship between "has actor" and "actor of". The relationship between "客车" and "得克萨斯州" is inferred from the rule that "if A has location B and A is in physical contact with C, then C has location B", the subsumption relation-

Figure 12. Matching results of Rose's query with Zhao's description. Boxes and arrows have the same meanings as in Figure 11.

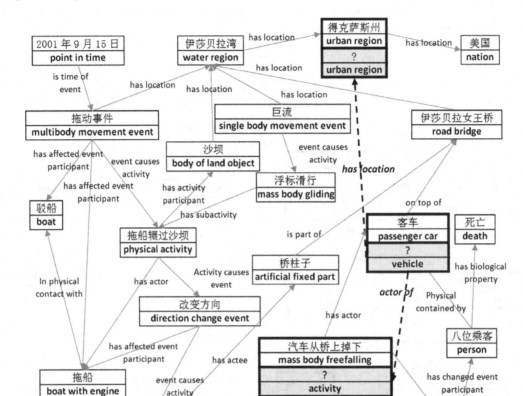

ship between property "underneath" and property "in physical contact with", the inverse relationship between property "underneath" and property "on top of", and the transitivity of property "has location". In detail, the relationship "伊莎贝拉女王桥 has location得克萨斯州" is inferred from the relationship "伊莎贝拉女王桥 has location 伊莎贝拉湾" and relationship "伊莎贝拉湾 has location得克萨斯州". The relationship "伊莎贝拉女王桥 is in physical contact with 客车" is inferred from the relationship "客车 is on top of 伊莎贝拉女王桥", the inverse relationship between "underneath" and "on top of", and the

subsumption relationship between "underneath" and "in physical contact with". Based on above rule, "伊莎贝拉女王桥 has location得克萨斯州" and "伊莎贝拉女王桥 is in physical contact with 客车", the relationship "客车 has location 汽得克萨斯州" is inferred. The properties (including implied ones) among these four instances in the description are matched with the properties of Rose's query. So Zhao's description matches with Rose's query.

However, Laura's description does not match with Rose's query (see Figure 13). Even though her description does mention a disaster event

Figure 13. Rose's query does not match with Laura' description. Arrows with dash lines show that the source entity in query is matched with the target instance in description. Other boxes and arrows have the same meanings as in Figure 6.

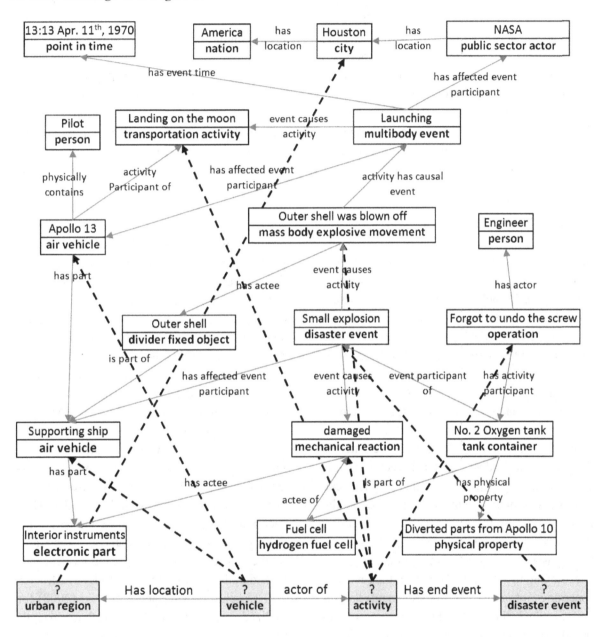

("Small explosion"), two vehicles ("Apollo 13" and "Supporting ship", class "air vehicle" is a direct sub class of "vehicle"), a urban region ("Houston", class "city" is a direct sub class of "urban region"), and four activities ("Landing on the moon", class "transportation activity" is a

sub class of "activity" through "human activity"; "Outer shell was blown off", class "mass body explosive movement" is a sub class of "activity" through "mass body transport", "mass transport", "transport phenomenon", "physical activity", "natural activity"; "Forgot to undo the screw", class "Operation" is a sub class of "activity" through "human activity"; "damaged", class of "mechanical reaction" is a sub class of "activity" through "physical activity", "natural activity"), the relationships between the four activities and the disaster event "Small explosion" are not "has end event", and the relationships "actor of" between the two vehicles and four activities cannot be inferred.

This example demonstrates how Model SEMCL supports cross-language knowledge sharing based on matching at the semantic predicate level.

RELATED WORK

In the previous section, we considered some other models for knowledge sharing. In this section, we compare Model SEMCL with some closely related work from the literature.

Littman et al. (1998) used Latent Semantic Indexing (LSI) to retrieve cross-language documents automatically. They treated a set of dual-language documents as training documents to create a dual-language semantic space in which terms from both languages are represented. Standard mono-lingual documents are represented as language-independent numerical vectors in this semantic space, so queries in either language can retrieve documents in either language without the need to translate the query. The LSI method is based on keywords. The semantic space contains the dual-language terms that form an index for speeding up the retrieval. However, the semantic space does not support classifications and relationships, so the LSI method cannot support retrieval based on matching at the semantic predicate level. For this method is based on NLP techniques essentially, we consider its knowledge sharing model is Model TEMCL.

Schonhofen et al. (2008) demonstrated a twofold use of Wikipedia for cross-language information retrieval. They exploited Wikipedia hyperlinkage for query term disambiguation.

They used bilingual Wikipedia articles for dictionary extension. As shown in Model TEMCL (Figure 2), the methods based on Information retrieval techniques translate query term into multi-languages. The big issue is the ambiguity. Their methods tried to disambiguate query term translation by exploiting of Wikipedia byperlink structure. Their methods increased the precision more than traditional text-based approaches, but still limited for the grammatical complexity and ambiguity of natural language.

Uschold et al. (2003) described a prototype implementation of a semantic filtering capability added to an existing XML-based publish and subscribe infrastructure. They created a domain ontology that represents the key concepts and relationships in the domain. Then they augmented the documents published with semantic annotations using concepts and relationships from the ontology. The semantic filters (queries) were created for subscriptions using the same ontology. An inference engine was used to determine which semantic annotations match with the semantic filters. Their knowledge sharing model can be considered as an example of Model SEM.

Wang et al. (2004) used a Publish/Subscribe system to share the knowledge. In their system, the knowledge descriptions, which they call Events, are represented with RDF. They also used a domain ontology as the domain basic knowledge which specifies the concepts involved in the Events, the relations between them, and the constraints on them. Their knowledge sharing model can be considered as an example of Model SEM.

Halaschek-Wiener and Kolovski (2008) formalized a syndication architecture that utilizes the OWL and description logic reasoning for selective content dissemination. Their methods provided finer grained control for filtering and automated reasoning for discovering implicit subscription matches. Their knowledge sharing model also is an example of Model SEM.

Kraines et al. (2006) used semantic web technologies to share expert knowledge. The basic knowledge of the domain is presented to knowledge users as domain ontologies. The Knowledge Providers create knowledge descriptions for their knowledge resources, and the Knowledge Seekers create queries to search for knowledge of interest to them. Therefore, this system is an implementation of Model SEM.

Tummarello and Morbidoni (2008) presented a Semantic Web application DBin platform that enables groups of users with a common interest to cooperatively create semantically structured knowledge bases. DBin platform provided specific tools, such as querying, viewing and editing facilities, based on Semantic Web techniques to users. It is also an example of Model SEM.

Lopez et al. (2007) created AquaLog, a portable question-answering system that takes queries expressed in natural language and an ontology as input, and returns answers drawn from one or more knowledge bases. We consider the knowledge sharing model of AquaLog is Model SEM augmenting with NLP techniques. AquaLog converted the query in natural language into semantic query by using NLP tools, and then inferred the semantic query in knowledge bases represented in semantic structure form.

Diaz-Galiano et al. (2008) used the Medical Subject Headings (MeSH) to expand queries in the task of multilingual image retrieval. The expansion consists of searching for terms from the topic query in the MeSH vocabulary and adding similar terms. MeSH has a hierarchical structure that provides a consistent way to retrieve information using different terms for the same concepts. However, the MeSH structure does not contain typed relationships. So, the MeSH-based method also does not support retrieval at the semantic predicate level. We consider their knowledge sharing model is Model SEMCL in thesaurus level.

In summary, while the first two related research works support cross-language knowledge sharing, because they do not handle semantics directly, the accuracy of the matching results is limited. The next six related research works support the seman-

tic search but do not handle the cross-language issue. The last research work support semantic search in thesaurus level, but does not support semantic search in predicate level. Our approach supports cross-language knowledge sharing at the semantic predicate level.

CONCLUSION

In today's age of information explosion, vast amounts of new knowledge are generated every day in a diversity of languages. How to share and search this knowledge efficiently is one of the most important problems in the information science community. Conventional cross-language knowledge sharing models that are based on natural language processing technologies suffer from the exacerbated effect of ambiguity and grammatical complexity over multiple languages. This paper began with an analysis of the task of knowledge sharing in the Internet environment. An approach to matching knowledge resources using Semantic Web Technologies, called Model SEM, was identified. A new model based on Model SEM, SEMCL, was then proposed for cross-language semantic sharing and searching of knowledge resources. We introduced the framework of our proposal for Model SEMCL, focusing on the knowledge representation and search aspects. We then used a scenario based on an implementation of Model SEMCL for general engineering knowledge to demonstrate how Model SEMCL supports disambiguation, semantic predicate level matching, and cross-language sharing. The original contribution of this work is the creation of a cross-language knowledge sharing model that uses Semantic Web technologies to enable searches across multiple languages at a semantic predicate level.

Our implementation of Model SEMCL is accessible on the EKOSS website (www.ekoss.org). Currently, the EKOSS knowledge sharing system supports three languages: English, Japanese and Chinese. To date, a number of different users of EKOSS have used their preferred languages to create semantic statements to describe their knowledge resources. Currently, we just consider the knowledge sharing in the same community, i.e., the knowledge providers and seekers use the same domain ontology to represent their knowledge resources and search queries. In our future work, we will study the knowledge sharing crossing communities that will address the problems of knowledge barriers.

ACKNOWLEDGMENT

The authors thank the President's Office of the University of Tokyo for funding support.

REFERENCES

Diaz-Galiano, M. C., Garcia-Cumbreras, M. A., Martin-Valdivia, M. T., Montejo-Raez, A., & Urena-Lopez, A. (2008). Integrating MeSH ontology to improve medical information retrieval. In C. Peters et al. (Eds.), *Advances in Multilingual and Multimodal Information Retrieval* (LNCS 5152, pp. 601-606). Berlin: Springer-Verlag.

GO. (1999). *The Gene Ontology*. Retrieved May 11, 2010, from http://www.geneontology.org

Goldschmidt, D. E., & Krishnamoorthy, M. (2008). Comparing keyword search to semantic search: A case study in solving crossword puzzles using the GoogleTM API. *Software, Practice & Experience*, *38*(4), 417–445. doi:10.1002/spe.840

Guo, W., & Kraines, S. (2008). Explicit scientific knowledge comparison based on semantic description matching. In *Proceedings of the American Society for Information Science and Technology: Vol. 45. People Transforming Information – Information Transforming People* (pp. 1-18). Hoboken: Wiley InterScience.

Guo, W., & Kraines, S. (2009). Cross-language knowledge sharing model based on ontologies and logical inference. In Chu, S., (Eds.), *Series on Innovation and Knowledge Management* (*Vol. 8*). Singapore: World Scientific.

Halaschek-Wiener, C., & Kolovski, V. (2008). Syndication on the Web using a description logic approach. *Web Semantics: Science. Services and Agents on the World Wide Web, 6*, 171–190. doi:10.1016/j.websem.2008.06.002

Hunter, L., & Cohen, K. B. (2006). Biomedical language processing: What's beyond PubMed? *Molecular Cell, 21*, 589–594. doi:10.1016/j.molcel.2006.02.012

Hunter, L., Lu, Z., Firby, J., Baumgartner, W. A. Jr, Johnson, H. L., Ogren, P. V., & Cohen, K. B. (2008). OpenDMAP: An open source, ontology-driven concept analysis engine, with applications to capturing knowledge regarding protein transport, protein interactions and cell-type-specific gene expression. *BMC Bioinformatics, 9*, 78. doi:10.1186/1471-2105-9-78

Kahan, J., & Koivunen, M. R. Prud'Hommeaux, E., & Swick, R. R. (2001). Annotea: An open RDF infrastructure for shared Web annotations. In *Proceedings of the 10th International Conference on World Wide Web* (pp. 623-632). New York: ACM.

Koivunen, M. R. (2005). Annotea and semantic web supported collaboration. In *Proceedings of the Workshop on User Aspects of the Semantic Web UserSWeb at European Semantic Web Conference* (pp. 5-16).

Kraines, S., Guo, W., Kemper, B., & Nakamura, Y. (2006). EKOSS: A knowledge-user centered approach to knowledge sharing, discovery, and integration on the Semantic Web. In I. Cruz et al. (Eds.), *The Semantic Web - ISWC 2006* (LNCS 4273, pp. 833-846). Berlin: Springer Verlag.

Lin, H. F. (2007). Effects of extrinsic and intrinsic motivation on employee knowledge sharing intentions. *Journal of Information Science*, *33*(2), 135–149. doi:10.1177/0165551506068174

Littman, M. L., Dumais, S. T., & Landauer, T. K. (1998). Automatic cross-language information retrieval using latent semantic indexing. In Grefenstette, G. (Ed.), *Cross-Language Information Retrieval*. Boston: Kluwer Academic Publishers.

Lopez, V., Uren, V., Motta, E., & Pasin, M. (2007). AquaLog: an ontology-driven question answering system for organizational semantic intranets. *Web Semantics: Science, Services and Agents on the World Wide Web*, *5*, 72–105. doi:10.1016/j.websem.2007.03.003

OWL. (2004). *OWL Web Ontology Language*. Retrieved April 15, 2010, from http://www.w3.org/TR/2004/REC-owl-features-20040210

Schonhofen, P., Benczur, A., Biro, I., & Csalogany, K. (2008). Cross-language retrieval with Wikipedia. In C. Peters et al. (Eds.), *CLEF 2007* (LNCS 5152, pp. 72-79). Berlin: Springer Verlag.

SUMO. (2003). *Suggested Upper Merged Ontology*. Retrieved May 11, 2010, from http://www.ontologyportal.org/

Tang, X. (2007). Towards meta-synthetic support to unstructured problem solving. *International Journal of Information Technology & Decision Making*, *6*(3), 491–508. doi:10.1142/S0219622007002630

Tang, X., & Zhang, Z. (2008). Paper review assignment based on human-knowledge network. In [Singapore.]. *Proceedings of IEEE SMC, 2008*, 102–107.

Tummarello, G., & Morbidoni, C. (2008). The DBin platform: a complete environment for Semantic Web communities. *Web Semantics: Science, Services and Agents on the World Wide Web*, *6*, 257–265. doi:10.1016/j.websem.2008.08.002

Uschold, M., Clark, P., Dickey, F., Fung, C., Smith, S., Uczekaj, S., et al. (2003). A semantic infosphere. In D. Fensel et al. (Eds.), *ISWC 2003* (LNCS 2870, pp. 882-896). Berlin: Springer Verlag.

Wang, J., Jin, B., & Li, J. (2004). An ontology-based publish/subscribe system. In H. A. Jacobsen (Ed.), *Middleware 2004* (LNCS 3231, pp. 232-253). Berlin: Springer Verlag.

Widen-Wulff, G., & Ginman, M. (2004). Explaining knowledge sharing in organizations through the dimensions of social capital. *Journal of Information Science*, *30*(5), 448–458. doi:10.1177/0165551504046997

Widen-Wulff, G., & Suomi, R. (2003). Building a knowledge sharing company – evidence from the Finnish insurance industry. In *Proceedings of the 36th Annual Hawaii International Conference on System Sciences (HICSS36)*, Big Island, HI. Washington, DC: Computer Society Press.

This work was previously published in the International Journal of Knowledge and Systems Science, Volume 1, Issue 3, edited by W.B. Lee, pp. 1-19 copyright 2010 by IGI Publishing (an imprint of IGI Global).

Chapter 12

A Collective–Intelligence View on the Linux Kernel Developer Community

Haoxiang Xia
Dalian University of Technology, China

ABSTRACT

With the rapid proliferation of all sorts of online communities, the knowledge creation and dissemination in these online communities have become a prominent social phenomenon. In this paper, one typical Open Source Software community—the online community of Linux kernel developers—is studied from the perspective of collective intelligence, to explore the social dynamics behind the success of the Linux kernel project. The Linux kernel developer community is modeled as a supernetwork of triple interwoven networks, namely a technological media network, a collaboration network of the developers, and a knowledge network. The development of the LDC is then an evolutionary process through which the supernetwork expands and the collective intelligence of the community develops. In this paper, a bottom-up approach is attempted to unravel this evolutionary process.

INTRODUCTION

In recent years, with the explosion of the Internet and the World Wide Web, online communities have become a prominent social phenomenon (Preece & Maloney-Krichmar, 2005); correspondingly, these

online communities are playing an increasingly vital role in society-wide knowledge developments. Typical examples include the Wikipedia community which produces high-qualified encyclopedia (Giles 2005), the open source software (OSS) developer communities which build complex software systems like Apache and Mozilla (Mockus et al., 2002), and "Science 2.0" communities for

DOI: 10.4018/978-1-4666-1782-7.ch012

scientific collaboration (Shneiderman, 2008). The proliferation of such knowledge-intensive online communities may raise a critical research issue, i.e. to study how knowledge is created and diffused in the online communities, and how the communities themselves grow during the collective actions of the participants. This issue is akin to the well-discussed research field of "Knowledge Management" (e.g., Nonaka & Takeuchi, 1995; Alavi & Leidner, 2001), which is usually focused on the "management" of knowledge assets and knowledge-related processes in a formal organization. Nevertheless, it can be argued that the existing theories and models for organizational knowledge management cannot be simply transplanted to the situation of online communities, since the processes of knowledge creation, dissemination and utilization in the online communities are fundamentally different from those in a formal organization. The creation, dissemination and utilization of knowledge in the online community are commonly accomplished by independent participants in a self-organizing and "autopoietic" (Varela et al., 1974) fashion, while in the formal organization such knowledge processes usually take place under the centralized managerial control to achieve some well-defined organizational objectives. New theories and models to explain the knowledge-related processes in online communities are required.

The Linux kernel developer community is one of the most famous online OSS communities; and this community may provide a fine case to study the knowledge processes in the online communities. The Linux kernel is the operating system kernel that underpins all distributions of Linux operating systems, which was initiated in 1991 by Finnish programmer Linus Torvalds and has thereafter been developed by thousands of part-time voluntary programmers scattered across the Internet without formal organization or centralized control. Along with the development of the Linux kernel, the online community of the contributors, or the Linux Kernel developer community, rapidly grows. In the Linux developer community, three phenomena are noticeable. First, the Linux operating system kernel, which is a software product of very-large-scale and complexity, is efficiently developed with high-quality in an unconventional way. Second, there is the self-organization of the online community of contributors throughout the development of the Linux kernel. Third, the development of the Linux kernel is a creative process. In this process, large amount of knowledge and skills are used to develop the software product; and on the other hand new knowledge about the development of the Linux operating system is also created. In this sense software development is inherently interwoven with the creation of knowledge of programming and software-project management; and we may then call this Linux kernel developer community as a "knowledge-creating community". Facing these intriguing phenomena, it is worthwhile to examine the underlying dynamics of the evolution of the Linux kernel developer community, as well as the collective action of software development and knowledge creation in this self-organized community.

Therefore, in this paper we try to explore the knowledge-intensive online communities by giving an analysis on the actual case of the Linux-kernel developer community (DC for short). In an earlier effort, we suggested that many online communities manifest some degree of community intelligence (Xia et al., 2008; Luo et al., 2009). Based on this idea, we in this paper try to explore the underlying dynamics for the evolution of the LDC as well as the development of this community's knowledge product, the Linux kernel.

A SHORT HISTORY OF THE LDC

To facilitate further discussion, the history of Linux is shortly introduced, with the focus being placed on the growth of the developer community in which the Linux kernel is collectively created and continually updated.

Linux was initially developed by Linus Torvalds in 1991, when he was a student in computer science at University of Helsinki. His initial motivation was to write programs in order to use some UNIX functions in his own PC with an 80386 processor; and he implemented a task-switching program, a disk driver and a small file system, which constituted Linux 0.01. On 25 August 1991, he announced this skeletal operating system in the newsgroup "comp.os.minix" and asked for suggestions for the preferable features. Then, his continuous efforts ended up to Linux 0.02, which came on October 5th. Together with the free release of the source code, he posted another message in the same newsgroup to seek feedbacks as well as possible contributors or co-developers. This was a critical event for Linux since it started the collective journey of Linux development. The response was instantly positive; of the first ten people to download Linux, five sent back bug fixes, code improvements, and new features. By the end of the year, when Linux finally became a stand-alone system in Version 0.11, more than a hundred people worldwide had joined the Linux newsgroup and the mailing list (Kurabawa, 2000). Since then, the Linux developer community rapidly expands, together with the rapid development of the Linux operation system.

One critical measure is the development of the Linux kernel in term of the source lines of code (SLOC). The actual SLOCs in some typical versions are listed in Table 1. This table shows that the Linux kernel rapidly expands in the past 18 years.

Another critical measure for the growth of the LDC is to count the community scale. Since its creation in 1991, this open operating system has attracted increasing numbers of developers worldwide. In the year of 1993, there were over 100 developers worked on the Linux Kernel. More recently, as reported by Koah-Hatman et al. (2008), each release since version 2.6.11 generally con-

Table 1. Growth of SLOC in linux kernel (some typical versions)

Release Year	Kernel Version	Source Lines of Code
1991	Linux 0.0.1	10,239
1994	Linux 1.0.0	176,250
1996	Linux 1.2.0	310,950
1999	Linux 2.2.0	1,800,847
2001	Linux 2.4.0	2,210,149
2003	Linux 2.6.0	5,929,913
2008	Linux 2.6.25	9,232,484

(Data Source from: Wikipedia article on "Linux Kernel", available at: http://simple.wikipedia.org/wiki/Linux_kernel, lastly accessed on July 15, 2009)

tains the work of nearly 1000 developers. Since 2005, about 3700 individual developers have contributed to the kernel. Their report also shows that the number of developers gradually increases from 483 in Version 2.6.11 to 1057 in Version 2.6.24.

The previous description reveals much information for the LDC. Linux had a somewhat haphazard starting-up, since Torvalds himself was not even aware that he was writing an operating system when he began programming the first task-switching system in 1991. He did not anticipate at that time that Linux would catch such persistent enthusiasms from so many developers and users, nor could he imagine that Linux would become such huge and complex software and such a successful product. From this haphazard starting-up, the community rapidly expands together with the explosion of the Linux (kernel) product. Behind the success of the Linux operating system and the growth of the Linux developer community, two questions naturally come to the fore: what are the mechanism underlying the evolution of this Linux developer community; and why this complex software product can be successfully created in this largely open community without thorough planning or centralized control.

SOME PREVIOUS VIEWS

The intriguing phenomena of the Linux operating system and the corresponding developer community have attracted great attention in the last decade. Here a few typical explanations are shortly introduced.

One well-noted work is given by Raymond (1999), who distinguished two different modes of software development, i.e., the "cathedral" model of most of the commercial world and the "bazaar" model of the Linux world. The success of the Linux project is then attributed to the inherent openness in the bazaar model. On one hand, Raymond believes one success factor of Linux is the frequent releasing and updating so that the users can quickly detect the bugs; one the other, with a large developer base, the project leader Linus Torvalds can safely rely on others to write and test the code for him. The openness is for sure an important factor for enhancing Linux development; however, it is farfetched to use the openness to explain everything.

Kuwabara (2000), by contrast, argued that the bazaar-analogy is too simplistic, and the success of the Linux project should be understood from an evolution and complex-adaptive-system (CAS) point of view. To him, behind the Linux project is a bottom-up engineering approach that effectively challenges the top-down worldview entrenched in the monolithic software engineering approach. We largely agree with his CAS view; our further argument is that the Linux developer community is not merely an evolutionary system, but also an evolutionary intelligent system, as the knowledge-and-problem-solving aspect is less stressed in Kuwabara's work. Another limitation of Kuwabara's work is that he points out that the Linux project should be considered as a CAS, but the underlying mechanisms of the formation of this CAS is not well-addressed.

Iannacci (2005), in his PhD dissertation, gave a social epistemological analysis for the LDC. The major focus is on the coordination mechanisms that

are emerged in the community. Three mechanisms are analyzed in his work, namely standardization, loose-coupling to form a "heterachical" structure, and partisan mutual adjustment. Lee and Cole (2003), from the knowledge-creation perspective, attempted to develop a community-based model of knowledge creation, adopting the evolutionary framework suggested by Campbell (1960) and emphasizing the role of criticism and critical evaluation as a key driver in the evolutionary processes.

The prior contributions, among many others, are no doubt valuable for deepening our understanding of the LDC. However, their work just reflects the partial facts of the LDC from different facets; more endeavors are still needed to obtain a more comprehensive view.

TOWARDS A COMMUNITY-INTELLIGENCE VIEW ON THE LDC

Based on the prior observations, in this section we give our analysis on the LDC, basically regarding this community as an evolutionary intelligent system in which the participants collectively create knowledge and solve problems. The LDC largely reflects the phenomenon of "community intelligence" (Xia et al., 2008; Luo et al., 2009) or the "collective intelligence" (Levy, 1997; Mataric, 1993; Heylighen, 1999; Malone & Klein, 2007; Bonabeau, 2009) of online communities. Subsequently, we try to explain the evolution of the LDC from the aspect of community intelligence.

THE LDC AS AN EXAMPLE OF COMMUNITY INTELLIGENCE

Our central point is that the development of the LDC shows a typical example for the formation of community intelligence. Under this view, the LDC contains a "supernetwork" (Nagurney & Wakolbinger, 2005) structure that consists of triple interwoven networks, as illustrated in Figure 1.

Figure 1. The "Supernetwork" of community intelligence in the LDC (Source: Xia et al., 2008)

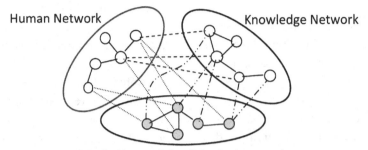

First, the LDC grows in the environment of computer networks, especially of the Internet. Thus there is a technological network which underpins the interactions of the LDC. The major role of this technological network in the LDC is to serve as communication media that enable information passing, knowledge diffusion, and interpersonal collaboration. Therefore, we can call this network "media network". Second, intermediated by the "media network", there is a "human network" of the participating programmers, in which the nodes are the programmers and the edges are the communications and collaborations between the programmers. The collaborations of the programmers on one hand create the product of Linux kernel, and on the other hand generate knowledge about the development of the Linux kernel. The knowledge about the Linux kernel development is logically structured in a networked form, and we can call it "knowledge network". As discussed in our earlier work, these three networks are intertwined to form a supernetwork. This supernetwork can be termed as a "knowledge supernetwork" since it is characterized by the knowledge network and the collaborative knowledge work in the human network to form the knowledge network.

Furthermore, this knowledge supernetwork is "intelligent" in the sense of problem-solving through the collective action of Linux development. In other words, this online community of the independent programmers manifests higher capabilities in the collective software development than any individual programmer per se. The collective intelligence of the LDC can be exhibited in two aspects. On one hand, the community contains a knowledge base (i.e., the "knowledge network" in the prior triad) superior to the member programmer's; on the other hand, the community is self-organized to form a collaboration network (i.e., the "human network" in the prior triad) so that the collective action of software development is well-coordinated and effective.

Corresponding to the prior supernetwork view of the LDC, a further research topic is to examine how this knowledge supernetwork grows through the collective work in Linux kernel development, more specifically to examine the co-evolution of the human network and the knowledge network. To carry out this investigation, the starting point is that the overall evolution of the LDC is not a monolithic process, compatible with the "bottom-up engineering" of Linux development as Kuwabara contended. Linux is developed by thousands of independent programmers without complete goal-setting, thorough planning, or top-down task-assignment. When Torvalds initially announced Version 0.01, he himself had no clear intention for the future of Linux; and he just asked for feedbacks and suggestions on the features which Linux should contain. During the entire process of Linux development, he also avoids imposing long-term plans and visions on the community:

That way I can more easily deal with anything new that comes up without having pre-conceptions of how I should deal with it. My only long-range plan has been and still is just the very general plan of making Linux better (Interview, cited from Kuwabara, 2000)

Instead, the stage-goals of development usually rise from collective efforts and discussions. Unlike a formally-organized software project, neither Torvalds nor any other sub-system maintainer authoritatively arranges a particular contributor to accomplish a particular task. From the very beginning, it has been left to each contributor to decide what to work on at the moment:

In developing Linux, you have complete freedom to do whatever you feel like doing. There's no specification anywhere of what the Linux kernel has to end up doing, and as such there is no requirement for anyone to do anything they are not interested in (Personal Interview, cited from Kuwabara, 2000)

Thus, the entire project is carried out in a spontaneous mode with no global coordination. In the project, nobody can anticipate what will be added or modified in the next release of the Linux kernel. Associated with this spontaneous and bottom-up development of the Linux operating system is the endogenous growth of the corresponding community of the developers. This LDC again grows from bottom up as the result of the free choices of the contributors. No one can exactly anticipate who will join the community by submitting patches and bug-fits at the next stage of work, or who will leave because of any reason. Without formal organization, up to now this community has somehow stabilized to be an effective community that efficiently creates complex software of high quality.

Accordingly, a "bottom-up" and generative approach (Epstein & Axtell, 1996) should be adopted to study the social dynamics of the LDC

evolution. Following this approach, we need to identify the local actions that eventually propel the overall evolution of the community, and then to examine how the global evolutionary processes can emerge from the local action.

AN EXPLORATION OF THE UNDERLYING DYNAMICS OF THE LDC EVOLUTION

In the previous sub-section, we argue that behind the development of the LDC is a spontaneous process of the evolution of community intelligence. In this sub-section, a bottom-up investigation is given to explore the underlying mechanisms.

Identifying the Local Force

With global project-planning and top-down task-assignment being absent in the Linux kernel development, the programmers have complete freedom to do whatever they feel like to do. The individual programmers' coding behavior is obviously one of the important local actions that are directly meaningful for the production of the Linux kernel. However, the coding behavior itself does not explain the social dynamics of the LDC since it ensures neither the interpersonal collaborations nor the assembly of different pieces of code to fulfill a complete system function. Then, the first question is: what is the key driven force to propel the evolution of the entire LDC and the creation of the Linux kernel?

Our answer to this question is that communication may serve as such local force. It can be easily observed in the Linux-kernel mailing list that there are dense communications within the Linux developer community. According to a report by Zack Brown (cited from Kuwabara, 2000), in the later 1990s the kernel traffic has reached up to six megabytes of posts in a week. In another research, Lee and Cole (2003) counted the total number of emails sent to the mailing list during

1995 to 2000. They found that 14,535 people had sent at least one e-mail to the mailing list; and each person has averagely sent 14 emails over 5 years, since there were 199,374 emails archived as of August 26, 2000. These communications cover wide-range of topics like bug-reports and -fixes, announcements of patches, discussions on technical problems, and debates about the development choices. The community members who write posts are surely the direct communicators and the communications are the key factor to link them together to accomplish their joint efforts in developing the Linux kernel code. In addition, these communications also attract more people who do not directly participate in the discussions on a particular thread. However, they read the posts, they read and test the programs, and they often learn a lot from these discussions and their future coding actions may be influenced. In this sense, they are the indirect participants of the communications. Consequently, these communications actually connect more people than it seems; and they play a critical role in the growth of the LDC as self-organization processes that eventually impels the global development of the entire community may be activated by the local communications.

Self-Organization Processes Impelled by Local Communications

Coordination is doubtlessly critical to the quality of Linux as well as to the growth of the community itself. Without coordination, the integrity of the Linux product would not be possible, nor could the developer community grow to be a coherent or creative one. However, as previously stated, the top-down coordination is generally absent in this community. Instead, coordination in the LDC is an emergent property generated from bottom up, where the local communications serve as the driving force. One simplest case of coordination is the task "assignment" (tasks not assigned really, as the tasks are voluntarily done). For one contributor,

the good performance in his past work reinforces his reputation and trustworthiness for the quality of his other contributions. Such coordination is indeed activated by the indirect communications. The contributor transfers knowledge by submitting the patches; and other community members simultaneously get "know-who" knowledge when obtaining the technical knowledge related to the submitted patch. As a result, such indirect knowledge communication impels possible future collective and collaborative work.

More direct technical communications are also pervasive in the LDC, basically via the Linux-kernel mailing-list. Randomly picking up a thread from the mailing-list archive, we often see intensive discussions on some particular technical problem. For example, Michael Zick reported a bug-fix on May 22nd, 2009 by posting the following message:

```
"Found in the bit-rot for 32-bit,
x86, Uni-processor builds:
diff --git a/arch/x86/include/asm/
alternative.h b/arch/x86/include/asm/
alternative.h
index f6aa18e..3c790ef 100644--- a/
arch/x86/include/asm/alternative.h
+++ b/arch/x86/include/asm/
alternative.h
@@ -35,7 +35,7 @@
"661:\n\tlock; "
#else /* ! CONFIG_SMP */
-#define LOCK_PREFIX ""
+#define LOCK_PREFIX "\n\tlock; "
#endif
/* This must be included *after* the
definition of LOCK_PREFIX */ Sub-
mitted: M. S. Zick" (Source: Linux-
kernel mailing list, archived at:
http://lkml.indiana.edu/hypermail/
linux/kernel/0905.2/02562.html)
```

Immediately, this message causes intensive discussion. Under this thread, there were 31

Figure 2. Feedback Process of a Contributor's Implicit Reputation in the LDC (Adapted from Kuwabara, 2000)

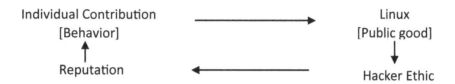

postings on that same day. At least 6 persons participated. Among them, Zick posted 13 messages, Andi Klein posted 4, Ingo Molnar posted 1, Peter Anvin posted 4, Samuel Thibault posted 4, Dreier posted 2, and there are 3 other anonymous postings (probably posted by the above-listed authors too). This is a common scenario of the technical discussions in the LDC. It is not unusual that such technical discussions give rise to the emergent collaborations among the participants. Iannacci (2005) terms this kind of coordination as "partisan mutual adjustment" and argues that collaboration teams or "social networks" may appear from such communications. These social networks are open to contributions from everybody. However, they usually contain strong ties among a limited number of participants because of their frequent interactions; and a stable core may form around the strongly-tied participants. From the view of social-network-analysis (SNA), such stable cores can usually be termed "cliques".

Besides facilitating the formation and adjustments of the collaborative teams or "cliques", the coordination through communications also plays a critical role in the advancement of the overall Linux kernel project. Kuwabara mentioned an example of the row I/O patch, submitted by Stephen Tweedle in 1998 and rejected by Torvalds several times before the final version was at last applied into the kernel. In the example, an iteratively-improved technical solution was achieved by collective work of the involved developers coordinated through communications.

From the prior description, it can be perceived that the emergent coordination is a key element that makes order grow from chaos in the LDC, as through such coordination the structuring of collaborative teams or cliques takes place and the patches with good quality are often the result of the coordinated work.

Closely related to the emergent coordination is the evolution of an implicit reputation system underlying the LDC. It is the common case that the highly-reputed or trusted persons play a central role in the communications and collaborations. They often become the primary coordinators (e.g., sub-system maintainers) in many collective efforts. However, their reputations are, in turn, the result of the performances of their previous contributions in submitting patches and in the discussions.

Kuwabara (2000) describes a feedback process for the self-reinforcement of the individual reputation, as shown in Figure 2.

In this process, the reputation of an individual increases according to the contributions he or she makes; and in turn, the increasing of his or her reputation may foster the further contributions from the same individual. Kuwabara uses such reinforcement process to explain the motivations for a community member to contribute. We argue that this process also has influences to the evolution of the community itself. With the increasing reputation, an individual may play an increasingly-important role in the development actions; thus the evolution of the implicit reputation system is a critical factor for the formation and variation of the overall structure of the community.

From another aspect, the communications also stimulate "stigmergic" processes (Theraulaz

& Bonabeau, 1999). The stigmergic processes basically function through the technical building of the Linux system. As previously cited from the project leader Linus Torvalds' assertion, "my only long-range plan has been and still is just the very general plan of making Linux better", the global goal-setting and long-range planning are absent in developing Linux. Moreover, the development of Linux is the collective work of massive autonomous contributors who also lack global sight of the project. With these two essential features, the development of Linux is the collective architecting without blueprint, resembling the nest-construction activities in the insect societies such as the termite colonies (Theraulaz & Bonabeau, 1995). Thus, it is natural to suppose that the stigmergic processes may exist in the Linux developer community, analogous to the collective nest-construction in a termite colony. Following this analogy, the general situation of Linux development is that the contributors decide what to do in terms of what they have done. Therefore, no one, including the defacto project leader Linus Torvalds, knows in advance what would be added or modified in the next release; and the overall development is always open-ended. But during this open-ended process, their product is increasingly complex, increasingly powerful, and increasingly fitted to the environment (i.e., to better satisfy user needs and to cope with the technology advances outside the Linux project).

Generally, there are two sources to stimulate the stigmergic interactions. One situation is the amplification of some personal ideas and suggestions inside the community. Another situation is the adaptation to environmental or external changes, especially technological innovations outside the Linux project. Responding to the internal and the external "stimuli", some member(s) may trigger a stigmergic process in the community, acting like a termite emits pheromones onto a site to call for other termites to continue building there. Such a stigmergic process is generally a self-reinforcement process. If one ongoing topic is active and

intriguing, and if it brings many open challenges, many contributors would be attracted to this topic; and more progresses may be made, bringing even more amount of further open issues…Gradually, when the "constructing" on this topic is going to complete, the contributors may step away because there is not so much work left.

Bringing the previous discussions together, we can conclude that the self-organizing processes around the emergent coordination, the evolving reputation system and the stigmergic interactions in constructing the software system cause the global effect that the overall process of the Linux kernel development has become an adaptive process of the evolution of community intelligence. The global property of the community intelligence of the LDC will be examined in the next sub-section.

Collective Intelligence of the LDC as Emergent Global Property

The previously-discussed self-organizing processes results in the global process of the development of collective intelligence in the LDC. In this sub-section, we take a look at such collective intelligence at the communal level.

The "intelligence" of the LDC is firstly and most-remarkably represented by the Linux operating system itself. Today the Linux kernel has become an extremely complex software system containing over 9 million source lines of code. Building such a system looks like a mission impossible to a collectivity of part-time hackers without any formal organization, as it is difficult task even for the largest corporations. The efficiency and effectiveness in the building of the Linux system have unquestionably proved the high "intelligence" of this online community. Kroah-Hatman et al. (2008) showed the rate of change of Linux kernel from Version 2.6.11 to 2.6.24.

On average within 100 days the community announces a new stable release, which contains thousands of pieces of changes from the previous

Figure 3. The Emergent Hierarchical Structure of the LDC (Adapted from a figure in: www.kernel.org/ pub/linux/kernel/people/gregkh/talks/kernel_devel-google-2008-06-05.pdf)

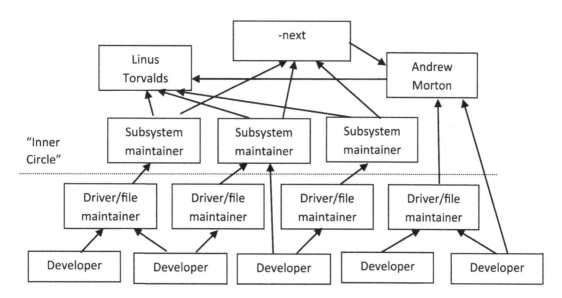

release. This figure convincingly illustrates the highly-efficient work done by the Linux developer community. For the effectiveness of the Linux contributors' work, it is difficult to get direct quantitative measurement; but the complexity of the system on one hand, and the adoption rate1 on the other hand have illustrated the effectiveness of their development.

In addition to the external measurement of the efficiency and effectiveness of the development work, the global regularity of the LDC can also been seen internally. As the internal measure, two properties are shortly discussed here, i.e., the global structuring of the community and the emergence of the norms of code quality and coding style.

One global consequence of the previously-discussed self-organization processes is the formation and evolution of the community structure. Most remarkably, a hierarchical structure gradually forms during the evolution of the community. This structure was described by Kroah-Hatman in his 2008 presentation at Google, as shown in Figure 3.

This hierarchical structure is actually a core-periphery structure. In this structure, the project leader Torvalds works closely with a limited number of lieutenants. They are core developers and subsystem maintainers and they constitute the "inner circle" of the community. The peripheral participants are the ad hoc patch-submitters and bug-reporters. Torvalds himself explained this structure in a post:

The fact is, we've had "patch penguins" pretty much forever, and they are called subsystem maintainers. They maintain their own subsystem, ie people like David Miller (networking), Kai Germaschewski (ISDN), Greg KH (USB), Ben Collins (firewire), Al Viro (VFS), Andrew Morton (ext3), Ingo Molnar (scheduler), Jeff Garzik (network drivers) etc etc. ...

A word of warning: good maintainers are hard to find. Getting more of them helps, but at some point it can actually be more useful to help the _existing_ ones. I've got about ten-twenty people I really trust, and quite frankly, the way people work is hardcoded in our DNA. Nobody "really trusts" hundreds of people. The way to make these things scale out more is to increase the network of trust not by trying to push it on me, but by making it more of a _network_, not a star-topology around me." (Source: Linux Kernel Mailing List Archive, at: http://lkml.indiana.edu/hypermail/linux/kernel/0201.3/1070.html)

In this post, Torvalds clearly stated that the structuring of the community relies on a "network of trust". He himself trusts a small number people in the "inner circle" or the subsystem maintainers, and each maintainer trusts a small number of other developers, and so on… This network of trust is in fact formed under the implicit reputation system underlying the community. Correspondingly, the evolution of this reputation system generally directs the adjustment of this working structure of the community. In short, the overall structure of the Linux developer community is emergent instead of organized top-down; and the subsystem maintainers grow, instead of being officially assigned. This structure is furthermore flexible. An active contributor who performs well in his previous contributions may play an increasingly vital role in the community; by contrast, if one contributor becomes less active, he might gradually become the peripheral participants.

The third measure is the formation of the global norms in the community. With the growth of the community, the formats of submitting patches and reporting-bugs become standardized. The standards on the code quality and the coding styles are also enforced. An example given by Kuwabara (2000) is the Italian programmer Andreas Arcangeli's patches for the printer code:

[Arcangeli] made substantial improvements, then branched out, but tended to do some pretty sloppy things - to the point where Linus said "go away." Andreas refused to go away, and eventually had major changes to the kernel accepted. All Linus did was enforce coding standard (Personal Interview 1999, cited from Kuwabara, 2000)

At the first glimpse, it looks like that this standardization attributes to the personal efforts of Torvalds and his close co-developers. But factually it is the result of the coordination of the entire community. Without the abundant base of contributors, this standardization is impossible; without the adoption of the standards by the contributors, this standardization is either impossible. In turn, this standardization is a means of the emergent coordination of the whole community; and the accepted norms or standards are actually become a proportion of the communal knowledge.

To sum up, in the prior analysis, a rough picture has been drawn to explain the social dynamics that underlie the LDC evolution. Generally, the LDC that develops the Linux software can somehow be analogous to a mound-building termite colony. In both cases, the building activities are accomplished by the individual agents without global planning or task-assignment; and the coordination is emergent from the "stigmergic" information exchange. The "stigmergic" information exchange in the LDC is realized by the direct and indirect communications and these communications eventually propel the overall evolution of the community. The overall evolution of the LDC is then a dualistic process in which the collaboration network of the human beings grows on one hand and the knowledge network about the Linux development expands on the other hand. The expansion of the knowledge network is partially manifested by the improvements of the Linux product itself.

CONCLUSION

In this paper, the social dynamics underlying the LDC evolution is explored from the aspect of community intelligence. It can be concluded from this investigation that the online community of the Linux kernel developers grows through a spontaneous self-organization process. In this process, the personal activities of programming and the interpersonal communications that stimulate knowledge transfer and coordination are the most fundamental local "force" that boosts the global evolution of the community. As a result, the LDC evolves as an "intelligent" social system that effectively and efficiently "solves" a complex problem, i.e. the development of the Linux kernel. The development of this collective intelligence of the LDC is embodied as the expansion of a supernetwork of three interwoven networks, where a knowledge network is embedded within a human network supported by a media network. This analysis of the LDC may, in turn, facilitate to enrich our understandings on the development of community intelligence in general. Subsequent to the present work, more elaborate exploration of the social mechanisms that underpin community intelligence will be a key subject of future research. On the other hand, this work may have practical implications for developing computer-support systems to enhance the knowledge creation and dissemination in the online communities like the Linux kernel developer community.

ACKNOWLEDGMENT

This work is partly supported by National Natural Science Foundation of China (NSFC) under Grant No. 70871016. Part of this work was presented in the 6th International Conference on Knowledge Management (ICKM, 2009) jointly with the 10th International Symposium on Knowledge and Systems Sciences (KSS 2009). The present work wouldn't be accomplished without the dense discussions with Prof. Taketoshi Yoshida and Dr. Shuangling Luo at Japan Advanced Institute of Science and Technology; but the mistakes or improper views that may appear in the paper are of the author's sole responsibility. The author is also grateful for the comments and suggestions from the anonymous reviewers, which help greatly to improve the quality of this paper.

REFERENCES

Alavi, M., & Leidner, D. (2001). Knowledge management and knowledge management systems. *Management Information Systems Quarterly*, *25*(1), 107–136. doi:10.2307/3250961

Bonabeau, E. (2009). Decision 2.0: The power of collective intelligence. *MIT Sloan Management Review*, *50*(2), 45–52.

Campbell, D. T. (1960). Blind variation and selective retention in creative thought as in other knowledge processes. *Psychological Review*, *67*, 380–400. doi:10.1037/h0040373

Epstain, J. M., & Axtell, R. L. (1996). *Growing artificial societies: social science from the bottom up*. Washington, DC: Brookings Institution Press.

Giles, J. (2005). Special report: Internet encyclopaedias go head to head. *Nature*, *438*, 900–901. doi:10.1038/438900a

Heylighen, F. (1999). Collective intelligence and its implementation on the Web: Algorithms to develop a collective mental map. *Computational & Mathematical Organization Theory*, *5*(3), 253–280. doi:10.1023/A:1009690407292

Iannacci, F. (2005). *The social epistemology of open source software development: the Linux case study*. Unpublished doctoral dissertation, University of London, London.

Kroah-Hatman, G., Corbet, J., & McPherson, A. (2008). How fast it is going, who is doing it, what they are doing, and who is sponsoring it. *Report at the Linux Foundation*. Retrieved December 15, 2008, from https://www.linuxfoundation.org/publications/linuxkerneldevelopment.php

Kuwabara, K. (2000). Linux: a bazaar at the edge of chaos. *First Monday, 5*(3). Retrieved July 8, 2009, from http://firstmonday.org/htbin/cgiwrap/bin/ojs/index.php/fm/article/view/1482/1397

Lee, G. K., & Cole, R. E. (2003). From a firm-based to a community-based model of knowledge creation: The case of Linux kernel development. *Organization Science, 14*(6), 633–649. doi:10.1287/orsc.14.6.633.24866

Levy, P. (1997). *Collective intelligence: mankind's emerging world in cyberspace (R. Bononno, Tran.)*. Cambridge, MA: Perseus Books.

Luo, S., Xia, H., Yoshida, T., & Wang, Z. (2009). Toward collective intelligence of online communities: A primitive conceptual model. *Journal of Systems Science and Systems Engineering, 18*(2), 203–221. doi:10.1007/s11518-009-5095-0

Malone, T. W., & Klein, M. (2007). Harnessing collective intelligence to address global climate change. *Innovations: Technology, Governance, Globalization, 2*(3), 15–26. doi:10.1162/itgg.2007.2.3.15

Mataric, M. J. (1993). Designing emergent behaviors: From local interactions to collective intelligence. In *Proceedings of the Second International Conference on Simulation of Adaptive Behavior* (pp. 432-441). Cambridge, MA: MIT Press.

Mockus, A., Filding, R. T., & Herbsleb, J. D. (2002). Two case studies of open source software development: Apache and Mozilla. *ACM Transactions on Software Engineering and Methodology, 11*(3), 309–346. doi:10.1145/567793.567795

Nagurney, A., & Wakolbinger, T. (2005). Supernetworks: An introduction to the concept and its applications with a specific focus on knowledge supernetworks. *International Journal of Knowledge, Culture and Change Management, 4*.

Nonaka, I., & Takeuchi, H. (1995). *The knowledge creating company: How Japanese companies create the dynamics of innovation*. New York: Oxford University Press.

Preece, J., & Maloney-Krichmar, D. (2005). Online communities: Design, theory, and practice. *Journal of Computer-Mediated Communication, 10*(4). Retrieved January 13, 2010, from http://jcmc.indiana.edu/vol10/issue4/preece.html

Raymond, R. (1999). The cathedral and the bazaar. *Knowledge, Technology & Policy, 12*(3), 22–49.

Shneiderman, B. (2008). Science 2.0. *Science, 319*, 1349–1350. doi:10.1126/science.1153539

Theraulaz, G., & Bonabeau, E. (1995). Coordination in distributed building. *Science, 269*, 686–688. doi:10.1126/science.269.5224.686

Theraulaz, G., & Bonabeau, E. (1999). A brief history of stigmergy. *Artificial Life, 5*, 97–116. doi:10.1162/106454699568700

Varela, F. J., Maturana, H. R., & Uribe, R. (1974). Autopoiesis: the organization of living systems, its characterization and a model. *Bio Systems, 5*, 187–196. doi:10.1016/0303-2647(74)90031-8

Xia, H., Wang, Z., Luo, S., & Yoshida, T. (2008). Toward a concept of community intelligence: A view on knowledge sharing and fusion in Web-mediated communities. In *Proceedings of the 2008 IEEE International Conference on Systems, Man, and Cybernetics* (pp.88-93). Washington, DC: IEEE Press.

ENDNOTE

[1] e.g., IDC's report for Q1 2007 says that Linux now holds 12.7% of the overall server market, source: Linux Watch, at http://www.linux-watch.com/news/NS5369154346.html

This work was previously published in the International Journal of Knowledge and Systems Science, Volume 1, Issue 3, edited by W.B. Lee, pp. 20-32 copyright 2010 by IGI Publishing (an imprint of IGI Global).

Chapter 13
Exploration and Exploitation in Parallel Problem Solving:
Effect of Imitation Strategy and Network Structure

Hua Zhang
Xi'an Jiaotong University, China

Youmin Xi
Xi'an Jiaotong-Liverpool University, China

ABSTRACT

In previous studies on coordinating exploration-exploitation activities, much attention has been paid on network structures while the roles played by actors' strategic behavior have been largely ignored. In this paper, the authors extend March's simulation model on parallel problem solving by adding structurally equivalent imitation. In this way, one can examine how the interaction of network structure with agent behavior affects the knowledge process and finally influence group performance. This simulation experiment suggests that under the condition of regular network, the classical trade-off between exploration and exploitation will appear in the case of the preferentially attached network when agents adopt structure equivalence imitation. The whole organization implicitly would be divided into independent sub-groups that converge on different performance level and lead the organization to a lower performance level. The authors also explored the performance in the mixed organization and the management implication.

DOI: 10.4018/978-1-4666-1782-7.ch013

INTRODUCTION

Since March's classical research, the terms "exploration" and "exploitation" have increasingly come to dominate organizational studies of organization design, organizational adaptation, organizational learning, competitive and so on (Gupta et al., 2006). The central thesis of James March's "Exploration and Exploitation in Organizational Learning" is that "maintaining an appropriate balance between exploration and exploitation is a primary factor in system survival and prosperity" (March, 1991). While the importance of pursuing both exploration and exploitation has been highlighted, much more remains to be understood about how organization coordinates the development of exploratory and exploitative activities (Jansen et al., 2006; He & Wong, 2004).

In this direction, prior researchers have paid much attention on the network structure variables. As in March' paper, the advice network among organization members is implicitly assumed to be a hub-like structure which is represented by the organization code. March use organization code to control the relative rates of exploration and exploitation (March, 1991). Miller et al. (2006) extended March's model by adding an interpersonal learning which replaces the mediation of an organizational code, and in their extending model fixed grid is represented as the interpersonal communication structure (Miller et al., 2006). David decentralized the organization code and extended the hub and fixed grid network structure to more general case under the context of the parallel problem solving (Lazer & Friedman, 2007). Four archetypical networks including linear network, totally connected network, random networks, and smallworld networks are examined in their simulations experiment. Besides simulation studies much empirical research has also been devoted on the research of network structure: Jansen et al examined how formal and informal organizational structure coordinates the development of exploratory and exploitative innovation in

organizational unites (Jansen et al., 2006); Mason et al. (2008) examined how different network structures affect the propagation of information in laboratory-created groups. Different types of networks were compared on speed of discovery and convergence on the optimal solution in Mason's research (Mason et al., 2008).

All the former research came to the very similar conclusion in terms of the relationship between network and organization performance. That is, dense network would drive out the personal heterogeneity, which results in lower long-run performance but higher short-run performance; sparse network, in contrast, keeps the personal heterogeneity, which leads to lower short-run performance but higher long-run performance. These studies suggest that there is an invert-U relationship between network density and organization performance.

The studies mentioned above have employed the traditional 'structuralist' perspective which advocates that the types of resources that can be acquired from a network depend on the structure of network relations (Adler & Kwon, 2002). According to the different definition on social capital, there is still controversy over the optimal structure of that over the relative benefits of brokerage network and cohesive network structure. The former refers to a particular network which occupies the sole intermediate position between others who are disconnected and can interact only through the broker; the latter refers to the situation in which all the members are connected each other. Proponents of brokerage argue for the benefits of unique information which is the valuable resource of innovation; proponents of cohesive network argue for the benefits of efficient information diffusion and normal trust which promotes co-operation (Coleman, 1988; Burt, 2004).

Research on this social capital debate has often focused on these two types of network affects without considering the network content. Next to structure, the network literature has recently showed increased attention for the influence of the content conveyed through ties on resource acquisition (Rodan et al., 2004; Fleming et al., 2007) and the individual's strategic orientation (Obstfeld, 2005). Tracing the development of organization study literature we can see that scholars have developed midrange theories of how organizational learning behavior impacts organizational performance (Argote et al., 1990; Epple et al., 1996). However, to date the bulk of this research has focused on declarative (know-what) or procedural (know-how) knowledge with little attention paid on organizational performance as a function of actor's knowledge about partner selections (know-who).

Drawing on the discussion above we propose that prior studies highly illuminate the passive role of network in adjusting the knowledge process in organization but neglect the active role that individual can play in keeping individual heterogeneity and linking to the different others. Without considering network content variables some plausible conclusions deduced from the above studies would be argued: dose diversity can always lead to a high performance level? How the interaction of network structure with agent behavior affects group performance? To address these questions and extend what has been, until now, peripheral attention to actor's behavior strategy in exploration-exploitation literature. This paper focuses on the individual's know-who knowledge, beginning with the assumption that advice network structure is a factor but not the only factor accounting for knowledge process. We contribute to a greater clarity and better understanding of how agent's partner selection affects the knowledge process and finally lead to different performance level. By considering the agent's know-who knowledge we can also explore how the interaction of network with agent behavior affects the group performance.

The organization of this paper is as follows. The related work on agent behavior in exploration-exploitation research is discussed. After proposing a formal model which describes the detailed

simulation model of the organization processes, we introduce the model and the design of the computational experiment. The intensive experimental results are discussed and the management implications are given.

LITERATURE REVIEW AND CONCEPT MODEL

The Trade-Off on Network Structure

Inherent to the social capital debate is a paradoxical trade-off between cohesive networks promoting cooperation and information diffusion efficiency and sparse networks flexible to heterogeneous knowledge and ideas. Since we cannot simultaneously maximize both facets of a network, this reflects a sharp trade-off between information diffusion and diversity in an efficient network (Figure 1).

In recent years the role of network content and its interaction effect with network structure has emerged as an important area of inquiry in our understanding of innovation and group performance. It is well recognized that network content variable including the attribute of actors and actors' behavior pattern complement network structure to promote creativity and innovation on the one hand and cooperation and coordination on the other. According to their surrey research, Rodan (2004) proposed that, while network structure matters, access to heterogeneous knowledge is of equal importance for overall managerial performance and of greater importance for innovation performance. Developing a social definition of creative success and tracing the development of creative ideas, Fleming propose that interaction of structure with the personal attributes affects the brokerage on generating the initial insight and future idea development (Fleming et al., 2007). Obstfeld introduced tertius iungens strategic orientation and propose that this orientation with dense social networks and diverse social

Figure 1. The trade-off between information diffusion and diversity in an efficient network (Source: Lazer, David; Friedman, Allan. Administrative Science Quarterly. 2007)

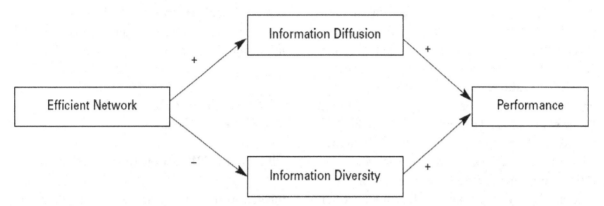

knowledge predict individual involvement in innovation (Obstfeld, 2005).

While prior work has demonstrated a relationship between network structure and group performance, inadequate attention has been paid to network content (Rodan et al., 2004). Our study draws on both structural and content perspectives in examining the way network structure affects knowledge process which contributes to group performance. Particularly, we focus on actor's partner selection. Contrasting to the 'know how' and 'know what' knowledge, 'know who' reflects another emergent important kind of knowledge in organization learning (Borgatti & Cross, 2003). By considering the agent's partner selection behavior in inquiring information in their advice network, we can examine how the interaction of network structure with agent behavior affects knowledge process (Figure 2).

AGENT BEHAVIOR IN EXPLORATION-EXPLOITATION RESEARCH

March and Miller's work only focused on agent learning rate (March, 1991; Miller et al., 2006). They suggested that learning too fast from either the organizational code or other actors can re-

duce knowledge diversity, which leads to lower knowledge levels in equilibrium. Their simulation experiment shows that slow learning by the individual members would produce the highest long-run performance. Actually they implicitly assumed that individual members are capable of searching for the best solutions given enough time. This assumption hardly corresponds with researcher's general understanding of individual creativity (Barron, 1981). We can hardly believe organization members would succeed in searching for the best solution without any help from others (Perry, 2006). This defect of agent behavior design is partially resolved in Lazer.D's model on parallel problem solving.

As a basic model of agent interaction on parallel problem solving, Lazer.D takes actor's myopia into consideration and based on which author design the behavior rule. To reflect myopia agent could only evaluate the solutions of those agents who are directly connected and totally copy the solution of the most successful neighbor (Lazer & Friedman, 2007). We argue that this imitation design is somewhat inadequate and neglects the consideration of agent's active selection when facing the heterogeneous solutions. There are many defects in this imitation design. For example, it is still in doubt that agents have enough cognitive capability to digest the new solution which may

Figure 2. Concept model: how partner selection influence the relationship between network structure and knowledge process

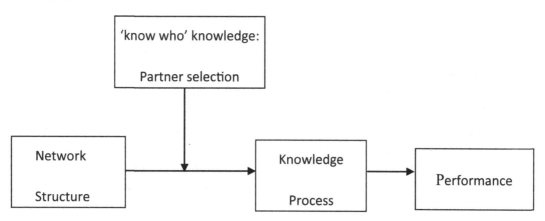

deviate greatly from their status quo solution. Furthermore, agents will explore new solutions based on current one, and the fact that the candidate solution is superior does not mean this candidate solution will outperform others all the time. The existing sunk-cost compels agents to think over before making the decision on whether to give up current solution to follow the temporarily better one or not.

Previous simulation research on agents' communication design mainly focuses on agents' neighbors (Nobuyuki et al., 2007; David & Friedman, 2007; Chang & Harrington, 2007). That is, agents could only communicate with those who are directly connected with them. Although this nearby imitation pattern reflects agent's some kind of myopia, this design can bring to some plausible conclusions. For instance, in Lazer's study, when agents only consider emulating their direct neighbors, regardless of what the network structure is, network density became the main factor affecting knowledge distribution. Network topological structure is supposed to play an important role in information diffusion (Cowan, 2004). We argue that different network structures would have different influence on coordinating exploration and exploitation although they may have the same density. Lazer.D also indicated that some differ-

ent assumptions on emulate process could have significant effects on organization performance (David & Friedman, 2007).

Following the preceding discussion on the potential risks of ignoring actor's other imitation behavior, rather than assuming agent emulating the directly connected neighbors, we assume that agents will keep their eyes on those who are structurally equivalent. Loosely speaking, structural equivalence refers to the extent to which two nodes are connected to the same others. The fact that two agents are structurally equivalent indicates that they may have the same social status, same role or they are even completely substitutable. Based on the similarity theory, agents are more likely to do the same thing as those who are similar to themselves. Structural equivalence also grasps agent's myopia perfectly. Because myopia agents are unable to directly evaluate all the potential solutions in the whole organization, besides emulating the directly connected people, imitation pattern of structurally equivalent is another heuristic partner selection rule when an agent faces complexity problem. Based on the discussion above, it is reasonable to assume that structurally equivalent people are the favorite target of imitation.

PARALLEL PROBLEM SOLVING

The concept of parallel problem solving was first proposed in Lazer's study, which portrays a context where all the agents are engaged in the same problem solving and the success of any one or subset of agents has no direct effect on other agents (David & Friedman, 2007). There are many phenomena belonging to parallel problem solving, as Lazer. D proposed, such as professor or doctors dealing with the similar professional problems, state governments formulating public policy and most knowledge-intensive research or development activities of NPD. There are two distinct characteristics in parallel problem solving. Firstly, problem space may vary in different levels of complexity. For a simple problem, there may be a few or even only one best solution, but for a complex problem there may be many plausible solutions and it is difficult to search for the best one. Secondly, agents can learn from each other about how their solutions work and each agent's performance is independent of the others. Each individual engaging in parallel problem solving can improve his performance by either innovate himself or emulate others. On the one hand, the network structure linking those individuals will determine who has access to what kind of information; on the other hand, agents do have access to active strategy to determine whether to emulate.

In conclusion, we extended March's model by adding agent's imitation strategies: know-who knowledge which focuses on whom did the agent emulate. In this paper we assume that imitation happens among those who are approximately structurally equivalent. We will explore how the interaction of network structure with this imitation strategy affects the organization performance under the context of parallel problem solving.

THE MODEL

As the previous studies, we view organization as a complex adaptive system, where individuals interact with each others. In March's model (1991) individuals learn from a "organization code" which represent the socialization process. In this way individuals are not allowed to interact with other individuals directly. In our work, however, we build on recent work by Miller et al. (2006) and model the agents' interaction happening in an advice network. Besides, we also model the agents' know-who knowledge which determines the partner selection process in interpersonal learning which makes our paper distinct from the seminal model of March's work. Our model has three main entities—an environment, the individuals, and an organization:

Environment

Like March (1991) and other seminal works, we describe the environment the agents face to as having m dimensions, each of which has a value of 1 or −1. The probability that any one dimension is randomly assigned, that is 0.5.

Individuals

There are n individuals in an organization. We regard the individuals as the carrier of knowledge, beliefs and practice. The value of the knowledge represents the beliefs agent hold against the environment. Each belief for an individual has a value of 1, 0, or −1. A value of 0 means that an individual is not sure about what the environment really is.

Organization

As mentioned above, we view organization as a complex adaptive system, where individuals interact with each other directly from the advice network rather from the organization codes. This assumption is carried out by model the agents'

Figure 3. Preferentially attached network and regular network

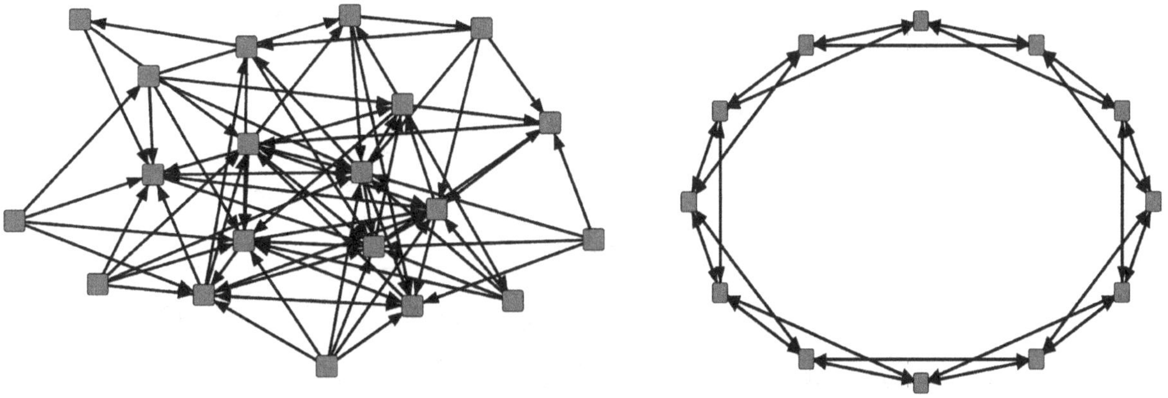

advice network which will be introduced in the next section.

AGENTS' DECISION PROCESS AND BEHAVIOR RULES

Similar to March's (1991) original work, individuals can observe the payoff of their overall belief set. They can also observe the payoff of their partners who are directly connected with them. The chosen partners are determined by know-who knowledge agents hold. If individuals ascertain that others have belief sets outperforming theirs, they may update their own beliefs to copy the higher-performing belief sets. Though individuals may be able to ascertain whether other individuals have belief sets that outperform their own, but the possibility of successful imitation is not 100 percent. This possibility reflects two practical implications: on the one hand it reflects the agent's preference of exploitation over exploration– bigger possibility means agents are more likely to adopt others' solution and smaller value means agents prefer to keep their own heterogeneity; on the other hand, this also reflects agent's learning ability: agents may not catch a potential belief set which deviates greatly from their current one. To address this, we model the possibility of successful copy is 0.5.

Network Structure

Our imitation pattern is based on the structural equivalence distinguished by degree distribution. In this case, not only network density but network structure will affect differently on system-level performance. Imagine that, asymmetry network and a regular network will exert significantly different influence on system-level performance even though they have the same density. Asymmetry in degree distribution refers to networks in which "a few highly connected nodes linking the rest of the less connected nodes to the system" (Jeong et al., 2000). To explore the influence of structural equivalence imitation pattern on performance, we employed an asymmetry network and a regular network. The former is represented by a scale-free network and the other is a fixed grid to represent the advice network, each with the constant number of out-agree and in-agree (Figure 3).

Partners Selection Rules

We assume that an agent is myopic, unable to detect the best solution in group. Agents cannot see the performance level of other agents in organization;

Table 1. Summary of model parameters

Parameter type	Name	Definition	Values
Environment	m	Num of dimensions	30
	v	Value of dimensions	1, -1
Organization	n	Num of organization people	50
	LA	Regular network	None
	PA	Preferal attach network	None
Individuals	b	Value of beliefs	1, -1, 0
	P	Learning ability	0.5
	SQ	Emulate the structurally equivalent peers	None
	NB	Emulate the connected neighbors	None

furthermore, agents don't have much incentive to public their solutions either. To improve their performance and explore at a higher level in the future agents have to interact with other agents and mimic the most successful one among the available candidates.

Besides the most adopted agent's communication pattern ---near neighbor selection, we introduce another heuristic partner selection rule: structurally equivalent selection. In our model, agents tend to emulate those who are structurally equivalent with them. The two agents are supposed to be exactly structurally equivalent if they have the same relationship to all other agents (Wasserman & Faust, 1994). Pure Structural equivalence can be quite rare in social relations but approximations to it may not be so rare. In network structure analysis researchers are often interested in examining the degree of structural equivalence. There are many ways in which agents could be defined as approximate structural equivalence. And some algorithms have been particularly useful in applying graph theory to define the structural equivalence, such as "Euclidean Distance", "Correlation" (Wasserman & Faust, 1994). Actually there are indeed a very large number of the algorithms we can classify group sets of agents into categories based on some commonality in their positions in network. For the sake of simplicity, we here only consider a relaxed criterion: agents will fall into

the same class if they have the same out-degree and in-degree. This criterion relaxes the conditions of the same agents actor connects to/with. Rather than connecting to the same agents, only the sum of degrees represents for structural equivalence.

Computational Experiment Design

The simulation experiment is conducted under the following conditions: we consider a organization of 50 agents. All the organization members are engaged in solving a problem including 30 dimensions. The initial beliefs set agents hold are randomly generated, and those 50 agents are randomly placed in their communication networks. Two network types and two imitation strategies mentioned above are summarized in Table 1 with the concrete network parameters.

We compared the performance over time of each of the communication networks summarized above and explored how the actor's imitation strategy varied with the network structure to determine group performance. The definitions of the parameters introduced in this section are provided in Table 1. The values of these parameters used in the computational experiments are also given in Table 1. The model was programmed in the Matlab7.0 language and the Matlab picture software toolkit. We let the each simulation run for 50 units of time, which we take to be repre-

Figure 4. The organization performance change under the condition of NB learning and SQ learning (LA network)

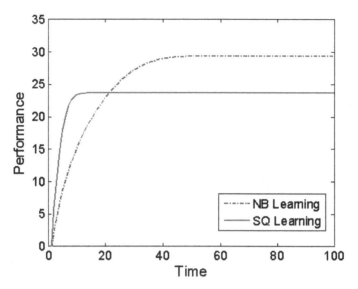

sentative of the organization's long-run state. All the results presented in this paper are averages based upon 100 runs of each simulation model. Equilibrium occurred when organization converged on a fixed performance levels and all the agents plunged into their optimal point.

RESULTS

Performance under the Regular Network

Our first concern is to examine the effect of know-who knowledge on organization performance. As mentioned above, when agents adopt the strategy of learning from their directly connected neighbors we label this know-who knowledge "NB Learning"; similarly, when agents adopt the strategy of learning from their structurally equivalent peers we label this know-who knowledge "SQ Learning". We specify agents' communication pattern is regular network, and under this condition we examine how these different learning types affect the organization performance. Figure 4 displays

the performance of organization as a function of increasing time under these two different learning types. And we can see the classical trade-off between exploitation and exploration: agents who adopt the "SQ learning" know-who knowledge outperform the "NB Learning" agents in the short run, but in the long run, the "NB Learning" agents perform better.

Why the performance contrail evolves in a very different way when agents face to the same advice network? There is our interpretation: according to our definition of the structural equivalence, all the agents are structurally equivalent. This means that all the agents in organization will be the potential candidates for the imitator, while only the directly connected neighbors (4 in this experiment) are the potential candidates for the imitator when agents hold the NB learning. In this situation SQ learning plays the very similar role like the dense network in previous work (Sze-Sze, 2008; Lazer & Friedman, 2007). SQ learning would drive out the personal heterogeneity, which results in lower long-run performance but higher short-run performance; NB learning, in contrast, keeps the personal heterogeneity,

Figure 5. The organization performance change under the condition of NB learning and SQ learning (PA network)

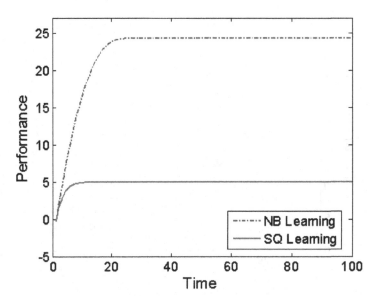

which leads to lower short-run performance but higher long-run performance. In a word, when organization adopt a regular network as the advice network among agents, SQ learning leads to organization knowledge overlap quickly but NB learning keeps organization knowledge diversity.

Performance under the Preferentially Attached Network

Figure 5 illustrates the effect of NB learning and SQ learning on the equilibrium performance level when the topological structure of advice network turn out to be a PA network. As shown in Figure 5 SQ learning quickly finds a good solution but NB learning outperforms all the time. This result can be explained by their substantively different communication.

All the agents are the structural equivalent in LA network while in PA network agents belong to a few structural sub-groups because of the structurally equivalent partner selection. That is, PA network is no longer a single-component network when agents adopt SQ learning but NB

learning still keeps the whole network connected. SQ learning brings both positive and negative effect on performance: on the one hand, agents only search the best solutions in the sub-group they belong to, the existence of sub-group keeps the information diversity from the whole organization's angle; on the other hand, there is no communication among agents belonging to different sub-group. Sub-groups in PA network are independent with each other. This structural obstacle cut off the information diffusion, which is negatively related to performance.

When agent chooses those who are structurally equivalent to emulate, the whole organization is partitioned to several independent sub-groups and agents belonging to different sub-groups have no opportunity to communicate each other at all. Just like the local search good solutions only spread in a close circle and can not diffuse over the whole organization. Structure equivalence keeps the diversity from the system-level angle at the mean time builds the bastions which stops good solutions diffusion. In this case, each sub-group will converge on different performance level.

Although these sub-groups keep diversity from the whole organization angle lack of communication among different structurally equivalent sub-group leads to a lower performance level the whole organization achieved. This explains why SQ learning achieves a very quick performance level but finally converge at a lower level than NB learning.

Performance in a Mixed Organization

Based on our earlier findings, we would expect that introducing NB learners into an organization of SQ learners would improve the performance achieved and shorten the convergent time. This proves to be the case; however, the former relation is linear but the later relation is nonlinear. As shown in Figure 6(a), the proportion of NB learners positively affects the final performance. And LA network outperforms PA network all the time because of the structural obstacle discussed above.

Figure 6(b) shows the different contrail of equilibrium time. When agents interact with each other by LA network, the proportion of NB learners positively affects the convergent time. But the situation in PA network is dramatically different. When SQ learners are in the minority, their "NB learning" colleagues drag down their convergent time. However, for combinations involving a majority of NB learners, the resulting time decreases. This inverse-U relation between proportion of NB learner and convergent time can be explained as follows. When the combinations involve a majority of NB learners or SQ learners, the whole organization is similar to a single-component network or some divided sub-groups. Both of which is easy to achieve the equilibrium state. However, when neither learns became the majority, the whole organization became a semi-small world structure, which includes some divided sub-group and there is some NB learner holds the bridge position. In this case it takes time to spread knowledge in and among the circle, which leads to a longer convergent time. Unfor-

tunately the existence of structural obstacle hinders this combination from achieving the highest performance.

CONCLUSION

According to the debate on the trade-off of information diffusion and diversity in a network, we add partner selection to the March's simulation model to examine how the individual's know-who knowledge affects knowledge process and finally influence group performance.

Given the current limited understanding of the relationship between actor's behavior and organization performance, and in the face of limited empirical data, the modeling undertaken here indicates that both advice network and individual know-who knowledge can affect organization performance by adjusting knowledge diffusion and diversity. Furthermore, we introduce another heuristic partner selection rule when agents face the complexity problem. Our simulation experiment suggests that imitation pattern determines the direction of knowledge flow. When agents try to emulate the directly connected people, a better solution can spread over the whole organization; but when agents see the structurally equivalent people as the learning resource, the whole organization will be divided into independent sub-groups which converge on different performance level.

We contribute to a greater clarity and better understanding of how advice network affects the system-level performance. Agents' selective imitation will keep knowledge diversity at individual level. Previous studies assuming that agents emulate the directly connected people get to the conclusion that network density attributes to the final organization performance regardless of what topological structure of advice network is. In our study we assume there is another heuristic partner selection rule which agents choose to emulate their structurally equivalent peer, under the condition that this agent imitation strategy

Figure 6. The organization performance in a mixed organization

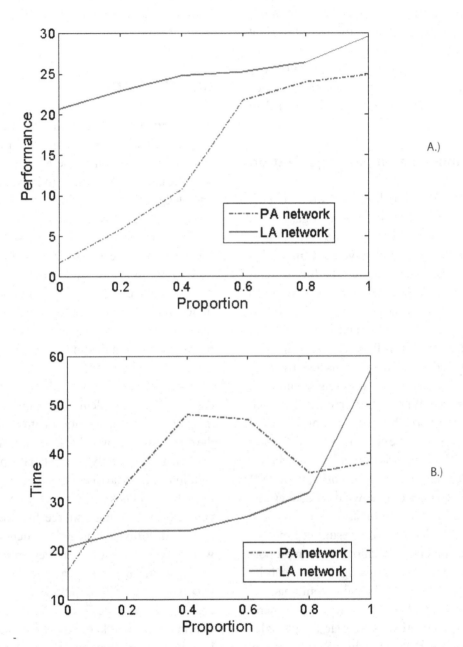

network topological structure (even with the same density) plays a significant role in knowledge flow and finally influences the convergent performance level. Agent's imitation pattern determines the direction of knowledge flow. When agents adopt the structurally equivalent imitation, the whole organization is no longer a single-component network but can be seen as many independent sub-groups. No communication happens among different sub-groups which lead to the different performance level they achieved. The influence

Figure 7. The trade-off between information diffusion and diversity in the interaction of network with agent imitation behavior

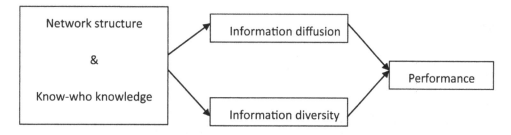

of interaction of network with agent behavior on organization performance is depicted in Figure 7.

Our simulation study has much management implication for NPD and R&D institution. In the situation of such an organization where all the engineers are solving the same complex problem which may have many plausible solutions, the challenge confronting to the manager is how to structure the advice network and induct engineers' behavior to achieve a high performance level both in the short-run and long-run, which means organization has to keep the balance between exploitation and exploration all the time.

Particularly, network configuration can be seen as the formal organization arrangement — the rigid institution, while agent's imitation decision reflects the result of organization's "soft control" – the influence of the organization culture or value on the organization members. We can picture how to employ these two rules in organization's different running stages. This circle arrangement can maintain the dynamic balance between exploration and exploitation in organization theoretically. Our simulation experiment suggests that both network configuration and actor behavior can be employed to achieve this goal. Notice that when granting more freedom to organization members they may actually choose to emulate their structurally equivalent peers. Over time, people may lock in to a limited set of people with whom they are familiar with and frequently interact, which might be efficient but yield suboptimal solution if other people are better sources, especially when

the sub-group is small, which has been proved by our experiment. Give the importance of people as critical sources of knowledge; our study indicates the needs to avoid people's structurally equivalent imitation and other path dependence actions.

In this paper, we have considered only a very simple rule to judge the structural equivalence----the sum of the in-degree and out-degree, and our design of imitation extent is equally simplistic; thus, many obvious extensions are easily conceivable. Furthermore, we didn't consider the co-evolution of actor behavior and network structure which will appear to have new and deep consequences for collective outcomes. This dynamic organization process would end up with finding a perfect institution and it is worthy of further development.

REFERENCES

Adler, P. S., & Kwon, S. W. (2002). Social capital: Prospects for a new concept. *Academy of Management Review*, *27*(1), 17–40. doi:10.2307/4134367

Argote, L., Beckman, S. L., & Epple, D. (1990). The persistence and transfer of learning in industrial settings. *Management Science*, *36*(2), 140–154. doi:10.1287/mnsc.36.2.140

Barron, F., & Harrington, D. M. (1981). Creativity, Intelligence, and Personality. *Annual Review of Psychology*, *32*(1), 439–476. doi:10.1146/annurev.ps.32.020181.002255

Borgatti, S. P., & Cross, R. (2003). A relational view of information seeking and learning in social networks. *Management Science*, *49*(4), 432–445. doi:10.1287/mnsc.49.4.432.14428

Burt, R. S. (2004). Structural Holes and Good Ideas. *American Journal of Sociology*, *110*(2), 349–399. doi:10.1086/421787

Chang, M. H., & Harrington, J. J. (2007). Innovators, imitators, and the evolving architecture of problem-solving networks. *Organization Science*, *18*(4), 648–666. doi:10.1287/orsc.1060.0245

Coleman, J. S. (1988). Social capital in the creation of human capital. *American Journal of Sociology*, *94*(S1), 95–120. doi:10.1086/228943

Cowan, R., & Jonard, N. (2004). Network structure and the diffusion of knowledge. *Journal of Economic Dynamics & Control*, *28*(8), 1557–1575. doi:10.1016/j.jedc.2003.04.002

Epple, D., Argote, L., & Murphy, K. (1996). An empirical investigation of the microstructure of knowledge acquisition and transfer through learning by doing. *Operations Research*, *44*(1), 77–86. doi:10.1287/opre.44.1.77

Fleming, L., & Mingo, S. (2007). Collaborative Brokerage, Generative Creativity, and Creative Success. *Administrative Science Quarterly*, *52*(3), 443–475.

Gupta, A. K., & Smith, K. E. (2006). The Interplay between Exploration and Exploitation. *Academy of Management Journal*, *49*(4), 693–706.

Hanaki, N., & Peterhansl, A. (2007). Cooperation in evolving social networks. *Management Science*, *53*(7), 1036–1050. doi:10.1287/mnsc.1060.0625

He, Z. L., & Wong, P. K. (2004). Exploration vs. exploitation: An empirical test of the ambidexterity hypothesis. *Organization Science*, *15*(4), 481–494. doi:10.1287/orsc.1040.0078

Jansen, J. J., & den Van, B. (2006). Exploratory Innovation, Exploitative Innovation, and Performance: Effects of Organizational Antecedents and Environmental Moderators. *Management Science*, *52*(11), 1661–1674. doi:10.1287/mnsc.1060.0576

Jeong, H., Tombor, B., & Albert, R. (2000). The large-scale organization of metabolic networks. *Nature*, *407*(6804), 651–654. doi:10.1038/35036627

Lazer, D., & Friedman, A. (2007). The Network Structure of Exploration and Exploitation. *Administrative Science Quarterly*, *52*(4), 667–694. doi:10.2189/asqu.52.4.667

March, J. G. (1991). Exploration and Exploitation in Organizational Learning. *Organization Science*, *2*(1), 71–87. doi:10.1287/orsc.2.1.71

Mason, W. A., & Jones, A. (2008). Propagation of innovations in networked groups. *Journal of Experimental Psychology. General*, *137*(3), 422–433. doi:10.1037/a0012798

Miller, K. D., & Zhao, M. (2006). Adding interpersonal learning and tacit knowledge to March's exploration-exploitation model. *Academy of Management Journal*, *49*(4), 709–722.

Obstfeld, D. (2005). Social Networks, the Tertius Iungens Orientation, and Involvement in Innovation. *Administrative Science Quarterly*, *50*(1), 100–130.

Perry-Smith, J. E. (2006). Social Yet Creative: The Role Of Social Relationships In Facilitating Individual Creativity. *Academy of Management Journal*, *49*(1), 85–101.

Rodan, S., & Galunic, D. C. (2004). More than network structure: how knowledge heterogeneity influences managerial performance and innovativeness. *Strategic Management Journal*, *25*, 541–556. doi:10.1002/smj.398

Sze-Sze, W. (2008). Task knowledge overlap and knowledge variety: the role of advice network structures and impact on group effectiveness. *Journal of Organizational Behavior, 29*(5), 591–614. doi:10.1002/job.490

Wasserman, S., & Faust, K. (1994). *Social network analysis: Methods and applications.* Cambridge, UK: Cambridge University Press.

This work was previously published in the International Journal of Knowledge and Systems Science, Volume 1, Issue 3, edited by W.B. Lee, pp. 55-67 copyright 2010 by IGI Publishing (an imprint of IGI Global).

Chapter 14
Exploring the Enterprise Value of Wikis through Media Choice Theories

Christian Wagner
City University of Hong Kong, China

Andreas Schroeder
Open University, UK

Wing Yan Wong
City University of Hong Kong, China

Anna Shum
City University of Hong Kong, China

ABSTRACT

Wikis are quickly emerging as a new corporate medium for communication and collaboration. They allow dispersed groups of collaborators to asynchronously engage in persistent conversations, the result of which is stored on a common server as a single, shared truth. To gauge the enterprise value of wikis, the authors draw on Media Choice Theories (MCTs) as an evaluation framework. MCTs reveal core capabilities of communication media and their fit with the communication task. Based on the evaluation, the authors argue that wikis are equivalent or superior to existing asynchronous communication media in key characteristics. Additionally argued is the notion that wiki technology challenges some of the held beliefs of existing media choice theories, as wikis introduce media characteristics not previously envisioned. The authors thus predict a promising future for wiki use in enterprises.

DOI: 10.4018/978-1-4666-1782-7.ch014

1. INTRODUCTION

A report by Gartner Group forecasted that by 2009, half of Fortune 500 firms would have adopted wiki technology (Atlassian, 2008). This prediction suggests a strong belief in the impact and desirability of the technology. Several proponents of wiki technology expect that wikis will become the internal communication media of choice for organizations and effectively replace email. Corporate examples such as Google's "Goowiki" intranet demonstrate the conviction held by some companies to replace traditional technologies with a wiki's open communication platform (Goowiki, 2008). Yet, what justifies these strong beliefs in wiki technology as a tool for communication and collaboration? This article attempts to answer this question by applying the lens of media choice theories.

Based on the empirical evidence provided by 43 published case studies and the defining characteristics of three media choice theories, the results show that wikis meet and even exceed capabilities of several other communication media. Our finding not only proves that Wiki technology is a highly credible replacement for email as the most popular business communication technology in use, but also assist us in broadening existing media choice theories.

2. WIKIS IN THE ENTERPRISE

Wiki technology and the principles of wiki-based collaboration have gained popularity through online encyclopedias such as Wikipedia (Wagner, 2006). However, in its original conceptualization wiki technology was not developed for the purpose of a public internet-based encyclopedia but as an internal collaboration platform. Ward Cunningham originally developed the c2 wiki, also known as "Ward's Wiki" (Wiki, 2009) to support the effort of his project team to maintain version control in a software development proj-

ect. The underlying principle was to create "the simplest database that might just work" (Leuf & Cunningham, 2001 p. 15). The c2 wiki quickly developed into an open knowledge sharing and collaboration environment. The use of wiki as an encyclopedia (Wikipedia, 2009) arose only several years later in 2000, when Nupedia creators Larry Sanger and Jimmy Wales were looking for a collaboration technology to overcome their stalling initiative to create a free, online encyclopedia (Timothy, 2005). As of 2009, Wikipedia is the world's largest encyclopedia, with over 2.9 Million entries in the English version alone. Wikipedia is also the 8th most popular Internet site, according to Alexa.com.

The design of wiki technology is based on eleven principles (Wagner, 2004). Among the most distinctive of these principles is openness which specifies that "any reader can edit [content] as he/she sees fit" (Wagner, 2004, p. 270). Based on this design principle wiki users can refactor (Fowler, 1999) content which has previously been posted and hereby modify, extend or adjust its meaning. The refactoring capability of wikis allows for a new form of collaboration. Instead of passively reading content which has previously been posted on the wiki, users actively edit content. The 'wiki way' of collaboration (Leuf and Cunningham, 2001) is characterized by users jointly editing content and thereby integrating their particular knowledge or perspectives. An example of wiki based collaboration is provided by Foremski (2005) who describes an effort at IBM corporation to promote corporate blogging through the creation of clear guidelines. Instead of developing the guidelines by corporate lawyers or other small expert groups, IBM asked its employees to participate in the guideline development for a period of 14 days, using a shared wiki. In the collaborative editing process users built up on each others' work which continuously improved the quality of the content. The resulting content represented a consensus of the individuals involved in the creation process, which is now used by IBM.

Wikis and the wiki way of working have been implemented in a range of organizational functions as shown in a recent survey by Majchrzak et al. (2006). Consistent with its initial development objective, wikis are often used in areas of software development where they are used for technical communication, issue tracking and internal workflow. However, further organizational functions have also been found to use wikis for ad-hoc collaboration, exchanging ideas and brainstorming. Other areas of application include general information and knowledge management, such as vacation schedules, personal blogs as well as repository for policies and guidelines. These functions highlight the inherent flexibility and adaptability of wikis.

Although numerous case studies attest to the enterprise value of wikis, there have been few formal evaluations, and to the authors' best knowledge none that considers the technology's capabilities and corresponding task fit. Enterprise wikis differ from open wikis such as Wikipedia or Wikitravel, based on their usually smaller user numbers, access restrictions, non-anonymity, and higher participation rates (Majchrzak et al., 2006). Hence, evaluating wikis with consideration of these unique factors is important. Thus, the purpose of this article is to take on this task, by evaluating wikis in the enterprise through the lens of media choice theories.

3. THEORIES OF MEDIA CHOICE

Media choice theories focus on two aspects: identifying and comparing communication media with regards to their core capabilities, and explaining the dynamic relationship between communication media and the communication task. Theories of media choice such as Media Richness Theory, Media Choice Theory and Common Ground Theory have established a catalogue of media capabilities to systematically characterize different media devices. These theories and their

method of characterizing communication media are subsequently reviewed.

Media Richness Theory

Media richness theory (MRT) has originally been introduced into the IS domain by Daft and Lengel (1986) to explain media choices of managers in an organizational context. MRT focuses on two core premises (Dennis, 1999). Communication media differ in richness (the ability to change the understanding of information) and performance improves when managers match the richness of the media to the communication task. Building on social presence theory (Short, 1976). MRT argues that richer media create higher social presence which facilitates understanding between the individuals involved in the communication process. Depending on the characteristics of the information processing task different levels of media richness are required.

Following this theoretical proposition MRT categorizes communication media with respect to their inherent richness (Daft & Lengel, 1986). Four media capabilities are used to determine the richness of communication media: multiplicity of cues, immediacy of feedback, language variety and personal focus. Multiplicity of cues describes the number of ways information can be communicated through the medium (e.g., text, voice, physical gestures). Immediacy of feedback describes the extent to which a medium facilitates rapid responses. Language variety refers to the ability of the medium to convey natural language (instead of only numeric information). The personal focus captures if a medium supports the personalization of messages. Table 1 indicates how different communication and collaboration media are categorized based on the MRT framework. As an example, email is classified as a relatively lean communication medium due to the low immediacy of feedback and low multiplicity of communication cues.

Table 1. Media assessment based on Media Richness Theory

Medium	Immediacy of feedback	Multiplicity of cues	Language variety	Personal focus
Face-to-face	High	High	High	High
Video conference	Med-High	Medium	Low	Medium
Telephone conference	High	Medium	Low	Medium
Synchronous instant messaging	Med-High	Low-Med	Low	Med-High
Synchronous electronic conferencing	Med-High	Low-Med	Low-Med	Medium
Asynchronous bulletin board	Low	Low-Med	Low-Med	Low
E-mail	Low	Low	Low	Medium
Written mail	Low	Low-Med	Low	Medium

Theory of Media Synchronicity

The theory of media synchronicity (TMS) provides a different perspective on media choice by focusing on the ability of media to synchronize communication and collaboration processes in groups (Dennis, 1999). In its core premise TMS argues that "the ability of a medium to change understanding within a time interval - is linked not only to its social factors but also to its information processing capabilities" (p. 49). TMS extends the range of media capabilities provided by MRT and also extends the notion of the information processing task. While MRT focuses on the relationship between media capabilities and characteristics of the information processing task, TMS focuses on the connection between media capabilities and the underlying communication processes required. Communication processes are characterized as conveyance (an exchange of information) or convergence (the development of shared meaning).

TMS categorizes communication media with regards to three information processing capabilities (parallelism, rehearsability, reprocessability) and two social capabilities (immediacy of feedback and symbol variety) (Dennis, 1999, p. 49) parallelism describes the number of simultaneous communication processes that can co-exist effectively; rehearsability refers to the ability to

refine messages before sending; reprocessability focuses on the ability to re-exam information after the communication event; immediacy of feedback follows its MRT based equivalent and symbol variety subsumes the multiplicity of cues and language variety of MRT.

For most task environments[1] the convergence process is best supported by a communication medium which provides low feedback and high parallelism to allow group members to autonomously obtain information and independently focus on the deliberation of its meaning. Email provides such capabilities as indicated in Table 2. The conveyance process is best supported by communication media which provide high immediacy of feedback and low parallelism to allow group members to synchronize their interaction and to integrate their deliberation process. Face-to-face interactions provide such a combination of capabilities.

Common Ground Theory

Common ground theory (CGT) (Clark & Brennan, 1991) introduces a different perspective in investigating communication. It focuses on the use of communication media in the presence or absence of common ground between communication partners. Common ground is established through shared experiences and knowledge but

Table 2. Media assessment based on Theory of Media Synchronicity

Medium	Immediacy of feedback	Symbol variety	Parallelism	Rehearsability	Reprocessability
Face-to-face	High	High	Low	Low	Low
Video conference	Med-High	Medium	Low	Low	Low
Telephone conference	High	Medium	Low	Low	Low
Synchronous instant messaging	Med-High	Low-Med	Low-Med	Medium	Med-High
Synchronous electronic conferencing	Med-High	Low-Med	Low-Med	Low-Med	Medium
Asynchronous bulletin board	Low	Low-Med	High	High	High
E-mail	Low	Low	High	High	High
Written mail	Low	Low-Med	High	High	High

also as an interactive process during the communication event. In this respect grounding can be compared to convergence – the development of shared meaning. While MRT and TMS focus on the alliance between media capabilities and information processing task or communication process, CGT places emphasis on the common ground of the interlocutors, as the theory suggests that it determines the communication media which can be effectively employed.

Individuals who are initially lacking common ground require a highly interactive medium which allows for the expression and joint negotiation of common ground. To determine the interactive capabilities, communication media are characterized with regard to their co-presence, visibility, audibility, contemporality, simultaneity, reviewability and revisability: co-presence, visibility and audibility describe aspects of media richness where co-presence relies on face-to-face interactions. Contemporality is comparable to immediacy of feedback in MRT and TMS; simultaneity describes the ability to send and receive information at the same time; sequentiality specifies that turns perform in sequence; reviewability refers to the ability to reexamine information after the communication event (cf., reprocessability in TMS). Revisability puts forth the idea of refining information before the communication event (cf., reprocessability in TMS). Based on this assessment email technol-

ogy is not appropriate for communication in the absence of common ground as it lacks all the other social and interactive media capabilities which support the grounding process (see Table 3).

4. CASE ANALYSIS AND FINDINGS

To fully understand the function of enterprise wikis it is necessary to systematically identify their media capabilities and to analyze their role in established media choice theories. To address these research objectives the present investigation has conducted a meta-analysis of publicly available case descriptions of enterprise wikis. Case descriptions of enterprise wikis were identified through academic databases (EBSCOhost, Business Source Complete, IEEE Xplore, SpringerLink, ScienceDirect), Google Scholar as well as Google web-search. Searches focused on the following terminologies: wiki, enterprise wiki, firm wiki, corporate wiki, workplace wiki. The criteria for accepting a case for analysis were: a detailed description of the actual use of the wiki and a clear identification of the organization and the context in which it was used. Excluded were generic sales descriptions, product reviews, critiques and generic reports about enterprise wikis.

Based on various researches, case descriptions of 43 enterprise wiki were identified and used

Table 3. Media assessment based on Common Ground Theory

Medium	Copresence	Visibility	Audibility	Contemporality	Simultaneity	Sequentiality	Reviewability	Revisability
Face-to-face	High	High	High	High	High	High	Low	Low
Video conference	Low	High	High	High	High	High	Low	Low
Telephone conference	Low	Low	High	High	High	High	Low	Low
Answering machine (asynchronous telephone conversation)	Low	Low	High	Low	Low	Low	High	Low
Synchronous instant messaging	Low	Low	Low	High	High	High	High	High
E-mail	Low	Low	Low	Low	Low	Low	High	High
Written mail	Low	Low	Low	Low	Low	Low	High	High

for further analysis. 17 case descriptions were obtained from academic sources (journal and conference proceeding), 17 descriptions from the trade press (online and print), four descriptions from companies using enterprise wikis and five provided by wiki vendors. All cases had been prepared between 2001 and 2008. While many cases are specifically cited as evidence vis-à-vis a particular media choice theory, others served as background for the understanding of enterprise wiki use (Atlassian, 2008b; Auer et al., 2007; Bock & Paxhia, 2008; Carlin, 2007; Cooney, 2006; Gilbane, 2005; Havenstein, 2007; Independent, 2008; Johnson et al., 2008; Kakizawa et al., 2007; Peirera & Soares, 2007; Rowe & Drew, 2006; Sarrel, 2007; Udell, 2004a; Udell, 2004b)

The case descriptions were analyzed by focusing on instances of the media capabilities described in the established media choice theories. The categorization was based on insights obtained through the case reviews, but it also included a comparison with other communication and collaboration media. Table 4 summarizes the media capability of enterprise wiki as identified in the case data.

The meta-analysis allowed for an identification of the particular media capabilities of enterprise

wikis. Most of the capabilities were clearly identified through a minimum of three case descriptions. On average, insights from about 8 cases were used to derive a categorization of the different media capability. Only with regard to the immediacy of feedback case descriptions were found misleading as they highlighted the quick interactions on a wiki platform. But a comparison to other communication media such as video-conferencing helped to put the immediacy of feedback characteristic of enterprise wiki into perspective. Only for two media capabilities (rehearsability, revisability) the available case information did not provide sufficient insights. In this case personal experience was used to derive categorization.

5. DISCUSSION

Wikis represent a new communication and collaboration technology for organizations. Interestingly, a comparison of the media proficiency of enterprise wikis with other communication media indicates surprising similarities with email technology. Emails and wikis exhibit similar capabilities across most categories, which indicate

Table 4. Analysis of enterprise wiki characteristics and capabilities against media theories

Media theory	Media characteristic	Assessment of wiki capability	Source
MRT	**Immediacy of feedback** Extent to which the wiki provides users with rapid responses	**Low - Medium** Several cases point to the high speed of wiki-based communication processes. But in comparison to chat- or face-to-face based interactions wikis do not provide a high immediacy of feedback.	Low: (Timothy, 2008; Venners, 2004; Wagner, 2004) Medium: (Daft & Lengel, 1986; Foremski, 2005; Fowler, 1999; Leuf & Cunningham, 2001; Majchrzak et al., 2006; Wikipatterns, 2008)
	Multiplicity of cues Number of ways information is communicated (e.g., text, verbal cues)	**Low - Medium** Wikis are largely text based but are increasingly integrated with pictures and videos to provide additional communication cues. But the multiplicity of cues for information exchange are still limited when compared to other tools such as video-conferencing	(Clark & Brennan, 1991; Dennis & Kinney, 1998; Dennis & Valacich, 1999; Hasan & Pfaff, 2006; Leuf & Cunningham, 2001; Majchrzak et al., 2006; Suarez, 2008; Szybalski, 2005; Wiki, 2008)
	Language variety Ability to convey natural language	**High** Wikis allows users to input natural language as well as tables and numbers.	(Clark & Brennan, 1991; Dennis & Kinney, 1998; Dennis & Valacich, 1999; Hasan & Pfaff, 2006; Leuf & Cunningham, 2001; Majchrzak et al., 2006; Olson & Olson, 2004; Suarez, 2008; Szybalski, 2005; Wiki, 2008)
	Personal focus Extent to which the wiki supports the personalization of messages.	**Low** Wikis are largely a many –to-many communication medium where messages are directed to groups and not the individual.	(Black & Kilzer, 2008; Bean & Hott, 2005; Daft & Lengel, 1986; Dove et al., 2005; Leuf & Cunningham, 2001; Majchrzak et al., 2006; Wiki, 2008; Wikipatterns, 2008)
TMS	**Symbol variety** → multiplicity of cues and language variety of MRT	**Low - Medium** Wikis are largely text based but are increasingly integrated with pictures and videos to provide additional communication cues. Multiplicity of cues for information exchange is still limited when compared to other tools such as video-conferencing.	(Clark & Brennan, 1991; Dennis & Kinney, 1998; Dennis & Valacich, 1999; Hasan & Pfaff, 2006; Leuf & Cunningham, 2001; Majchrzak et al., 2006; Olson & Olson, 2004; Suarez, 2008; Szybalski, 2005; Wiki, 2008)
	Immediacy of feedback → immediacy of feedback of MRT	**Low - Medium** Several cases point to the high speed of wiki-based communication processes. But in comparison to chat or face-to-face based interactions wikis do not provide a high immediacy of feedback.	Low: (Timothy, 2008; Venners, 2004; Wagner, 2004; Wiki, 2008) Medium: (Daft & Lengel, 1986; Foremski, 2005; Fowler, 1999; Leuf & Cunningham, 2001; Majchrzak et al., 2006; Wikipatterns, 2008)
	Parallelism Amount of communication processes that can co-exist effectively	**High** Wiki-users can collaborate on the same document simultaneously. Probably among the highest level of parallelism among all communication tools.	(Daft & Lengel, 1986; Havenstein, 2008; Leuf & Cunningham, 2001; Mader, 2008; O'Leary, 2008; Olson, 2004; Venners, 2004; Wikipatterns, 2008)
	Rehearsability Ability to fine-tune messages before sending	**High** Every edit and posting can be reviewed on the screen before it is submitted to the wiki.	- - -
	Reprocessability Ability to re-exam information after the communication event	**High** Wiki–based content remains a reference point. Even deleted or modified messages can be reverted to identify previous content.	(Daft & Lengel, 1986; Dennis & Valacich, 1999; Dove et al., 2005; Fowler, 1999; Littlefield, 2005; Short et al., 1976; Thoeny, 2005; Wikipatterns, 2008)

Continued on following page

Table 4. Continued

CGT	Co-presence, Visibility, Audibility Face-to-face inter-actions and media richness	**Low** Wiki users are largely dispersed.	(Daft & Lengel, 1986; Ebersbach et al., 2008; Goowiki, 2008; Hasan & Pfaff, 2006; Havenstein, 2008; Heck, 2005; Mayfield, 2008; Wikipatterns, 2008)
	Simultaneity ability to send and receive information at the same time	**Low** Wiki users editing content are not simultaneously reviewing changes and other postings	(Black & Kilzer, 2008; Clark & Brennan, 1991; Fowler, 1999; Lio et al. 2005; Majchrzak et al., 2006; Short et al., 1976; Wikipatterns, 2008)
	Contemporality → immediacy of feed-back of MRT, TMS	**Low - Medium** Several cases point to the high speed of wiki-based communication processes. But in comparison to chat or face-to-face based interac-tions wikis do not provide a high immediacy of feedback.	Low: (Timothy, 2008; Venners, 2004; Wagner, 2004; Wiki, 2008) Medium: (Daft & Lengel, 1986; Foremski, 2005; Fowler, 1999; Leuf & Cunningham, 2001; Majchrzak et al., 2006; Wikipatterns, 2008)
	Reviewability → reprocessability of TMS	**High** Wiki–based content remains a reference point. Even deleted or modified messages can be re-verted to identify previous content.	(Delio, 2005; Dennis & Valacich, 1999; Dove et al., 2005; Fowler, 1999; Lynch, 2008; Short et al., 1976; Szybalski, 2005; Wikipatterns, 2008)
	Revisability → rehearsability of TMS	**High** Every editing and posting can be reviewed on the screen before it is submitted to the wiki.	- - -

that they share the same niche in the corporate media landscape asynchronously and lean media draws their strengths from rehearsability and re-processability. Both forms of media assist people in carefully formulating what they mean, and in thoroughly decoding the communication they have received (Olson, 2000). This observation is confirmed by a number of reports describing how wiki adoption has reduced the use of internal emails in organizations (Suarez, 2008). However, in addition to these similarities, wikis offer a distinct set of advantages for internal communication needs. Email is a client-based technology which distributes independent copies of identical messages to all receivers, clocking up email servers and leading to versioning prob-lems. A wiki, on the other hand, is a server-based technology which allows users to view the same single document, relieving the communication infrastructure from duplicated messages, and preventing the circulation of multiple versions. This underlying structural difference makes wiki a better choice for enterprises that depend heav-ily on internal communication. Based on their media capabilities, the only significant difference between wiki and email is the ability of email to personalize messages. Based on this ability it can be assumed that emails will remain the media of choice for communication tasks which require personalization. However, currently only a small fraction of the email messages currently within organizations require personalization (Lynch, 2008). Unfortunately, by choosing email over wikis, enterprises still fall victim to "corporate spam" (unwanted messages) that accumulate in employee mailboxes. Adopting wikis instead could result in communication savings of 30% or more (Mayfield, 2008).

The analysis has also revealed a shortcom-ing in the specific media capabilities currently considered in media choice theories, which do not consider the refactoring of content. However, this clearly constitutes an important capability of wikis: users continuously modify content after the initial communication event. This capabil-ity is significant as it turns a discreet text-based communication event into an ongoing communication process which continually increases the information quality. In order to address this issue, future media choice studies should include the refactoring capability in their theorizing and media assessment as it constitutes a capability which has a significant impact on two established media choice theories.

The refactoring capability of wikis challenges some of the core assumptions of CGT which focuses on the development of common ground among communication partners. CGT stipulates that the development of common ground requires rich media since lean, text-based media does not provide the verbal or non-verbal cues required. However, the refactoring capability and the wiki way of collaboration seem to challenge this assumption. During the refactoring process users continuously negotiate meaning and assumptions, and the jointly developed content eventually represents the shared knowledge of the participants. Evidence collected from Wikipedia shows how large numbers of users collaboratively edit content until consensus is reached. Wiki technology thus seems to challenge CGT as the refactoring capability enables users to develop common ground even though wikis are text-based, lean media which do not convey additional verbal or non-verbal cues.

The refactoring capability has also significant implications for TMS. TMS posits that the communication processes of conveyance and convergence require different sets of technologies with a distinct combination of media capabilities. However, the present analysis suggests that wiki technology is able to successfully support both of these communication processes. Convergence – the development of shared meaning – is very well supported through the refactoring capability and the subsequent development of common ground among users. Conveyance – the presentation of information – is supported through the rehearsability and reprocessability which allows users to effectively publish content to a large audience. By effectively supporting both information processing tasks, wikis challenge some of the core assumptions of TMS and thus require an extension of the theory.

6. IMPLICATIONS AND CONCLUSION

Enterprise wikis have only recently received attention from information system research and organizational practice. Wikis constitute a new tool which is used for a large variety of communication and collaboration purposes. To better understand the role of wikis in organizations and to compare wikis with other communication and collaboration media it is necessary to understand its underlying capabilities.

In order to identify the media capabilities of enterprise wikis, we have collected and reviewed case descriptions of enterprise wikis. We have based our analysis on the media capabilities provided by three established media choice theories (MRT, MST, CGT). The analysis allowed us to systematically identify the media capabilities and to compare enterprise wikis with other communication and collaboration media.

Our investigation has created a number of contributions to theory and practice. From a theoretical perspective, we have grounded enterprise wikis and their capabilities in established media capability frameworks. We have discussed enterprise wikis in the light of established IS theories and have identified how the unique features of enterprise wikis challenge some of their core theoretical assumptions. From a practical perspective, we have introduced enterprise wikis as a flexible enterprise tool which offers unique opportunities for communication and collaboration in organizations.

Despite a particular focus on rigor and objectivity, the particular methodology adopted for the study has created a number of limitations of the present research. Our study is based on secondary data which also include non-academic case-descriptions of enterprise wiki use. Although we cannot assure the validity of these secondary data, by including a larger number of cases and by focusing on general trends among the case descriptions we assume that the introduced bias is negligible. However, future research could address this limitation by directly investigating enterprise wikis and their particular use in organizations.

ACKNOWLEDGMENT

The research reported in this article was supported in part by GRF grant 9041292 and CityU SRG grant 7002346, as well as the Centre for Applied Knowledge and Innovation Management.

REFERENCES

Atlassian. (2008a). *JavaPolis*. Retrieved from http://www.atlassian.com /software/confluence/casestudies/javapolis.jsp

Atlassian. (2008b). *Johns Hopkins University*. Retrieved from http://www.atlassian.com/software/confluence/casestudies/ johnhopkins.jsp

Auer, S., Jungmann, B., & Schönefeld, F. (2007). Semantic Wiki Representations for Building an Enterprise Knowledge Base. In Antoniou, G., Aßmann, U., Baroglio, C., Decker, S., Henze, N., Patranjan, P.-L., & Tolksdorf, R. (Eds.), *Reasoning Web* (pp. 330–333). Berlin: Springer. doi:10.1007/978-3-540-74615-7_7

Bean, L., & Hott, D. D. (2005). Wiki: A Speedy New Tool to Manage Projects. *Journal of Corporate Accounting & Finance, 16*(5), 3–8. doi:10.1002/jcaf.20128

Black, E. L., & Kilzer, R. D. (2008). Web 2.0 Tools Ease Renovation Service Disruptions at the Ohio State University Libraries. *Public Services Quarterly, 4*(2), 93–109. doi:10.1080/15228950802202317

Bock, G., & Paxhia, S. (2008). 2008 Taking Stock of Today's Experiences and Tomorrow's Opportunities. In *Gilbane Group Research Report*. Collaboration and Social Media.

Carlin, D. (2007). Corporate Wikis Go Viral. *BusinessWeek*.

Clark, H. H., & Brennan, S. A. (1991). *Perspectives on Socially Shared Cognition*. Washington, DC: APA Books.

Cooney, L. (2006). Wiki as a Knowledge Management Tool. In *Proceedings of CERAM Sophia-Antipolis*.

Daft, R. L., & Lengel, R. H. (1986). Organizational Information Requirements, Media Richness and Structural Design. *Management Science, 32*(5), 554–571. doi:10.1287/mnsc.32.5.554

Delio, M. (2005). *The Enterprise Blogosphere*. InfoWorld.

Dennis, A. R., & Kinney, S. T. (1998). Testing Media Richness Theory in the New Media: The Effects of Cues, Feedback, and Task Equivocality. *Information Systems Research, 9*(3), 256–274. doi:10.1287/isre.9.3.256

Dennis, A. R., & Valacich, J. S. (1999). Rethinking Media Richness: Towards a Theory of Media Synchronicity. In *Proceedings of the 32nd Hawaii International Conference on System Sciences*.

Dove, M. T., Calleja, M., Bruin, R., Wakelin, J., Tucker, M. G., & Lewis, G. J. (2005). The eMinerals collaboratory: tools and experience. *Molecular Simulation, 31*(5), 329–337. doi:10.1080/08927020500066163

Ebersbach, A., Glaser, M., & Heigl, R. (2008). *Installing Confluence in Wiki Web Collaboration* (pp. 337–349). Berlin: Springer.

Foremski, T. (2005, August 5). *IBM is preparing to launch a massive corporate wide blogging initiative*. Retrieved from http://www.siliconvalleywatcher.com/mt/archives/2005/05 /can_blogging_bo.php

Fowler, M. (1999). *Refactoring, Improving The Design of Existing Code*. Boston: Addison-Wesley.

Gilbane, F. (2005). Technologies for Enterprise Applications? In *The Gilbane Report*. Blogs & Wikis.

Goowiki. (2008, August 8). *The Unofficial Google Wiki*. http://google.wikia.com /wiki/Goowiki

Hasan, H., & Pfaff, C. C. (2006). The Wiki: an environment to revolutionise employees' interaction with corporate knowledge. In *18ᵗʰ ACHI International Conference Proceeding Series* (Vol. 206, pp. 377-380).

Havenstein, H. (2007). *Top secret: DIA embraces Web 2.0 Analysts are turning to wikis, blogs, RSS feeds and enterprise "mashups"*. ComputerWorld.

Havenstein, H. (2008). CIA explains its Wikipedia-like national security project. In *ComputerWorld*. Top Secret.

Heck, M. (2005). *TWiki: Open Source with a Corporate Following*. InfoWorld.

Independent. (2008, August 9). Retrieved from http://www.independent.co.uk/news/science/the-end-of-email-discover-new-ways-to-stay-in-touch-458638.html

Johnson, N. F., Clarke, R. J., & Herrington, J. (2007). The potential affordances of enterprise wikis for creating community in research network*s*. In *Proceedings of the Emerging Technologies Conference*.

Kakizawa, Y. (2007). In-house Use of Web 2.0: Enterprise 2.0. *NEC Technical Journal*, *2*(2), 46–49.

Leshed, G., Haber, E. M., Matthews, T., & Lau, T. (2008). CoScripter: Automating & Sharing how-to Knowledge in the Enterprise. In *Proceedings of the 26ᵗʰ annual SIGCHI Conference on Human Factors in Computing Systems*.

Leuf, B., & Cunningham, W. (2001). *The Wiki Way: quick collaboration on the Web*. Reading, MA: Addison-Wesley.

Lio, E. D., Fraboni, L., & Leo, T. (2005). TWiki-based facilitation in a newly formed academic community of practice. In *Proceedings of the International Symposium on Wikis (Wikisym)*.

Littlefield, D. (2005). Share and enjoy... Building Design. *Computer Weekly*, *1678*, 24–25.

Lynch, C. G. (2008). *Enterprise Wikis Seen As a Way to End 'Reply-All' E-Mail Threads*. Retrieved from http://www.cio.com/article/197101/Enterprise_Wikis_Seen_As_a_Way_to_End_Reply_All_E_Mail_Threads

Mader, S. (2008). *Wikipatterns*. New York: Wiley.

Majchrzak, A., Wagner, C., & Yates, D. (2006). Corporate Wiki Users: Results of a Survey. In *Proceedings of the International Symposium on Wikis (Wikisym)*.

Mayfield, R. (n. d.). Retrieved from http://www.forbes.com/2008/10/15/cio-email-manage-tech-cio-cx_rm_1015email.html

O'Leary, D. E. (2008). Wikis: From Each According to His Knowledge. *Computer*, *41*(2), 34–41. doi:10.1109/MC.2008.68

Olson, G. (2004). From information to knowledge: Recommendations for Wikis as Enterprise Solutions for Collaborative Work.

Olson, G. M., & Olson, J. S. (2000). Distance Matters. *Human-Computer Interaction*, *15*(2-3), 139–178. doi:10.1207/S15327051HCI1523_4

Pereira, C. S., & A. L. (2007). Soares. Improving the quality of collaboration requirements for information management through social networks analysis. *International Journal of Information Management, 27*(2), 86–103. doi:10.1016/j.ijinfomgt.2006.10.003

Rowe, D., & Drew, C. (2006). The Impact of Web 2.0 on Enterprise Strategy. *Cutter IT Journal, 19*(10), 6–13.

Sarrel, M. D. (2007). *Wicked Productive Wikis* (p. 88). PC Magazine.

Short, J., William, E., & Christie, B. (1976). *The Social Psychology of Telecommunications*. London: John Wiley and Sons.

Suarez, L. (2008). *Can Social Tools Really Replace Email?* Retrieved from http://it.toolbox.com/blogs/elsua/can-social-tools-really-replace-email-they-already-are-part-ii-25793

Szybalski, A. (2005). *Why it's not a wiki world (yet)*. Retrieved from http://www.andy.bigwhitebox.org/papers/wiki_world.pdf

Thoeny, P. (2005). *TWiki Success Story of Wind River*. Retrieved from http://www.twiki.org/cgi-bin/view/Main/TWikiSuccessStoryOfWindRiver

Timothy, L. (2008, August 3). *The Early History of Nupedia and Wikipedia: A Memoir*. Retrieved from http://features.slashdot.org/article.pl?sid=05/04/18/164213

Udell, J. (2004a). *The social enterprise*. InfoWorld.

Udell, J. (2004b). *Year of the enterprise Wiki*. InfoWorld.

Venners, B. (2004). *The Simplest Thing that Could Possibly Work*. Retrieved from http://www.artima.com/intv /simplest.html

Wagner, C. (2004). Wiki: A Technology for Conversational Knowledge Management and Group Collaboration. *Communications of the Association for Information Systems, 13*, 265–289.

Wagner, C. (2006). Breaking the Knowledge Acquisition Bottleneck Through Conversational Knowledge Management. *Information Resources Management Journal, 19*(1), 70–83.

Wiki. (2009). Retrieved from http://c2.com

Wikipatterns.com. (2007). *Wiki Not Email*. Retrieved from http://www.wikipatterns.com /display/wikipatterns/Wiki+Not+Email

Wikipedia. (2009). Retrieved from http://wikipedia.org.

ENDNOTE

[1]   The fit of media capabilities depends on particular combinations of communication processes and task environment.

This work was previously published in the International Journal of Knowledge and Systems Science, Volume 1, Issue 2, edited by W.B. Lee, pp. 15-26 copyright 2010 by IGI Publishing (an imprint of IGI Global).

Chapter 15
Enhancing On-Line Conferencing Ba with Human-Machine Interaction CorMap Analysis

Bin Luo
Chinese Academy of Sciences, China

Xijin Tang
Chinese Academy of Sciences, China

ABSTRACT

Recently, information is being used to enhance supporting technologies in conference management systems, which greatly improves the efficiency of conference organizing affairs and promotes extensive communication and cooperation between researchers. The on-line conferencing ba (OLCB) serves as a conference management system and provides an environment for knowledge creation. CorMap analysis is a technique for qualitative meta-synthesis, which can carry out series mining from qualitative data. The early OLCB system pushes the visualized results of CorMap analysis to users by images. In this paper, the authors introduce an interactive CorMap analysis to enhance the OLCB system, which enables users to conduct the conference mining process directly and acquire more clear and structured information. The working process of interactive CorMap analysis is shown with the application of the 7th International Workshop on Meta-synthesis and Complex Systems (MCS'2007).

DOI: 10.4018/978-1-4666-1782-7.ch015

1. INTRODUCTION

According to the statistics of organized meeting in 2008 by the International Congress & Convention Association (ICCA), there were 7,300 events organized by international associations (Sirk, 2009). These events took place on a regular basis and rotated between a minimum of three countries in the year 2008, a rise of approximately 800 over 2007. With the fast-growth in both scale and frequency of conferences and advances in communication and information technologies, digital revolutions are happening to conference management. As more ubiquitous computing technologies are applied, conference management systems are no longer limited to basic functions such as paper submission and information presentation, but extend well to in-depth analysis of conference data, which may help the conference organizers make appropriate programs and the participants find interesting topics and draw a rough scenario about the latest developments of the concerned topics (Pesenhofer, Mayer, & Rauber, 2006; Tang, Zhang, & Wang, 2007). Conference mining, which generates indepth exploratory analysis results that are pushed to users for stimulating their further thinking and friends making, before, during and after formal conference activities, is now becoming the most valuable auxiliary feature of the conference management system (Matsuo, Tomobe, Hasida, et al., 2006; Tang, Zhang, & Wang, 2007).

The concept of on-line conferencing ba (OLCB) was firstly coined in 2006 during the interdisciplinary research of meta-synthesis system approach to complex problem solving and knowledge science, and then exhibited in organizing international conference with a demo system using some relevant technologies (Tang, 2006). OLCB system not only has the basic functions of information release, paper submission, paper review assignment and paper review, but also is expected to be considered as a creative support system by integrating a series of statistical methods to conduct the mining of the fundamental con-ference data such as submissions and registered authors, and post those visualized mining results to stimulate on-line discussions among participants and other target groups.

At the early OLCB system, users can drop their comments for discussion at the BBS area with the static pictures about the mining visualization which may stimulate imaginations and but also is incapable to meet the users' desire for further exploration themselves. In this paper, we report our endeavors of this improvement to enable interested people to manipulate the CorMap analysis directly by Web application. With recent studies on conference mining (Tang & Zhang, 2007; Tang, Liu, & Zhang, 2008), human-machine interaction of the CorMap analysis in OLCB system is greatly improved to exhibit human-machine interaction process of approaching the meta-synthesis from qualitative hypothesis to quantitative validation. Then the OLCB system may enhance the facilitation of knowledge sharing and creation, stimulation of participants' imagination and creativity to a greater extent, in short, provide better service for the conference participants.

2. ON-LINE CONFERENCING BA (OLCB)

Japanese Professor Nonaka has once adopted a Japanese word ba, to refer to a shared space which is of physical, virtual or even mental context, to achieve the spiral SECI process of knowledge conversion. An academic conference is a platform for information and knowledge exchange, through which the organizer actually provides a physical ba for dynamic knowledge sharing and new idea emergence. In adoption of the idea of ba, the on-line conferencing ba (OLCB) is designed for conferecing affairs as a supplementary virtual platform which is unhindered by time and space. OCLB engages in idea exchange, knowledge sharing and inspiration emergence by integrating the qualitative meta-synthesis technologies, CorMap

Figure 1. Framework of OLCB

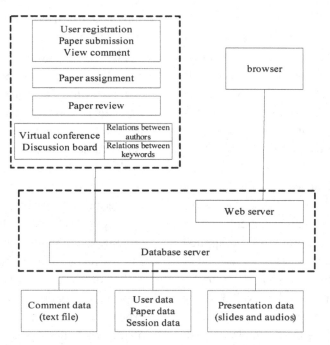

and iView to conduct the conference mining for hidden patterns and setting up a forum for users discussion. CorMap and iView analysis are proposed by meta-synthesis and knowledge science research group in Academy of Mathematics and Systems Science, Chinese Academy of Sciences, have been applied to textual data analysis for diverse problems, such as group discussion process analysis, conference mining, experts' knowledge essence elicitation and social psychological analysis, etc. (Tang, 2007, 2008, 2009; Tang & Zhang, 2007; Tang, Zhang, & Wang, 2008). After carrying out both CorMap and iView analysis toward the fundamental conference data, OLCB pushes the visualized mining results in pictures to users.

Figure 1 shows the framework of OLCB. The system was firstly applied to the 7th International Symposium on Knowledge and Systems Sciences (KSS'2006). The visualized analysis results were posted at the virtual conference board area and somewhat helpful to answer the basic questions for those people who are unfamiliar with knowledge science studies, such as "what are the current

major topics?", "who are principal explorers in this field?", "who are the major research interest groups?" etc. Thus a knowledge conversion and upgrading environment may be generated for users' awareness and idea generation. Figure 2 shows an author network of KSS'2006 and users' comments on the mining results.

As a virtual conferencing environment, OLCB aims to be a creative support system. The idea of "ba" requires dynamic and interrelated knowledge and human involvement. The active human-machine interaction is the key to OCLB system. Then CorMap analysis is implemented as a Web-based application and integrated into OLCB directly instead of those selected CorMap images posted by the organizers. The Web-based CorMap analysis may attract more users to undergo the mining process and discuss with other people at the commenting area, and then may promote more information sharing and idea emergence. Next the details of such an improvement of OLCB are depicted.

Figure 2. Author network of KSS'2006

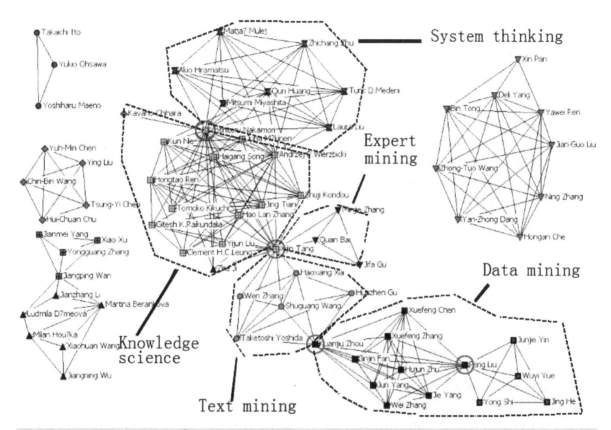

Medeni, T commented on "Topic 4: Knowledge creation: creativity support, awareness support, etc" at 2006-10-19 23:50:03
Together with the slides and audio provided in the "virtual conference," and other conference information, this "funny thing" is stimulating. Thanks a lot for all your great work to develop the conference ba!

3. CorMap ANALYSIS TOOL

CorMap analysis tool is a qualitative modeling and visualization tool developed independently by meta-synthesis and knowledge science research group. The core technique of the analysis tool is CorMap analysis which is a technology for qualitative meta-synthesis using a series of statistic methods towards processing the qualitative (textual) data with the meta structure as <thesis, author, paper title, keyword set> (Tang, 2007, 2008a, 2009). Those statistic methods mainly include correspondence analysis and k-means clustering together with other techniques. The

main functions of CorMap analysis tool are as follows.

(1) Open data set. The tool can read MS Excel and MS Access documents with data structure organized with the format as <thesis, author, paper title, keyword set>. In a specified analysis, users can see all the processed qualitative data of the "thesis" such as the thesis MCS'2007, the first data is ("mcs'2007", "chtian", "Extensive Epidemic Spreading Model based on Multi-Agent System Framework", "epidemic spreading model, simulation, multi-agent system"). According

to the data set dialog, we can also know the number of records, authors and keywords in the thesis.

(2) Conduct exploratory analysis (correspondence analysis). Use Correspondence Analysis algorithm to analyze data, and map all the authors and keywords and their corresponding relationships to the coordinate system of the same two-dimensional plane to show a visualization result. The keywords are articulated as attributes of authors and papers. A relation between authors and keywords may be acquired directly from the visualization results. People may easily find who may pay close attention to the same ideas (keywords) and then hold active communication and further discussion.

(3) Conduct idea clustering. Provide k-means clustering analysis with the authors and the keywords of conference data on the basis of the exploratory analysis. Then work out the distance between the keywords and center keywords (marked with larger font) among categories. Different categories are distinguished by different colors. With each cluster, the keyword which is close to the centroid is referred to as the representative of the affiliated cluster.

(4) Show the fittest clustering number: Use algorithms to calculate the best cluster number based on the current exploratory analysis where K corresponds to the maximum distance, it is the best cluster number.

(5) Show dominance, consistency and differences analysis. This function allows users to analyze the contributions or investigate the roles of the participants to the concerned topics or the conference, and thus serves as a variety of measures of the participants' behaviors. This function is especially useful to evaluate the human's performance during a divergent group discussion process

(6) Select experts. Users can choose authors with a higher degree of correlation to analyze,

to obtain a clearer visualization result and also can select the authors to analyze if he/she likes.

(7) Show/Hide authors or keywords. This function makes it easy for users to understand more structured information. Sometimes the visualization results are unharnessed because the authors and keywords in the visualization result are overlapped, and then users can hide the authors or keywords for a better vision.

(8) Save results. The user can save the visualized analytical results every step as they conduct the above-mentioned CorMap analysis into images in bmp or jpeg format.

4. IMPLEMENTATION OF INTERACTIVE CorMap ANALYSIS FOR THE OLCB SYSTEM

In accordance with the idea of ba, CorMap on-line analysis tool is developed with the Web technology to achieve the Web-based human-machine interaction for OLCB, which is expected to help users conduct the CorMap analysis themselves with their own desires and then contribute more to the on-line discussion, which may trigger the emergence of a virtual ba for more association and deep thinking.

4.1 Enhancing the Human-Machine Interaction Feature of CorMap Analysis in the OLCB System

As a Web-based system, OLCB system is developed by JSP+Servlet+JavaBean technologies. Both Java applet and servlet technologies are applied to enable users to fulfill CorMap analysis interactively. Java applet is a small program written in Java language and usually is embedded in html document to run inside a Web browser. It is now designed to perform some tasks such as animated graphics and interactive tools (http://java.sun.com/applets/). Java servlet is a small program written

Figure 3. The work flow of CorMap analysis applet

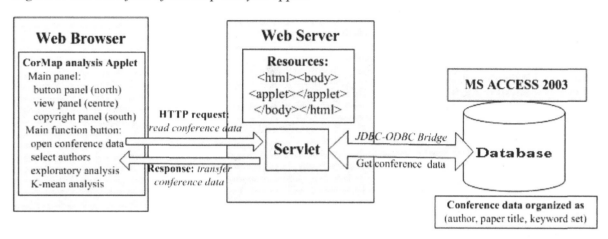

in Java language, which can be thought of as an applet that runs on the Web server. Java servlet provides Web developers with a simple, consistent mechanism for extending the functionality of a Web server and for accessing existing business systems (http://java.sun.com/products/servlet). Both applet and servlet can communicate with each other to implement the data transfer.

To enable the human-machine interactive Cor-Map analysis at the OLCB system, the key point of implementing the Web-based CorMap analysis is to read data from the Web server to the browser. And so CorMap analysis applet is designed to access and exchange conference data from Java servlet, whose data come from the conference database by the JDBC-ODBC bridge. Figure 3 shows the main structure and work flow of interactive Web-based CorMap analysis application.

The main panel of applet includes three parts, the top panel includes the functional buttons; the central panel is designed to dynamically show the visualization results and the bottom panel displays the time of the conducted tasks and the copyright information. The function buttons correspond to program blocks that perform the function. Those buttons fulfill the functions addressed at Section 3, i.e. "*DataSet*" for open conference data, "*Cor-Map*" for exploratory analysis, "*Keyword Cluster*" for keyword clustering, "Fittest K" to acquire the

fittest cluster number, "*Select Authors*" for exploratory analysis of authors combination, "*Show/ Hide Author*" and "*Show/Hide Keyword*" for better visions of CorMap analysis results. The interface is as shown in Figure 4(a). Usually the visualization results are soon acquired; the response of the server for the functional request, especially the displaying the visualized results depends on the quality of network and the client-side browser.

The visualization mining results of the interactive or directly manipulated CorMap analysis show authors (papers) with no background and keywords with white background at the 2D space based on their correspondence relations. As the mouse move and remains in the position of an author's label, the title of the paper written by that author will pop up. As the mouse moves to a keyword, the coordinates of that keyword will be displayed.

4.2 Applying Interactive CorMap Analysis of OLCB System to MCS'2007

Figure 4 shows the application of the Web-based interactive CorMap analysis of OLCB system to the 7th International Workshop on Meta-synthesis and Complex Systems (MCS'2007) affiliated with

Figure 4. Applying the interactive CorMap analysis of OLCB to MCS'2007 (a) Main Interface (b) Correspondence Analysis For MCS'2007 (c) K-mean cluster analysis (k=3) (d) author selection (e) correspondence analysis of the selected authors.

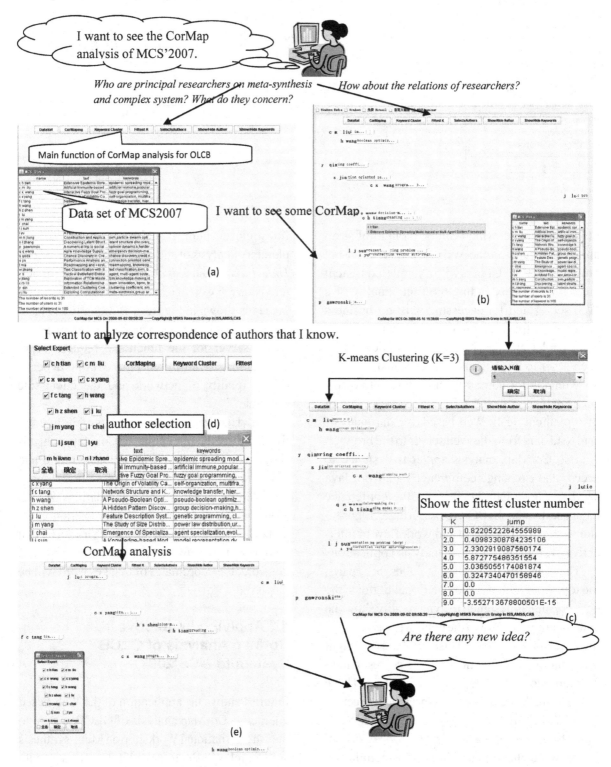

the 7th International Conference on Computational Sciences (ICCS'2007) held in Beijing during May 28-30, 2007. User clients can dynamically select to show full-scale conference data, and acquire steady conference mining results. Figure 4(a) shows the data set of MCS'2007 and the number of authors and keywords. Figure 4(b) displays the exploratory analysis result of the MCS'2007, all authors and keywords of the MCS'2007 and in particular show the paper's title of the author C.H. Tian. Some authors and keywords are unseen due to overlapping of keywords and authors. Figure 4(c) shows the result of K-means clustering analysis when k=3 and based on the exploratory analysis of MCS'2007. We can know from the dialog box that the fittest k is 4. Figure 4(d) shows the dialog of author selection. We selected 8 authors (Tian, Liu, Wang, Yang, Tang, Wang, Shen, and Lu) for exploratory analysis and Figure 4(e) shows the CorMap of the selected authors. For people who are interested in the meta-synthesis and complex system (MCS), it may be somewhat helpful to grasp the fundamental concepts of MCS by using the CorMap analysis of MCS'2007 OLCB system. Users may get a basic or possible association between authors and their academic thoughts represented by keywords from those visualization results.

With such an interactive tool, users can experience the conference mining process according to their own analysis, such as accessing the conference data and selecting experts and cluster numbers. Visualized results of conference mining allow users to access the perceptual knowledge and then go to further analysis. Enhancing the OLCB system with such kind of human-machine interaction may arouse users' interest to use the OLCB system and then drop messages at the on-line discussion area. Besides the enhanced OLCB system provides an effective exchange of information support for the physical meeting. Clustering analysis may help observers find some research groups from the visualization information, understand the perceptual knowledge of MCS, acquire

some rational understanding, and thus trigger the exploration of tacit knowledge. The functions of showing/hiding authors or keywords help users to access more structured information.

The OLCB systems may not be evaluated in a quantitative way, but to a certain extent, users' comments and ideas at the on-line discussion area may show the effectiveness of the developed systems to some extent.

5. CONCLUSION

In this paper, we present the improvement of the early OLCB system by the implementation of the Web-based interactive CorMap analysis application. Such an endeavor may increase the users' experience of drill-down the conference data under their own interests and viewpoints for more scenarios of the research topics, and then promote the higher-level communication and information sharing among the participants and the other researchers. Through the process of dynamic human-machine interaction, the virtual conferencing ba may serve as a better supplement to the physical convening as a more humanized platform for knowledge creation to stimulate either deeper or wider thinking in addition to the improvement of information sharing and the users' enhanced experiences.

Improving the on-line conference ba system is still ongoing, and many functions will be further developed. Current interactive CorMap analysis application at the OLCB only analyzes the existing conference data. Some possible endeavors may include to achieve the human-machine interaction function of iView analysis and to conduct both analytical tools toward the on-line discussion data. Moreover, it is also worth explorations of expanding the application of OLCB to daily network exchanges such as BBS and blog.

Furthermore, if open environments are implemented to enable more applications dynamically integrated or manipulated, for example, to allow access to a simulation application reported at one paper at the conference, then the OLCB not only provides the basic ideas of the concerned topics relevant to the conference themes using the qualitative meta-synthesis technologies, such as CorMap and iView analysis, but also may enable interactive validating by interesting people for those hypotheses usually off-line validated by the authors themselves. Such a way may show the process from open qualitative hypothesis to quantitative validation under a consensus level, which just exhibits the practice of meta-synthesis approach (Tang, 2008b). Such a style is happening during the era of Science 2.0.

ACKNOWLEDGMENT

This research is supported by National Natural Science Foundation of China (NSFC) under grant No. 70571078.

REFERENCES

Matsuo, Y., Tomobe, H., Hasida, K., et al. (2006). POLYPHONT: an advanced social network extraction system from the Web. In *Proceedings of 15th International World Wide Web Conference (WWW2006)*, Edinburgh International Conference Centre, Scotland (pp. 397-406).

Nonaka, I., Konno, N., & Toyama, R. (2001). Emergence of 'Ba. In Nonaka, I., & Nishiguchi, T. (Eds.), *Knowledge emergence* (pp. 13–29). New York: Oxford University Press.

Pesenhofer, A., Mayer, R., & Rauber, A. (2006, December 6-8). Improving scientific conferences by enhancing conference management system with information mining capabilities. In *Proceedings of the 1st International Conference on Digital Information Management (ICDIM 2006)*, Bangalore, India (pp. 359-366). Washington, DC: IEEE Press.

Sirk, M. (2009). *ICCA 2008 Statistics Report preface: international association meetings: genuine recession-busters?* Retrieved July 08, 2009, from http://www.iccaworld.com/npps/story.cfm?ID=1915

Tang, X. J. (2006). *Meta-synthesis and Complex System (2005-2006)* (Tech. Rep. No. MSKS-2006-03). Beijing, China: AMSS.

Tang, X. J. (2007). Towards meta-synthetic support to unstructured problem solving. *International Journal of Information Technology & Decision Making, 6*(3), 491–508. doi:10.1142/S0219622007002630

Tang, X. J. (2008a). Approach to detection of community's consensus and interest. In Y. Ishikawa, et al. (Eds.), *APWeb'2008 Workshops* (LNCS 4977, pp. 17-29). Heidelberg, Germany: Springer Verlag.

Tang, X. J. (2008b, December 9-12). Enabling a meta-synthetic discovery workshop for social consensus process. In Proceedings of the *IEEE/WIC/ACM International Conference on Web Intelligence and Intelligent Agent Technology* (pp. 436-441), Sydney. Washington, DC: IEEE Press.

Tang, X. J. (2009). Qualitative meta-synthesis techniques for analysis of public opinions for in-depth study. In J. Zhou (ed.), *Proceedings of the 1st International ICST Conference on Complex Sciences: Theory and Applications (Complex'2009)* (Part 2, LNICST 5, pp. 2338-2353). Heidelberg, Germany: Springer Verlag.

Tang, X. J., Liu, Y. J., & Zhang, W. (2008). Augmented analytical exploitation of a scientific forum. In Iwata, S., (Eds.), *Communications and discoveries from multidisciplinary data* (pp. 65–79). Heidelberg, Germany: Springer-Verlag. doi:10.1007/978-3-540-78733-4_3

Tang, X. J., Zhang, N., & Wang, Z. (2007). Augmented support for knowledge sharing by academic conference - on-line conferencing ba. In *Proceedings of IEEE WiCOM'2007 the Management Track of IEEE International Conference on Wireless Communications, Networking and Mobile Computing* (pp. 6400-6403). Washington, DC: IEEE Press.

Tang, X. J., Zhang, N., & Wang, Z. (2008). Exploration of TCM masters knowledge mining. *Journal of Systems Science and Complexity, 21*(1), 34–45. doi:10.1007/s11424-008-9064-3

Tang, X. J., & Zhang, W. (2007). How knowledge science is studied - a sision from conference mining of the relevant knowledge science symposia. *International Journal of Knowledge and Systems Science, 4*(4), 51–60.

This work was previously published in the International Journal of Knowledge and Systems Science, Volume 1, Issue 2, edited by W.B. Lee, pp. 62-70 copyright 2010 by IGI Publishing (an imprint of IGI Global).

Section 4
Applications

Chapter 16
Expert Mining and Traditional Chinese Medicine Knowledge

Gu Jifa
Chinese Academy of Sciences, China

Song Wuqi
Dalian University of Technology, China

Zhu Zhengxiang
Dalian University of Technology, China

Gao Rui
China Academy of Chinese Medical Sciences, China

Liu Yijun
Chinese Academy of Sciences, China

ABSTRACT

Expert mining is an emergent theory and technique that is useful for collecting the ideas, experiences, knowledge and wisdom from experts. Thus, in this paper, the authors have applied expert mining to solve problems related to social system and knowledge systems pertaining to specific types of information. TCM (Traditional Chinese Medicine) masters accumulated useful knowledge in medicine from ancient China paying close attention to collecting and maintaining the ideas, experiences, knowledge and wisdom from famous elder masters in TCM. In collecting this information, a large project was conducted from 100 famous elder masters in TCM supported by the Ministry of Science and Technology of China, State Administration of Traditional Chinese Medicine. Due to the enormity of this project, subprojects have been established using advanced IT technology, Artificial Intelligence, Knowledge Science and Systems Science to analyze and express these masters' experiences and theories. One of the subprojects uses expert mining and other techniques to analyze both individual and group ideas and knowledge. This paper will describe results and future planning in how this subproject will be conducted while introducing methods and tools used for expert mining.

DOI: 10.4018/978-1-4666-1782-7.ch016

1. INTRODUCTION

In the middle of 1980's when Gu dealt with some problems related to the regional development strategy system for Beijing, besides of collecting the data, information and knowledge and constructing a series of mathematical models we found that the expert opinions are very important for solving the problems. In order to determine the objectives, constraints and possible alternatives for development strategies we had designed a detailed questionarries and sending to 400 experts for collecting their opinions about the objectives, constraints and possible alternatives for development strategies in Beijing (Gu & Yang, 1987). The selected 400 experts consisted from the top leaders from Beijing municiapality (20), carderes with middle rank from Beijing municiapality (180), experts from research institutions and experts from universities and others (200). After data processing we had obtained the statistical resultes about development strategy in line of Delphi method. But when we submitted the final results to the top leaders from Beijing municiapality, results were not accepted by them. After then we wished to find the reasons, Gu had asked his graduated student to run a cluster analysis for all responders in 400 questionnares, finally we found that with the decreasing of the λ there appeared one large clusters and two small clusters. The large cluster consisted of carderes with middle rank from Beijing municiapality and experts from research institutions,whose consideration were more practical The first small cluster of experts came from universities, whose considerations were more academic and the last small cluster from the top leaders from Beijing municiapality, whose considerations were more political and applicable. It was understandble that the top leaders had their own considerations on base of more higher political perspective and more practical managerable manupilation. Since then we think the more justic Delphi method for all experts maybe inpractical we'd better use the

weighted summuation to process our data statistics, it means we should give different weights to peoples with different rank.

In the 90's we had met with some technical system with heavy human factors, the first case related to the water resource management in Qinhuangdao city. When we wish to establish some satisfaction criterion to determine what level of water in reservior will be better for operation. The criterion function we chosed had five parameters which were very difficult for us to estimate, finally we ask an appropriate expert who gave the estimation for three parameters directly according to his experience (Gu & Tang, 2006). The second case was how can we construct the diagram of standards of commerce on base of a little number of existed standards. In paper (Gu, Tang, Wang et al., 1997) we proposed a set of methods to collect the expert's opinions., such as Brainstorming, Delphi, AHP, cluster analysis etc. In the brainstorming stage we usually invited 4-8 experts in giving the framwork for our study and designing the questionnarie. We invited 30 experts from different department stores to fill the questionnarie. Finally we convened the expert meeting with different knowledge background from department stores, research institutions and management organization around 20 persons and we used the majority principle and decision power from higher leaders in making final decision.

In 2004 Gu started involve in studying the social harmony problems. The social system is an open giant complex system. There are three kinds of channels to obtain information: formal society, informal society and network society. In order to collect and process useful information we have to use different mining techniques: data mining, text mining, web mining, model mining, psychology mining, and expert mining: The first four mining techniques deal with mainly the explicit data and information. The later two techniques mainly deal with the tacit information. In recent years we pay much attention to develop the expert mining (Gu, Tang, & Niu, 2005; Gu, 2006).

Just two years ago we involved in the study of Traditional Chinese Medicine(TCM) from the system science and knowledge science view. The main aim is to accumulate and carry forward the experience and thoughts from elder and famous TCM doctors and try to find their good knowledge and find some new knowledge, here again we wish use the expert mining to fulfill this task. The total number of elder and famous TCM doctors are 100. This time the quality of knowledge and wisdom in these experts are obvious, so then we call these experts as Masters in deferentiating with general experts and TCM doctors (Song, Liu, & Gu, 2007; Tang, Zhang, & Wang, 2007).

2. EXPERT MINING

The terminology of expert mining appeared just in recent five-ten years around. We wish use expert mining to collect, analyze and use expert's opinions, thoughts, idea, knowledge and wisdom for accumulating, carrying forward their useful knowledge, especially for solving the realistic complex problem. With the development of data mining, text mining and web mining people find that to mine the live, tacit and unstructured thoughts, idea, knowledge and wisdom from experts become more challenged but important affairs. To facilitate expert mining, the new theory and methods have to be developed. The computerized tools for mining expert's ideas and group work will be applied

2.1 What is Expert and Expert Mining?

For solving some problems the people who may contribute their opinion, knowledge and wisdom to us is expert. We may differentiate experts into different dimension, such as the number of experts, the degree of education, title of job, the domain of knowledge, which more related to the problem solving. The one dimension is the number of experts: 1) if we wish deal with the number of experts with huge amount (say, 10^3- 10^6), the each expert just looks like one sample in population, in this case usually we often use statistical methods, we care the opinions from experts just their trends and some simple values in some attributes we are interesting; 2) if we wish deal with the number of experts with middle amount (say, 10^2-10^3), in this case we will care the trends and some insights; 3) if we wish deal with the number of experts with few amount (say 10-10^2), in this case we will care the trends and more insights, we will care of not only the opinions they express explicitly, but also tacit, their knowledge background and their benefit delegated. Especially some of experts we may call them Master, it means their knowledge are much wider and deeper compared with the common experts; 4) if we wish deal with the number of experts just several, one, two or three, in this case we will care their specific insights and wisdom, such experts we may call them Guro, great leader. Another dimensions we may list, like the degree of education, title of job etc.

Expert mining is a method and tool for collecting, storing, analyzing opinion, thoughts, experiences, knowledge and wisdom from the experts and extracting useful and innovative knowledge and idea by using IT technology, computing technology, human-computer interaction and group discussion. It not only cares the explicit knowledge and thoughts, but also the tacit and unstructured knowledge and thoughts behind experts. Usually the experts express their knowledge and thoughts in several types:

Speak explicitly (language, word)-explicit;
Speak implicitly-tacit;
Express by gesture (expression in eyes, gesticulation, tone);
Speak on Web-web;
Speak lie(speak insincerely, false intelligence, rumour)-intelligence.

In defferent cases we shall use different methods and tools.

2.2 Some Ways to Expert Mining

We wish mention some ways going to expert mining:

(1) From data mining to expert mining:
  1) Kovalerchuk et al (Department of Computer Science, Central Washington University) assumed: Traditional numeric statistical data mining methods have relatively limited applicability in IA, because data are often not numeric and have a very asymmetric pattern representation. For instance, there are only a few terrorism messages in the stream of normal ones. New relational data mining and link discovery have significant potential to address these challenges. Also, relational methods have important advantages over traditional methods for linking, integrating, and conflating images of different resolutions, sensor modalities, viewing angles, and geometric projections. Especially during solving the medicine diagnostic they use the terminalogy- expert mining (Kovalerchuk & Vityaev, 2000; Kovalerchuk, 2005; Kovalerchuk, Vityaev, & Ruiz, 2001).
  2) Lemke et al (Script Software, Germany) used self-organizing data mining technologies in medical data analysis, which may select automatically useful knowledge for medical decisions, such as diagnosis of heart disease. "Knowledge Miner" was designed to support the knowledge extraction process on a highly automated level. Implemented are 3 different GMDH-type self-organizing modeling algorithms to make knowledge extraction

systematically, fast, successful and easy-to-use even for large and complex system such as one of the most complex systems: the human (Lemke & Muller, n.d.).

(2) From web mining to expertise oriented search:
  1) Tang et al (Department of Computer and Technology, Tsinghua University) proposed Expertise Oriented Search, which aims at providing comprehensive analysis and mining for people from distributed sources. They give an overview of the expertise oriented search system (ArnetMiner). The system addresses several key research issues in extraction and mining of the researcher social network. The system is in operation on the internet for about one year and receives accesses from about 1,500 users per month. Feedbacks from users and system logs also indicate that users consider the system can really help people to find and share information in the web community (Tang, Zhang, Zhang, Yao, Zhu, & Li, n.d.).
  2) Quan et al(School of Computing Engineering., Nanyang Technological Univ., Singapore) proposed a web mining approach for finding expertize in research areas. Indexing Agents search and download scientific publications from web sites that typically include academic web pages, then they extract citations and store them in a Web Citation Database. In addition, researcher information is also saved into the Researcher Database. Data mining techniques are applied to the Web Citation Database on citation keywords and authors to form document clusters and author clusters. The Multi-Clustering technique is proposed

to mine the combined information of document clusters and author clusters for information on expertise in specified research areas (Quan, Siu, & Fong, 2003).

(3) From synthesizing expert's opinion to expert mining

Dai, Yu and Gu et al run a large project under the support of National Natural Science Foundation of China (NSFC), titled "Man-Computer Cooperated HWME Supporting Macro-Economy Decision-Making". The one of key problems in project is how to synthesize the opinions. For this problem Gu and his colleagues had proposed the various methods for synthesizing the expert opinions, the concepts and theory of consensus building, the tools for collecting, analyzing and visualizing the expert's opinion- Electronic Common Brain (ECB), Group Argumentation Environment (GAE) and Attributed Directed Graph Model. Especially in Institute of Systems Science, CAS we develop the expert mining and run a series of experiments (Dai, Yu, & Gu, 2003; Gu, 2001; Gu & Tang, 2001; Gu, 2002; Gu, 2002; Gu, Wang, & Tang, 2007; Cui, Li, Xia, & Zhang, 2003).

(4) Ontology-based approach to expert mining

Zhang et al proposed complex multi-agent systems to combine the MAS and expert agent to discover knowledge of heterogeneous experts. An ontology-based approach for knowledge and expert mining in hybrid multi-agent system is introduced (Zhang, Tang, Bai, & Gu, 2007).

2.3 Some Basic Ideas for Mining the Expert Thoughts

We may list some basic ideas for mining the thoughts:

1) Transferring expert knowledge from tacit to explicit(SECI model);
2) Combining abilities of human and machine;
3) Complementary using 6 mining(Data mining, Text mining, Web mining, Psychology mining, Model mining, Expert mining);
4) Using Meta-synthesis approach to integrate various data, information, model, experiences, wisdom and computer capacity

2.3.1 Meta-synthesis of Opinions

(1) Meta-synthesis of Opinions by text
   1).Simple survey (narrative); 2).Meta-analysis; 3). Qualitative Meta-synthesis
(2) Meta-synthesis of Opinions by meeting

Expert meeting could serves as to acquire more information from human experts directly.

1). Types of meeting;
   a) Brainstorming type for collecting the vivid and frank opinions;
   b) Studying type for collecting and studying some opinions on the base of deep investigation;
   c) Decision type for concentrating the opinions. In order to obtain the consensus from experts we also studied different methods, tools for getting the consensus
2) Three new discussion types
   a) Syntegration (Beer);
   b) Meeting on Web(WebScope);
   c) Nominal Group meeting;
   3). Ba, Facilitation, Mediation;
   4). DMTMC-system;
   5) M-A-M'(Meeting I-Analysis- Meeting II)
3) Meta-synthesis of Opinions by interview deeply: Psychology mining (Gu, Liu, & Song, 2007).

Table 1. The comparisions of expert mining with data mining, text mining

	Data mining, Text mining	Expert mining
1.the object for mining	Data and information	Expert's knowledge and expertice
2. number of samples	Huge amount	Few samples
3. Combination of human and machine	Based on machine mainly	Based on human
4.Thinking method	Logical, image	Logical, image and inspiration
5.Mode of analysis	Quantitative analysis mainly	Combination of qualitative and quantitative analysis, qualitative mainly
6.the expression of knowledge	Explicit knowledge mainly	Tacit knowledge mainly
7.Relation with the feeling and personality	Not related	Related
8. the result of mining	Knowledge and useful information	Systemic knowledge,new idea
9. Psychology and atomsphere around	Not related	Related
10.World view,Culture and philosophy	Not considered mainly or just a few	Need to consider

4) Meta-synthesis of Opinions by modeling: Multi-agent simulation(MAS)(Luo, Si, Hu, & Yang, 2004; Liu, Niu, & Gu, 2007).

Mentioned concepts and theory we had introduced in some other papers here we don't want touch too much detail (Gu, Tang, & Niu, 2005; Gu, 2006; Gu, 2001; Gu, 2002; Gu, Wang, & Tang, 2007).

2.3.2 The Comparisons of Expert Mining with Data Mining, Text Mining and Web Mining

We may compare the main specific features within the data mining (DM), text mining (TM) and expert mining illustrated in Table 1

2.3.3 Combination of Expert Mining and Other Different Methods for Mining

We may use the data mining to analyze a huge amount of data to discovery some useful knowledge.

We may use the Text mining to extract some useful textual information from many texts in documents.

We may use the Web mining to extract useful information from the internet, intranet etc.

We may use the model mining to obtain some new results which human will obtain only by simple mind calculation with difficulties, e.g. results from calculation derived from complicated equations, result from forecasting model, results for agent-based model simulation etc.

We may use the psychology mining to dig the deep thoughts behind the surface of mind

Besides of the mentioned five mining we may use expert mining to ask opinion and thoughts directly from experts. Finally after using mentioned other mining techniques we will ask experts to analyze the all results which are sometimes contradicted each with other and also need expert to make final judgment for the obtained results, even more we will ask experts to create some new idea, methods, techniques and theory, new alternatives for decision, it means to use the wisdom to create something which originally does not exist.

2.4 Some Examples for Expert Mining

Ex.1. Forecasting the GDP growth rate- JAIST test 2003.1(2003, JAIST)(Pathmaker)(Gu, Wang, & Tang, 2007; Gu & Tang, 2003)

Ex.2. Agora test for ISSS(2003.7,Crete) (Cogni-Scope) (Crete, 2003)

Ex.3. Forecasting the GDP growth rate under the impact of SARS- IIASA test (2003.9, IIASA) (Pathmaker, Model integration) (Gu, Wang, & Tang, 2007)

Ex.4. Surveying Xiangshan Scientific Conference (2005-2006) (Web mining, GAE) (Gu, Wang, & Tang, 2007; Zhang & Tang, 2006)

Ex.5. Discussion on social harmony problems-MBA test (2006, 7, Beijing) (Pathmaker, GAE, Psychology interview) (Gu, Liu, & Song, 2007)

Ex.6. Taxi test (2007.7, Beijing) (Psychology interview, MAS) (Liu, Niu, & Gu, 2007)

Ex.7. TCM Master test (2007, Beijing) (Pathmaker, GAE, Ucinet, TCM Master Miner) (Song, Liu, & Gu, 2007; Tang, Zhang, & Wang, 2007)

Ex.8. A collective discussion on the designing the regulation law for research projects (2004, Beijing) (GAE) (Tang & Liu, 2004)

Ex.9. Group Argumentation and its Analysis on a highlighted social event (2005,Beijing) (GAE) (Tang & Liu, 2007)

3. EXPERT MINING AND TCM KNOWLEDGE

From 2006 year we have engaged in a large project in "Ten Five plan" National supported to Science and Technology organized by Ministry of Science and Technology and Administration bureau of Traditional Chinese Medicine in China. This project had collected the academic thoughts and experiences from 100 Chinese masters in TCM based on IT technology and Database. We just analyze these processed primary data further more and got some theoretical and experiment results.

Following the macro philosophy of disease, traditional Chinese diagnostics are based on overall observation of human symptoms rather than "micro" level laboratory tests. There are four types of TCM diagnostic methods: observe, hear and smell, ask about background and touching. Modern TCM practitioners in China often use a traditional system in combination with Western methods. TCM is considered to require considerable diagnostic skill. This often depends on the ability to observe what are described as subtle differences. This may be contrasted with a straightforward laboratory test, which indicates an unambiguous cause. A training period of years or decades is said to be necessary for TCM practitioners to understand the full complexity of symptoms and dynamic balances.

From September of 2007 Ministry of Science and Technology and Administration bureau of Traditional Chinese Medicine in China started continue the similar project on methods for mining the academic thoughts and diagnose experiences of famous and elder TCM doctors as one project in "Eleven Five plan" State supported to Science and Technology. This new project will be lasted three years and consisted of five subprojects. The four subprojects use such as data mining, machine learning, SVM, implicit structure model, network analysis etc. (Zhang, Wang, Zhou, Liu, Yao, & Li, 2008; Ren, Wang, Liu, Zhang, Wang, Zhang, Liu, & Sun, 2006; Zhang & Yuan, 2006; Liu, Zhang, Aziguli, & Liu, 2008; Zhu, Song, & Gu, 2008), most of them try to find the deep and new knowledge based on the TCM Doctors' experience which are usually stored already in the special database in some structured way. Xiyuan Hospital and Academy of Mathematics and Systems Science jointly run a fifth subproject within them. The more complete title of our project is the study on the mining methods for the analyzing collective law of academic thoughts from famous and elder TCM doctors. Our project is based on the expert mining. We not only pay the attention on the structured knowledge, but also unstructured and tacit knowledge. We will use the information and knowledge from common database, but also pay much attention to the live expert knowledge, so we will use expert meeting with supporting by

Figure 1. Roadmap for TCM project

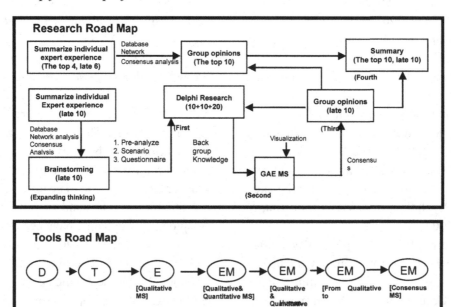

Figure 2. Relationships between the 13 experts and diagnosis by Zhu et al. (2009)

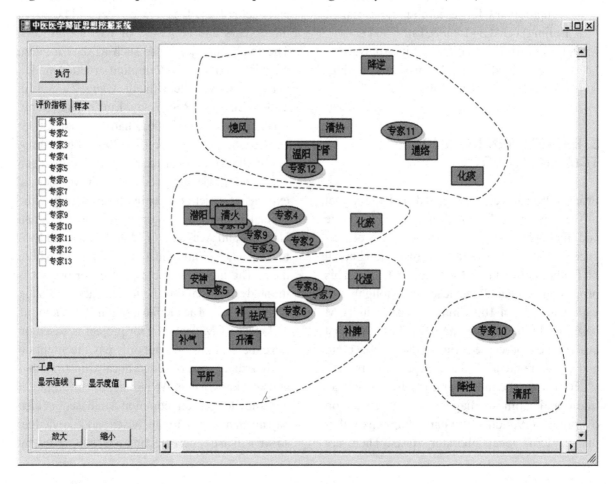

some computer tool, consensus methods, network analysis and multi-agent simulation. We will study not only individual knowledge from expert, but also their collective law. Since this new project is just undergoing, here we wish only show the roadmap for studying this project (see Figure 1). In this project we will use brainstorming in Xiyuan hospital and a series of methods for converging the collective thinking from a group of experts with support of experting mining and some visualization tools. Finally an example was given to show the feasibility of expert mining (Zhu, Gu, & Song, 2009). We collected 148 cases on high blood pressure involved 13 elder and famous TCM doctors, used the correspondence analysis to research the relationships between the experts and diagnosis.

(see Figure 2, Figure 3, and Figure 4), also used GAE to find some relationship between the diagnosis and Chinese medicine on the liver disease (see Figure 5). According to master mining method, we constructed software named Meta-synthesis Master Knowledge Mining Platform (MIMP) in order to process the data and information from expert mining (Song & Gu, 2009).

4. CONCLUSION

Expert mining like data mining, text mining is a good method and tool for collecting the data, information and knowledge, but based mainly on the tacit knowledge from expert directly. Since the

Figure 3. Principle of treatment by Song (2008)

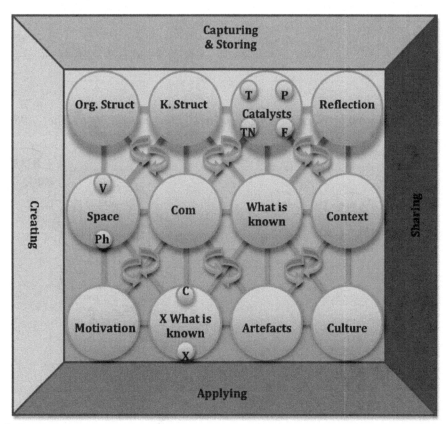

KM The Knowledge Core

Griffiths (2009) Edinburgh

Figure 4. Experts and treatment by Song (2008)

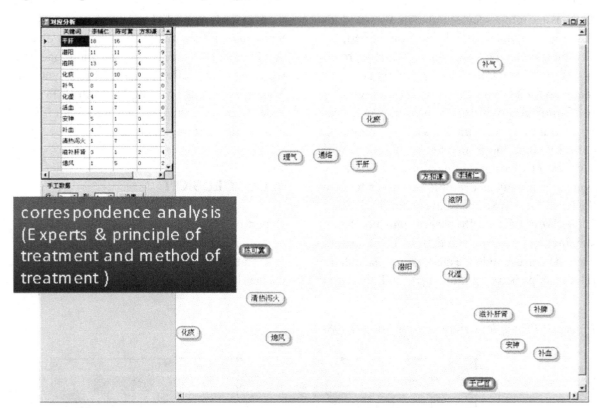

Figure 5. Relationship between the diagnosis and Chinese medicine by Liu (2008)

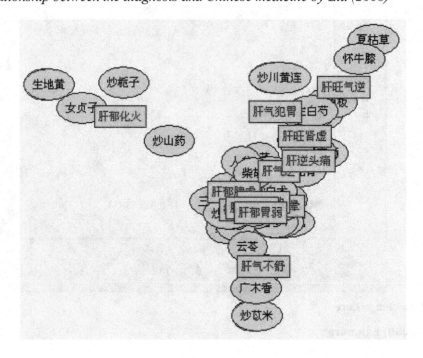

information, knowledge for expert mining usually not so vividly like the explicit knowledge used by data mining and text mining, so it requires some new idea, thoughts and techniques to deal with. We have chance to meet two practical complex systems, social system and human body system in recent years, the practical trouble for finding the appropriate models and solution and hard to get the useful information directly force us to use the meta-synthesis system approach and the combination of six mining including the expert mining. Certainly we shall do more research and practices on the expert mining

ACKNOWLEDGMENT

This paper is supported by Ministry of Science and Technology of China, State Administration of Traditional Chinese Medicine (TCM) 2007BAI10B06

REFERENCES

Crete. (2003). *Proceedings of the 47th Annual Meeting of the International Society for the Systems Sciences*. Retrieved from http://www.isss. org/world/en/conferences/crete2003

Cui, X., Li, Y. D., Xia, L. M., & Zhang, J. C. (2003, September 1). *An attributed directed graph model of HWME based on internet* (pp. 8-9). Paper presented at the 17th JISR-IIASA Workshop on Methodologies and Tools for Complex System Modeling and Integrated Policy Assessment.

Dai, R., Yu, J. Y., & Gu, J. F. (2003, September 8-10). A meta-synthetic approach for decision support system. In Proceedings of *CSM'03, the 17th JISR-IIASA Workshop on Methodologies and Tools for Complex System Modeling and Integrated Policy Assessment* (pp. 10-12). Retrieved from www.iiasa.ac.at/~marek/ftppub/Pubs/csm03/abst.ps

Gu, J. F. (2001). On synthesizing opinions-how can we reach consensus. *Journal of Systems Engineering*, *16*(5), 340–348.

Gu, J. F. (2002, March 25-27). Consensus building and meta-synthesis. In Proceedings of VEAM2002. Kobe, Japan: JAIST.

Gu, J. F. (2002, July 15-18). Study on the meta-synthesis of data, information model and expert Opinions. In Proceedings of CMS2002. Austria: IIASA.

Gu, J. F. (2006). Expert mining for solving the social harmony problems. *COE News*, *2*(4), 1–3.

Gu, J. F., Liu, Y. J., & Song, W. Q. (2007, August 5-10). A scientific discussion test on some social harmony problems. In *Proceedings of the 51st meeting of the International Society for the Systems Sciences (ISSS2007)*, Tokyo (pp. 2007-2056).

Gu, J. F., & Tang, X. J. (2001). Metasynthesis, WSR and consensus. In *Proceedings of Intern. Symposium on Knowledge and Systems Sciences: Challenges to Complexity* (pp. 12-16).

Gu, J. F., & Tang, X. J. (2003). A test on meta-synthesis system approach to forecasting the GDP growth rate in china. In J. Wiley & J. K. Allen (Eds.), *Proceedings of 47th Annual Conference of the International Society for the Systems Sciences*.

Gu, J. F., & Tang, X. J. (2006). *Wuli-Shili-Renli system approach: Theory and applications*. Shanghai, China: Shanghai Science and Technology, Education Publisher.

Gu, J. F., Tang, X. J., & Niu, W. Y. (2005). Meta-synthesis system approach for solving social complex problems. In J. F. Gu & G. Chroust (Eds.), *Proceedings of 1st World Congress of the International Federation for Systems Research*. Kobe, Japan: JAIST Press.

Gu, J. F., Tang, X. J., Wang, L., et al. (1997). Wuli-Shili-Renli Approach to preparing the diagram of standard system for the commercial accommodations and facilitation in China. In *Systems Methodology III: Possibilities for Cross-cultural Learning and Integration* (pp. 21-32). Hull, UK: the University of Hull.

Gu, J. F., Wang, H. C., & Tang, X. J. (2007). *Meta-synthesis Method System and Systematology Research*. Marrickville, Australia: Science Press.

Gu, J. F., & Yang, J. L. (1987). MCDM and strategic development. In Sawaragi, Y. (Ed.), *Towards Interactive and Intelligent DSS* (pp. 280–287). Berlin: Springer Verlag.

Kovalerchuk, B. (2005, May). Advanced data mining, link discovery and visual correlation for data and image analysis. In *Proceedings of Tutorial Notes International Conference on Intelligence Analysis (IA '05)*. Retrieved from http://analysis.mitre.org

Kovalerchuk, B., & Vityaev, E. (2000). *Data Mining in Finance: Advances in Relational and Hybrid Methods*. Dordrecht, The Netherlands: Kluwer.

Kovalerchuk, B., Vityaev, E., & Ruiz, J. F. (2001). Consistent and complete data and "expert" mining in medicine. *Studies in Fuzziness and Soft Computing, 60*, 238–281.

Lemke, F., & Müller, J.-A. (n.d.). *Medical Data Analysis Using Self-Organizing Data Mining Technologies*. Retrieved from http://www.knowledgeminer.net/pdf/medical.pdf

Liu, J. M., & Zhang, D. Z., Aziguli, & Liu, J. H. (2008). Centrality Research Based on Traditional Medicine Network. *Computer Simulation, 25*(5), 317–320.

Liu, Y. J., Niu, W. Y., & Gu, J. F. (2007). Exploring computational scheme of complex problem solving based on meta-synthesis approach. In *Proceedings of the International Conference on Computational Science, Lecture Notes in Computer Science* (pp. 9-17).

Luo, P., Si, G. Y., Hu, X. F., & Yang, J. Y. (2004). Swarm & discussion of the method of constructing the special public opinion model. *Journal of System Simulation, 16*(1), 5–7.

Quan, T. T., Siu, C. H., & Fong, A. C. M. (2003, December 3-5). A Web mining approach for finding expertise in research areas. In *Proceedings of the 2003 International Conference on Cyberworlds (CW'03)* (pp. 310-317).

Ren, T. G., Wang, Q. G. L. Y., Liu, X. F., Zhang, F., Wang, Y., & Zhang, Y. H. (2006). Study on information of syndrome standard based on data. *Journal of Beijing University of Traditional Chinese Medicine, 29*(7), 442–444.

Song, W. Q., & Gu, J. F. (2009). Experience Mining. In *Proceedings of IKM2009*. Application of Information Visualization Technologies in Masters.

Song, W. Q., Liu, Y. J., & Gu, J. F. (2007). *Mining TCM experiences of TCM masters based on the medical cases data* (Tech. Rep. No. 3). Beijing, China: Xi Yuan Hospital, Chinese Academy of Sciences.

Tang, J., Zhang, J., Zhang, D., Yao, L. M., Zhu, C. L., & Li, J. Z. (n.d.). *ArnetMiner: An expertise oriented search system for academic researcher social network*. Retrieved from http://keg.cs.tsinghua.edu.cn/persons/tj/arnetminer/arnetminer.html

Tang, X. J., & Liu, Y. J. (2004). A test of pooling the wisdom of the experts-A collective discussion on the designing the regulation law for research projects. In *Proceedings of the Well-off Society Strategies and Systems Engineering* (pp. 339-345). Hong Kong, China: Global-Link Publisher.

Tang, X. J., & Liu, Y. J. (2007). Group argumentation and its analysis on a highlighted social event - Practice of Qualitative Meta-synthesis. *Systems Engineering: Theory and Practice, 27*(3), 42–49. doi:10.1016/S1874-8651(08)60023-X

Tang, X. J. N., Zhang, N., & Wang, Z. (2007). Exploration of TCM masters knowledge mining. In *Proceedings of Computational Science (ICCS2007)* (LNCS 4490, pp. 35-42). Berlin: Springer Verlag.

Zhang, L. W., & Yuan, S. H. (2006). Implicit structure model and research on syndrome differentiation of Chinese medicine (I): Basic thought and analytic tool of implicit structure. *Journal Of Beijing University of Traditional Chinese Medicine, 29*(6), 365–369.

Zhang, M., Tang, X. J., Bai, Q., & Gu, J. F. (2007, June). Expert discovery and knowledge mining in complex multi-agent systems. *Journal of Systems Science and Systems Engineering, 16*(2), 222–234. doi:10.1007/s11518-007-5043-9

Zhang, R. S., Wang, Y. H., Zhou, X. Z., Liu, B. Y., Yao, N. L., & Li, P. (2008). Integration of Famous TCM Doctors' Experience and Data Mining Technology. *World science and technology-modernization of traditional Chinese medicine and materia medica, 10*(1), 45-52, 63.

Zhang, W., & Tang, X. J. (2006). Web text mining on xssc, in Knowledge and Systems Sciences: Toward Knowledge Synthesis and Creation. In *Proceedings of the 7th International Symposium on Knowledge and Systems Sciences (KSS'2006)* (LNCS 8, pp. 167-175). Hong Kong, China: Global-Link Publishers.

Zhu, Z. X., Gu, J. F., & Song, W. Q. (2009). From Data Mining to Expert Mining. *Systems Engineering, 27*(1), 1–7.

Zhu, Z. X., Song, W. Q., & Gu, J. F. (2008). A Multi-agent and Data Mining Model for TCM Cases Knowledge Discovery. In *Proceedings of the International Colloquium on Computing, Communication, Control and Management (CCCM 2008)* (Vol. 3, pp. 341-346). Retrieved from www.iita-conference.org/isecs/index_files/cccm2008content.pdf

This work was previously published in the International Journal of Knowledge and Systems Science, Volume 1, Issue 2, edited by W.B. Lee, pp. 27-38 copyright 2010 by IGI Publishing (an imprint of IGI Global).

Chapter 17

Semantic Interoperability for Enhancing Sharing and Learning through E-Government Knowledge-Intensive Portal Services

Ching-Chieh Kiu
Multimedia University, Malaysia

Lai-Yung Yuen
The Hong Kong Polytechnic University, China

Eric Tsui
The Hong Kong Polytechnic University, China

ABSTRACT

E-Government emerges from web sites that offer static information, documents and forms for employees and citizens, enquiries, and process automations to many types of stakeholders. Increasingly, different layers of government services are being consolidated into a knowledge portal, providing on time and online services. Such knowledge portals not only provide a platform for integrating applications and information from all government sources, but also provide platforms for knowledge sharing and learning to the public with the objective to improve the efficiency and the quality of E-Government processes and services. However, due to the heterogeneity of applications and information across different levels of government agencies, a significant amount of work is needed to re-configure such applications and services into a new platform. However, semantics are often deficient, which results in problems establishing effective knowledge sharing and learning in E-Government. This paper confers how knowledge intensive portals can be used for enhancing sharing and learning in E-Government. The authors discuss innovative information on how the Semantic Web and Web 2.0 technologies can be applied in providing interoperability to leverage knowledge sharing and learning activities.

DOI: 10.4018/978-1-4666-1782-7.ch017

Figure 1. Page count of selected E-Government sites available through Google on June 2005 vs. May 2008

Country	Government domain	Number of web pages		% Increment number of web pages	Website link
		June 2005[1]	May 2008		
USA	.gov	368,000,000	855,000,000	132%	http://www.usa.gov/
Canada	.gc.ca	12,100,000	22,400,000	85%	http://www.canada.gc.ca/
UK	.gov.uk	9,280,000	62,200,000	570%	http://www.direct.gov.uk/
Australia	.gov.au	7,200,000	37,300,000	418%	http://www.gov.au/
China	.gov.cn	2,630,000	184,000,000	6896%	http://www.gov.cn/
New Zealand	.gov.nz*	1,290,000	14,900,000	1055%	http://newzealand.govt.nz/
South Africa	.gov.za	816,000	1,810,000	122%	http://www.gov.za/
Hong Kong	.gov.hk	887,000	4,430,000	399%	http://www.gov.hk/
Thailand	.gov.th*	728,000	20,400,000	2702%	http://www.thaigov.go.th/
Slovenia	.gov.si	388,000	1,080,000	178%	http://www.gov.si/

Remark: * indicated the government domain has changed (May, 2008).
.gov.nz changed to **.govt.nz** and **.gov.th** changed to **.go.th**

1. INTRODUCTION

With the advent of the Internet, E-Government has developed immensely since the end of the 90s. Most countries all over the world are implementing E-Government services to facilitate a range of services to citizens, public sectors and other authorities. E-Government provides a convenient way for citizens to access and obtain the information they desire, without having manually to locate and filter out the content that is not needed (Wagner et al., 2006). Hence, E-Government encompasses the largest volume of web documents over the Internet as shown in Figure 1 and the volume of web documents has indeed grown within 3 years from 2005 to 2008. The rapid increase of E-Government web documents over the Internet has been partly due to the government of China; its documents have increased from 2.6 million to 184 million, following China in the proliferation of web documents is the Thailand government and the New Zealand government with increases of 2702% and 1055% of increments respectively. With such a massive build-up of codified assets, the problem of "information overlook" can no doubt easily occur, leading to valuable information being ignored and missed by the citizens (Misra, 2006).

One approach to solve this problem is to develop a *one-stop knowledge-intensive government portal service* to unify all government agency websites, and to allow access to all government agencies' webpage services and information. Such a knowledge portal enables the public to access the Government's knowledge sharing and learning activities. Knowledge sharing and learning are important activities in E-Government which enhance and improve the efficiency and quality of E-Government processes and services and also improve interaction and the relationship between the public and government. Despite the recent uptake in the adoption of service-oriented architectures (SOA) (Bloomberg, 2003) among enterprise applications, much of the needed contextual knowledge about the provided application, which is crucial for providing concise and personalized knowledge, is still lacking. The core focus of SOA has been, up to now, on issues concerned with business and IT alignments.

Semantic interoperability in E-Government remains a crucial issue in E-Government due to the heterogeneity problem which has arisen in applications and knowledge repositories in different levels of agencies in government. Hence, knowledge sharing and learning activities have failed to take place in government processes and services. A potential solution can be the use of Semantic Web and Web 2.0 technologies for effective knowledge sharing and learning in an E-Government environment.

In Section 2 of this paper, we discuss the evolution, (including interoperability), of E-Government towards knowledge sharing and learning through knowledge-intensive portal services. The semantic interoperability issues of E-Government are discussed in Section 3. Meanwhile, the use of Semantic Web and Web 2.0 technologies to support knowledge sharing and learning in E-Government are discussed in Section 4 and 5, respectively. The challenges and issues in adopting Semantic Web and Web 2.0 technologies are presented in Section 6. The final section provides our conclusions.

2. E-GOVERNMENT EVOLUTION AND INTEROPERABILITY

2.1 Evolution of E-Government

E-Government is the use of ICT to unify the services of government agencies into a portal which we refer to as, ideally speaking, a *one-stop knowledge-intensive government portal service* to improve the efficiency, convenience and accessibility of services to the public. The impact of E-Government services and processes is increasingly important to the public as is evidenced by the increasing number of visitors to E-Government portals for accessing services. For example, the Malaysian Government (Steven, 2008) reported that there has been a threefold increase in the number of visitors in these two years and it had

recorded 6.5 million visitors as at May 15 2008 and 9.9 million visitors as at 04 Jun 2008.

E-Government is being deployed not only to provide citizen services such as driving license renewal, business registration, electronic income tax returns, form downloading etc., but also as a knowledge repository for information searching to leverage knowledge sharing and learning activities. A survey by (Estabrook et al. 2007) revealed nearly four out of five American Internet users have visited government websites to seek information or assistance for problem solving and decision-making. They usually visit local, state or federal government websites for information and a total of 71% has done this in the last 12 months compared to 66% in the past year.

Knowledge-intensive portal services not only offer customization or personalization functions, static content and electronic transactions, but they are able to collect and disseminate information and knowledge to the public. Such a portal can automatically connect the public to the right government agency, to answers and information through FAQs. It then rates information content based on collective preferences. Various efforts on developing such portals have been reported in (Paralic, 2003); (Sidoroff & Hyvnon, 2005); (Klischewski, 2003); (Fraser et al., 2003); (Daddieco, 2004); (Wimmer, 2006); (Overeem et al., 2006); (Gugliotta et al., 2005).

According to United Nations E-Government Survey (2008), E-Government has gone through five phases. In the first phase, information on government operations and services was published in a static way. In the next phase, more information on public policy and governance was provided with links to archived information. Moving to the third phase, an interactive portal to deliver online services to enhance the convenience of citizens is evident. Interactions between public and government are established and online transactions are provided in the fourth phase. In the fifth phase, which no E-Government has achieved so far, integration between E-Government and back office infrastructure is established to enable involvement of the public in government decision-making, in particular, through e-participation. Interoperable services and applications are integrated in E-Government at this phase.

2.2 Interoperability in E-Government

The aim of E-Government is to develop a *one-stop knowledge-intensive government portal service* to enable the public to access all services at different levels of agencies where the users need have no knowledge or direct interaction with the government agencies. Therefore, services need to be interoperable in order to allow for data and information to be exchanged and processed seamlessly within or across government agencies. However, in E-Government development and implementation, there are challenges ahead and the following questions were raised in (Ojo & Janowski, 2005):

- How can systems from different agencies exchange information and messages meaningfully?
- How can information be integrated from various agencies, while guaranteeing semantic accuracy?
- How can government intranets capture and use the knowledge about the government itself (e.g., services, resources, etc.)?
- How can government services be dynamically configured based on the specifications of citizens, the private sector and public authorities?

Commonly, government organizations have a very distributed structure; whereas different agencies are organized in different levels (e.g., federal vs. state vs. local) and provide different services to the citizens. The operation of each of these agencies is supported by proprietary legacy systems. Due to the diversified level of government organizations, various issues related to technological heterogeneity, Organisational heterogeneity and information heterogeneity have arisen. Therefore, Organisational, semantic and technical interoperability as shown in Table 1 need to be established in order to resolve the heterogeneity problems in E-Government deployment (Brusa1 et al., 2007).

3. SEMANTIC INTEROPERABILITY

Interoperability is the ability to make information from one system semantically and syntactically accessible to another system. According to (Tripathi et al., 2007), "semantic interoperability is concerned with ensuring that the precise meaning of exchanged information is understandable by any other application that was not initially developed for the current purpose. Semantic interoperability enables distributed systems to combine received information with other information resources and to process it in a meaningful manner. Semantic interoperability is therefore a prerequisite for the front-end multilingual delivery of services to the user".

As depicted in Table 1, semantic interoperability is used to resolve information heterogeneity which resulted from structural heterogeneity and semantic heterogeneity. Examples of semantic heterogeneity are *synonymy*, *polysemy*, *acronym*, and *abbreviation*. These terms are further explained below:

- Synonymy refers to two different words with similar meaning, e.g., *reservation* and *booking* are synonymous.
- Polysemy are words which take on different meanings in different contexts, e.g., in a *military* context, *hardware* means military weaponry while in an *information technology* context, *hardware* refers to electrical components making up a computer system.
- Acronym is a word formed from the initial letters of a multi-word name. For example,

Table 1. Heterogeneity and interoperability in e-government

Heterogeneity	Interoperability
Organisational heterogeneity arises when the elements have different features that must be taken into consideration to solve problems in the State, such as processes, decisions, guidelines, criteria, work actors, among others.	*Organisational interoperability* refers to defining business goals, modeling business processes and bringing about the collaboration of administrations that wish to exchange information and may have different internal structures and processes.
Information heterogeneity arises from structural heterogeneity and semantic heterogeneity. Structural heterogeneity occurs when data are kept in different data structures; meanwhile semantic heterogeneity occurs when different data have the same meaning or when unique data refers to two different concepts.	*Semantic interoperability* concerns ensuring that the exact meaning of the exchanged information is understandable by any other application within or between administrations, either locally or across countries and with the enterprise sector.
Technological heterogeneity arises when there is technical diversity, such as different methodologies, platforms, protocols, equipments and work environments, among others.	*Technical interoperability* refers to the technical issues of linking computer systems and services, defining standard protocols and data formats.

the acronym for *grade point average* is *GPA*.

- Abbreviation is a shortened form of a word or phrase. For example, *technical* is abbreviated as *tech*.

Semantic interoperability needs to be achieved in order to integrate heterogeneous, distributed information and applications of different agencies so as to provide a comprehensive E-Government service as well as a knowledge sharing and learning platform for citizens. (Abecker et al. 2006) emphasize the importance of such an environment and succinctly summarize it as a "combination of information and process integration facilitating a variety of objects with specific semantics which seems to be quite natural: the E-Government domain can provide an ideal test bed for existing semantic web research, and semantic web technologies can be an ideal platform to achieve the vision of a knowledge-based, user-centric, distributed and networked E-Government."

4. SEMANTIC WEB TECHNOLOGIES

The Semantic Web technologies allow for publishing information to the public. They gather information through usable forms, react online to specific requests from the public, manage the on-

line exchange of items of high-value and integrate services (Paralic et al., 2003) for E-Government. In addition, the Semantic Web provides an effective and transparent E-Government. The web pages are defined with semantic meanings and metadata to enhance machine understanding and interpretation during information exchange as well as facilitate the integration of applications and information from many different sources (Klischewski, 23).

The Semantic Web aims to alleviate integration and interoperability problems of heterogeneous knowledge repositories across a network. The Semantic Web provides a common framework for developing an infrastructure to allow efficacious knowledge sharing and learning through the Semantic Web layer stack, whereas the lowest three layers (Unicode, URI, namespace and XML) act as a basis for defining semantics for a range of web resources. The RDF (Resource Description Framework) layer can be viewed as the first layer of the Semantic Web that provides metadata to web resources. Additional meta-information for annotating semantics to web resources is provided by the ontology layer and above.

According to Gruber (1993), an ontology is an "explicit specification of a conceptualization". Ontology is used to give explicit meaning to stored information, making it easier for machines to automatically process and integrate information. Commonly, semantic interoperability is achieved through the implementation of existing ontologies into a E-Government knowledge portal. In such portals, different ontologies have been developed in order to resolve the issue of semantic interoperability among various government agencies and departments. Through the use of these ontologies, integration of otherwise heterogeneous information and applications from various agencies into an E-Government portal has been made possible. For instance, (Fraser et al., 2003) developed the SmartGov E-Government ontology to provide the public authority with a knowledge-based core repository for government transaction services; (Daddieco 2004) has developed an ontology for the subject domain of export controls in the US government for effective knowledge retrieval and sharing. (Wimmer 2006) has developed an ontology for a knowledge map (semantic net) to support search and navigation via the net to enhance learning about government.

Ontology has also been used in conjunction with Semantic Web Services for enhancing semantic interoperability to E-Government services as illustrated in the work by (Overeem et al. 2006) and (Gugliotta et al., 2005). However, the use of ontology in defining knowledge services for E-Government services is still immature, and this topic of research will be quite a challenge for the E-Government movement as appropriate knowledge services from diversified types of services provided by different levels of government agencies need to be defined.

5. WEB 2.0 TECHNOLOGIES

5.1 Leveraging Web 2.0 in E-Government

In the world of Web 2.0, problems of interoperability are essentially issues about the quality of service. The public want to discover, access, organize, utilize whatever is available at the E-Government portal to help generate the results they desire, with minimal effort. This solution entails semantics in the user interface on the development of E-Government services Semantic Interoperability Community of Practice. Semantic interoperability is needed in order to provide the much needed semantics (i.e., meaning and context) to Web 2.0 services in the E-Government portal. Through semantic interoperability, "in-context" meaning among users can be better harnessed and shared leading to a richer user experience and a more user-friendly operating environment.

The Web 2.0 technologies provide a new infrastructure for government to interact with the public. Web 2.0 technologies such as blogs, wikis, content syndication, content tagging services, podcasting and multimedia sharing services (Anderson, 2007) are dramatically improving the knowledge sharing and learning capability of the public through (collective and collaborative) e-participation in government decision-making. Web 2.0 technologies increase the public awareness of the government processes and also provide a greater two-way communication between the government and the public.

The role of the Web 2.0 technologies in E-Government can be categorized into three distinct levels of use, which are: communication-focused, interaction-focused and services-focused (Chang & Kannan, 2008).

- *Communication-focused uses*: Government disseminates information that is relevant to citizens in a broad manner through blogs, RSS, wikis, enterprise social networks and podcasts and vlogs. In this way citizens have easy access to the information and gain more awareness of the content than they did previously.

- *Interaction-focused uses*: Government interacts with employees, other agencies and citizens to get their feedback on service design, new ideas, policies, plans, services and other government issues. Mash-ups of content and application are created to ben-

Figure 2. Media used for knowledge sharing and learning in e-government

Country	News	Email	RSS	Mobile	Blog	Chat
USA	x	x	x	x	x	x
Canada	x	x	x	x		
UK	x			x		
Australia	x	x	x			
China	x	x				
New Zealand	x	x	x			
South Africa	x	x				
Hong Kong	x		x	x		
Thailand	x					
Slovenia	x	x				

efit citizens. Web 2.0 technologies such as online community chat, blogs, social tagging, social networking, wiki are commonly leveraged in an E-Government portal.

- *Services-focused uses*: Government allows intermediaries to mash-up content and applications of government organizations to provide items of value to citizens. For example, banks can combine their customers' information with government information to help their customers file taxes and make the process more efficient for citizens. Virtual world experimentation to get feedback from citizens on service designs is another example of a useful application.

5.2 Web 2.0 Applications in E-Government

As can be seen from the E-Government portals shown in Figure 2, news, email, RSS feeds, mobile, blogs and chats are the media used by the government to stay connected with the public. These are particularly useful for disseminating up-to-date information on government services and activities.

As shown in Figure 2, Web 2.0 services are not yet widely adopted in E-Government. The most common Web 2.0 service used in the E-Governments to channel update information to public is RSS feeds. RSS (Really Simple Syndication) feeds allow the public to obtain up-to-date information automatically from RSS-enabled E-Government portals without having to constantly go and visit the sites.

In Table 2, other Web 2.0 technologies that can positively contribute to the way the public can leverage their knowledge sharing and learning activities as well as participate in E-Government decision-making are listed.

Leveraging Web 2.0 technologies into Semantic Web E-Government knowledge-intensive portal services can be an effective way for knowledge and information exchange and can enhance the learning process through collaborative effort as demonstrated in Wagner et al.'s (2006) work. They have developed Semantic Webs for E-Government using the Wiki technology, namely the semantic Wiki web. Through such portals, knowledge sharing can be more successful and

Table 2. Web 2.0 technologies, descriptions and e-government websites

Application	Descriptions	Examples of E-Government websites with such features (if available)
Blogs	A Blog is a simple webpage consisting of information, opinion or links, called posts which are arranged chronologically with the most recent first. Blog facilitates critical feedback from the public by letting them express their opinion on topics by adding comments.	http://www.egovni.com/ http://blog.usa.gov/roller/ http://www.pueblo.gsa.gov/http://www.openmass.org/
Wikis	The best known Wiki is Wikipedia, the world's largest online encyclopedia, it allow users to read and edit the information in the wiki web document. It can be referred to as a collaborative tool for the community. Wiki can store plain texts with a limited degree of formatting support.	http://www.govitwiki.com/ http://utahegov.wikispaces.com/ http://oim.modernisering.dk/StartSide
Podcasts	Podcasts are audio or video recordings of talks, interviews etc. that play on wide range of handheld MP3 devices. These content are usually tagged for easy and automatic download into consumer devices for replay.	http://utahsciencecenter.org/uscprograms.php http://www.polity.org.za/
Mash-ups	Mash-ups are web services that pull together data from different sources to create a new service. Increasingly, business users are empowered to produce their own mash-ups without support from IT staff.	http://www.dhs.alabama.gov/ http://rru.worldbank.org/businessplanet/
Social bookmarking	Social bookmarking allows users to create lists of bookmarks which can be tagged with keywords. A bookmark can belong in more than one category.	http://www.ico.gov.uk/ http://www.usa.gov/
Social networking	Social networking builds links with relevant social networks through interaction and by posting tailored information.	http://twitter.com/egovrc

knowledge learning can be fostered in more effective and collaborative way.

6. CHALLENGES AND ISSUES

Designing a Semantic Web for E-Government poses several challenges. Firstly, there is the difficulty of extracting knowledge and information from documents and people and identifying the semantic relationships between these knowledge objects in order to design ontologies for E-Government. Secondly, integration often is a bottleneck and poses severe difficulties due to the highly heterogeneous structure of diversified applications across different levels of government. Thirdly, there is also the shortage of expertise and resources to verify the content and the semantic links in indexed web documents. Lastly, rapid change of web documents and their semantic

relationships compromise the review efforts mentioned above.

In the world of Web 2.0, one key challenge for E-Government is how to select and implement the right Web 2.0 technologies to positively enhance and leverage knowledge sharing and learning capabilities for improving government services and processes, and also to increase participation from the public for better government decision-making. There is also the common challenge of Knowledge Management (KM) which is to entice people to use these services and share their knowledge in a sustained way.

More complications exist. With the use of social bookmarking in tagging, folksonomy has emerged from the practice and this has resulted in inconsistent and ambiguous terms that prevent knowledge sharing and learning activities from taking place efficiently. Resolving the ambiguity and inconsistent meanings of the tags poses another challenge for E-Government. Current research on integrating taxonomy and folksonomy tags is nevertheless being carried out by the authors (Kiu & Tsui, 2009).

Without proper control and coordination, E-Government might have difficulty in maintaining the fast growing repository of knowledge through the widely used Web 2.0 services.

7. CONCLUSION

The E-Government knowledge-intensive portal services extend knowledge management by enabling different groups of users (civil servants and citizens alike) to organize and share information from heterogeneous applications of government agencies. Such a portal is highly advantageous to the public because it offers great opportunities for quality service delivery and interaction in an easy and convenient way, and can deliver a range of government information and services.

Deployment of E-Government knowledge-intensive portal services with a combination of the Semantic Web and Web 2.0 technologies can ensure semantic interoperability to integrate heterogeneous applications and information from different levels of government agencies in order to share knowledge and enable learning to take place efficaciously. Such an accomplishment can improve public participation in government decision-making. In addition, an appropriately devised knowledge service enables governments to provide appropriate and efficient services to the public through the E-Government knowledge portals. However, significant challenges still need to be overcome before the above aim can be achieved.

ACKNOWLEDGMENT

The authors gratefully acknowledge the support of The Hong Kong Polytechnic University (under grant account 1-45-37-0542) for carrying out this piece of research.

REFERENCES

Abecker, A., Sheth, A., Mentzas, G., & Stojanovic, L. (2006). The Semantic Web meets eGovernment. In *Proceedings of the 2006 AAAI Spring Symposium* Series, Stanford University, Stanford, CA. Retrieved August 28, 2008, from http://www.aaai.org/Press/Reports/Symposia/Sprin g/ss0606.php

Anderson, P. (2007). *What is Web 2.0? Ideas, technologies and implications for education.* JISC Technology and Standards Watch.

Arroyo, S., Ding, Y., Lara, R., Stollberg, M., & Fensel, D. (2004). Semantic Web Languages - Strengths and Weakness. In *Proceedings of the International Conference in Applied computing (IADIS04)*, Lisbon, Portugal.

Bloomberg, J. (2003). The role of the service-oriented architect. *The Rational Edge*. Retrieved August 28, 2008, from http://www.therationaledge.com/conte nt/may_03/ PDF/bloomber g.pdf

Brusa1, G., Caliusco, M. L., & Chiotti, O. (2007). Enabling Knowledge Sharing within E-Government Back-Office Through Ontological Engineering. *Journal of Theoretical and Applied Electronic Commerce Research, 2*(1), 33-48.

Chang, A., & Kannan, P. K. (2008). *Leveraging Web 2.0 in Government, E-Government/ Technology Series*. IBM Center for The Business of Government.

Daddieco, R. J. (2004). *Retrieving knowledge in E-Government: the prospects of ontology for regulatory domain record keeping systems*. Wimmer.

Di, A. M. (2007). *What Does Web 2.0 Mean to Government?* Stamford, CT: Gartner.

Estabrook, L., Witt, E., & Rainie, L. (2007). *Information searches that solve problems - How people use the Internet, libraries, and government agencies when they need help*. Pew Internet & American Life Project.

Fraser, J., Adams, N., Macintosh, A., McKay-Hubbard, A., Lobo, T. P., Pardo, P. F., et al. (2003). Knowledge Management Applied to E-Government Service: The Use of an Ontology. In M. Wimmer (Ed.), *Proceedings of Knowledge Management in E-Government (KMGov 2003)* (LNCS 2645, pp. 116-126). New York: Springer.

Gruber, T. R. (1993). A Translation Approach to portable Ontology Specifications. *Knowledge Acquisition*, *5*, 199–220. doi:10.1006/knac.1993.1008

Gugliotta, A., Cabral, L., Domingue, J., & Roberto, V. (2005). A semantic web service-based architecture for the interoperability of E-Government services. In *proceedings of International Workshop on Web Information Systems Modeling (WISM 2005)*, Sydney, Australia.

Kiu, C. C., & Tsui, E. (2009). Taxonomy - Folksonomy Integration for Knowledge Navigation through Unsupervised Data Mining Techniques. Knowledge Management Research & Practice. *Knowledge Management Research and Practice*, *8*, 24–32.

Klischewski, R. (2003). Semantic Web for E-Government. In R. Traunmuller (Ed.), *Proceedings of EGOV 2003* (LNCS 2739). New York: Springer.

Misra, D. C. (2006). *E-Government: The State of Art Today-2*. Paper presented at the Official Launching of the Government-to-Government System and CIO Workshop, Ebene Cyber Tower, Rose Hill, Mauritius.

Nagarajan, M., Verma, K., Sheth, A. P., Miller, J., & Lathem, J. (2006) Semantic Interoperability of Web Services - Challenges and Experiences. In *Proceedings of the IEEE International Conference on Web Services (ICWS 2006)*.

Niemann, B. (2008). Getting to SOA and Semantic Interoperability for DoD Architectures. In *Proceedings of the 6th Annual DoD Architectures Conference*. Retrieved August 28, 2008, from http://semanticcommunity.wik.is/@api/deki/files/569/=BNiemannIDGA03032008.ppt?revision=2

Ojo, A., & Janowski, T. (2005). *Ontology, Semantic Web and Electronic Government*. Retrieved August 1, 2008, from http://www.emacao.gov.mo/documents/14/13/seminar1 3.pdf

Overeem, A., Witters, J., & Peristeras, T. (2006). *Semantic Interoperability in pan-European eGovernment services*. Retrieved July 6, 2008, from http://www.semantic-gov.org/ind ex.php?Name=UpDownload&req=getit&cid=2&lid=246

Paralic, J., Sabol, T., & Mach, M. (2003). *Knowledge Enhanced E-Government Portal. Knowledge Management in Electronic Government*. Berlin: Springer.

Reichling, K. (2009). *Semantic interoperability for public administrations in Europe – challenges and solutions, iDABC European eGovernment Services*. Retrieved July 1, 2009, from https://www.posccaesar.org/svn/pub/SemanticDays/2009/Session_1_Klaus_Reichling.pdf

Semantic Interoperability Community of Practice (SICoP). (2006). *Semantic Wave 2006*. Retrieved August 1, 2008, from http://web-services.gov/SICOPsemwave2006v1.0.doc

Sidoroff, T., & Hyvonen, E. (2005). Semantic E-Government portals - a case study. In *Proceedings of the ISWC-2005 Workshop Semantic Web Case Studies and Best Practices for eBusiness (SWCASE05)*.

Steven, P. (2008). Govt portal wins global award. *The Star Online*. Retrieved May 21, 2008, from http://thestar.com.my /news/story.asp?file=/2008/5/21/nation/200805211819&sec=nation

Tripathi, R., Gupta, M. P., & Bhattacharya, J. (2007). Selected Aspects of Interoperability in One-stop Government Portal of India. In *Proceedings of the 5th International Conference on E-Government*, Hyderabad, India.

United Nations E-Government Survey. (2008). *From E-Government to Connected Governance*. New York: United Nations.

Wagner, C., Cheung, K. S. K., Ip, R. K. F., & Böttcher, S. (2006). Building Semantic Webs for E-Government with Wiki technology. *Electronic Government*, *3*(1), 36–55. doi:10.1504/EG.2006.008491

Wimmer, M. A. (2006). Implementing a knowledge portal for egovernment based on semantic modelling: The E-Government intelligent portal (eip.at). In *Proceedings of the 39th Annual Hawaii International Conference on System Sciences (HICSS'06)*.

This work was previously published in the International Journal of Knowledge and Systems Science, Volume 1, Issue 2, edited by W.B. Lee, pp. 39-48 copyright 2010 by IGI Publishing (an imprint of IGI Global).

Chapter 18
A Formalised Approach to the Management of Risk:
A Conceptual Framework and Ontology

Mike Brownsword
Atego, UK

Rossitza Setchi
Cardiff University, UK

ABSTRACT

Taking pragmatic, systems engineering approach, this paper identifies a number of fundamental issues that presently arise in risk management, primarily as a result of the overly complex approach convention- ally taken in process definition and a lack of coherence within the current risk management vocabulary. The aim of the paper is to enable a fundamental simplification of the risk management process and an improved understanding of the associated terminology. The outcome of this work is a formalised but pragmatic approach to risk management resulting in the development of a conceptual framework and an associated ontology, which emphasises the understanding of people and their environment as part of risk management. The approach has been validated in a number of case studies of varying depth and breadth from the IT domain, defence, rail industry, and education, covering health and safety, business, project and individual needs.

DOI: 10.4018/978-1-4666-1782-7.ch018

INTRODUCTION

Background

The consideration of risk is a day-to-day phenomenon used by individuals and Small to Medium Enterprises (SMEs) as well as large national, multinational and global organisations. Although in many instances risks may be 'mitigated' this does not mean that all complex issues have been well understood.

Risk management proposes to be a solution to understanding and removing the worry associated with issues which may arise in the future. As a discipline it has existed since the 1960s, emerging from an historic need and desire to insure. From the 1980s clear reference can be made to a process for risk management which has remained relatively unchanged.

There are many tools available to assist in the modelling of complex systems. Modelling allows simplification of the system to allow the complexity to be understood or at least to aid the recognition that there is a complex issue. These tools vary from high level business strategy identification to Failure Modes and Effects Analysis (FMEA) examining the detail associated with failures of components in a system.

Many industries recognise the need for risk management. The UK railway industry for example has a defined and documented regime for addressing risk. This regime is documented and controlled through the use of standards such as EN 50126 (1999). It introduces risk as a safety concept which can be seen to run throughout a project lifecycle. However many industries have not recognised either the importance of formalising risk management and the surrounding issues or that the technology they are working with has associated risk. This lack of recognition may have legal, personal and technological impact.

Context and Scope

Observations made whilst working with aerospace, rail, defence and government organisations have shown a number of issues with the implementation of current risk management best practice. In some cases these issues arise due to a lack of willingness to carry out thorough risk management or to react when risks are revealed. However in many cases these managerial issues are compounded by fundamental issues of complexity and lack of pragmatism associated with the risk management process. Inhibiting the resolutions of many of these issues is the lack of understanding and agreement on terminology used to describe and discuss risk. As a result, the word 'risk' means something different almost every time it is used.

The aim of the paper is to propose a conceptual framework and an ontology enabling a fundamental simplification of the risk management and an improved understanding of the associated terminology. The outcome of this work is a formalised but pragmatic approach to risk management, which emphasises the understanding of people and their environment as part of risk management.

The paper introduces generic risk management frameworks, standards and terminology, providing a critical analysis of the risk terminology and definitions. Next, a conceptual framework and an associated ontology is proposed, followed by a conclusion.

LITERATURE REVIEW

Much of the literature relating to risk management is specific to industry, applications and tools. Instead, this literature review is focused on generic risk management frameworks, standards and associated terminology.

Frameworks

One of the first frameworks for risk management is Boehm's spiral model (1986) which is risk driven and reflects the incremental nature of most software development projects. Boehm (1989) defines software risk management as a discipline whose objectives are to "identify, address, and eliminate software risk items before they become either threats to successful software operation or major sources of software rework" (p. 1). He defines two primary steps within risk management: risk control and risk assessment. Three sub-steps exist within each; risk control covering management, monitoring and resolution and risk assessment involving identification, analysis and prioritisation. Boehm's approach provides a differentiation between risk assessment and risk control, and a useful delineation between identifying and fully defining risks and the plans and controls which need to be in place to ensure that risks are dealt with effectively.

Hughes and Cotterell (1999) have extended Boehm's model by defining risk engineering as involving risk analysis and risk management. The management area groups all planning, staffing, directing, monitoring and control activities whilst the analysis area focuses on the identification, estimation and evaluation of risk. It is believed that many of the changes are in the meaning of the word 'management'. In Boehm's work, the term 'risk management' is used to signify the whole area of risk assessment, analysis and control whereas Hughes and Cotterell are using management to specify only the control, planning and resource issues leaving identification, estimation and evaluation to risk analysis. Kirchsteiger (2008) takes a similar view when he explains risk assessment as the 'fact finding', and the administrative follow up measures as risk management.

Redmill (2002) highlights the three stages most consider to be included in risk analysis: hazard identification, hazard analysis and risk assessment (or evaluation). Furthermore, he expands these steps by adding a 'definition of scope' concerned with the planning of the work to be carried out during the risk analysis. Jenkins et al. (2009), Mohaghegh et al (2009) and Olsen and Lindoe (2009) all employ the concept of context or viewpoints. Olsen and Lindoe use context to understand the implications of transferring technology between contexts. Jenkins et al utilise dimensions to develop a management framework and Mohaghegh uses perspectives and multilevel framing to ensure the relevant aspects are included in the analysis.

Redmill's contribution is that he reflects on project management issues in terms of cost and time in relation to the detail required from a technique used to define hazards within the risk analysis stages. However, Redmill is predominantly concerned with hazards or causes. According to him, risk is the end point of understanding hazards where others including Boehm (1989) focus on effects rather than causes. Woodruff (2005) argues that the focus on consequence and hazard ensures that decisions are not based on overall risk which he suggests is leading to risk adverse stakeholders defining the level of acceptable or tolerable risk.

This lack of consistency is symptomatic of the lack of connectivity across disciplines when it comes to the understanding of risk. The variation in definition between Boehm and Redmill, including the focus on cause or effect, highlights a need to consider standard practice. It will be important to note whether the standards are industry specific or cross discipline. The next section investigates whether standards have provided a common understanding and approach to risk management.

Standards

Many professional bodies and industry organisations provide guidance, codes of practice and principles for risk management. These include the Institute of Chartered Accountants in England and Wales (ICAEW), the Institute of Risk Management (IRM), the Association of Insurance and Risk

Managers (AIRMIC) and the Canadian Information Processing Society (CIPS) to name a few.

In its briefing on risk management for SMEs, ICAEW (2002) identifies the need to apply risk management across the organisation expanding from the previous narrow financial view it took. Their recommendation is to consider five categories of risk: strategic, operational, financial, compliance and environmental. The risk management process defined by ICAEW normally involves:

- identifying and ranking the risks inherent in the company's strategy,
- selecting the appropriate risk management approaches,
- implementing controls to manage the remaining risks,
- monitoring the effectiveness of risk management approaches and controls, and
- learning from experience and making improvements.

This document defines the activities that the process must deliver and enforces the view that risk should be cross business rather than purely financial. It however does not explain whether 'business' is only the management side of an organisation or whether it is intended to include technical project and development.

The IRM (2002) have defined 'A risk management standard' with the purpose of providing an agreed terminology, process by which risk management can be carried out, organisation structure for risk management, and objective for risk management. The standard defines the drivers of risks, in terms of internal and external factors and further categorises these into types of risk which are financial, strategic, operational, and hazards. Much of the terminology used in the standard is adopted by ISO/IEC Guide 73 (2009) which is a positive move to ensure that a shared set of terminology is used within risk management.

Standards normally describe risk management as a lifecycle, process or a variation of the two. This section investigates four standards to understand the associated issues and the approach each standard takes.

IEC 61508 does not discuss risk management explicitly. Its focus is on the equipment being used to provide specific functions and its potential to cause harm. It highlights the need for hazard and risk analysis for which it defines a number of objectives including determining:

- the hazards and hazardous events of the equipment and its control system for all reasonably foreseeable circumstances, including fault conditions and misuse,
- the event sequences leading to the hazardous event, and
- the risks associated with the hazardous event.

Next, the standard defines a set of requirements for the hazard and risk analysis ensuring that the hazards and hazardous events are defined, event sequences determined, hazard eliminations considered, likelihood of hazardous events evaluated, and potential consequences determined. The standard discusses the relationship between hazard, hazardous event and risk. A hazardous event is defined as the situation where a person is harmed; risk is the probability of the harm and its severity. The standard states that risk shall be evaluated, or estimated, for each hazardous event.

The approach the standard takes, only defining the requirements to be fulfilled, leaves an organisation to select and implement its own choice of risk management approaches or indeed to define its own. This can be advantageous for those with multiple approaches dependant on project or product, but can make demonstration of compliance complicated. The standard provides a good overall set of ideas for the consideration of safety related systems. It does not consider risk management but does feed forward into many domain specific standards including EN 50126 (1999), focused on the rail industry, which like IEC 61508 does not define a specific risk management approach or process but a lifecycle which has an element of risk analysis integrated within.

ISO 15288 (2002), the second standard discussed in this section, is arguably the most widely used systems engineering standard in the world. It is considered the key standard for understanding systems lifecycles by many including the International Council on Systems Engineering (INCOSE) who's Systems Engineering Handbook (2007) is based on the standard. ISO 15288 prescribes processes for systems engineering and a structure in which they can be applied. The framework also provides detail of the risk management process in the form of expected outcomes and tasks.

ISO 15288 is not a risk specific standard. However it still considers risk management a necessary part of a system life cycle and as such defines the outcomes and tasks which should be performed. It does not in any way define a flow for these tasks leaving it to the organisation to tailor as applicable. The standard provides a very good overall framework for understanding system lifecycles and presents an approach to defining them which enables processes to be re-used throughout the lifecycle rather than used once as some authors would suggest. Although ISO 15288 does not provide a deep and all encompassing explanation of risk management, it offers a good overview to work from within a framework which can be applied in most situations and organisations. The risk management process it describes is commensurate with those from other standards and best practice models including those already discussed. This standard is aimed at providing capability for the whole organisation rather than a single risk management focus.

The third standard considered, AS/NZS 4360 (2004) provides a generic set of guidance focused on improving identification of opportunities and threats, pro-active management, incident management, stakeholder confidence and trust, compliance with legislation and corporate governance. Alongside this breadth of objectives it is

aimed at many different activities, organisations and communities. It defines terminology, a risk management process, a detailed version of the process and provides some thoughts on assessing current practices and planning. This standard provides a set of goals aimed at supporting and guiding organisations through risk management. Even though this is considered one of the best examples of a risk management standard in the world, the detail it presents leaves questions and confusion as to which way the user of the standard should proceed. This coupled with the volume of unconnected terminology can only lead to different interpretations of the standard.

As a new overarching risk management standard ISO 31000 (2009a) is in a position to clearly define risk management, its needs and processes. The standard claims to recognise the variety of the nature, level and complexity of risks and provide generic guidelines on principles and implementation of risk management. It aims to describe the relationship between the principles for managing risk, the risk management framework and the risk management process. It provides a framework which enables a business level view of risk management. The framework is designed to enable a business to implement the risk management process whilst integrating risk management into its existing management systems. The framework is comprised of five components:

- mandate and commitment,
- design of framework for managing risk,
- implementing risk management,
- monitoring and review of the framework, and
- continual improvement of the framework.

The risk management process includes five activities: communication and consultation, establishing the context, risk assessment, risk treatment and monitoring and review. The risk assessment activity is further defined by three sub-activities:

risk identification, risk analysis and risk evaluation as defined in the ISO Guide 73 (2007).

The framework defined by the standard adds a level of business integration which has not been observed previously in other standards, although it is similar in style to the spiral model defined by Beohm (1986) which provides a project level framework for software risk management. The ISO 31000 framework enables a level of senior management involvement which has not been in evidence previously at an organisational level. The use of Guide 73 provides a single reference point for risk terminology. The next section investigates further the clarity of the terms and their relationships.

CRITICAL ANALYSIS OF RISK TERMINOLOGY AND DEFINITIONS

The AS/NZS 4360 standard defines twenty seven terms, some of which have cross references to other terms within the list. Each term is accompanied by explanatory text and notes giving some context to the term presented. Figure 1 a shows a diagrammatic interpretation of the definitions and the relationships between the terms proposed in AS/NZ 4360 (2004). These definitions and relationships highlight some fundamental issues:

- Some terms are not related to any of the other terms defined (e.g., 'hazard' and 'monitor').
- Where they are related it is not always clear what the relationship is (e.g., 'risk' and 'risk management framework').
- Ambiguous relationships also exist. For instance, 'risk avoidance' is related to 'risk' although the definition describes a 'risk situation'. It is not clear in this case whether it is the risk or the situation which is being withdrawn from. In addition, 'risk reduction' references 'risk' as being associated with 'consequence' and 'likelihood'

but this association is not mentioned in the definition of risk, 'consequence' or 'likelihood' causing confusion as to the nature of the relationship.

- A number of terms which would generally be related to risk have not been, specifically 'consequence' and 'likelihood', although the 'risk reduction' definition does suggest that there may be a relationship between them.
- The definitions of 'risk reduction' and 'risk treatment' either lessen or modify 'risk'; the difference between them seems to be only the level at which they are applied; one to 'risk', the other to 'likelihood' and 'consequence'.

The ISO Guide 73 provides the basic definitions of risk management generic terms, which are split into four groups: basic terms, terms related to people or organisation affected by risk, terms related to risk assessment, and terms related to risk treatment and control. This paper focuses on the basic terms referencing specific relationships where relevant (Figure 1 b). The guide defines seventeen basic terms many of which have multiple definitions including 'risk' which has one main definition and two variations. Each definition provides references to other defined terms used within.

Figure 1 b shows that more than half of the terms defined relate directly to the definition of risk. The number of direct relationships to the definition of risk presents an issue when factoring in the general lack of relationship from these terms to any other definition. This concern is supported by the repetition of relationships (e.g., 'directs and controls' risk and 'provides intentions, policies, procedures or decisions relating to the management of risk'). Figure 1 b also shows relationships marked as <<implied>> which are not stated by reference but are suggested by the notes associated with the definition.

Figure 1. Risk management terminology

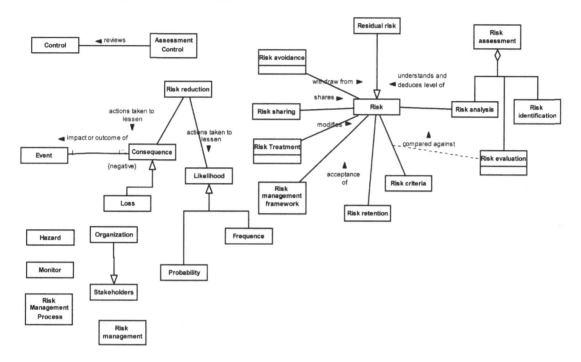

a. AS/NZS 4360 Risk Management Terminology

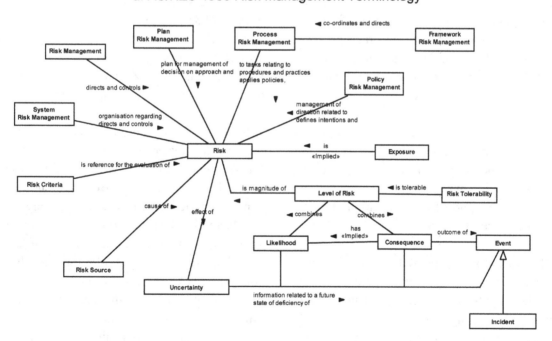

b. ISO Guide 73 Risk Management Terminology

Figure 2. QoS UML profile

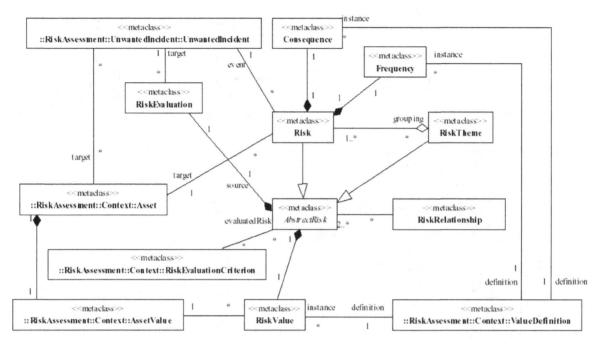

Each of these two standards has its own advantages. ISO 31000 uses relationships from all of its terms. AS/NZS 4360 incorporates process terminology where ISO 31000 separates it into a different set of definitions. There are similarities which may be useful to note:

- The relationships between 'consequence' and 'event' are almost identical.
- Both standards provide detail regarding the composition of risk.
- They both ignore the composition of most terms other than risk.

The fact that both standards have similar issues with the definition of risk and the direct relationships they try to assert between management terms and risk highlight the need for a formalised approach to the definition of domain terminology. When the same modelling principle is applied to other sets of terminology similar results are achieved. 'Risk treatment' for example is referred

to as a process, activity and a measure (solution) in ISO 16085 (2006).

The UML profile for modelling quality of service (QoS) (OMG, 2008b) shown in Figure 2 is based on the AS/NZS 4360 (2004) terminology. It defines 'risk' through 'frequency' and 'consequence'. It can be seen by the clarity and volume of relationships between the terms in Figure 2 that this profile provides a better related set of terminology than either standard considered above. This approach may be of use in supporting a more generic model of risk terminology.

Mazouni and Aubry (2007) use the UML in a similar way but rather than defining a profile they have defined an ontology for Preliminary Hazard Analysis (PHA). PHA is a specific tool used for hazard identification, in this case applied in the rail industry. This work again improves the clarity of the use and relationships between terms.

The numerous definitions of risk and its surrounding terminology alongside the lack of consistency in the relationships between terms is a complex issue. To further understand the root cause of this problem focus will be placed on the central term 'risk'. This work considers a number of risk definitions from texts and standards (see Figure 3) prior to drawing conclusions regarding overall issues with the definition of risk.

The Harvey's financial definition of risk (2010) contains a succinct definition focused on the loss of money; the *Asset* is providing a return and it is the uncertainty of the return that is a concern.

Leveson (1995) provides a number of definitions including risk and hazard. He defines risk as the hazard level combined with (i) the likelihood of the hazard leading to an accident (sometimes called danger) and (ii) hazard exposure or duration (sometimes called latency). In this definition, *Hazard exposure* requires an understanding of how long something will be exposed. The point Leveson is trying to make is that the longer one is in a hazardous state, the more likely an accident is to occur.

Roland and Moriarty (1990) state that risk is associated with likelihood or possibility of harm; it is the expected value of loss. The empty diamond in Figure 3 denotes that *Risk* may still exist if either *Possibility* or *Value* is not present. This definition shows two very different ideas of what risk is. Moreover, Roland and Moriarty imply that the *Value of Loss* is equivalent to *Possibility* of *Harm*.

Storey (1996) in his book on safety critical computer systems defines risk as is a combination of the frequency or probability of a specified hazardous event, and its consequence. It is the frequency of an event combined with the consequence that makes up risk. The problem, which can be seen in this diagram (Figure 3), is the use of the word 'combination' as there is no explanation of how to combine the relevant information.

BS 6079-3 (2000) describes risk as the uncertainty inherent in plans and the possibility of something happening that can affect the prospects of achieving business or project goals. This definition uses vague terminology - it is not difficult to agree that there is a possibility of something

happening. This definition is bordering on the possibilistic discussed by Clarke (2007).

BS 8444 (1996) defines risk as the combination of the frequency, or probability, of occurrence and the consequence of a specified hazardous event. The interpretation of this definition in Figure 3 provides an understanding of a strong relationship between *Hazardous event* and *Occurrence and consequence*. It is strange however that occurrence and consequence are combined as there could be many possible consequences for any one occurrence.

EN 50126 (1999) defines risk as the probable rate of occurrence of a hazard causing harm and the degree of severity of the harm. Figure 3 shows a level of separation between the probability (*Probable rate*) and the harm. This separation raises questions as to which probability is specified in the definition. It is not clear whether it is the probability of the hazard occurring or the harm.

Seven definitions of risk have been considered and a number of similarities can be identified including the use of probability, focus on outcomes, use of hazard, dependency on timing and multiple interpretations.

The first of these similarities, the use of probability, can be seen in many of the definitions through the use of words like frequency, likelihood and uncertainty. These terms all infer the use of probability in risk. For probability to mean something in terms of risk it must be relevant to its mathematical definition and therefore the sum of all probabilities must equal one.

The definitions above all in some way refer to an outcome. Some consider this to be harm, accident or consequence. The problem with accident and harm is that they only take into account one view of the argument – the negative effect. To gain a fuller picture future (Hollnagel, 2008) and positive (Flage & Aven, 2009) consequences must also be considered.

A number of the definitions incorporate 'hazard', a word which could be considered to have as many definitions as risk. In general it is used to

Figure 3. Definitions of risk

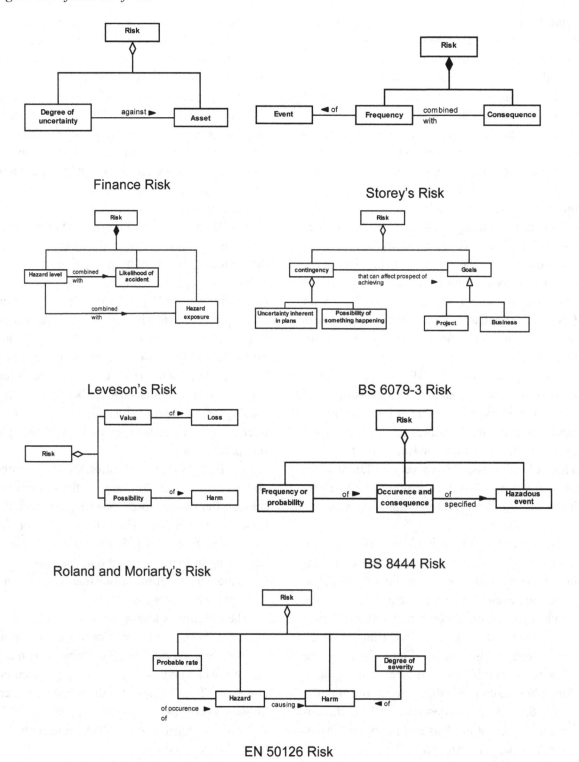

Figure 4. Framework requirements

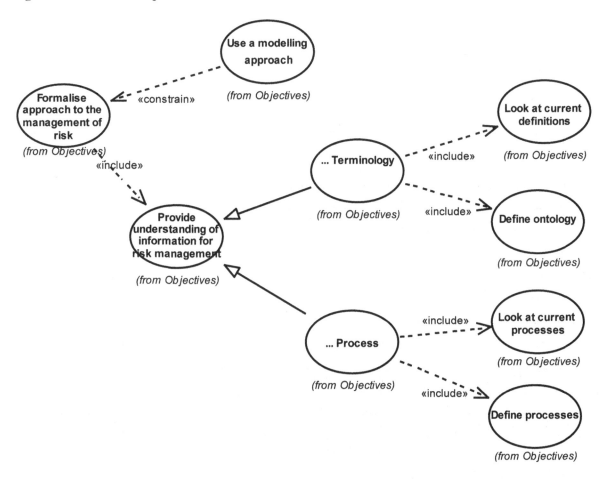

signify an event preceding the outcome or consequence under scrutiny (Gamper & Turcanu, 2009; Stevens & Thevaranjan, 2009; Woodruff, 2005).

CONCEPTUAL FRAMEWORK FOR THE FORMALISATION OF RISK MANAGEMENT

The framework must fulfil the needs of formalisation including enabling consistency, repeatability, multiple views and pragmatism. Furthermore, to provide a consistent understanding of risk management it is desirable to have a common approach to the consideration of all concepts being investigated and defined. The conceptual framework must (Figure 4):

- use a modelling approach
- be capable of providing an understanding of the current terminology of risk management
- be applicable to the definition of ontologies and taxonomies, and
- be an accepted approach for the definition of processes.

Options to be considered for the provision of the framework required focus on modelling languages as languages provide an abstraction from specific applications. Table 1 lists ten graphical

Table 1. Framework options

Name/Ref.	Description	Terminology		Process		Formal Output
		Current	Defn.	Current	Defn.	
Business Process Modeling Notation (BPMN) (OMG 2008a)	A general process modelling language.	N	N	Y	Y	N
EXPRESS and EXPRESS-G (ISO 2004)	An international standard general-purpose data modelling language.	Y	Y	N	N	Y
Extended Enterprise Modeling Language (EEML) (Krogstie 2008)	A multi layer approach to modelling business processes including goals and resources.	Y	Y	Y	Y	?
Flowchart (ISO 5807 1985)	A schematic representation of an algorithm or process.	N	N	Y	Y	N
IDEF (1994)	A family of modelling languages, including IDEF3 for business process modelling and IDEF5 for modelling ontologies.	Y	Y	Y	Y	N
Object Role Modeling (ORM) (Halpin and Morgan 2008)	A method for relational modelling that can be used for information and rules analysis.	Y	Y	N	N	N
Petri nets (Girault and Rudiger 2002)	A technique for the description and analysis of processes, specifically focused on concurrent processes in distributed systems.	N	N	Y	Y	Y
Specification and Description Language(SDL) (ITU-T 1999)	A specification language targeted at the behaviour of distributed systems.	N	N	Y	Y	Y
Systems Modelling Language (SysML) (OMG 2008c)	A domain-specific modelling language for systems engineering that is defined as a profile of the UML.	Y	Y	Y	Y	Y
Unified Modeling Language (UML) (OMG 2007)	A general-purpose modelling language that is an industry standard for specifying software-intensive systems. UML 2.0, the current version, supports thirteen different diagram techniques, and has widespread tool support.	Y	Y	Y	Y	Y

modelling languages showing their ability to model and define terminology and processes, and provide a formal output. Based on the information shown in Table 1 the UML and SysML are the only languages able to fulfil the requirements stated above, specifically the ability to define both processes and terminology. As the SysML is a profile of the UML with some specific additions it is possible to select both. The main work of defining ontology and processes will be carried

out using the UML. Concepts from the SysML will be used where relevant.

To further support the use of the UML a number of example applications have been investigated. These example applications have been categorised by industry and are related to a general set of terms which can be used to describe concepts within a systems understanding. The two major concepts to which this paper relates the applications it describes are *Life cycle concept* and *Development*. The *Life cycle concept* provides

Figure 5. Conceptual framework

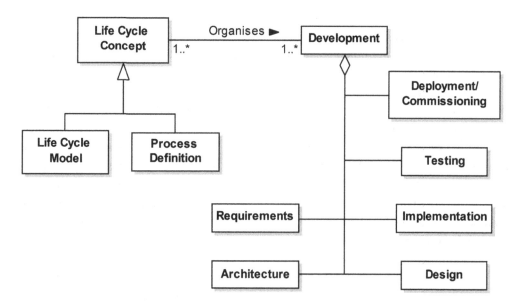

all of the organisation tools including life cycles, life cycle models and the processes which are executed within them. The need for the *Life cycle concept* lies in the need to organise the work being carried out, this work has been captured with the use of the term 'development'. *Development* in this case is the activity of the people carrying out the work whether organised by life cycle and process or not.

Development can be considered a wide concept, a statement with which NATO agrees based on its definition of the software development process, from their standard AQAP-150 (1997), the process by which user need/requirements are translated into a software product. Somerville (2007) suggests that software development is where the software is designed and programmed. However he surrounds this definition with the concepts of specification, validation and evolution.

Using these definitions as a basis, a set of activities likely to occur within a development is proposed. These abstracted activities are: requirements, architectures, design, implementation, testing and deployment. The activities may sound like processes or life cycle phases: in this case they represent the natural practices which people will carry out even without a process or lifecycle in place.

The diagram in Figure 5 showing the concepts and the activities within a development is used to relate example applications to the life cycle concepts and development. The examples will firstly be taken from the IT/IS domain followed by defence, rail industry and then science/education. Each application will have a brief explanation outlining its work and highlighting the areas that were aided through formalisation using the UML.

The first area to be investigated is the IT/IS domain. Five IT applications of the UML have been considered including associations with the life cycle concepts and development activities. These five applications apply to different aspects of the development and life cycle concepts: code generation and software patterns, the Semantic Web, the unified process, use case based requirements, and security-critical IT systems.

- Peckham and MacKellar (2001) use the UML to record design patterns from the database community, once recorded the known good patterns were incorporated into high level conceptual models for new software. The re-use of design patterns enabled speedier design and implementation.

- Baclawski et al. (2001) investigate the use of the UML as an ontology development language by comparing it with existing markup languages. They conclude that incompatibility issues can be resolved through the definition of a UML profile.

- Jacobson et al. (1999) define the unified process as an iterative and incremental life cycle model where the stages in the life cycle are carried out once, with the processes being run many times within each stage.

- Some (2005) defines an approach using use cases along side a number of domain models (class diagrams) to provide a formalisation of the requirements engineering process. This has been carried out to improve the link between customer need and the system design and implementation.

- Vraalsen et al. (2004) apply the UML to risk analysis of security-critical IT systems and provide a tool-supported methodology for model-based analysis. This tool has been designed to apply across all development activities.

From these examples it is reasonable to conclude that the UML is accepted across the IT/IS domain as a tool which provides a level of formalisation and consistency which is not inherent in other system definition tools.

This section discusses a number of non-IT/IS applications of the UML. For each example it describes how the UML has been used to aid in formalisation, consistency and communication. The first of these areas is defence where, with so many organisations contracting for and supplying equipment, a clear consistent approach to communication and system definition is imperative. Three defence applications are considered in this work. These applications apply to different aspects

of the development and life cycle concepts: process formalisation, architectural framework, and conceptualisation. The main points from each of these applications are detailed below.

- Company A uses the UML to define its life cycles and processes. When following the processes for system development all relevant information and artefacts are also developed and delivered through the medium of UML. This company is doing this to improve its systems engineering capability. It sees the use of the UML as providing consistency and formalisation to the work they are carrying out.

- MODAF (2007) provides an architectural framework for the UK Ministry of Defence (MOD). This framework is used to format information which in turn supports communication between the MOD and its suppliers. The MOD has suggested that the UML and SysML can be used to deliver a number of the views within the framework due to the level of formalisation offered by the UML.

- Nicola et al. (2007) discuss the development of a conceptual modelling framework-ontology, aimed to support effective training programs through simulations of mission operations. It uses Mission Space Models (MSMs) which are conceptual models that describe the real world abstractions capturing not only the semantics of a static scenario but also the dynamics, behavioural patterns and the pragmatics of each defence action involved.

The use of the UML in military acquisition shows that there is an appreciation of the breadth of application which the UML can have. It is not only being applied to IS/IT projects but to any system delivery project within the MOD.

The rail industry has been an established industry for over 200 years. Its safety culture is a result of a long history of rail accidents. As the world moves forward with both technology and expectation the rail industry must also improve. This work considers three example applications from the rail industry which apply to different aspects of the development and life cycle concepts.

- Company W use the UML for their system development which enables them to produce the minimum number of external artefacts by holding all of the system information in one central project repository.
- Bayley (2004) discusses an abstract model of the European Rail Traffic Management System (ERTMS) and the modelling of the interlocking system requirements using UML. This work enables communication through the formalisation of the understanding of the ERTMS.
- Mazouni and Aubry (2007) use the UML as a tool to define an ontology for Preliminary Hazard Analysis (PHA). This provides terminology which may be used to describe accident scenarios, risk calculation, severity calculation and risk reduction.
- Barrow (2005) applies UML to the modelling of standards to show the benefits that can be gained through a more formal structure and common communications medium. In these example standards modelling is applied to train activated warning systems and ERTMS.

The UML has been used in the rail industry to improve clarity, abstract multiple views and improve communications with suppliers effectively shortening supply time.

Four science and education applications of the UML and their associations with the life cycle concepts and development activities are considered. These are formalisation, understanding and teaching.

- Webb and White (2005) use the UML to develop models and improve understanding of cell biology.
- McNellis (2005) use the UML to represent cognitive mapping methods improving the consistency within the maps.
- The seven views approach to process modelling defined by Holt (2005) is adopted by the BSI as the best practice approach for modelling processes. This approach, defined using the UML, provides a formalisation and completeness to process modelling.
- Holt (2004) uses the UML to provide a tailored life cycle complete with life cycle processes. This approach enables university students to understand the importance of life cycles and processes before carrying out their degree projects following a defined life cycle model.

The overview of the four application domains indicates that the formalisation framework in Figure 5 can be used to define both terminology and approach. The UML provides a multi view language based on the use of up to 13 different types of diagram. The diagrams are inter-related; the relationships provide the ability to carry out consistency checks between diagrams enabling confidence in the concepts defined to grow. The use of object orientation providing multiple views, consistency and repeatability enables the UML to be used as a framework for formalisation. The following section describes the way in which the UML will be applied to the visualisation and formalisation of ontology and process.

ONTOLOGY MODELLING

Examples of domain specific uses of the UML for defining ontologies have already been shown in the applications above. What is required in this case is an approach which in not related to a particular domain.

IDEF 5 (1994) provides a generic approach to the definition of ontology using its own schematic and elaboration languages which enable the definition of initial visual versions of ontologies. However, it provides a large number of detailed constructs which could be considered too complicated for any initial version. The IDEF approach provides three schematic views: classification, object state and composition along with symbols which can be deployed onto the schematics. The main symbols are 'kind', 'individual', 'referent', 'relation', 'state' and 'process'.

Others including Cranefield and Purvis (1999) have been investigating the use of the UML as an ontology modelling language. Cranefields approach is to use the UML to describe an ontology and compare this with the advantages and disadvantages of existing ontology representation languages used for knowledge based reasoning. Cranefield uses UML class and object diagrams to obtain what he describes as both a highly structured model that could support automated reasoning and an expressive language that it would not be practical to attempt general-purpose reasoning with. The ontology developed in this work capitalises on the approaches taken by Cranefield's use of class diagrams and IDEF5's definition of kinds and relationships.

A generic definition of an ontology, as presented in Figure 6, includes *Concepts* which may be *Terms* or *Relationships*: the relationships relate terms to each other. The stereotypes, shown within the chevrons, define the UML elements which will be used to represent these Concepts on an Ontology.

The risk ontology shown in Figure 7 is generic and can be applied to any situation or industry. The definition of risk shows that for a risk to exist there must be a *Chance to occur* and an *Outcome*. The *Chance to occur* provides the probability of the *Outcome* occurring. The Outcome described refers to the unwanted event. Outcome

Figure 6. Ontology concepts and realisation

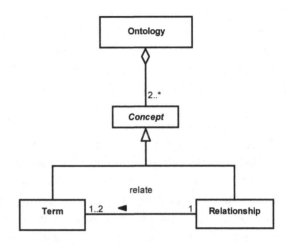

in many cases including Hollnagel (2008) and Aven and Kristensen (2005) is used interchangeably with consequence. Therefore a risk is an outcome and a chance for that outcome to occur.

This definition has been purposely kept simple and, more importantly, singular. The singularity is to provide more clarity and consistency; if discussing a risk then it must be one risk. It would be counter intuitive to then refer to multiple outcomes in a risk. The *Chance to occur* is also singular as it is logical that there can only be one chance to occur for any one outcome. This singularity adds an orthogonal view when asking if all outcomes been considered. For all outcomes to have been considered the sum of all the associated *Chance to occur* must equal 1, assuming that it is presented as a probability. This suggests that a set of risks will be collated creating a *Risk set* which itself would need to be verified. A full investigation into the verification of completeness of a *Risk set* is beyond the scope of this work.

Once a risk has been defined it is possible to apply a *Classification* to the *Outcome*. Classification in most cases is related to the idea of the severity of the Outcome. When considering people and injuries, classifications are likely to include insignificant, marginal, critical and catastrophic. Classifications such as these are often related to the

Figure 7. Risk ontology

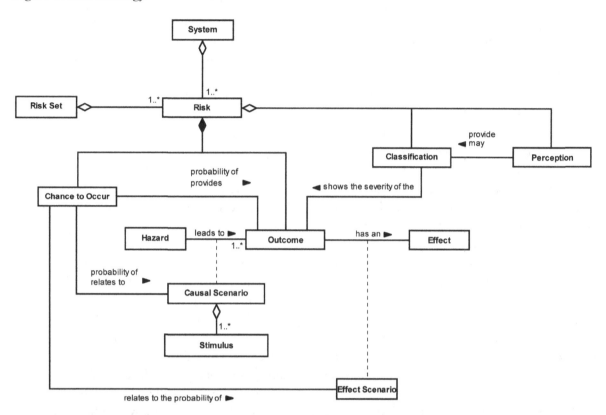

effect on people or a system and tend to focus on industry specific issues (Kristensen et al., 2006). Where people are concerned classification is rarely the only consideration. It may also be necessary to understand stakeholder feelings towards the *Outcome* and *Classification* these feelings are known as the *Perceptions*.

Perceptions may help to define classifications but are one of the most dangerous aspects to understanding and treating risk. A perception is a view of the severity of the outcome from a specific stakeholder's understanding. It is discussed in depth by Belzer (2001), Pezzullo and De Filippo (2009), and Clarke (2007).

One approach to categorising systems and the type of risk that relate to them is to categorise the outcome:

- Firstly, is the outcome positive or negative? Most will no longer consider an outcome to be part of a risk once they have established that this outcome will benefit them (Hessami, 1999). Also Flage and Aven (2009) discuss the need to balance positive and negative outcomes through the use of portfolios.

- Once a risk has been defined as negative, the question is if it is critical or non-critical. Again non-critical outcomes tend to be forgotten.

- The next question is if there is a safety implication. This is where most start to consider outcomes as risks.

In many areas critical systems or safety critical systems are discussed. In these cases it is the classification of the outcome which is being used to select the category of risk. In many cases the category will then be transposed onto the name of the system to highlight possible outcomes and therefore the need for a more rigorous approach to the system definition and development.

One problem here is that in many instances there is no differentiation between the categorisation of a system and the classification of an outcome. Classifications may be assumed due to the categorisation of the system. Therefore, there is a need to be consistent about classification and categorisation of risk. Classification relates to the severity of outcome. Categorisation on the other hand refers to separating out types of outcome, i.e., financial, marketing etc. Figure 7 has linked these categorisations of the outcome to terminology which is used to describe systems. It must be remembered that there is no hard and fast rule as to how a system and an outcome are related, the words are generally used interchangeably and hence, one should be extremely careful with their use.

This work has not set out to define all of the terminology associated with risk. However, there are concepts which need to be considered to ensure the scope of risk management can be understood. The following defines relationships between risk and some of the broader terms, such as 'hazard' and 'effect') which are often associated and sometimes confused with risk. In this work, hazard is used to cover the idea of events leading up to the occurrence of an outcome.

Figure 7 also shows that the relationship between the *Hazard* and the *Outcome* is via *Causal scenarios*, the use of scenarios means that there could be many hazards leading up to the outcome and it is important that these are recorded as they will be required for both causal analysis and definition of mitigations. The two salient points to be remembered about hazards are that they must be recorded and they must happen before the *Outcome*, the *Effect* will happen afterwards as characterised by the bow tie model (Delvosalle et al., 2005). Consequences or effects are all of

the things that happen or need to happen after an outcome has occurred. Effect analysis is in essence opposite to the hazard or causal analysis. It provides an understanding of what happens after an outcome has occurred. Again it is important to record effects as they will, for those outcomes which can't be removed, become the basis for the policies and procedures acting as mitigation.

There are already many definitions of risk; any new definition will need to have a justifiable difference. The difference in this case is that using the UML as a common language highlights similarities across existing standards and approaches enabling a dialogue to be held between risk experts in different industries. It may also provide a common base knowledge of risk before specialising in one area. This section presents four mappings between the definitions presented in the risk ontology and those discussed. Mappings will be separated in to those which map directly to the definition of risk and wider mappings to the associated terminology. The mappings will highlight the differences between the terminology within the definitions which had previously been considered to be commensurate. The definitions which have been mapped include financial, project and technical. The technical definitions cover both safety and non-safety categorisations.

Two direct mappings can be made from Harvey's financial definition (2010) to the generic definition: (i) *Degree of uncertainty* and *Chance to occur*, and (ii) *Return* and *Outcome*. Return is the only outcome that the financial definition is concerned with. The wider mapping is between *Asset* and *System*. System has been added from the wider model to show the relationship to Asset. The concept of an asset has not been included in the generic definition in this way as it suggests ownership related to the outcome where other definitions may be concerned with outcomes relating to people or property which is not owned. This mapping shows some interesting points regarding the financial definition of risk. Firstly the sector has included the outcome that it is concerned about in its definition. This means in terms of the generic definition that there is only ever one outcome to be considered and that is return. Secondly the definition includes the system; this focuses the view to be taken of the system to purely financial, although this is not a problem in the financial sector but would be for example in the railways where the safety consideration is key.

Two direct mappings are possible between the project related risk definition from BS6079 (2000), and the generic; there is also one wider mapping. The direct mappings are: (i) *Possibility of something happening* to *Chance to occur* and (ii) *Goals* to *Outcome*. The wider mapping is between *Uncertainty Inherent in plans* and *Hazard*. In this case 'hazard' has been included from the wider model to show the relationship of uncertainty to the causal effects of risks. The fact that hazards are included in the definition shows that there is a dynamic aspect to the definition. It is telling you to consider the events leading up to the outcome as part of the definition of the outcome itself. The usage of the word goal in the definition is interesting as it provides a positive view of the outcome, a desired achievement, rather than the negative view which is taken in most cases where risk is considered.

There are three direct mappings between the safety based definition from EN 50126 (1999) and the generic definition and one wider mapping. The direct mappings are: (i) *Probable rate* to *Chance to occur*, (ii) *Harm* to *Outcome* and (iii) *Degree of severity* to *Classification*. The wider mapping is *Hazard* to *Hazard*. Similarly to the project definition, hazard is incorporated here, again giving a dynamic complication to the definition. Severity which is also included provides classifications for the outcome; this has been included as a nonmandatory part of the generic definition. It is much easier to define a relevant set of classifications within a well established industry. However, if setting out on a risk management exercise for the first time it is unlikely to add value to the initial work.

There are two direct mappings and one mapping to the wider concept when considering a non-safety based risk defined in BS8444 (1996). The two direct mappings are between: (i) *Frequency* or *Probability* and *Chance to occur,* (ii) *Occurrence and consequence* to *Outcome* (this is only a partial mapping as the non-safety definition also relates to the effect of the outcome after it has occurred) and (iii) *Occurrence and consequence* and *Effect* maps specifically to the consequence element. The wider mapping is between *Hazardous event* and *Hazard*. This definition considers both the hazards and the effects of the outcome which makes a risk something almost impossible to consider as it includes all possible pre- and post- scenarios. This definition is closer to a definition of risk analysis rather than risk.

Many of these definitions have inherent time considerations within them; these are generally seen through the use of the term 'hazard' or 'consequence' which focuses the reader on the preceding and post outcome happenings. The definition presented here has removed this time consideration from the basic risk definition to focus the reader on the main issue the problem outcome. Obviously timing is still important and will be incorporated through relationships with the wider terminology and implementation of the associated processes.

Hazard is a recurring theme in the mappings but does not play such a central role in the definition of risk. This work has chosen to eliminate the complexity of timing within the definition of risk, hence the relationship to hazards which can then be investigated through causal evaluation. There is still an unresolved issue with the term 'hazard' which may need to be replaced with a more general term which does not imply a negative. In many situations there is a level of synergy between hazard and risk which needs to be investigated further but is outside the scope of this work.

Having defined the terms within risk and the relationships to surrounding terms, Figure 7 highlights the relationships between the terms and concepts already discussed and can be considered as a generic ontology for risk.

A clear definition of terminology of risk including the relationships between the terms is imperative. Without understanding these relationships it is impossible to consistently discuss or manage risk. When compared with the Risk submodel within the OMG quality of service and fault tolerance profile for IT (OMG, 2008b) provides a clear and usable set of terms and relationships for any industry or application.

CONCLUSION

The aim of this paper was to define risk and present an ontology for risk management. Using the UML as a formalisation tool this paper has presented a generic definition of risk and placed it within ontology for risk management. The ontology provides the relationships between the definition and associated terminology.

The ontology is central to understanding the relationships between other risk standards. To aid with this understanding mappings have been developed between the generic risk definition and the standards discussed. From these mappings a number of salient points were highlighted including the over complication of the definition.

The paper has also shown mappings between various definitions of risk discussed. This has enabled further clarity and questioning of the meanings of terminology from specific industries and how they relate to each other.

Understanding the terminology and ontology of risk and risk management provides a good grounding for understanding more of the risk domain; mappings provide an understanding of relationships to specific domains.

REFERENCES

AQAP. 150. (1997). *Quality assurance requirements for software development*. Brussels, Belgium: NATO.

AS/NZS 4360. (2004). *Risk management*. Standards Australia and New Zealand.

Aven, T., & Kristensen, V. (2005). Perspectives on risk: review and discussion of the basis for establishing a unified and holistic approach. *Reliability Engineering & System Safety*, *90*, 1–14. doi:10.1016/j.ress.2004.10.008

Baclawski, K., Kokar, M., Kogut, P., Hart, L., Smith, J., Holmes, W., et al. (2001). *Extending UML to support ontology engineering for the Semantic Web* (LNCS 2185, pp. 342-360). New York: Springer.

Barrow, R. (2005). Setting new boundaries - applying the UML to railway standards. In *Proceedings of the IEE Seminar on UML Systems Engineering*. Washington, DC: IEEE.

Bayley, C. (2004). Modelling interlocking systems with UML. In *Proceedings of the IEEE Seminar on Railway System Modelling - Not Just for Fun*. Washington, DC: IEEE.

Belzer, R. B. (2001). Getting beyond 'grin and bear it' in the practice of risk management. *Reliability Engineering & System Safety*, *72*(2), 137–148. doi:10.1016/S0951-8320(01)00015-1

Boehm, B. W. (1986). A spiral model of software development and enhancement. *ACM SIGSOFT Software Engineering Notes*, *11*(4), 14–24. doi:10.1145/12944.12948

Boehm, B. W. (1989). S*oftware risk management* (LNCS 387, pp. 1-19). New York: Springer.

BS 6079-3. (2000). *Project management - Part 3: Guide to the management of business related project risk*. London: British Standards Institution.

BS 8444-3. (1996). *Risk Management - Part 3: Guide to risk analysis of technical systems*. London: British Standards Institution.

Clarke, L. (2007). Thinking possibilistically in a probabilistic world. *Significance Statistics Making Sense, 4*(4), 190–192.

Cranefield, S., & Purvis, M. (1999). UML as an ontology modelling language. In *Proceedings of the Workshop on Intelligent Information Integration, 16th International Joint Conference on Artificial Intelligence (IJCAI-99)*, Stockholm, Sweden.

Delvosalle, C., Fievez, C., Pipart, A., Casal Fabreg, J., Planas, E., Christou, M., & Mushtaq, F. (2005). Identification of reference accident scenarios in SEVESO establishments. *Reliability Engineering & System Safety, 90*, 238–246. doi:10.1016/j.ress.2004.11.003

EN 50126. (1999). *Railway applications - The specification and demonstration of reliability, availability, maintainability and safety (RAMS)*. European Standards.

Flage, R., & Aven, T. (2009). On treatment of uncertainty in system planning. *Reliability Engineering & System Safety, 94*, 884–890. doi:10.1016/j.ress.2008.09.011

Gamper, C. D., & Turcanu, C. (2009). Can public participation help managing risks from natural hazards? *Safety Science, 47*, 522–528. doi:10.1016/j.ssci.2008.07.005

Girault, C., & Rudiger, V. (2002). *Petri nets for systems engineering: a guide to modelling, verification and applications*. New York: Springer.

Harvey, C. R., & Campbell, R. (2010). *Finance Glossary*. Retrieved October 6, 2010, from http://www.duke.edu/~charvey

Hessami, A. (1999). Risk - A missed opportunity? *Risk and Continuity, 2*, 17–26.

Hollnagel, E. (2008). Risk + barriers = safety? *Safety Science, 46*, 221–229. doi:10.1016/j.ssci.2007.06.028

Holt, J. (2005). *A Pragmatic Guide to Business Process Modelling*. BCS.

Holt, J. D. (2004). Those who can - use ISO IEC 15288. In *Proceedings of the INCOSE Spring Conference*.

Hughes, B., & Cotterell, M. (1999). *Software project management*. New York: McGraw-Hill.

ICAEW. (2002). *Risk management is now a core business process*. The Institute of Chartered Accountants in England and Wales.

IDEF5. (1994). *IDEF5 method report*. College Station, TX: Knowledge Based Systems Inc.

IEC 61508. (1998). *Functional safety of electrical/electronic/programmable electronic safety-related systems*. European Electrotechnical Standardisation Organisation CENELEC.

INCOSE. (2007). *Systems engineering handbook*. INCOSE.

IRM. (2002). *A risk management standard*. London: The Institute of Risk Management.

ISO 15288. (2002). *Systems engineering - system life cycle processes*. Geneva, Switzerland: International Organization for Standardization.

ISO 16085. (2006). *ISO systems and software engineering - life cycle processes - risk management*. Geneva, Switzerland: International Organization for Standardization.

ISO 31000 (2009a). *BS ISO risk management - principles and guidelines on implementation*. Geneva, Switzerland: International Organization for Standardization.

ISO 31010 (2009b). *Risk management - risk assessment techniques*. Geneva, Switzerland: International Organization for Standardization.

ISO 5807. (1985). *Information processing – documentation symbols and conventions for data, program and system flowcharts, program network charts and system resources charts*. Geneva, Switzerland: International Organization for Standardization.

ISO EC Guide 73. (2007). *ISO/IEC risk management – vocabulary*. Geneva, Switzerland: International Organization for Standardization.

ITU-T. (1999). *Series Z: languages and general software aspects for telecommunication systems, formal description techniques (FDT) – specification and description language (SDL)*. Geneva, Switzerland: International Telecommunications Union.

Jacobson, I., Booch, G., & Rumbaugh, J. (1999). *The unified software development process*. Reading, MA: Addison-Wesley Professional.

Jenkins, R. E., Brown, R. D. H., & Phillips, M. R. (2009). Harbour Porpoise (Phocoena Phocoena) conservation management: a dimensional approach. *Marine Policy, 33*(5), 744–749. doi:10.1016/j.marpol.2009.02.003

Kirchsteiger, C. (2008). Carbon capture and storage desirability from a risk management point of view. *Safety Science, 46*, 1149–1154. doi:10.1016/j.ssci.2007.06.012

Krogstie, J. (2008). Using EEML for combined goal and process oriented modeling: a case study. In *Proceedings of the EMMSAD, the Thirteenth International Workshop on Exploring Modeling Methods in Systems Analysis and Design*, Montpellier, France (pp. 112-129).

Leveson, N. G. (1995). *Safeware, system safety and computers*. Reading, MA: Addison-Weslyey Professional.

Mazouni, M., & Aubry, J. (2007). A PHA based on a systemic and generic ontology. In *Proceedings of the IEEE/INFORMS International Conference on Service Operation and Logistics and Informatics, the IEEE – ITS international conference (SOLI'2007)*, Philadelphia.

McNeillis, P. (2005). Cognitive mapping and UML modelling comparing book and mind. In *Proceedings of the IEE Seminar on UML Systems Engineering*, London.

MODAF. (2007). *The MOD architecture framework (MODAF)*. London: The British Ministry of Defence.

Mohaghegh, Z., Kazemi, R., & Mosleh, A. (2009). Incorporating organizational factors into Probabilistic Risk Assessment (PRA) of complex sociotechnical systems: a hybrid technique formalization. *Reliability Engineering & System Safety, 94*, 1000–1018. doi:10.1016/j.ress.2008.11.006

Nicola, A., Kabilan, V., Missikoff, M., & Mojtahed, V. (2007). Practical issues in ontology modeling: the case of defence conceptual modelling framework-ontology. In Müller, G., Morel, J. P., & Vallespir, G. (Eds.), *Enterprise Interoperability*. New York: Springer. doi:10.1007/978-1-84628-714-5_25

Olsen, O. E., & Lindoe, P. H. (2009). Risk on the ramble: the international transfer of risk and vulnerability. *Safety Science, 47*(6), 743–755. doi:10.1016/j.ssci.2008.01.012

OMG. (2007). *OMG UML specification*. Needham, MA: Object Management Group.

OMG. (2008a). *Business process modeling notation*. Needham, MA: Object Management Group.

OMG. (2008b). *UML(TM) profile for modeling quality of service and fault tolerance characteristics and mechanisms specification*. Needham, MA: Object Management Group.

OMG. (2008c). *OMG SysML specification*. Needham, MA: Object Management Group.

Peckham, J., & MacKellar, B. (2001). Generating code for engineering design systems using software patterns. *Artificial Intelligence in Engineering*, *15*, 219–226. doi:10.1016/S0954-1810(01)00018-8

Pezzullo, L., & De Filippo, R. (2009). Perceptions of industrial risk and emergency management procedures in hazmat logistics: a qualitative mental model approach. *Safety Science*, *47*, 537–541. doi:10.1016/j.ssci.2008.07.006

Redmill, F. (2002). Risk analysis - a subjective process. *Engineering Management Journal*, *12*(6), 91–96. doi:10.1049/em:20020206

Roland, H. E., & Moriarty, B. (1990). *System safety engineering and management*. New York: Wiley. doi:10.1002/9780470172438

Some, S. S. (2006). Supporting use case based requirements engineering. *Information and Software Technology*, *48*(1), 43–58. doi:10.1016/j.infsof.2005.02.006

Somerville, I. (2007). *Software engineering*. Reading, MA: Addison-Wesley.

Stevens, D. E., & Thevaranjan, A. (2008). *A moral solution to the moral hazard problem*. Retrieved October 6, 2010, from http://ssrn.com/abstract=1138279

Storey, N. (1996). *Safety critical computer systems*. Reading, MA: Addison-Wesley.

Vraalsen, F., den Braber, F., Hogganvik, I., Soldal Lund, M., & Stølen, K. (2004). The CORAS tool-supported methodology for UML-based security analysis. In *SINTEF ICT*.

Webb, K., & White, T. (2005). UML as a cell and biochemistry modelling language. *Bio Systems*, *80*(3), 283–302. doi:10.1016/j.biosystems.2004.12.003

Woodruff, J. M. (2005). Consequence and likelihood in risk estimation: a matter of balance in UK health and safety risk assessment practice. *Safety Science*, *43*, 345–353. doi:10.1016/j.ssci.2005.07.003

This work was previously published in the International Journal of Knowledge and Systems Science, Volume 1, Issue 4, edited by W.B. Lee, pp. 1-21 copyright 2010 by IGI Publishing (an imprint of IGI Global).

Chapter 19
VPRS–Based Group Decision–Making for Risk Response in Petroleum Investment

Gang Xie
Chinese Academy of Sciences, China

Wuyi Yue
Konan University, Japan

Shouyang Wang
Chinese Academy of Sciences, China

ABSTRACT

From the perspective of risk response in petroleum project investment, the authors use a group decision-making (GDM) approach based on a variable precision rough set (VPRS) model for risk knowledge discovery, where experts were invited to identify risk indices and evaluate risk exposure (RE) of individual projects. First, the approach of VPRS-based GDM is introduced. Next, while considering multiple risks in petroleum project investment, the authors use multi-objective programming to obtain the optimal selection of project portfolio with minimum RE, where the significance of risk indices is assigned to each of corresponding multi-objective functions as a weight. Then, a numerical example on a Chinese petroleum company's investments in overseas projects is presented to illustrate the proposed approach, and some important issues are analyzed. Finally, conclusions are drawn and some topics for future work are suggested.

DOI: 10.4018/978-1-4666-1782-7.ch019

INTRODUCTION

In petroleum industry, project investment is characterized by irreversible decision-making with uncertainty (Chapman & Ward, 2004; Chorn & Shokhor, 2006), and risk response measures should be adopted (Aven & Vinnem, 2007). During the life cycle of a petroleum project, there are multiple risks, such as political and economic risks (Pandian, 2005; Stephens et al., 2008), environmental risks (Bowonder, 1981; Ferreira et al., 2003; Norberg-Bohm, 2000), price volatility and financial risks (Chorn & Shokhor, 2006), and geological and technical risks (Asrilhant et al., 2007). Hence, it is necessary to implement risk response measures for corresponding risks in petroleum projects.

Many researchers have investigated petroleum project risk management, and some of risk management process and tools have been designed. Aven and Pitblado (1998) discussed the practices in petroleum project risk management, focusing on risk analysis, interpretation, acceptance criteria, and risk communication, besides emergency preparedness. Some decision support tools are developed to support risk management. Proposing a set of multi-disciplinary elements structured with the balanced scorecard's rationale, Asrilhant et al. (2004) explored ways to increase understanding of best practices of decision-making in petroleum project risk management. Kravis and Irrgang (2005) developed a case-based system to support risk assessment in oil and gas well design. In project risk management, risk response measure portfolio was adopted for multiple risks (Xie et al., 2006a), which will be used for risk response in petroleum project investment in this study.

In the practice of petroleum investment, proper portfolio selection is an effective way to reduce nonsystematic risk (Walls, 2004; Ross, 2004). In general terms, portfolio selection is a multi-attribute decision-making (MADM) problem. As a consequence, usually, multi-objective programming methods are used in petroleum project selec-

tion (Memtsas, 2003), where we further consider risk preferences and weights of decision-makers in the group decision-making (GDM). Then, managers can implement risk response measures for selected projects.

In general terms, due to relativity and complexity of risk management, the risks are usually identified and analyzed by group of managers and experts (Walls & Dyer, 1996). Moreover, petroleum investment is a so important issue that multiple objectives should be involved in. As a result, GDM is a usual way for petroleum project investment (Van Groenendaal, 2003). In the methodology proposed in this paper, experts are invited to identify risk indices and to evaluate the risk exposure (RE) of the petroleum projects in a region. In GDM, decision-makers often have different risk preferences (Walls & Dyer, 1996) and weights (Xie et al., 2006b, 2008). However, how to measure the risk preference and the weight of experts in GDM is a problem yet.

The rough set theory (RST) is a good tool to measure risk preferences of the decision-maker. RST extracts the knowledge based on quality of classification (QoC), and can discover knowledge from data sets automatically (Pawlak, 1982, 1991). In particular, RST does not need any priori information such as probability distribution in statistics, which is suitable for the rather small sample size of the available petroleum projects in this paper. However, due to uncertainty, ambiguity, and complexity that exist in project risk management (Ross, 2004; Goumas & Lygerou, 2000), it is hard to avoid misclassification caused by decision-makers, which cannot be treated well by RST. Variable precision rough set (VPRS) is an extension of RST with a confidence threshold value set at $\beta(0.5 < \beta \leq 1)$, which means misclassification rate of up to $1 - \beta$ is tolerated in decision tables (Ziarko, 1993; Xie et al., 2006c). Though a VPRS model has been used for petroleum project investment risk management (Xie et al., 2010), a group decision-making scenario has not been considered as yet. Therefore, we propose an application of VPRS-based GDM for risk response in petroleum project investment.

For the above problems, we design a mechanism that knowledge is discovered for risk response in petroleum project investment based on VPRS-based GDM. Firstly, we introduce the approach of VPRS-based GDM. Next, we use multi-objective programming to obtain the optimal selection of projects with minimum RE. Then, a numerical example on a Chinese petroleum company's investments in overseas projects is presented to illustrate the proposed approach. Moreover, some important issues are analyzed in the following discussion. Finally, conclusions are drawn and some topics of future work are suggested.

The remainder of the paper is organized as follows. The approach of VPRS-based GDM is introduced. Then, risk based project selection model is designed. We then illustrate the proposed approach by using a numerical example of overseas petroleum project investment of a Chinese petroleum company, and some related issues are analyzed.

VPRS-BASED GROUP DECISION-MAKING

In this section, we introduce basic concepts associated with the VPRS model, as well as application of the VPRS model in GDM. Let C be the condition attribute set and D be the decision attribute set. O is the object set, i.e. the universe. Suppose that there are L equivalence classes in

$E(P)$ and
$$E(P) = \{X_1, X_2, \cdots, X_L\}(l = 1, 2, ..., L).$$

Let $\text{card}(O)$ represent the number of objects in set O.

With a given confidence threshold value β, if $Z \subseteq O$ and $P \subseteq C$, then O is partitioned into three

regions: a positive region $\text{POS}_P^\beta(Z)$, a negative region $\text{NEG}_P^\beta(Z)$, and a boundary region $\text{BND}_P^\beta(Z)$, as follows (Ziarko, 1993; Xie, et al, 2008):

$$\text{POS}_P^\beta(Z) = \bigcup_{\Pr(Z|X_l) \geq \beta} \{X_l \in E(P)\}, \tag{1}$$

$$\text{NEG}_P^\beta(Z) = \bigcup_{\Pr(Z|X_l) \leq 1-\beta} \{X_l \in E(P)\}, \tag{2}$$

$$\text{BND}_P^\beta(Z) = \bigcup_{\Pr(Z|X_l) \leq 1-\beta} \{X_l \in E(P)\} \tag{3}$$

where $E(P)$ denotes a set of equivalence classes decided by condition attribute set P. Then, the quality of classification (QoC), denoted by $\gamma^\beta(P, D)$, is defined as

$$\gamma^\beta(P, D) = \frac{\text{card}(\text{POS}_P^\beta(Z))}{\text{card}(O)} \tag{4}$$

where $\text{card}(\text{POS}_P^\beta(Z))$ is the number of objects in the universe divided into the positive region.

In a VPRS-based GDM for petroleum project investment, expert group are invited to identify the risk indices and evaluate risk exposure (RE) of individual projects in a same region, where similar external risk character is assumed. Suppose there are m petroleum projects, n risk indices and K DMs participating in VPRS-based GDM. Let o_i be the ith petroleum project (i=1, 2, ..., m). The index set $C = \{C_1, C_2, ..., C_n\}$ (j=1, 2, ..., n) is used to describe the petroleum projects, where the indices are independent. In evaluating results of DM_k (k=1, 2, ..., K), C_{kj} is the condition attribute set consisting of the jth index, D_k is the decision attribute set, C_{kij} and D_{ki} are values of C_{kj} (j=1, 2, ..., n) and D_k in object o_i(i=1, 2, ..., m), respectively. The condition attribute set denoted by $C_{ki} = \{C_{ki1}, C_{ki2}, ..., C_{kin}\}$ and decision attribute set D_{ki} evaluated by DMs form a group deci-

Table 1. Group decision table on RE of projects

o_i	DM$_1$						DM$_2$						DM$_3$					
	C_{11}	C_{12}	C_{13}	C_{14}	C_{15}	D_1	C_{21}	C_{22}	C_{23}	C_{24}	C_{25}	D_2	C_{31}	C_{32}	C_{33}	C_{34}	C_{35}	D_3
1	2	3	1	2	1	2	2	1	1	2	1	1	2	2	2	2	2	2
2	2	1	1	2	1	1	1	2	1	2	2	2	2	2	2	1	2	2
3	1	2	1	1	1	1	1	1	1	1	2	1	1	3	2	1	1	2
4	2	2	2	2	2	2	2	2	1	2	1	1	3	2	3	2	2	2
5	3	2	2	2	2	2	2	2	1	2	2	2	1	3	1	2	2	1
6	3	3	2	3	2	3	2	2	2	3	2	2	3	3	3	3	3	3
7	3	3	3	3	3	3	3	3	2	3	2	3	3	3	4	3	2	4
8	3	3	3	3	3	3	3	3	3	3	2	3	3	1	1	3	2	1
9	3	2	3	3	2	3	3	3	3	3	4	3	4	4	4	3	3	4
10	4	2	4	3	3	3	3	3	3	3	4	3	4	4	4	3	3	4
11	4	4	4	4	4	4	3	4	4	3	3	3	3	3	3	4	3	3
12	4	3	4	4	3	4	3	4	4	4	3	4	3	3	3	4	3	3

sion table (see Table 1). Then, QoC of C_{kj} on D_k is defined as

$$\gamma^{\beta_k}(C_{kj}, D_k) = \frac{\text{card}(\text{POS}^{\beta_k}_{C_{kj}}(Z))}{\text{card}(O)} \tag{5}$$

where β_k is the confidence threshold value of DM$_k$ given by GDM moderator.

As a usual function of the Analytical Hierarchy Process (AHP), a judgment matrix is constructed for assigning weights to index sets (readers can refer to Xie, Zhang, Lai & Yu, 2008, for more details). In this paper, AHP is used to construct relationships among QoC coefficients, and to realize pairwise comparisons between relative significance of condition attribute sets; we construct a judgment matrix S_k as follows:

$$S_k = \begin{pmatrix} s_{k,11} & s_{k,12} & \cdots & s_{k,1n} \\ s_{k,21} & s_{k,22} & \cdots & s_{k,2n} \\ \vdots & \vdots & & \vdots \\ s_{k,n1} & s_{k,n2} & \cdots & s_{k,nn} \end{pmatrix}$$

where $s_{k,jt}$ is the element of jth row and tth column in S_k, and denotes the relative significance of C_{kj} to C_{kt} ($j,t = 1, 2, \ldots, n$), that is

$$s_{k,jt} = \frac{\gamma^{\beta_k}(C_{kj}, D_k)}{\gamma^{\beta_k}(C_{kt}, D_k)}. \tag{6}$$

Let w_{kj} be the weight of condition attribute set C_{kj}, evaluated by DM$_k$, and then it can be denoted as

$$w_{kj} = \frac{(\prod_{t=1}^{n} s_{k,jt})^{\frac{1}{n}}}{\sum_{j=1}^{n} (\prod_{t=1}^{n} s_{k,jt})^{\frac{1}{n}}}. \tag{7}$$

Therefore, for a given β_k of DM$_k$, weight vector w_k consisting of w_{kj} ($j = 1, 2, \ldots, n$) is

$$w_k = (w_{k1}, w_{k2}, \ldots, w_{kn}). \tag{8}$$

For another decision-maker DM$_p$ ($p = 1, 2, \ldots, K$, $p \neq k$), the degree of deviation $D(w_k, w_p)$ between weight vectors w_k and w_p is defined as

$$D(w_k, w_p) = \frac{1}{n} \sum_{j=1}^{n} \left| w_{kj} - w_{pj} \right|. \qquad (9)$$

In VPRS-based GDM, after β_k is given by moderator for DM_k, we define weight α_k of DM_k as

$$\alpha_k = \frac{\sum\limits_{p=1, p \neq k}^{K} 1 / D(w_k, w_p)}{\sum\limits_{k=1}^{K} \sum\limits_{p=1, p \neq k}^{K} 1 / D(w_k, w_p)} \qquad (10)$$

where α_k decreases in its deviation with other DMs.

In a GDM environment, we integrate REs, as evaluated by all individual DMs, into single integrated risk exposure (IRE). Then the IRE vector of o_i is expressed as follows.

$$A_i = (A_{i1}, A_{i2}, ..., A_{in}) \qquad (11)$$

where A_{ij} ($i=1, 2, ..., m, j=1, 2, ..., n$) is defined as

$$A_{ij} = \sum_{k=1}^{K} C_{kij} w_{kj} \alpha_k. \qquad (12)$$

On the basis of RE evaluation by group DMs, we investigate selection of an optimal petroleum project investment in the following section.

RISK-BASED PROJECT SELECTION

In this section, we use the multi-objective programming approach to obtain optimal project selection in petroleum investment. The objective is to select a petroleum project portfolio with minimum RE. In petroleum project selection, $x_i \in \{0,1\}$ ($i=1, 2, ..., m$) is used as the decision variable. When $x_i = 0$, it means project o_i should not be selected. Otherwise, i.e. when $x_i = 1$, it

means project o_i should be selected. Let I_i be the proportion of project o_i in the total investment and r_i be the rate of return of project o_i. As risk indices are of the same dimension, we can summarize RE for multiple risks directly.

Just like Xie, Yue, Wang & Lai (2010), we use w_{kj} in Eq. (7) to reflect the risk preference of DM_k for risk index C_{kj}. Therefore, the single objective function for petroleum project selection is developed as follows:

$$\begin{cases} \min \sum\limits_{k=1}^{K} \sum\limits_{i=1}^{m} \sum\limits_{j=1}^{n} (C_{kij} w_{kj} + D_{ki}) x_i \alpha_k, \\ \text{subject to:} \\ \sum\limits_{i=1}^{m} I_i x_i \leq 1, \\ \sum\limits_{i=1}^{m} I_i r_i x_i \geq r, \\ \sum\limits_{j=1}^{n} w_{kj} = 1, \\ \sum\limits_{k=1}^{K} \alpha_k = 1, \\ x_i \in \{0,1\} \end{cases} \qquad (13)$$

where r is the threshold value of total rate of return.

After the single objective function is solved, the optimal petroleum project selection is available. Then, risk response measures could be adopted for each project in a portfolio way. Therefore, we design a risk response procedure as follows.

Step 1: K DMs, m possible petroleum projects and an index set $C=\{C_1, C_2, ..., C_n\}$ are determined;

Step 2: REs of risk index set C of each petroleum project are evaluated by DM_k ($k=1, 2, ..., K$) and a group RE decision table is established;

Step 3: Set parameter β_k for DM_k by the moderator;

Table 2. Investment proportion, rate of return of projects

o_i	o_1	o_2	o_3	o_4	o_5	o_6	o_7	o_8	o_9	o_{10}	o_{11}	o_{12}
I_i	0.08	0.03	0.10	0.12	0.15	0.07	0.11	0.12	0.17	0.13	0.03	0.08
r_i	1.20	1.82	0.83	0.50	1.28	1.05	2.10	2.50	2.10	1.60	4.00	6.20

Step 4: Compute QoC $\gamma^{\beta_k}(C_{kj}, D_k)$ by Eq. (5), thus obtaining the significance w_{kj} of risk index C_{kj} by Eq. (7). When $w_{kj}=0$, it means that C_{kj} is not important and should be removed. However, if C_{kj} is necessary, then return to *Step 2*;

Step 5: Weight α_k is assigned to DM_k with respect to the degree of deviation $D(w_k, w_p)$ between weight vectors by Eqs (9)-(10);

Step 6: IRE is calculated by Eq. (12);

Step 7: Multi-objective programming is used to form a single objective function by Eq. (13).

Step 8: Solve the single objective function and obtain the optimal portfolio selection set $X=(x_1, x_2, ..., x_m)$.

Step 9: Risk response measures are adopted with risk response strength sorting based on IRE.

Then, we continue to use a numerical example to illustrate the approach of risk response in petroleum project investment in the following section.

A NUMERICAL EXAMPLE

In recent years, petroleum companies in China have been investing heavily in overseas projects. Their investments cover five continents, and business scope includes sectors such as exploration and production (E&P), refining and chemicals (R&C), and pipeline and transportation (P&T). However, as new entrants to global markets, Chinese petroleum companies usually confront such risks as estimates of reserves, technology, business, construction, production and politics (Shen, 2006; Jing, 2007). As a consequence, risk response is important for Chinese petroleum companies' overseas investments.

In this section, the proposed approach of VPRS-based GDM is used for one of the biggest petroleum companies in China to support risk response in overseas investments. The company organizes meetings to discuss risk management of its overseas projects periodically. In these meetings, some petroleum managers and experts are invited to identify risk indices and to evaluate risk exposure (RE) of a number of petroleum projects which are distributed in several main regions around the world.

Taking one of the serial meetings as an example, we illustrate the approach. Five risk indices, capability risk (C_1), geological and technology risk (C_2), financial risk (C_3), environment risk (C_4) and political risk (C_5), make up the risk index set $C=\{ C_1, C_2, C_3, C_4, C_5\}$. RE is divided into four levels: 1, 2, and 3, where 1 denotes low, 2 denotes common and 3 denotes high.

For convenience, we use subscript i of o_i to substitute project o_i in the following tables. Twelve eligible petroleum project samples are selected, and RE of them is evaluated to form a group decision table as in Table 1.

RE of a project consists of six numbers; for example, 132333, which means capability risk is low, geological and technology risk is high, financial risk is common, environment risk is

Table 3. Petroleum project selection

o1	o2	o3	o4	o5	o6	o7	o8	o9	o10	o11	o12
1	0	1	0	1	0	0	1	1	0	0	1

high, political risk is high, and total risk of the project is high.

Risk Assessment

Let β_1=0.8, β_2=0.9 and β_3=0.75. Using Eq. (5) to process the data in Table 1, we can obtain the weight vectors of risk indices decided by DMs as follows:

w_1 = (0.30, 0.10, 0.15, 0.40, 0.05),
w_2 = (0.00, 0.40, 0.20, 0.13, 0.27),
w_3 = (0.15, 0.22, 0.44, 0.15, 0.04).

In a GDM, there may be great diversity among DMs' weight vectors, which reflects the preference of DMs for different types of risks. From the application of VPRS-based GDM, we can see that risk indices considered important by DM_1, DM_2 and DM_3 are environment risk, geological and technology risk and financial risk more, respectively. As a result, preference of a DM for a particular kind of risk decreases in significance of the corresponding risk index.

Project Selection

On the basis of weight vectors of risk indices decided by DMs, we obtain weight of DMs: α_1 = 0.31, α_2=0.31 and α_3=0.37. The investment proportion and rate of return of the selected 12 projects are shown in Table 2.

The company requested that the total rate of return r of the selected project portfolio should be no less than 150%. Therefore, the single objec-

tive function for petroleum project selection is as follows:

$$\begin{cases} \min \sum_{k=1}^{3}\sum_{i=1}^{12}\sum_{j=1}^{5}(C_{kij}w_{kj}+D_{ki})x_i\alpha_k, \\ \text{subject to:} \\ \sum_{i=1}^{12}I_ix_i \leq 1, \\ \sum_{i=1}^{12}I_ir_ix_i \geq 1.5, \qquad (14) \\ \sum_{j=1}^{5}w_{kj}=1, \\ \sum_{k=1}^{3}\alpha_k=1, \\ x_i \in \{0,1\} \end{cases}$$

After solving the objective function, we obtain the optimal project selection for petroleum investment as shown in Table 3.

In addition, we make use of Eq. (12), and obtain the IRE for each selected petroleum project as shown in Table 4.

Risk Response

Assuming that R_j is the risk response measure for risk index C_j, we obtain the risk response measure for selected petroleum projects with strength sorting in the region as in Table 5, where the strength increases in IRE of the corresponding risk indices.

Table 4. IRE of selected petroleum projects

O_i	A_1	A_2	A_3	A_4	A_5
1	0.30	0.38	0.43	0.44	0.13
3	0.15	0.43	0.43	0.22	0.20
5	0.33	0.55	0.32	0.44	0.23
8	0.45	0.55	0.49	0.66	0.24
9	0.50	0.76	0.98	0.66	0.41
12	0.54	0.83	0.92	0.88	0.34

CONCLUSION

In this paper, we made use of the GDM approach based on a variable precision rough set (VPRS) model for risk response in petroleum project investment. Firstly, we introduce the approach of a VPRS-based GDM, where risk preferences and weights of DMs are considered. Next, considering multiple risks in petroleum project investment, we use multi-objective programming to obtain the optimal selection of projects with minimum RE, where the significance of risk indices is assigned to each of corresponding multi-objective functions as a weight. Then, a numerical example on a Chinese petroleum company's investments in overseas projects is presented to illustrate the proposed approach, and some important issues are analyzed.

The contribution of this study is that significance of risk indices in weight vectors can be used to represent the risk preferences of the DMs in the VPRS-based GDM. Moreover, by deriving the degree of deviation among weight vectors, we can assign a weight to each DM.

In future studies, risk management, including behavioral operations management, in petroleum projects, the approach for new applications, and VPRS model combined with other theories are aspects that would be worth further exploration.

Table 5. Risk response measures with strength sorting

O_i	Risk response measures with strength sorting
1	$R_4 \succ R_3 \succ R_2 \succ R_1 \succ R_5$
3	$R_2 \succ R_3 \succ R_4 \succ R_5 \succ R_1$
5	$R_2 \succ R_4 \succ R_1 \succ R_3 \succ R_5$
8	$R_4 \succ R_2 \succ R_3 \succ R_1 \succ R_5$
9	$R_3 \succ R_2 \succ R_4 \succ R_1 \succ R_5$
12	$R_3 \succ R_4 \succ R_2 \succ R_1 \succ R_5$

ACKNOWLEDGMENT

This work was supported by the National Natural Science Foundation of China (Nos. 70871107, 70731003) and China Postdoctoral Science Foundation (Grant No. 20060400103), and was in part by GRANT-IN-AID FOR SCIENTIFIC RESEARCH (No. 21500086) and MEXT, Japan.

REFERENCES

Asrilhant, B., Dyson, R., & Meadows, M. (2007). On the strategic project management process in the UK upstream oil and gas sector. *Omega, 35*, 89–103. doi:10.1016/j.omega.2005.04.006

Asrilhant, B., Meadows, M., & Dyson, R. G. (2004). Exploring decision support and strategic project management in the oil and gas sector. *European Management Journal, 22*(1), 63–73. doi:10.1016/j.emj.2003.11.017

Aven, T., & Pitblado, R. (1998). On risk assessment in the petroleum activities on the Norwegian and UK continental shelves. *Reliability Engineering & System Safety, 61*(1-2), 21–29. doi:10.1016/S0951-8320(98)80002-1

Aven, T., & Vinnem, J. E. (2007). *Risk Management: With Applications from the Offshore Petroleum Industry*. Berlin, Germany: Springer Verlag.

Bowonder, B. (1981). Environmental risk assessment issues in the third world. *Technological Forecasting and Social Change, 19*(1), 99–127. doi:10.1016/0040-1625(81)90051-2

Chapman, C., & Ward, S. (2004). Why risk efficiency is a key aspect of best practice projects. *International Journal of Project Management, 22*, 619–632. doi:10.1016/j.ijproman.2004.05.001

Chorn, L. G., & Shokhor, S. (2006). Real options for risk management in petroleum development investments. *Energy Economics, 28*, 489–505. doi:10.1016/j.eneco.2006.03.002

Ferreira, D., Suslick, S., & Moura, P. (2003). Analysis of environmental bonding system for oil and gas projects. *Natural Resources Research, 12*(4), 273–290. doi:10.1023/B:NARR.0000007806.90842.8f

Goumas, M., & Lygerou, V. (2000). An extension of the PROMETHEE method for decision making in fuzzy environment: Ranking of alternative energy exploitation projects. *European Journal of Operational Research, 123*, 606–613. doi:10.1016/S0377-2217(99)00093-4

Jing, D. (2007). Risk analysis of Chinese overseas petroleum investment. *Land and resources information, 4*, 44-47.

Kravis, S., & Irrgang, R. (2005). A case based system for oil and gas well design with risk assessment. *Applied Intelligence, 23*, 39–53. doi:10.1007/s10489-005-2371-7

Memtsas, D. P. (2003). Multiobjective programming methods in the reserve selection problem. *European Journal of Operational Research, 150*(3), 640–652. doi:10.1016/S0377-2217(02)00519-2

Norberg-Bohm, V. (2000). Creating incentives for environmentally enhancing technological change: Lessons from 30 years of U.S. energy technology policy. *Technological Forecasting and Social Change, 65*(2), 125–148. doi:10.1016/S0040-1625(00)00076-7

Pandian, S. (2005). The political economy of trans-Pakistan gas pipeline project: Assessing the political and economic risks for India. *Energy Policy, 33*, 659–670. doi:10.1016/j.enpol.2003.09.011

Pawlak, Z. (1982). Rough sets. *International Journal of Computer and Information Science, 11*(5), 341–356. doi:10.1007/BF01001956

Pawlak, Z. (1991). *Rough Sets: Theoretical Aspects of Reasoning about Data*. Boston: Kluwer Academic Publishers.

Ross, J. G. (2004). Risk and uncertainty in portfolio characterization. *Journal of Petroleum Science Engineering, 44*(1-2), 41–53. doi:10.1016/j.petrol.2004.02.004

Shen, Q. (2006). Risk analysis of international petroleum construction project. *Chinese Petroleum Corporation, 1*, 59–61.

Stephens, J. C., Wilson, E. J., & Peterson, T. R. (2008). Socio-Political Evaluation of Energy Deployment (SPEED): An integrated research framework analyzing energy technology deployment. *Technological Forecasting and Social Change, 75*(8), 1224–1246. doi:10.1016/j.techfore.2007.12.003

Van Groenendaal, W. (2003). Group decision support for public policy planning. *Information & Management, 40*, 371–380. doi:10.1016/S0378-7206(02)00044-7

Walls, M. R. (2004). Combining decision analysis and portfolio management to improve project selection in the exploration and production firm. *Journal of Petroleum Science Engineering, 44*, 55–65. doi:10.1016/j.petrol.2004.02.005

Walls, M. R., & Dyer, J. (1996). Risk propensity and firm performance: a study of the petroleum exploration industry. *Management Science, 42*(7), 1004–1021. doi:10.1287/mnsc.42.7.1004

Xie, G., Yue, W., Wang, S., & Lai, K. K. (2010). Dynamic risk management in petroleum project investment based on a variable precision rough set model. *Technological Forecasting and Social Change*. doi:10.1016/j.techfore.2010.01.013

Xie, G., Zhang, J., & Lai, K. K. (2005). A group decision-making model of risk evasion in software project bidding based on VPRS. *Lecture Notes in Artificial Intelligence, 3642*, 530–538.

Xie, G., Zhang, J., & Lai, K. K. (2006a). Risk avoidance in bidding for software projects based on life cycle management theory. *International Journal of Project Management, 24*(6), 516–521. doi:10.1016/j.ijproman.2006.03.004

Xie, G., Zhang, J., & Lai, K. K. (2006b). Using VPRS to mine the significance of risk factors in IT project management. *Lecture Notes in Artificial Intelligence, 4062*, 750–757.

Xie, G., Zhang, J., & Lai, K. K. (2006c, December 18). Web-based risk avoidance group decision support system in software project bidding. In *Proceedings of the 3rd International Workshop on Web-Based Support Systems (WSS'06), WI-IAT 2006 Workshops*, Hong Kong, China (pp. 180-183).

Xie, G., Zhang, J., Lai, K. K., & Yu, L. (2008). Variable precision rough set for group decision-making: An application. *International Journal of Approximate Reasoning, 49*(2), 331–343. doi:10.1016/j.ijar.2007.04.005

Ziarko, W. (1993). Variable precision rough set model. *Journal of Computer and System Sciences, 46*(1), 39–59. doi:10.1016/0022-0000(93)90048-2

This work was previously published in the International Journal of Knowledge and Systems Science, Volume 1, Issue 3, edited by W.B. Lee, pp. 45-54 copyright 2010 by IGI Publishing (an imprint of IGI Global).

Chapter 20
A Rough–Sets Approach to Kansei Evaluation Modeling and Design Support

Hongli Ju
Japan Advanced Institute of Science and Technology, Japan

Yoshiteru Nakamori
Japan Advanced Institute of Science and Technology, Japan

ABSTRACT

This paper proposes a Kansei modeling technique by using the Rough-sets Theory based on a set of evaluation data for Kutani-ware coffee cups. Kutani-ware is a famous traditional craft that is a very important traditional industry in Japan. However, it has been shrinking recently because of the changes in lifestyle or the appearance of more functional modern products. To reactivate this industry by developing and recommending products that attract people's feelings, this study develops a modeling technique for identifying relations between design and feeling by obtaining some if-and-then rules. An important contribution of the paper is that the proposed technique can suggest new designs by analyzing customers' Kansei requirements, which are not used in the evaluation experiment. This makes the recommendation successful by determining people's Kansei into data instead of attempts.

DOI: 10.4018/978-1-4666-1782-7.ch020

Figure 1. The production of traditional crafts in Japan

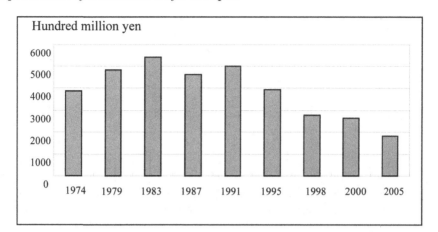

INTRODUCTION

Kansei

Kansei is the impression somebody gets from a certain artifact, environment or situation using all of their senses of sight, hearing, feeling, smell, taste as well as their reorganization (Schütte & Eklund, 2003), (Nagamachi, 1994). Kansei incorporates the meaning of the words sensitivity, aesthetics, feelings, emotions affection and intuition (Lee et al., 2002). Shimizu sees Kansei as being closely related to sophisticated human abilities such as sensibility, recognition, identification, relationship, making and creative action, where the process of biding together these concepts also is part of the Kansei (Shimizu et al., 2004). As the performance of commodities is not the only factor people focus on when they merchandise, therefore, it is important for manufacturers to have a customer-focused approach in order to improve attractiveness in development of new products, which should satisfy not only requirements of physical quality, but also consumers' psychological needs, by essence subjective (Petiot & Yannou, 2004).

Kutani-Ware

Kutani-ware is a representative traditional craft in Ishikawa Prefecture, which is based on advanced techniques, and has priceless cultural value. The Kutani-ware industry was promoted by Syoza Kutani, who pushed the mass production of Kutani-ware for export. The trade activities in the 1980s included developing new commodities, opening up oversea markets, developing new techniques and proposing new designs. According to the statistics, there are more than 1,000 kinds of traditional crafts in Japan. All of these crafts have been important not only from the economic perspective, but also particularly important from the culture perspective in maintaining a spiritual heritage which makes the country unique. Because of the development of Japanese economy after the war and the westernization of people's lifestyle, the traditional industries achieved splendid results in the 1980s. However after the bubble economy collapsed, the production volume decreased notably, and the number of staff was also reduced sharply (see Figure 1 and Figure 2).

Kansei Engineering

Kansei Engineering is a method for systematically exploring people's feeling about a product and

Figure 2. The number and the age of traditional industry staff in Japan

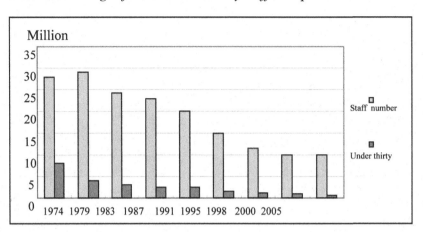

translating them into design parameters (Schütte & Eklund, 2003). Kansei Engineering is also a method for product development, which based on customers' impressions and feelings (Nagamachi, 1994; Jodon, 2006). Kansei Engineering is adaptable to a wide range of product applications. According to Nagamachi (2002), there are two directions of flow in Kansei Engineering: one of which is "from design to diagnosis" and the other one is "from context to design". The first one involves manipulating individual aspects of product's formal properties in order to test the effect of the alteration on user's overall response to the product. The other one involves looking at the scenarios and contexts in which the product is used and then drawing conclusions about the implications of this for the design. A great benefit of Kansei Engineering is that it can be used to link a variety of product properties to omit emotions. Studies have been done on things like micro level surface finishes of glass materials (Barnes et al., 2004), and music genres for mobile phone ads (Deng & Kao, 2003). There are many works done with Kansei Engineering methodology development within the period between fall 2000 and spring 2005. Someone studied how to apply Kansei Engineering in an European context (Schütte & Eklund, 2004), someone proposed model on Kansei Engineering to allow the identification

of development needs and the definition of new instruments for the methodology, and someone proposed a conceptual model for spanning the space of product properties and tested it in a application study on laminate flooring (Schütte et al., 2004).

Rough-Sets Theory

Frequently used technique in Kansei Engineering is factor analysis (Dillon & Goldstein, 1984), which is a technique that reduces a large number of variables into a smaller number of groups, the so-called factors. Within these groups, all variables are related to each other. Using factor analysis provides a possibility to identify the underlying basic variables and the correlations between them. In Kansei Engineering this tool can be used for group semantic descriptions within a certain product domain, label them, and give mathematical relations between the factors. This study uses the Rough-sets Theory for identifying relations between design and feeling, by which craftsmen could produce products that attract the feeling of people. The rough-sets theory was introduced by Pawlak in the early 1980s as a mathematical tool to deal with vagueness and uncertainty (Pawlak, 1992). It has been applied in many fields such as machine learning, knowledge acquisition,

Figure 3. Our method

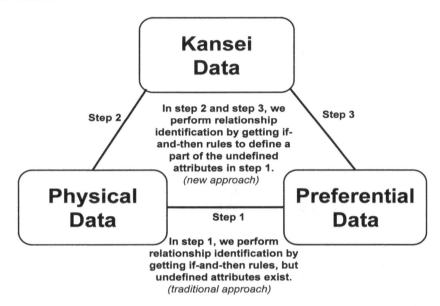

decision analysis, information retrieval, pattern recognition, and knowledge discovery recently (Nakamura, 1996), (Polkowski, 1998). Since many databases contain fuzzy, incomplete or identical datasets, certain tools must be deployed. The rough-sets theory is one of these tools, which contains three vague concepts: "lower approximation", "upper approximation" and "Covering Index", which is abbreviated as CI (Mori, 2002).

Objectives

We have two objectives in this study: *First,* to propose a new method for getting some new recommendations out of the samples we used in the evaluation experiment through getting new rules. Using the previous method we can just identify the relationship between customers' preferences and the physical data of the samples. In this paper we put the Kansei data of the customers' into the steps of evaluation in order to make the selection more close to the feelings of the users; and then get new recommendations. *Second,* to support for the designers of the Kutani-ware industry by performing simulations using the new rules. Our

new method is shown in Figure 3. In the first step we do relationship identification between the physical data and the prefecture data, and get a lot of rules. Within these rules, there are lots of indefinite attributes. In the second and the third step we do relationship identification among the Kansei data, the prefecture data and the physical data, and finally we identified the attributes which are indentified in the first step by getting a lot of new rules. The process is complex, and in this paper we just show you the process of two new rules.

Data Collection

In our study, except the physical data about the coffee cups, the Kansei data and the prefecture data which from the evaluators are also required. We gathered 45 evaluators who are not familiar with Kutani-ware but desirable to purchase some traditional craft. We used 35 prepared Kutani-ware coffee cups (we call them sample 1, sample 2… sample 35 in this paper), and 10 pairs of adjectives (like simple and rich) are prepared to use the semantic differential method (7 grades). We

Figure 4. Pictures of Kutani-ware coffee cups

Figure 5. Questionnaire sheet used in the experiment

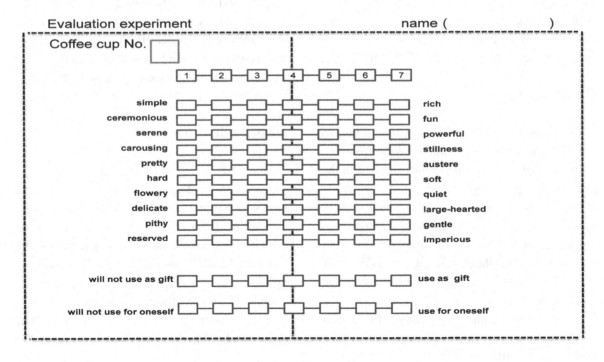

Table 1. Physical data of the samples

Samples	A (Color)	B(Inside)	C (Pattern)	D (Mouth)	E (Handle)	F(volume)	G(weight)
1	blue	white	plant	curve	vertical	middle	300g
2	sliver	color	plant	curve	vertical	big	350g
3	red	white	figure	circular	vertical	middle	300g
4	white	flower	plant	circular	sideways	middle	150g
5	sliver	color	nature	circular	sideways	middle	300g
6	white	white	plant	circular	sideways	big	350g
7	white	white	plant	circular	sideways	big	350g
8	white	white	plant	circular	vertical	middle	300g
...	...	...	...	...	...	...	...
34	white	white	plant	circular	vertical	big	400g
35	white	flower	plant	curve	sideways	big	350g

Table 2. Simplified physical data

Samples	A (Color)	B(Inside)	C(Pattern)	D(Mouth)	E (Handle)	F(Volume)	G(Weight)
1	A7	B4	C1	D3	E1	F2	G4
2	A8	B3	C1	D3	E1	F3	G5
3	A4	B4	C4	D1	E1	F2	G4
4	A2	B2	C1	D1	E2	F2	G1
5	A8	B3	C2	D1	E2	F2	G4
6	A2	B4	C1	D1	E2	F3	G5
7	A2	B4	C1	D1	E2	F3	G5
8	A2	B4	C1	D1	E1	F2	G4
...	...	...	...	...	...	...	...
34	A2	B4	C1	D1	E1	F3	G6
35	A2	B2	C1	D3	E2	F3	G5

show the pictures of them in Figure 4, and he questionnaire used in the experiment in Figure 5.

Before the experiment we analyzed the physical data of the samples which is shown in Table 1 and the simplified one is shown in Table 2. Through the evaluation experiment we finally obtained the average data of all the evaluators which is shown in Table 3, the evaluated one is shown in Table 4, and the simplified one is shown in Table 5.

Data Analysis

As mentioned above, we do relationship identifications in 3 steps using our new method of developing new recommendations by using software as bellow. Figure 6 and Figure 7 show the input data, and Figure 8, Figure 9 and Figure 10 show the process. In the first step we identify the relationship between the physical data and the prefecture data like almost researchers and we obtain a lot rules but pay attention to the rules

Table 3. Average data

Samples	a (Rich)	b (Fun)	c (Powerful)	g (Stillness)	...	i (Gentle)	j (Imperious)	Use as gift	Use oneself
1	5.89	3.64	4.44	2.51	...	3.02	4.87	4.31	3.09
2	3.51	4.07	2.91	5.42	...	3.89	3.80	4.47	4.36
3	5.11	4.62	4.51	2.69	...	3.47	3.60	2.82	1.98
4	2.53	4.09	2.22	4.87	...	6.00	3.49	5.20	4.96
5	3.36	3.09	2.58	5.62	...	4.16	4.38	4.13	3.47
6	4.22	5.56	4.47	2.91	...	4.67	3.20	3.58	2.93
7	1.80	4.76	2.69	4.87	...	5.38	3.49	3.53	3.33
8	2.20	4.71	2.53	4.44	...	5.96	3.53	4.69	3.47
...	...	...	...	...	...	...	...	...	...
34	5.09	3.24	3.53	4.22	...	3.44	4.53	3.73	2.93
35	5.11	4.18	3.69	3.78	...	4.87	3.98	5.16	3.64

Table 4. Evaluated average data

Samples	a (Rich)	b (Fun)	c (Powerful)	g (Stillness)	...	i (Gentle)	j (Imperious)	Use as gift	Use oneself
1	Yes	Middle	Middle	No	...	Middle	Middle	Yes	No
2	Middle	Middle	No	Yes	...	Middle	Middle	Yes	Yes
3	Yes	Middle	Middle	No	...	Middle	Middle	No	No
4	No	Middle	No	Middle	...	Yes	Middle	Yes	Yes
5	Middle	Middle	No	Yes	...	Middle	Middle	Yes	No
6	Middle	Yes	Middle	No	...	Middle	Middle	No	No
7	No	Middle	No	Middle	...	Yes	Middle	No	No
8	No	Middle	No	Middle	...	Yes	Middle	Yes	No
...	...	...	...	...	...	...	...	...	...
34	Yes	Middle	Middle	Middle	...	Middle	Middle	No	No
35	Yes	Middle	Middle	Middle	...	Middle	Middle	Yes	No

like "A2G4" and "A2E2G4". The attributes B, C, D, and E are undefined. In order to define the attributes which are undefined we perform the relationship identifications in step 2 and step 3 and finally we obtained the new rule "A2B3G4" and "A2B3C1E2G4" by defining the attribute B as B3, the attribute C as C1, the attribute E as E2, and the attribute G as G4.

Simulations

In order to make the new rules more easily and clearly to be understood, we performed simulation to support for the designers. Concretely, we changed some attributes of the samples according to the new rules "A2B3G4" and "A2B3C1E2G4" which mean "white outside, color inside and 150g weight", and "white outside, color inside, plant pattern, sideways handle and 150g weight". For instance, we changed B2 to B3 about cup NO.15,

Table 5. Simplified average data

Samples	a (Rich)	b (Fun)	c (Powerful)	g (Stillness)	...	i (Gentle)	j (Imperious)	Use as gift	Use oneself
1	a1	b2	c2	g3	...	i2	j2	1	2
2	a2	b2	c3	g1	...	i2	j2	1	1
3	a1	b2	c2	g3	...	i2	j2	2	2
4	a3	b2	c3	g2	...	i1	j2	1	1
5	a2	b2	c3	g1	...	i2	j2	1	2
6	a2	b1	c2	g3	...	i2	j2	2	2
7	a3	b2	c3	g2	...	i1	j2	2	2
8	a3	b2	c3	g2	...	i1	j2	1	2
...	...	...	...	...	...	...	...	...	...
34	a1	b2	c2	g2	...	i2	j2	2	2
35	a1	b2	c2	g2	...	i2	j2	1	2

Figure 6. The input data 1

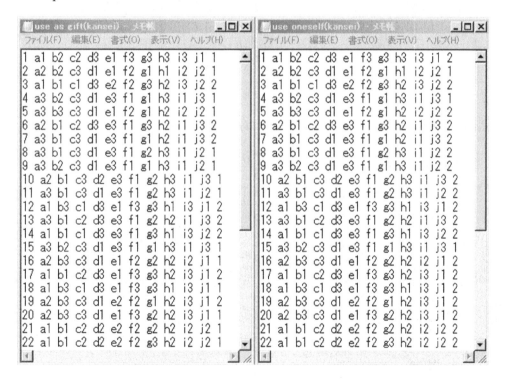

changed A4B4 to A2B3 about cup NO.3, and changed B4 to B3 about cup NO.11. We also performed reevaluation experiment and got a good result. Here is the detail described in Figure 11 and 12.

CONCLUSION

In this study we performed a new method to identify the relationships between people's preferences and the physical data of the samples. We

Figure 7. The input data 2

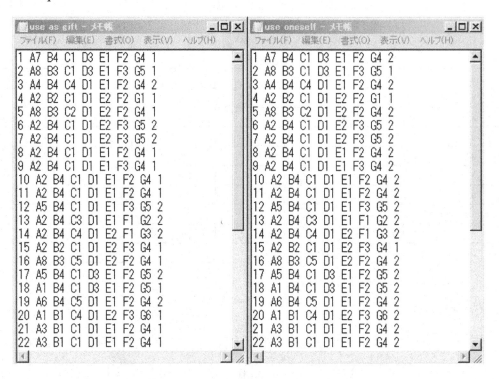

Figure 8. Relationship between preferential data and physical data

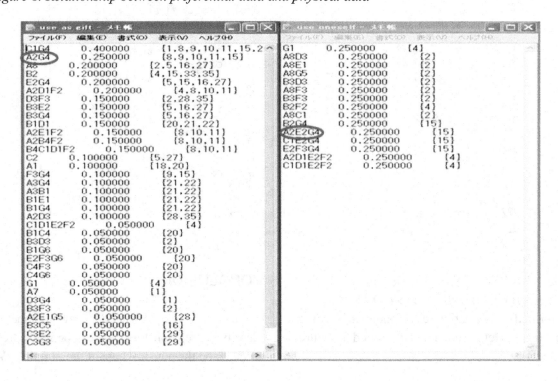

Figure 9. Relationship between preferential data and Kansei data

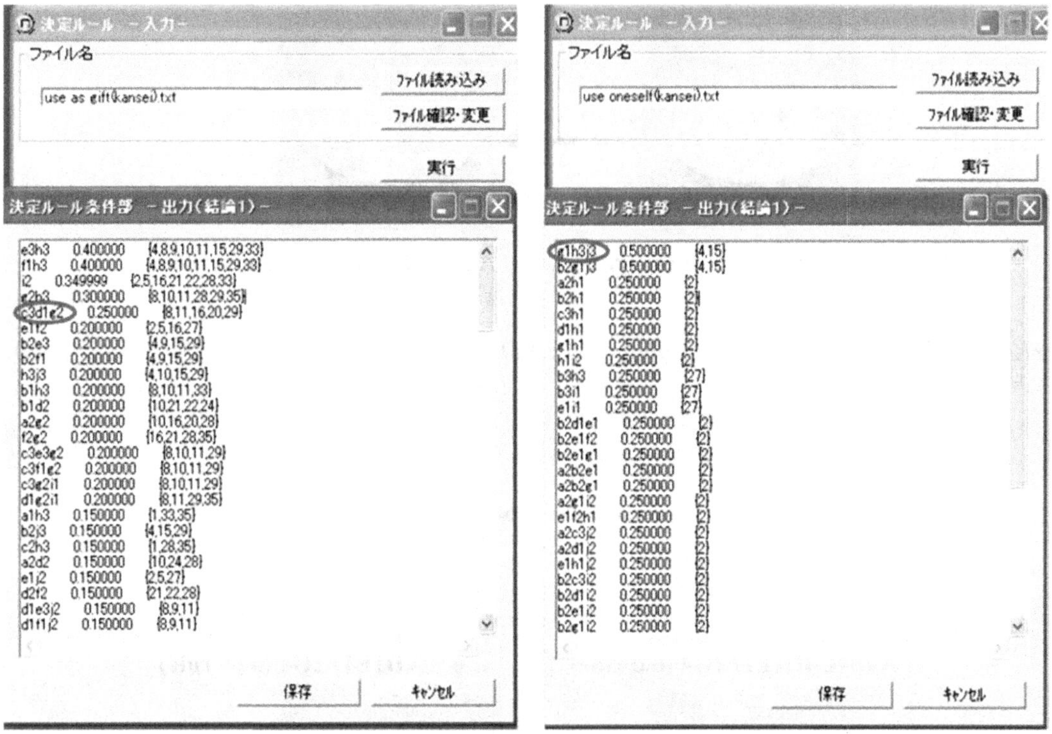

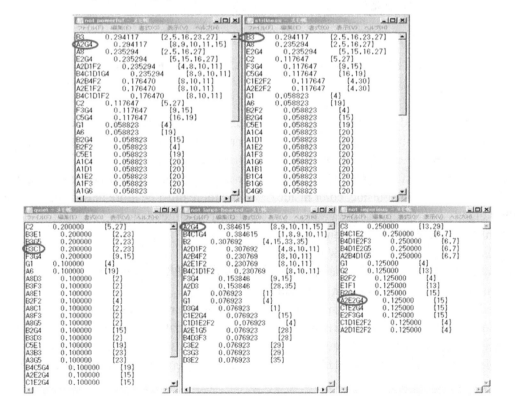

Figure 10. Relationship between physical data and Kansei data

Figure 11. Simulation by rule A2B3C1E2G4 about cup NO. 15

A2B2C1D1E2F3G4 (old rule)   **A2B3C1D1E2F3G4 (new rule)**

Figure 12. Simulation by rule A2B3G4 about cups NO. 3 and 11

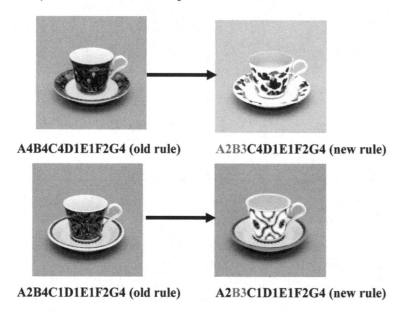

A4B4C4D1E1F2G4 (old rule)   **A2B3C4D1E1F2G4 (new rule)**

A2B4C1D1E1F2G4 (old rule)   **A2B3C1D1E1F2G4 (new rule)**

showed two new rules and performed some new recommendations. One is: "if A2 and B3 and C1 and E2 and G4 then preferential". The other one is "if A2 and B3 and G4 then preferential". In other words, if the cup has "white outside, color inside and 150g weight", then it would be preferential. If it has a "white outside, color inside, plant pattern, sideways handle and 150g weight", it would also be preferential. Thus if we change the attribute B in cups numbers 3, 11, 15, and then they will be preferred by customers. We did a simulation which is shown above and evaluated the new cups, which were reputed by 80% of the evaluators. In this paper, when we identified relationships among the physical data, the Kansei data and prefectures, we just chose the top 3 of the CI from the large number of rules. In further research we plan to develop software to process all the rules, and there must be more new combined rules and new recommendations.

ACKNOWLEDGMENT

Part of this work was originally presented in the 10th International Symposium on Knowledge and Systems Sciences (KSS, 2009) jointly with the 6th International Conference on Knowledge

Management (ICKM, 2009) in Hong Kong in December of 2009.

REFERENCES

Barnes, C. J., Childs, T. H. C., Henson, B., & Southee, C. H. (2004). Surface finish and touch-a case study in a new human factors tribology. *Wear*, *257*(7-8), 740–750. doi:10.1016/j.wear.2004.03.018

Deng, Y., & Kao, Y. P. (2003). *The development of musical selection plan based on Kansei similarity*. China: National Chiao Tung University, Institute of Applied Art.

Dillon, W. R., & Goldstein, M. (1984). *Multivariate Analysis*. New York: John Wiley & Sons Inc.

Jodon, P. W. (2000). *Designing pleasurable products*. London: Taylor and Francis.

Lee, S., Harada, A., & Stappers, P. J. (2002). Pleasure with Products: Design based Kansei. In Green, W., & Jordon, P. (Eds.), *Beyond Usability* (pp. 219–229). New York: Taylor and Francis.

Mori, N. (2002). Rough Set Approach to product Design Solution for the Purposed Kansei. *Bulletin of Japanese Society for Science of Design*, *150*, 85–94.

Nagamachi, M. (1994). Kansei Engineering: An ergonomic technology for a product development. In *Proceedings of IEA*, *94*, 1220–122.

Nagamachi, M. (2002). Kansei Engineering as a powerful consumer-oriented technology for product development. *Applied Ergonomics*, *33*(3), 289–294. doi:10.1016/S0003-6870(02)00019-4

Nakamura, A. (1996). A rough logic based on incomplete information and its application. *International Journal of Approximate Reasoning*, *15*(4), 367–378. doi:10.1016/S0888-613X(96)00075-8

Pawlak, Z. (1982). Rough Sets. *International Journal of Computer and Information Sciences*, *11*, 341–356. doi:10.1007/BF01001956

Petiot, J.-F., & Yannou, B. (2004). Measuring consumer perceptions for a better comprehension. *IJIE (Norwalk, Conn.)*, *33*(6), 507–525.

Polkowski, L. (2002). *Rough Sets: mathematical foundations*. New York: Physica Verlag.

Schütte, S. (2004). Developing the Space of Properties Supporting Kansei Engineering Procedure. *Theoretical Issues in Ergonomics Science*, *5*(3), 214–232.

Schütte, S., & Eklund, J. (2003). *Product Development for Heart and Soul*. Sweden: Linkoping University, Department for Quality and Human System Engineering.

Schütte, S., Eklund, J., Axelsson, J., & Nagamachi, M. (2004). Concepts, methods and tools in Kansei Engineering. *Theoretical Issues in Ergonomics Science*, *5*(3), 214–232. doi:10.1080/1463922021000049980

Shimizu, Y., Sadoyama, T., Kamijo, M., Hosaya, S., Hashimoto, M., & Otani, T. (2004). On-demand production systems of apparel on basis of Kansei Engineering. *International Journal of Clothing Science and Technology*, *16*(1/2), 32–42. doi:10.1108/09556220410520333

This work was previously published in the International Journal of Knowledge and Systems Science, Volume 1, Issue 3, edited by W.B. Lee, pp. 33-44 copyright 2010 by IGI Publishing (an imprint of IGI Global).

Chapter 21
A Knowledge–Based System for Sharing and Reusing Tacit Knowledge in Robotic Manufacturing

Lei Wang
Kyoto University, Japan

Yajie Tian
Kyoto University, Japan

Tetsuo Sawaragi
Kyoto University, Japan

Yukio Horiguchi
Kyoto University, Japan

ABSTRACT

A critical problem in robotic manufacturing is that the task of teaching robotics is rather time-consuming. This has become a serious problem in the present age of cost reduction. Collaboration with a company in the field has revealed that the root cause of this problem is that there is not a common knowledge base in this domain, which can serve as shared and reused knowledge. In robotic manufacturing, the skills and experiences of skilled workers are a form of tacit knowledge that is difficult to be acquired and transferred to other workers and robots. This paper proposes a knowledge-based system for sharing and reusing tacit knowledge in the robotic assembly domain. In this system, a modified EBL (Explanation-based Learning) method is proposed to generalize tacit knowledge from specific robotic programs made by skilled workers. A newly operational criterion is proposed for the generalized tacit knowledge, which demands that it should be expressed understandably by human workers and be reusable by robots to generate programs automatically.

DOI: 10.4018/978-1-4666-1782-7.ch021

INTRODUCTION

Robots are being deployed in more and more industrial sectors. However, a critical problem in robotic manufacturing is that the task of teaching robots is too time-consuming (Brogårdh, 2007; Blomdell et al., 2005; Haegele et al., 2005). This has become a bottleneck to improving the flexibility of robotic manufacturing systems, which keeps small and medium size enterprises (SMEs) away from robotic automation. This problem is especially severe in the robotic assembly domain.

Therefore, various methods have been proposed to facilitate the task of teaching robots (Argall et al., 2009). Many researchers have applied virtual reality technologies (Aleotti, 2004; Li, 2000; Chong, 2009), while others have used intuitive teaching methods such as leading robots directly by human hands (Maeda, 2008) or instructing robots by voice (Pires, 2006). Although these methods indeed simplify the task of teaching robots, they overlooked the essential fact the task of teaching robots is to transfer knowledge from human workers to robots.

By teaching robots a series of assembly tasks, it can be seen that the repetitive teaching of similar tasks and the repetitive revising of a new task are the main causes of the slowness of the task. To solve this problem, it is important to be able to share and reuse the skills and experiences of skilled workers. Thus, this paper proposes a knowledge based system (KBS) for sharing and reusing knowledge in robotic manufacturing. The fundamental issue in this approach is how to acquire and accumulate the knowledge of skilled workers into a knowledge base, i.e., a knowledge infrastructure.

Generally, the skills and experiences of skilled workers are a kind of tacit knowledge that is difficult to clearly articulate and transfer to others. Nevertheless, skilled workers can do implement such tacit knowledge in their demonstrations of teaching robots. As a result, the robotic programs of skilled workers are products of the skills they used, and contain their tacit knowledge. The problem herein is how to identify such an essential part that is implementing their skills and reusable to other similar cases. In this paper, a method based on explanation-based learning (EBL) is used to selectively acquire the knowledge of skilled workers by analyzing their robotic programs.

EBL is a deductive learning method for acquiring generalized knowledge from a single specific observation (DeJong & Mooney, 1986; DeJong, 2006). In contrast to other learning methods, such as artificial neural networks (ANN) that require many training examples, EBL can learn new knowledge from a single example, with the aid of a knowledge intensive analysis using a domain theory (i.e., a pre-encoded knowledge base) (Mitchell et al., 1986; Wang et al., 2008). Because it enables learning without repetitive human tutoring, EBL is an appropriate method for learning the tacit knowledge of skilled workers. Sawaragi et al. (2006) have applied EBL in container loading problems to capture the tacit knowledge of experts. Levine and DeJong (2006) have used EBL to generalize operation skills in the flight domain. In this paper, a modified EBL is proposed to design the knowledge based system.

In the following of this paper, we introduce the background of robotic assembly and the EBL method, and the related works. We present the proposed KBS and its knowledge acquisition mechanism and present experiments on reusing the acquired knowledge along with analyzed results. Next, we compare the proposed method with other methods and discuss the importance of tacit knowledge sharing. Finally, a conclusion is presented.

BACKGROUND DESCRIPTION

Problem in Robotic Assembly

As shown in Figure 1, robotic assembly refers to using two or more robots in a work cell to complete the assembly of a wide variety of products that are made of various workpieces.

Robot teaching is the most important and difficult work in robotic assembly. Workers teach a robot in the following steps: 1. making a program for the task of assembling a workpiece; 2. Setting the robot in teaching mode, and teaching the robot the coordinates of points in the program with a teaching pendant; 3. checking the effectiveness of the teaching by letting the robot execute the commands one by one; 4. setting the robot in playback mode to check the automatic execution of the robotic program.

Robot teaching is awfully time-consuming for the following two main reasons. First, workers have to teach robots repeatedly even for similar assembly tasks, because there is no way for knowledge to be shared and reused. For example, to screw four bolts into four holes in a box, human workers have to teach the robot four times, although the mechanics of screwing are common each time. If the screwing skill of workers is acquired and saved in a knowledge base, and the KBS has the ability to recognize in which situations to reuse it, then the KBS will be able to help the robot automatically deal with similar screwing situations. In this way, workers will only need to teach the robot each basic assembly task once.

Second, workers often have to revise the robotic program for a new assembly task repeatedly in response to the occurrence of errors in the playback mode, which are due to lack of experiences. This is because, in teaching mode, the actions of the robot are discrete, and the speed of motion is very slow. However, in playback mode, the robot's actions are executed continually at high speed. Thus, unexpected errors that did not happen in teaching mode may occur in playback mode. In this case, the workers have to revise the corresponding part of the robotic program to correct such errors. In addition, while teaching a robot a new assembly task, many new decisions need to be made, such as how to grasp or place the workpiece, whether and where to insert an intermediate point, when

Figure 1. Robotic assembly work cell (Noda et al., 2009)

and how long to add a time delay, and so on. If skills and experiences were available to be shared and reused, then many errors could be avoided, and the time required to teach the robots could also be reduced.

Tacit Knowledge in Robotic Assembly

In the robotic assembly domain, whether workers are moving a robotic arm to pick up or place a workpiece, the task is non-trivial, and a number of contingencies could arise, each affecting the applicability or outcome of the robotic program. Thus, the nuances of the real world necessitate that workers have to be familiar with the physical properties of workpieces in a particular situation as well as their kinematic characteristics when they are moved by robots in high speed. In addition, workers have to deal with various environment situations. For example, suppose that the task is to palletize a group of blocks in a plate, as shown in Figure 2. When placing the first block into the plate, to make a stable insertion, the approach position of the block should be close to the target hole. In placing the second block, the robotic operation seems to be the same as the first one. However, to avoid collision with the first palletized block, an intermediate approach point is added, which makes the second block first approach the target hole at a position above the palletized block before approaching at a closer position to its destination.

It is difficult to observe these types of knowledge explicitly in robotic operations. However, such knowledge is indeed implemented in the form of robotic programs by inserting intermediate points, by adjusting the specific positions and velocities of the robots, by inserting extra commands to adjust the timing of the operations, and so on. Experienced workers could interpret such programs and selectively recognize which parts of the program are critical for its successful performance. However, for less-experienced workers, it would be quite difficult to understand robotic programs made by skilled workers, which gives rise to the problem of skill-succession.

Such assembly skills and experiences that are implemented within robotic programs are the tacit knowledge owned by skilled workers. The efficiency of a robotic assembly work cell could be dramatically improved if the tacit knowledge of skilled workers could be shared with other workers and transferred to robots. In this paper, we propose a knowledge-based system based on EBL to share and reuse the tacit knowledge of skilled workers.

EBL

The basic idea of EBL is that with sufficient background knowledge, humans appear to learn quite a lot from one example and use the learned results to guide their problem solving efforts next time around.

An EBL system requires four inputs: 1. Goal: a concept describing what is supposed to learn; 2. Training example: a specific example of the goal demonstrating what is to be observed and learned; 3. Domain theory: a set of rules and facts to be used in explaining how the training example satisfies the goal, i.e., the background knowledge in a domain; 4. Operationality criterion: a set of

Figure 2. Example: adding an intermediate point

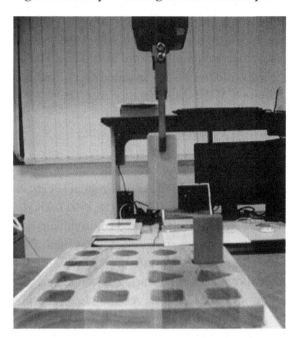

predicates specifies the form in which the learned concept definition must be expressed. The output is a new definition of the goal, which is represented in terms of the training example.

There are two steps in the EBL learning process: 1. Analysis: analyzing the training example, and explaining why the training example is an example of the goal or how the operator schema in the training example realizes the goal. The result of the analysis is an explanation tree. 2. Generalization: the explanation tree is generalized according to the operationality criteria. The output is a new definition of the goal.

Two features of EBL make it appropriate for learning tacit knowledge in the robotic assembly domain: 1. EBL can learn from a single example. This feature is very important, because it is difficult to obtain many training examples in the robotic assembly domain due to the long teaching time. Moreover, each robot teaching example usually contains distinguished knowledge, specific to its unique assembly situation. 2. EBL can generalize from an example without human tutoring. This feature makes EBL appropriate for learning tacit knowledge. However, in the proposed KBS, to adapt EBL to acquiring knowledge from robotic programs, two modifications should be made to the construction of the domain theory, and the definition of the operationality criterion.

Related Works

Segre has first applied EBL in the robotic manufacturing domain in his ARMS system (Segre & DeJong, 1985; Segre, 1988; Segre, 1991). ARMS was developed on a simulated environment, and aimed to construct an autonomous system. Different from the ARMS system, our system is built on real robotic manufacturing systems. Furthermore, our system emphasizes knowledge sharing between human workers and robots, besides the function of automatically reusing the learned knowledge in similar tasks.

In addition to EBL, many other methods have also been applied in a variety of robotic manufacturing problems for acquiring and reusing expert knowledge. According to the way how the expert knowledge is reused, we classify these methods into three types: self-adapting (SA) method, learning from demonstration (LfD) method, and knowledge based (KB) method.

In the recent 2 decades, the SA method has prevailed in the AI area and in the robotic manufacturing domain. Nuttin and Brussel (1997) and Prabhu and Garg (1997) used reinforcement learning (RL) and artificial neural networks (ANN) in designing learning controllers respectively for peg-into-hole assembly task and deburring task. Lopez-Juarez and Howarth (2002) and Chen and Naghdy (2002) applied ANN and online-learning method in peg-into-hole assembly. Noda and Nagatani (2008), Noda, Nagatani, and Nagano (2008) developed an active search algorithm based on active learning for optimizing robot motion trajectory. In the SA method, the researchers use their prior knowledge to model the objective system/ problem. Then the parameters in their models are refined or optimized by responding to feedback of the online robot operations.

Within LfD method, a state-action mapping policy is learned from examples or demonstrations provided by a teacher. Then the learned policy is reused to guide the robot operation in future tasks. Argall (Argall et al., 2009) made a survey on LfD and categorized LfD research in terms of demonstrator, problem space, policy derivation and performance. Hovland et al. (1996) employed hidden Markov model (HMM) to transfer human peg-into-hole assembly skill to robot based on a set of training data gathered from human. Friedrich and Dillmann (1995) developed an extended programming by demonstration method (PbD) to create a plan for a given task not only on the basis of the given demonstration data. Additionally the user is asked for the intention he followed with the demonstration. Therewith a generalized plan from a single demonstration can be reused for a whole set of tasks. The idea is the same as EBL. Dillmann et al. (1999) improved the PbD method, in which the goal is to modify information gained by the demonstration in that way that different target systems are supported.

In the KB method, human knowledge is encoded as facts and rules in a knowledge base. And task plans can be generated based on the knowledge base. Hwang and Ho (1996) developed a knowledge based framework to support task-level programming and operational control of robots. Fujita et al. (2008) employed the KB method in the assembly shop process design support system of his company.

Generally, the SA method requires a large number of training data or experiments; the LfD method concentrates on making a robot mimic human operations without explaining the know-how in the operations; the KB method focuses on planning for a task by existing rules in a knowledge base. In our research, the aim is to acquire the tacit know-how from a single robot teaching example of human workers. This is because each robot teaching example contains the unique know-how

Figure 3. The structure of the knowledge-based system

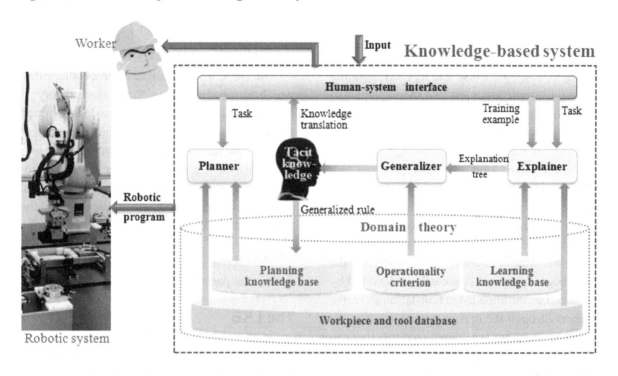

of the human teacher. Therefore, in the proposed method, a modified EBL is used to explain the operation of the human worker and to generalize it as a rule, and the KB method is used to generate program for new similar tasks. We will compare the above methods with our method after presenting our method.

THE KNOWLEDGE-BASED SYSTEM

Structure of The KBS

As Figure 3 shows, the proposed KBS works as a medium between workers and the robotic system in a work cell. Workers interact with the KBS through a human-system interface. The KBS is mainly composed of the learning part, the planning part, and the domain theory.

The Learning Part

The learning part consists of the explainer and the generalizer. The function of the learning part is to acquire knowledge from robotic teaching demonstrations of skilled workers. The inputs of the learning part are a task and its corresponding training example, i.e., the robotic program for the task. Its output is the acquired knowledge for the task.

In the KBS, the tasks are classified into 2 types: 1. Pick-up, and 2. Placing. This classification is based on the following considerations. The assembly process of any workpiece can be segmented into the pick-up phase and the placing phase. In factories, workers also program and teach robots for the pick-up and the placing operations of a workpiece separately. In fact, this classification of the tasks is the classification of the knowledge implemented by workers. Thus, classifying the tasks in this way can make the acquired knowledge more flexible and reusable for workers in actual factory environments.

As Figure 3 shows, a task and its corresponding training example are input into the explainer of the learning part. The explainer explains how the training example accomplishes the task by using the rules in the learning knowledge base and the data retrieved from the workpiece and tool database. Its result is an explanation tree. Then the generalizer generalizes knowledge from the explanation tree according to the operationality criterion. The generalizer outputs the generalized knowledge in two ways. One represents the knowledge in terms that is easily understood by workers, i.e., the knowledge translation shown to workers through the human-system interface in Figure 3. The other is a generalized rule that can be used by the planning part, and is saved into the planning knowledge base.

The Planning Part

The planning part is the planner in Figure 3. Its function is to generate robotic programs for input tasks. The planner generates robotic programs by using rules in the planning knowledge base and data in the workpiece and tool database. The output robotic programs will be sent to the robotic system.

The Domain Theory

The domain theory, i.e., the knowledge base, is the most important part of the KBS. It is composed of the learning knowledge base (LKB), the operationality criterion (OC), the planning knowledge base (PKB), and the workpiece and tool database (WTD).

The WTD provides data on workpieces and robot tools that can be used by both the learning part and the planning part. For example, the block data are given in the form:

wp(ID,Type-Subtype,[Height,Length,Width])[1].

The following is a specific example:
wp(5,block-1,[49.5,24.5,14.5]).

The OC is a set of language processing rules, which is pre-encoded in the domain theory. It defines the terms in which the knowledge learned from the learning part should be expressed. It requires the learned knowledge to be expressed in two ways: 1. a representation in natural language that can be easily understood by workers; and 2. a rule formulated with predicates from the planning part, i.e., a rule that can be reused by the planning part.

The LKB and the PKB is the core of the KBS, as they the parts that contain knowledge.

The LKB

The LKB is composed of a base of basic learning rules and a base of analysis rules.

The training example is composed of robotic commands and parameters. To analyze the training example, the learning part must understand the meanings of the robotic commands. The basic learning rules are the rules that explain each robotic command or each commonly used combination of robotic commands. For example, consider the rule

```
grip(T1,HN,T2):-
cmd(N1,dly(T1)),
cmd(N2,hclose(HN)),
cmd(N3,dly(T2)),
T1>0.2, T2>0.2,
N2=:=N1+1,
N3=:=N2+1.
```

It means that the action of gripping is realized by a combination of three commands 'dly(T1)', 'hclose(HN)', and 'dly(T2)'. 'T1>0.2', 'T2>0.2' mean that the delay time should be longer than 0.2 second. 'N2=:=N1+1', 'N3=:=N2+1' mean that the sequence of the three commands is 'dly(T1)', 'hclose(HN)', and 'dly(T2)'. In other words, the gripping action is achieved by closing a robot tool, and there should be delays both before and after closing the robot tool. This combination of commands is a rule/operation that is commonly used in writing robotic programs for seizing workpieces. Thus it is pre-encoded in the domain theory.

The analysis rules are used to analyze the work cell state of a task and the corresponding tacit knowledge of skilled workers implemented in the training example. There are three main kinds of rules in the base of analysis rules:

1. Rules for analyzing work cell state data, which are mainly used to analyze the robot movement speed in automatic mode, the relationship between robot tool and target workpiece, and the environment state nearby the assembly destination.
2. Rules for analyzing parameters, which are used to explain how human workers chose the coordinates of the seizing, placing, and approach points for a workpiece.
3. Rules for analyzing robot commands, which are used to analyze which operation strategy (i.e., robotic program schema) is used in the robot program in a training example.

There are four types of operation strategies:

1. Essential strategies – There are two essential strategies for pickup and placing tasks respectively. They are almost the same, and the only one difference is whether the command to the robot tool is 'close gripper' or 'open gripper': "move to safe point, approach the target point, get at the target point, close/open gripper, retreat to approach point, move back to safe point."
2. Time-delay strategies – To make an assembly operation stable, or to coordinate cooperation between a robot and other facilities, sometimes it is necessary to add time delays 'dly N' into an essential strategy. These are the time-delay strategies. For example, if a

pickup task requires high precision, to make the robot tool stable in high-speed motion, it needs to delay 1 second before the tool gets to the target point.

3. Speed-changing strategies – These strategies are used for adjusting the speed of a robot tool by adding a speed-changing command 'ovrd' into an essential strategy. For example, in a placing task 'screw a pin', to make the pin align precisely with the target hole, the robot tool must move the pin at a very low speed from the approach point to the hole. However, in other parts of the trajectory, the robot tool does not need to move at such a low speed. In other words, to accomplish a task both stably and efficiently, speed-changing strategies play an important role.
4. Intermediate-point-adding strategies – Usually, the environment state in a work cell is complicated. In any a pick-up or placing task, to avoid collisions, it is often necessary to add intermediate points into an essential strategy.

All of the rules and strategies in the LKB are explicit knowledge that we can generalize from the operation manual of robots or common sense. Thus, we summarize them and encode them to construct the LKB, which is the most important part of the KBS.

On the other hand, the tacit knowledge of skilled workers is contained in their robotic programs, i.e., the training examples. It is how skilled workers selectively combine the above rules and strategies to construct a complicated operation strategy for a pickup/placing task. In most cases, the pickup/placing task is given in a particular environment or with particular requirements. In other words, the tacit knowledge of skilled workers can be generalized as a rule: Given the features/requirements of a particular pickup/placing task, the rule determines which type of complicated operation strategy should be selected.

In brief, the LKB provides general knowledge of robotic assembly in the form of discrete rules and strategies. It is used by the learning part to analyze the input tasks and training examples. The output of the learning part is the acquired tacit knowledge, which is generalized as a rule and saved in the PKB.

The PKB

The PKB is composed of a basic planning base and a planning rule base.

The basic planning base is composed of 2 parts:

1. Robotic program schemata – Most robotic programs are composed of several staple commands (e.g., 'mov', 'mvs', 'dly', 'ovrd', 'hclose', 'hopen', etc.). In addition, robots are often operated within routine schemata. Thus, it is possible to summarize all the potential complicated operation strategies for the pickup/placing tasks in the robotic assembly domain. Hence, the robotic program schemata of the potential complicated operation strategies are generalized and encoded in the basic planning base.

2. Parameter calculation rules – These rules are used to calculate the exact coordinates of point parameters in the robotic program.

The planning rule base contains two main kinds of rules:

1. Rules for analyzing tasks – When a task is input into the planning part, the planning part first analyze the features or requirements of the task with these rules. Then, it uses the rules learned from the learning part to select a robotic program schema from the planning basic base. Subsequently, given the state data in the input task, it uses the parameter calculation rules to calculate the point coordinates, and generates the robotic program that can be used by the robotic system. The features

and requirements of a task refer to the type of the target workpiece, the type of the robot tool, the relationship between the workpiece and the tool, the speed with which the robot is required to run in automatic mode, etc.

2. Rules learned from the learning part – In fact, most of the complicated operation strategies (i.e., robotic program schemata) in the robotic assembly domain can be generalized and encoded in the domain theory of the KBS. They are explicit knowledge. The tacit knowledge of skilled workers is in knowing how to select an appropriate operation strategy and use it flexibly for a particular task. Thus, the tacit knowledge must be learned from training examples. To make the tacit knowledge reusable, it is generalized as indexing rules for robotic program schemata in the planning rule base.

LEARNING MECHANISM OF THE KBS

In this section, a specific example is given to illustrate how the tacit knowledge is generalized as a rule and shared with workers by the learning part of the KBS in Figure 3.

As shown in Figure 4, there are two queues of blocks with the same frictional properties and density but different weights. The same color blocks have the same heights, but have different size cross-sections. The blocks in the right queue are thinner than the blocks in the left queue. The green blocks are the highest, while the blue ones are the lowest. The red blocks are higher than the yellow ones. Note that the width of the blocks, but not the color, is the key feature that affects the operation strategies.

In the example, four tasks and their corresponding training examples are given in turn to be learned by the KBS. They are picking up and placing the blue and the yellow blocks in the right queue in Figure 4. Because the learning mechanism

Figure 4. Example: palletizing blocks

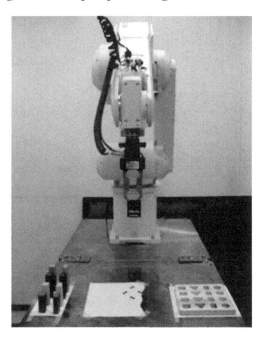

is the same for the four tasks, only the learning process for picking up the blue block is presented in details. The other three are only given to compare the learning results.

In learning from picking up the blue block, the task input to the learning part of the KBS is as follows:

Task goal: pickup.
Robot motion speed in automatic mode: auto_ovrd(80).
Initial position of the target block:
ini_pos(5, block-1, [691.27, -219.85, 49.5, -179.89, 0.38, 0.02]).

The fact 'auto_ovrd(80).' indicates that the robot's motion speed in automatic mode is 80% of its maximum motion speed. In the fact 'ini_pos(5, block-1, [691.27, -219.85, 49.5, -179.89, 0.38, 0.02]).', '5' is the ID number of the blue block. 'block-1' is its type. '[691.27, -219.85, 49.5, -179.89, 0.38, 0.02]' is the coordinate of the point that indicates its initial position, at the center of the upper side of the target block.

The other input, the training example is as follows:

Robot commands and parameters:
cmd(1,mov(phome)). %Mov Phome
cmd(2,mov(p5,50)).   %Mov P5,-50
cmd(3,mvs(p5)). %Mvs P5
cmd(4,dly(0.3)). %Dly 0.3
cmd(5,hclose(1)).   %HClose 1
cmd(6,dly(0.3)). %Dly 0.3
cmd(7,mvs(p5,50)). %Mvs P5,-50
cmd(8,mov(phome)). %Mov Phome
point(phome, [612.390, 0.180, 463.520, -179.890, 0.380, 0.020]).
point(p5, [691.270, -219.850, 210.000, -179.890, 0.380, 0.02]).

In the above, the elements in the right column (Mov Phome, etc.) are the primitive robotic commands in the robotic program. The left column (cmd(1,mov(phome))., etc.) is the transformation of the primitive robotic commands. The primitive robotic commands are transformed into facts of the training example, which can be understood by the KBS. Each robotic command is tagged with a number to indicate its order in the robotic program. In this way, the repeated commands can be distinguished by their sequence numbers.

After the above two inputs are input into the learning part, the "explainer" starts to explain how the training example accomplishes the pickup task. The explaining process is a search through the rules in the LKB, as shown in Figure 5.

The search tries rules one by one to construct an explanation tree, and terminates when all the leaf nodes of the explanation tree have been proved by the facts of the training example and the task, or by facts in the LKB. Such facts are the underlined terms in Figure 5. Because of limitations of space, Figure 5 cannot show the whole explanation tree. Thus, the sub-trees of seize_point and pickup_act are not shown completely. After all the leaf nodes are proved, the arguments in the searched rules (i.e., the terms above the dashed

Figure 5. Explanation tree of the example: picking up the blue block in the right queue.

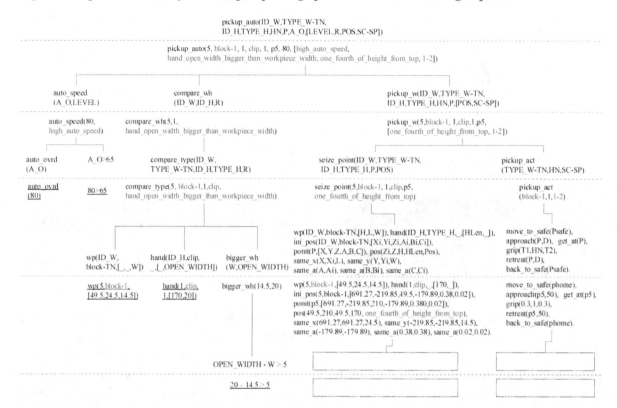

lines in Figure 5) are instantiated with the values in the facts. In this way, as the terms under the dashed lines in Figure 5 shows, an instantiated explanation tree is obtained.

Then, according to the operationality criterion, the "generalizer" generalizes tacit knowledge from the instantiated explanation tree by selecting key arguments and transforming them into an understandable knowledge translation and a reusable generalized rule. In Figure 5, the red arguments are the selected key arguments, which present the features/requirements of the pickup task, the seizing position of the blue block, the pickup operation strategy, etc.

The learning result is made up of two parts. The first is the knowledge translation for workers:

IF:
The automatic running speed is: high_auto_speed;
The workpiece type is: block-1;

The robot tool type is: clip;
The robot hand open width is: hand_open_width_bigger_than_workpiece_width;
THEN:
The seizing position on the workpiece is: one_fourth_of_height_from_top;
The pickup operation is:

move to a safe point, approach the seizing point at a distant position (to avoid collision with nearby workpieces), move to the seizing point, seize the target workpiece, retreat to the approach point, move back to the safe point.

The second is a generalized rule for the planning part:

pickup_plan(ID_W,block-1, ID_H,clip,P_name,hand_open_width_bigger_than_workpiece_width,high_auto_speed, [P_Coordinate,Command_Sequence]):-

seizeponit(ID_W,block-1,ID_H,one_fourth_of_
height_from_top,P_name,P_Coordinate),
pickupact(ID_W,block-1,clip,1-2,P_
name,Command_Sequence).

The above generalized rule does not include the detailed pickup operation actions. Instead, it contains the code for the pickup strategy used in the training example, which is '1-2'. In the planning part, this is a rule to transform '1-2' into robotic commands by using the robotic program schema whose code is '1-2' in the basic planning base. In '1-2', '1' indicates the type of the operation strategy, and '2' indicates its sub-type.

The pickup strategy used here is an essential one, since picking up the blue block is a simple task. The tacit knowledge in this example is that the robot tool should approach the blue block at a distant position. Because there are other blocks near the blue one, approaching it from a distance can avoid collisions in moving it after picking it up.

In placing the blue block, the placing strategy used is also an essential one, whose code is '1-1'. The tacit knowledge in this task is that the robot should approach at a position near the destination to make the blue block align with the target hole. In addition, the releasing point is at half the depth of the hole to make the blue block slide smoothly into the hole. (In the palletizing example in Figure 4, the cross-sections of the target holes are bigger than the cross-sections of their corresponding blocks. Thus the placing tasks are loose insertions.)

For picking up the yellow block in the right queue, the tacit knowledge learned is the same as that of picking up the blue block. Thus, the KBS does not need to save the generalized rule learned from this task in the PKB, while it simply presents the knowledge translation for the workers.

However, for placing the yellow block, the tacit knowledge learned is different from that of placing the blue block. For this task, the placing strategy used is '2-1':

move to a safe point, approach the releasing point at a distant position (to avoid collision with obstacles nearby destination), approach at a position near the releasing point, move to the releasing point, release the target workpiece, retreat to the distant approach point, move back to the safe point.

This is a complicated placing strategy, which is formulated by adding a distant approach point (i.e., an intermediate point) into the essential placing strategy '1-1'. In placing the yellow block, the previously placed blue block is taken as an obstacle near the destination as shown in Figure 2. To avoid collision with the blue block, a distant approach point should be added. The generalized rule learned from this task is different from that of placing the blue block, thus the KBS will save it in the PKB.

The four tasks given in this section illustrated the learning mechanism of the KBS. In the next section, we show how the learned knowledge is reused by the planning part of the KBS.

EXPERIMENTS AND ANALYSIS

As mentioned above, the KBS learned the knowledge of palletizing the blue and the yellow blocks in the right queue in Figure 4, and the learned knowledge is generalized as reusable rules to palletize the remaining blocks without being taught by the human. Through this learning procedure, the PKB of the KBS can be updated, since new generalized rules are added into its planning rule base.

In this section, experiments are conducted by using the planning part of the KBS to generate robotic programs for palletizing the other six blocks. The purpose is as follows: 1. to show how the planning part works, 2. to test the integrity and consistency of the domain theory, and 3. to show the boundaries of reuse implied by the generalized rules.

We present three aspects of the experimental analysis. Aspect 1 shows how the planning part works and that the generalized rule is valid for similar tasks. Aspects 2 and 3 show cases in which

Figure 6. Tree of searched rules for picking up the red block in the right queue

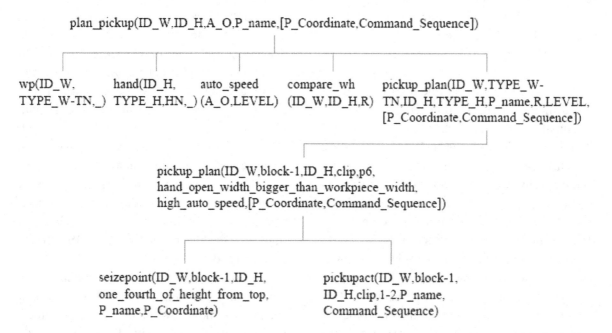

the generalized rule is not valid, that is, problems that can occur in the PKB.

Aspect 1: How the Planning Part Works

To generate the robotic program of picking up the red block in the right queue, the task input into the "planner" is:

Task goal: pickup.
Robot motion speed in automatic mode: auto_ovrd(80).
Initial position of the target block:
ini_pos(7, block-1, [691.27, -219.85, 70, -179.89, 0.38, 0.02]).
The "planner" first uses rules in the PKB to analyze the features/requirements of the task.

Then it matches these feature/requirements with those in the premises of the generalized rules. In other words, the planning process is also a search of the rules. Unlike learning, it is

a search through the PKB. Figure 6 shows the searched rules.

Finally, the generalized rule learned from picking up the blue block matches with the input task. This rule retrieves the pickup robotic program schema '1-2' and the corresponding parameter calculation rule from the basic planning base. In this way, the "planner" outputs the robotic program for picking up the red block as follows:

The seize point coordinate is
[691.27, -219.85, 204.5, -179.89, 0.38, 0.02]
The pickup command sequence is:
mov(psafe), mov(p6, 50), mvs(p6), dly(0.3), hclose(1), dly(0.3), mvs(p6, 50), mov(psafe).

This robotic program can be executed successfully to pick up the red block in the right queue. In the same way, the "planner" generates a valid program for placing the red block. By reusing the learned knowledge in this way, the robot-teaching time can be reduced.

Aspect 2: Inconsistent Theory Problem

In Figure 4, the blocks in the right queue belong to the same type 'block-1'. This is because their widths are almost the same. However, the "planner" fails to generate a program for picking up the green block in the right queue. This is caused by a confliction between the rules in the domain theory. In WTD, the "planner" finds that the width of the green block is 15, its type is 'block-1', and the open width of the robot tool is 20. In the planning rule base, there is a rule 'compare_wh' saying that:

If:

robot_tool_open_width − workpiece_width > 5,
Then: hand_open_width_bigger_than_workpiece_width;

If:

robot_tool_open_width − workpiece_width =< 5,
Then: similar_hand_open_width_and_workpiece_width.

This rule is used for analyzing the relationship between a robot tool and the target workpiece. Therefore, for the green block, the task features/requirements analysis result is as follows:

The workpiece type is: block-1;
The robot hand open width is: similar_hand_open_width_and_workpiece_width.
However, in the planning rule base, the rule learned from picking up the blue block is:

IF:

The automatic running speed is: high_auto_speed;
The workpiece type is: block-1;
The robot tool type is: clip;

The robot hand open width is: hand_open_width_bigger_than_workpiece_width;

THEN:

The seize position on the workpiece is: one_fourth_of_height_from_top;
The pickup operation is:

move to a safe point, approach the seizing point at a distant position (to avoid collision with nearby workpieces), move to the seizing point, seize the target workpiece, retreat to the approach point, move back to the safe point.

This means that there is no rule in the PKB that can be used for picking up the green block. This failure is caused by the conflict between the rule 'compare_wh' and the learned rule for picking up the blue block.

In this example, the learned rule determines the pickup strategy by considering both the type of the block and the comparison between its width and the open width of the tool. The comparison is decided by the pre-encoded rule 'compare_wh', which dose a calculation with the data (i.e., the width) of the block and the tool. In this case, a minor variance of the block data will lead to completely different comparison result. If the width of the green block was not 15, but was 14.99, then there would be no such 'planner' failure.

Or on the other hand, assume that we change the 'compare_wh' rule to be
If:

robot_tool_open_width − workpiece_width >=5,
Then: hand_open_width_bigger_than_workpiece_width;

If:

robot_tool_open_width − workpiece_width < 5,
Then: similar_hand_open_width_and_workpiece_width.

In this case, there also would be no conflict between the rule 'compare_wh' and the learned rule. Then, the "planner" will be able to reuse the learned rule successfully to generate a robotic program for picking up the green block.

This experiment reveals that due to real-time uncertainty factors (e.g., the minor variance of the workpiece data); it is difficult to make the pre-encoded rules to be completely consistent with the new learned rules. This is the inconsistent theory problem that may exist in any knowledge-based system. In the proposed KBS, the method of solving this problem is that an expert manually revises the rules to resolve their contradiction. Another method is to introduce a feature weighing mechanism to compare the importance/influences of the conflicting features in the rules. Then the KBS uses the rules by respecting the feature of the greatest importance/influence. The feature weighing mechanism will be the subject of our future research.

Aspect 3: Incomplete Theory Problem

In Figure 4, the blocks in the left queue belong to type 'block-2', because their widths are almost the same. After the task of picking up the blue block in the left queue is input into the KBS, the "planner" finds that there is no rule in the PKB available for picking it up. This is the incomplete theory problem of the PKB. In the KBS, the method of solving this problem is to give a training example of this task. Then the KBS can learn from the training example and update the PBK.

In this experiment, a training example of picking up the blue block in the left queue is given to the KBS. The KBS learns the following rule:

IF:

The automatic running speed is: high_auto_speed;
The workpiece type is: block-2;
The robot tool type is: clip;

The robot hand open width is: similar_hand_open_width_and_workpiece_width;

THEN:

The seize position on the workpiece is: one_fourth_of_height_from_top;
The pickup operation is:

move to a safe point, approach the seizing point at a distant position (to avoid collision with nearby workpieces), slow down the speed (to avoid collision between the robot tool and the target workpiece), approach the seizing point, move to the seizing point, seize the target workpiece, retreat to the approach point at the distant position, resume normal speed, move back to the safe point.

In the basic planning base, the code for the pickup strategy used in this training example is '3-2'. This pick-up strategy is a complicated one, which is formulating by adding an intermediate approach point and a speed change into the essential pickup strategy. Because the width of the blue block is similar to the open width of the robot tool, in the high speed automatic mode, the robot tool is prone to collide with the block. Therefore, the speed of the robot tool should slow down when it moves to the seizing point. In addition, an approach point that is close to the block should be added to align the robot tool with the block. In the following experiments, the rules learned from picking up and placing the blue block are reused successfully in picking up and placing the rest blocks in the left queue.

DISCUSSION

Compared with Other Methods

In this section, we compare our method with other methods, i.e., the SA method, the LfD method and the KB method that we introduced earlier from the perspective of the ability of sharing and reusing expert knowledge.

In the SA method, the expert knowledge is used to model the objective system or to define the feed-back/reward function. Then the system is optimized through online learning from its exploration. Thus, the SA method is an unsupervised learning method. Within the SA method, the knowledge is inductively learned from multiple/repetitive explorations by the system itself, but is not learned from human experts. Therefore, the limitation of the SA method is that it sacrifices the communication with human so as to lack expressiveness and inferential richness of the learned knowledge. It makes the SA method lose the chance that expert knowledge may help it converge within less exploration times. On the other hand, our method emphasizes knowledge sharing. The knowledge acquired by our method can not only be reused by the system, but also can be understood and reused by human.

The LfD method acquires human knowledge from demonstrations given by human. However, it just learns the state-action mapping policy, but ignores the analysis of the demonstrations. Thus, the quality of the learned knowledge is limited by the quality of the given demonstrations. Moreover, the LfD method often requires a set of training demonstrations for learning. Our method can learn from a single training example by analyzing it with the LKB and generalizing the explanation with the OC. The analyzing ability makes our method can critically learn from an example instead of learning a state-action mapping policy in a passive way. In addition, the ability of learning from a single example is important in that each example has the particular knowledge of the expert who gave the example. Especially in real robotic manufacturing, it is difficult to provide many training examples.

The KB method is the method we used in the planer of our system. Compared to other KB system, our KBS uses a modified EBL to update its PKB, which

makes the KB method enhance the extendibility and practicability.

Importance of Sharing Tacit Knowledge

Within factory automation, many kinds of automations like robotic technologies are introduced and did contribute to improving the productivity of manufacturing. However, these trends are causing another novel problem, the so-called de-skilling hypothesis of human workers induced by the automation (Braverman, 1974). In other words, the more automation is incorporated into the manufacturing process, the less the worker understands the process; the more sophisticated the machine becomes, and the less control and comprehension of the machine the worker has.

In the current factories, skills on how to operate and maintain the automation, e.g., robots, to keep them work continuously without failures are tacit knowledge. The tacit knowledge is of importance because the technical hitches caused by the wrong instructions to the robot do make the production lead time longer, but there is no way to share and reuse the tacit knowledge needed to avoid those kinds of technical hitches that are currently grasped in mind by only few experienced workers. Thus, construction of a novel knowledge infrastructure is needed that can support the maintenance and the transfer of the tacit knowledge of manufacturing among the human workers.

As for knowledge management and knowledge creation, the SECI model proposed by Nonaka and Takeuchi (1995) is well known. He mentioned that the creation of knowledge is a continuous process of dynamic interactions between tacit and explicit knowledge. We completely agree with this idea, but so far few discussions have been made on how to realize that knowledge creation cycle technically with the support of machine learning methodologies and how to design an entire system from a perspective of human-machine collaborative systems. Therefore, in this paper, based on the considerations above, we propose the KBS based on a modified EBL method to facilitate tacit knowledge sharing and reusing between human workers and robots.

CONCLUSION

In this paper, we have proposed a KBS to acquire tacit knowledge for sharing and reusing in the robotic assembly domain. The original EBL has been modified to acquire tacit knowledge from the robotic programs of skilled workers. A new operationality criterion is proposed, which demands that the learned tacit knowledge should be understandable by workers and reusable by robots. With the KBS, workers can learn the tacit knowledge implemented in robotic programs made by other workers. In this way, robotic programs become a vehicle for transferring tacit knowledge of skilled workers. This enables skill-succession even after the original skilled workers have retired. In addition, the KBS can generate robotic programs for assembly tasks in similar cases. Thus, it enables human workers to avoid repeatedly teaching robots similar assembly tasks. This reduces the robot teaching time dramatically. The KBS thus helps share tacit knowledge in the robotic assembly domain, and improves the efficiency and flexibility of robotic manufacturing.

However, there are also limitations to the proposed KBS, such as the inconsistent theory problem, which is a typical limitation that almost all knowledge-based systems encounter. Our future research will be on strengthening the human-system interaction function of the KBS to solve this problem.

ACKNOWLEDGMENT

This research is partially supported by Grant-in-Aid for Creative Scientific Research No.19GS0208 of the Ministry of Education, Culture, Sports, Science and Technology (MEXT) of Japan. The authors would also like to thank Akio Noda and Haruhisa Okuda, Mitsubishi Electric, Japan for their help and support of the experimental facilities and technical suggestions.

REFERENCES

Aleotti, J., Caselli, S., & Reggiani, M. (2004). Leveraging on a virtual environment for robot programming by demonstration. *Robotics and Autonomous Systems, 47*, 153–161. doi:10.1016/j.robot.2004.03.009

Argall, B. D., Chernova, S., Veloso, M., & Browning, B. (2009). A survey of robot learning from demonstration. *Robotics and Autonomous Systems, 57*(5), 469–483. doi:10.1016/j.robot.2008.10.024

Blomdell, A. (2005). Extending an industrial robot controller: implementation and applications of a fast open sensor interface. *Robotics & Automation Magazine, IEEE, 12*(3), 85–94. doi:10.1109/MRA.2005.1511872

Braverman, H. (1974). *Labour and Monopoly Capital: The Degradation of Work in the Twentieth Century*. New York: Monthly Review Press.

Brogårdh, T. (2007). Present and future robot control development — an industrial perspective. *Annual Reviews in Control, 31*, 69–79. doi:10.1016/j.arcontrol.2007.01.002

Chen, Y., & Naghdy, F. (2002, December). *Skill acquisition in transfer of manipulation skills from human to machine through a haptic virtual environment*. Paper presented at the 2002 IEEE International Conference on Industrial Technology, Bangkok, Thailand.

DeJong, G. (2006, September). *Toward robust real-world inference: a new perspective on explanation-based learning*. Paper presented at the 17th European Conference on Machine Learning, Berlin.

DeJong, G., & Mooney, R. (1986). Explanation-based learning: an alternative view. *Machine Learning, 1*, 145–176. doi:10.1007/BF00114116

Dillmann, R., et al. (1999, October). *Learning robot behaviour and skills based on human demonstration and advice: the machine learning paradigm*. Paper presented at the 9th International Symposium of Robotics Research, Snowbird, UT.

Friedrich, H., & Dillmann, R. (1995, April). *Robot programming based on a single demonstration and user intentions*. Paper presented at the 3rd European Workshop on Learning Robots EWLR-3, Heraklion, Crete, Greece.

Fujita, T., et al. (2008, August). *Robot control cell production system of senju (thousand-handed) kannon model that demonstrated optimality to the multi-product production in varying volumes for eight years*. Paper presented at the 4th IEEE Conference on Automation Science and Engineering, Key Bridge Marriott, DC.

Haegele, M., et al. (2005). *White paper - industrial robot automation. European Robotics Network*. Retrieved from http://www.euron.org/miscdocs/docs/euron2/year2/dr-14-1-industry.pdf

Hovland, G., Sikka, P., & McCarragher, B. (1996, April). *Skill acquisition from human demonstration using a hidden markov model*. Paper presented at the 1996 IEEE International Conference on Robotics and Automation, Minneapolis, MN.

Hwang, C. P., & Ho, C. S. (1996). A knowledge-based task-level programming and execution environment for robots. *Robotics and Computer-integrated Manufacturing, 12*(4), 329–351. doi:10.1016/S0736-5845(96)00020-8

Levine, G., & DeJong, G. (2006, June). *Explanation-based acquisition of planning operators*. Paper presented at the 2006 International Conference on Automated Planning and Scheduling, the English Lake District, Cumbria, UK.

Li, Y. F., Ho, J., & Li, N. (2000). Development of a physically behaved robot work cell in virtual reality for task teaching. *Robotics and Computer-integrated Manufacturing, 16*, 91–101. doi:10.1016/S0736-5845(99)00042-3

Lopez-Juarez, I., & Howarth, M. (2002). Knowledge acquisition and learning in unstructured robotic assembly environments. *Information Sciences, 145*, 89–111. doi:10.1016/S0020-0255(02)00225-6

Maeda, Y., Ushioda, T., & Makita, S. (2008, May). *Easy robot programming for industrial manipulators by manual volume sweeping*. Paper presented at the 2008 IEEE International Conference on Robotics and Automation, Pasadena, CA.

Mitchell, T. M., Keller, R. M., & Kedar-Cabelli, S. T. (1986). Explanation-based generalization: a unifying view. *Machine Learning, 1*, 47–80. doi:10.1007/BF00116250

Noda, A., et al. (2009, December). *Intelligent robotic technologies for cell assembly system*. Paper presented at the 10th SICE System Integration Division Annual Conference, Tokyo, Japan.

Noda, A., & Nagatani, T. (2008, September). *Motion learning for industrial robots with an active search algorithm*. Paper presented at the 26th Annual Conference of the Robotics Society of Japan, Kobe, Japan.

Noda, A., Nagatani, T., & Nagano, H. (2008, December), *Active search algorithm on motion learning of industrial robots*. Paper presented at the 9th SICE System Integration Division Annual Conference, Gifu, Japan.

Nonaka, I., & Takeuchi, H. (1995). *The Knowledge-Creating Company*. New York: Oxford University Press.

Nuttin, M., & Van Brussel, H. (1997). Learning the peg-into-hole assembly operation with a connectionist reinforcement technique. *Computers in Industry*, *33*, 101–109. doi:10.1016/S0166-3615(97)00015-8

Pires, J. N. (2006). *Industrial robots programming: building applications for the factories of the future*. New York: Springer.

Prabhu, S. M., & Garg, D. P. (1997, May). *Fuzzy logic based reinforcement learning of admittance control for automated robotic manufacturing*. Paper presented at the 1st International Conference on Knowledge-Based Intelligent Electronic Systems, Adelaide, South Australia.

Sawaragi, T., Liu, Y., & Tian, Y. (2006). Human-machine collaborative knowledge creation: capturing tacit knowledge by observing expert's demonstration of load allocation. *International Journal of Knowledge and Systems Science*, *3*(2), 9–19.

Segre, A. (1988). *Machine learning of robot assembly plans*. Norwell, MA: Kluwer Academic Publishers.

Segre, A. (1991). Learning how to plan. *Robotics and Autonomous Systems*, *8*, 93–111. doi:10.1016/0921-8890(91)90016-E

Segre, A., & DeJong, G. (1985, March). *Explanation based manipulator learning: acquisition of planning ability through observation*. Paper presented at the 1985 IEEE International Conference on Robotics and Automation, St. Louis, MO.

Wang, L., Tian, Y., & Sawaragi, T. (2008, July). *Explanation-based manipulator learning: acquisition of assembling technique through observation*. Paper presented at the 17th World Congress the International Federation of Automatic Control, Seoul, South Korea.

ENDNOTE

[1]   In the following descriptions of predicates, characters initiated with capital letters or upper case characters represent variables, while lower case characters are constants.

This work was previously published in the International Journal of Knowledge and Systems Science, Volume 1, Issue 4, edited by W.B. Lee, pp. 61-78 copyright 2010 by IGI Publishing (an imprint of IGI Global).

Compilation of References

Abecker, A., Sheth, A., Mentzas, G., & Stojanovic, L. (2006). The Semantic Web meets eGovernment. In *Proceedings of the 2006 AAAI Spring Symposium* Series, Stanford University, Stanford, CA. Retrieved August 28, 2008, from http://www.aaai.org/Press/Reports/Symposia/Sprin g/ss0606.php

Adler, P. (2001). Market, hierarchy and trust: The knowledge economy and the future of capitalism. *Organization Science*, 214–234.

Adler, P. S., & Kwon, S. W. (2002). Social capital: Prospects for a new concept. *Academy of Management Review*, *27*(1), 17–40. doi:10.2307/4134367

Akkerman, S. (2006). *Strangers in dialogue. Academic collaboration across organizational boundaries*. Unpublished doctoral dissertation, University of Utrecht, The Netherlands.

Alasoud, A., et al. (2009). An Empirical Comparison of Ontology Matching Techniques. *Journal of Information Science, 35*(4), 379-397. Retrieved October 18, 2010, from http://jis.sagepub.com/cgi/content/abstract/35/4/379

Alavi, N., & Leidner, D. (1999). Knowledge management systems: emerging views and practices from the field. In *Proceedings of the 32ⁿᵈ Hawaii international conference on system science*. Retrieved October 22, 2008, from http://www2.computer.org/portal/web/csdl/doi/10.1109/HICSS.1999.77 2754

Alavi, M., & Leidner, D. (2001). Knowledge management and knowledge management systems. *Management Information Systems Quarterly*, *25*(1), 107–136. doi:10.2307/3250961

Alavi, M., & Leidner, D. E. (1999). Knowledge management systems: Issues, challenges and benefits. *Communications of the Association for Information Systems*, *1*(7).

Alavi, M., & Leidner, D. E. (2001). Review: Knowledge management and knowledge management systems: Conceptual foundations and research issues. *Management Information Systems Quarterly*, *25*(1), 107–136. doi:10.2307/3250961

Aleotti, J., Caselli, S., & Reggiani, M. (2004). Leveraging on a virtual environment for robot programming by demonstration. *Robotics and Autonomous Systems*, *47*, 153–161. doi:10.1016/j.robot.2004.03.009

Allee, V. (2002). *The future of knowledge: Increasing prosperity through value networks*. Boston: Butterworth-Heinemann.

Alvesson, M., & Karreman, D. (2002). Odd couple: coming to terms with knowledge management. *Journal of Management Studies*, *38*(7), 995–1018. doi:10.1111/1467-6486.00269

Amidon, D. (2003). *The innovation superhighway: Harnessing Intellectual Capital for sustainable collaborative advantage*. New York: Butterworth and Heinemann.

Anderson, P. (2007). *What is Web 2.0? Ideas, technologies and implications for education*. JISC Technology and Standards Watch.

Anderson, R. C., Nguyen-Jahiel, K., McNurlen, B., Archodidou, A., So-young, K., & Reznitskaya, A. (2001). The Snowball Phenomenon: Spread of ways of talking and ways of thinking across groups of children. *Cognition and Instruction*, *19*(1), 1–46. doi:10.1207/S1532690XCI1901_1

Andriessen, D., & van den Boom, M. (2007). East is East, and West is West, and (n)ever its intellectual capital shall meet. *Journal of Intellectual Capital*, *8*(4), 641–652. doi:10.1108/14691930710830800

Angus, J. (2003). KM's father figure: Robert Buckman. *Infoworld Magazine*. Retrieved December 18, 2008, from www.infoworld.com

Antonacopoulou, E. P. (2006). Modes of Knowing in Practice: The Relationship between Learning and Knowledge Revisited . In Renzl, B., Matzler, K., & Hinterhuber, H. (Eds.), *The Future of Knowledge Management*. London: Palgrave.

AQAP. 150. (1997). *Quality assurance requirements for software development*. Brussels, Belgium: NATO.

Arbnor, I., & Bjerke, B. (2009). *Methodology for creating business knowledge* (3rd ed.). London: Sage Publications.

Archer, M. S. (1995). *Realist social theory: The morphogenetic approach*. Cambridge, UK: University of Cambridge Press.

Argall, B. D., Chernova, S., Veloso, M., & Browning, B. (2009). A survey of robot learning from demonstration. *Robotics and Autonomous Systems*, *57*(5), 469–483. doi:10.1016/j.robot.2008.10.024

Argote, L. (1999). *Organizational Learning: creating, retaining and transferring knowledge*. Norwell, MA: Kluwer Academics.

Argote, L., Beckman, S. L., & Epple, D. (1990). The persistence and transfer of learning in industrial settings. *Management Science*, *36*(2), 140–154. doi:10.1287/mnsc.36.2.140

Argyris, C., & Schon, D. (1982). *Reasoning, learning and action: Individual and organisational*. Reading, MA: Addison-Wesley.

Aries, S., Le Blanc, B., & Ermine, J.-L. (2008). MASK: Une méthode d'ingénierie des connaissances pour l'analyse et la structuration des connaissances (MASK: A Knowledge Engineering Method for Analysing and Structuring Knowledge) . In *J.-L. Ermine (Dir.), Management et ingénierie des connaissances, modèles et méthodes* (pp. 261–306). Paris: Hermes Lavoisier.

Armstrong, M. (2006). *A handbook Of Human Resource Management Practice* (10th ed.). Cambridge, UK: Cambridge University Press.

Arroyo, S., Ding, Y., Lara, R., Stollberg, M., & Fensel, D. (2004). Semantic Web Languages - Strengths and Weakness. In *Proceedings of the International Conference in Applied computing (IADIS04)*, Lisbon, Portugal.

AS/NZS 4360. (2004). *Risk management*. Standards Australia and New Zealand.

Asgeirsdottir, B. (2005). OECD work on knowledge and the knowledge economy. In *Proceedings of the OECD/NSF conference on 'Advancing knowledge and the knowledge economy*. Retrieved November 15, 2007, from http://www.flacso.edu.mx/openseminar/downloads/ocde_knowledge_speech.pdf

Ash, J. (2004). Knowledge works. *Inside knowledge magazine*, *8*(2). Retrieved October 1, 2007, from http://www.ikmagazine.com/xq/asp/txtSearch.CRM/exactphrase.1/sid.0/articleid.9F1AD936-E784-4833-A566-E92BF3B92B6C/qx/display.htm

ASLIB. (1952). Harnessing knowledge. *Nature*, *170*, 698–699. doi:10.1038/170698a0

Asrilhant, B., Dyson, R., & Meadows, M. (2007). On the strategic project management process in the UK upstream oil and gas sector. *Omega*, *35*, 89–103. doi:10.1016/j.omega.2005.04.006

Asrilhant, B., Meadows, M., & Dyson, R. G. (2004). Exploring decision support and strategic project management in the oil and gas sector. *European Management Journal*, *22*(1), 63–73. doi:10.1016/j.emj.2003.11.017

Atherton, J. S. (2005). *Learning and Teaching, Theories of Learning*. Retrieved January 19, 2005, from http://www.learningandteaching.info/learning/theories.htm

Atlassian. (2008a). *JavaPolis*. Retrieved from http://www.atlassian.com /software/confluence/casestudies/javapolis.jsp

Atlassian. (2008b). *Johns Hopkins University*. Retrieved from http://www.atlassian.com/software/confluence/casestudies/ johnhopkins.jsp

Auer, S., Jungmann, B., & Schönefeld, F. (2007). Semantic Wiki Representations for Building an Enterprise Knowledge Base . In Antoniou, G., Aßmann, U., Baroglio, C., Decker, S., Henze, N., Patranjan, P.-L., & Tolksdorf, R. (Eds.), *Reasoning Web* (pp. 330–333). Berlin: Springer. doi:10.1007/978-3-540-74615-7_7

Aven, T., & Kristensen, V. (2005). Perspectives on risk: review and discussion of the basis for establishing a unified and holistic approach. *Reliability Engineering & System Safety*, *90*, 1–14. doi:10.1016/j.ress.2004.10.008

Aven, T., & Pitblado, R. (1998). On risk assessment in the petroleum activities on the Norwegian and UK continental shelves. *Reliability Engineering & System Safety*, *61*(1-2), 21–29. doi:10.1016/S0951-8320(98)80002-1

Aven, T., & Vinnem, J. E. (2007). *Risk Management: With Applications from the Offshore Petroleum Industry*. Berlin, Germany: Springer Verlag.

Babcock, P. (2004). Shedding light on knowledge management. *HRMagazine*, *49*(5), 46–50.

Bacharach, S. B. (1989). Organizational theories: some criteria for evaluation. *Academy of Management Review*, *14*(4), 496–515. doi:10.2307/258555

Baclawski, K., Kokar, M., Kogut, P., Hart, L., Smith, J., Holmes, W., et al. (2001). *Extending UML to support ontology engineering for the Semantic Web* (LNCS 2185, pp. 342-360). New York: Springer.

Bak, P. (1997). *How nature works. The science of self-organized criticality*. Oxford, UK: Oxford University Press.

Bandura, A. (1997). *Self-efficacy. The exercise of control*. New York: W. H. Freeman and Company.

Barabási, A.-L. (2003). *Linked. How everything is connected to everything else and what it means for business, science, and everyday life*. New York: Penguin Group.

Barab, S., & Kirshner, D. (2002). Rethinking methodology in the learning sciences. *Journal of the Learning Sciences*, *10*, 5–15. doi:10.1207/S15327809JLS10-1-2_2

Barkham, P. (2008, July). What is the knowledge economy. *The Guardian Newspaper*. Retrieved January 18, 2009, from http://www.guardian.co.uk/business/2008/jul/17/economics.economicgrowth

Barnard, C. (1938). *The function of the executive*. Cambridge, MA: Harvard University Press.

Barnes, C. J., Childs, T. H. C., Henson, B., & Southee, C. H. (2004). Surface finish and touch-a case study in a new human factors tribology. *Wear*, *257*(7-8), 740–750. doi:10.1016/j.wear.2004.03.018

Barron, F., & Harrington, D. M. (1981). Creativity, Intelligence, and Personality. *Annual Review of Psychology*, *32*(1), 439–476. doi:10.1146/annurev.ps.32.020181.002255

Barrow, R. (2005). Setting new boundaries - applying the UML to railway standards. In *Proceedings of the IEE Seminar on UML Systems Engineering*. Washington, DC: IEEE.

Bayley, C. (2004). Modelling interlocking systems with UML. In *Proceedings of the IEEE Seminar on Railway System Modelling - Not Just for Fun*. Washington, DC: IEEE.

Bean, L., & Hott, D. D. (2005). Wiki: A Speedy New Tool to Manage Projects. *Journal of Corporate Accounting & Finance*, *16*(5), 3–8. doi:10.1002/jcaf.20128

Beccerra-Fernandez, I., & Sabherwal, R. (2006). ICT and knowledge management systems . In Schwartz, D. G. (Ed.), *Encyclopedia of Knowledge Management* (pp. 230–236). Hershey, PA: IGI Global.

Bellah, R. N., Madsen, R., Sullivan, M. M., Swidler, A., & Tipton, S. M. (Eds.). (1985). *Habits of the heart*. Berkeley, CA: University of California Press.

Bell, D. (1973). *The coming of post-industrial society: A venture in social forecasting*. New York: The Basic Press.

Belzer, R. B. (2001). Getting beyond 'grin and bear it' in the practice of risk management. *Reliability Engineering & System Safety*, *72*(2), 137–148. doi:10.1016/S0951-8320(01)00015-1

Benbya, H., Passiante, G., & Belbaly, N. A. (2004). Corporate portal: a tool for knowledge management synchronization. *International Journal of Information Management*, *24*, 201–220. doi:10.1016/j.ijinfomgt.2003.12.012

Benmahamed, D., & Ermine, J.-L. (2007). Knowledge Management Techniques for Know-How Transfer Systems Design. The Case of Oil Company . In *Creating Collaborative Advantage through Knowledge and Innovation* (pp. 15–34). New York: World Scientific Publishing Company. doi:10.1142/9789812707482_0002

Bennet, A., & Bennet, D. (2007). *Knowledge mobilization in the social sciences and humanities: Moving from research to action*. Frost, WV: MQI Press.

Bhatt, G. (2001). Knowledge management in organizations: examining the interaction between technologies, techniques and people. *Journal of Knowledge Management*, *5*(1), 68–75. doi:10.1108/13673270110384419

Biesta, G. (2006). *Beyond Learning. Democratic Education for a Human Future*. Boulder, CO: Paradigm Publishers.

Black, E. L., & Kilzer, R. D. (2008). Web 2.0 Tools Ease Renovation Service Disruptions at the Ohio State University Libraries. *Public Services Quarterly*, *4*(2), 93–109. doi:10.1080/15228950802202317

Blacker, F. (1995). Knowledge, knowledge workers and organizations: an overview and interpretation. *Organization Studies*, *16*(6), 1021–1046. doi:10.1177/017084069501600605

Blackman, D., Connelly, J., & Henderson, S. (2004). Does double loop learning create reliable knowledge. *The Learning Organization*, *11*(1), 11–27. doi:10.1108/09696470410515706

Blomdell, A. (2005). Extending an industrial robot controller: implementation and applications of a fast open sensor interface. *Robotics & Automation Magazine, IEEE*, *12*(3), 85–94. doi:10.1109/MRA.2005.1511872

Bloomberg, J. (2003). The role of the service-oriented architect. *The Rational Edge*. Retrieved August 28, 2008, from http://www.therationaledge.com/conte nt/may_03/PDF/bloomber g.pdf

Bock, G., & Paxhia, S. (2008). 2008 Taking Stock of Today's Experiences and Tomorrow's Opportunities . In *Gilbane Group Research Report*. Collaboration and Social Media.

Boehm, B. W. (1989). S*oftware risk management* (LNCS 387, pp. 1-19). New York: Springer.

Boehm, B. W. (1986). A spiral model of software development and enhancement. *ACM SIGSOFT Software Engineering Notes*, *11*(4), 14–24. doi:10.1145/12944.12948

Bohm, D., & Peat, D. (2000). *Science, order & creativity* (2nd ed.). London: Routledge.

Boland, R. J., & Tenkasi, R. V. (1995). Perspective making and perspective taking in communities of knowing. *Organization Science*, *6*, 350–372. doi:10.1287/orsc.6.4.350

Bonabeau, E. (2009). Decision 2.0: The power of collective intelligence. *MIT Sloan Management Review*, *50*(2), 45–52.

Borgatti, S. P., & Cross, R. (2003). A relational view of information seeking and learning in social networks. *Management Science*, *49*(4), 432–445. doi:10.1287/mnsc.49.4.432.14428

Borgo, S., & Lesmo, L. (2008). Formal Ontologies Meet Industry . In *Frontiers in Artificial Intelligence and Applications Series (Vol. 174)*. Amsterdam, The Netherlands: IOS Press.

Boughzala, I., & Ermine, J.-L. (Eds.). (2006). *Trends in Enterprise Knowledge Management*. London: Hermes Penton Science. doi:10.1002/9780470612132

Boulding, K. (1956). General systems theory: The skeleton of science. *Management Science*, *2*, 197–208. doi:10.1287/mnsc.2.3.197

Bourdelais, P. (1993). *L'âge de la vieillesse. Histoire du vieillissement (Age of ageing, the history of ageing)*. Paris: Odile Jacob.

Bourdieu, P. (1985). The forms of capital. In J.G. Richardson (Ed.), *Handbook of theory and research for the sociology of dducation* (pp. 241-258). New York: Greenwood.

Bournemann, M., et al. (2003). *An illustrated guide to Knowledge Management*. Paper presented at the Wissenmanagement forum, Graz. Retrieved December 18, 2008, from www.wm-forum.org

Bouthiller, F., & Shearer, K. (2002). Understanding knowledge manageent and information management: the need for an empirical perspective. *Information research*, *8*(1). Retrieved January 4, 2008, from http://informationr.net/ir/8-1/paper141.html

Bowonder, B. (1981). Environmental risk assessment issues in the third world. *Technological Forecasting and Social Change, 19*(1), 99–127. doi:10.1016/0040-1625(81)90051-2

Boxall, P. (1996). The strategic HRM debate and the resource-based view of the firm. *Human Resource Management Journal, 6*(3), 59–75. doi:10.1111/j.1748-8583.1996.tb00412.x

Boxall, P., & Steeneveld, M. (1999). Human Resource strategy and competitive advantage: a longitudinal study of engineering consultancies. *Journal of Management Studies, 36*(4), 443–463. doi:10.1111/1467-6486.00144

Braverman, H. (1974). *Labour and Monopoly Capital: The Degradation of Work in the Twentieth Century*. New York: Monthly Review Press.

Brogårdh, T. (2007). Present and future robot control development—an industrial perspective. *Annual Reviews in Control, 31*, 69–79. doi:10.1016/j.arcontrol.2007.01.002

Bruner, J. (1987). Foreword. In R. W. Rieber & A. S. Carton (Eds.), *The collected works of L. S. Vygotsky, Vol. 1. Problems of general psychology* (pp. 1-16). New York: Plenum Press.

Bruner, J. (1996). *The Culture of Education*. Cambridge, MA: Harvard University Press.

Brusa1, G., Caliusco, M. L., & Chiotti, O. (2007). Enabling Knowledge Sharing within E-Government Back-Office Through Ontological Engineering. *Journal of Theoretical and Applied Electronic Commerce Research, 2*(1), 33-48.

BS 6079-3. (2000). *Project management - Part 3: Guide to the management of business related project risk*. London: British Standards Institution.

BS 8444-3. (1996). *Risk Management - Part 3: Guide to risk analysis of technical systems*. London: British Standards Institution.

Buckley, W. (1967). *Sociology and modern systems theory*. Englewood Cliffs, NJ: Prentice-Hall.

Buller, D. J. (2005). *Adapting minds. Evolutionary Psychology and the persistent quest for human nature*. Cambridge, MA: MIT Press.

Burt, R. S. (2004). Structural Holes and Good Ideas. *American Journal of Sociology, 110*(2), 349–399. doi:10.1086/421787

Bush, V. (1945). As we may think. *The Atlantic Magazine.* Retrieved October 7, 2008, from http://www.theatlantic.com/magazine/archive/1969/12/as-we-may-think/3881/

Buzan, B., & Buzan, T. (2003). *The Mind Map Book: Radiant Thinking - Major Evolution in Human Thought (Mind Set)* (3rd ed.). London: BBC Active.

Campbell, D. T. (1960). Blind variation and selective retention in creative thought as in other knowledge processes. *Psychological Review, 67*, 380–400. doi:10.1037/h0040373

Carlin, D. (2007). Corporate Wikis Go Viral. *BusinessWeek.*

Carr, W. (2006). Philosophy, methodology and action. *Journal of Philosophy of Education, 40*(4), 421–435. doi:10.1111/j.1467-9752.2006.00517.x

Carter, L. F. (1968). Knowledge production and utilisation in contemporary organisations. In T. L. Eidell & J. M. Kitchel (Eds.), *Knowledge production and utilisation in educational administration 1969* (pp. 1-20). Columbus, Ohio: University council for educational administration.

Carter, R., Martin, J., Mayblin, B., & Munday, M. (1986). *Systems, management and change*. London: The Open University.

Castillo, O., Matta, N., Ermine, J.-L., & Brutel-Mainaud, S. (2004). Knowledge Appropriation from Profession Memories. In *Proceedings of 16th European Conference on Artificial Intelligence, Workshop Knowledge Management and Organizational Memories*, Valencia, Spain.

Cepeda, G. (2006). Competitive advantage of knowledge management . In Schwartz, D. G. (Ed.), *Encyclopedia of Knowledge Management* (pp. 34–43). Hershey, PA: IGI Global.

Chadwick, J. (1990). *The decipherment of linear B* (2nd ed.). Cambridge, UK: Cambridge University Press.

Chang, A., & Kannan, P. K. (2008). *Leveraging Web 2.0 in Government, E-Government/ Technology Series*. IBM Center for The Business of Government.

Chang, M. H., & Harrington, J. J. (2007). Innovators, imitators, and the evolving architecture of problem-solving networks. *Organization Science, 18*(4), 648–666. doi:10.1287/orsc.1060.0245

Chapman, C., & Ward, S. (2004). Why risk efficiency is a key aspect of best practice projects. *International Journal of Project Management, 22*, 619–632. doi:10.1016/j.ijproman.2004.05.001

Chauvel, D., & Desprs, C. (2002). A review of survey research in knowledge management: 1997-2001. *Journal of Knowledge Management, 6*(3), 207–223. doi:10.1108/13673270210434322

Checkland, P. (2000). Soft systems methodology: A thirty year retrospective. *Systems Research and Behavioral Science, 17*, S11–S58. doi:10.1002/1099-1743(200011)17:1+<::AID-SRES374>3.0.CO;2-O

Chen, Y., & Naghdy, F. (2002, December). *Skill acquisition in transfer of manipulation skills from human to machine through a haptic virtual environment.* Paper presented at the 2002 IEEE International Conference on Industrial Technology, Bangkok, Thailand.

Chia, R. (2004). Strategy-as-practice: Reflections on the research agenda. *European Management Review, 1*, 29–34. doi:10.1057/palgrave.emr.1500012

Chiva, R., & Alegre, J. (2005). Organisational learning and organisational knowledge. *management learning, 36*(1) 49-68.

Chiva, R., & Alegre, J. (2005). Organisational learning and organisational knowledge. *Management Learning, 36*(1), 49–68. doi:10.1177/1350507605049906

Choi, N., et al. (2006). A Survey on Ontology Mapping. *ACM SIGMOD Record, 35*(3), 34-41. Retrieved October 18, 2010, from http://citeseerx.ist.psu.edu/viewdoc/download?doi=10.1.1.107.4316&rep=rep1&type=pdf

Chorn, L. G., & Shokhor, S. (2006). Real options for risk management in petroleum development investments. *Energy Economics, 28*, 489–505. doi:10.1016/j.eneco.2006.03.002

Chowdhury, M. S. (2006). Human behaviour in the context of training: An overview of learning theories as applied to training and development. *Journal of knowledge management, 7*(2). Retrieved January 10, 2008, from http://www.tlainc.com/articl12.htm

Chun, M., Sohn, K., Arling, P., & Granados, N. F. (2008). Systems theory and knowledge management systems: The case of Pratt-Whitney Rocketdyne. In *proceedings of the 41st Hawaii International Conference on Systems Sciences* (pp. 1-10).

Churchman, C. W. (1970). Operations research as a profession . *Management Science, 17*, 37–53.

Cilliers, P. (2005). Complexity, deconstruction and relativism. *Theory, Culture & Society, 22*(5), 255–267. doi:10.1177/0263276405058052

CIRET-centre. (n.d.). Retrieved January 18, 2009, from http://nicol.club.fr/ciret/english/visionen.htm

Clarke, L. (2007). Thinking possibilistically in a probabilistic world. *Significance Statistics Making Sense, 4*(4), 190–192.

Clarke, T. (2001). The knowledge economy. *Education + Training, 43*(4/5), 189–196. doi:10.1108/00400910110399184

Clark, H. H., & Brennan, S. A. (1991). *Perspectives on Socially Shared Cognition.* Washington, DC: APA Books.

Clement, J. (1994). Use of physical intuition and imagistic simulation in expert problem solving . In Tirosh, D. (Ed.), *Implicit and Explicit Knowledge.* Hillsdale, NJ: Ablex Publishing.

Cohen (Eds.), *Boston Studies in the philosophy of science, Vol. 200.* Dordrecht, The Netherlands: Kluwer Academic Publishers.

Coleman, J. S. (1988). Social capital in the creation of human capital. *American Journal of Sociology, 94*(S1), 95–120. doi:10.1086/228943

Comte, A. (1844). *A general view of positivism.* London: Reeves and Turner.

Conroy, C. (2008). *Towards Ontology Mapping for Ordinary People*. Paper presented at the European Semantic Web Conference, Tenerife, Spain. Retrieved October 18, 2010, from http://people.csail.mit.edu/pcm/ESW-C08PHD/conroy.pdf

Cooney, L. (2006). Wiki as a Knowledge Management Tool. In *Proceedings of CERAM Sophia-Antipolis*.

Corbetta, P. (2003). *Social Research: Theory, Methods and Techniques*. London: Sage.

Correndo, G., & Alani, H. (2007). *Collaborative Ontology Mapping and Data Sharing*. (Tech. Rep. No. SO17 1BJ). Southampton, UK: University of Southampton, Electronic and Computer Science Department. Retrieved October 18, 2010, from http://eprints.ecs.soton.ac.uk/16676/1/correndo-Collaborative.pdf

Cowan, R., & Jonard, N. (2004). Network structure and the diffusion of knowledge. *Journal of Economic Dynamics & Control*, *28*(8), 1557–1575. doi:10.1016/j.jedc.2003.04.002

Cranefield, S., & Purvis, M. (1999). UML as an ontology modelling language. In *Proceedings of the Workshop on Intelligent Information Integration, 16th International Joint Conference on Artificial Intelligence (IJCAI-99)*, Stockholm, Sweden.

Crease. (2002). Finding the flaw in falsifiability. *Physics world online magazine*. Retrieved April 8, 2009, from www.physicsworld.com/cws/article/print/16478

Creech, H. (2005). Mobilising IUCN's knowledge to secure a sustainable future. *The IUCN knowledge management study*. Retrieved December 18, 2008, from http://www.iisd.org/pdf/2008/km_study_full_report.pdf

Creswell, J. (1994). *Research Design: Quantitative and Qualitative Approaches*. Thousand Oaks, CA: Sage.

Crete. (2003). *Proceedings of the 47th Annual Meeting of the International Society for the Systems Sciences*. Retrieved from http://www.isss.org/world/en/conferences/crete2003

Cruywagen, M., Swart, J., & Gevers, W. (2008). One size does not fit all – towards a typology of knowledge centric organisations. *Electronic Journal of Knowledge Management*, *6*(2), 101–110.

Cui, X., Li, Y. D., Xia, L. M., & Zhang, J. C. (2003, September 1). *An attributed directed graph model of HWME based on internet* (pp. 8-9). Paper presented at the 17th JISR-IIASA Workshop on Methodologies and Tools for Complex System Modeling and Integrated Policy Assessment.

Daddieco, R. J. (2004). *Retrieving knowledge in E-Government: the prospects of ontology for regulatory domain record keeping systems*. Wimmer.

Daft, R. L., & Lengel, R. H. (1986). Organizational Information Requirements, Media Richness and Structural Design. *Management Science*, *32*(5), 554–571. doi:10.1287/mnsc.32.5.554

Dai, R., Yu, J. Y., & Gu, J. F. (2003, September 8-10). A meta-synthetic approach for decision support system. In Proceedings of *CSM'03, the 17th JISR-IIASA Workshop on Methodologies and Tools for Complex System Modeling and Integrated Policy Assessment* (pp. 10-12). Retrieved from www.iiasa.ac.at/~marek/ftppub/Pubs/csm03/abst.ps

Damm, D., & Schindler, M. (2002). Security issues of a knowledge medium for distributed project work. *International Journal of Project Management*, *20*(1), 37–47. doi:10.1016/S0263-7863(00)00033-8

Davenport, T. H., & Prusak, L. (2000). *Working Knowledge: How Organizations Manage What They Know*. Boston, MA: Harvard Business School Press.

Davies, J., Struder, R., Sure, Y., & Warren, P. W. (2005). Next generation knowledge management. *BT Technology Journal*, *23*(3), 175–189. doi:10.1007/s10550-005-0040-3

Davis, B. (2004). *Inventions of teaching. A genealogy*. Mahwah, NJ: Lawrence Erlbaum.

Davis, B., & Sumara, D. (2006). *Complexity and education. Inquiries into learning, teaching, and research*. Mahwah, NJ: Lawrence Erlbaum.

Davis, B., Sumara, D., & Luce-Kapler, R. (2000). *Engaging minds. Learning and teaching in a complex world*. Mahwah, NJ: Lawrence Erlbaum.

Dawn, J., Bodorik, P., & Dhaliwal, J. (2002). Supporting the e-business readiness of small and medium sized enterprises: approaches and metrics. *Internet research: Electronic networking applications and policy, 12*(2), 139-164.

DeJong, G. (2006, September). *Toward robust real-world inference: a new perspective on explanation-based learning*. Paper presented at the 17th European Conference on Machine Learning, Berlin.

DeJong, G., & Mooney, R. (1986). Explanation- based learning: an alternative view. *Machine Learning, 1,* 145–176. doi:10.1007/BF00114116

Delio, M. (2005). *The Enterprise Blogosphere*. InfoWorld.

DeLong, D. W. (2004). *Lost knowledge. Confronting the threat of an aging workforce*. Oxford, UK: Oxford University Press.

Delvosalle, C., Fievez, C., Pipart, A., Casal Fabreg, J., Planas, E., Christou, M., & Mushtaq, F. (2005). Identification of reference accident scenarios in SEVESO establishments. *Reliability Engineering & System Safety, 90,* 238–246. doi:10.1016/j.ress.2004.11.003

Deng, H., & Martin, B. (2003). A framework for intelligent organizational knowledge management. In *Proceedigns of Integrated Design and Process Technology, the 7th World Conference on Integrated Design and Process Technology*, Austin, TX.

Deng, Y., & Kao, Y. P. (2003). *The development of musical selection plan based on Kansei similarity*. China: National Chiao Tung University, Institute of Applied Art.

Dennett, D. C. (2003). *Freedom evolves*. New York: Viking.

Dennis, A. R., & Valacich, J. S. (1999). Rethinking Media Richness: Towards a Theory of Media Synchronicity. In *Proceedings of the 32nd Hawaii International Conference on System Sciences*.

Dennis, A. R., & Kinney, S. T. (1998). Testing Media Richness Theory in the New Media: The Effects of Cues, Feedback, and Task Equivocality. *Information Systems Research, 9*(3), 256–274. doi:10.1287/isre.9.3.256

Desforges, C. (2001). Educational research and educational practice. 'What does educational research have to offer to education?' In A. Wald & H. Leenders (Eds.), *Wat heeft onderwijs-onderzoek het onderwijs te bieden?* Den Haag, The Netherlands: NWO.

Desouza, K. C. (2003). Janaury-February). Knowledge management barriers: Why the technology imperative seldom works. *Business Horizons,* 25–29. doi:10.1016/S0007-6813(02)00276-8

Detlor, B. (2000). The corporate portal as information infrastructure: towards a framework for portal design. *International Journal of Information Management, 20*(2), 91–101. doi:10.1016/S0268-4012(99)00058-4

Di, A. M. (2007). *What Does Web 2.0 Mean to Government?* Stamford, CT: Gartner.

Diakoulakis, I. E., Georpopoulos, N. B., Koulouriotis, D. E., & Emeris, D. M. (2004). Towards a holistic knowledge management model. *Journal of Knowledge Management, 8*(1), 32–46. doi:10.1108/13673270410523899

Diaz-Galiano, M. C., Garcia-Cumbreras, M. A., Martin-Valdivia, M. T., Montejo-Raez, A., & Urena-Lopez, A. (2008). Integrating MeSH ontology to improve medical information retrieval. In C. Peters et al. (Eds.), *Advances in Multilingual and Multimodal Information Retrieval* (LNCS 5152, pp. 601-606). Berlin: Springer-Verlag.

Dick, B. (2003). Action research and grounded theory. In *Proceedings of Refereed paper ALARPM/SCIAR conference*. Retrieved February, 8, 2009 from http://www.uq.net.au/~zzbdick/dlitt/DLitt_P60andgt.pdf

Dicken, P. (2007). *Global shift: Mapping the changing contours of the world economy* (5th ed.). London: Sage Publications.

Dillmann, R., et al. (1999, October). *Learning robot behaviour and skills based on human demonstration and advice: the machine learning paradigm*. Paper presented at the 9th International Symposium of Robotics Research, Snowbird, UT.

Dillon, W. R., & Goldstein, M. (1984). *Multivariate Analysis*. New York: John Wiley & Sons Inc.

Dills, C. R., & Romiszowski, A. J. (Eds.). (1997). *Instructional developmental paradigms*. Englewood Cliffs, NJ: Educational Technology Publications.

Dove, M. T., Calleja, M., Bruin, R., Wakelin, J., Tucker, M. G., & Lewis, G. J. (2005). The eMinerals collaboratory: tools and experience. *Molecular Simulation, 31*(5), 329–337. doi:10.1080/08927020500066163

Drucker, P. F. (1959). *Landmarks of tomorrow*. New York: Harper.

Drucker, P. F. (1997, September-October). The future that has already happened. *Harvard Business Review*, 20–24.

Duncan, W. J. (1972). The knowledge utilisation process in management and organisation. *Academy of Management Journal, 15*(3), 273–287. doi:10.2307/254853

Earl, M. (2001). Knowledge management strategies: Toward a taxonomy. *Journal of Management Information Systems, 18*(1), 215–233.

Ebersbach, A., Glaser, M., & Heigl, R. (2008). *Installing Confluence in Wiki Web Collaboration* (pp. 337–349). Berlin: Springer.

Ebrahimi, M., Saives, A. L., & Holford, W. D. (2008). Qualified ageing workers in the knowledge management process of high-tech businesses. *Journal of Knowledge Management, 12*(2), 124–140. doi:10.1108/13673270810859569

Eckert, K., et al. (2009). Improving Ontology Matching using Meta-level Learning. In *Proceedings of the 6th European Semantic Web Conference on the Semantic Web (ESWC-2009)* (pp. 158-172). Berlin: Springer Verlag. Retrieved October 18, 2010, from http://ki.informatik. uni-mannheim.de/fileadmin/publication/Eckert09meta-level.pdf

Edelman, G. (1992). *Bright Air, Brilliant fire. On the Matter of the Mind*. London: Penguin Books.

Edelman, G. (2004). *Wider than the sky. A revolutionary view of consciousness*. London: Penguin Books.

Edelman, G., & Tononi, G. (2000). *Consciousness. How matter becomes imagination*. London: Penguin Books.

Edvinsson, L., & Kivikas, M. (2007). IC or Wissensbilanz process: Some German experiences. *Journal of Intellectual Capital, 8*(3), 376-385. Edvinsson, L., & Yu, A. (2008, December 11-12). *Some Intellectual Capital (IC) perspectives from a Chinese point of view*. Paper presented at the 4th Asia-Pacific International Conference on Knowledge Management (KMAP 2008), Guangzhou, China.

Edvinsson, L. (2002). *Corporate longitude: Navigating the knowledge economy*. Stockholm, Sweden: Bookhouse & Pearson.

Edvinsson, L., & Malone, M. A. (1997). *Intellectual Capital: Realizing your company's true value by finding its hidden brain power*. New York: Harper.

Edward, T., & Rees, C. (2006). *International Human resource Management: Globalization, national systems and multinational companies* (pp. 151–167). Upper Saddle River, NJ: Pearson Education Limited.

Egan, K. (1997). *The educated mind. How cognitive tools shape our understanding*. Chicago: University of Chicago Press.

Eidoon, Z., et al. (2007). A vector based method of ontology matching. In *Proceedings of Third International Conference on Semantics, Knowledge and Grid* (pp. 378-381). Retrieved October 18, 2010, from http://ro.uow.edu.au/cgi/viewcontent.cgi?article=1008&context=dubaipapers

Elkana, Y. (2000). Rethinking – not Unthinking – the Enlightenment. In W. Krull (Ed.), *Debates on Issues of Our Common Future*. Weilerswist, Germany: Velbruck Wissenschaft. Retrieved from http://www.ceu.hu/yehuda_rethinking_enlightnment.pdf

EN 50126. (1999). *Railway applications - The specification and demonstration of reliability, availability, maintainability and safety (RAMS)*. European Standards.

Epple, D., Argote, L., & Murphy, K. (1996). An empirical investigation of the microstructure of knowledge acquisition and transfer through learning by doing. *Operations Research, 44*(1), 77–86. doi:10.1287/opre.44.1.77

Epstain, J. M., & Axtell, R. L. (1996). *Growing artificial societies: social science from the bottom up*. Washington, DC: Brookings Institution Press.

Epstein, J. M. (2006). *Generative social science: Studies in agent-based computational modelling*. Princeton, NJ: Princeton University Press.

Ermine, J.-L. (2005). A Theoretical and formal model for Knowledge Management Systems. In Remenyi, D. (Ed.), *ICICKM'2005* (pp. 187–199). Reading, UK.

Ermine, J.-L., Boughzala, I., & Tounkara, T. (2006). Critical Knowledge Map as a Decision Tool for Knowledge Transfer Actions. *Electronic Journal of Knowledge Management, 4*(2), 129–140.

Estabrook, L., Witt, E., & Rainie, L. (2007). *Information searches that solve problems - How people use the Internet, libraries, and government agencies when they need help.* Pew Internet & American Life Project.

Euzenat, J., & Shvaiko, P. (2007). *Ontology matching.* New York: Springer. Retrieved October 18, 2010, from http://www.springerlink.com/content/xl5g3g1774h84536/

Euzenat, J., et al. (2004). *D2.2.3: State of the art on ontology alignment* (IST Project IST-2004-507482). *Knowledge Web Consortium.* Retrieved October 18, 2010, from http://starlab.vub.ac.be/research/projects/knowledgeweb/kweb-223.pdf

Euzenat, J., et al. (2007). *Deliverable 1.2.2.2.1: Case-based recommendation of matching tools and techniques* (IST-2004-507482). *Knowledge Web Consortium.* Retrieved October 18, 2010, from http://knowledgeweb.semanticweb.org/semanticportal/deliverables/D1.2.2.2.1.pdf

Farradane, J. E. L. (1970). Analysis and organisation of knowledge for retrieval. In *Proceedings of the 44th Aslib conference, University of Aberdeen.* Retrieved October 8, 2008, from http://www.emeraldinsight.com.ezproxy.webfeat.lib.ed.ac.uk/Insight/viewPDF.jsp?Filename=html/Output/Published/EmeraldFullTextArticle/Pdf/2760221203.pdf

Fayyad, U., Piatetsky-Shapiro, G., & Smyth, P. (1996). From data mining to knowledge discovery: an overview. In Fayyad, U., & Piatetsky-Shapiro, G. (Eds.), *Advances in Knowledge Discovery and Data Mining* (pp. 1–34). Cambridge, MA: MIT Press.

Feldman, S. (2009). *Worldwide search and discovery software 2009-2013 Forecast update and 2008 vendo shares (Doc. No. 219883).* International Data Corporation.

Ferreira, D., Suslick, S., & Moura, P. (2003). Analysis of environmental bonding system for oil and gas projects. *Natural Resources Research, 12*(4), 273–290. doi:10.1023/B:NARR.0000007806.90842.8f

Feynman, R. P. (1974). *Cargo Cult Science.* Retrieved from http://www.lhup.edu/~DSIMANEK/cargocul.htm

Fisher, A. G. B. (1933). Capital and the growth of knowledge. *The Economic Journal, 43*(71), 379–389. doi:10.2307/2224281

Flage, R., & Aven, T. (2009). On treatment of uncertainty in system planning. *Reliability Engineering & System Safety, 94,* 884–890. doi:10.1016/j.ress.2008.09.011

Fleming, L., & Mingo, S. (2007). Collaborative Brokerage, Generative Creativity, and Creative Success. *Administrative Science Quarterly, 52*(3), 443–475.

Flood, R. L. (1999). *Rethinking the Fifth Discipline. Learning within the unknowable.* London: Routledge.

Flood, R. L., & Jackson, M. C. (1991). *Creative problem solving: Total systems intervention.* New York: John Wiley & Sons.

Foray, D. (2004). *The Economics of Knowledge.* Cambridge, MA: MIT Press.

Foremski, T. (2005, August 5). *IBM is preparing to launch a massive corporate wide blogging initiative.* Retrieved from http://www.siliconvalleywatcher.com/mt/archives/2005/05 /can_blogging_bo.php

Foucault, M. (1972). *The order of things: An archeology of human sciences.* New York: Routledge.

Fowler, M. (1999). *Refactoring, Improving The Design of Existing Code.* Boston: Addison-Wesley.

Foy, P. S. (1999). Knowledge management in industry. In Liebowitz, J. (Ed.), *Knowledge Management Handbook.* Boca Raton, FL: CRC Press.

Fraser, J., Adams, N., Macintosh, A., McKay-Hubbard, A., Lobo, T. P., Pardo, P. F., et al. (2003). Knowledge Management Applied to E-Government Service: The Use of an Ontology. In M. Wimmer (Ed.), *Proceedings of Knowledge Management in E-Government (KMGov 2003)* (LNCS 2645, pp. 116-126). New York: Springer.

Frawley, W. (1997). *Vygotsky and cognitive science. Language and the unification of the social and computational mind.* Cambridge, MA: Harvard University Press.

Freddo, A., & Tacla, C. (2009). Evaluation of a method for partial ontology alignment in multi-agent system. [from http://inderscience.metapress.com/app/home/contribution.asp?referrer=parent&backto]. *International Journal of Reasoning-based Intelligent Systems, 1*(3/4), 132–146. Retrieved October 18, 2010. doi:10.1504/IJRIS.2009.028013

Freeman, R. R. (1977). Ocean and environmental information: The theory, policy and practice of knowledge management. *Marine Policy, 1*(3), 215–229. doi:10.1016/0308-597X(77)90028-8

Friedrich, H., & Dillmann, R. (1995, April). *Robot programming based on a single demonstration and user intentions.* Paper presented at the 3rd European Workshop on Learning Robots EWLR-3, Heraklion, Crete, Greece.

Fujita, T., et al. (2008, August). *Robot control cell production system of senju (thousand-handed) kannon model that demonstrated optimality to the multi-product production in varying volumes for eight years.* Paper presented at the 4th IEEE Conference on Automation Science and Engineering, Key Bridge Marriott, DC.

Gamper, C. D., & Turcanu, C. (2009). Can public participation help managing risks from natural hazards? *Safety Science, 47*, 522–528. doi:10.1016/j.ssci.2008.07.005

Garavan, T. N. (1991). Strategic Human Resource Development. *Journal of European Industrial Training, 15*(1), 17–31. doi:10.1108/EUM0000000000219

Garavan, T. N. (2007). A strategic perspective on human resource development. *Advances in Developing Human Resources, 9*(1), 11–21. doi:10.1177/1523422306294492

Garud, R., Jain, S., & Kumaraswamy, A. (2002). Institutional entrepreneurship in the sponsorship of common technological standards: The case of Sun Microsystems and Java. *Academy of Management Review, 45*(1), 196–214. doi:10.2307/3069292

Gherardi, S. (2009). The critical power of the 'practice lens'. *Management Learning, 40*(2), 115–128. doi:10.1177/1350507608101225

Gibson, J. (2005). *Community resources: Intellectual property, international trade and protection of traditional knowledge.* Burlington, VA: Ashgate Publishing.

Giddens, A. (1979). *Central problems in social theory: Action, structure and contradiction in social analysis.* London: Macmilian.

Gilbane, F. (2005). Technologies for Enterprise Applications? In *The Gilbane Report.* Blogs & Wikis.

Giles, J. (2005). Special report: Internet encyclopaedias go head to head. *Nature, 438*, 900–901. doi:10.1038/438900a

Girault, C., & Rudiger, V. (2002). *Petri nets for systems engineering: a guide to modelling, verification and applications.* New York: Springer.

Giunchiglia, F., & Shvaiko, P. (2003). Semantic Matching. *Knowledge Engineering Review journal, 18*(3), 265-280. Retrieved October 18, 2010, from http://citeseerx.ist.psu.edu/viewdoc/download?doi=10.1.1.69.8108&rep=rep1&type=pdf

Giunchiglia, F., et al. (2007). Semantic matching: Algorithms and implementation. *Journal on Data Semantics, 9*, 1-38. Retrieved October 18, 2010, from http://www.cisa.inf.ed.ac.uk/OK/Publications/Algorithms%20and%20Implementation.pdf

Globus, G. (1995). *The postmodern brain.* Amsterdam, The Netherlands: John Benjamins Publishing.

GO. (1999). *The Gene Ontology.* Retrieved May 11, 2010, from http://www.geneontology.org

Gold, A. H., Malhotra, A., & Segars, A. H. (2001). Knowledge Management: An organisational capabilities perspective. *Journal of Management Information Systems, 18*(1), 185–214.

Goldschmidt, D. E., & Krishnamoorthy, M. (2008). Comparing keyword search to semantic search: A case study in solving crossword puzzles using the GoogleTM API. *Software, Practice & Experience, 38*(4), 417–445. doi:10.1002/spe.840

Goowiki. (2008, August 8). *The Unofficial Google Wiki.* http://google.wikia.com /wiki/Goowiki

Goumas, M., & Lygerou, V. (2000). An extension of the PROMETHEE method for decision making in fuzzy environment: Ranking of alternative energy exploitation projects. *European Journal of Operational Research, 123*, 606–613. doi:10.1016/S0377-2217(99)00093-4

Granott, N. (1998). Unit of Analysis in Transit. From the Individual's Knowledge to the Ensemble Process. *Mind, Culture, and Activity, 5*(1), 42–66. doi:10.1207/s15327884mca0501_4

Greenwood, D. J., & Levin, M. (2005). Reform of the social sciences and of universities through action research . In Denzin, N. K., & Lincoln, Y. S. (Eds.), *The sage handbook of qualitative research* (3rd ed., pp. 33–64). Thousand Oaks, CA: Sage.

Griffiths, D. A., & Morse, S. M. (2009). Knowledge Management: Towards overcoming dissatisfaction in the field. *World Academy of Science Engineering and Technology, 57*(2), 724–735.

Grover, V., & Davenport, T. H. (2001). General perspectives on knowledge management: Fostering a research agenda. *Journal of Management Information Systems, 18*(1), 5–21.

Gruber, T. R. (1993). A Translation Approach to portable Ontology Specifications. *Knowledge Acquisition, 5,* 199–220. doi:10.1006/knac.1993.1008

Gu, J. F. (2002, July 15-18). Study on the meta-synthesis of data, information model and expert Opinions. In Proceedings of CMS2002. Austria: IIASA.

Gu, J. F. (2002, March 25-27). Consensus building and meta-synthesis. In Proceedings of VEAM2002. Kobe, Japan: JAIST.

Gu, J. F. (2007). From hard to soft, from West to East. Panel discussion, Tokyo. In *Proceedings of ISSS2007,* Tokyo, Retrieved from http://isss.org/conferences/tokyo2007/20070807-isss-1100-gu.pdf

Gu, J. F. (2008, March 9-10). *Meta-synthesis knowledge system: Basics and practice.* Paper presented at the International Workshop on Knowledge Integration and Innovation, Dalian, China.

Gu, J. F., & Tang, X. J. (2001). Metasynthesis, WSR and consensus. In *Proceedings of Intern. Symposium on Knowledge and Systems Sciences: Challenges to Complexity* (pp. 12-16).

Gu, J. F., & Tang, X. J. (2001a, September 21-23). *Meta-synthesis knowledge system (MSKS).* Paper presented at MCS2001, Beijing, China.

Gu, J. F., & Tang, X. J. (2001b). *Meta-Synthesis knowledge system for complex system* (Tech. Rep. AMSS-2001-11). Beijing, China: Academy of Mathematics and System Sciences, Chinese Academy of Sciences.

Gu, J. F., & Tang, X. J. (2003). A test on meta-synthesis system approach to forecasting the GDP growth rate in china. In J. Wiley & J. K. Allen (Eds.), *Proceedings of 47th Annual Conference of the International Society for the Systems Sciences.*

Gu, J. F., Liu, Y. J., & Song, W. Q. (2007, August 5-10). A scientific discussion test on some social harmony problems. In *Proceedings of the 51st meeting of the International Society for the Systems Sciences (ISSS2007),* Tokyo (pp. 2007-2056).

Gu, J. F., Song, W. Q., & Zhu, Z. X. (2008a, October). Meta-synthesis and expert mining. In *Proceedings of the 2008 IEEE International Conference on Systems, Man, and Cybernetics* (pp. 467-471).

Gu, J. F., Song, W. Q., Zhu, Z. X., Gao, R., & Liu, Y. J. (2008b, December 11-13). *Expert mining and TCM knowledge.* Paper presented at KSS2008, Guangzhou, China.

Gu, J. F., Tang, X. J., & Niu, W. Y. (2005). Meta-synthesis system approach for solving social complex problems. In J. F. Gu & G. Chroust (Eds.), *Proceedings of 1st World Congress of the International Federation for Systems Research.* Kobe, Japan: JAIST Press.

Gu, J. F., Tang, X. J., Wang, L., et al. (1997). Wuli-Shili-Renli Approach to preparing the diagram of standard system for the commercial accommodations and facilitation in China. In *Systems Methodology III: Possibilities for Cross-cultural Learning and Integration* (pp. 21-32). Hull, UK: the University of Hull.

Gu, J. F., Wang, H. C., & Tang, X. J. (2007). *Meta-synthesis method system and systematology research.* Beijing, China: Science Press.

Guba, E. G., & Lincoln, Y. S. (1985). *Naturalistic Enquiry.* Beverly Hills, CA: Sage.

Gugliotta, A., Cabral, L., Domingue, J., & Roberto, V. (2005). A semantic web service-based architecture for the interoperability of E-Government services. In *proceedings of International Workshop on Web Information Systems Modeling (WISM 2005),* Sydney, Australia.

Gu, J. F. (2001). On synthesizing opinions-how to reach consensus. *Journal of Systems Engineering, 16*(5), 340–348.

Gu, J. F. (2006). Expert mining for solving the social harmony problems. *COE News, 2*(4), 1–3.

Gu, J. F., & Tang, X. J. (2002). Meta-synthesis and knowledge science, Systems engineering. *Theory into Practice, 22*(10), 2–7.

Gu, J. F., & Tang, X. J. (2005). Meta-synthesis approach to complex system modeling. *European Journal of Operational Research*, *166*(3), 597–614. doi:10.1016/j.ejor.2004.03.036

Gu, J. F., & Tang, X. J. (2006). *Wuli-Shili-Renli system approach: Theory and applications*. Shanghai, China: Shanghai Science and Technology, Education Publisher.

Gu, J. F., & Tang, X. J. (2007). Meta-synthesis system approach to knowledge science. *International Journal of Information Technology and Decision Making*, *6*(3), 559–572. doi:10.1142/S0219622007002629

Gu, J. F., Wang, H. C., & Tang, X. J. (2007). *Meta-synthesis Method System and Systematology Research*. Marrickville, Australia: Science Press.

Gu, J. F., & Yang, J. L. (1987). MCDM and strategic development . In Sawaragi, Y. (Ed.), *Towards Interactive and Intelligent DSS* (pp. 280–287). Berlin: Springer Verlag.

Guo, W., & Kraines, S. (2008). Explicit scientific knowledge comparison based on semantic description matching. In *Proceedings of the American Society for Information Science and Technology: Vol. 45. People Transforming Information – Information Transforming People* (pp. 1-18). Hoboken: Wiley InterScience.

Guo, W., & Kraines, S. (2009). Cross-language knowledge sharing model based on ontologies and logical inference . In Chu, S., (Eds.), *Series on Innovation and Knowledge Management* (*Vol. 8*). Singapore: World Scientific.

Gupta, A. K., & Smith, K. E. (2006). The Interplay between Exploration and Exploitation. *Academy of Management Journal*, *49*(4), 693–706.

Haegele, M., et al. (2005). *White paper - industrial robot automation. European Robotics Network*. Retrieved from http://www.euron.org/miscdocs/docs/euron2/year2/dr-14-1-industry.pdf

Halaschek-Wiener, C., & Kolovski, V. (2008). Syndication on the Web using a description logic approach. *Web Semantics: Science . Services and Agents on the World Wide Web*, *6*, 171–190. doi:10.1016/j.websem.2008.06.002

Hamel, G., & Prahalad, C. K. (1990). The Core Competence of the Corporation. *Harvard Business Review*, *68*(3), 79–9.

Hanaki, N., & Peterhansl, A. (2007). Cooperation in evolving social networks. *Management Science*, *53*(7), 1036–1050. doi:10.1287/mnsc.1060.0625

Handzic, M., Lagumdzija, A., & Celjo, A. (2008). Auditing knowledge management practices: model and application. *Knowledge management research and practice*, *6*, 90-99.

Harper, S. (2006). *Ageing Societies: Myths, Challenges and Opportunities*. London: Hodder.

Harvey, C. R., & Campbell, R. (2010). *Finance Glossary*. Retrieved October 6, 2010, from http://www.duke.edu/~charvey

Hasan, H., & Pfaff, C. C. (2006). The Wiki: an environment to revolutionise employees' interaction with corporate knowledge. In *18th ACHI International Conference Proceeding Series* (Vol. 206, pp. 377-380).

Hasan, H., & Crawford, K. (2003). Codifying or enabling: the challenge of knowledge management systems. *The Journal of the Operational Research Society*, *54*, 184–193. doi:10.1057/palgrave.jors.2601388

Havelock, R. G. (1968). Dissemination and translation roles. In T. L. Eidell & J. M. Kitchel (Eds.), *Knowledge production and utilisation in educational administration 1969* (p. 64-119). Columbus, OH: University council for educational administration.

Havenstein, H. (2007). *Top secret: DIA embraces Web 2.0 Analysts are turning to wikis, blogs, RSS feeds and enterprise "mashups"*. ComputerWorld.

Havenstein, H. (2008). CIA explains its Wikipedia-like national security project . In *ComputerWorld*. Top Secret.

Hayduk, L. A. (1987). *Structural Equation Modeling with LISREL: Essentials and advances*. Baltimore, MA: John Hopkins University Press.

Hayduk, L. A. (1996). *LISREL issues, debates, and strategies*. Baltimore, MA: John Hopkins University Press.

Hebel, M. (2007). Light bulbs and change: Systems Thinking and organisational learning for new ventures. *The Learning Organization*, *14*(6), 499–509. doi:10.1108/09696470710825114

Heck, M. (2005). *TWiki: Open Source with a Corporate Following*. InfoWorld.

Heisig, P. (2009). Harmonisation of knowledge management – comparing 160 KM frameworks around the globe. *Journal of Knowledge Management, 13*(4), 4–31. doi:10.1108/13673270910971798

Henkin, L. (1953). Some notes on nominalism. *Journal of Symbolic Logic, 18*, 19–29. doi:10.2307/2266323

Henry, N. L. (1974). Knowledge Management: A new concern for public administration. *Public Administration Review, 34*(3), 189–196. doi:10.2307/974902

Hessami, A. (1999). Risk - A missed opportunity? *Risk and Continuity, 2*, 17–26.

Heylighen, F. (1999). Collective intelligence and its implementation on the Web: Algorithms to develop a collective mental map. *Computational & Mathematical Organization Theory, 5*(3), 253–280. doi:10.1023/A:1009690407292

He, Z. L., & Wong, P. K. (2004). Exploration vs. exploitation: An empirical test of the ambidexterity hypothesis. *Organization Science, 15*(4), 481–494. doi:10.1287/orsc.1040.0078

Hillman, D. J. (1977). Model for the on-line management of knowledge transfer. *On-line Review, 1*(1), 23-30.

Hollnagel, E. (2008). Risk + barriers = safety? *Safety Science, 46*, 221–229. doi:10.1016/j.ssci.2007.06.028

Holsapple, C. W. (2004). *Handbook on knowledge management: Knowledge Matters*. Berlin: Birkhauser.

Holsapple, C. W., & Joshi, K. D. (2004). A formal knowledge management ontology: conduct, activities, resources, and influences. *Journal of the American Society for Information Science and Technology, 55*(7), 593–612. doi:10.1002/asi.20007

Holt, J. D. (2004). Those who can - use ISO IEC 15288. In *Proceedings of the INCOSE Spring Conference*.

Holt, J. (2005). *A Pragmatic Guide to Business Process Modelling*. BCS.

Hori, K., Kakakaji, K., Yamamoto, Y., & Ostwald, J. (2004). Organic perspectives of knowledge management: Knowledge evolution through a cycle of knowledge liquidisation and crystallisation. *Journal of universal computer science, 10*(3), 252-261.

Houghton, L. (2008). Generalization and systemic epistemology: Why should it make sense? *Systems Research and Behavioral Science, 26*, 99–108. doi:10.1002/sres.929

Hovland, G., Sikka, P., & McCarragher, B. (1996, April). *Skill acquisition from human demonstration using a hidden markov model*. Paper presented at the 1996 IEEE International Conference on Robotics and Automation, Minneapolis, MN.

Hughes, B., & Cotterell, M. (1999). *Software project management*. New York: McGraw-Hill.

Hunter, L., & Cohen, K. B. (2006). Biomedical language processing: What's beyond PubMed? *Molecular Cell, 21*, 589–594. doi:10.1016/j.molcel.2006.02.012

Hunter, L., Lu, Z., Firby, J., Baumgartner, W. A. Jr, Johnson, H. L., Ogren, P. V., & Cohen, K. B. (2008). OpenDMAP: An open source, ontology-driven concept analysis engine, with applications to capturing knowledge regarding protein transport, protein interactions and cell-type-specific gene expression. *BMC Bioinformatics, 9*, 78. doi:10.1186/1471-2105-9-78

Husserl, E. (1928). *Logische untersuchungen. Erster Band: Prolegomena zur reinen Logik. Text der 1. und der 2. Auflage (Husserliana: Edmund Husserl Gesammelte Werke)*. Berlin, Germany: Springer.

Husserl, E. (1973). *Cartesianische Meditationen und Pariser Vorträge* [Cartesian meditations and the Paris lectures]. The Hague, The Netherlands: Martinus Nijhoff.

Husserl, E. (1982) Ideas Pertaining to a Pure Phenomenology and to a Phenomenological Philosophy, First Book: General Introduction to a Pure Phenomenology (Kersten, F., Trans.). In Husserl, E., *Collected Works: Volume 2*. The Hague, Netherlands: Martinus Nijhoff.

Husserl, E. (1984). *Logische untersuchungen. Zweiter Band: Untersuchungen zur Phänomenologie und Theorie der Erkenntnis. In zwei Bänden*. Berlin, Germany: Springer.

Hwang, C. P., & Ho, C. S. (1996). A knowledge-based task-level programming and execution environment for robots. *Robotics and Computer-integrated Manufacturing, 12*(4), 329–351. doi:10.1016/S0736-5845(96)00020-8

IAEA. (2006). *Risk Management of Knowledge Loss in Nuclear Industry Organizations.* Vienna, Italy: IAEA Publications. Retrieved from http://www.iaea.org/inisnkm/nkm/nkmPublications.html

Iannacci, F. (2005). *The social epistemology of open source software development: the Linux case study.* Unpublished doctoral dissertation, University of London, London.

ICAEW. (2002). *Risk management is now a core business process.* The Institute of Chartered Accountants in England and Wales.

IDEF5. (1994). *IDEF5 method report.* College Station, TX: Knowledge Based Systems Inc.

IEC 61508. (1998). *Functional safety of electrical/electronic/programmable electronic safety-related systems.* European Electrotechnical Standardisation Organisation CENELEC.

INCOSE. (2007). *Systems engineering handbook.* IN-COSE.

Independent. (2008, August 9). Retrieved from http://www.independent.co.uk/news/science/the-end-of-email-discover-new-ways-to-stay-in-touch-458638.html

Information services advisory council. (1998). *Managing information as a strategic asset: corporate intranet development and the role of the company library.* Retrieved from www.conference-board.org/products/intranet-white-paper.cfm

Inkpen, A. C., & Tsang, E. W. K. (2005). Social capital, networks, and knowledge transfer. *Academy of Management Review, 30*(1), 146–165. doi:10.5465/AMR.2005.15281445

IRM. (2002). *A risk management standard.* London: The Institute of Risk Management.

ISO 15288. (2002). *Systems engineering - system life cycle processes.* Geneva, Switzerland: International Organization for Standardization.

ISO 16085. (2006). *ISO systems and software engineering - life cycle processes - risk management.* Geneva, Switzerland: International Organization for Standardization.

ISO 31000 (2009a). *BS ISO risk management - principles and guidelines on implementation.* Geneva, Switzerland: International Organization for Standardization.

ISO 31010 (2009b). *Risk management - risk assessment techniques.* Geneva, Switzerland: International Organization for Standardization.

ISO 5807. (1985). *Information processing – documentation symbols and conventions for data, program and system flowcharts, program network charts and system resources charts.* Geneva, Switzerland: International Organization for Standardization.

ISO EC Guide 73. (2007). *ISO/IEC risk management – vocabulary.* Geneva, Switzerland: International Organization for Standardization.

ITU-T. (1999). *Series Z: languages and general software aspects for telecommunication systems, formal description techniques (FDT) – specification and description language (SDL).* Geneva, Switzerland: International Telecommunications Union.

Jackson, M. C. (2003). *Systems thinking: Creative holism for managers.* Chichester, UK: John Wiley & Sons.

Jackson, M. C. (2001). critical Systems Thinking and practice. *European Journal of Operational Research, 128*(2), 233–244. doi:10.1016/S0377-2217(00)00067-9

Jackson, M. C., & Keys, P. (1984). Towards a system of systems methodologies. *The Journal of the Operational Research Society, 35*, 473–486.

Jacobson, I., Booch, G., & Rumbaugh, J. (1999). *The unified software development process.* Reading, MA: Addison-Wesley Professional.

Jansen, J. J., & den Van, B. (2006). Exploratory Innovation, Exploitative Innovation, and Performance: Effects of Organizational Antecedents and Environmental Moderators. *Management Science, 52*(11), 1661–1674. doi:10.1287/mnsc.1060.0576

Jenkins, R. E., Brown, R. D. H., & Phillips, M. R. (2009). Harbour Porpoise (Phocoena Phocoena) conservation management: a dimensional approach. *Marine Policy, 33*(5), 744–749. doi:10.1016/j.marpol.2009.02.003

Jennex, M. E., & Olfman, L. (2004). Assessing knowledge management success/effectiveness models. In *Proceedings of the 37th Hawaii international conference on system sciences.* Retrieved February 18, 2008, from http://ieeexplore.ieee.org/xpl/freeabs_all.jsp?arnumber=1265571

Jeong, H., Tombor, B., & Albert, R. (2000). The large-scale organization of metabolic networks. *Nature, 407*(6804), 651–654. doi:10.1038/35036627

Jing, D. (2007). Risk analysis of Chinese overseas petroleum investment. *Land and resources information, 4*, 44-47.

Jodon, P. W. (2000). *Designing pleasurable products.* London: Taylor and Francis.

Joe, C., & Yoong, P. (2006). Harnessing the expert knowledge of older workers: Issues and challenges. *Journal of Information and Knowledge Management, 5*(1), 63–72. doi:10.1142/S0219649206001323

Johnson, N. F., Clarke, R. J., & Herrington, J. (2007). The potential affordances of enterprise wikis for creating community in research networks. In *Proceedings of the Emerging Technologies Conference.*

Jörg, T. (1998). *The development of a complex dynamic causal model for cyclically organized processes of cumulative advantage and disadvantage in education.* Paper presented at the annual meeting of the American Educational Research Association, San Diego, CA.

Jörg, T. (2003). Towards a Complex Generative Pedagogy. A European perspective. In *Proceedings of SIG Chaos and Complexity Theories, AERA Conference,* Chicago. Retrieved from http://ccaerasig.com/papers/03/JorgEuropean.htm

Jörg, T. (2004). A theory of Reciprocal Learning in dyads. *Cognitive Systems, 6-2*(3), 159-170.

Jörg, T. (2004). Complexity Theory and The Reinvention of Reality of Education. In B. Davis, R. Luce-Kapler, & R. Upitis (Eds.), *Proceedings of the Complexity Science and Educational Research Conference* (pp. 121-146). Edmonton, Alberta, Canada: University of Alberta. Retrieved from http://www.complexityandeducation.ca

Jörg, T. (2005). A generative complexity theory of minds evolving in peer interaction. In P. Bourgine, F. Képès, & M. Schoenauer (Eds.), *Towards a science of complex systems*: *Proceedings of the European Complex Systems Society. Abstracts Book* (p. 210). Paris: European Complex Systems Society.

Jörg, T. (2006). Minds in Evolution through Human Interaction. *Cognitive Systems, 6-4*, 363-386.

Jörg, T. (2007a). Visiting the future of learning and education from a complexity perspective. In C. Stary, F. Bacharini, & S. Hawamdeh (Eds.), *Knowledge management: Innovation, technology and cultures* (pp. 227-241). Singapore: World Scientific Publishing Company.

Jörg, T. (2008). *Rethinking the Learning Organization as a complex, generative learning network.* Paper presented at the conference on Small Business Networks, Beijing, China.

Jörg, T. (2009). Thinking in complexity about learning and education – A programmatic view. *Complicity, 6*(1). Retrieved from http://www.complexityandeducation.ualberta.ca/COMPLICITY6/Complicity6_TOC.htm

Jörg, T. (in press). *New thinking in complexity for the social sciences and humanities. A generative, trans-disciplinary approach.* New York: Springer.

Jörg, T., Davis, B., & Nickmans, G. (2007b). Towards a new, complexity science of learning and education. *Educational Research Review, 2*(2), 145–156.

Jörg, T., Davis, B., & Nickmans, G. (2008). About the outdated Newtonian paradigm in education and a complexity science of learning: How far are we from a paradigm shift? *Educational Research Review, 3*(1), 77–100. doi:10.1016/j.edurev.2008.02.002

Kahan, J., & Koivunen, M. R. Prud'Hommeaux, E., & Swick, R. R. (2001). Annotea: An open RDF infrastructure for shared Web annotations. In *Proceedings of the 10th International Conference on World Wide Web* (pp. 623-632). New York: ACM.

Kakabadse, N. K., Kakabadse, A., & Kouzmin, A. (2003). Reviewing the knowledge management literature: Towards a taxonomy. *Journal of Knowledge Management, 7*(4), 75–91. doi:10.1108/13673270310492967

Kakizawa, Y. (2007). In-house Use of Web 2.0: Enterprise 2.0. *NEC Technical Journal, 2*(2), 46–49.

Kalfoglou, Y., & Schorlemmer, M. (2005). Ontology Mapping: The State of the Art. *The Knowledge Engineering Review, 18*(1), 1-31. Retrieved October 18, 2010, from http://eprints.ecs.soton.ac.uk/10519/1/ ker02-ontomap. pdf

Kaneko, K. (2006). *Life: An introduction to complex systems biology*. Berlin, Germany: Springer.

Kannan, S., & Madden-Hallet. (2006). Population ageing challenges knowledge management and sustaining marketing culture. *International Journal of Knowledge. Culture and Change Management, 6*(3), 57–70.

Kaplan, R. S., & Norton, D. P. (2004). *Strategy Map: converting intangible assets into tangible outcomes*. Boston: Harvard Business School Press.

Kauffman, S. (1993). *The origins of order. Self-organization and selection in evolution*. New York: Oxford University Press.

Kauffman, S. (1995). *At home in the universe*. New York: Oxford University Press.

Kawano, S., & Nakamori, Y. (2000, September 25-27). *Environment knowledge management using the framework model*. Paper presented at the International Symposium on Knowledge and Systems Sciences: Challenges to Complexity (KSS'2000), Ishikawa, Japan.

Kemmis, S., & McTaggart, R. (2005). Participatory Action Research: Communicative Action and the Public Sphere . In Denzin, N., & Lincoln, Y. (Eds.), *Handbook of Qualitative Research* (3rd ed., pp. 559–603). Thousand Oaks, CA: Sage Publications.

Kirchsteiger, C. (2008). Carbon capture and storage desirability from a risk management point of view. *Safety Science, 46*, 1149–1154. doi:10.1016/j.ssci.2007.06.012

Kirshner, D. (2002). *Anh Linh's Shapes as an Instance of "Complex Pedagogy", A Historical Perspective*. Paper presented at the Annual Meeting of the AERA, New Orleans, LA.

Kiu, C. C., & Tsui, E. (2009). Taxonomy - Folksonomy Integration for Knowledge Navigation through Unsupervised Data Mining Techniques. Knowledge Management Research & Practice. *Knowledge Management Research and Practice, 8*, 24–32.

Klein, D. B., & Romero, P. P. (2007). Model building versus theorising: The paucity of theory in the journal of economic theory. *Econ Journal Watch, 4*(2), 241–271.

Klischewski, R. (2003). Semantic Web for E-Government. In R. Traunmuller (Ed.), *Proceedings of EGOV 2003* (LNCS 2739). New York: Springer.

Knowlton, L. W., & Phillips, C. C. (2009). *The Logic Model Guidebook – Better strategies for great results*. London: Sage publications.

Kogut, B., & Zander, U. (1996). What do firms do? Coordination, identity, and learning. *Organization Science, 7*, 502–518. doi:10.1287/orsc.7.5.502

Kohlbacher, F., Güttel, W. H., & Haltmeyer, B. (2009). Special Issue on the Ageing Workforce and HRM – Challenges, Chances, Perspectives. *International Journal of Human Resources Development and Management, 9*(2/3).

Koivunen, M. R. (2005). Annotea and semantic web supported collaboration. In *Proceedings of the Workshop on User Aspects of the Semantic Web UserSWeb at European Semantic Web Conference* (pp. 5-16).

Koizumi, H. (2001). Trans-disciplinarity . *Neuroendocrinology Letters, 22*, 219–221.

Kolda, T., Brown, D., & Corones, J. (2005). *Data Sciences Technology for homeland security information management and knowledge discovery* (Sandia Rep. SAND2004-6648). Livermore, CA: Sandia National Laboratories.

Koneko, K. (2004). *Life as a Complex System*. Paper presented at the First European Conference on Complex Systems, Torino, Italy.

Konno, N. (2008, October). Knowledge workplace: Knowledge management and office design. *Happy Workplace*. Retrieved October 2008, from http://www. happyworkplace.jp/en/

Kovalerchuk, B. (2005, May). Advanced data mining, link discovery and visual correlation for data and image analysis. In *Proceedings of Tutorial Notes International Conference on Intelligence Analysis (IA '05)*. Retrieved from http://analysis.mitre.org

Kovalerchuk, B., & Vityaev, E. (2000). *Data Mining in Finance: Advances in Relational and Hybrid Methods*. Dordrecht, The Netherlands: Kluwer.

Kovalerchuk, B., Vityaev, E., & Ruiz, J. F. (2001). Consistent and complete data and "expert" mining in medicine. *Studies in Fuzziness and Soft Computing, 60*, 238–281.

Kraines, S., Guo, W., Kemper, B., & Nakamura, Y. (2006). EKOSS: A knowledge-user centered approach to knowledge sharing, discovery, and integration on the Semantic Web. In I. Cruz et al. (Eds.), *The Semantic Web - ISWC 2006* (LNCS 4273, pp. 833-846). Berlin: Springer Verlag.

Kravis, S., & Irrgang, R. (2005). A case based system for oil and gas well design with risk assessment. *Applied Intelligence, 23*, 39–53. doi:10.1007/s10489-005-2371-7

Kroah-Hatman, G., Corbet, J., & McPherson, A. (2008). How fast it is going, who is doing it, what they are doing, and who is sponsoring it. *Report at the Linux Foundation*. Retrieved December 15, 2008, from https://www.linux-foundation.org/publications/linuxkerneldevelopment.php

Krogstie, J. (2008). Using EEML for combined goal and process oriented modeling: a case study. In *Proceedings of the EMMSAD, the Thirteenth International Workshop on Exploring Modeling Methods in Systems Analysis and Design*, Montpellier, France (pp. 112-129).

Król, Z. (2007b). Is Science About Power and Money? In Y. Nakamori, Z. Wang, J. Gu, & T. Ma (Eds.), *Proceedings of the 8ᵗʰ International Symposium on Knowledge and Systems Sciences (KSS2007), 2ⁿᵈ International Conference on Knowledge, Information and Creativity Support Systems (KICSS2007)* (pp. 364-371). Nomi, Japan: Japan Advanced Institute of Science and Technology and International Society for Knowledge and Systems Sciences.

Król, Z. (2005). Intuition and history: Change and the growth of mathematical knowledge. *International Journal of Knowledge and Systems Science, 2*(3), 22–32.

Król, Z. (2007a). The emergence of new concepts in science . In Wierzbicki, A. P., & Nakamori, Y. (Eds.), *Creative Environments: Issues for Creativity Support for the Knowledge Civilization Age* (pp. 415–442). Berlin-Heidelberg, Germany: Springer Verlag. doi:10.1007/978-3-540-71562-7_17

Kuhn, T. S. (1962). *The structure of scientific revolutions*. Chicago: Chicago University Press.

Kuhn, T. S. (1970). *The structure of scientific revolutions* (2ⁿᵈ ed.). Chicago: University of Chicago Press.

Kulkarni, U. R., Ravindran, S., & Freeze, R. (2006). A knowledge management success model: Theoretical development and empirical validation. *Journal of Management Information Systems, 239*(3), 309–347.

Kuwabara, K. (2000). Linux: a bazaar at the edge of chaos. *First Monday, 5*(3). Retrieved July 8, 2009, from http://firstmonday.org/htbin/cgiwrap/bin/ojs/index.php/fm/article/view/1482/1397

Laera, L., et al. (2007). Argumentation over Ontology Correspondences in MAS. In *Proceedings of the 6ᵗʰ International Conference on Autonomous Agents and Multi-Agent Systems*. Retrieved October 18, 2010, from http://citeseerx.ist.psu.edu/viewdoc/download?doi=10.1.1.97.3394&rep=rep1&type=pdf

Lakoff, G. (1987). *Women, fire, and dangerous things*. Chicago: University of Chicago Press.

Lazer, D., & Friedman, A. (2007). The Network Structure of Exploration and Exploitation. *Administrative Science Quarterly, 52*(4), 667–694. doi:10.2189/asqu.52.4.667

Lee, W. B. (2008). On the relationship between innovation, Intellectual Capital and Organizational Unlearning. In G. Ahonen (Ed.), *Inspired by knowledge organizations: Essays in honour of Professor K Sveiby on his 60 Birthday*. The Swedish School of Management, Helsinki, Finland. Lin, Y. Y., & Edvinsson, L. (2008). National intellectual capital: Comparison of the Nordic Countries. *Journal of Intellectual Capital, 9*(4), 525-545.

Lee, G. K., & Cole, R. E. (2003). From a firm-based to a community-based model of knowledge creation: The case of Linux kernel development. *Organization Science, 14*(6), 633–649. doi:10.1287/orsc.14.6.633.24866

Lee, S., Harada, A., & Stappers, P. J. (2002). Pleasure with Products: Design based Kansei . In Green, W., & Jordon, P. (Eds.), *Beyond Usability* (pp. 219–229). New York: Taylor and Francis.

Lehaney, B., Clarke, S., Coakes, E., & Jack, G. (2004). *Beyond Knowledge Management*. Hershey, PA: IGI Global.

Lemke, F., & Müller, J.-A. (n.d.). *Medical Data Analysis Using Self-Organizing Data Mining Technologies*. Retrieved from http://www.knowledgeminer.net/pdf/medical.pdf

Leonard, A. (1999). A viable systems model: consideration of knowledge management, *Journal of knowledge management practice*. Retrieved October 2007, from http://www.tlainc.com/articl12.htm

Leshed, G., Haber, E. M., Matthews, T., & Lau, T. (2008). CoScripter: Automating & Sharing how-to Knowledge in the Enterprise. In *Proceedings of the 26th annual SIGCHI Conference on Human Factors in Computing Systems*.

Leuf, B., & Cunningham, W. (2001). *The Wiki Way: quick collaboration on the Web*. Reading, MA: Addison-Wesley.

Leveson, N. G. (1995). *Safeware, system safety and computers*. Reading, MA: Addison-Weslyey Professional.

Levine, G., & DeJong, G. (2006, June). *Explanation-based acquisition of planning operators*. Paper presented at the 2006 International Conference on Automated Planning and Scheduling, the English Lake District, Cumbria, UK.

Levy, P. (1997). *Collective intelligence: mankind's emerging world in cyberspace (R. Bononno, Tran.)*. Cambridge, MA: Perseus Books.

Li, J., et al. (2009). RiMOM: A Dynamic Multistrategy Ontology Alignment Framework. *IEEE transactions on knowledge and data engineering, 21*(10). Retrieved October 18, 2010, from http://dit.unitn.it/~p2p/RelatedWork/Matching/RiMOM_TKDE.pdf

Liao, S. H. (2003). Knowledge management technologies and applications-literature review from 1995 to 2002. *Expert Systems with Applications, 25*(2), 155–164.

Limone, A., & Bastias, L. E. (2006). Autopoiesis and knowledge in the organisation: Conceptual foundation for authentic knowledge management. *Systems Research and Behavioral Science, 23*, 39–49. doi:10.1002/sres.745

Lin, H. F. (2007). Effects of extrinsic and intrinsic motivation on employee knowledge sharing intentions. *Journal of Information Science, 33*(2), 135–149. doi:10.1177/0165551506068174

Linstone, H. A. (1984). *Multiple perspectives for decision making*. Amsterdam, The Netherlands: North-Holland.

Lio, E. D., Fraboni, L., & Leo, T. (2005). TWiki-based facilitation in a newly formed academic community of practice. In *Proceedings of the International Symposium on Wikis (Wikisym)*.

Littlefield, D. (2005). Share and enjoy... Building Design. *Computer Weekly, 1678*, 24–25.

Littman, M. L., Dumais, S. T., & Landauer, T. K. (1998). Automatic cross-language information retrieval using latent semantic indexing . In Grefenstette, G. (Ed.), *Cross-Language Information Retrieval*. Boston: Kluwer Academic Publishers.

Liu, Y. J., Niu, W. Y., & Gu, J. F. (2007). Exploring computational scheme of complex problem solving based on meta-synthesis approach. In *Proceedings of the International Conference on Computational Science, Lecture Notes in Computer Science* (pp. 9-17).

Liu, J. M., & Zhang, D. Z., Aziguli, & Liu, J. H. (2008). Centrality Research Based on Traditional Medicine Network. *Computer Simulation, 25*(5), 317–320.

Li, Y. F., Ho, J., & Li, N. (2000). Development of a physically behaved robot work cell in virtual reality for task teaching. *Robotics and Computer-integrated Manufacturing, 16*, 91–101. doi:10.1016/S0736-5845(99)00042-3

Locoro, A., & Mascardi, V. (2009). A Correspondence Repair Lgorithm Based On Word Sense Disambiguation And Upper Ontologies. In *Proceedings of the International Conference on Knowledge Engineering and Ontology Development (KEOD-09)*. Retrieved October 18, 2010, from http://didisi.disi.unige.it/person/MascardiV/Download/LocoroMascardiKeod2009.pdf

Lopez-Juarez, I., & Howarth, M. (2002). Knowledge acquisition and learning in unstructured robotic assembly environments. *Information Sciences, 145*, 89–111. doi:10.1016/S0020-0255(02)00225-6

Lopez, V., Uren, V., Motta, E., & Pasin, M. (2007). Aqua-Log: an ontology-driven question answering system for organizational semantic intranets. *Web Semantics: Science . Services and Agents on the World Wide Web, 5*, 72–105. doi:10.1016/j.websem.2007.03.003

Luhmann, N., & Schorr, K.-E. (2000). *Problems of reflection in the system of education*. In European studies in education (Vol. 13). Münster, Germany: Waxmann.

Lundvall. (2006). *Knowledge management in the learning economy* (Danish Research Unit for Industrial Dynamics working paper 06-6). Retrieved May 16, 2008, from http://www.druid.dk/wp/pdf_files/06-06.pdf

Luo, P., Si, G. Y., Hu, X. F., & Yang, J. Y. (2004). Swarm & discussion of the method of constructing the special public opinion model. *Journal of System Simulation, 16*(1), 5–7.

Luo, S., Xia, H., Yoshida, T., & Wang, Z. (2009). Toward collective intelligence of online communities: A primitive conceptual model. *Journal of Systems Science and Systems Engineering, 18*(2), 203–221. doi:10.1007/s11518-009-5095-0

Lusty, I. (1942). Air-line engineering management. *Aircraft engineering*, 201-202.

Lynch, C. G. (2008). *Enterprise Wikis Seen As a Way to End 'Reply-All' E-Mail Threads*. Retrieved from http://www.cio.com/article/197101/Enterprise_Wikis_Seen_As_a_Way_to_End_Reply_All_E_Mail_Threads

Machlup, F. (1962). *The production and distribution of knowledge in the United States*. Princeton, NJ: Princeton University Press.

Mack, R., Ravin, Y., & Byrd, R. J. (2001). Knowledge portals and the emerging digital knowledge workplace. *IBM Systems Journal, 40*(4), 925–955. doi:10.1147/sj.404.0925

Mader, S. (2008). *Wikipatterns*. New York: Wiley.

Maeda, Y., Ushioda, T., & Makita, S. (2008, May). *Easy robot programming for industrial manipulators by manual volume sweeping*. Paper presented at the 2008 IEEE International Conference on Robotics and Automation, Pasadena, CA.

Maier, R. (2004). *Knowledge Management Systems: Information and Communication Technologies for Knowledge Management*. Berlin: Springer.

Maier, R., & Hadrich, T. (2006). Knowledge management systems . In Schwartz, D. G. (Ed.), *Encyclopaedia of Knowledge Management* (pp. 442–450). Hershey, PA: IGI Global.

Mainzer, K. (2004). *Thinking in complexity. The computational dynamics of matter, Mind, and mankind*. Berlin, Germany: Springer.

Majchrzak, A., Wagner, C., & Yates, D. (2006). Corporate Wiki Users: Results of a Survey. In *Proceedings of the International Symposium on Wikis (Wikisym)*.

Malone, T. W., & Klein, M. (2007). Harnessing collective intelligence to address global climate change. *Innovations: Technology, Governance, Globalization, 2*(3), 15–26. doi:10.1162/itgg.2007.2.3.15

March, J. G. (1991). Exploration and Exploitation in Organizational Learning. *Organization Science, 2*(1), 71–87. doi:10.1287/orsc.2.1.71

Markov, S. (2009). *Markov Network based Ontology Matching. Israel: Ben-Gurion University, Dept. of Computer Science*. Retrieved October 18, 2010, from http://ijcai.org/papers09/Papers/IJCAI09-312.pdf

Markus, L. M. (2001). Toward a theory of knowledge reuse: Types of knowledge reuse situations and factors in reuse success. *Journal of Management Information Systems, 18*(1), 57–93.

Martensson, M. (2000). A critical review of knowledge management as a management tool. *Journal of Knowledge Management, 4*(3), 204–216. doi:10.1108/13673270010350002

Martin, B., & Deng, H. (2003, December 17-19). Managing organizational knowledge in a socio-technical context. In P. Santiprabhob & J. Daengdej (Eds.), *Proceedings of the Fourth International Conference on Intelligent Technologies*, Chiangmai, Thailand.

Maruyama, M. (1963). The second cybernetics, deviation amplifying mutual causal Processes. *American Scientist, 51*, 179.

Mascardi, V., et al. (2009). Automatic Ontology Matching Via Upper Ontologies: A Systematic Evaluation. *IEEE Transactions on Knowledge and Data Engineering, 22*(11). Retrieved October 18, 2010, from http://doi. ieeecomputersociety.org/10.1109/TKDE.2009.154

Mason, W. A., & Jones, A. (2008). Propagation of innovations in networked groups. *Journal of Experimental Psychology. General, 137*(3), 422–433. doi:10.1037/a0012798

Massey, A. P., & Montaya-Weiss, M. M. (2003). Enhancing performance through knowledge management. In *Handbook of business strategy* (pp. 147-151). New York: Thomson publishing.

Mataric, M. J. (1993). Designing emergent behaviors: From local interactions to collective intelligence. In *Proceedings of the Second International Conference on Simulation of Adaptive Behavior* (pp. 432-441). Cambridge, MA: MIT Press.

Matsuo, Y., Tomobe, H., Hasida, K., et al. (2006). POLYPHONT: an advanced social network extraction system from the Web. In *Proceedings of 15th International World Wide Web Conference (WWW 2006),* Edinburgh International Conference Centre, Scotland (pp. 397-406).

Matta, N., Ermine, J.-L., Aubertin, G., & Trivin, J.-Y. (2002). Knowledge Capitalization with a knowledge engineering approach, the MASK method. In *Proceedings of the Knowledge Management and Organisational memories* (pp. 17-28). Boston: Kluwer Academic Press.

Maturana, H. R. (1978). Biology of language. The epistemology of reality. In G. A.

Maxwell, R. (1968). Presentation speech. *Information storage and retrieval, 4*(2), 87-90.

Mayfield, R. (n. d.). Retrieved from http://www.forbes.com/2008/10/15/cio-email-manage-tech-cio-cx_rm_1015email.html

Mazouni, M., & Aubry, J. (2007). A PHA based on a systemic and generic ontology. In *Proceedings of the IEEE/INFORMS International Conference on Service Operation and Logistics and Informatics, the IEEE – ITS international conference (SOLI'2007)*, Philadelphia.

McCracken, M., & Wallace, M. (2000). Towards a redefinition of strategic HRD. *Journal of European Industrial Training, 24*(5), 281–290. doi:10.1108/03090590010372056

McElroy, M. W. (2000). The new knowledge management. *Knowledge and innovation: Journal of the knowledge management consortium international, 1*(1), 43-67.

McNeillis, P. (2005). Cognitive mapping and UML modelling comparing book and mind. In *Proceedings of the IEE Seminar on UML Systems Engineering*, London.

Meadows, D. H. (1982). Whole systems – Whole Earth models and systems. *The Coevolution Quarterly*, 98–108.

Mehta, N. (2007). The value creation cycle: moving towards a framework for knowledge management implementation. *Knowledge management research and practice, 5*, 126-135.

Meilicke, C. (2008). The Relevance of Reasoning and Alignment Incoherence in Ontology Matching. In *Proceedings of the ESWC 2009 PhD Symposium*, Heraklion, Greece. Retrieved October 18, 2010, from http://www.springerlink.com/index/p56133140356v70g.pdf

Meilicke, C., Stuckenschmidt, H., & Tamilin, A. (2008). Reasoning support for mapping revision. *Journal of Logic and Computation*. Retrieved October 18, 2010, from http://logcom.oxfordjournals.org/content/19/5/807.short

Mekhilef, M., & Flock, C. (2006). Knowledge Management: A multidisciplinary survey . In Cunningham, P., & Cunningham, M. (Eds.), *Exploiting the knowledge economy: Issues, applications, case studies*. Amsterdam, The Netherlands: IOS Press.

Memtsas, D. P. (2003). Multiobjective programming methods in the reserve selection problem. *European Journal of Operational Research, 150*(3), 640–652. doi:10.1016/S0377-2217(02)00519-2

Mestrovic, S. G. (1998). *Anthony giddens: The last modernist*. London: Routledge.

Metaxiotis, K., Engazakis, K., & Psarras, J. (2005). Exploring the world of Knowledge management: agreements and disagreements in the academic/practitioner community. *Journal of Knowledge Management, 9*(2), 6–18. doi:10.1108/13673270510590182

Midgley, G. (2000). *Systems intervention: Philosophy, methodology and practice*. New York: Kluwer/Plenum.

Midgley, M. (2001). *Science and Poetry*. London: Routledge.

Midgley, M. (2004). *The myths we live by*. London: Routledge.

Midgley, G. (2004). Systems thinking for the 21st century. *International Journal of Knowledge and Systems Science, 1*(1), 63–69.

Miller & E. Lenneberg (Ed.). *Psychology and Biology of Language and Thought. Essays in honor of Eric Lenneberg* (pp. 27-63). New York: Academic Press.

Miller, K. D., & Zhao, M. (2006). Adding interpersonal learning and tacit knowledge to March's exploration-exploitation model. *Academy of Management Journal, 49*(4), 709–722.

Mingers, J. (2008). Management knowledge and knowledge management: realism and forms of truth. *Knowledge management research and practice, 6*, 62-76.

Mingers, J. (2002). Can social systems be autopoietic? Assessing Luhmann's social theory. *The Sociological Review, 50*, 278–299. doi:10.1111/1467-954X.00367

Misra, D. C. (2006). *E-Government: The State of Art Today-2*. Paper presented at the Official Launching of the Government-to-Government System and CIO Workshop, Ebene Cyber Tower, Rose Hill, Mauritius.

MIT. (2005). *Mission statement*. Retrieved at June 10, 2006, from http://learning.media.mit.edu/mid_mission.html

Mitchell, T. M., Keller, R. M., & Kedar-Cabelli, S. T. (1986). Explanation-based generalization: a unifying view. *Machine Learning, 1*, 47–80. doi:10.1007/BF00116250

Mockus, A., Filding, R. T., & Herbsleb, J. D. (2002). Two case studies of open source software development: Apache and Mozilla. *ACM Transactions on Software Engineering and Methodology, 11*(3), 309–346. doi:10.1145/567793.567795

MODAF. (2007). *The MOD architecture framework (MODAF)*. London: The British Ministry of Defence.

Mohaghegh, Z., Kazemi, R., & Mosleh, A. (2009). Incorporating organizational factors into Probabilistic Risk Assessment (PRA) of complex socio-technical systems: a hybrid technique formalization. *Reliability Engineering & System Safety, 94*, 1000–1018. doi:10.1016/j.ress.2008.11.006

Mokyr, J. (2002). *The gifts of Athena: Historical origins of the knowledge economy*. Princeton, NJ: Princeton University Press.

Morgan, G. (1997). *Images of organization*. Thousand Oaks, CA: Sage.

Morin, E. (1997). *Reformé de pensée, transdisciplinarité, réforme de l'Université*. Retrieved January 15, 2006, from http://nicol.club.fr/ciret/bulletin/b12/b12c1.htm

Morin, E. (2001). *Seven Complex Lessons in Education for the Future*. Paris: UNESCO.

Morin, E. (2002). *A propos de la complexité*. Retrieved January 15, 2006, from http://www.litt-and-co.org/philosophie/philo.textes.htm

Mori, N. (2002). Rough Set Approach to product Design Solution for the Purposed Kansei. *Bulletin of Japanese Society for Science of Design, 150*, 85–94.

Morin, E. (2002). From the Concept of System to the Paradigm of Complexity. *Journal of Social and Evolutionary Systems, 15*(4), 371–385. doi:10.1016/1061-7361(92)90024-8

Mulej, M. (2007). Systems theory - a world view and/or a methodology aimed at requisite holism/realism of human's thinking, decisions and action. *Systems Research and Behavioral Science, 24*(3), 347–357. doi:10.1002/sres.810

Nagamachi, M. (1994). Kansei Engineering: An ergonomic technology for a product development. In . *Proceedings of IEA, 94*, 1220–122.

Nagamachi, M. (2002). Kansei Engineering as a powerful consumer-oriented technology for product development. *Applied Ergonomics, 33*(3), 289–294. doi:10.1016/S0003-6870(02)00019-4

Nagarajan, M., Verma, K., Sheth, A. P., Miller, J., & Lathem, J. (2006) Semantic Interoperability of Web Services - Challenges and Experiences. In *Proceedings of the IEEE International Conference on Web Services (ICWS 2006)*.

Nagurney, A., & Wakolbinger, T. (2005). Supernetworks: An introduction to the concept and its applications with a specific focus on knowledge supernetworks. *International Journal of Knowledge, Culture and Change Management, 4*.

Nagy, M. (2008). DSSim Results for OAEI 2008. In *Proceedings of 7th International Semantic Web Conference Ontology Matching (OM 2008)* (pp. 147-160). Retrieved October 18, 2010, from http://citeseerx.ist.psu.edu/viewdoc/download?doi=10.1.1.142.8474&rep=rep1&type=pdf#page=143

Nagy, M., et al. (2007). *DSSim: managing uncertainty on the semantic Web* (Tech. Rep.). Poznan, Poland: Poznan University of Economics, Department of Information Systems. Retrieved October 18, 2010, from http://citeseerx.ist.psu.edu/viewdoc/download?doi=10.1.1.104.9963&rep=rep1&type=pdf

Nakamori, Y. (2000, September 25-27). Knowledge management system toward sustainable society. In *Proceedings of the 1st International Symposium on Knowledge and System Sciences,* Ishikawa, Japan (pp. 57-64).

Nakamori, Y. (2003). Systems methodology and mathematical models for knowledge management. *Journal of Systems Science and Systems Engineering, 12*(1), 49–72. doi:10.1007/s11518-006-0120-z

Nakamori, Y., & Zhu, Z. C. (2004). Exploring a sociologist understanding for the i-System. *International Journal of Knowledge and Systems Science, 1*(1), 1–8.

Nakamura, A. (1996). A rough logic based on incomplete information and its application. *International Journal of Approximate Reasoning, 15*(4), 367–378. doi:10.1016/S0888-613X(96)00075-8

Nicola, A., Kabilan, V., Missikoff, M., & Mojtahed, V. (2007). Practical issues in ontology modeling: the case of defence conceptual modelling framework-ontology . In Müller, G., Morel, J. P., & Vallespir, G. (Eds.), *Enterprise Interoperability*. New York: Springer. doi:10.1007/978-1-84628-714-5_25

Niemann, B. (2008). Getting to SOA and Semantic Interoperability for DoD Architectures. In *Proceedings of the 6th Annual DoD Architectures Conference*. Retrieved August 28, 2008, from http://semanticcommunity.wik.is/@api/deki/files/569/=BNiemannIDGA03032008.ppt?revision=2

Noda, A., & Nagatani, T. (2008, September). *Motion learning for industrial robots with an active search algorithm*. Paper presented at the 26th Annual Conference of the Robotics Society of Japan, Kobe, Japan.

Noda, A., et al. (2009, December). *Intelligent robotic technologies for cell assembly system*. Paper presented at the 10th SICE System Integration Division Annual Conference, Tokyo, Japan.

Noda, A., Nagatani, T., & Nagano, H. (2008, December), *Active search algorithm on motion learning of industrial robots*. Paper presented at the 9th SICE System Integration Division Annual Conference, Gifu, Japan.

Nonaka, I., & Takeuchi, H. (1995). *The knowledge-creating company: How Japanese companies create the dynamics of innovation*. New York: Oxford University Press.

Nonaka, I. (1991). The knowledge-creating company. *Harvard Business Review, 69*(6), 96–104.

Nonaka, I. (1994). A dynamic theory of organizational knowledge creation. *Organization Science, 1*, 14–37. doi:10.1287/orsc.5.1.14

Nonaka, I. O., & Takeuchi, H. (1995). *The knowledge-creating company: how Japanese companies create the dynamics of innovation*. New York: Oxford University Press.

Nonaka, I., & Konno, N. (1998). The concept of 'Ba': Building a foundation for knowledge creation. *California Management Review, 40*(3), 40–54.

Nonaka, I., Konno, N., & Toyama, R. (2001). Emergence of 'Ba . In Nonaka, I., & Nishiguchi, T. (Eds.), *Knowledge emergence* (pp. 13–29). New York: Oxford University Press.

Nonaka, I., & Takeuchi, H. (1995). *The knowledge creating company: How Japanese companies create the dynamics of innovation*. New York: Oxford University press.

Nonaka, I., & Toyama, R. (2002). A firm as a dialectic being: toward the dynamic theory of the firm. *Industrial and Corporate Change*, *11*, 995–1109. doi:10.1093/icc/11.5.995

Nonaka, I., & Toyama, R. (2007). Why do firms differ? The theory of the knowledge creating firm . In Ichijo, K., & Nonaka, I. (Eds.), *Knowledge creation and management 2007* (pp. 13–31). New York: Oxford University Press.

Nonaka, I., Toyama, R., Hirata, T., & Kohlbacher, F. (2008). *Managing flow: A process theory of the knowledge-based firm*. Basingstoke, UK: Palgrave Macmillan.

Nonaka, I., Toyama, R., & Konno, N. (2000). SECI, ba and leadership: A unified model of dynamic knowledge creation. *Long Range Planning*, *33*, 5–34. doi:10.1016/S0024-6301(99)00115-6

Norberg-Bohm, V. (2000). Creating incentives for environmentally enhancing technological change: Lessons from 30 years of U.S. energy technology policy. *Technological Forecasting and Social Change*, *65*(2), 125–148. doi:10.1016/S0040-1625(00)00076-7

Normann, R. (2001). *Reframing business: When the map changes the landscape*. Chichester, UK: John Wiley & Sons.

Nowotny, H. (2005). The increase of complexity and its reduction: Emergent interfaces between the Natural Sciences, Humanities and Social Sciences. *Theory, Culture & Society*, *22*(5), 15–31. doi:10.1177/0263276405057189

Nutting, P. G. (1918). The application of organised knowledge to national welfare. *The Scientific Monthly*, *6*(5), 406–416.

Nuttin, M., & Van Brussel, H. (1997). Learning the peg-into-hole assembly operation with a connectionist reinforcement technique. *Computers in Industry*, *33*, 101–109. doi:10.1016/S0166-3615(97)00015-8

O'Leary, D. E. (1998). Knowledge management systems: converting and connecting. *IEEE Intelligent Systems*, *13*(3), 30–33. doi:10.1109/MIS.1998.683179

O'Leary, D. E. (2008). Wikis: From Each According to His Knowledge. *Computer*, *41*(2), 34–41. doi:10.1109/MC.2008.68

Obstfeld, D. (2005). Social Networks, the Tertius Iungens Orientation, and Involvement in Innovation. *Administrative Science Quarterly*, *50*(1), 100–130.

OECD. (1996). *Ageing in OECD Countries, a Critical Policy Challenge*. Paris: OECD Publishing.

OECD. (2007). *Ageing and the Public Service, Human Resource Challenges*. Paris: OECD Publishing.

Ojo, A., & Janowski, T. (2005). *Ontology, Semantic Web and Electronic Government*. Retrieved August 1, 2008, from http://www.emacao.gov.mo/documents/14/13/seminar1 3.pdf

Olsen, O. E., & Lindoe, P. H. (2009). Risk on the ramble: the international transfer of risk and vulnerability. *Safety Science*, *47*(6), 743–755. doi:10.1016/j.ssci.2008.01.012

Olson, G. (2004). From information to knowledge: Recommendations for Wikis as Enterprise Solutions for Collaborative Work.

Olson, G. M., & Olson, J. S. (2000). Distance Matters. *Human-Computer Interaction*, *15*(2-3), 139–178. doi:10.1207/S15327051HCI1523_4

OMG. (2007). *OMG UML specification*. Needham, MA: Object Management Group.

OMG. (2008a). *Business process modeling notation*. Needham, MA: Object Management Group.

OMG. (2008b). *UML(TM) profile for modeling quality of service and fault tolerance characteristics and mechanisms specification*. Needham, MA: Object Management Group.

OMG. (2008c). *OMG SysML specification*. Needham, MA: Object Management Group.

Ou, S., et al. (2008). *Development and Alignment of a Domain-Specific Ontology for Question Answering*. Retrieved October 18, 2010, from http://www.lrecconf.org/proceedings/lrec2008/pdf/561_paper.pdf

Overeem, A., Witters, J., & Peristeras, T. (2006). *Semantic Interoperability in pan-European eGovernment services*. Retrieved July 6, 2008, from http://www.semantic-gov.org/ind ex.php?Name=UpDownload&req=getit&cid=2&lid=246

OWL. (2004). *OWL Web Ontology Language*. Retrieved April 15, 2010, from http://www.w3.org/TR/2004/REC-owl-features-20040210

Pandian, S. (2005). The political economy of trans-Pakistan gas pipeline project: Assessing the political and economic risks for India. *Energy Policy, 33*, 659–670. doi:10.1016/j.enpol.2003.09.011

Paralic, J., Sabol, T., & Mach, M. (2003). *Knowledge Enhanced E-Government Portal. Knowledge Management in Electronic Government*. Berlin: Springer.

Pasteur, K., Pettit, J., & van Schagen, B. (2006). *Knowledge management and organisational learning for development* (Workshop background paper). Retrieved January 11, 2009, from www.km4dev.org

Pawlak, Z. (1982). Rough sets. *International Journal of Computer and Information Science, 11*(5), 341–356. doi:10.1007/BF01001956

Pawlak, Z. (1991). *Rough Sets: Theoretical Aspects of Reasoning about Data*. Boston: Kluwer Academic Publishers.

Peckham, J., & MacKellar, B. (2001). Generating code for engineering design systems using software patterns. *Artificial Intelligence in Engineering, 15*, 219–226. doi:10.1016/S0954-1810(01)00018-8

Pereira, C. S., & A. L. (2007). Soares. Improving the quality of collaboration requirements for information management through social networks analysis. *International Journal of Information Management, 27*(2), 86–103. doi:10.1016/j.ijinfomgt.2006.10.003

Perry-Smith, J. E. (2006). Social Yet Creative: The Role Of Social Relationships In Facilitating Individual Creativity. *Academy of Management Journal, 49*(1), 85–101.

Pesenhofer, A., Mayer, R., & Rauber, A. (2006, December 6-8). Improving scientific conferences by enhancing conference management system with information mining capabilities. In *Proceedings of the 1st International Conference on Digital Information Management (ICDIM 2006)*, Bangalore, India (pp. 359-366). Washington, DC: IEEE Press.

Peters, M. (2005). Editorial. New approaches in the philosophy of learning. *Educational Philosophy and Theory, 37*(5), 627–631. doi:10.1111/j.1469-5812.2005.00146.x

Petiot, J.-F., & Yannou, B. (2004). Measuring consumer perceptions for a better comprehension. *IJI . E (Norwalk, Conn.), 33*(6), 507–525.

Pezzullo, L., & De Filippo, R. (2009). Perceptions of industrial risk and emergency management procedures in hazmat logistics: a qualitative mental model approach. *Safety Science, 47*, 537–541. doi:10.1016/j.ssci.2008.07.006

Pires, J. N. (2006). *Industrial robots programming: building applications for the factories of the future*. New York: Springer.

Polanyi, M. (1958). *Personal knowledge: Towards a post-critical philosophy*. London: Routledge & Kegan Paul.

Polanyi, M. (1969). Knowing and Being . In Grene, M. (Ed.), *Essays by Michael Polanyi*. Chicago: University of Chicago.

Polanyi, M. (1974). *Personal knowledge: Towards a post-critical philosophy*. Chicago: University of Chicago Press.

Polkowski, L. (2002). *Rough Sets: mathematical foundations*. New York: Physica Verlag.

Popper, K. R. (1934). *Logik der Forschung*. Vienna, Austria: Julius Springer Verlag.

Popper, K. R. (1972). *Objective knowledge*. Oxford: Oxford University Press.

Prabhu, S. M., & Garg, D. P. (1997, May). *Fuzzy logic based reinforcement learning of admittance control for automated robotic manufacturing*. Paper presented at the 1st International Conference on Knowledge-Based Intelligent Electronic Systems, Adelaide, South Australia.

Prat, N. (2006). A hierachical model for knowledge management . In Schwartz, D. G. (Ed.), *Encyclopaedia of Knowledge Management* (pp. 848–854). Hershey, PA: IGI Global.

Preece, J., & Maloney-Krichmar, D. (2005). Online communities: Design, theory, and practice. *Journal of Computer-Mediated Communication, 10*(4). Retrieved January 13, 2010, from http://jcmc.indiana.edu/vol10/issue4/preece.html

Prigogine, I., & Stengers, I. (1984). *Order out of chaos. Man's new dialogue with nature*. Glasgow, Scotland: Fontana Paperbacks.

Prusak, L. (2006). Foreword . In Schwartz, D. G. (Ed.), *Encyclopaedia of Knowledge Management*. Hershey, PA: IGI Global.

Prusak, L., & Weiss, L. (2007). Knowledge in organisational settings . In Ichijo, K., & Nonaka, I. (Eds.), *Knowledge creation and management 2007* (pp. 32–43). New York: Oxford University Press.

Qian, X. S., Yu, J. Y., & Dai, R. W. (1990). A New Discipline of Science: Open Complex Giant System and Its Methodology. *Chinese Journal of Nature, 13*(1), 3–10.

Quan, T. T., Siu, C. H., & Fong, A. C. M. (2003, December 3-5). A Web mining approach for finding expertise in research areas. In *Proceedings of the 2003 International Conference on Cyberworlds (CW'03)* (pp. 310-317).

Quine, W. V. O. (1947). On universals. *Journal of Symbolic Logic, 12*, 74–84. doi:10.2307/2267212

Quine, W. V. O. (1951). Semantics and abstract objects. *Proceedings of the American Academy of Arts and Sciences, 80*, 90–96. doi:10.2307/20023638

Qureshi, S., Briggs, R. O., & Hlupic, V. (2006). Value creation from intellectual capital: convergence of knowledge management and collaboration in the intellectual bandwidth model. *Group Decision and Negotiation, 15*(3), 197–220. doi:10.1007/s10726-006-9018-x

Rahe, M. (2009). Subjectivity and cognition in knowledge management. *Journal of Knowledge Management, 13*(3), 102–117. doi:10.1108/13673270910962905

Rasli, M. D. (2004). *Knowledge management framework for the Malaysian constructing companies* (IRPA Project No. 74320). Retrieved December 18, 2008, from http://eprints.utm.my/4121/

Ray, T. (2005). Making Sense Of Managing Knowledge. In S. Little & T. Ray (Eds.), *Managing Knowledge: An Essential Reader 2005* (pp. 1-6, 10). London: Sage.

Raymond, R. (1999). The cathedral and the bazaar. *Knowledge . Technology & Policy, 12*(3), 22–49.

Redmill, F. (2002). Risk analysis - a subjective process. *Engineering Management Journal, 12*(6), 91–96. doi:10.1049/em:20020206

Reichling, K. (2009). *Semantic interoperability for public administrations in Europe – challenges and solutions, iDABC European eGovernment Services*. Retrieved July 1, 2009, from https://www.posccaesar.org/svn/pub/SemanticDays/2009/Session_1_Klaus_Reichling.pdf

Ren, T. G., Wang, Q. G. L. Y., Liu, X. F., Zhang, F., Wang, Y., & Zhang, Y. H. (2006). Study on information of syndrome standard based on data. *Journal of Beijing University of Traditional Chinese Medicine, 29*(7), 442–444.

Rescher, N. (1998). *Complexity. A philosophical overview*. New Brunswick, NJ: Transaction Publishers.

Rigby, D., & Bilodeau, B. (2007). Management tools and trends 2007. *A survey from Bain and Company*. Retrieved June 17, 2008, from http://www.bain.com/management_tools/Management_Tools_and_Trends_2007.pdf

Rigby, D., & Bilodeau, B. (2009). *Management Tools and Trends 2009*. Retrieved October 8, 2009, from www.bain.com

Riley, T. B. (2003, August 4). An overview of the knowledge economy. *egov Monitor Weekly*. Retrieved February 22, 2009, from http://www.egovmonitor.com/features/riley07.html

Robbins, G. (1999). Prologue. In *The collected works of L.S. Vygotsky, Vol.6*. New York: Plenum Press.

Rodan, S., & Galunic, D. C. (2004). More than network structure: how knowledge heterogeneity influences managerial performance and innovativeness. *Strategic Management Journal, 25*, 541–556. doi:10.1002/smj.398

Roland, H. E., & Moriarty, B. (1990). *System safety engineering and management*. New York: Wiley. doi:10.1002/9780470172438

Rose, S. (1997). *Lifelines. Biology beyond determinism*. Oxford, UK: Oxford University Press.

Ross, J. G. (2004). Risk and uncertainty in portfolio characterization. *Journal of Petroleum Science Engineering, 44*(1-2), 41–53. doi:10.1016/j.petrol.2004.02.004

Roth, J. (2003). Enabling knowledge creation: Learning from an R+D organisation. *Journal of Knowledge Management, 7*(1), 32–48. doi:10.1108/13673270310463608

Rowe, D., & Drew, C. (2006). The Impact of Web 2.0 on Enterprise Strategy. *Cutter IT Journal, 19*(10), 6–13.

Rubenstein-Montano, B., Liebowitz, J., Buchwalter, J., McCaw, D., Newman, B., & Rebeck, K. (2001). The Knowledge Management Methodology Team. A Systems Thinking framework for knowledge management. *Decision Support Systems, 31*, 5–16. doi:10.1016/S0167-9236(00)00116-0

Ruggles, R. (1998). The state of the notion: knowledge management in practice. *California Management Review, 40*, 80–89.

Ryle, G. (1949). *The concept of the mind.* Chicago: University of Chicago press.

Ryle, G. (1984). *Intensionality: An essay in the philosophy of mind.* New York: Cambridge University Press.

Sabou, M., et al. (2008). Exploring the Semantic Web as Background Knowledge for Ontology Matching. *Journal on Data Semantics, 9*, 156-190. Retrieved October 18, 2010, from http://kmi.open.ac.uk/people/marta/papers /JoDS_2008.pdf

Salmon, W. C. (1993). Causality: Production and propagation. In E. Sosa, & M. Tooley *Causation* (pp. 154-171). Oxford: Oxford University Press.

Sandelowski, M., & Barroso, J. (2006). *Handbook for Synthesizing Qualitative Research.* New York: Springer.

Sarah, R., & Haslett, T. (2003). *Learning is a process which changes the state of knowledge of an individual or organisation* (Tech. Rep. No. 72/03). Melbourne, Australia: Monash University. Retrieved February 16, 2008, from http://www.buseco.monash.edu.au/mgt/research/working-papers/2003/wp72-03.pdf

Sarrel, M. D. (2007). *Wicked Productive Wikis* (p. 88). PC Magazine.

Sassone, L. A. (1996). Philosophy across the curriculum: A democratic Nietzschean pedagogy. *Educational Theory, 46*(4), 511–524. doi:10.1111/j.1741-5446.1996.00511.x

Sawaragi, T., Liu, Y., & Tian, Y. (2006). Human-machine collaborative knowledge creation: capturing tacit knowledge by observing expert's demonstration of load allocation. *International Journal of Knowledge and Systems Science, 3*(2), 9–19.

Schon, D. A. (1983). *The reflective practitioner: How professionals think in action.* New York: Basic books.

Schön, D. A. (1987). *Educating the reflective practitioner.* San Francisco, CA: Jossey-Bass.

Schonhofen, P., Benczur, A., Biro, I., & Csalogany, K. (2008). Cross-language retrieval with Wikipedia. In C. Peters et al. (Eds.), *CLEF 2007* (LNCS 5152, pp. 72-79). Berlin: Springer Verlag.

Schreiber, G., Akkermans, H., Anjewierden, A., de Hoog, R., Shadbolt, N., Van de Velde, W., & Wielinga, B. (1999). *Knowledge Engineering and Management, The CommonKADS Methodology.* Cambridge, MA: MIT Press.

Schutt, P. (2003). The post Nonaka knowledge management. *Journal of universal computer science, 9*(6), 451-462.

Schütte, S. (2004). Developing the Space of Properties Supporting Kansei Engineering Procedure. *Theoretical Issues in Ergonomics Science, 5*(3), 214–232.

Schütte, S., & Eklund, J. (2003). *Product Development for Heart and Soul.* Sweden: Linkoping University, Department for Quality and Human System Engineering.

Schütte, S., Eklund, J., Axelsson, J., & Nagamachi, M. (2004). Concepts, methods and tools in Kansei Engineering. *Theoretical Issues in Ergonomics Science, 5*(3), 214–232. doi:10.1080/1463922021000049980

Schwaninger, M. (2009). Complex versus complicated: The how of coping with complexity. *Kybernetes, The international journal of systems and cybernetics, 38*(1-2), 83-92.

Segre, A., & DeJong, G. (1985, March). *Explanation based manipulator learning: acquisition of planning ability through observation.* Paper presented at the 1985 IEEE International Conference on Robotics and Automation, St. Louis, MO.

Segre, A. (1988). *Machine learning of robot assembly plans.* Norwell, MA: Kluwer Academic Publishers.

Segre, A. (1991). Learning how to plan. *Robotics and Autonomous Systems, 8*, 93–111. doi:10.1016/0921-8890(91)90016-E

Semantic Interoperability Community of Practice (SICoP). (2006). *Semantic Wave 2006*. Retrieved August 1, 2008, from http://web-services.gov/SICOPsemwave2006v1.0.doc

Senge, P., Scharmer, C. O., Jaworski, J., & Flowers, B. S. (2005). *Presence. Exploring profound change in people, organizations and society*. London: Nicholas Brealey Publishing.

Senge, M. (1997). *The fifth discipline*. London: Century Business Publishing.

Sergiovanni, T. J. (1996). *Leadership for the schoolhouse*. San Francisco: Jossey-Bass.

Sewell, W. H. Jr. (1992). A theory of structure: Duality, agency, and transformation. *American Journal of Sociology, 98*(1), 1–29. doi:10.1086/229967

Shanks, G., Tansley, E., & Weber, R. (2003). Using ontology to validate conceptual models. *Communications of the ACM, 46*(10), 85–89. doi:10.1145/944217.944244

Sharif, A. M. (2006). Knowledge management: A neuro-hemispherical view of the field. *Knowledge management research and practice, 4*, 70-72.

Shen, Q. (2006). Risk analysis of international petroleum construction project . *Chinese Petroleum Corporation, 1*, 59–61.

Shimizu, Y., Sadoyama, T., Kamijo, M., Hosaya, S., Hashimoto, M., & Otani, T. (2004). On-demand production systems of apparel on basis of Kansei Engineering. *International Journal of Clothing Science and Technology, 16*(1/2), 32–42. doi:10.1108/09556220410520333

Shneiderman, B. (2008). Science 2.0. *Science, 319*, 1349–1350. doi:10.1126/science.1153539

Short, J., William, E., & Christie, B. (1976). *The Social Psychology of Telecommunications*. London: John Wiley and Sons.

Sidorkin, A. M. (2002). *Learning relations: Impure education, deschooled schools & dialogue with evil*. New York: Counterpoints.

Sidoroff, T., & Hyvonen, E. (2005). Semantic E-Government portals - a case study. In *Proceedings of the ISWC-2005 Workshop Semantic Web Case Studies and Best Practices for eBusiness (SWCASE05)*.

Silva, N., et al. (2006). *An approach to ontology mapping negotiation*. Paper Presented at the Third International Conference on Knowledge Capture Workshop on Integrating Ontologies, Banff, Canada. Retrieved October 18, 2010, from http://www.citeseerx.ist.psu.edu/viewdoc/download?doi=10.1.1.106.6079&rep=rep1&type=pdf#page=56

Siorpaes, K., & Hepp, M. (2008). Games with a Purpose for the Semantic Web. [from http://www.heppnetz.de/files/gwap-semweb-ieee-is.pdf]. *IEEE Intelligent Systems, 23*(3), 50–60. Retrieved October 18, 2010. doi:10.1109/MIS.2008.45

Sirk, M. (2009). *ICCA 2008 Statistics Report preface: international association meetings: genuine recession-busters?* Retrieved July 08, 2009, from http://www.iccaworld.com/npps/story.cfm?ID=1915

Slagter, F. (2007). Knowledge management among the older workforce. *Journal of Knowledge Management, 11*(4), 82–96. doi:10.1108/13673270710762738

Smith, P. A. C. (2003). *Successful knowledge management: The importance of relationships* (Tech. Rep.). Santiago, Chile: Universidad Central de Chile. Retrieved February 2, 2008, from www.tlainc.com/S&C%20A1%20N1%2003.doc

Snowden, D. J. (2002). Complex acts of knowing, paradox and descriptive self-awareness. *Journal of Knowledge Management, 6*(2), 100–111. doi:10.1108/13673270210424639

Solintander, M., & Solintander, N. (2010). The sharing, protection and thievery of intellectual assets: The case of the formula 1 industry. *Management Decision, 48*(1), 37–57. doi:10.1108/00251741011014445

Somerville, I. (2007). *Software engineering*. Reading, MA: Addison-Wesley.

Some, S. S. (2006). Supporting use case based requirements engineering. *Information and Software Technology, 48*(1), 43–58. doi:10.1016/j.infsof.2005.02.006

Song, H., Deng, H., & Martin, B. (2005). Technological approach to knowledge management. In *Proceedings of the Second International conference on Information Management and Science*, Kunming, China.

Song, W. Q., Liu, Y. J., & Gu, J. F. (2007). *Mining TCM experiences of TCM masters based on the medical cases data* (Tech. Rep. No. 3). Beijing, China: Xi Yuan Hospital, Chinese Academy of Sciences.

Song, W. Q., Liu, Y. J., Zhu, Z. X., & Gu, J. F. (2008). A Framework of Meta-Synthesis Consensus Support System for Group Decision-Making Problems. In *Proceedings of the 2008 Fifth International Conference on Fuzzy Systems and Knowledge Discovery* (Vol. 3, pp. 319-324).

Song, W. Q., & Gu, J. F. (2009). Experience Mining . In *Proceedings of IKM2009*. Application of Information Visualization Technologies in Masters.

Spender, J. C. (2005). An overview: What's new and important about knowledge management? Building new bridges between managers and academics . In Little, S., & Ray, T. (Eds.), *Managing Knowledge: An essential reader 2005* (2nd ed., pp. 126–128). Thousand Oaks, CA: Sage Publications.

Spiegler, I. (2003). Technology and knowledge: bridging a "generating" gap. *Information & Management, 40*(6), 533–539. doi:10.1016/S0378-7206(02)00069-1

Stacey, R. D. (2003). *Complexity and group processes. A radically social understanding of individuals*. Hove, UK: Brunner-Routledge.

Starobinski, J. (2003). *Action and reaction. The life and adventures of a couple*. New York: Zone books.

Stephens, J. C., Wilson, E. J., & Peterson, T. R. (2008). Socio-Political Evaluation of Energy Deployment (SPEED): An integrated research framework analyzing energy technology deployment. *Technological Forecasting and Social Change, 75*(8), 1224–1246. doi:10.1016/j.techfore.2007.12.003

Steven, P. (2008). Govt portal wins global award. *The Star Online*. Retrieved May 21, 2008, from http://thestar.com.my /news/story.asp?file=/2008/5/21/nation/200805211819&sec=nation

Stevens, D. E., & Thevaranjan, A. (2008). *A moral solution to the moral hazard problem*. Retrieved October 6, 2010, from http://ssrn.com/abstract=1138279

Stewart, T. A. (2002). The case against Knowledge management. *Business 2.0 magazine*. Retrieved August 20, 2007, from http://money.cnn.com/magazines/business2/articles/mag/print/0,1643,36747,00.html

Storey, N. (1996). *Safety critical computer systems*. Reading, MA: Addison-Wesley.

Streb, C. K., Voelpel, S. C., & Leibold, M. (2008). Managing the aging workforce: Status quo and implications for the advancement of theory and practice. *European Management Journal, 26*, 1–10. doi:10.1016/j.emj.2007.08.004

Suarez, L. (2008). *Can Social Tools Really Replace Email?* Retrieved from http://it.toolbox.com/blogs/elsua/can-social-tools-really-replace-email-they-already-are-part-ii-25793

SUMO. (2003). *Suggested Upper Merged Ontology*. Retrieved May 11, 2010, from http://www.ontologyportal.org/

Supyuenyong, V., & Islam, N. (2006). Knowledge management architecture: building blocks and their relationships. In *Proceedings of the IEEE PICMT 2006 technology management for the global future* (pp. 1210-1219).

Sveiby, K. E. (1997). *The new organizational wealth: Managing and measuring knowledge-based Assets*. San Francisco: Berrett-Koehler Publishers.

Sveiby, K. E. (2008). East and West do meet – that is the real issue! *Journal of Intellectual Capital, 9*(2).

Sveiby, K. E., & Lloyd, T. (1987). *Managing knowhow – Add value by valuing creativity*. New York: Bloomsbury.

Sze-Sze, W. (2008). Task knowledge overlap and knowledge variety: the role of advice network structures and impact on group effectiveness. *Journal of Organizational Behavior, 29*(5), 591–614. doi:10.1002/job.490

Szulanski, G. (2000). The Process of Knowledge Transfer: A Diachronic Analysis of Stickiness. *Organizational Behavior and Human Decision Processes, 82*(1), 9–27. doi:10.1006/obhd.2000.2884

Szybalski, A. (2005). *Why it's not a wiki world (yet)*. Retrieved from http://www.andy.bigwhitebox.org/papers/wiki_world.pdf

Tan, H., & Lambrix, P. (2007). A method for recommending ontology alignment strategies. In *Proceedings of the 6th international semantic web and 2nd Asian conference on Asian semantic web conference*, Busan, Korea (pp. 494-507). Retrieved October 18, 2010, from http://www.ida.liu.se/~patla/publications/ISWC07-preprint.pdf

Tang, J., Zhang, J., Zhang, D., Yao, L. M., Zhu, C. L., & Li, J. Z. (n.d.). *ArnetMiner: An expertise oriented search system for academic researcher social network*. Retrieved from http://keg.cs.tsinghua.edu.cn/persons/tj/arnetminer/arnetminer.html

Tang, X. J. (2006). *Meta-synthesis and Complex System (2005-2006)* (Tech. Rep. No. MSKS-2006-03). Beijing, China: AMSS.

Tang, X. J. (2008a). Approach to detection of community's consensus and interest. In Y. Ishikawa, et al. (Eds.), *APWeb'2008 Workshops* (LNCS 4977, pp. 17-29). Heidelberg, Germany: Springer Verlag.

Tang, X. J. (2008b, December 9-12). Enabling a meta-synthetic discovery workshop for social consensus process. In Proceedings of the *IEEE/WIC/ACM International Conference on Web Intelligence and Intelligent Agent Technology* (pp. 436-441), Sydney. Washington, DC: IEEE Press.

Tang, X. J. (2009). Qualitative meta-synthesis techniques for analysis of public opinions for in-depth study. In J. Zhou (ed.), *Proceedings of the 1st International ICST Conference on Complex Sciences: Theory and Applications (Complex'2009)* (Part 2, LNICST 5, pp. 2338-2353). Heidelberg, Germany: Springer Verlag.

Tang, X. J. N., Zhang, N., & Wang, Z. (2007). Exploration of TCM masters knowledge mining. In *Proceedings of Computational Science (ICCS2007)* (LNCS 4490, pp. 35-42). Berlin: Springer Verlag.

Tang, X. J., & Liu, Y. J. (2004). A test of pooling the wisdom of the experts-A collective discussion on the designing the regulation law for research projects. In *Proceedings of the Well-off Society Strategies and Systems Engineering* (pp. 339-345). Hong Kong, China: Global-Link Publisher.

Tang, X. J., Zhang, N., & Wang, Z. (2007). Augmented support for knowledge sharing by academic conference - on-line conferencing ba. In *Proceedings of IEEE WiCOM'2007 the Management Track of IEEE International Conference on Wireless Communications, Networking and Mobile Computing* (pp. 6400-6403). Washington, DC: IEEE Press.

Tang, X. J. (2007). Towards meta-synthetic support to unstructured problem solving. *International Journal of Information Technology & Decision Making, 6*(3), 491–508. doi:10.1142/S0219622007002630

Tang, X. J., & Liu, Y. J. (2007). Group argumentation and its analysis on a highlighted social event - Practice of Qualitative Meta-synthesis. *Systems Engineering: Theory and Practice, 27*(3), 42–49. doi:10.1016/S1874-8651(08)60023-X

Tang, X. J., Liu, Y. J., & Zhang, W. (2008). Augmented analytical exploitation of a scientific forum . In Iwata, S., (Eds.), *Communications and discoveries from multidisciplinary data* (pp. 65–79). Heidelberg, Germany: Springer-Verlag. doi:10.1007/978-3-540-78733-4_3

Tang, X. J., Zhang, N., & Wang, Z. (2008). Exploration of TCM masters knowledge mining. *Journal of Systems Science and Complexity, 21*(1), 34–45. doi:10.1007/s11424-008-9064-3

Tang, X. J., & Zhang, W. (2007). How knowledge science is studied - a sision from conference mining of the relevant knowledge science symposia. *International Journal of Knowledge and Systems Science, 4*(4), 51–60.

Tang, X., & Zhang, Z. (2008). Paper review assignment based on human-knowledge network. In [Singapore.]. *Proceedings of IEEE SMC, 2008*, 102–107.

Tatsiopoulos, C., & Boutsinas, B. (2009). *Ontology mapping based on association rule mining*. Paper Presented at 11th International Conference on Enterprise Information Systems, Milan, Italy. Retrieved October 18, 2010, from http://episgr.net23.net/docs/ontology_mapping_based_on_association_rule_mining.pdf

Teece, D. J., Pisano, G., & Shuen, A. (1997). Dynamic Capabilities and Strategic Management. *Strategic Management Journal, 18*(7), 509–533. doi:10.1002/(SICI)1097-0266(199708)18:7<509::AID-SMJ882>3.0.CO;2-Z

Teleos. (2004). 2004 *Global Most Admired Knowledge Enterprises (MAKE) Report Executive Summary.* Retrieved from www.knowledgebusiness.com

Teleos. (2006). *2006 Global Most Admired Knowledge Enterprises (MAKE) Report Executive Summary.* Retrieved from www.knowledgebusiness.com

Teram, E., Schachter, C. L., & Stalker, C. A. (2005). The case for integrating grounded theory and participatory action research: Empowering clients to inform professional practice. *Qualitative Health Research, 15*(8), 1129–1140. doi:10.1177/1049732305275882

The Lancet. (1908, January 4). The Diffusion of Medical Knowledge. *Lancet*, 33–34.

The Science Newsletter. (1940). Defense requires knowledge, organised and implemented. *Science News, 38*(3), 47. doi:10.2307/3916486

Theraulaz, G., & Bonabeau, E. (1995). Coordination in distributed building. *Science, 269*, 686–688. doi:10.1126/science.269.5224.686

Theraulaz, G., & Bonabeau, E. (1999). A brief history of stigmergy. *Artificial Life, 5*, 97–116. doi:10.1162/106454699568700

Thoeny, P. (2005). *TWiki Success Story of Wind River.* Retrieved from http://www.twiki.org/cgi-bin/view/Main/TWikiSuccessStoryOfWindRiver

Timothy, L. (2008, August 3). *The Early History of Nupedia and Wikipedia: A Memoir.* Retrieved from http://features.slashdot.org/article.pl?sid=05/04/18/164213

Tiwana, A. (2000). *The Knowledge management Toolkit: practical techniques for building a knowledge management system.* Upper Saddle River, NJ: Prentice Hall.

Toffler, A. (1984). Science and change. Foreword. In I. Prigogine & I. Stengers (Eds.), *Order out of chaos. Man's new dialogue with nature* (pp. xi-xxxi). Glasgow, Scotland: Fontana Paperbacks.

Tripathi, R., Gupta, M. P., & Bhattacharya, J. (2007). Selected Aspects of Interoperability in One-stop Government Portal of India. In *Proceedings of the 5th International Conference on E-Government*, Hyderabad, India.

Trojah, C., et al. (2009). An Argumentation Framework based on strength for Ontology Mapping. In *Argumentation in Multi-Agent Systems* (LNCS 5384, pp. 57-71). Retrieved October 18, 2010, from www.di.uevora.pt/~pq/papers/argmas08.pdf

Tsui, E. (2003). Tracking the role and evolution of commercial Knowledge Management software. In Holsapple, C. W. (Ed.), *Handbook on Knowledge Management* (pp. 5–25). Heidelberg, Germany: Springer.

Tummarello, G., & Morbidoni, C. (2008). The DBin platform: a complete environment for Semantic Web communities. *Web Semantics: Science . Services and Agents on the World Wide Web, 6*, 257–265. doi:10.1016/j.websem.2008.08.002

Tuomi, I. (2000). Data is more than knowledge: implications of the reversed hierarchy for knowledge management and organizational memory. *Journal of Management Information Systems, 16*(3), 103–117.

Tushman, M. L., & Anderson, P. (1986). Technological discontinuities and organizational environments. *Administrative Science Quarterly, 31*, 439–465. doi:10.2307/2392832

Udell, J. (2004a). *The social enterprise.* InfoWorld.

Udell, J. (2004b). *Year of the enterprise Wiki.* InfoWorld.

Ulrick, D. (1997). Organising around capabilities . In Hesselbein, F., Goldsmith, M., & Beckhard, R. (Eds.), *The organisation of the future.* San Francisco: Jossey-Bass.

Ulrick, D. (1998). The new mandate for HR. *Harvard Business Review*, 124–134.

UNFPA. (2002). *Population Ageing and Development.* UNFPA Publishing. Retrieved from http://www.unfpa.org/publications/detail.cfm?ID=67&filterListType=3

United Nations E-Government Survey. (2008). *From E-Government to Connected Governance.* New York: United Nations.

Uschold, M., Clark, P., Dickey, F., Fung, C., Smith, S., Uczekaj, S., et al. (2003). A semantic infosphere. In D. Fensel et al. (Eds.), *ISWC 2003* (LNCS 2870, pp. 882-896). Berlin: Springer Verlag.

Vallacher, R. R., & Nowak, A. (Eds.). (1994). *Dynamical systems in social psychology*. San Diego, CA: Academic Press.

Valsiner, J. (1998). *The Guided Mind*. Cambridge, MA: Harvard University Press.

Van Berten, P., & Ermine, J.-L. (2006). Applied Knowledge Management: a set of well-tried tools. *VINE: The Journal of Information and Knowledge Management Systems, 36*(4), 423–431.

van den Hoof, B., & de Ridder, J. A. (2004). Knowledge sharing in context: the influence of organizational commitment, communication climate and CMS use on knowledge sharing. *Journal of Knowledge Management, 8*(6), 118.

Van der Veer, R., & Valsiner, J. (Eds.). (1994). *The Vygotsky reader*. London: Blackwell.

Van Geert, P. (1994). *Dynamic systems of development: Change between complexity and Chaos*. New York: Harvester Wheatsheaf.

Van Groenendaal, W. (2003). Group decision support for public policy planning. *Information & Management, 40*, 371–380. doi:10.1016/S0378-7206(02)00044-7

Varela, F. J., Maturana, H. R., & Uribe, R. (1974). Autopoiesis: the organization of living systems, its characterization and a model. *Bio Systems, 5*, 187–196. doi:10.1016/0303-2647(74)90031-8

Varga, C., & Ugrin, E. (2008). *New theory of state and democracy*. Budapest, Hungary: Institute for Strategic Research.

Venners, B. (2004). *The Simplest Thing that Could Possibly Work*. Retrieved from http://www.artima.com/intv/simplest.html

Vico, G. (1744). *The new science of Giambattista Vico*. Ithaca, NY: Cornell University Press.

Von Bertalanffy, L. (2006). *General System Theory: Foundations, Development, Applications* (Revised ed.). George Braziller.

Von Foerster, H. (1993). *Understanding understanding*. New York: Springer-Verlag.

Vraalsen, F., den Braber, F., Hogganvik, I., Soldal Lund, M., & Stølen, K. (2004). The CORAS tool-supported methodology for UML-based security analysis. In *SINTEF ICT*.

Vygotsky, L. (1987). In R. W. Rieber & A. S. Carton (Eds.), *Vol. 1: Problems of general psychology*. New York: Plenum Press.

Vygotsky, L. (1997). In R. W. Rieber & A. S. Wollock (Eds.). *Vol. 3: Problems of the theory and history of psychology*. New York: Plenum Press.

Wagner, C. (2004). Wiki: A Technology for Conversational Knowledge Management and Group Collaboration. *Communications of the Association for Information Systems, 13*, 265–289.

Wagner, C. (2006). Breaking the Knowledge Acquisition Bottleneck Through Conversational Knowledge Management. *Information Resources Management Journal, 19*(1), 70–83.

Wagner, C., Cheung, K. S. K., Ip, R. K. F., & Böttcher, S. (2006). Building Semantic Webs for E-Government with Wiki technology. *Electronic Government, 3*(1), 36–55. doi:10.1504/EG.2006.008491

Wallerstein, I. (1996). *Opening the Social Sciences. Report of the Gulbenkian Commission on the restructuring of the Social Sciences*. Palo Alto, CA: Stanford University Press.

Walls, M. R. (2004). Combining decision analysis and portfolio management to improve project selection in the exploration and production firm. *Journal of Petroleum Science Engineering, 44*, 55–65. doi:10.1016/j.petrol.2004.02.005

Walls, M. R., & Dyer, J. (1996). Risk propensity and firm performance: a study of the petroleum exploration industry. *Management Science, 42*(7), 1004–1021. doi:10.1287/mnsc.42.7.1004

Wang, J., Jin, B., & Li, J. (2004). An ontology-based publish/subscribe system. In H. A. Jacobsen (Ed.), *Middleware 2004* (LNCS 3231, pp. 232-253). Berlin: Springer Verlag.

Wang, L., Tian, Y., & Sawaragi, T. (2008, July). *Explanation-based manipulator learning: acquisition of assembling technique through observation*. Paper presented at the 17th World Congress the International Federation of Automatic Control, Seoul, South Korea.

Wang, P., & Xu, B. (2008). Lily: Ontology Alignment Results for OAEI 2008. In *Proceedings of the 7th International Semantic Web Conference Ontology Matching (OM 2008)* (pp. 167-176). Retrieved October 18, 2010, from http://citeseerx.ist.psu.edu/viewdoc/download?doi= 10.1.1.142.8474 &rep=rep1&type=pdf#page=143

Wasserman, S., & Faust, K. (1994). *Social network analysis: Methods and applications*. Cambridge, UK: Cambridge University Press.

Watson, S., & Hewett, K. (2006). A multi-theoretical model of knowledge transfer in organisations: determinants of knowledge contribution and knowledge reuse. *Journal of Management Studies, 43*(2), 141–173. doi:10.1111/j.1467-6486.2006.00586.x

Webb, K., & White, T. (2005). UML as a cell and biochemistry modelling language. *Bio Systems, 80*(3), 283–302. doi:10.1016/j.biosystems.2004.12.003

Webster, G., & Goodwin, B. (1996). *Form and Transformation. Generative and Relational Principles in Biology*. Cambridge, UK: Cambridge University Press.

Wenger, E., McDermott, R., & Snyder, W. (2002). *Cultivating communities of practice: A guide to managing knowledge*. Boston: Harvard Business School Press.

Wertsch, J. V. (1998). *Mind as action*. New York: Oxford University Press.

Widen-Wulff, G., & Suomi, R. (2003). Building a knowledge sharing company – evidence from the Finnish insurance industry. In *Proceedings of the 36th Annual Hawaii International Conference on System Sciences (HICSS36)*, Big Island, HI. Washington, DC: Computer Society Press.

Widen-Wulff, G., & Ginman, M. (2004). Explaining knowledge sharing in organizations through the dimensions of social capital. *Journal of Information Science, 30*(5), 448–458. doi:10.1177/0165551504046997

Wierzbicki, A. P., & Nakamori, Y. (2006). *Creative space: Models of creative processes for the knowledge civilization Age*. Springer-Verlag: Berlin-Hidelberg.

Wierzbicki, A. P., & Nakamori, Y. (2007). The episteme of knowledge civilization. In Y. Nakamori, Z. Wang, J. Gu, & T. Ma (Eds.), *Proceedings of the 8th International Symposium on Knowledge and Systems Sciences (KSS2007), 2nd International Conference on Knowledge, Information and Creativity Support Systems (KICSS2007)* (pp. 8-21). Nomi, Japan: Japan Advanced Institute of Science and Technology and International Society for Knowledge and Systems Sciences.

Wierzbicki, A. P., & Nakamori, Y. (2007, July 23-27). *Testing knowledge creation theories*. Paper presented at IFIP-TC7 Conference, Cracow, Poland.

Wierzbicki, A. P., Zhu, Z. C., & Nakamori, Y. (2006). A new role of systems science: informed systems approach. In A. P. Wierzbicki & Y. Nakamori (Eds.), *Creative space: Models of creative processes for the knowledge civilization Age* (pp. 161-215). Berlin-Heidelberg: Springer-Verlag.

Wierzbicki, A. P., & Nakamori, Y. (Eds.). (2006). *Creative space: Models of creative processes for the knowledge civilization age*. Berlin-Heidelberg, Germany: Springer-Verlag.

Wiig, K. M. (1997). Knowledge management: where did it come from and where will it go. *Expert Systems with Applications, 13*(1), 1–14. doi:10.1016/S0957-4174(97)00018-3

Wiki. (2009). Retrieved from http://c2.com

Wikipatterns.com. (2007). *Wiki Not Email*. Retrieved from http://www.wikipatterns.com/display/wikipatterns/ Wiki+Not+Email

Wikipedia. (2008). *Oldowan*. Retrieved May 21, 2009, from http://en.wikipedia.org/wiki/Oldowan

Wikipedia. (2009). Retrieved from http://wikipedia.org.

Wikipedia. (2009a). *Epistemology*. Retrieved May 26, 2009, from http://en.wikipedia.org/wiki/Epistemology

Wikipedia. (2009b). *Nominalism*. Retrieved May 22, 2009, from http://en.wikipedia.org/wiki/Nominalism

Wikipedia. (2009c). *Cargo cult science*. Retrieved May 7, 2009, from http://en.wikipedia.org/wiki/Cargo_cult_science

Wikipedia. (2009d). *Small_stellated_dodecahedron*. Retrieved June 7, 2009, from http://en.wikipedia.org/wiki/Small_stellated_dodecahedron

Williams, S. R. (1931). The collection and creation of knowledge. *The Journal of Higher Education, 2*(8), 415–419. doi:10.2307/1974428

Wilson, T. D. (2002). The nonsense of knowledge management. *Information research, 8*(1).

Wimmer, M. A. (2006). Implementing a knowledge portal for egovernment based on semantic modelling: The E-Government intelligent portal (eip.at). In *Proceedings of the 39th Annual Hawaii International Conference on System Sciences (HICSS'06)*.

Wittgenstein, L. (1922). *Tractatus logico-philosophicus*. Cambridge, UK: Cambridge University Press.

Woodruff, J. M. (2005). Consequence and likelihood in risk estimation: a matter of balance in UK health and safety risk assessment practice. *Safety Science, 43*, 345–353. doi:10.1016/j.ssci.2005.07.003

Wozniak, R. H. (1996). Qu'est-ce que l'intelligence? Piaget, Vygotsky, and the 1920s crisis in psychology. In A. Tryphon & J. Vonèche (Eds.), *Piaget – Vygotsky. The social genesis of thought*. Hove, UK: Psychology Press.

Wright, S. (1932). The role of mutation, inbreeding and crossbreeding and selection in Evolution. In *Proceedings of the Sixth International Congress of Genetics* (Vol. 1, pp. 356-366).

Wright, S. (1934). The method of path coefficients. *Annals of Mathematical Statistics, 5*, 161–215. doi:10.1214/aoms/1177732676

Wright, S. (1960). The treatment of reciprocal interaction, with or without lag, in path analysis . *Biometrics, 16*(3), 423–445. doi:10.2307/2527693

Xia, H., Wang, Z., Luo, S., & Yoshida, T. (2008). Toward a concept of community intelligence: A view on knowledge sharing and fusion in Web-mediated communities. In *Proceedings of the 2008 IEEE International Conference on Systems, Man, and Cybernetics* (pp.88-93). Washington, DC: IEEE Press.

Xie, G., Zhang, J., & Lai, K. K. (2006c, December 18). Web-based risk avoidance group decision support system in software project bidding. In *Proceedings of the 3rd International Workshop on Web-Based Support Systems (WSS'06), WI-IAT 2006 Workshops,* Hong Kong, China (pp. 180-183).

Xie, G., Yue, W., Wang, S., & Lai, K. K. (2010). Dynamic risk management in petroleum project investment based on a variable precision rough set model. *Technological Forecasting and Social Change.* .doi:10.1016/j.techfore.2010.01.013

Xie, G., Zhang, J., & Lai, K. K. (2005). A group decision-making model of risk evasion in software project bidding based on VPRS. *Lecture Notes in Artificial Intelligence, 3642*, 530–538.

Xie, G., Zhang, J., & Lai, K. K. (2006a). Risk avoidance in bidding for software projects based on life cycle management theory. *International Journal of Project Management, 24*(6), 516–521. doi:10.1016/j.ijproman.2006.03.004

Xie, G., Zhang, J., & Lai, K. K. (2006b). Using VPRS to mine the significance of risk factors in IT project management. *Lecture Notes in Artificial Intelligence, 4062*, 750–757.

Xie, G., Zhang, J., Lai, K. K., & Yu, L. (2008). Variable precision rough set for group decision-making: An application. *International Journal of Approximate Reasoning, 49*(2), 331–343. doi:10.1016/j.ijar.2007.04.005

Yang, B., Zheng, W., & Viere, C. (2009). Holistic views of knowledge management models. *Advances in Developing Human Resources, 11*(3), 273–289. doi:10.1177/1523422309338584

Yolles, M. I. (1996). Critical Systems Thinking, paradigms, and the modelling space. *Systems Practice, 9*(6), 549–570. doi:10.1007/BF02169213

Yves, R., et al. (2008). ASMOV: Results for OAEI 2008, Monterrey. In *Proceedings of the 7th International Semantic Web Conference Ontology Matching (OM 2008)* (pp. 132-140). Retrieved October 18, 2010, from http://citeseerx.ist.psu.edu/viewdoc/download?doi=10.1.1.142.8474&rep=rep1&type=pdf#page=143

Yves, R., et al. (2009). Ontology matching with semantic verification. *Journal of Web Semantics: Science, Services and Agents on the World Wide Web*. Retrieved October 18, 2010, from http://www.dit.unitn.it/~p2p/RelatedWork/Matching/ontology_matching_with_semantic_verification.pdf

Zhang, R. S., Wang, Y. H., Zhou, X. Z., Liu, B. Y., Yao, N. L., & Li, P. (2008). Integration of Famous TCM Doctors' Experience and Data Mining Technology. *World science and technology-modernization of traditional Chinese medicine and materia medica, 10*(1), 45-52, 63.

Zhang, S., & Bodenreider, O. (2007). Hybrid Alignment Strategy for Anatomical Ontologies Results of the Ontology Alignment Contest. In *Proceedings of ISWC 2007 Ontology Matching Workshop,* Busan, Korea. Retrieved October 18, 2010, from http://mor.nlm.nih.gov/pubs/pdf/2007-oaei-sz.pdf

Zhang, W., & Tang, X. J. (2006). Web text mining on xssc, in Knowledge and Systems Sciences: Toward Knowledge Synthesis and Creation. In *Proceedings of the 7th International Symposium on Knowledge and Systems Sciences (KSS'2006)* (LNCS 8, pp. 167-175). Hong Kong, China: Global-Link Publishers.

Zhang, L. W., & Yuan, S. H. (2006). Implicit structure model and research on syndrome differentiation of Chinese medicine (I): Basic thought and analytic tool of implicit structure. *Journal Of Beijing University of Traditional Chinese Medicine, 29*(6), 365–369.

Zhang, M. J., & Zhang, C. Q. (1999). Potential cases, methodologies and strategies of synthesis of solutions in distributed expert systems. *IEEE Transactions on Knowledge and Data Engineering, 11*(3), 498–503. doi:10.1109/69.774105

Zhang, M., Tang, X. J., Bai, Q., & Gu, J. F. (2007, June). Expert discovery and knowledge mining in complex multi-agent systems. *Journal of Systems Science and Systems Engineering, 16*(2), 222–234. doi:10.1007/s11518-007-5043-9

Zhao, L. Y., & Gu, J. F. (2000). The application of probabilistic risk assessment approach to the safety analysis of one specific type of launch vehicle in China. *Systems Engineering: Theory & Pratice, 20*(6), 91–97.

Zhdanova, A., & Shvaiko, P. (2006). Community-Driven Ontology Matching. In *Proceedings of ESWC '06* (LNCS 4011, pp. 34-49). New York: Springer. Retrieved October 18, 2010, from http://dit.unitn.it/~p2p/RelatedWork/Matching/eswc06_ontology_matching.pdf

Zhu, Z. X., Song, W. Q., & Gu, J. F. (2008). A Multi-agent and Data Mining Model for TCM Cases Knowledge Discovery. In *Proceedings of the International Colloquium on Computing, Communication, Control and Management (CCCM 2008)* (Vol. 3, pp. 341-346). Retrieved from www.iita-conference.org/isecs/index_files/cccm2008content.pdf

Zhu, Z. C. (1998). Conscious mind, forgetting mind: Two approaches in multimethodology. *Systemic Practice and Action Research, 11*(6), 669–690. doi:10.1023/A:1022140405046

Zhu, Z. C. (1999). The practice of multimodal approaches, The challenge of cross-cultural communication, and the search for responses. *Human Relations, 52*(5), 579–607.

Zhu, Z. C. (2000). Dealing with a differentiated whole: The philosophy of the WSR approach. *Systemic Practice and Action Research, 13*(1), 21–57. doi:10.1023/A:1009519505326

Zhu, Z. X., Gu, J. F., & Song, W. Q. (2009). From Data Mining to Expert Mining. *Systems Engineering, 27*(1), 1–7.

Ziarko, W. (1993). Variable precision rough set model. *Journal of Computer and System Sciences, 46*(1), 39–59. doi:10.1016/0022-0000(93)90048-2

Zilsel, E. (2000). The social origins of modern science. In D. Raven, W. Krohn, & R. S.

About the Editor

W.B. Lee is the Chair Professor and Director of the Knowledge Management Research Centre, of The Hong Kong Polytechnic University. He is currently a council member of the Hong Kong Productivity Council and a member of the assessment panel of the Innovation and Technology Fund of the Hong Kong SAR Government. He established the Knowledge Solution Laboratory, the first of its kind in Hong Kong, and pioneered the research and practice of knowledge management in various organisations in manufacturing, trading, public utilities, various government departments, and healthcare. Professor Lee and his team have launched Asia's first online MSc Programme in Knowledge Management. His research interests include manufacturing strategy, knowledge management, organisational learning, and intellectual capital-based management.

Index